Microsoft® Exchange Server V5.5

Planning, Design, and Implementation

Microsoft® Exchange Server V5.5

Planning, Design, and Implementation

Tony Redmond

Digital Press
Boston • Oxford • Johannesburg • Melbourne • New Delhi • Singapore

Digital Press™ is an imprint of Butterworth–Heinemann.

 Recognizing the importance of preserving what has been written, Butterworth–Heinemann prints its books on acid-free paper whenever possible.

Butterworth–Heinemann supports the efforts of American Forests and the Global ReLeaf program in its campaign for the betterment of trees, forests, and our environment.

Library of Congress Cataloging-in-Publication Data

Redmond, Tony, 1959–
    Microsoft Exchange server V5.5 : planning, design, and implementation / Tony Redmond.
        p.   cm.
        Includes index.
        ISBN 1-55558-213-3 (pbk. : alk. paper)
        1. Microsoft Exchange server. 2. Client/server computing.
    I. Title.
    QA76.9.C55R425   1998
    005.7 '13769--dc21   98-21457
                                                                              CIP

British Library Cataloguing-in-Publication Data
A catalogue record for this book is available from the British Library.

The publisher offers special discounts on bulk orders of this book.
For information, please contact:

    Manager of Special Sales
    Butterworth–Heinemann
    225 Wildwood Avenue
    Woburn, MA 01801–2041
    Tel: 781-904-2500
    Fax: 781-904-2620

For information on all Digital Press publications available, contact our World Wide Web home page at: http://www.bh.com/digitalpress

10 9 8 7 6 5 4

Designed and composed by ReadyText, Bath, UK
Printed in the United States of America

Dedication

Clearly I couldn't write books about e-mail systems without an enormous amount of support from my wife and children. They continue to provide that support in a usually uncomplaining manner, although I know that when I write they suffer the pains generated by a concentrated author. They deserve every dedication I can muster.

Contents

(For cards outside the US please affix a postage stamp)

BUSINESS REPLY MAIL

FIRST CLASS MAIL   PERMIT NO. 78   WOBURN, MA

POSTAGE WILL BE PAID BY ADDRESSEE

DIRECT MAIL DEPARTMENT
BUTTERWORTH-HEINEMANN
225 WILDWOOD AVE
PO BOX 4500
WOBURN MA 01888-9930

At Butterworth-Heinemann, we are dedicated to providing you with quality service. So that we may keep you informed about titles relevant to your field of interest, please fill in the information below and return this postage-paid reply card. Thank you for your help, and we look forward to hearing from you!

What title have you purchased?

Where was the purchase made?

Name

Job Title

Institution

Address

Town/City

State/County

Zip/Postcode

Country

Telephone

email

☐ Please keep me informed about other books and information services on this and related subjects.

(FOR OFFICE USE ONLY)

BUTTERWORTH-HEINEMANN IS ON THE WEB – http://www.bh.com/

US1 US1

Foreword

It is now almost two years since Exchange V4.0, the first version of Exchange, was finally born on March 13th 1996. In that time another two versions have arrived, Exchange V5.0 in February 1997 and now Exchange V5.5 in November 1997. The product has certainly filled out fast! But after fast and furious updates we now enter a period of consolidation. The Exchange development team is now building for NT 5.0 with a publicly stated commitment that the next version of Exchange will ship within 90 days of the ship of NT 5.0. So we will not see a version of Exchange in 1998. Instead, we will all have the chance to build on the platform that has already been established.

One of the key strengths of Exchange that is often missed in press and analyst reviews is that it was designed as a platform product and nowhere is that more evident than in the speed of the subsequent releases. Exchange V4.0 represents 500 man years worth of design and development over a five year period. Yet within a year the team was able to add another 300 man years, and nine months after that another 250 man years. So in the twenty months subsequent to release the team was able to supercede the development effort of the previous five years. This is one of the key benefits of the architecture that was established in the first place. Its goal was to enable very rapid subsequent development and it certainly has delivered on that task.

So we are really are now in Phase Two of Exchange implementation. Phase One was a time of aggressive messaging deployment. Enormous pent-up demand for a single messaging infrastructure had been building in the marketplace. Many large corporate customers had "ended up" with a whole spider web of departmental messaging systems and enormous maintenance fees were being paid on switch products whose sole purpose in life was to provide gateways and a single directory to link together all these products.

The requirement for consolidation was obvious. The CIO of one of the top companies in the UK demanded it no matter what the cost when he tried one day to send a message to somebody on a different departmental mail system which failed to get through. The CIO of a global oil company personally originated a memo to the entire company announcing a project simply called "OMS", or "One Messaging System". Both of these companies chose Exchange as their platform three years before it shipped and spent those years preparing to do a global deployment as soon as the product was ready. These are but two of many hundreds of companies, large and small, who looked to Exchange V4.0 to provide the integration at the desktop and the single interface to an wealth of collaborative applications that only a true platform can provide.

We knew that many companies had been tracking our progress, in tune with our design goals, but in our wildest dreams we could not have imagined just how many. Ten million licenses sold, mass deployments taking place all over the world. Ten contracts signed for the delivery of over one hundred thousand desktops inside a single company. Two of those already realized with over one hundred thousand desktops existing inside both companies. This makes them the largest single messaging platform deployments ever. Both global rollouts achieved within one hundred weeks of the golden code being built, necessitating a deployment rate of a minimum of one thousand desktops a week.

But although all of these existing customers are deriving great communication benefit from the unification achieved from the delivery of a single platform, the true vision emerges in Phase Two: Beyond Messaging. Where the single platform can be assumed by a rich variety of application vendors who can build Workflow, Document Management and other collaborative products directly into the Office desktop that is the end user experience of Exchange and use the strength of that hard won architecture to provide core back end services such as the Directory and the Object Store.

Analysts have predicted that the third party marketplace that is emerging around the Exchange platform will grow to be seven times the size of its software sales, and those sales are already greater than any other Microsoft Server product at this stage of its lifecycle. Once the Outlook client was included in Office 97, it marked the point where two previous separate group of ISVs, (Office and NT) now combine to create a wide variety of both client and server applications for Exchange.

For those of you who have already deployed your end user desktop becomes empowered as never before. Collaboration has previously done well at the departmental level but the intrusive nature and price per desktop of the software has prevented more widespread take-up. Workflow and Document Management products have always found their deployments limited to less than 2% of the available desktops within a company.

End users want to live inside their primary application and not have to leave it to activate other applications. Now with Exchange those applications can be run from the Outlook menus using all the same commands that the users have already learnt.

In 1998 we will see an explosion of Phase Two deployments, both in customers utilizing the Exchange desktop they already implemented and in customers deploying applications as they deploy the Exchange desktop. Even if only one of these two groups became active the results would be dramatic. With both groups implementing, the marketplace will be unrecognizable by the end of the year.

Once again, DIGITAL is well ahead of the curve. The company that was the first to commit to Windows NT now has more NT experts inside their company than Microsoft does, as Bill Gates recently pointed out.

DIGITAL then went on to commit to and internally deploy Exchange well before it shipped, and a result DIGITAL (as at May 1998) has contracted to deploy nearly 3 million Exchange seats. In fact, over 20% of the seats already sold are being deployed by DIGITAL, and many of these contracts are with the companies who are undertaking the largest deployments of Exchange. Obviously customers feel very comfortable deploying with a company whose Exchange implementation was the first global deployment to be completed after Microsoft, and remained the largest for over a year after Exchange shipped. DIGITAL was only overtaken when companies who simply had more employees completed their deployments. In fact, in the top ten of the largest existing worldwide Exchange deployments there is only one company who was not part of the Early Adopters program that I ran to help Exchange customers design their deployments before we shipped. That company is only there because they engaged DIGITAL to manage their worldwide deployment.

And now as Phase Two implementations are kickstarted all over the world DIGITAL is already there with its Worldwide Solutions Alliance. Early on, DIGITAL recognized the huge opportunity for solutions built on Exchange and established a separate consulting practice to focus on Exchange deployment and implementation. DIGITAL now has their own Workflow and Document Management product (DIGITAL Work Expeditor), as well as other Exchange-related software products like the DIGITAL Enterprise Archive and Communiqué, and has forged alliances with a wide range of other application vendors to provide a complete suite of software opportunities.

So while the Exchange development team build for NT 5.0, we will build on top of the platform they have already given us. This year at Tech-Ed and the annual Exchange Deployment Conference the main focus will be on the collaboration that has been achieved on top of the infrastructure. The architecture that took us so long to develop and took you so little time to deploy because of the strength of what we did.

We left the marketplace for three years to come back with the best design possible. As the Worldwide Messaging Server Product Manager I shipped MS Mail 3.2 in April of 1993 and did not return until we shipped Exchange Server 4.0 in March of 1996. I thought it would take much longer to reclaim the market that we lost in those three years. I could not have imagined that we would celebrate Christmas 1997 with the third version released, ten million seats sold and with two 100 thousand plus deployments, Exchange holding the Number One and the Number Two top single messaging implementations in the world.

So we are all set for 1998. Plenty of stuff to do as we watch Exchange for NT 5.0 emerge. Exchange V5.5 brings the unlimited data store enabling the choice of server design to be totally unconstrained by any limitations other than the hardware itself. Many customers including Microsoft are using this feature to consolidate servers. Microsoft now operates 13 Exchange V5.5 systems that support more than one thousand users. And as I write Outlook 98 is about to join the Exchange V5.5 stable with some great new features particularly for the remote user. Even those of you who are fully deployed do not need to stay still unless you want to.

Some critics have pointed to the speed of which versions have been released as somehow reflecting a failure of the original design. It is actually a reflection of how closely Microsoft has been monitoring and learning from the reality of the product as it is actually deployed. That and the intense nature of the competitive marketplace has resulted in a very rapid response to customer feedback. If you are a customer we care about what you have to say and we listen. I estimate that at least 90% of the features delivered in each release represents functionality requested by the customers. So never stop telling us where you think we could do better. In a year's time Tony will be writing about Exchange for NT 5.0 and there is still time for you to impact the final feature set.

If you are a customer make your voice heard. Exchange is your product too.

Elaine K Sharp

Elainesh@Microsoft.com
Worldwide Messaging Server Product Manager
Microsoft Corporation, March 1992 to October 1996

Preface

A practical approach

Microsoft, along with many other attributes, is probably the world's best marketing company when it comes to PC software. It is very easy to fall into the habit of believing everything that comes out of Microsoft HQ in Redmond, Washington (I think the name of the town is so appropriate...), and sometimes I feel that the books written about Microsoft products occasionally (or even a lot) fall into the trap of wearing rose-tinted glasses.

This is not a book lauding the virtues and benefits of Exchange V5.5. It is, I hope, a hard-nosed and practical look at what the server is good at along with some views on the places where the server, in my view, falls down. All furnished with a pragmatic approach to the business of implementing Exchange and its clients within corporate messaging infrastructures.

All software products need time to mature. Two years hard experience in the cauldron of day-to-day use by real people plus considerable effort on the part of its developers has helped to evolve Exchange to the stage where it can claim to be the world's most functional messaging system. This is not a claim I would have subscribed to for Exchange V4.0, nor indeed for Exchange V5.0. It's certain that Exchange V5.0 was a major step forward and that it marked the incorporation of a number of key Internet messaging technologies into the product. Exchange V5.5 has gone much further in a short time and has now achieved a stage where it can justifiably claim that it surpasses its major competitors. There are gaps, unique features offered by other products, but the overall package of the Windows NT operating system and Exchange is hard to ignore if you're looking for an e-mail system today.

Books need time to mature too. Especially books intended to offer advice about how to design for and then deploy a software product like an e-mail system. The advice and guidance offered to customers has changed as Exchange evolved, and as experience with Exchange in real-life production environments grew. This book reflects experience gained since 1996, from some of the earliest customer deployments using beta versions of Exchange V4.0 right through to projects rolling out in 1998 based on Exchange V5.5. The intention is to reflect best practice in the aspects of design, planning, and operations for Exchange. The target audience is, I think, composed of system administrators and planners, consultants, and anyone else who's interested in making their own assessment of Exchange. I will definitely not satisfy people who want a set of detailed "how do I do that" lists covering every aspect of the operation and deployment of Exchange. There are many other books that document how every option on a menu works or prepares people to take the Microsoft certification exam on Exchange.

I have not discarded all of the information and advice given in my previous books covering Exchange V4.0 and V5.0. Much of the content from those books has been retained, but larger amounts have been cut or rewritten. In some places I was just plain wrong. In others I wasn't definite or specific enough about the advice being given. Elsewhere changes in Exchange V5.5 have rendered text obsolete or incorrect in some aspect. And, of course, all of the new functionality in V5.5 needs to be dissected. Instead of rushing out an update to cover V5.5 immediately the new software was released in November 1997, I opted to wait a few months to see how things developed through the first deployments.

DIGITAL and Exchange

I work for Digital Equipment Corporation (referred to as DIGITAL from here on). I like to think that I'm a practical kind of person and I believe customers come to DIGITAL looking for clear and unbiased advice about all sorts of products including Exchange, and expect our consulting staff to deliver. A lot of the content in this book comes from that background. My intention is to help customers to evaluate how well Exchange fits into their plans, with or without an existing messaging system in place, and then proceeding from that point to implement solutions working with Exchange in one way or another. The fact that DIGITAL now has one of the largest Windows NT and Exchange deployments in the world, has added a great deal of experience and knowledge contained in this book. When I starting writing about Exchange, DIGITAL, like so many of the early adopters, was still struggling with issues like its network and the Windows NT domain infrastructure. Since mid-1996 the rollout of Exchange has progressed smoothly within DIGITAL, albeit with some hiccups. Knowledge of those problems and my personal observations gained from being a consumer of the Exchange implementation inside DIGITAL has helped form a definite view on the right way to approach large-scale deployments. The internal view, allied to the experience gained from many customer projects, is presented in this book as a set of best practices for deployment projects.

I strongly believe that the experience gained through working with many other messaging systems in the last two decades is tremendously valuable during enterprise-scale implementations of Exchange. The longer I work with Exchange the more apparent it is that many of the lessons learnt from other corporate messaging products, like DIGITAL ALL-IN-1, can be taken over and applied to Exchange. There are obvious differences, such as the interaction between Windows NT and Exchange, but establishing a good base for the deployment of any system is a good initial step to take, and using experience to avoid the potholes waiting along the road to trap the unwary is only sensible.

I imagine that some of the views expressed in this book will conflict with those held by others. I'm not always positive about Exchange, but then again, I'm not always positive about any product (software and others) that I use. You've just got to make the best of what you've got.

My own Exchange environment

It's difficult to write a book in a pure vacuum. Day-to-day experience with any system or product is a great trainer. I work within a consulting organization (called NSIS, or Network and Integration Services) that is focused on large-scale messaging deployments for major corporate customers. The majority of our projects involve Exchange and DIGITAL's own messaging technologies, including ALL-IN-1, Office-Server, MailWorks for UNIX, TeamLinks, MAILbus 400, and X.500 Directory Services as well as systems such as PROFS, Lotus Notes, HP Open Mail, and many others. To back up our consultants we have our own operational environment maintained separately from the "official" DIGITAL Exchange implementation that currently supports 55,000 employees. The DIGITAL Exchange environment is composed of an organization that spans multiple sites (31 at last count) across the world. The NSIS Exchange organization incorporates 15 additional sites from Australia to Finland and uses all of the technology we implement for customers. The two organizations are linked by SMTP. The screen shots used for illustrations throughout this book come from the Exchange servers and connectors that I use for day-to-day messaging. There are no pilot, test, or prototype servers featured. Everything is based on the experience gained of putting Exchange to work as a production messaging system.

If you look carefully at the screen shots you'll realize that our servers are sometimes imperfect. In other words, they don't fully reflect the way that we might have liked to bring the systems into production had we the time and luxury of a fully planned and designed implementation. The names given to our Windows NT servers, for instance, follow no naming convention. In acknowledging such imperfections I suspect that our systems are not too far removed from many others in use throughout the world. The important thing is that we have learn from the mistakes we made putting Exchange into production, and most of the mistakes are noted here so that you can avoid the same pitfalls.

Building towards success

There's little doubt in my mind that Exchange is and will continue to be a successful product. In 1996 Microsoft estimated that there were between seven and nine million users of Microsoft Mail and three million users of the original Schedule+ product. Using these figures, (albeit in the knowledge that creating a truly accurate count of the users of any product is nearly impossible once sales go past the million mark), a quick calculation reveals that if there is an average of 25 clients connected to each Microsoft Mail Post Office some 280,000 post offices might potentially migrate to Exchange. It seems that a lot of Microsoft Mail sites have already moved over. Most of the migrations we see today involve Lotus cc:Mail or Novell GroupWise.

The whole world of electronic mail is going through a boom period right now, and the success generated by Exchange in the corporate sphere is shared by other messaging systems. The technical community has nearly always been comfortable with electronic mail and the benefits it could bring to businesses. People within the technical community have been using electronic mail to overcome the barriers imposed by distance or time since the late 1970's, and a whole sub-culture built up around mail, but it's taken time for the concept to spread. Prompted by the explosive success of the Internet, everyone outside the IT community now has a basic understanding of electronic mail and are willing to try it out for themselves. Many millions of new mailboxes are added to the Internet every year. Of course, no-one can physically count all the mailboxes in active use, so any numbers you see must be treated as estimates that have been arrived at using deduction and a fair amount of "finger in the air" calculation.

Apart from making electronic mail more available to ordinary people, the Internet has also greatly driven down the investment required to go on-line with the Web or access other Internet resources. In most cases a simple low monthly payment is sufficient to enable connectivity into the big bad world of electronic communications. All of this makes electronic mail an exciting area to work in right now, and I hope that some of the excitement filters through the pages of this book.

Acknowledgments

Many people within DIGITAL and Microsoft who helped in one way or another as I struggled to come to grips with Exchange and assemble the information contained in the book. There's a long list of people to acknowledge and I'm sure that I will miss someone along the line. With this in mind I'd like to thank Frank Clonan, Pierre Bijaoui, Jens Trier Rasmussen, Geoff Robb, Bill Rafferty, John Rhoton, Kieran McCorry, John B. Horan, Eric Purcell, Peter McQuillan, Chris Brownstone, Nick Powell, and Pat Baxter. In particular, I would like to acknowledge the special contribution made by Stan Foster. Stan is one of the internal messaging architects for DIGITAL and has been up to his neck in the ins and outs of the DIGITAL implementation of Exchange. As such he has accumulated a wide range of practical knowledge about the good and bad in Exchange and has been very willing to share his experience with me. Stan also corrected many of the mistakes I made as the book was written.

Elaine Sharp was the voice of Exchange for many people in the 1993–96 period when she managed the Exchange early adapters program. Elaine and I didn't get on so well at first, and certainly clashed over the content of my Exchange V4.0 book. Since then our relationship is much improved and I was delighted when she accepted the challenge to write the forewords for my V5.0 and V5.5 books. We may not still agree on everything, but at least the arguments are good humored now. Paul Bowden of Microsoft Consulting Services in the UK provided invaluable insight into directory replication. At least I now have a glimmering of what might be going on inside all those replication messages.

Brian Valentine, the General Manager of the Exchange development group, handled my queries with patience and made sure that most were answered. There are still a few outstanding! Other people in the Exchange development group helped too, and I'd like to acknowledge the assistance of Mark Ledsome, Steve Townsend, Iain McDonald, Chris Williams, Jim Reitz, David Howell, Charles Eliot,

Stan Sorensen, Chris Larson, Vanessa Feliberti, David Madison, Derik Stenerson, Brian Murphy, Holly Grabowski, and many others from Building 16 in the Microsoft campus who answered individual questions. On a historical note, the Exchange development group relocated to Building 43 in February 1998. Judging by some of the stories of wild release parties told at the Exchange conferences, Building 16 probably needed a rest.

Elizabeth McCarthy and Pam Chester, my editors at Digital Press, agreed to do the book very quickly, and co-ordinated everything in a most efficient manner. Finally, Graham Douglas of *ReadyText* handled all the complexities of taking a book from Word for Windows files into print. He also made sure that all the changes I wanted to make while the book was in production were inserted in the right place.

In closing let me note that all the errors in the book are mine. No one else can claim responsibility. All I can offer in defense of any error is the simple fact that they are honest mistakes generated during my own experience gained working with Exchange. Exchange is a big product with lots of interesting (and some not so interesting) challenges for people interested in deploying it into a networked, heterogeneous messaging environment. I hope you have as much fun meeting that challenge as I've had. Whatever you do, keep the thought in mind that Exchange is only a software product and life is much more interesting than any one product can be. Let's go forward on that note.

Tony Redmond
May 1998

The author invites comments on the content of the book.
Please send e-mail to:

`Tony.Redmond@digital.com`

Introducing Microsoft Exchange Server

I.I   The Exchange program

When it was launched in 1996, Microsoft Exchange Server represented a new departure for Microsoft messaging products. Instead of a situation where it is enough to be able to send electronic messages to other users connected to a common system, Microsoft promised an "Information Exchange", the ability for people to share and manage information they need with anyone, anywhere, anytime. Of course, you need to be connected into the program before you can do all this, and, in one way, that's what this book is all about.

"Exchange" is often applied as a general catch-all title for the integrated suite of client and server electronic mail products released by Microsoft. It's important to differentiate between the clients and server because each can be operated independently of the other. A strong link is forged between Microsoft clients and servers through a common application programming interface (MAPI, Microsoft's Messaging Application Programming Interface). You don't have to use clients created by Microsoft with Exchange, and you can connect Microsoft clients to other servers. In these instances the API used to connect the client to the server varies from POP3 through IMAP4 to HTTP/HTML, as we'll see in chapter 2.

Exchange is viewed as a very strategic and successful product within Microsoft. Developing a high-capacity robust mail server with client and gateway connections is not an easy task. Providing good migration facilities to accommodate the needs of a large installed base (in this case, Microsoft Mail) adds complexity to the task, as does the requirement to build for an international market. To the end of 1995 some 800 man-years had been used to develop the many millions of lines of code necessary to build Exchange Server and its clients. In her foreword, Elaine Sharp reports that the total effort expended to date now amounts to over 1,050 man years. As of early 1998, the code libraries for Exchange server contained some 9 million lines of code. A massive development effort continues to keep Exchange ahead of its competitors. Sometimes, as we'll discuss later on, the rate of change enforced by the rapid pace of development poses a unique challenge for deployment teams.

As large as it is, the massive Exchange code base does not represent the work done in associated development groups within Microsoft, such as that to develop other BackOffice components or make changes like adding cluster support to the Windows NT operating system itself. All in all, the whole effort to bring Exchange to market has been enormous.

It's fair to say that Exchange was just about to ship for quite a long time. Never has a messaging product gone through quite such a long gestation, although I think it fair to say that the delay in the release date allowed both Windows NT and Exchange to mature to a point where both exhibit the qualities necessary for deployment in heavy-duty sites. Microsoft first started to reveal its plans for a high-end messaging and information server to the industry in 1993, but the complexities encountered during the development process contributed to the delayed release. Exchange was in beta test for 2.5 years and through seven different beta versions released to an ever-growing set of customers willing to undergo the trials and tribulations of working with beta software. To complete the trivial pursuit section I'll note in passing that during development Exchange had an array of code names including Spitfire, Touchdown, Firefox, and Mercury. The first version of Exchange eventually shipped in March 1996.

Exchange is designed to compete in corporate electronic mail markets. By their very nature corporate implementations tend to be international, so the fact that Exchange can run in English, French, German, and Japanese, and support clients running in 24 different languages is important. Any Exchange server can support any Exchange client no matter what language the client operates in, so a single Exchange server running English could, for instance, support the requirements of a Swiss installation where clients might run in English, French, German, and Italian. The internationalization of Exchange is based on the UNICODE base established by Windows NT itself.

1.2   The Exchange value proposition

New products coming to market for the first time must create a value proposition before customers will consider a purchase. This fact is as true about software applications as it is in respect of any other product. If it weren't then any new product which appeared would instantly gain market share and acceptability. As we all know, while marketing executives might hope that their products would succeed, not all products do.

The value proposition put forward by Exchange can be broken down into a small number of succinct points:

- A strong set of electronic mail functionality for users, system administrators, and programmers
- Good security
- Highly integrated system administration
- A wide range of easily installed and configured connectors (gateways) to other messaging systems
- A building block approach to messaging infrastructures beginning with individual servers and growing right up to distributed networks of servers accommodating many thousands of users
- A distributed and largely self-managing directory
- A distributed document repository (public folders)
- Exploitation of the electronic mail infrastructure through mail-enabled applications and electronic forms
- All provided in a reasonably priced, easy to install package.

The growing influence of Windows NT as a major operating system provides one of the major reasons why the value proposition put forward by Exchange is attractive to customers. Windows NT has developed rapidly over the last few years to a stage where it can provide a single-login, location-independent infrastructure onto which enterprises can layer and deploy distributed applications such as Exchange.

The evolution of TCP/IP to become the de facto protocol for networking is also an important point because much of the fundamental building blocks for TCP/IP-based distributed computing are included in the base Windows NT operating system. Off-site access for users is also facilitated by in-built standard remote access services (RAS). Microsoft's obvious dedication to the task of making Windows NT the operating system of choice for corporate computing is evident by the speed in which new and important technologies are built into Windows NT.

Apart from the growing feature list incorporated into the operating system, a number of trends have emerged in the recent past to support Windows NT. Amongst the most important of these are:

- The level of technical difficulty experienced in the migration of Novell NetWare V3.11 LANs to NetWare V4.0 (or above) has caused many companies to review their methods of providing shared file and print services to PC users. Windows NT provides excellent file and print services and quite a number of NetWare V3.11 installations have moved over to Windows NT, figuring that the move to NT is easier than an upgrade to NetWare V4.

- The opportunity exists to replace some large database applications running on mainframe and mini-computers with equivalent applications built around high-end Windows NT servers. Because of the huge disparity in hardware purchase and maintenance costs the financial equation is usually if not always highly favorable, even when the cost of migrating the application is factored in.

- Applications designed around the client/server model mean that the power of PC desktops can be leveraged in a much more powerful and cost-effective manner than the situation where PCs act as expensive terminal emulators for monolithic centralized application systems.

- Generally, PCs (using the broadest possible definition of the term) have become all pervasive on the desktop. Video terminals and workstations still exist and there's a good population of low-end older PCs to deal with as well, but steadily dropping hardware costs and escalating performance levels mean that users receive much more "bang for their buck" than ever before. System management and administration must follow the dispersed PCs to regain control over applications and user environments before they disappear from sight.

The combination of Windows NT, which provides a common software platform for clients and servers, and highly functional applications, such as Exchange and the other components of the Microsoft BackOffice program, offers the potential to achieve great benefits for companies. Achieving those benefits and realizing the real potential of Windows NT is the challenge for those charged with the planning, design, and implementation of Windows NT and Exchange deployments.

1.3   A quick overview of Exchange

Exchange Server is tightly integrated into the Windows NT operating system, taking full advantage of the multitasking and multithreaded attributes of the operating system. System management and administration is integrated directly into base system components to make life easier all round. You can, for example, create a mailbox for a new or existing user directly from the Windows NT account administration tool. Possibly more important are the facts that Exchange is layered directly on top of the Windows NT network and security models, so clearly if you haven't managed to get these items sorted out you won't be in a position to even think about implementing Exchange anytime soon.

We're just a couple of pages into the book but already the most fundamental and important point about any Exchange implementation has been made. That is, of course, the complete and total reliance on the Windows NT operating system. Anyone intending to do anything serious with Exchange must understand that Windows NT is the foundation stone the messaging infrastructure is built upon. A quickly put-together or ill-considered implementation of Windows NT will result in a structure like a house built of cards—pretty to look at, but liable to complete, sudden, and catastrophic collapse. Microsoft cannot be blamed for not telling people to create a solid Windows NT infrastructure before attempting to implement Exchange. The message is repeated time and time again in very clear terms in all the technical white papers on the subject issued by Microsoft since 1994.[1]

The close working relationship between Windows NT and Exchange implies that a certain degree of competence with Windows NT is required from anyone associated with the design or implementation of Exchange. This experience is not acquired by running SETUP.EXE, the ubiquitous Windows installation program to perform the 30-minute installation of Exchange, followed by a quick client upgrade for a Windows 95 PC. These activities will result in an operational server and client pair, but that's hardly the same as a corporate-standard messaging system. Ideally in-house staff or external consultants should be certified as Windows NT system engineers through the Microsoft Certified Professional[2] program.

While this book discusses many operational concepts relating to the successful deployment of Windows NT, more careful consideration and planning is needed before a full-scale implementation of Exchange can be approached with confidence. The Windows NT Resource Kit (an optional extra available from Microsoft) is particu-

---

1.   Copies of the white papers are available from http://www.microsoft.com/exchange/ or from the Microsoft Technet (Technical Information Network) CD-ROM. Technet CD-ROMs are issued monthly to subscribers. The subscription fee is not high and the information gained is well worthwhile.
2.   Classes covering Exchange server are available from Microsoft ATECs (Authorized Training and Education Centres). A certification exam covering Exchange server is included in the Microsoft Certified Professional curriculum and exam schedule.

larly useful in this respect. The Resource Kit is issued from time to time, so make sure you have the latest copy.

Of course, tight integration into the Windows NT operating system is a double-edged sword. The advantages gained (largely integrated system management) can only be achieved if Windows NT is going to be your preferred platform. If you want to use anything else like OpenVMS or any variant of UNIX then Exchange is not going to be very interesting at all.

The major pieces or services that collectively make up Exchange Server are listed below. The name of the executable of each component is shown in parenthesis.

- The Message Transfer Agent or MTA (EMSMTA.EXE) used to route messages to other MTAs, either another Exchange server or what Microsoft charmingly terms "foreign" X.400 (1984 or 1988) MTAs. While its basic role is to interchange messages with other Exchange servers, the MTA also serves as a connectivity engine to link Exchange to other different types of mail systems. The connectivity engine uses a series of "connectors" that understand the interconnectivity and formatting requirements of other mail systems to bridge between the raw database format used internally by Exchange. Out-of-the-box connectors are available for X.400, SMTP, Lotus Notes, Lotus cc:Mail, IBM PROFS, IBM SNADS, and Microsoft Mail systems. And of the connectors are included in the Exchange Server "Enterprise Edition".

- The Directory Store (DSAMAIN.EXE), a collection of all the data (names and connection information) relating to the Exchange organization (a collection of sites and servers, or individual computers running Exchange) together with user account information and shared resources such as distribution lists and "custom recipients". All Exchange servers in the same organization share a single replicated directory. There is no chaining or referral as would be found in the more traditional model of a distributed directory. All queries are resolved against a local copy of the distributed directory.

- The Information Store (STORE.EXE), a structured repository broken down into two distinct sections. The first stores personal data for users, grouped into folders, while the second holds all the information available in public folders. The repositories are implemented as relational databases, optimized to store the type of non-structured data classically found in messaging or electronic file cabinet systems. The Information Store is not a passive repository. It takes care of public folder replication and delivers any messages addressed to users located on the same server. The database technology used by the Information Store is similar in many respects to that applied to transaction processing applications and provides advanced features such as the capability to automatically recover transactions (messages) from logs should problems occur with the database. On-line backup is also incorporated, allowing users to work while system administrators take care of daily housekeeping. To my knowledge, these features are not found in the file system or database used by any other high-end messaging system, and are, in effect, a significant competitive advantage for Exchange. See the discussion covering how the Information Store works beginning on page 249 for more detailed information.

- The Exchange Administrator (ADMIN.EXE) and System Attendant (MAD.EXE) programs provide system management facilities for an Exchange server. These can be broadly defined in activities such as creating new user accounts (mailboxes) that require manual intervention, and those that are carried out in the background, for instance the monitoring of connections between different servers. Manual tasks are performed with the Administrator program, but one of Exchange's most impressive features is the level of automated management carried out by the System Administrator.

- The Internet Mail Service (MSEXCIMC.EXE). Once separated from the standard Exchange kit, the Internet Mail Service has become a fundamental part of Exchange.

- The Internet News Service (EXCHINS.EXE) connects Exchange public folders to Internet news groups. The connection is bi-directional. Exchange is able to provide an outgoing feed from public folders to news groups as well as accepting incoming information.

All of these components run as multi-threaded Windows NT services executing their functions independently of each other. A service is basically a program that executes in the background, without direct user intervention. All of the Exchange services are managed like other standard Windows NT services, using the "Services" applet that can be invoked from the Control Panel. Other aspects of Exchange, such as the management of the contents of the Directory and Information Stores, are managed through the Exchange administration program.

In addition to the base services Exchange can make use of a number of optional components, not all of which will be operational on every server. These include the Directory Synchronizer, the Key Management server (to control message encryption and decryption), the Microsoft Mail connector, the Lotus cc:Mail connector, the Lotus

Notes connector, and so on. Third party gateways (called connectors in Exchange-speak), such as those that link Exchange to other messaging types like fax and voice mail complete the comprehensive functionality line-up.

Figure 1.1 *The basic structure of the Microsoft Exchange Server*

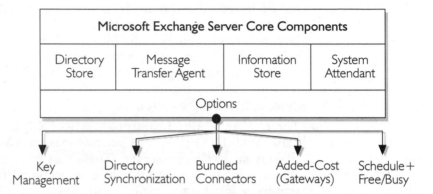

Clearly sites running existing mail systems will have to pay special attention to directory synchronization. Microsoft provides synchronization tools for Microsoft Mail systems, but, as we'll discuss later on, synchronizing with other sources of directory data is not accomplished as easily.

1.3.1   Packaging

Microsoft has adopted a building block approach for Exchange packaging to allow people to purchase only the parts of the server that they really need. An overview of the different packages available for Exchange Server are described in Table 1.1. Microsoft is a global company and local market conditions may dictate different packaging. For example, different packages exist for the academic market, and varying numbers (from 5 to 20) of client access licenses are also bundled with certain packages. Pricing also differs from country to country and special offers may be made available from time to time, particularly in regard to upgrades from previous versions of Exchange or competitor products. Contact your local Microsoft office or reseller for up-to-date information.

Over time Microsoft has greatly simplified the choice of editions. You can start off with the standard edition and remain with it unless you need an X.400 or IBM connector, or indeed wish to build large Information Stores. The enterprise edition is also required if you want to use Exchange in an NT cluster. Many corporate project teams opt to use the enterprise edition straightaway, if only because the enterprise edition is a very convenient way of getting all the base functionality required by large-scale deployments in a single package. Corporate deployments always seem to require some special items, so the enterprise edition doesn't hold the solution to all problems, but it's a great start.

Table 1.1   *The different packages available for Microsoft Exchange Server*

Package	Functionality
Microsoft Exchange Server V5.5, Standard Edition	Basic server package including all the components necessary to install a single server—public and Private Information Stores, Schedule+, directory service, the MTA, Microsoft Mail connector, Internet Mail Server, Lotus cc:Mail connector, Lotus Notes Connector, Site Connector, Active Server components, Key Management Server, Internet News Service, Electronic Forms Designer, the administration program, and the migration wizard. Outlook clients for Windows (16 and 32 bit) and Apple Macintosh are included.
Microsoft Exchange X.400 connector	The connector can be used to link Exchange sites together, or to connect to other X.400-compliant messaging systems.
Microsoft Exchange Server V5.5, Enterprise Edition	A package designed for corporate messaging deployments. All of the functionality included in the standard edition is included along with the X.400 connector, the IBM PROFS connector, and the IBM SNADS connector. In addition, the enterprise edition supports the unlimited store.

Remember that client access licenses are required before any client can connect to an Exchange server. Some of the packages include a number of client access licenses, but it's unlikely that there'll be enough for all the clients you want to operate.

1.3.2   Small Business Server

Exchange is full of functionality and able to connect to almost every other messaging system in use on the planet. Sometimes connectivity isn't required because all you need is a simple mail system. In these instances even the standard edition of Exchange is overkill, both in terms of its capabilities and the knowledge required to install and configure the server.

Microsoft's answer is the BackOffice Small Business Server (SBS), which includes Exchange. The code used in SBS is very different to other versions of Exchange. Its major advantage is the ease of configuration, where wizards are used to guide the installer through a number of simple setup screens that collect some basic information and then proceed to configure the server. Aside from easier installation, here are the major differences between "regular" Exchange and its SBS variant.

- SBS is based on the Exchange V5.0 code base. None of the enhancements in V5.5 are included.

- SBS is limited to 25 client connections. If you want to connect more clients you need to upgrade.

- SBS is installed as a single-server, single-site organization. It is able to communicate with other Exchange servers, but only via SMTP (a variant of the Internet Mail Service). Directory and public folder replication does not exist in the SBS world.

SBS is targeted at the small business that might have been running a single Microsoft Mail or Lotus cc:Mail post office. Given the restricted functionality, it is unlikely that SBS will often be encountered in corporate messaging circles.

1.3.3   New versions of Exchange on the horizon

The development of Exchange continues at a frantic pace. New versions of the server can be expected to appear at frequent intervals and the complete versions issued at these times are supplemented by the release of service packs (patch kits). At one stage Exchange V4.0 had a new service pack released every 90 days or so, but this pace has slowed down dramatically as the software matures. Some people get worried about service packs appearing at such a frequent interval, looking at this fact as evidence that the software is bug-ridden and unstable, and also worrying about how they can deploy updates to all the server computers that may be operating across their enterprises.

Such worries are understandable. The issue of how to plan for frequent software updates for servers is not something that can be swept underneath a carpet without some thought, and a plan to allow for cross-organization upgrades should be included in any plan for corporate implementations of Exchange. You don't have to install every service pack, but it may be necessary to install a specific service pack in order to move to a new version of Exchange in the future.

The requirement to upgrade may extend to Windows NT too. Exchange V5.5 is the first release to require systems to upgrade to NT V4.0—no accommodation exists for NT V3.51. Current directions publicly announced by Microsoft indicate that the next functionality release of Exchange (codenamed "Platinum") is tied to NT V5.0, so a further upgrade will be needed there. Indeed, because the next major version of Exchange is dependent on NT V5.0 it is fair to assume that Exchange V5.5 will have the longest lifetime of any version to date.

Exchange V4.0 was first available in March 1996, and is due to be formally retired (the date when support is no longer available) in September 1998, a 30-month lifespan. Based on this, Exchange V5.5, which shipped in November 1997, will be a fully supported version until at least April 2001.

You may agree or disagree with Microsoft's policy that requires you to install a service pack before upgrading to a new version, but I suggest that you accept this as a fact of life, part of the cost of doing business in this space, and move on. The more important thing to remember is to always carefully review the full list of bug fixes in each service pack to allow for an intelligent, informed decision as to whether it is good and wise to deploy an optional service pack to all servers. Remember that all the bug fixes have reference numbers that can be used to check against the Microsoft Knowledge Base (via the Web or TechNet CDs). The Knowledge Base includes a full description of each problem and the fix that was made. Reviewing a selection of the relevant articles will give you a flavor of the contents of the service pack.

I don't worry about the number of bug fixes that appear in service packs. All software has bugs. Anyone who tells you otherwise is either lying or has never engineered any large and complex software project. The fact that service packs (a collection of bug fixes that can be applied to a software product such as Exchange or Windows NT) appear at regular intervals tells you that Microsoft are serious about developing a quality product. At the end of the day Microsoft don't want to delay the availability of bug fixes to customers. A cynical view asks the question why didn't they test for or otherwise find these bugs in the first place, but some bugs just don't appear until they're put under the spotlight of production use within customer messaging environments. Some of the bugs found in the Internet Mail Service (largely fixed in service pack 2 for Exchange V4.0) are classic examples of how a component used across a wide variety of different production environments suddenly exhibits problems that need to be fixed. The fixes were made, the service pack issued, the product's quality improved.

Because of the intensely competitive nature of the e-mail market Microsoft need to come up with new product releases at regular intervals. Full product releases typically concentrate on a theme or central focus that addresses a particular segment of the overall e-mail market. Based on product delivery and plans announced to date I believe that three distinct themes can be seen in Exchange development.

- *Achieve market share* (Exchange V4.0): This version of Exchange focused on how to migrate the vast population of Microsoft Mail clients and post offices over to Exchange. The reason is simple—achieve market share and presence.

- *Embrace the Internet* (Exchange V5.0): Support for POP3 and web clients and the addition of key Internet protocols such as HTML, HTTP, and NNTP marked the start of a movement towards Internet protocols as the base for new functionality within Exchange. The Lotus cc:Mail connector made migration to Exchange much easier for cc:Mail installations.

- *Performance and Scalability* (Exchange V5.5): Technical advances such as clustering for Windows NT, removing the 16GB limit for the Information Store, and better support for multi-processor systems allow very large Exchange servers to be built. The theoretical vision of a 20,000+ user system demonstrated at trade shows becomes closer, especially as high-end processors such as the Pentium Pro and Alpha continue to crank out ever-increasing chip speeds.

- *Unification with Windows NT* (Exchange V.*next*). Using common services becomes a theme as Exchange seeks to take advantage of basic Windows NT features such as the Active Directory, Management Console, and Server-Side scripting (or Windows Scripting Host). Functionality from the Exchange-specific components are merged into the standard services and then dropped. The net result is an even tighter integration into Windows NT.

These themes represent my view of Microsoft's development strategy for Exchange. When Microsoft are asked to outline their strategy they break things down slightly differently. Brian Valentine, general manager of the Exchange development group, broke the development strategy for Exchange into four main areas as follows (1996 Exchange Deployment Conference):

- Architectural-level improvements
    - Continual enhancement of the level of reliability, scalability, and security provided by Exchange
    - Easing the load placed on system administrators for day to day operations, especially in small offices
- Compliance with standards
    - Build around native Internet protocols
    - Deliver native-format content to Internet systems

- Integrated groupware
  - Develop and deliver groupware and workflow based on native Internet standards
- Common development
  - Build and deploy e-forms and other applications based on Internet standards

The Exchange engineering team has lived up to these commitments since they were outlined in 1996, and the direction stated then still holds sway. Microsoft believe that one of Exchange's major strengths is its solid architecture, mostly because the architecture allows Exchange to expand and accommodate new protocols and standards as they become important within the messaging market. Over the past few years we've seen fluctuations in protocol popularity as X.400, SMTP/MIME and other standards find new supporters and detractors, and the situation is complicated by the appearance of new protocols such as POP3, IMAP4, SSL, HTML, and so on. Exchange has been designed and built from scratch to be a multi-standard server. Dual messaging protocols were used in V4.0 (the server is equally happy to talk to other messaging systems via either SMTP or X.400), expanded in V5.0 to bring in POP3, HTML, HTTP, and then taken on with IMAP4 in V5.5. The desire to incorporate new standards can be expected to continue, and Exchange is well poised to move forward precisely because of its solid architectural base.

Through its sheer burgeoning mass, the Internet exerts the most important current influence on messaging today. In essence, Exchange is Microsoft's Internet mail server. Look at the Microsoft statements about building on "native Internet protocols" or delivering "native Internet content" in Exchange and you'll get a good idea of how Microsoft view the future. The Internet is great, but a lot of the information presented or available within the Internet is relatively unstructured and difficult to find. Through the absorption and integration of Internet protocols Exchange is well positioned to become a provider of structured, well-organized information for Internet users. The ability to use a Web client to browse through the data held and managed on an Exchange server is a compelling example of how structured data can be provided to Internet users; the fact that the same data is available to many other clients just adds value.

1.3.4   Planning for change

In such a turbulent and fast-changing world it's important that you should plan for change. As explained above, Exchange will evolve, but you also need to include Windows NT in the equation. Exchange and Windows NT should really be viewed as single units that will become more tightly coupled as the years go by. At the end of the day the wise system planner factors in server software upgrades at least once a year and sets aside time, money, and personnel to review developments as they are delivered by Microsoft. Failure to do so could result in an organization not getting the advantages they seek from the Windows NT/Exchange combination. On the other hand, being too focused on upgrading may lead to problems that you definitely don't want to get into, such as the premature deployment of immature (even beta) software into the production environment. Look for a comfortable compromise between rushing in to install the latest and greatest code and getting behind the development curve.

1.4   Building an implementation plan for Exchange

Implementing a computer system is not always easy. Good implementations require a structure to build on, and Exchange is no different. Successful projects are built on a foundation established by a well-thought out implementation plan that breaks the essential tasks required to complete the implementation down into a number of important stages. An implementation plan is not a project plan because there's much more focus on design, making decisions that have a huge effect on the overall shape the project will take. Eventually the implementation plan serves as input into the project plan. At this stage the design decisions have been taken and documented and the project plan can break the individual sections of the implementation plan into the tasks and schedule that will lead to the deployment of Exchange servers and clients.

The essential elements of an implementation plan vary from company to company and installation to installation. For example, the choice made about the Windows NT domain model to use or the server hardware to install Exchange on may already have been decided and can't be changed, even if you know that things would flow a little more smoothly if just a little alteration was made. In all cases it's good to review the items that could feature in an implementation plan, just to make sure that everything is covered in your deployment.

Table 1.2 lists the major headings that I use within the implementation plans I write for Exchange.

As stated above, you don't have to use all of these headings. Use whatever makes sense in your situation, adding or subtracting headings as you see fit. Remember, you know more about your own requirements than anyone else!

Table 1.2   *Elements of an Exchange implementation plan*

Major heading	Sub-headings
Windows NT design	■ The domain model to use ■ Deployment of domain controllers ■ Deployment of other applications on NT servers where Exchange will be installed
Network infrastructure	■ Existing network traffic patterns and available bandwidth. ■ Impact of Exchange-related network load ■ Impact of other applications that may be introduced along with Exchange ■ Current implementation of the TCP/IP infrastructure, including DNS, DHCP, and WINS. ■ Predicted growth rate in network traffic over the next three years.
Exchange organization	■ Location of sites ■ Number of servers within sites ■ Workload allocated to servers ■ Allocation of users to servers
Server Hardware	■ Hardware platform for Exchange servers (Intel or RISC) ■ Impact of other applications such as SMS, SQL Server, or file and print services ■ Configuration details including RAID and UPS
Client desktop environment	■ Operating system ■ Other applications that will be run with Exchange ■ Choice of client software to connect to Exchange ■ Hardware platform, including any requirement to introduce new PCs or upgrade existing PCs.
Connectivity	■ Connections to other messaging systems, including the determination of the exact degree of interoperability (simple text or compound messages). ■ Directory synchronization with other messaging systems ■ Connections to other information sources such as NNTP, FAX, voice mail, or pagers.
Extensions	■ Third party add-ons ■ Electronic forms ■ Client extensions developed with MAPI

Table 1.2   *Elements of an Exchange implementation plan (continued)*

Major heading	Sub-headings
Operational procedures	■ Backup and Restore procedures ■ Disaster recovery plan ■ Allocation of privileges and permissions ■ Document retention policy, including the policy for the creation and maintenance of public folders. ■ Plan for distribution of software upgrades (new versions and service packs) to clients and servers. ■ Operation of Advanced Security, if desired ■ Virus checking for Exchange
Training	■ System administrators ■ System designers ■ Help Desk and support staff ■ Programmers ■ Users
Pilot systems to verify all aspects of the previous plans	■ More than 3 servers, using the same hardware platform as will be used in production. ■ Connected in more than one site ■ Using network infrastructure ■ Featuring range of client platforms ■ Including more than 50 users ■ Including all third party products and client extensions.

1.5   One-stop system management

Market analysts have rightly criticized PC LAN-based e-mail systems over the years for the high cost per seat associated with these systems. Once a decision is reached to move towards a client/server model there's not much that can be done about the cost of the PC hardware and software, including network cards and other items required to link a user into the corporate network. All of these costs are based on items that have largely moved into the commodity category and similar expense is incurred no matter which vendor's e-mail system is used.

While hardware and software costs have descended in real terms people costs have risen. Due to the number of parts contributing to the whole system and the complexities involved in connecting all the parts together PC LAN-based e-mail systems require more hands-on maintenance time per user than older mainframe or mini-based systems. A lot of time is spent in fire-fighting mode getting users' mail through rather than proactive preventative maintenance. Where two or three full-time people might administer a large centralized system serving a thousand users it is common to find the same number taking care of a hundred users. Even worse, valuable user time is absorbed doing work that they are not trained for, such as PC software installation or printer maintenance. Overall, it is the human factor that has contributed more than any other to the overall high cost per seat in the PC environment.

Exchange is designed to permit a single point of contact for system administrators for all components that might require management intervention through the Exchange administration program. All of the servers in a site can be managed from a single workstation, and each individual server can cope with far more users than a single older-style post office. Using a highly graphical, point-and-click interface for system administration is most appropriate when not too many items need to be displayed or manipulated. The Exchange administration program is wonderful for low-end or medium-sized systems, but information can be slow to find and then displayed in situations where there are, for example, thousands of mailbox entries in a single recipients container.

In much the same way just occasionally the graphical design limits the information about an item that can be viewed. For instance, when tracking a message it would be nice to be able to view more information about a selected message, but because the graphical interface is designed to show a particular set of data you can't. These comments are mild criticisms of the administration program, which is, in general, a very commendable step forward in messaging administration.

Some of the safeguards built into the graphical interface of the Exchange administration program can be circumvented by running the program in "raw mode". Raw mode is invoked by specifying the /R switch when ADMIN.EXE is started. Using raw mode is like playing around with explosives. If you know what you're doing and you take care there's a fair chance that you won't do any damage. On the other hand, you've got to remember that raw mode gives you direct control over the directory structures normally safeguarded by the graphical interface, and that if your finger slips when typing a command (or when responding to a prompt) it's entirely possible to wreak havoc. In this context havoc means causing enough internal damage to necessitate a complete restore of the Exchange Directory Store. Deleting a container or other important structure in the directory is a pretty good example of what I mean. Raw mode certainly isn't intended for day-to-day use.

Because its use carries such a high potential for accidents it cannot be recommended unless you proceed with great care.

1.5.1   Managing connections to other systems

The majority of corporate messaging systems are heterogeneous in nature. In other words, you don't have a single mail system deployed throughout the different departments, groups, and work teams that collectively form the enterprise. A lot of the reasons for this situation are historical. Different people installed different systems at different times, and the systems have become embedded into the body of the enterprise. Connecting all of the different systems is skilled work, and it's usually something that takes a reasonably high percentage of the available system administration effort.

Generally speaking, because a wide range of well-integrated off-the-shelf connectors is available for Exchange, it is relatively easy to link Exchange into corporate messaging environments. If you're upgrading from a DOS-based post office you'll find that the combination of Windows NT, Exchange, and the Exchange connectors deliver a far more stable, robust and powerful base for the messaging system than you had before. The net result is that less connectivity problems are encountered on a day to day basis, reducing the overall workload for the people who have to manage the e-mail system and releasing skilled people for more useful activities. Because the connections are up and running all the time users also benefit through the much more predictable and reliable nature of the service.

On the other side of the coin, those upgrading from mini- or mainframe e-mail systems will experience the same type of reliability in multi-system connectivity they probably enjoy today. In these cases the added value delivered by Exchange is ease of setup and maintenance. I have never experienced connectors that are quite so easy to install and configure as those that are integrated into Exchange or the optional connectors available as add-ons afterwards. Again, the net effect is to ease the load on system administrators. The data to back up these assertions of ease of use and maintenance is described in Chapter 7.

1.5.2   Software upgrades, patches, and service packs

Any step that contributes to high system availability and a consistent level of service is good. The advances in one-stop system management delivered in Exchange server will be welcomed by system administrators. But the nature of software technology and the demands of both users and the market mean that new hardware and software appear on a very regular basis. A system will therefore never be fixed in time and plans must be made to evolve the system in a planned manner in order that advantage can be taken of the advances and new technology. You can be sure that faster and more capable hardware will be available; new versions of Exchange server and clients will ship; and the desktop applications such as word processors and spreadsheets will evolve. Over a three-year period you can expect to see at least two new releases of Windows NT, Exchange server and clients, and the desktop applications. Will this new software feature in your plans? How will the new software be made available to users without undue disruption and while maintaining the advances in system reliability achieved through the deployment of Windows NT and Exchange?

A number of solutions to enable client software distribution are available today. Microsoft System Management Server (SMS) is the best known, probably due to the common membership in the BackOffice suite SMS shares with Exchange. SMS has been used to distribute and maintain client software in many large deployments and is effective providing that SMS itself is implemented correctly. In the future SMS is scheduled to be replaced by a base feature in Windows NT V5.0 called policy based management, part of Microsoft's initiative to reduce the total cost of ownership of Windows-based systems. However, this feature will only be viable when Windows NT V5.0 is deployed and can only deal with 32-bit desktops. SMS will continue to provide an answer for environments that remain with Windows NT V4.0 or need to accommodate 16-bit desktops.

Handling server upgrades is a problem that is easier in one respect (because there are less servers than client systems to be updated), but harder in another (because the effect of a bad upgrade is felt by multiple clients). The Microsoft Exchange developers appear resolute in their determination to make software updates quickly available to customers, and they are to be commended for the way that they provide fixes for software that has been obsoleted by new versions. Exchange V4.0 is scheduled to be retired in September 1998 and two complete new versions have appeared since V4.0 first appeared, yet Microsoft continues to support and fix the software, which is reassuring for customers who can't arrange for fast upgrades.

As shown in Table 1.3, three service packs[3] were issued fairly rapidly after Exchange V4.0 was released in 1996. At that time, presentations delivered at the 1996 Exchange Conference set the expectation

---

3.   A service pack is a collection of bug fixes, sometimes referred to in Microsoft-speak as the latest mature build of a product. Service packs are usually cumulative, but this is not always the case. In other words, if you install Service Pack 3 you are in fact installing all the fixes included in Service Packs 1 and 2. Look at the properties of a server to discover the build number and service pack level installed on that server. The operation must be repeated for each server within a site, and each site within an organization.

that service packs would be issued at roughly 90-day intervals. The delay in issuing service pack 4 for Exchange V4.0 can easily be explained. The engineering group was, after all, fully occupied getting Exchange V5.0 out the door.

Table 1.3   *Exchange Software version numbers*

Exchange Build Number	Meaning
837	Exchange V4.0 RTM ("Release to Manufacturing"), March 1996
838	Exchange V4.0 Service Pack 1, May 1996 (SP1)
993	Exchange V4.0 Service Pack 2, August 1996 (SP2)
994.64	Exchange V4.0 Service Pack 3, November 1996 (SP3)
995.54	Exchange V4.0 Service Pack 4, April 1997 (SP4)
996	Exchange V4.0 Service Pack 5, February 1998
1389.7	Exchange V5.0 Release Candidate 1[a], December 1996
1457.11	Exchange V5.0 RTM, February 1997
1458.48	Exchange V5.0 Service Pack 1, June 1997
1460.11	Exchange V5.0 Service Pack 2, February 1998
1461	Exchange V5.0 Service Pack 3, April 1998
1960.7	Exchange V5.5 RTM, November 1997
2100 (estimated)	Exchange V5.5 Service Pack 1, May 1998

a. You shouldn't run Release Candidate software in production after the release to manufacturing variant is available. Apart from anything else, you'll get very little sympathy from Microsoft support should anything go wrong.

As the Exchange code base matured the need to push out bug fixes has lessened. The release rate for V5.0 service packs was far less than V4.0. The first three service packs for V4.0 appeared in 8 months whereas the first 3 for V5.0 arrived in 14. The same, or a slightly slower rate, can probably be expected for V5.5. Even if service packs appear rarely, it is not an excuse to omit the time to review service packs regularly from an implementation plan. All software has bugs, so make sure that you have time set aside to review available service packs at a six-month interval.

1.5.3   Should I install a service pack?

Normally there's no great harm in installing a service pack quickly. After all, they contain fixes to problems that the Exchange developers have tracked down and rectified. Microsoft PSS representatives generally urge customers to apply any available service packs as the first step when a problem is detected. However, service packs do not get the benefit of the extensive external beta test program that most Microsoft products are subjected to, and bugs can lurk beneath the surface, ready to explode at the most inconvenient times. Two such situations have already occurred with the service packs issued for Exchange V4.0. Service Pack 2 included many important or even essential fixes for the MTA, but it introduced a problem with the Internet Mail Service. Service Pack 3 addressed many of the reported issues with the Internet Mail Service, but it introduced a bug that stopped some third party products working, such as Cheyenne's ArcServe backup utility. The problems in the service packs were addressed through quick fixes issued from Microsoft and made available through their FTP site[4], but the sheer fact that these bugs arrived through service packs made many system administrators uneasy.

The situation is compounded by the close inter-relationship between Exchange and Windows NT. Service packs are also issued for Windows NT, so what's the correct and safest combination of Windows NT, Exchange, and the various service packs? At the beginning we all knew that the answer was Windows NT V3.51 SP4 and Exchange V4.0, but as software evolves, bugs are found and fixed, and service packs appear, the waters get murkier and murkier.

Exchange V5.0 and V5.5 both use Windows NT V4.0 SP3 as their base platform (a number of hot fixes are required for clustered servers). A new version helps because a firm statement can be made as to what revision levels for Windows NT should be used. We can all start off again from Windows NT V4.0 SP3, but the merry-go-round recommences with the appearance of the first service pack afterwards for either Exchange or Windows NT. Life was certainly never meant to be easy, at least not for system administrators.

It's worth noting that Exchange V5.5 is the first version to require installations to move to a new version of NT (rather than a service pack).

---

4.   Ftp://ftp.microsoft.com/bussys/exchange/exchange-public/fixes is a good starting point for Exchange bug fixes released by Microsoft.

The need to upgrade from V3.51 to V4.0 may delay some deployments of Exchange V5.5. Fortunately the combination of Windows NT V4.0 and Exchange V5.5 offer bullet-proof protection against any Year 2000 problems, lifting an undoubted worry off the shoulders of some system administrators. Table 1.4 is my attempt to list the valid or recommended combinations of Windows NT and Exchange.

Table 1.4   *Valid combinations of Windows NT and Exchange Server*

Exchange →	V4.0	V4.0 SP1	V4.0 SP2	V4.0 SP3	V4.0 SP4	V5.0	V5.5
Windows NT V3.51 SP4	Base Platform	OK	OK	OK	OK	OK	Not supported
Windows NT V3.51 SP5	OK	OK	OK	OK	OK	OK	Not supported
Windows NT V4.0	Not supported	Not supported	OK	OK	OK	Not supported	Not supported
Windows NT V4.0 SP1	Not supported	Not supported	OK	OK	OK	Not supported	Not supported
Windows NT V4.0 SP2	Not supported	Not supported	OK	OK	OK	OK	Not supported
Windows NT V4.0 SP3	Not supported	Not supported	OK	OK	OK	Base Platform	Base Platform

Will the situation improve in the future? Some trends are emerging that will affect the attitude we take towards service packs. First, since mid-1997, Microsoft runs beta tests for service packs instead of rushing to issue code to anyone who cares to request it. This step has been forced on Microsoft by the debacle of Windows NT Service Pack 2, a collection of bug fixes that introduced some nice new bugs of its own. We should therefore expect that any future service pack has at least been through some degree of extensive testing in the field, albeit not to the same extent as with a full software release.

The second trend is more interesting. Issuing a new software release costs a lot of money (sources inside Microsoft put the cost around the $1 million mark). There is a constant pressure to keep software competitive by including new features, yet there is matching pressure not to force the pace of software development because some customers can't keep up. From an Exchange perspective its development group relies on Windows NT, yet exerts no real pressure on the Windows NT development group. Exchange is just another product for Windows NT, one that has to join the push forward to new releases like Windows NT V5.0. There is, however, a commitment for Exchange to support new releases of Windows NT very soon after those releases are provided to customers. If this wasn't done then Exchange would potentially be in the ludicrous position where it couldn't support a new release of Windows NT, but competing products could.

1.5.4   Is Exchange V5.5 SP1 a "Feature Pack"?

The next major release of Exchange is codenamed "Platinum", and is, according to Microsoft, dependent on Windows NT V5.0. There's no doubt that Platinum marks a major step in the evolutionary path, but it also delivers a dilemma for the Exchange developers. They must ensure that Exchange remains competitive and delivers features requested by customers, most of whom won't want to rush to deploy a brand new version of Windows NT.

One solution is to deliver new functionality in service packs, and indicate to customers that the service pack is optional. In other words, it doesn't contain any essential bug fixes. At the time of writing, based on early views of Exchange V5.5 SP1, this approach may well be the one that's been taken. Microsoft has delivered new functionality in service packs for both Windows NT and Exchange before. For example, the first Exchange clients for the Apple Macintosh appeared in Exchange V4.0 SP2.

Here are some of the features scheduled to be in Exchange V5.5 SP1. As always, things may change between the time I write this and the date when the actual code is delivered. However, the list shows that SP1 contains a number of interesting features. I have commented further on the different features in appropriate chapters:

- The User Interface is provided to control the "anti-spam" features built into Exchange V5.5.
- The Advanced Security subsystem uses X.509 V3 certificates issued by the Windows NT Certificate Server, and supports S/MIME encryption for messages and digital signatures.
- Message Archiving (also known as journalling) is introduced to help companies meet the requirements of authorities such as the US SEC.
- Alpha versions of the Lotus Notes, PROFS, and SNADS connectors.
- Outlook Web Access is updated to support access to the contacts folder, and be able to change a user's Windows NT password.

None of the new features are especially earth-shattering. You need to review the list and decide whether any justify the upgrade. Certainly, if you work in the financial industry and come under the authority of the SEC, message archiving might be an essential feature, but other companies, who are not compelled to keep copies of e-mail, will not rush to accept the performance hit that the feature requires.

1.5.5   Deploying new software

Many large companies that I work with have rules that prohibit the introduction of new software versions until they have been tested for between 60 to 90 days. Testing means that the software is installed on servers that are closely monitored. Ideally, the test servers replicate the production environment and should: have third-party products (like a backup product) installed, use all the different connectors, and include the spectrum of clients operated by users connected to the server. I recommend that the test environment be established as a site within the production Exchange environment, so that the test servers can fully participate with all the other (non-upgraded) servers.

It may seem dangerous to introduce a test site into the production environment, but this is the only real way to isolate and identify any potential interoperability problems that might otherwise show up when the first few live servers are upgraded. Keeping the test servers in a separate site isolates them and allows easy disconnection, if required, from the rest of the organization. A certain degree of control has to be exerted. For example, new connectors that will take over routing of messages for the rest of the organization to destinations like the Internet should not be installed on test servers; thousands of test entries should not be imported into the directory (and thereafter replicated around the organization), and so on. It is relatively easy to create a set of guidelines where the differing needs of the operations and planning staffs are met. Remember that any reasonably sized organization (more than 10 servers) will have to engage in rolling upgrades when the time comes to install new versions of Exchange or Windows NT. During the upgrade period a mixture of "old" and "new" servers will be in production. Creating and operating a test site within the production organization only brings the inevitable forward.

Usually it's only large companies that can afford the relative luxury of operating such a comprehensive test. But then again, it's a lot more serious to introduce a new bug via updated software to multiple, often geographically-dispersed servers, a scenario that is more relevant to large companies than their smaller counterparts.

Seeking to minimize the disruption of service levels delivered to users is definitely a good tactic for everyone to adopt. This means that you shouldn't try and upgrade at every opportunity. Instead, try and group upgrades together so that you don't have to intervene with the servers too often. Twice a year is more than enough. Remember, each time someone has to perform a software installation it will cost money.

People won't be able to use the systems so they'll be less productive, each server has to be manually upgraded, and the servers must be closely monitored immediately after the upgrade to make sure that everything works right. All of this activity can cost thousands of dollars, so it's wise to try and balance the need to be up to date with software revisions with the demands of the business to provide a cost-effective service.

The best advice I can give is:

- Keep in touch with the current software revision levels for Windows NT, Exchange, and any other product you use. The Microsoft Web site (www.microsoft.com/exchange) is updated with details of new service packs as soon as the packs are released.

- Review the contents of the service packs and make a decision whether you need to install the update. The README.TXT file normally lists the bugs that have been fixed and references an article in the Microsoft Knowledge Base for each bug. You can review the articles to discover more details about the bug fixes, if desired. It is difficult to realize the value of the patches from a quick browse through README.TXT, so be warned that it can take a considerable effort to research each Knowledge Base article and compare its contents against your experience of your own operating environment. This is work that should be done while the service pack is tested.

- Always test service packs before deploying them into production. Some people like to let others take any heat generated by bugs in service packs by waiting at least a month before upgrading anything. During this period monitor sources like the Internet mailing list for Exchange to see if anyone else has hit a problem.

- Upgrade all servers as quickly as possible after the decision is made to proceed. There's no point in having some servers running a different software version. All it does is make support more difficult.

- Take backups (of both Exchange and Windows NT) both before *and after* the upgrade is performed. The reason for taking a backup before any software upgrade is obvious; the reason for taking it afterwards is because it is entirely possible that the internal structures (or schemas) of the Directory and Information Stores may have been changed when the service pack was applied. Any attempt to restore a store using a backup taken before the upgrade may not succeed! There is no need to backup Windows NT after the software upgrade, unless you feel paranoid (or more secure if it's taken).

- Plan the upgrade. Make sure that users are aware that the systems may be unavailable for stated periods and that the help desk and other system administrators are understand why the upgrade is being performed.

Remember that installing a new server is only the start of a journey. Along the way you'll spend a lot of time and money keeping the server running. Your goal should be to expend minimum effort for maximum return.

1.5.6   Upgrading to Exchange V5.5

Upgrading a computer from either Exchange V4.0 or V5.0 to V5.5 is a relatively painless process. Like everything else to do with Windows NT and Exchange, proper planning is an absolute pre-requisite. Coming into work and suddenly deciding "it's a great day to upgrade a server" is not the right thing to do. New software must be tested to validate that it will work properly in your production environment in association with any specialized or third party software you operate.

Most system administrators have their own recipe for software upgrades. It's good to have a basic checklist to follow, so here's mine:

1.   The initial step is to select the first server within a site to upgrade. Because the directory is altered during the upgrade process you must perform the upgrade on the bridgehead server first. Note that there can be several bridgehead servers in a site, see page 510 for an explanation of the bridgehead concept. The preferred order for upgrades is: bridgehead servers, any other server that hosts a connector (like the Lotus cc:Mail connector), dedicated public folder servers, and finally, mailbox servers. Of course, if you only have one or two servers each of which supports a mixture of mailboxes, connectors, and public folders, you may not have the luxury of choice.

2.   Make sure that the computer is at the correct revision level of Windows NT by installing any service packs that are required (for example, service pack 3 for Windows NT V4.0). If upgrading from Windows NT V3.51 to V4.0 make sure that this is done first, and give the system at least a couple of days (weeks is more preferable) to stabilize before proceeding with the Exchange upgrade. Upgrade the Internet Information Server to the required revision level (V3.0 or above) if you're interested in supporting Web clients.

3.   Take a full backup of the Exchange Directory and Information Stores. Shut down the Exchange services afterwards and

then take a file-level backup of the Windows NT and Exchange directory structures. Windows NT is backed up to make sure that you can roll back to a set of system files and registry in the state before the upgrade occurred. The Exchange directory structure is copied for the same reason. Remember that Exchange files can be spread across a number of disks, so make sure that all relevant disks are copied to tape.

4.   Stop all applications and other services to ensure that the installation procedure can upgrade any files it needs to. Many applications now use MAPI in one way or another, and if they are active they will lock a file and prevent the upgrade proceeding. MAPI32.DLL is a good example of a file that is often locked by an active application.

5.   The Exchange databases (Public, Private, and Directory Stores) are converted to a new format during the V5.5 upgrade. It is possible that minor inconsistencies exist inside these files or that they have become inefficient in terms of their internal structures through use over an extended period of time. Running the EDBUTIL (to compact the databases) or the ISINTEG utilities (to check and repair inconsistencies) are strictly optional steps. The conversion process will proceed more quickly if the databases are compact, but the time taken to run EDBUTIL is often longer than any time saved during the installation.

6.   Install Exchange V5.5 using the normal setup program. To avoid contention with files moved onto the system during the installation, make sure that all mail-enabled programs and services (anything that might possibly use MAPI) are stopped before beginning the upgrade. Everything happens quite quickly—a Pentium 166 MHz system with a 1GB Information Store is usually upgraded from V5.0 in under an hour. The larger the Information Stores the slower the upgrade will be, and upgrades from Exchange V4.0 take roughly twice as long as from V5.0 because the databases are converted twice (to V5.0 format and then to V5.5). Updating the stores is often the longest part of the upgrade procedure, and the time required depends on the speed of the CPU and disk I/O subsystem on any particular computer. Large servers that support stores greater than a few megabytes may take a couple of hours to get through the store upgrade phase.

7.   If the system runs the Exchange Key Management Server component it must be upgraded using its separate installation program.

8.   Test the server by connecting a client to it and verifying that
     everything works. Because a standard mechanism (RPC) is
     used to connect MAPI clients to Exchange, any Exchange or
     Outlook client is quite happy to connect to an Exchange V5.5
     server. Conversely, newer Outlook or Exchange clients are
     able to connect to an Exchange V4.0 or V5.0 server.

9.   Notify users that the server is back on the air and available for
     use. Ideally the users should receive some information about
     the server's new capabilities if they are interested in items
     such as newsfeeds, Web access, or POP3/IMAP4 clients.

10. Upgrade any client install share points with Exchange V5.5
     client installation kits (for Outlook V8.03 or Outlook 98).
     Notify the personnel assigned to perform client upgrades that
     the install points are available.

Reports exist that some third party extensions which add email
addresses to the directory can cause an upgrade to fail because the
upgrade process is unable to create new objects with the third-party
address. In most instances the problem has occurred with FAX connectors, so if you operate a FAX connector that adds addresses to the
directory, install it on a test system and attempt an upgrade. One
workaround is to temporarily disable all third-party email address
generation before the upgrade commences by clearing the check box
for each address type in the Site Addressing property page for the Site
Configuration object.

After an Exchange V5.5 server is introduced into a site, either as a
new server or as the result of an upgrade, special procedures (provided
as part of the Exchange V5.5 kit) must be followed if a decision is
made to create a new server running Exchange V4.0. I must say that I
cannot see the point of installing Exchange V4.0 software on a new
server in a site where an Exchange V5.5 server is already active. It
seems better to me to use the new version of Exchange everywhere
once you've begun using it. Once an Exchange V5.5 server is operational within a site let it settle in and allow the new directory schema
to replicate to the other servers before you upgrade the next server in
the site. There is no good reason to rush to upgrade servers one after
the other unless you want to set a new speed record for upgrades.

Servers upgraded to V5.5 correspond quite happily with older
counterparts. Because all communications between servers in a site are
accomplished through RPCs it is valid to upgrade only one server to
V5.5 and keep all other at V4.0 or V5.0. For example, you might decide
to upgrade the server that supports the X.400 and Internet connectors
in a site, but leave the servers that just provide messaging (private fold-

ers). Another valid reason is a wish to introduce the new Lotus Notes connector into a new server within a site. Finally, sites distributed across large geographic areas inevitably need time to arrange the basic logistics of an upgrade and it would be impossible not to envisage a situation where you'd want to perform a rolling upgrade. In a similar vein, because communications between sites can be made by RPCs or SMTP or X.400 messages there is no requirement (apart from Microsoft's desire to have everyone run the very latest software) to uplift all servers to V5.5 in the shortest possible time.

1.5.7   Do clients need to be updated too?

Planning to upgrade a set of servers, even when there are 50 or more to do and they're spread across a large number of different countries, is a project that shouldn't cause too many problems. It's a totally different manner to plan the upgrade of several thousand clients, especially when the upgrade issue wasn't considered too carefully when the clients were first deployed.

If client software is accessed from a shared file service then the upgrade is straightforward. The file service is upgraded and everyone proceeds to work, perhaps not even noticing the new options available to Outlook V8.03 or Outlook 98 clients. On the other hand, if temptation has won out and client software is cheerfully spread across the hard disks of hundreds or thousands of individual PCs, the upgrade challenge takes on a new dimension. Just how will you arrange to visit all the PCs? How long will it take to upgrade each client? Does anything else have to be upgraded at the same time? Are all the PCs physically available? Who takes care of notebook PCs—their owners or the PC support team? How will the new client software be distributed to everyone who needs it?

Given the challenge, and the cost involved in rolling out new client software to lots of PCs, the question "do the clients really have to be upgraded to use the new version of Exchange?" must be asked. The first thing to understand is that aside from the POP3, IMAP4 and Web clients, Exchange clients communicate with the server using RPCs. The RPC mechanism between clients and servers is not changed, so it is totally feasible to connect the very oldest MAPI client (Exchange V4.0) client to an Exchange V5.5 server, or the very latest Outlook 98 client to an Exchange V4.0 server. Basic messaging functionality will work, but (very logically) any new feature supported by the Exchange V5.5 server cannot be used by older clients. This fact is brutally obvious, and is included here for the sake of completeness.

In practice running a slightly outdated client isn't very harmful and I think that it's perfectly acceptable to consider running with a mixture of older clients and Exchange V5.5 for a couple of months after the Exchange V5.5 server is installed. Deleted items recovery is a new feature in Exchange V5.5 and is designed to allow users to recover items deleted in error without the need to bother system administrators. If you don't upgrade clients administrators will have to recover deleted items by logging on to user mailboxes with an Outlook V8.03 or 98 client, something that can rapidly become a very boring activity. Deleted items recovery is so important that I recommend that you consider client upgrades more quickly than you might otherwise.

Microsoft, of course, would prefer you to upgrade because it's easier for them to support the latest version of any software. If you experience problems with clients and contact Microsoft support you'll probably be told that you must upgrade before they can help you, so at this stage you can proceed to upgrade any client affected by the problem (bug) that you've found.

Operating a production environment composed of a mismatch of client/server versions isn't a recommended strategy. It is far better to bite the bullet and take whatever steps are necessary to ensure that you can deploy new client software easily and quickly. As we've seen with the server, new versions and service packs appear all the time, so it is a wise investment to install the infrastructure, such as SMS, to support automated client upgrades.

1.5.8   International versions

Although this book is written in English it is an undeniable fact that Exchange is a popular e-mail server throughout the world. Following the success of the international versions of Windows 95 and Windows NT, Exchange and its clients are available in a number of different languages. You can connect a client running in any language to a server running in another language. User communities can operate clients in multiple languages and connect to a server running in another language. The sole issue is whether or not clients can read the content of messages created in different languages.

For example, if you create a message using the Greek client, can it be read with the German client, or the Japanese client, or even the Russian client? Or, as shown in Figure 1.2, can messages generated with the standard (US English) Outlook client be read after they've been transferred across to a server that's running the Japanese editions of both Windows NT and Exchange. The fact that Windows NT uses Unicode to store characters guarantees that message content and other data can be transferred and recognized by servers running different language editions, so problems only tend to occur at the client end.

Figure 1.2
Interoperability. A Japanese Outlook client reads an English language message

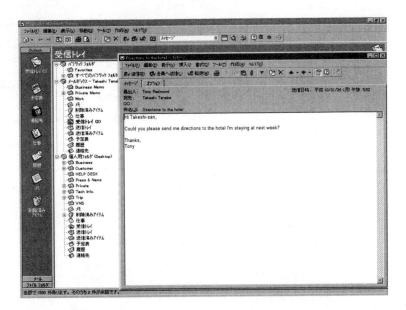

Interoperability across international versions is not an issue specific to Exchange. Instead, it is all to do with the code pages installed on client computers. People running computers in Greece use a different code page to represent and display the Greek character set to that used for the Russian character set. If you receive a message that has been composed in Greek and attempt to read it without loading the Greek character set you probably won't make very much sense of what you see. The rule is, if you expect to read messages composed in a particular character set, make sure that the relevant code page is installed on your PC.

The English-language server CD includes software for many different language clients, while the French, German, and Japanese servers offer a more restricted choice. The range of client languages outlined in Table 1.5 is not definitive. It merely represents language availability at the time of writing. Check with your local Microsoft office for the current situation.

Table 1.5   *International availbility of Exchange Server and Outlook clients*

	Exchange Server V5.5	**Outlook 8.03 client**
English[a]	🖴	🖴
French	🖴	🖴
German	🖴	🖴
Japanese	🖴	🖴

Table 1.5   *International availbility of Exchange Server and Outlook clients (continued)*

	Exchange Server V5.5	Outlook 8.03 client
Spanish		▣
Swedish		▣
Italian		▣
Dutch		▣
Portuguese		▣
Brazilian		▣
Korean		▣
Traditional Chinese		▣
Simplified Chinese		▣
Norwegian		▣
Danish		▣
Finnish		▣
Czech		▣
Hungarian		▣
Polish		▣
Russian		▣
Greek		▣
Turkish		▣

a. English language versions are available in "International" and "US & Canada" editions. The difference is the type of encryption technology bundled into the client.

1.6   Is Exchange just email or is it groupware?

"Groupware" is a strange term, which means very different things to different people, but it's basically all about helping groups of people to work together in more intelligent ways. In terms of application software groupware is very different to electronic mail because the focus tends to be more on widening information sharing rather than the often purely singular interchange involved in the sending and receipt of an electronic mail message.

Software vendors vary in their definitions of just what groupware is exactly. Much depends on the aspect of groupware that their products excel in. Microsoft's edge in messaging leads to an assertion that electronic mail is the most important groupware application, with electronic forms and good interpersonal scheduling close afterwards. Lotus, on the other hand, considers information sharing and bespoke application development to be at least as important as electronic mail. Both can be right, because each customer situation poses different requirements. I think groupware can be broken down into a number of discrete areas of functionality or user requirements as described in Table 1.6 below. For each area I've indicated my view on whether Exchange provides a solution to the requirement.

Table 1.6   *Exchange groupware capabilities*

Groupware applications		Exchange capabilities
Interpersonal messaging	Used by almost everyone in an organization. Can be thought of as one to one communications.	Very strong, the basic function of an Exchange server.
Structured document repository (file cabinet)	Location available to applications to store objects. Usually accessible from multiple client applications and often network-enabled, allowing access to documents from points distributed across a WAN.	Medium, based on mixture of public and private folders.
Bulletin boards	Used to make relatively static information from central sources that are available to users on a read-only basis. Can be thought of as one to many communications.	Strong, using read-only public folders.
Workflow/ electronic forms	Structured form of messaging where "intelligent" items are routed from user to user, following rules that determine the processing steps taken at each stage.	Medium. Electronic forms do not provide the type of comprehensive workflow functionality available in workflow-specific applications, but the advent of the Event Service in V5.5 offers increased potential. See note on Exchange and workflow.
Interactive conferencing	Many to many communication where users have the ability to post their ideas in electronic forums.	Strong, using writeable public folders or NNTP.

Table 1.6   *Exchange groupware capabilities (continued)*

Groupware applications		Exchange capabilities
Time management/ scheduling	Applications that allow users to schedule meetings and appointments with each other. Often includes requests to schedule fixed items such as conference rooms, projectors, or white boards. Electronic mail is commonly used to transport meeting requests between users or across a network.	Strong (Schedule+ or Outlook calendaring)

Remember that the assessments offered in Table 1.6 are mine, and you will probably have different views on the subject. From the table you can see that Exchange offers a great deal of potential in most areas of groupware. The weakest area for Exchange is unquestionably workflow processing, and this is where competing products will no doubt stress their own capabilities. In rebuttal there are many third-party software developers who are able to provide more sophisticated workflow solutions that can be integrated into Exchange.

1.6.1   Exchange electronic forms

If Exchange is primarily a mail server, albeit one that includes notable attributes like an X.400-compliant MTA, would there be any reasons to consider Exchange to be an advance on the previous Microsoft messaging system? Of course, the answer is yes, mostly because Exchange is far more reliable and scaleable than any Microsoft Mail post office, but perhaps a more compelling reason is rooted in its groupware capabilities. Exchange V5.5 scales new heights though its support of a wide array of new clients and protocols, moving even further away from the "just a mail server" label.

In any demonstration of Exchange you're bound to run into electronic forms somewhere along the line. Electronic forms are positioned as the way to accomplish groupware applications, capable of meeting many different needs. Groupware applications fall into many categories. Some groupware applications use intelligent document routing functionality enabled by a messaging infrastructure to move business documents around an organization. Exchange certainly has the messaging infrastructure and can move documents around, but its workflow capabilities are limited in comparison to specialized workflow products (see page 36). Other groupware applications focus on collaborative working, functionality enabling people to share information in a more developed and intuitive manner than they can through the simple exchange of mail messages. Lotus Notes has built a huge market around replicated document-oriented databases that allow easy sharing, and its market share has established Lotus Notes as the de facto groupware standard in many people's eyes.

Exchange approaches groupware from a messaging perspective rather than building applications around document databases. Public folders provide the foundation for Exchange's groupware functionality. These are repositories whose contents can be automatically replicated to "replicas" located on other Exchange sites. Exchange servers sharing a common location (a site in Exchange terminology, with the caveat that a site can expand over a wide geographical area as long as the requisite network bandwidth is available) share public folders. A user connecting to any server within a site can look at the same set of public folders, access controls permitting, of course.

Public folders can store any type of object. Electronic forms are an intelligent form of object, which contain code that can be executed when users access the forms. A set of sample forms applications is provided with Exchange to form a toolkit that can be drawn upon by programmers to develop site-specific applications. The toolkit contains commonly required applications such as electronic conferences, bulletin boards, and a range of intelligent forms like travel requests.

Originally, Exchange electronic forms were based around a utility called the Electronic Forms Designer (EFD), a variant of Visual Basic. The forms produced were slow and couldn't be used on some platforms. HTML has solved the platform issue and the introduction of the Exchange Event service, which allows code to be associated with folders and then be automatically invoked when specific events occur in a folder offers a great deal of potential for groupware applications to be built in the future.

1.6.2   Client and Server Extensions

Visual Basic or Vbscript can be used for many things, but not perhaps for heavy-duty or time-critical applications. Exchange addresses this requirement through the MAPI interface which can be used with Visual C++ to build client or server extensions for Exchange.

Client extensions add menu options or command buttons to the interface, and provide the code behind the interface. Third party products, like Fulcrum Find!, a text search and retrieval package, usually have to build client extensions to integrate their code with Exchange clients. Server extensions perform background processing, for example, to gather statistics or perform maintenance operations on mailboxes. The Exchange Resource Kit includes examples of both client and server extensions, albeit without the actual source code. You'll have to buy a book such as "Inside MAPI[5]" for detailed explanations of how to approach MAPI development and see some solid examples of source code that can be loaded directly into Visual C++.

Microsoft themselves are busy seeking opportunities to add value to Exchange and create the utmost degree of synergy by weaving Exchange into the fabric of as many applications as possible. One obvious example is to mail-enable the Microsoft desktop "Office" applications like Word for Windows and Excel. Another is the integration between the Microsoft Internet Explorer and Exchange. The setup wizard for the Internet Explorer is able to install "Internet Mail" as a valid MAPI service provider.

Outside Microsoft a wide range of Independent Software Vendors (ISVs) are engaged in the task of writing extensions for Exchange. Quite logically, most extensions focus on the concept of the Universal Inbox, extending its capabilities to accommodate technologies other than electronic mail.

1.6.3   Exchange and workflow

It's possible to implement simple workflow with electronic forms, but not to accomplish the more complex and complicated routing steps that are usually associated with workflow applications. These routing steps include parallel and serial routing, joins and splits, quorum voting, intelligent decision points and branching, and other features.

Microsoft announced a plan to add workflow capabilities to Exchange in April 1996 with the unveiling of MAPI-Workflow Framework (MAPI-WF), engineered in conjunction with Wang Computers. Documentation and sample code appeared during 1996 but MAPI-WF has still not yet been included in shipping releases of Exchange at the time of writing. Software has a habit of bypassing initiatives with new developments, and the advent of some basic routing features in the Collaborative Data Objects library makes me wonder whether MAPI-WF will ever appear.

MAPI-WF is a Microsoft-centric extension to an API. Since its announcement, Internet protocols have exerted a lot of influence over the Exchange V5.0 and V5.5 releases. The Internet Engineering Task Force is working on extensions to the MIME standard to allow workflow and other data to be carried around in MIME-encoded documents. There's a lot of value in this approach because MIME is a stan-

---

5.   Authored by De Cruz/Thayer. Published by Microsoft Press (1996).

dard that isn't owned by any one company. Thus, there is every chance that many different companies will support the MIME workflow extensions in their mail servers, allowing workflow applications to flow between different mail servers.

Paper business documents have never been really threatened by electronic versions. Up to this point in time there has never been a generally agreed standard for workflow or the intelligent exchange of application data, so if you wanted to create workflow applications within an enterprise everyone who participated in workflow cycles had to use the same mail server. The closest to an agreed standard so far is EDI, but it favors highly structured documents such as purchase orders and isn't really appropriate to build rather less structured documents like vacation requests. In a heterogeneous messaging environment where departments quite often selected and deployed their own choice of mail server it is still impossible to implement workflow applications and their popularity decreased after the initial flush of enthusiasm. The only people who have really succeeded with workflow were those who succeeded in creating largely homogeneous environments, with just one mail server deployed everywhere. Not many large companies are in this category.

Microsoft's current vision for workflow within Exchange is embodied in Exchange Routing Objects, first shipped as part of Exchange V5.5 SP1. Routing Objects are an extension of Collaborative Data Objects. The Event Service (see chapter 12) and public folders are used to process workflow code and provide a repository for workflow items respectively. It's still early days for Routing Objects, so it's difficult to know where the boundaries of workflow applications built with them lie. The first release is very email-centric, in that the different stages within a workflow cycle are accomplished through email messages sent to and from the routing engine. In itself, email routing applications are enough to satisfy the vast majority of simple routing requirements found in typical office environments, and from a competitive perspective, the advent of Routing Objects is enough for Microsoft to claim that Exchange offers the same type of out-of-the-box workflow capability as Lotus Notes.

Companies that need advanced workflow solutions must consider third party products like KeyFile, JetForm, Eastman Software, Staffware, and the DIGITAL Work Expeditor workflow product. All of these products are integrated (albeit to varying degrees) with Exchange, so it is totally possible to create full-featured workflow applications for Exchange today. Most of the third party workflow products support other mail systems so it is even feasible to meet the challenge of heterogeneous messaging environments.

I.7   Integration with other Microsoft products

There are several different office product suites available for Windows. If you select Exchange as the basis for your messaging system does it matter if you choose a word processing, spreadsheet, or presentation graphics application, or an integrated suite from another vendor?

All the current releases of desktop applications from the major vendors such as Lotus and Corel/WordPerfect support the major aspects of Windows integration such as OLE. On the conceptual level there should be no difficulties attaching files generated by common Windows applications such as Lotus 1-2-3 or WordPerfect to messages created by an Exchange client, or storing similar files in public folders for replication throughout an Exchange organization.

However, while things may work on a purely practical level it's safe to assume that Microsoft desktop applications will enable a more complete degree of integration. For instance, look at ability to use Word for Windows as the message creation editor for the Windows 95 Exchange client. You'll need Word for Windows (but only from Office 95[6] onwards) before "WordMail" is possible, but it's a nice example of how you can take a standard word processing editor and utilize it for as many tasks as possible, including message composition. The integration isn't perfect and users need to be aware that some of the advanced features of the Word editor are stripped out when the message text is saved or sent.

This is because all messages are sent in Rich Text Format (RTF) to assure that any client can read the content. I've forgotten that the conversion will happen at times and let myself send messages that are badly formatted, leading the recipients to wonder whether I was drunk when I composed the text. It's all too easy to insert a table into a message, input all the data, and then find that the content is "rearranged" when the table is converted to simple text when the message is sent. In line with developments in other Microsoft office applications, the message editor in future clients will probably use HTML instead of RTF as the basic storage format. In fact, this evolution has already started, because Outlook 98 allows users to select HTML as their editor of choice. I've been using HTML in this way for a couple of months now, and the changeover is largely transparent. HTML is, of course, much more capable of transmitting complex formatting instructions than RTF, and when this happens the problem I've referred to

---

6.   You need a patch for Office 95 to upgrade it to Office 95a before some of the advanced features such as "Post to Exchange folder" from Word or Excel work properly.

will go away. In a purely practical sense it's more important to consider whether your PC is capable of invoking Word for Windows every time you want to create a new message. Word, after all, is quite a heavy-duty application.

Sites that use versions prior to Office 97 must be content with the standard message creation editor. The standard editor is perfectly capable in its own way but lacks the extended range of features available to a full-function word processor like Word.

Other features that can be gained from a purely Microsoft desktop environment include the ability to use a personal address book as the source for mail merge operations carried out by Word for Windows. The Outlook contacts folder can also be used. Applications can also use MAPI functions to post documents or worksheets directly into a public or private folder. It's difficult to see other applications creating an integration with Exchange that goes to the length of accommodating address books for mail merges, but it should be possible to build code to bridge the gap between an application and Exchange folders. MAPI is, after all, a publicly documented interface.

Exchange extracts and displays OLE properties from objects created by OLE-compliant applications when those objects are imported into Exchange. For instance, the author, title and summary information for an Excel worksheet are stored as OLE properties, so if a worksheet is dragged from the DOS file system and dropped into an Exchange folder, the user is not prompted for a title as it's extracted automatically. Of course, this magic is only viable if users care to fill in the information held as OLE properties. The feature is not restricted to Microsoft applications either, as any application is able to support OLE if they desire. However, it's fair to say that the most complete implementation of OLE across a complete suite of applications is found in the Microsoft Office suite.

If you are going to switch to a purely Microsoft desktop environment it may be best to do so in conjunction with a change to the desktop operating system as this will concentrate all the changes in a single operation. Switching to the latest version of Windows and the Microsoft Office suite at the same time is something that many corporate installations are considering today, but remember that such a changeover may have other impacts like hardware upgrades.

At the end of the day the decision about which desktop applications are going to be used depend on many factors, including some historical aspects and how the people who actually use the applications feel about things. An attempt to change someone's word processor or spreadsheet can be taken as a personal insult, especially if people have accumulated personal libraries of useful macros or other shortcuts. The retraining requirement plus the cost of switching applications, no matter how tempting the trade-in offers seem, are other points to bear in mind.

1.8   Exchange and the Internet

The Internet has been around for years, but over the past few years there has been an explosive growth in interest from both the computing and non-computing communities in the potential possible from a global information highway. The establishment of the World Wide Web (WWW) and easy availability of WWW browsers such as Netscape, Mosaic, and Microsoft's Internet Explorer has brought the power of distributed computing home to many people. The ease by which anyone with an Internet presence can make information available to others by establishing a WWW site is stunning when considered against the problems that the same exercise would have met a few short years ago. Look at the number of newspaper and magazine advertisements published today that include URLs[7] for Web sites. If you pick up a magazine from 1995 or before you'd perhaps find one or two examples. Now URLs are everywhere, despite their technical and non-user friendly nature.

Another interesting aspect to consider is the influence that Internet-evolved standards are having within corporate computing networks. Once the focus was on using functionality like the World Wide Web or TCP/IP as a basis for presenting a corporate external face to the world, but now there's more and more use of technology from the Internet within internal networks to form the Intranets[8]. Developments such as secure tunneling (the ability to make a direct connection from the Internet through a firewall to an internal network via an encrypted communication channel) meld the Internet with Intranets to present what's apparently a single seamless network to users. Indeed, the real growth over the next few years are likely not to be in the Internet itself, but rather in the development and deployment of Internet-originated technologies within corporations as people move towards a more distributed way of working.

---

7.   URL = Universal Resource Locator, a network pointer to a page on a Web site. Enterprises commonly publish the URL for their "home page", the entry point to their Web site. For example, Http://www.digital.com is the URL pointing to the home page for Digital Equipment Corporation.

8.   An Intranet is a network built from Internet-type components (World Wide Web, TCP/IP networks, etc.) but which operates purely within the boundaries of a single company or enterprise.

In terms of electronic mail it's a sobering thought that the numbers of people equipped with Internet mail accounts may already have passed or will soon pass the number of mail accounts operating in corporate systems[9]. The Internet has truly delivered e-mail to the masses. Metcalfe's Law, part of the lore of the computer industry and named after Bob Metcalfe, the inventor of the Ethernet networking protocol and founder of 3Com Corporation, states that the power of a network increases with the square of the nodes installed in the network. In other words, as PCs are added to a network people have more and more opportunity to share information using those PCs via e-mail, the Web, traditional file and print services, and other mechanisms. All of this means that the available network bandwidth had better increase in line with the extra nodes else the performance delivered to users will steadily degrade over time. This fact is as true for private networks as it is for the Internet.

Some observers of computing trends have pointed to the evolution of WWW browsers to include e-mail functionality and asked whether a compelling case exists for enterprises to consider jettisoning their messaging and information distribution infrastructures in favor of a move to an Internet-based solution. Cost is a major reason for such a move even being considered. Comparing the cost of Internet connections together with WWW software versus the costs of installing and operating networks, servers, and clients internally appears to make a great case for a move to do business on the Internet because, generally speaking, everything can be done much more cheaply. Today the degree of functionality available in Internet-centric e-mail systems is lower than a fully-fledged system such as Exchange. These systems will never be as functional as long as they are based on protocols such as POP/3, where clients pull messages down from the server for local processing. These systems work, but only as long as you are content to use the same PC all the time and never want to move from PC to PC within an organization. IMAP4, a more developed version of an Internet client/server messaging protocol, delivers more functionality than POP3, but still not as much as a system based on proprietary standards, like Exchange or Lotus Notes.

The promise of low-cost connectivity seems compelling but while the costs involved in connecting a single individual to the Internet are cheap, the costs of achieving consistent, secure, and reliable messaging across the Internet for hundreds or thousands of people aren't necessarily so low. The costs of scaling a system up for thousands of users

---

9.   "Electronic Mail and Message Systems" (April 29, 1996) reports 47,260,000 LAN-based mailboxes and 30,810 host-based mailboxes installed as at March 31, 1996.

increase dramatically if a high value is placed on system availability, data security, and 100% guaranteed message delivery. Internet messaging tools exist, but other applications like scheduling, workflow, and collaborative authoring don't. The Internet already creaks and groans (in an electronic sense) during heavy processing periods, chiefly when the working hours for people on the east and west coasts of the United States overlap. Perhaps moving to a structure that's already having problems handling the load isn't such a wise move for a corporation?

Even if a general move isn't going to be made to use the Internet as a corporate infrastructure the desire still exists within corporations to achieve whatever leverage is possible from the resources available within the Internet. Seeking to create close links between the information held in internal systems and the information available externally (subject always to the installation of a good firewall to prevent unauthorized access) is a good strategy to take.

1.8.1   How Exchange supports the Internet

Exchange is a good Internet citizen. By this I mean that Exchange V5.5 supports all of the most common Internet protocols for messaging, directory, and data access. Look at the list of the ways Exchange can interact with the Internet:

- POP3 and IMAP4 mail clients are able to connect to an Exchange server and use Exchange to send and receive messages.

- Any Web browser that supports frames and Vbscript or Java-Script can connect to Exchange and use even more of the server's functionality. Where POP3 clients are interested in a very simple exchange of messages, Web clients can send and receive mail, browse any folder in a mailbox, access public folders, and look peoples' names up in the Exchange directory. Anonymous access to public folders is also supported, so Exchange can act as a repository for documents published to external people. These features are enabled through the support of the HTML and HTTP protocols, JavaScript and Microsoft's own ActiveX technology. LDAP is supported for directory access.

- The SSL (Secure Sockets Layer) protocol is supported to allow Web clients to log-on to Exchange in an encrypted manner.

- The Internet Mail Service (connector) is a highly capable SMTP mail server that supports all the important protocols required to send messages to Internet recipients—SMTP, MIME, UUEN-CODE, and BINHEX.

- The NNTP (Network News Transport Protocol) protocol is used to allow Exchange users to read the content of Internet news-groups through public folders. Automatic feeds come in from

NNTP to public folders, relieving the necessity for multiple people within a company to subscribe to and track newsgroups, thus making better use of valuable network connections.

Details of how the various protocols are implemented in Exchange are distributed throughout this book, with chapter 2 containing most information. All of this goes to prove that you should have no doubt in the capabilities of Exchange to play a full role within a company Intranet or the general Internet. The server is certainly as capable as anything else that is available today, and it scores highly on usability to create a combination that is a compelling solution for many people. Of course, Exchange will never be regarded as a "true" Internet server because it runs on Windows NT and not UNIX (a totally facetious view is that a server must be able to awk, grep, and ls with the best to score 100% as an Internet citizen). From a practical and pragmatic view Exchange delivers everything most people want in an Internet mail and information server.

Introducing so many new protocols in a single release is certainly accompanied by a degree of risk. The engineering team must now focus effort across multiple protocols and sources of data, many of which they have no control over. Dealing with independently defined (open) protocols is both a joy and hardship for companies like Microsoft, and I expect that some of the new Internet components in Exchange will need time to become as robust as other parts of the server. If we look at other core components like the MTA, the store, and the Internet Mail Service, experience with earlier versions of Exchange shows that problems were detected as soon as people put Exchange into real-life production environments. This is inevitable for any product that is used on a global basis in thousands of different companies, and Microsoft moved quickly to fix the problems, albeit with multiple service packs. Nevertheless the fact remains that the problems were addressed and the core components are now very solid. The same profile can be expected for the new Internet components.

Above all, the comprehensive support of Internet protocols within Exchange is a great pointer to the future. MAPI will continue to be the essential foundation for Exchange, at least for the foreseeable future, but Internet protocols are now a pervasive part of the server and possibly the most important piece of the client jigsaw. Internet protocols will prosper inside Exchange and anyone interested in this product needs to become fully conversant with HTTP, HTML, POP3, IMAP4, NNTP, SMTP, MIME, and so on.

1.9   Challenges for Microsoft Exchange server

Every new software product that arrives on the technology scene faces challenges that must be overcome before the software is deemed to be successful. Some of the challenges are inherited from the environment the software is deployed into; others arise from people who work with the software or in the links to other products established by APIs or network connections. Exchange is not built with magic, nor can the server perform tricks. Along with its own set of challenges the eventual success of Exchange is influenced by many of the same challenges that face other messaging products. This section outlines, in fairly broad strokes, the most important challenges. Details of how you might face those challenges and how to be successful in your implementation follows in later chapters.

1.9.1   The Microsoft legacy

When Exchange V4.0 first shipped the immediately obvious obstacle in the way of success for the product was the fact that Microsoft has no history in the design and implementation of enterprise-level messaging systems. In fact, Exchange can be described as the first family of e-mail products that Microsoft has engineered from scratch. The previous generation of e-mail clients, post offices, and connectors was largely bought in from an external company in the form of a product called "Network Courier", and then released as Microsoft Mail. The fundamental principles of LAN-based e-mail systems established in products like Network Courier and Lotus cc:Mail are preserved to this day in Microsoft Mail, and I think it's fair to say that the evolution of Microsoft Mail since its purchase has been in a series of small steps rather than a total redesign.

It's important to realize that the Microsoft Mail clients and its Post Office (server) are far removed from the Exchange program and, apart from the fact that Microsoft Mail clients can be incorporated in an Exchange environment via the Microsoft Mail connector, there is no direct link between the two. It would therefore be unfair to draw any conclusion about Exchange from past experience with Microsoft Mail.

Moving on from a basic e-mail client, Exchange is intended to be much more than a "mail user agent"[10]. Bundled into Exchange is a messaging server, a messaging backbone, a directory service, and the connections that enable the "universal inbox". Implementations from

---

10.   A very basic definition of a mail user agent is a program that allows users to compose, read, and send messages. Many additional options can be built on top of this basic set of functionality.

other vendors have not attempted to build all this functionality into a single product, preferring instead to spread it across several products that can, if required, be interconnected to form a logical MTA. The fact that Microsoft has little or no background in this type of messaging technology allows a fresh and brand new look at MTA designs, and maybe it's the right way to go! Certainly the level of integration established across the different components of Exchange have set a new standard for the electronic mail industry.

1.9.2   Competing in the corporate messaging market

One fundamental truth of client-server computing is that older methods of piloting system implementations are obsolete and invariably produce inaccurate results. When I started working with mainframe computer systems we used to pilot new software by running test suites against a limited set of users, carefully recording results as we went. Those results were then used as the basis to determine the likely sizing for full-scale implementations of whatever system we had in mind. In simple terms, if the pilot was run for 20 terminals (users) then roughly 5 times the resources were required to support 100 users, and so on.

The "test then multiply" methodology survived the mainframe era. Suitably modified I have seen it used to size PC LANs. For example, how much disk to attach to a server, and so on. The same methodology just does not work in client-server implementations because it is so hard to accurately predict what will happen when the system goes live.

In working with e-mail systems over the last fifteen years or so I have found that users learn more about the system every day they're connected. People keep on trying to do new things and learn through a process of trial and experiment. Where users might start by sending two messages a day soon they're up to ten, and then on to twenty. Where once someone would limit themselves to a few brief lines in an electronic memo, tomorrow they write their life story. Where two or three addresses are the norm on messages numbers grow to a stage where large (200+) distribution lists become the norm. Where users would never consider rich text attachments they progress to attach anything and everything that can exist on their hard drive, including multi-megabyte files. Overall, the average size of messages is going up and up and some large organizations have experienced a ten-fold increase in average message size (from approximately 4K to 40K) in the period 1991–1995. This trend can be expected to increase and the average message size may well reach 100K in some networks by the year 2000, or even sooner if the artistic side of users finds fulfillment in the increasingly graphic capabilities of today's desktop applications. Some software vendors are trying to help the situation by building compression capabilities into their products. Microsoft Office 97, for example, is able to create much smaller files in comparison to its predecessors, especially if graphics are incorporated into documents. This book was a 22MB document in Word 95, but decreased to 5MB when I upgraded to Office 97. The same effect is seen for PowerPoint presentations, which often contain graphics. The efforts of the software vendors are laudable, but I fear it's a race against the desire of users to create even more richly graphical documents. The day of the plain typewritten document is long gone.

What affect will it have on your e-mail system if someone attaches a 20-megabyte video or multimedia presentation to a message and sends it to all their friends throughout the network? You may think that a fifteen or twenty megabyte file is never going to be circulated via e-mail within your organization, but I have seen larger files than this sent out across a number of customer networks many times already. Large PowerPoint presentations originating from marketing departments are particular culprits. Most mail servers receiving such large messages don't perform quickly or smoothly, and some collapse under the load.

The increasing volume and size of messages mean that messaging systems are becoming more and more loaded as time goes on. If systems are not monitored and tuned on a continual basis the old adage that all performance always degrades over time (the best performance you ever see is immediately after a new system is switched on for the first time) comes into play and service levels for users degrade.

Running an Exchange server is not the same as running a Post Office on a LAN. There is more to think about, Windows NT is a more complex operating system than DOS, Windows, or Novell NetWare (or Intranetware), and connectivity with other messaging environments is more of an issue than ever before. Exchange servers will support larger user communities than any LAN-based Post Office, so more users are affected at one time if anything goes wrong with the server. There's a whole new skill set to learn to, littered with masses of new acronyms calculated to wear out valuable system management brain cells. Hopefully the remainder of this book provides some illumination to guide the way.

1.9.3   A maturing product

In earlier versions of this book I asked the question "when will Exchange be stable?" The flood of service packs and new versions issued by Microsoft provided one very good reason for the question. Given the vastly increased stability of Exchange server and the ever-increasing depth of experience in implementation and design perhaps the question that should now be asked is "how long can an Exchange design last without change"?

Microsoft is selling Exchange to the corporate sector, a place where people fondly remember the stability of mainframe and mini-computer messaging systems (one software release a year, no massive changes, and so on). Those days are gone now. Stability is an interesting question, because it's not just Exchange that has to be taken into the equation. A messaging environment is constructed from the underlying operating system, the mail server, and its clients. There is no doubt that the combination of Windows NT, Exchange, and the ever-increasing family of clients that can be connected to Exchange are collectively in a state of flux today. The bad news is that the period of flux will continue for at least two years; the good news is that if proper planning is done it should be possible to minimize the impact of change and maximize the leverage that can be achieved from the new developments.

Among the major changes that will occur in the next two years are:

- Windows NT V5.0; in particular, the advent of the Active Directory.

- First support for Microsoft Cluster Manager (the "Wolfpack" API) is included in Exchange V5.5 and allows two Exchange servers to be connected in a loose cluster. Future versions should enable servers to load-balance user demands as well as include more servers in the cluster.

- Exchange V5.5 supports the capability to build Information Stores, with all the associated knock-on effects on the file system and backup products. It will take some time for many people to build a store up to the stage where its sheer size (greater than 100GB) poses significant management challenges. It will be interesting to see how system administrators cope with the demands of such large files.

- 64-bit Windows NT.

- Rationalization of client options.

The impact of all of these developments is discussed throughout this book. I don't pretend to have the answers. At this stage all I can do is describe what I think is going to happen and why I think it's important. After that it's up to you to get the planning right, and make sure that your company is prepared for change.

1.9.4   Planning leads to success

Interestingly, it was reported that Exchange exceeded the number of licenses sold by Lotus Notes for the first time in the first quarter of 1998. The battle is hotting up all the time. Judged on the number of companies considering its deployment and the number of clients that have been installed Exchange is already a successful product. In September 1996 IDC estimated that 750,000 Exchange clients were already operational, six months after the product first shipped, the fastest ramp-up achieved by any new messaging product. When Exchange V5.0 shipped on March 11, 1997, Microsoft announced that 2 million client licenses had been sold. A huge increase was seen after the release of Exchange V5.0 and Microsoft announced that Exchange had attained 7.2 million clients by the time Exchange V5.5 was released at Comdex on November 18, 1997. The next landmark was reached at the end of January, 1998 when Microsoft said that Exchange had gained 10 million clients. The leap from 2 million to 10 million over roughly 11 months indicated that over 750,000 clients were being added each month. In the first quarter of 1998 Microsoft sold 3.05 million Exchange seats, surpassing the number sold by Lotus for Notes for the first time. At that time the total number of Exchange seats was over 13 million. The battle is hotting up all the time. IDC, and other consulting companies, have predicted that Exchange and Lotus Notes will both have over 18 million users by the end of 1998. Given the current run rate it's safe to say that Exchange will attain this user population.

Statistics tell the story you want. Getting to 13 million or whatever number of clients is certainly an impressive achievement, but maybe the impact of the number is lessened when you consider the huge size of the Microsoft Mail installed base, allied to the pent-up demand created by the long waiting period for Exchange V4.0 to be shipped. I prefer to say that only 13 million clients have been installed so far because major corporate customers had fully realized the amount of careful and detailed planning required before large-scale global deployments can be successful. Everyone should learn from this caution. To be successful we need to do the right amount of planning proportional to the size of your company. That's what the remainder of this book is all about—planning for success with Microsoft Exchange Server.

2

Exchange Clients

2.1   Introduction

Building a robust and reliable server infrastructure is only one part of the messaging story. Clients are equally important. The good news is that Exchange is able to support a wider variety of clients as time goes by. The bad news is that there's possibly too much choice today. From a user perspective it's nice to be able to pick and choose between lots of different clients so that literally everyone could have a different client program on their desktop. In this scenario the server is the point of unification for all the different clients, making sure that everyone can communicate together. Unfortunately diversity of clients is often a support nightmare, so some intelligent decisions need to be taken up front to select the clients for deployment.

MAPI, or Messaging Application Programming Interface, is used by Microsoft to build high-end clients such as Outlook. MAPI was the only interface available to clients to communicate with Exchange V4.0, but the range of available interfaces expanded to accommodate popular non-proprietary (largely Internet) standards in Exchange V5.0 and V5.5 through the support of protocols such as POP3, IMAP4, HTTP, HTML, and LDAP.[1]

The seamless introduction of these protocols is a tribute to the internal architecture of Exchange, built from the start to support multiple protocols and present them as external interfaces for other programs. It's also a fair indication of a trend that is likely to continue in the future when Exchange may expand its range of protocols to incorporate new

---

1.   POP3 is the third version of the Post Office Protocol, commonly used to connect Internet mail clients to mail servers. It is a basic interface in that it does not support the range of features commonly offered by high-end interfaces like MAPI. HTTP, the Hypertext Transfer Protocol, and HTML, the Hypertext Mark Up Language, are the interfaces used by Web browsers and servers to communicate together. IMAP4 is the Internet Mail Access Protocol, a successor to POP3. LDAP, the Lightweight Directory Access Protocol, is used by mail clients to access X.500-like or compliant electronic directory services.

standards as they become established in the electronic mail market. With the increase in supported protocols a number of questions present themselves. These questions need to be assessed carefully within the context of an implementation and deployment plan:

- What client platform should be used? The choice here ranges from DOS through Windows V3, Windows 95, Windows 98, Windows NT and Apple Macintoshes.

- What client interface is used? Perhaps MAPI to gain full access to all of the features of Exchange, or maybe POP3 or IMAP4 because there's an installed base of active Internet mail clients already?

- How will traveling or roving users be supported? Maybe using the normal client that people use when they're in the office, or maybe something like a Web browser when they're on the road and a low-capacity network connection is all that's available.

- What hardware will clients use? Maybe the client hardware in place can't support the demands that will be made by certain client types, limiting options to something like a Web browser. How will UNIX workstations, OS/2 systems and 80386-class Intel systems be incorporated into the environment?

- Perhaps some exciting new technology like the "Hydra" project for Windows NT can be used to meet certain client demands?

In this chapter I look at these and other questions in an attempt to understand what's really important and help you make intelligent decisions. One thing's for sure: the area of client technology is rapidly evolving and will change between the time this text is committed to a page and the time you read it. Always check to see what's currently available before making your mind up.

2.2   MAPI: The rock Exchange server is built on

Over the last few years great attention has been paid by the computer industry to application programming interfaces, mostly because programming to a set of well-documented and understood functions which are supported by multiple products is very much easier than having to create different interfaces for each product.

MAPI is part of a general set of APIs that form WOSA, or the Windows Open Systems Architecture. Each API within WOSA is designed to address a specific need. MAPI takes care of messaging, TAPI (the T stands for Telephony) caters for telephone-based applications, and so on. None of these APIs are formally sponsored or co-ordinated by an industry standards body. It is the sheer market force generated by Microsoft that has moved the WOSA APIs into the lead position for PC development. Other competing interfaces in the messaging area, such as VIM (Vendor Independent Messaging), an interface chiefly espoused by Lotus Development and implemented in their Lotus cc:Mail product, have long been bypassed by MAPI, which was the de facto interface used by any PC applications to integrate messaging functionality. The growing importance and features available in Internet client protocols means that MAPI might be surpassed in the future. It is not yet clear, however, when that time will be.

It could be construed that MAPI is yet another example of where Microsoft have imposed a standard on the computer industry. While it's true that the sheer number of Microsoft clients allied to the company's marketing ability has helped MAPI gain prominence, in this case there are many benefits in having a single pre-eminent standard for desktop messaging. The most obvious benefit is reduced cost, achievable because software developers now only have to code to a single standard rather than supporting many. Paradoxically, the single standard could also lead to increased choice for system implementers and users because more products may decide to make themselves "mail-enabled" through MAPI, figuring that if everyone is including support for messaging functions in their product they should too.

2.2.1   The different faces of MAPI

The first implementations of MAPI were incorporated into Microsoft Mail from 1993. These implementations were not complete in that the full power and scope of the interface had not been built. In fact, just enough functions were available to build a basic messaging system such as Microsoft Mail, leading to the implementation being referred to as "Simple MAPI", "sMAPI", or "MAPI-0". Simple MAPI is composed of a total of twelve functions including those necessary to log onto a server and then to create, address, send, and read messages. Even the biggest Microsoft fan cannot claim that Microsoft Mail is anything but a simple e-mail client, and indeed this is a strong selling point for the product as users don't tend to need very much training before they become productive. However, it is also a weakness because a lot of functionality available in competing products from other vendors (for example Lotus cc:Mail or DIGITAL TeamLinks) is not supported by the Simple MAPI interface.

Simple MAPI can be viewed as a first step towards the full MAPI interface. Extended MAPI, or MAPI V1.0 is far more comprehensive and capable of accommodating the needs of many different messaging systems.

MAPI can be described as a multi-layered architecture. From top to bottom the different layers are:

1. Client applications. For example, the Exchange client, Outlook, Schedule+.

2. Client Interface, or the mechanism by which client applications make calls to the MAPI subsystem. Four MAPI interfaces are offered to allow client programs to connect:

- The original Simple MAPI interface.
- CMC, or Common Mail Calls.
- OLE Messaging.
- Extended MAPI.

 Only the last of these interfaces can be regarded an implementation of the full range of MAPI functionality as envisaged by its designers, and this is the interface used by the Exchange server and clients. OLE messaging follows the general trend of Microsoft application programming interfaces towards well-defined object-oriented interfaces. Exchange server and clients use extended MAPI, which is the most flexible and powerful interface.

3. The MAPI run time system and the message spooler.

4. The Service Provider Interface.

5. The individual Service Providers. The Service Provider Interface and the three major service providers are discussed in detail on the next page.

The run time component and the message spooler form the layer between MAPI client interfaces and service providers. The run time component is a DLL that contains a set of base objects and the APIs used by other components. The API contains all the functions necessary to establish a client session with MAPI, to initialize everything correctly, to read profiles to determine what services a user normally connects to, and how to retrieve information such as folders, messages, and other items from a MAPI service provider. The message spooler is an independent process that manages the flow of messages in and out of the system. On Windows 95 and Windows NT systems you'll see a process called MAPISP32 running when the message spooler is active. Not all MAPI service providers use the message spooler, but it is certainly used by Exchange.

As MAPI is an open interface or at least one that's published into the public domain, doesn't this mean that anyone can write a client and connect it to an Exchange server? The answer is that it all depends on what you want to do. The interface between MAPI clients and Exchange fully exploits the power of the API. The interface to Exchange includes a number of MAPI extensions to enable functionality like public folders. So where it's true that building a client using MAPI will allow a connection to be made, the degree of integration afterwards depends on much of the MAPI interface and any particular extensions are supported by a specific implementation. Certainly there shouldn't be much difficulty in sending and reading messages, but dealing with public folders or electronic forms requires a lot more work on the client side.

It is probably safe to assert that MAPI clients will have the edge in features and functionality when connected to Exchange over the next couple of years. Microsoft will continue to use MAPI until an independent protocol that is capable of the same (or preferably wider) feature set. The most capable Internet client protocol available today (IMAP4) cannot yet match MAPI, but I expect that it will be interesting to observe developments in this space in the next few years.

2.2.2 MAPI Service Providers and clients

Applications have very different messaging needs. Most popular desktop applications only want to be able to send copies of documents they produce as attachments to messages created and dispatched without requiring users to leave the application. This is the approach taken by produces such as Word, Excel, and PowerPoint. It's a highly functional approach because it lets users get on with their job without having to start up a separate mail application.

Full-blown e-mail applications such as Outlook typically deliver a lot more functionality. They can read, forward, and reply to messages as well as being able to simply generate and send messages. MAPI provides the messaging subsystem for Windows PCs, and facilitates the requirements of desktop and mail applications through the set of interfaces we've just discussed. The different interfaces—Simple MAPI, CMC, OLE Messaging, and Extended MAPI—are all layered on top of MAPI itself. In effect MAPI is the collection point for all messaging commands issued by applications on a Windows PC.

A set of Service Providers, or SPIs, is arrayed beneath the MAPI layer. Service Providers are the implementations of driver programs which action the commands issued by clients through the MAPI layer. You can think of Service Providers as the glue connecting MAPI clients to services that are, in turn, physically represented by software running on a server computer somewhere in the network. Microsoft and other software vendors may provide a single service, or collect together a number of different services that can be provided to clients by a mail server. Exchange delivers all of the services necessary for a high-end messaging system. The most important services are:

- *Message Store:* how are messages organized and accessed in a structured repository. For example, the set of folders in an Exchange mailbox. Message stores are defined as a well-organized hierarchy of folders and messages, where folders are objects that can contain other folders as well as messages. Message store providers also handle the creation and submission of messages.

- *Message Transport:* how are messages physically dispatched to their eventual destination.

- *Address Books:* sources of addressing information that can be made available to end users. Exchange provides an on-line address book (the Directory Store) and off-line address book (the OAB and PAB).

MAPI takes the responsibility of deciding whether its own subsystem is able to handle a client request, or which service provider should take on the task. Table 2.1 outlines how MAPI and the different Exchange service providers might interact during a simple client session. On Windows PCs MAPI service providers come as one or more Dynamic Link Libraries. This implementation allows the code for each service provider to be loaded as required by clients.

Table 2.1   *Interaction between service providers*

Client action	Responsible components
Start up an Exchange client and connect to an Exchange server	MAPI
Display the list of folders in the server mailbox	Message store provider
Create a new message	Message store provider
Respond to CTRL/K keystroke to validate some addresses added to message header	Address book provider
Send the message	Message store provider, then message spooler, then transport provider
Delete the message from the outbox folder	Message store provider
Exit from Exchange and Log Off	Message store provider, then MAPI

When a MAPI client initializes it consults its "profile" to discover what set of services it is configured for. Profiles are named lists of message services and configuration data that are created and managed by users. Users may have multiple profiles configured on a single PC. For example, you might configure a profile for use in the office when a wide range of messaging servers are available, and another for use when you're traveling, when the only server that can be connected to is Exchange (via a RAS dial-up connection).

The installation procedure for service providers writes details about the capabilities that can be offered to clients into the system registry. Clients are then able to browse through the set of available services when they configure a profile. Figure 2.1 illustrates the set of MAPI services typically configured for a MAPI client. Details of the Dynamic Link Libraries can be gained by viewing a service provider's properties.

Figure 2.1 *MAPI Services and Providers*

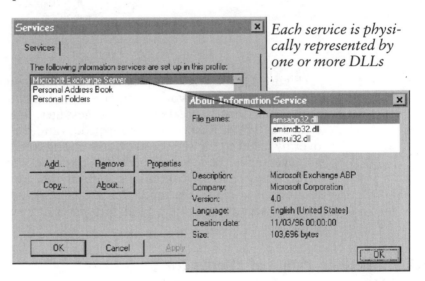

Each service is physically represented by one or more DLLs

The standard Windows 95 kit contains MAPI service providers for Microsoft Mail, FAX, and the Microsoft Network. You can also add an Internet (POP3) provider from the Windows 95 Plus! kit. When you configure an Exchange client in this environment you are able to select one or all of these service providers to use. And when Exchange is available you can install the Exchange service provider and use it to connect to the server. Third parties provide MAPI service providers to allow clients to connect to their servers and if these are available you can configure a client for them as well. The resulting profile might well contain entries for four or more providers, all of which will be connected to when the client starts up.

Figure 2.2 The
Windows
Messaging
subsystem

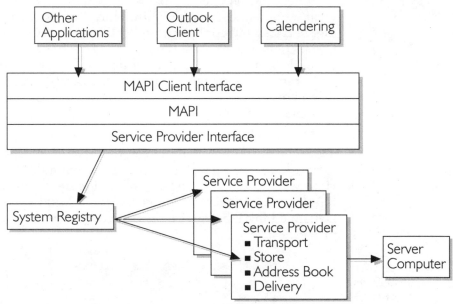

Figure 2.2 illustrates how all of the components in the Windows messaging subsystem work together. At the top clients use calls to messaging functions to create and send messages. The functions are processed by MAPI. Responsibility for processing the messages is handed over by MAPI to the service providers configured in the user's profile, and eventually the messages arrive at a server computer that takes care of delivery. Extended functions such as the address book, meeting requests, or e-forms are handled in the same way, the difference being that the service providers (and the server) must be able to process these type of messages.

2.3   A wide range of clients for Exchange

A huge array of clients can connect to Exchange. Outlook clients for Windows 95, Windows NT, Windows 16-bit, and Apple Macintosh can be found on the Exchange CD. However, the Outlook client is only available for PowerPC-based Macintoshes. Other Macintosh computers must be satisfied with the older Exchange client, a browser, or a POP3 or IMAP4 client.

A DOS client is also provided as a short-term tactical solution to cater for organizations that have considerable populations of low-end PCs still in place. The client is limited by the basic functionality available to any DOS application. Don't expect to be able to handle embedded OLE objects, for instance. Of course, a purely cynical view of the situation is that providing someone with the DOS client is possibly one good way of convincing them that life could be a lot richer and that they should really start using a more modern platform! Of course, some people don't get the opportunity to make a choice of the technology they use. I'm not necessarily referring to people who lack the financial resources to buy faster computers. Many packages exist to relay the output from the 80 × 25 displays commonly used by DOS software to people who are visually impaired, providing a good reason for DOS to remain part of the client line-up.

A UNIX client is notable for its absence in the client line-up. Primarily due to their understandable focus on Windows, Microsoft has never provided a solution for UNIX workstations. UNIX is a popular and powerful platform for mail servers used by many millions of people. However, the total market for UNIX workstations, although popular with their users, is very small when compared to the total installed base of Windows clients.

With these points in mind the lack of a native UNIX client from Microsoft is not at all surprising. However, corporate messaging environments demand accommodation for all the different platforms typically found on user desktops, including UNIX workstations. Two options are available:

1.   Connect UNIX workstations via web browsers

2.   Install a POP3 or IMAP4 client on the workstation and connect using an Internet mail protocol

Using web browsers to access information on an Exchange server is covered later in this chapter. Many web browsers incorporate support for the POP3 or IMAP4 protocols, so this is an alternative approach. The second option is to use a separate POP3 or IMAP4 client. Both approaches work, although the UNIX community may be frustrated by the fact that not all features available to Windows clients are accessible by them. Encrypted messaging is a good example of such a missing feature, rendered inaccessible through gaps in the protocol used to connect or in the client's user interface. However, you should be able to read information and create and send messages, which is all that many people are really interested in. The situation certainly isn't as good as would pertain if a true native UNIX client were available, but at least you are able to connect UNIX users in.

While it's undeniable that Windows has grabbed the lion's share of the desktop market there are considerable and often influential groups of Apple Macintosh users in most major corporations. In comparison to their undoubted success with Microsoft Mail for Windows, Microsoft hasn't had a good record in the Macintosh messaging space over the years. In late 1995 Microsoft transferred Microsoft Mail for Macintosh (and some 750,000 clients) to Starnine Technologies, who were promptly taken over by Quarterdeck (the company made famous by its QEMM memory management product). Quarterdeck Mail for Macintosh shipped in 1996 and has reasonable interoperability between it, Microsoft Mail for the PC and Exchange.

Microsoft's own Exchange client for the Macintosh was not released with Exchange V4.0, eventually arriving some four months afterwards with Service Pack 2 (August 1996), and was updated though the addition of Schedule+ support in the Macintosh client provided with Exchange V5.0. A full Outlook client for the Macintosh is now provided with Exchange V5.5.

An important improvement from previous LAN-based mail systems is the provision of out-of-the-box remote (modem-enabled) access. In the previous Microsoft Mail product users had to purchase a separate add-on module to upgrade their client for remote access. The most common way to establish remote connections is via RAS dial-up connections to Exchange, a good example of how Exchange has leveraged off a standard component of the Windows NT operating system.

OS/2 systems, the great unwashed of the Windows community (in Microsoft's eyes), are able to run the Exchange 16-bit client under the OS/2 Windows subsystem. Communication with the server is accomplished via TCP/IP. I have never attempted to set up and operate such a configuration so I am unable to add any other value other than noting that such a combination exists. The question of whether an OS/2 client will ever work happily in an Exchange environment is left for experimentation on the part of those of you who have an OS/2 installed base to support. Given that browsers are available for OS/2 I think I would look in those directions for a solution rather than trying to convince OS/2 to run a Windows client.

2.3.1   Windows Messaging and the Original Exchange client

While I'm discussing clients, let me take the opportunity to pour a judicious amount of cold water on one of the biggest fables around Exchange, the "free" client that first appeared in Windows 95 and then in Windows NT V4.0. Building on the precedent established by the provision of the Microsoft Mail client in Windows for Work-Groups and Windows NT V3.x, basic messaging functionality is provided in all Windows 95 and Windows NT systems. The basic client was originally called the "Universal Inbox". Some fog and confusion is introduced into the picture when the Universal Inbox boldly called itself "Microsoft Exchange" when the client started up. The situation wasn't clarified when the original clients provided with Exchange V4.0 were called the "Exchange" client.

The basic client and the Exchange client shared almost the same user interface, with the major (and important) exception that the Exchange client knew about server-specific features like public folders. Most people now know that the basic client cannot be connected to Exchange because the necessary MAPI updates need to be applied first.

Figure 2.3
The original Exchange client for Windows 95

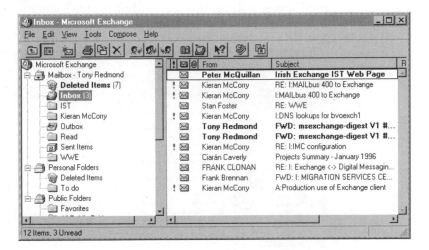

The concept behind the Universal Inbox—to provide a single consistent location for all electronic communications to arrive into—is a compelling vision, and Microsoft have done a good job in defining the structure for the single location, especially in Windows 95. As well as acting as a single location for incoming communications, the client is able to act as a fully-fledged message user agent, creating and sending messages via a variety of systems, each of which is defined as a messaging service provider. However, the standard Universal Inbox isn't as comprehensive a mail client as a full-blown Outlook client as it provides only the same degree of send/receive/process messaging capabilities as the older Microsoft Mail clients.

Microsoft renamed the Universal Inbox and began to refer to it as "Windows Messaging" in June 1996. The client included with Windows NT V4.0 is also called Windows Messaging. A separate Exchange client (Figure 2.3) continued to be included with Exchange Server through V5.0. Development has now ceased, and Outlook is the only client now shipped with the server.

2.3.2   The advent of Outlook

The Office 97 application suite introduced Outlook, the next generation of Exchange clients (Figure 2.4). Outlook takes a different view of the world. Instead of focusing primarily on e-mail, Outlook attempts to apply the same basic user interface to a whole range of information sources to form a desktop information manager, something that people can use to access and manage all of the different data sources they need to work with. Overall, Outlook is a much more comprehensive client than the Exchange V5.0 client, but it is only available for 32-bit Windows desktops. Exchange still figures very much as the preferred mail server behind the scenes, but again, Exchange is only one of the information sources for Outlook, albeit the most important one.

Figure 2.4 *The Outlook 98 client*

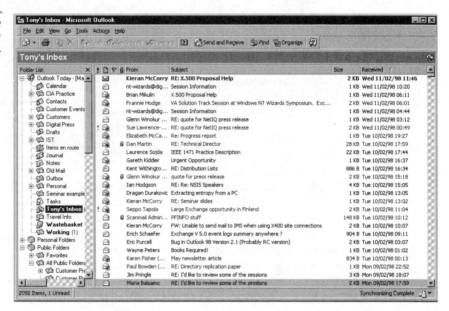

Lots of people will buy Office 97 and won't necessarily have an Exchange server at their disposal. They can still use Outlook as their mail client by connecting it to another mail server, such as an Internet messaging system via POP3 or IMAP4. Expect to see Microsoft put considerable effort into Outlook add-ons and enhancements to make the client work as smoothly as possible with Internet mail systems. Just as Exchange wants to become the server of choice for as many different types of mail clients as possible, the Outlook client wants to be the client of choice for as many different mail servers as possible. Delivering the widest range of functionality is the best way to ensure user loyalty, although the tactic of providing a free mail client along with every Microsoft Office kit will also be a great help in achieving the "client for the masses" goal.

There still is a large population of Microsoft Mail clients in use today. It is probable that Microsoft Mail Post Offices will serve a growing population of Outlook clients until the post offices can migrate to Exchange. There is a reasonable case to advise people using the Microsoft Mail client today to migrate to Outlook immediately to use it along with the rest of Microsoft Office. The clients can then switch their messaging focus to Exchange when the necessary infrastructure (network, Windows NT, and so on) has been put in place. This approach delivers more functionality to users quickly, relieving pressure on the implementation team and hopefully leading to more satisfied users.

A new version of calendaring software is included in Outlook, one that focuses on server-based folders rather than the mixture of server and local resources that powered Schedule+.

Remember that Outlook can be bought separately from the rest of the Microsoft Office applications, so there's no reason to wait until you're ready to upgrade from earlier versions of Word, Excel, and so on. Outlook works quite happily with Office 95 applications, or even earlier versions like Word for Windows V6.0.

2.3.3   Connecting different versions of Outlook to Exchange

At the time of writing there are five known versions of Outlook, as shown in Table 2.2.

Table 2.2   *Versions of Outlook*

Version	Released
Outlook V8.0	Original version released with Microsoft Office 97
Outlook V8.01	Version released with Exchange V5.0
Outlook V8.02	Bug fix release
Outlook V8.03	Version released with Exchange V5.5
Outlook 98	Version released with Microsoft Office 98

The number of versions indicates that Outlook has had an extremely fast development path. Some versions were produced to align with the Office application suite, others to align with Exchange, others to fix bugs. It is only now that the Outlook and Exchange development teams have truly managed to synchronize development plans and priorities. This doesn't mean that the current versions of Outlook are bad, just that at times small gaps appear between the client and Exchange.

The connection between Outlook and Exchange continues to evolve. Outlook V8.03 introduced the user interface to leverage the much-needed deleted items recovery feature in Exchange V5.5. Apart from its enhanced user interface, Outlook 98 includes the ability to synchronize the contents of off-line and server folders, something that road warriors will find invaluable. The original version of Outlook was not optimized for Exchange, so you should not use it in conjunction with the server. Apart from this, there's no requirement to upgrade to the newest version unless you need to use one of the new features. In passing, I should note that Outlook 98 requires Internet Explorer V4.01 (or later) to be installed on a PC because both products share the same HTML rendering engine. Sharing software components reduces the overall size of products, so it's a welcome step. However, some companies may be reluctant to install Internet Explorer just to share a rendering engine.

Sites that upgrade from the older Exchange client to Outlook should consider using the CHNGINBX utility[2] to remove the icon for the old client and replace it with Outlook. This does not remove the executables, such as EXCHNG32.EXE. It merely prevents user confusion arising through having two icons with broadly similar purpose on their desktop.

2.3.4   No luck for older terminals

"Green screen e-mail" is the term used by a certain Microsoft sales representative of my acquaintance to describe host-based messaging systems. The term accurately describes the green (or other color) glow of the 24×80 screen used to log onto mainframe or mini-based computers to access older messaging systems.

There's no method to connect unintelligent clients like IBM 3270s or the other classic Video Terminals (VTs) to Exchange. If you want to deploy Exchange you have to face the fact that PC clients are the only way forward. Most installations have gone a long way to sorting out their desktop infrastructure over the past few years and there has been a steady decline in the number of VTs in use. However, I know of quite a few sites where VTs are still counted in hundreds, mostly because they are cheap to install and support and many users only require simple text-based messaging. If you have a substantial VT population you'll either have to remove Exchange from your list of potential messaging solutions or pay the ante and replace VTs with PCs, with all the attendant costs involved.

----

2.   Available from http://www.microsoft.com/outlook/enhancements/chnginbx.asp

2.3.5   **Basic client functionality**

How many features of your word processor or spreadsheet do you actually use? How many have you mastered to a degree where you can use the feature without reaching for a manual or conducting a frantic search through the application's help file? If you're anything like me you'll only ever use about 20% of an application's features, unless it's something that you use every day. Electronic mail is an application accessed by most users every day, so the range of features offered by the application are important and it's more likely than even esoteric features will be discovered and used by quite a few people.

MAPI clients are highly functional. There are probably more options available on menus, especially if the long versions of the menus are turned on, than most people will ever care about. All of the options are presented in an attractive user interface that is utterly consistent with the rest of the Microsoft office applications. If you're accustomed to using Word, Excel, PowerPoint, and Access you'll be totally at home with Outlook. Even the more esoteric options hidden away on the farther reaches of Tools.Options, such as the feature which allows messages to be sent after a certain delay, show evidence of careful research into the finer points of graphical user interfaces.

While I like the overall functionality delivered in the Outlook client, all is not sweetness and light. The ability for a user to autoforward or redirect messages from a client option is a startling gap, mostly because this is a feature that's commonly found on other high-end messaging clients. Autoforward usually means that the server automatically forwards messages on to a different address after they are delivered in a mailbox, normally leaving a copy of the forwarded message in the mailbox. Redirection occurs on the server, with messages being intercepted and never reaching the original recipient's mailbox, so no trace of the redirected messages will be found. The system administrator can redirect messages on behalf of a user by setting the redirect property on a mailbox. The Inbox Assistant can help by providing a sort of autoforward, but I think that most people who have ever used an auto-forward feature would agree that it would be much better to be able to do this without fiddling around with rules or boring system administrators. The ability to update directory information such as a user's postal address or personal telephone number from the client is another omission that causes additional workload for administrators.

Figure 2.5 *MAPI*
Clients and
Providers
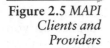

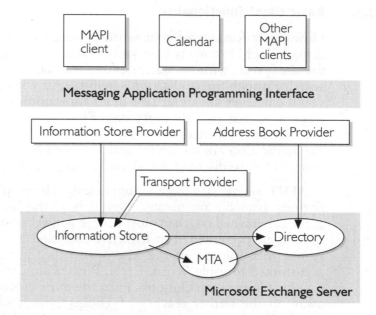

2.3.6 Non-Microsoft MAPI extensions

We've already discussed how the user configurations for the Windows messaging subsystem are defined in terms of a profile. A profile describes the services the user wishes to access and the MAPI providers that enable such access. A graphic illustrating typical components configured within a MAPI profile is shown in Figure 2.6.

If multiple users share a PC a separate profile is quite probably defined for each. It is quite possible for a user to maintain several profiles, each of which describes a totally different environment. For example, one profile might detail a connection to Exchange for use when transporting new messages while another specifies that a Microsoft Mail Post Office is to be used instead. Each of the different providers might be capable of making different features available to clients, so these differences can be configured as part of the profile too.

The attractive notion of having a single universal client as the access point to many different messaging services has encouraged many vendors to consider building the necessary software components to link Microsoft clients to their own mail servers via MAPI. DIGITAL has built two separate products (called Digital Drivers for MAPI[3]) to connect Exchange clients to DIGITAL MailWorks for UNIX or OfficeServer/ALL-IN-1 (OpenVMS) servers, allowing enterprises to

---

3.   The first version of the Digital MAPI driver (for MailWorks for UNIX) shipped in November 1995. The first version of the OfficeServer/ALL-IN-1 driver shipped in summer 1996.

deploy UNIX-based or OpenVMS-based messaging servers while continuing to use the well-integrated desktop functionality available in the Windows 95 clients.

The DIGITAL drivers are good examples of full MAPI service providers. The MAPI Service Providers enable DIGITAL mail servers to be defined to MAPI clients in terms they understand. As a message store (in DIGITAL messaging terms a store is referred to as a file cabinet), the transport by which messages pass between the client and server, and a directory of mail subscribers to replace or supplement the Exchange Global Address List. Apart from incorporating a huge new range of potential clients, building a MAPI service provider conveys a number of advantages to vendors. For example, changes normally don't have to be made on the server as all the work to translate MAPI functions to server-specific calls can be encapsulated in the service provider DLL that's installed on each client. This fact alone means that existing servers can continue to operate, in effect gracefully evolving to support new client connections without realizing the fact. While the server side is insulated from change, using MAPI means that a whole client user interface is picked up free of charge, giving the vendor the option of concentrating solely on the server if that makes commercial sense.

Figure 2.6
*DIGITAL's
ALL-IN-1 server
accessed by the
Exchange client
for Windows 95*

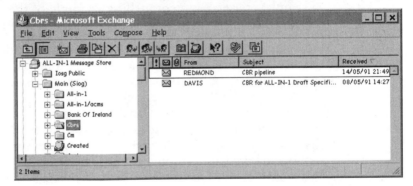

Figure 2.6 shows the original Exchange client for Windows 95 connected to a DIGITAL ALL-IN-1 server running on an OpenVMS system. Outlook clients are also supported. As far as the user is concerned all they see is the Exchange user interface. The only hints that it mightn't be an Exchange server humming in the background is a few discrete mentions of ALL-IN-1 when mailbox contents are listed or when users configure the services they wish to connect to. Even Lotus Notes, the major competitor for Exchange in the battle to win the hearts and minds of people for selection for corporate groupware and messaging deployments, provides a MAPI service provider for Exchange. The Lotus Notes service provider allows an Exchange client to connect to a mailbox on a Lotus Notes server (Release 4.0 or later). Once con-

nected you're able to drag and drop from one server to the other, preserving the data as well as most of the attributes of messages and other items.

Another good example of how MAPI can be used to build extensions for the Exchange client environment is the provision of an additional directory service that can be shared between Exchange and other clients. See the discussion and screen shot beginning on page 620.

While a general movement towards a common client for all sorts of electronic communications makes sense in many aspects, especially when client software is bundled with the desktop operating system there will be situations when a Microsoft client doesn't fully exploit the capabilities that a third party server can offer. Perhaps the MAPI specification doesn't completely accommodate features of other servers and no amount of magic programming can make the client work with the server. Or maybe the server offers more in terms of features such as workflow or document management. In these cases vendors, such as DIGITAL, will continue to supply their own client software.

Utilizing MAPI to permit enterprises to select clients from one source and servers from other, while all the time presenting users with a seamless service, is a compelling example of the power of the MAPI concept.

In general I think it's fair to say that mixing different MAPI clients with different MAPI servers is great as long as you're interested in purely messaging functionality. In other words, all you want to do is create, send, and read messages. However, if a particular client or server offers specific functionality you may not be able to access it with all possible combinations. Some testing may be required to establish exactly what's possible with what combination in your particular environment. For example, will public folders be accessible from non-Microsoft clients that connect to an Exchange server? Will Microsoft clients be able to utilize the mail delegation functionality as implemented in another vendor's MAPI-enabled server?

Another issue to consider is that third party service providers need to keep up to date with developments in the Exchange program. For example, when the Outlook client arrived with Exchange V5.0, software vendors had to issue new versions of their service providers. In 1997 DIGITAL updated their code to add new functionality in Open-VMS mail servers as well as to support Outlook, while Lotus has also upgraded code to allow Exchange and Outlook clients access to Lotus Notes (Domino) servers.

A purely cynical view of the situation, which is perhaps accurate in many respects, is that open systems work best as long as you buy all the open components from a single vendor. Along this line it may well be inevitable that MAPI components originating from Microsoft will always offer the highest degree of integration and interoperability with Exchange. This is somewhat inevitable where client and server components are built by a single vendor. The Microsoft clients will also look and feel exactly like other Microsoft applications, again hardly surprising because all the desktop applications make use of common programming libraries. Vendors selling alternate clients for connection to Exchange servers or servers for Microsoft clients have to make a compelling case and provide significant added value before a real case can be made for those alternate solutions to be considered. Better integration with other messaging systems installed within an organization, an integrated set of converters and viewers, or better customization capabilities are all good arguments to go towards another client, especially if you want to establish a situation where a common client (one that's capable of connecting to all servers) is used throughout your organization.

I do not recommend that you consider using client-level software such as service providers as the primary tools for migration from other mail systems to Exchange. It is attractive to imagine that you might be able to ask users to shoulder the burden for the migration of data to Exchange. However, the sheer amount of work and number of repetitions required to drag and drop messages from the old system to Exchange is too onerous in most cases. Remember that you're asking people to review all the messages in the old system, decide whether they want to take them to Exchange, and then perform the physical action of dragging and dropping. Users also have to create a new folder structure in Exchange to receive the messages they wish to move. It may take a user an hour or two (probably more) to review and process their old mailbox, but a very large number of hours is required if you scale the number of hours up across the entire user population. You won't be popular when you explain to upper management that several thousand people hours are going to be lost (in terms of other productivity).

In essence, MAPI service providers are coexistence tools, not for migration. Use the service providers to introduce Exchange to client desktop. Service providers span the gap between the introduction of Exchange within your messaging systems and whenever the Exchange client/server combination becomes the primary user environment. Other migration tools do a better, cleaner job of bulk movement of user files to Exchange.

2.4   Lightweight clients

Outlook provides a very high level of functionality, but it's not a client that's suitable for everyone. As we've just discussed, these full-function clients require a fairly modern and well-specified hardware platform before they can be used, and there are no Microsoft clients available for some operating systems, such as any variant of UNIX.

Many corporate environments have hundreds or even thousands of low-powered PCs still in use. It is common to find 80386- and early 80486-class systems that have been happily running DOS, Windows V3, old versions of Windows applications that don't take up quite as much system resources as today's editions, and maybe even terminal emulators to access mainframe or mini-computer e-mail systems. On such PCs it is difficult to achieve an acceptable degree of performance with Outlook. The DOS client is a notable exception, but I cannot think of a single corporate project I have worked with that has regarded the DOS client as anything other than an interesting side street, certainly not something suitable for deployment on user desktops. Old Apple Macintoshes (basically anything that's not powered by the PowerPC CPU) are often in the same situation, especially if they don't have a lot of memory or local hard disk.

Without unlimited finance, no one can propose a complete replacement of these systems, yet a solution must be found as otherwise a block is placed on Exchange implementation projects. Without client desktops capable of connecting to the server there's no point in installing the server. Without client desktops to use there's no point in replacing the current e-mail system. The desire to implement Exchange, or any high-end messaging system that uses a graphical user environment, founders on the rock of a low hardware base.

Another common situation is to find that plans exist for a complete overhaul of user hardware, normally as part of an effort to move desktops from Windows V3 to Windows 95 or Windows NT. Both Windows 95 and Windows NT require a great deal more hardware than Windows V3, so the need to invest in some new hardware is a well-recognized part of the upgrade effort. Application upgrades are usually factored into the deployment of a new version of Windows, and Outlook can be included in this set of tasks. The Exchange implementation project is contingent on new hardware being deployed as part of the general desktop upgrade. It is an advantage that the upgrade will eventually occur, but the implementation of Exchange can be slowed if the general upgrade does not progress quickly.

Lack of support for a certain operating system, limited finance and dependency on other projects are therefore three significant challenges for implementation project managers to overcome. Microsoft's answer is to allow "lightweight clients" to access and use the resources of an Exchange server, and so act as an alternative to Outlook. Microsoft is not generally associated with the engineering or provision of lightweight clients. The exception that proves the rule is the Internet Explorer, which can connect to Exchange as a browser or using a messaging protocol. Today, the protocols used by lightweight clients include:

- Post Office Protocol (POP3)
- Internet Mail Access Protocol (IMAP4)
- Hypertext Mark Up Language (HMTL)
- Hypertext Transmission Protocol (HTTP)
- Lightweight Directory Access Protocol (LDAP)
- Secure Sockets Layer (SSL)

Anyone can write software that uses one or more of these protocols to access the messaging and other capabilities of an Exchange server. The lightweight clients are broken down into two major families:

1. Messaging-only clients, those that use the POP3 or IMAP4 protocols to access an Exchange server.

2. Web browsers that use a combination of active pages and the HTTP/HTML protocols to access messaging, public folder, and scheduling functionality from an Exchange server.

Both families of lightweight clients can use LDAP to access the Exchange directory, providing the individual implementation of the client software supports the LDAP protocol.

There are a wide variety of e-mail clients that use POP3 or IMAP4 to connect to a mail server. Some clients are of a much higher quality than others, but the sheer number of available clients is testimony to the popularity of Internet messaging protocols. Netscape and Microsoft have made the provision of web browsers a two-horse race. The latest generation of either browser is capable of acting as Exchange clients. Given the option between using a messaging protocol or general-purpose browser I'd always go with the protocol. As we'll see later on, browsers are invaluable in some circumstances, but a client purpose designed for messaging will always enable a greater range of functionality.

A large proportion of browsers and Internet e-mail clients are given away free or provided on a shareware basis so they are undeniably cheap to deploy. Best of all, versions are available that will run quite happy on low-end Apple Macintoshes, any variant of a UNIX workstation, as well as the most basic Windows-capable PC. All lightweight clients interoperate happily with Outlook, so deployments of Exchange can therefore proceed released from dependencies imposed by software unavailability, low hardware base or lack of finance. From a marketing perspective the ability to connect Internet clients and browsers with Exchange expands the potential client market quite dramatically. How many browsers are in use today? No one knows—the only sure thing is that the number is already measured in the tens of millions and increasing all the time. Apart from the pure marketing element there's also a great deal of strategy being played out as Exchange expands the set of clients that are able to access and use its services. In competitive situations, where Exchange is head to head with other products, comparisons between the different products under review are made across a wide variety of points. If Exchange tops the list of servers in terms of the breath and variety of clients it supports, then the server is shown up in a very good light. Also, the initial implementation of the server may be very much easier if supported clients are already being used on peoples' desktops.

Free or shareware software is one thing, but there's no such thing as a free lunch and client connectivity is no different. According to Microsoft software licensing policy all clients, Exchange or lightweight, require a Client Access License (CAL). By selecting Internet clients or browsers you can certainly avoid paying for Microsoft client software, but licenses must be registered on the server.

We'll discuss the good and bad points of the specific lightweight clients over the next few pages. Before moving to specific details it's worth noting that all the lightweight clients share a common attribute, that of maintaining a passive rather than active connection to the server. Outlook clients connect to servers via RPCs so communication is two-way. Active clients are able to accept and react to the instructions sent out by the server. For example, a dialog should be displayed because it is the result of a rule being executed or the contents of a folder updated because a message has just been deleted. The simplest example is the broadcast announcing that a new message has arrived. All of this work is done through RPCs. Passive clients merely make demands of a server and do not react to server attempts to have intelligent conversations. Thus, whereas a browser is capable of displaying the contents of the Inbox, it is unable to maintain an active count of new messages. If a user wishes to discover how many new messages are in the Inbox they must make an explicit "refresh new mail count" request to the server.

2.5 Internet Mail clients

Exchange V5.0 began the process of opening Exchange up to different mail clients. Initial support was for POP3 clients, and Exchange V5.5 has now expanded the total potential client community through IMAP4.

2.5.1 The Post Office Protocol (POP3)

POP3 clients are the simplest (or even lightest) clients capable of connecting to an Exchange server. A wide range of POP3 client software is available on the market. Some of this software is free, yours for the expense of a download from a Web site somewhere. Other clients are available as commercial products, and clearly the degree of sophistication and functionality that's available from any client depends on the amount of work that's been put into it. The commercial products, like Eudora Pro, Pegasus, or DIGITAL TeamLinks, are complete in terms of functionality, and usually offer more features than those just devoted to message retrieval and sending. But if all you want is a simple mail program that can handle messages in a basic manner then one of the free (or shareware) programs will probably do the job.

The messaging functionality that can be built for any POP3 client is constrained by the limitations of the POP3 protocol, defined, like SMTP, by the Internet Engineering Task Force (IETF). The protocol concentrates on simple messaging and ignores high-end features like public folders or scheduling. Simplicity has its benefits too. Generally speaking, POP3 clients impose the lightest load on the server of any client. The model used involves off-line work to process messages followed by quick connections to the server to send any messages waiting and fetch any messages that have arrived since the last connection. The process of downloading messages from the server inbox to the client is rather charmingly referred to as "scraping". The table below lists points of client functionality and indicates whether these are available to POP3 clients.

As POP3 is a protocol in the public domain there are many different visions of what a client interface should look like. The protocol makes no demands on software designers; it merely states how a client can connect to a server and retrieve messages from it. The design of the user interface is left completely in the hands of software engineers, who are only limited by their own ingenuity and the constraints applied by the simplicity of the protocol. POP3 clients therefore vary greatly in terms of style, content, and quality. There are acknowledged market leaders who count their users in millions, such as Eudora or Pegasus, but there are other products too that are deserving of consideration.

Table 2.3   *Functionality available to POP3 clients*

Feature	Available to POP3 client
Access to any messages and attachments delivered into a user mailbox (inbox folder)	Yes
Can read Rich Text Format content in messages	Yes (contents are MIME-encoded)
Access and browse Exchange directory	Yes—via LDAP
Create new folders or otherwise manipulate folder hierarchy	No—POP3 only supports a simple inbox
Browse private folders on server	No—POP3 has no concept of private folders.
Browse public folders on server	No—POP3 has no concept of shared or public folders
Use Outlook electronic forms	No—POP3 has no concept of anything but a simple message
Set Out of Office Assistant	No client option available to set conditions for Out of Office Assistant.
Set AutoSignature text	No client options available to define text for addition to end of messages.
Use Outlook calendar or Schedule+ features to accept, view or create meetings	No—POP3 has no concept of scheduling
Use Exchange rules	No—POP3 has no concept of rule processing

Figure 2.7 shows the shareware version of Eudora[4] after a number of messages have been downloaded from an Exchange server. During a download messages may be removed from the server inbox, so if you use an Exchange client to connect to the same mailbox immediately after a POP3 download there might be no trace of any of the messages that the POP3 client now has control over. In addition, all formatting and rendering information in the messages are removed, leaving simple text content. Attachments are preserved and can be accessed. Most

---

4.   The shareware version is called Eudora Lite. It can be downloaded from http://www.eudora.com. The latest version of the Eudora clients support both POP3 and IMAP4.

POP3 clients move attachments into a download directory where the attachments can be dealt with in the same manner as DOS files. Format tagging and file names might be lost, depending on how the client deals with attachments and whether they can process long (32-bit) file names.

Figure 2.7
*The Eudora Lite
client after
downloading
some messages
from Exchange*

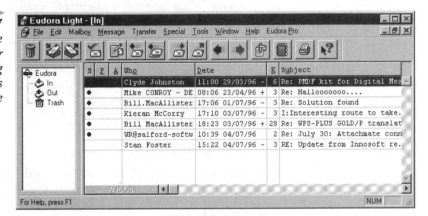

In terms of simple messaging POP3 clients work well with Exchange. Difficulties arise when you look at any extended functionality. Table 2.3 lists some of the extended messaging features that you'll miss by using a POP3 client rather than Outlook, but there are other things too to consider. For example, there is no option in a POP3 client to set a new password for a user account in a Windows NT domain. What happens when an account password expires? The technology answer is simple—there's a passwords applet available in the control panel of Windows 32-bit clients, but it's an extra step that users have to take. Training needs to be altered to reflect this fact, and the help desk prepared to take calls from users who have just discovered that they can't access their mailbox because their account password is expired.

In theory (only because we don't yet have real-world experience of connecting hundreds of POP3 clients to a server), Exchange can support more POP3 than Outlook clients. Certainly, the test results achieved by Microsoft in their test laboratories indicate that very large POP3 user communities (numbered in the thousands) can be supported by a medium-range Exchange server. Indeed, the "Scalability Day" demonstration by Microsoft in New York in May 1997 included a single Exchange server handling the simulated load of 50,000 POP3 clients.

Microsoft compares the number of POP3 clients supported by Exchange with the results of other POP3 servers, and Exchange looks pretty good. As always, the results achieved in a software laboratory must be taken with a large pinch of salt. Even so, because of the intermittent nature of the pull and push mechanism used to retrieve and send messages, it is reasonable to expect that POP3 clients will place less demand on the server. The number of inbound connections to the Internet Mail Service is the notable exception. Each POP3 client connects to the Internet Mail Service to send messages, so a server dealing with a population of POP3 clients needs to be configured to handle the increased number of connections. The default value (set through the Advanced tab of the Connections properties for the service) was 20 in V4.0. The value remains the same after an upgrade, so if you want to support a lot of simultaneous POP3 client connections you should increase the value.

2.5.2   Who are you getting mail from?

From time immortal, an SMTP client has been able to give itself any identity it wishes. In this instance, identity is the SMTP address displayed to people who receive messages from the client—I can connect to Netscape mail and announce myself as bgates@microsoft.com, and merrily generate messages as such. You can't do this from all clients, but the vast majority of Internet mail clients certainly permit it, including Netscape, Eudora, and even Outlook Express. Clients that generate SMTP messages through a connector or gateway, as in the case of Outlook clients, are not given the opportunity to misrepresent themselves because the server stamps all outgoing messages with the sender's true identity.

Of course, sophisticated recipients who understand messaging generally have mistrust messages that come in from people they don't know, and are likely to examine the information in the message header. The routing a message has taken within the network is clearly obvious from its header, so the true identity of a sender can be revealed.

Look at the example in Figure 2.8. Is the message really from Bill Gates? Of course it isn't. The message was generated by customizing the personal preferences for Netscape Communicator to insert Bill Gates as the sender for all messages. Unwary recipients would only detect the problem if they browsed through the message header to find out exactly where the message came from, and even still, if the originator was cunning, they would have included some SMTP header lines (as defined in RFC 822) to indicate that the message came from somewhere else. In this instance the originator didn't go to the trouble of messing with headers, so we get some value from our examination. You'd expect a true message from Bill Gates to come through a server somewhere in the Microsoft domain, but that isn't the case here. Instead, the message was sent from a PC called VORLON somewhere in the local domain. Clearly a case of someone having fun at my expense!

Figure 2.8 *A message from Bill Gates? Not likely!*

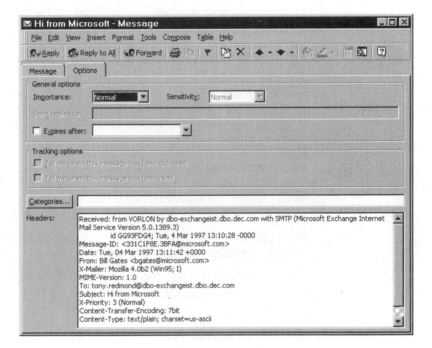

Normal human beings don't tend to look too closely at message headers. In fact, they never do. The mail server therefore takes an almost moral responsibility to protect people against SMTP crooks. Exchange can't force good behaviour on client software that it doesn't control, so any protection must come at the point where SMTP messages enter the Exchange environment—the Internet Mail Server.

Exchange attempts to match addresses in any incoming message against the directory. This is an attempt to create a user-friendly feature, because the unfriendly SMTP addresses are resolved into more readable display addresses fetched from the directory. Users can work with resolved addresses in the same way as they can with any other directory entry. For example, you can right-click on an address to see its properties, and if the address has been resolved in the directory, you'll be able to view other directory information (like manager, telephone number, e-mail addresses, and so on).

Let's assume that a message apparently comes from Peter.McQuillan@xyz.com and that there's a matching entry (custom recipient or mailbox) in the directory. In this case, if directory resolution is enabled, the server changes the display address to Peter McQuillan, or whatever the display name was in the directory. Matching is, of course, performed against the list of mail addresses that can be maintained for each directory entry.

Friendliness is fine when everyone plays by the rules. But we have to defend against the antics of people who might use the weak points of SMTP to insert rogue messages. Exchange V5.0 made a major change to help solve the problem. The default behavior of the Internet Mail Server is now to no longer attempt to resolve incoming SMTP addresses against the directory. Instead, addresses are left as they come in, unless you explicitly instruct the server to perform resolution. Given the world we live in this is probably the best way for the Internet Mail Server to behave.

All servers installed from scratch do not perform name resolution. Servers upgraded from V4.0 maintain their previous behavior. If you want to change the server to be in line with latest practice you'll need to amend the system registry by changing the following key:

```
HKEY_LOCAL_MACHINE\System\CurrentControlSet\Services\
MSExchangeIMC\Parameters\ResolveP2
```

Set the value to 0 to stop the Internet Mail Service performing name resolution. The registry value needs to be added if it is not already present.

2.5.3   Internet Mail Access Protocol (IMAP4)

While POP3 is a messaging protocol supported by many mail servers and clients it is relatively simple and not really suitable to meet the needs of a sophisticated messaging community. The deficiencies in POP3 were recognized long ago and efforts have been ongoing to replace it with IMAP4, the Internet Mail Access Protocol. Perhaps more mail servers and clients support POP3 today, but the situation is expected to change very quickly over the 1998–1999 period.

Like POP3, the user interface of IMAP4 clients is left totally to the software designer. The protocol defined in RFCs 1734 and 2060[5] lays out the set of more than 30 functions supported by IMAP4 (revision 1), and after that it's up to the software designer to construct a user interface around the functions. Because of the different possible interpretations of the protocol outlined in RFC 1734, Microsoft has based its implementation on the newer RFC 2060. Older IMAP4 clients built to support RFC 1734 may not work as expected with Exchange. However, the majority of these clients have now been superseded by newer software.

---

5.   See http://www.internic.net/ds/rfc-index.html for the latest RFC definitions.

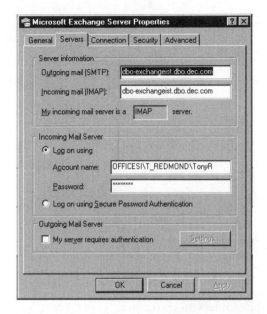

Unlike POP3, the IMAP4 protocol allows for server-based folders other than the inbox, and accommodates the concept of shared folders. It is therefore possible for IMAP4 clients to access public folders on an Exchange server, much like the browser and NNTP interfaces can today. A brief outline of the functionality available to IMAP4 clients is contained in Table 2.4. This table is based on the combination of Exchange Server and the Microsoft Outlook Express client.

Table 2.4 *Functionality available to IMAP4 clients*

Feature	Available to IMAP4 client
Access to any messages and attachments delivered into a user mailbox (any folder)	Yes
Can read Rich Text Format content in messages	Yes (RTF and HTML)
Access and browse Exchange directory	Yes—via LDAP
Create new folders	Yes
Change folder properties	No
Server storage of messages	Yes
Anonymous access	Yes (with permissions)

Table 2.4   *Functionality available to IMAP4 clients (continued)*

Feature	Available to IMAP4 client
Send encrypted messages to other IMAP4 users	Yes—using S/MIME
Synchronize server and client folders	Yes
Set message properties (flags, etc.)	Yes
Send encrypted messages to other MAPI users	No
Access attachments on mail messages	Yes
Access non-message items in public folders	No
Work with tasks, notes, and journal items	View only (via OWA)
Browse public folders on server (see Figure 2.13)	Yes
Set Out of Office Assistant	No
Set AutoSignature text	Yes
Use Outlook calendar or Schedule+ features to accept, view or create meetings	No
Use Exchange rules	No

Clearly, the list of features is much more comprehensive than those available to a POP3 client. However, when connected to Exchange, a POP3 client is less functional than a MAPI client. There are also some interesting "features" that will become obvious as we look at Outlook Express, the premier IMAP4 client for Exchange.

2.5.4   Microsoft Outlook Express

Microsoft Outlook Express (Figure 2.10), supplied as part of the Internet Explorer suite, is able to connect to Exchange via POP3 or IMAP4. Despite the fact that Outlook Express shares no code with the MAPI-based Outlook client, the naming reflects Microsoft's desire to create a common identity across all its clients (Outlook, Outlook Web Access, and Outlook Express).

Figure 2.10
*Outlook Express
accessing an
item in a Public
Folder*

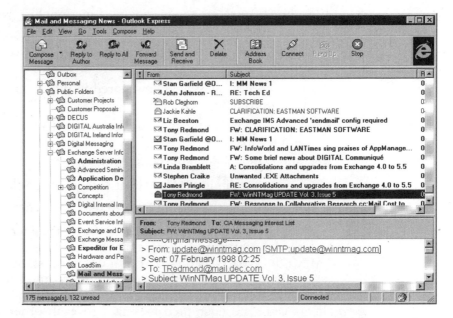

Microsoft claims that Outlook Express offers the most features of
any freeware client. The list of supported protocols is certainly impressive, incorporating POP3, SMTP, MIME, S/MIME, NNTP, HTML,
IMAP4, and LDAP. Together with the straightforward and attractive
user interface, the rich protocol list prompts people to ask why they
shouldn't just use this client instead of Outlook. Consider this list of
reasons why Outlook Express might be deployed rather than the
MAPI-based Outlook client:

- The same development group that works on the MAPI version of
  the Outlook client engineers Outlook Express.

- It can be expected that Microsoft will keep Outlook Express competitive with similar clients from Netscape and other vendors.

- Because there's less features to cover, it is easier to train people
  to use Outlook Express.

- Outlook Express is integrated with web browsing capabilities, so
  we have two important application areas integrated into one
  program.

- Best of all, Outlook Express is (currently) free. However, remember that you still need an Exchange CAL to connect any client to
  an Exchange server.

Quite a compelling case can be argued for Outlook Express! But before
we all rush to return unused copies of Outlook clients to Microsoft, let's
reflect on some of the functionality that you'd be giving up.

- Richer feature set for messaging functionality (recall message, deferred mail, inbox assistant, etc.)

- Calendaring (apart from viewing items previously scheduled into a calendar)

- Access to non-message items stored in public folders (including message attachments)

- Access to public folders on servers other than the one a mailbox is not located on

- Contact management/PIM functionality

- Client extendibility (MAPI client extensions or electronic forms)

- Advanced security (as implemented by Exchange V5.5)

With respect to advanced security (message encryption/decryption and digital signatures), new code in Exchange V5.5 SP1 supports S/MIME bodyparts as the basis of a common standard to implement these functions across multiple email systems and clients. Through the personal exchange of public keys, Outlook 98 and Outlook Express clients can send encrypted messages to each other already, and the advent of S/MIME support in Exchange V5.5 SP1 will make the whole situation easier to support. More information on the changes to the advanced security subsystem in Exchange V5.5 SP1 can be found starting on page 457.

Some interesting steps are taken to accommodate items that might be stored in Exchange folders. For example, tasks, journal items, notes, and calendar entries do not use the standard IPM.Message form that Outlook clients display to view normal messages. Each item type has its own form that incorporates some additional processing to display the item properly. If Outlook Express fetches one of these items it cannot access the necessary electronic form, so it turns to the active server technology used by Outlook Web Access (or OWA, see page 85) and invokes a browser to display the item.

Figure 2.11 is a good example of this and shows how an entry for St. Patrick's Day is displayed by the combination of Outlook Express and OWA. A separate log-on to OWA is required before the item can be displayed. This approach is functional insofar as it gains access to the data, but it is hardly a satisfying graphical experience. A similar approach is used when Outlook Express opens something like an Access database that's been stored in a folder: some code from OWA is called to download the item and launch the application. As we proceed towards the implementation of HTML (instead of RTF) as the basic cross-platform format for storage and display these minor irritations will be relieved.

Figure 2.11
*Outlook Web
Access is called
to process a
calendar item*

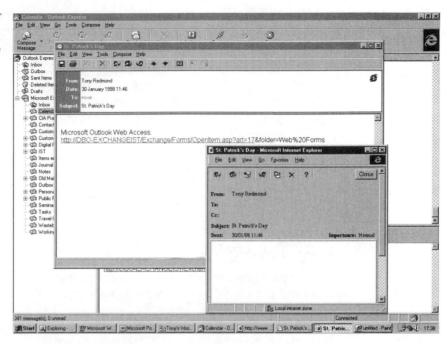

The major advantage of Outlook Express is the fact that Microsoft is engineering the product, making Outlook Express the preferred POP3 client for Exchange server. Outlook Express should remain very competitive, largely because Microsoft needs it to be so to maintain pressure on Netscape. It's undeniable that Outlook Express will always be handicapped by the constraints of the POP3 and IMAP4 protocols and so lag behind the full Outlook client in terms of functionality. However, even with these limitations, it should always be a more than adequate client for people who are just starting with e-mail, or those who really don't require the features of a high-end client. Also, if you need a solution that works on low-end hardware that might struggle with the demands of Outlook and the rest of the Office 97 suite, Outlook Express is an excellent way to help to introduce Exchange.

2.5.5 Secure connections?

The POP3 and IMAP4 protocols do not specify any particular means of enforcing secure communications between server and client. This allows great flexibility for designers to incorporate common security mechanisms such as Kerberos, or leverage specific authentication methods provided by a server. Including a mechanism like Kerberos is not automatic and the majority of POP3 or IMAP4 clients don't support anything except basic clear text authentication as defined in RFC 1225.

Clear text authentication isn't very secure. All the information necessary to establish a connection to the server is dispatched in clear, 7-

bit ASCII text, available to anyone who cares to monitor the network using a tool such as the SMS Network Monitor. As an example of what I mean, let's look at how a client notifies a POP3 server that it would like to connect to a mailbox.

POP3 clients communicate with server over a TCP/IP link to port number 110 (IMAP4 clients use port 143). In either case, the server responds to the initial query to indicate that it is able to accept client connections, and the client sends the name of the mailbox it wishes to connect to.

```
User <username> <CR> <LF>
```

POP3 servers respond with either +OK or –ERR to indicate that the mailbox name is known. The client then proceeds to send the password associated with the mailbox. Again, this data is sent in clear text.

```
Pass <password> <CR> <LF>
```

If the password is correct the server locks the mailbox for exclusive access and the client can proceed to issue the necessary commands to retrieve and send mail. In an Exchange context account names and passwords are exchanged under the control of the Windows NT authentication service, but the fact remains that the protocol determines that everything is dispatched from the client to the server in clear text. Also, because POP3 clients need to make a series of connections to fetch and send messages, the password information is cached by the server so that users aren't constantly bothered with log-in screens. Some consider password caching a potential security risk, but this implementation is somewhat inevitable given the way POP3 works.

Like POP3, IMAP4 supports clear text authentication. However, like browser access, IMAP4 clients can also use NTLM (Windows NT Challenge/Response, the type of log-on used when MAPI clients connect to Exchange). Both forms of authentication support channel encryption using SSL over port 933 to protect password information as it passes between client and server. The full set of authentication options made available by Exchange for IMAP4 clients is shown in Figure 2.12.

IMAP4 also allows for anonymous access. This feature is turned off by default. If activated, anonymous connections can be made using a stated account. The account can be anything you like except blank, and it may or may not be associated with an Exchange mailbox. No password is required. Anonymous access is possible only through clear text authentication, which is supported for the anonymous account even if clear text authentication is not enabled for the server as a whole. Anonymous IMAP4 users are able to access the same set of public folders available to anonymous web connections, unless the anonymous account has an Exchange mailbox, in which case the permissions held by the mailbox are used. A separate anonymous account must be maintained for every server that supports anonymous access. For comparison's sake, Outlook clients use the standard Windows NTLM challenge/response mechanism.

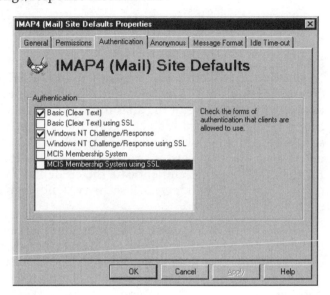

2.5.6 Testing connections

Configuring and testing new types of clients always presents a challenge to system administrators. The POP3 connection is easy to test using a TELNET connection to port 110. The connection essentially mimics the interaction between a client and the server. Instead of client software driving the connection by issuing a series of commands to connect, authenticate, and retrieve messages, the POP3 commands are issued manually. You can monitor the response to the commands and determine whether the link is operating as expected.

In the example, we'll assume that the server name (DBO-EXCHANGEIST) is known to the local DNS. We'll connect to my own mailbox. First, use TELNET to connect to port 110 on the server. Make sure that local echo is turned on for the TELNET session, otherwise you won't see characters you type echoed back to the screen.

After a successful connection is made Exchange announces its presence, together with the build number. Now enter the user name. Because Exchange uses Windows NT and there is a potential difference between the Windows NT account name and the Exchange mailbox name you may have to pass a fully specified name. That is, pass the Windows NT domain name, the Windows NT account name, and the alias for the Exchange mailbox.

```
+OK Microsoft Exchange POP3 Server 5.0.1389.6 ready
User OFFICESI\T_Redmond\TonyR
+OK
pass abc1238658
+OK User successfully logged on
```

In this set of commands we have:

Connected to port 110 on server DBO-EXCHANGEIST in the OFFICESI Windows NT domain, and issued a request to connect to my mailbox. Note the use of the alias for my mailbox (TonyR). The characters in the password are echoed to the screen, which isn't great if someone is looking over your shoulder. A short pause may be experienced after the password is provided. This is accounted for the need for the POP3 server to authenticate the credentials with a domain controller. Standard Windows NT security is not bypassed by POP3 clients.

Once a connection is made we can issue other commands to manipulate the contents of the mailbox. Remember that the POP3 server only deals in terms of an inbox folder, so that's exactly what you'll be working with. For example, to list the contents of the inbox (not a good idea with a big inbox), type:

```
List
```

Each message is listed sequentially together with an id number. No other attributes (title, author, etc.) are listed. Messages have to be retrieved from the server before a client is able to discover attributes. To retrieve a message, type the RETR command and the number of the message. For example, the command:

```
RETR 1
```

Retrieves the first message in the inbox. This is not the latest message. Rather, it is more likely to be the oldest message in the inbox. The connection has been adequately tested so we can close it off with a QUIT command.

Testing the POP3 connection in this way is quick and direct. Any potential client-specific configuration issues are eliminated and if successful, you've proved that Exchange is configured correctly and able to serve clients.

Telnet can also be used to test IMAP4 connections. In this instance you'll connect to port 143 and connect with a login command.

```
Login Windows NT domain name\Windows NT Account\Exchange mailbox alias
```

or

```
Login OFFICESI\T_Redmond\TonyR
```

After a successful logon, you can proceed to use IMAP4 functions to test the connection.

2.6   Browsing the Web with Exchange

We all know the impact of the Web. Acknowledging that impact and accommodating the huge spread of browsers as clients for Exchange is clearly a strategic step for Microsoft to take. It's also one of the most interesting aspects of Exchange, if only because of the way that the technology now being put in place may point the way to future desktops.

2.6.1   Active Technology

Web pages began life as passive entities. You clicked on a page, followed hyperlinks around the Web, but basically everything was quite static. The CGI (Common Gateway Interface) marked the next steps along the Web evolutionary path, allowing people to build scripts and link commands into pages so that some real processing could be performed when requested by users. However, the interaction between CGI scripts and users is asynchronous and still relatively passive. The advent of Java changed the way developers looked at Web pages because now there was a way to build code (or intelligence) into pages. Suddenly a rush began to understand where the limits for Java-enabled pages lay, what applications could be built, and how the ever growing Web could be harnessed for commercial advantage.

Sun Microsystems are the originators of Java and have been the chief proponents of a general move to Web-enabled applications, facilitated by new network-capable devices engineered by Sun and other vendors. After a slow start Microsoft began to catch up with the quantum leap in Web technology and have now formulated a strategy known as the Active Platform. Exchange is an important part of the Active Platform simply because email is immediately useful to many people. Solving a Microsoft problem with non-Windows clients is a side effect of enabling Exchange for browser access, albeit one that will help Exchange gain acceptance in some companies that it couldn't previously be deployed.

As with all new technologies the Active Platform promises something to everyone. Developers get an easy-to-use platform to build new Web applications. Users get a "seamless browsing experience, regardless of the operating system being used" (a phrase taken from a

Microsoft market bulletin, and one that I don't really understand!). Anyway, three core parts form the Active Platform:

- *Active Desktop*: Technology that will be built in at the operating system level (in other words, initially incorporated into Windows 95 and Windows NT) to leverage the capabilities of other Active Platform components.

- *Active Server*: Built into all versions of the Internet Information Server from V3.0, this is the server component of Active Platform, responsible for handling client requests generated by applications such as connecting browsers to Exchange. Collectively, the set of application components used to connect to Exchange is known as Active Messaging.

- *ActiveX*: A set of reusable development components including controls, documents, scripts, and a Java Virtual Machine (a software-based machine to run Java code). ActiveX controls are possibly the most famous component, mostly because of the wide exposure of the Windows development community to Visual Basic VBX and OCX controls. Two immediate advantages are gained from this background. First, ActiveX can be regarded as mature technology with a lot of developers who know the broad concepts. Second, there are a lot of controls that started life as VBX or OCX files that have now been converted to ActiveX controls.

The value of controls that can be dropped into a project and immediately add functionality is obvious to anyone who has ever programmed with Visual Basic, and the same approach is being taken with ActiveX. The difference is, of course, in this case the target environment is composed of Web pages that include ActiveX controls (active pages), with each control taking responsibility for a particular task. Today, ActiveX controls can only be used by Windows 95 and Windows NT desktops. Also, ActiveX is only natively supported by Internet Explorer, Microsoft's own browser, and requires an add-in before it can be used by other browsers. These facts presented a challenge for the Exchange development team, who have a goal to be the server of choice for the widest possible client population, so the connection between web browsers and Exchange is accomplished without the need for any ActiveX controls. Active pages (containing VBscript) are used instead, an approach that allows support for OS/2, Macintosh, and UNIX desktops. The decision to use Vbscript instead of ActiveX necessitated some false starts during the development of the web interface. For example, a prototype of the calendaring component was demonstrated at the 1996 Exchange Conference. The prototype had to be rewritten to use Vbscript and didn't appear until it was included in Exchange V5.5.

As mentioned above, the Active Messaging application bridges the gap between Exchange and the Internet Information Server. Let's see how this is done.

2.6.2   How Web browsers connect to Exchange

Figure 2.12 illustrates how Exchange supports Web browsers. The server-side application is called Active Messaging, which relies on V1.0b of the Active Server Pages component for Internet Information Server (IIS) V3.0. Access to Exchange can be gained through either IIS V3.0 or IIS V4.0, the latest available version at the time of writing.

Figure 2.13
*Components
of the Web
connection*

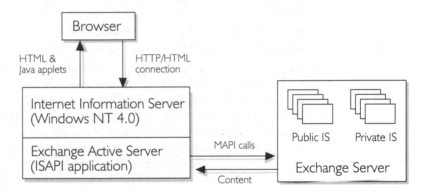

Active Messaging provides the interface between IIS and Exchange and is implemented as two dynamic link libraries. The functions contained in these libraries allow client requests to be interpreted and dispatched to Exchange for execution. In a similar manner the results of these requests are returned to Active Messaging and transformed into HTML instructions that can be displayed by a browser. Note the emphasis on processing performed by servers.

Today, the communication between a browser and Exchange is rather passive when compared to a MAPI client. The browser merely serves as a display device for whatever output is generated by the Active Messaging application on the server. All of the processing required to interpret the code contained in the active pages is performed on the server. Future developments such as Dynamic HTML, which allow web browsers to cache and manipulate data that originated from a server, may split processing between clients and servers a little more evenly, but not today.

The user interface created by Active Messaging is called Outlook Web Access (OWA), which we've already briefly encountered in conjunction with Outlook Express. You may have heard of it referred to as Outlook WebView, the original name introduced with Exchange V5.0. The name seeks to associate the functionality and interface delivered to browsers with the more comprehensive functionality delivered by the "real" Outlook client (which, of course, uses MAPI).

Let's review the components used in OWA:

- Any browser can be used, as long as it supports JavaScript and frames. Netscape Navigator V3.0 or later, or Microsoft Internet Explorer V3.02 (with the appropriate patches) or later are good choices[6]. Frames are used extensively to divide the browser screen into a user interface which somewhat approximates to the interface you'd see if you used an Exchange client. Java-Script, or more correctly, VBscript is used in association with Active Pages (pages that have embedded ActiveX controls) to accomplish complex processing, such as executing a lookup against the directory or creating a new message.

- Browsers connect to Exchange using the HTTP protocol through a standard URL (like http://myserver/exchange). The URL points to the Active Messaging application and eventually leads to an active page (.ASP file) that begins the connection process. It's possible to run Internet Information Server on a Windows NT V3.51 system, but this configuration does not support Active Pages. Internet Information Server V3.0 or later running on Windows NT V4.0 SP3 (or later) are required to support browser connections to Exchange. Apart from anything else, a higher degree of security is possible with Windows NT V4.0 because it supports SSL for network authentication.

- The initial page for Exchange offers users an option to either connect to their own mailbox or connect anonymously. All of the processing on this page is controlled by Vbscript code embedded in the active pages. The Internet Information Server converts VBscript to byte code on an as-needed basis. Anonymous connections are restricted to viewing a subset of public folders. Mailbox access is only available after a dialog is conducted to establish which mailbox to connect to and the user has provided the Windows NT account and password for that mailbox. SSL can be used to send encrypted password information to the server, otherwise the standard NTLM mechanism can be used. Clear text authentication is also supported, but perhaps this is only suitable for deployment in pilot projects.

- Dialog between the Active Messaging application and Exchange is conducted using MAPI. Requests from browsers are translated into equivalent MAPI function calls. Exchange sees requests

---

6.   Earlier versions of Netscape Navigator (2.02 onwards) supported Javascript and frames but don't support OWA, mostly because the implementation of the technology is incomplete.

from browsers in exactly the same way as if they were MAPI function calls generated by an Outlook client. Exchange responds with MAPI output, and this data is taken and rendered into HTML by Active Messaging before being sent to browser. Because active pages are all processed on the server and additional work is required to render the content returned by Exchange into HTML, each OWA "client" generates roughly twice the load of an Outlook client that's directly connected.

Active pages are basically the same as normal HTML pages. The big difference is the fact that they contain embedded code written in a language that will be very familiar to any Visual Basic programmer. For example, the code necessary to display the current time in an active page is:

```
<HTML>
Hallo World! The current time is <%= time() %>
</HTML>
```

Combined into a text file with an .ASP extension this code is enough to make a browser proclaim:

```
Hallo World! The current time is 6:13 PM
```

Not awe-inspiring, but enough to illustrate the point.

The source code for Active Messaging is split across a set of HTML pages, GIF graphics, and active pages. Some sample code is illustrated in Figure 2.14. The code is organized into a set of directories, one for each language (USA, Germany, Japan) supported by the server. Each language root directory has a set of sub-directories, and you'll find the actual source code here. For example, the \anon directory contains all the code used to connect anonymous clients to Exchange whereas the \inbox directory has the code to display the contents of an inbox folder.

The code in active pages is not compiled. Instead, .ASP pages hold interpreted scripts that are processed by the server upon request from a client. Interpreted scripts are easier to change than compiled code, even if they are slower. The speed issue is largely addressed by the fact that scripts are executed on the server, masking any great difference from a client perspective. Interpreted code also allows the same application to run across multiple client platforms. The same script runs on the server no matter how many client platforms are used. It is the responsibility of the clients (browsers) to display the data returned by the server. In the case of an active server application, clients receive HTML formatting instructions that result from scripts being run on the server.

Figure 2.14
*Source code for
an Exchange
active page*

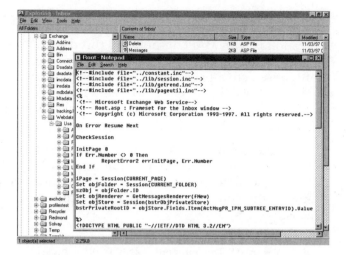

Figure 2.14
*Source code for
an Exchange
active page*

Some magic is required to make active server applications work. As well as installing the active pages, both the LDAP and HTTP protocols must be enabled on the target Exchange server. When this is done the server is ready to process incoming HTTP requests to open the active pages that form OWA. Active pages are processed in much the same way that those which contain only normal HTML. When the server processes simple, static pages that only contain HTML instructions the data is passed untouched to a client browser.

Figure 2.15
*Opening the
LOGON.ASP
active page
activiates the
logon screen*

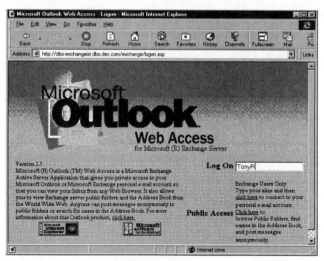

Activating an active page causes the server to pause, interpret the script commands and then execute them. The results of the commands are then returned to the browser. In the case of Exchange the Vbscript functions in the active pages interact with Active Messaging to log-on to the server, fetch inbox contents, and other details like the count of new messages. For example, opening the LOGON.ASP active page causes Active Messaging to begin the process of logging on to an Exchange mailbox, as can be seen in Figure 2.15.

Web browsers typically start an Exchange session by pointing to a URL like this:

```
http://server_name/Exchange
```

You can insert a URL pointing to Exchange in any HTML page. For example:

```
<a href=http://myserver/Exchange></a>
```

When the page is accessed IIS looks at its list of registered applications (services) to see where to find the root directory for Exchange (Figure 2.16). Normally the root is \EXCHSRVR\WEBDATA, and a file called GLOBAL.ASA is located there. GLOBAL.ASA initializes the application and calls LOGON.ASP, the active page controlling the log-on process. The other active pages used by Active Messaging are distributed across a set of sub-directories.

Figure 2.16
Defining for IIS where the Exchange active pages are located on a server

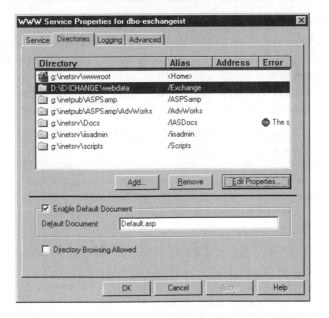

To connect, a user must enter their mailbox name (the alias or directory name is enough) and click on the link to Exchange. A password prompt is then displayed. Depending on the browser you have a choice of basic (clear text) authentication or NTLM. NTLM protects passwords by encrypting the exchange between client and server during the authentication process.

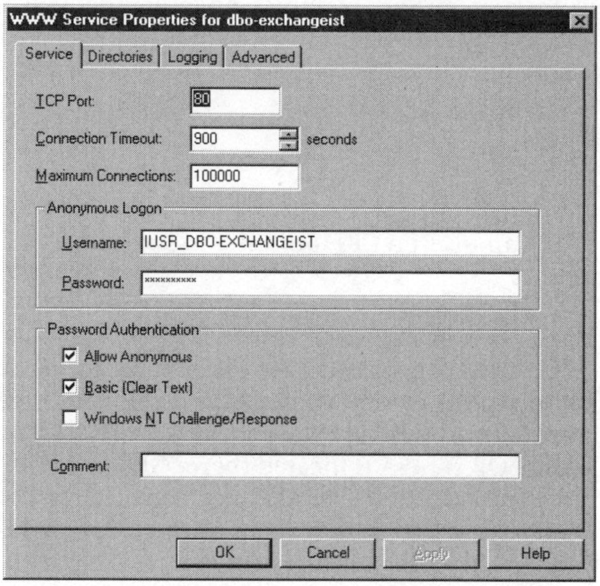

Figure 2.17
*Properties for
the IIS*

Out of the box, Netscape Navigator supports basic authentication whilst Internet Explorer (3.0 or later) supports both. You can update Navigator to support NTLM if the Authentication Proxy for Netscape browsers is loaded on the client (see http://backoffice.microsoft.com/ DownTrial/mapn.asp). Make sure that the password authentication properties for the IIS are set appropriately, as shown in Figure 2.17.

Use of NTLM requires that IIS is run on every Exchange server that wishes to support browser access to mailboxes. If you want to run a single IIS to provide access to many Exchange servers you're limited to basic authentication. Also, domain users need the right to log on locally to the system hosting IIS. Log-on capabilities may change as browser technology evolves so it's always best to check before rushing to implement.

The Rendering Object Engine (see page 94) helps to create a good looking client interface, even given some of the obvious limitations of browser-based user interfaces. The resulting pages are always dynamically generated and reflect the current state of the data stored by Exchange. As noted earlier, the relationship between a browser and Exchange is passive. Any updates must be explicitly requested before a browser can display them.

Some questions have been asked whether the use of active pages represents a potential security hole. Could hackers break into Exchange and access unauthorized data because they can "see" the script code that drives the active pages? The answer is "no". The script code is public, and merely contains the instructions necessary to control the connection to Exchange. Data is provided by the server according to the same permissions and rules that any other client is governed by. All of the data passing between a browser and Exchange is invisible to the active page and cannot therefore be intercepted or otherwise affected by the act of a hacker.

From the perspective of software engineering, building a link between browsers and a server through the generation of HTML-formatted output is not new. Lotus does much the same thing in their Domino server, and DIGITAL created similar features in the ALL-IN-1 Web Gateway in 1995. However, Microsoft has developed the concept to a new degree of integration and has created a remarkably usable and visually attractive client. Figure 2.18 shows the contents of my inbox folder being listed, while Figure 2.19 illustrates a week's schedule in my diary. The layout and appearance of OWA looks remarkably similar to Outlook, and as noted earlier, now that Microsoft has concentrated client development into a single development group, the clients should grow closer over time.

In addition, the components used to build OWA can be used to create other Web-centric applications. It will be interesting to see how developers manipulate the CDO messaging, calendaring, and workflow objects in future applications.

Figure 2.18
Using Outlook Web Access to access my mailbox

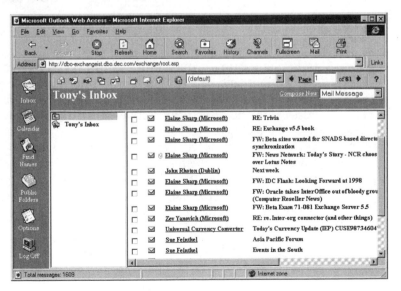

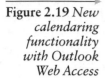

Figure 2.19 *New calendaring functionality with Outlook Web Access*

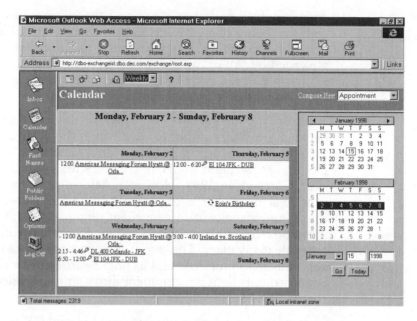

2.6.3   Subsets of Active Messaging

There are two major subsystems within Active Messaging:

1. The Messaging Object Library or Collaborative Data Objects

2. The HTML Rendering Object Library

The messaging object library looks after client requests to connect to Exchange (log-in and authentication) and navigation within folders, both public and private. All of the functions necessary for messaging operations (send, read, delete, attach or detach documents, look up an address in the directory). Active Messaging is now part of Collaborative Data Objects (CDO); a complete set of messaging, calendaring, and workflow objects that can be manipulated by languages such as VBscript. CDO is the basis of the Event Service, and has the potential to be very important to the future evolution of workflow capabilities (in particular) in Exchange over the next few years. The Event Service is reviewed in chapter 12. Full details of CDO can be found in the Microsoft Platform SDK.

The HTML rendering object library provides a set of functions to render outputs from Exchange into the HTML and VBscript suitable for processing by browsers. The rendering library is used to build the OWA user interface, but its functions could obviously be used for other applications. The library includes functions to create columns, groups, sorting, filtering, and conversation threads.

2.6.4   Outlook Web Access features

There's much that can be done with OWA, but there are some things that can't. Table 2.5 compares the features available from MAPI and OWA clients.

Table 2.5   *Feature comparison between MAPI and OWA clients*

Feature	MAPI client	OWA
Access any folder in a mailbox	Yes	Yes
Access public folders	Yes	Yes
Create and send new messages	Yes	Yes
Reply to message	Yes	Yes
Read RTF text in messages	Yes	Yes
Read attachments	Yes	Yes
Forward message	Yes	Yes
Set Inbox Assistant Rules	Yes	No
Set Out of Office Assistant	Yes	Yes
Change folder permissions	Yes	No
Use Personal Stores	Yes	No
Use Off-line stores	Yes	No
Set and apply auto-signature text	Yes	No
Use Calendaring	Yes	Yes
Access the PAB	Yes	No
Access the GAL	Yes	Yes
Create new folder	Yes	Yes
Delete folder	Yes	Yes
Move/Copy folder	Yes	Yes
Move/Copy items	Yes	Yes
Check email addresses (Control/K)	Yes	No (*)[a]

Table 2.5   *Feature comparison between MAPI and OWA clients (continued)*

Feature	MAPI client	OWA
Delete items	Yes	Yes
Personal folder views	Yes	No
Post new item in folder	Yes	Yes
Encrypt or decrypt messages	Yes	No
Add attachments to messages	Yes	Yes
Apply digital signatures to messages	Yes	No
Use Outlook contacts	Yes	No (*)
Create user-specific folder views	Yes	No
Process electronic forms	Yes	No (*)
Change Windows NT account password	Yes	No (*)
Auto-archiving	Yes (Outlook)	No

a. Features marked with an asterisk are provided in Exchange V5.5 SP1

There isn't too much missing, and it's certainly possible that future iterations of OWA will add missing features or address some of the reduced functionality. For example, Exchange V5.5 allowed access to user calendars for the first time (see Figure 2.19). Exchange V5.5 SP1 rounds off browser support by adding features like the ability to check email addresses on a message before it is sent, view the contents of the contacts folder, and change the password for a user's Windows NT account. At the same time, a wizard is provided to translate Outlook forms into a set of active pages that can be deployed for browsers.

2.6.5   Reasons for Outlook Web Access

Why have Microsoft developed and delivered browser access to Exchange? Here are a number of potential reasons to consider:

- First, OWA delivers a solution for UNIX workstations. UNIX workstations are nowhere near as numerous as Windows PCs, but their users are usually a pretty vocal bunch. Microsoft haven't a good record in integrating the UNIX community into their software applications, but the need is greater than ever before now as Microsoft seek to deliver truly enterprise solutions.

- Second, OWA can help deployment projects to roll out faster. It can take a long time to install large numbers of Windows 95 or Windows NT clients in a company, especially if the whole user desktop is being redesigned. Almost everyone has access to a browser, so they can now be given an Exchange mailbox and start working with the server. Later on, when planning is complete and the new desktops are ready, a full-feature MAPI client can be provided. At this stage users can continue working with all the messages and public folders they had used with OWA.

- Third, OWA delivers a solution for low-end Apple Macintosh and Windows (or even DOS) clients. Not everyone has a Pentium PC or PowerPC Macintosh, yet they may be required to use Exchange because everyone else is going to use Exchange. The department or cost center may not be able to pay for new hardware immediately, so OWA allows people to continue using older hardware until the necessary budget is available. The same point can be made in favour of POP3 or IMAP4 clients.

- Fourth, it's difficult to get the infrastructure necessary to transparently support roving users in place if you don't lay the foundations from the start. If the organization is in a situation where people have Windows or Windows NT installed on the hard disk of their PC the PC is very "personal". It is difficult for people arriving at a remote office to use a PC without having to create a new profile. Not everyone is happy to create a new profile or mess with other PC settings, so OWA allows quick and easy access to mailboxes without any great effort.

- Finally, it is conceivable that some people will want to pop into their local cybercafe to quickly read their e-mail back home. Web terminals are appearing in the most unlikely places—airports, shopping malls, maybe even drive-in restaurants soon. Should we all expect to be able to get back to a server to check our mail? Maybe, maybe not. The technology is certainly available to make this happen, but Exchange is only one piece in the jigsaw. Security across the Internet is a more fundamental challenge, and any Web connection from a public place must be controlled and secure. The advent of technologies such as PPTP (Point to Point Tunneling Protocol, available with Windows NT V4.0 Server) and encrypted tunnels through firewalls (like DIGITAL's Alta Vista Tunnel) make such connections more feasible. Once we have a secure connection to the home server the sole issue to solve is network capacity. There is no magic in the Active Server to relieve Internet bottlenecks and deliver great response to a waiting browser, and while the Internet remains a touch clogged this issue will always be there.

I doubted the ability of any Web browser to allow people to process mail across an Internet connection until Microsoft proved me wrong by setting up a "test-drive" site that anyone could connect to. I was able to log-in to a test account there, browse through an inbox, and create and send messages nearly as easily as I can within my own company's network. Given a fast server (Microsoft used an Alpha computer), and good access to the Internet (with suitable firewalls in place) it is entirely conceivable that people access their mail using browsers anywhere in the world.

Occasionally RAS dial-in connections are made over telephone lines that don't allow RPCs to complete successfully. In these situations you'll be told that Exchange cannot be reached by Outlook, even if you have used PING to establish that the network link is available and the server is running. HTTP is a much simpler protocol than MAPI and it doesn't depend on sensitive RPCs. It is often possible to connect using a browser when Outlook stubbornly insists that the server cannot be contacted. The robustness of the browser/Exchange combination has helped me access email on a number of times when all other methods failed.

Searching for an altogether more cynical reason one can't help looking at OWA as a pre-emptive strike against Netscape. Why bother with a Netscape mail server when you can use the very best of Netscape client technology in conjunction with Exchange? Just point a Netscape browser at the URL for Exchange and connect!

2.6.6 Anonymous access

Putting items into public folders allows Exchange users to share the information, but access is restricted to the Exchange community. You must own a mailbox and possess a set of Windows NT security credentials before the server is happy to allow you to view the contents of public folders. Restrictions like this aren't at all important if you operate in an Exchange-pure environment, but they can be very frustrating during migrations, when people haven't fully moved across to Exchange, or if a set of cross-platform clients are operated. Imagine the frustration for a user who receives a message saying that a presentation can be found in a certain public folder, or learns that some valuable marketing data has been posted in a spreadsheet in another folder?

Anonymous access means that a client is able to connect to Exchange without providing a set of security credentials. Access must be limited because the client making the connection has no identity and cannot possess the normal rights and privileges attributed to mailboxes. Normally, the right to access a folder is controlled by an access control list composed of mailbox names (or more precisely, the X.500-like directory name for the mailbox). Exchange permits anonymous access by creating a pseudo-name called "Anonymous" which allows administrators to nominate which folders they'd like unidentified clients to be able to view. Anonymous access is not granted by default. You must select each folder that you want to allow access to and modify its access control list to allow anonymous clients into the world of public folders. Reviewing and modifying the access control list for a large hierarchy of public folders is quite a task, but it's better to do this rather than granting anonymous access by default.

Restricting access to a nominated set of folders is one step, but it needs to be supplemented through special arrangements for Web clients. Outlook clients see the full public folder hierarchy when they access public folders. This is possible because the full hierarchy is replicated to all servers in an organization. However, you definitely don't want to allow anonymous clients to browse the complete public folder hierarchy because:

1.   The names of some public folders may contain hints to the contents, and those contents may be commercially sensitive.

2.   Publicly-available folders are most likely going to be used as repositories for documents and other information you'd like people outside (or inside) the company to access. You don't want people to be distracted when they access public folders, a possibility that certainly exists if they could browse through the complete hierarchy. Focusing on a selected set of folders serves as signpost to the information you want to disseminate.

3.   Browsers would have to download all of the hierarchy before it could be displayed. Clients accessing organizations with large public folder hierarchies might encounter performance problems.

Exchange provides a simple solution to the issue by allowing system administrators to build a set of shortcuts to the public folders they'd like to make available to anonymous clients. As shown in Figure 2.20, the shortcuts are configured as properties of the HTTP protocol object within a site. Shortcuts are specific to a site, so clients that connect to one site will not necessarily see the shortcuts to folders on another site unless the local system administrator has created a shortcut to a local replica. OWA accesses public folders in exactly the same way as mailboxes through a similar user interface, as you can see from Figure 2.21.

Figure 2.20
*Configuring
Public Folders
for anonymous
access*

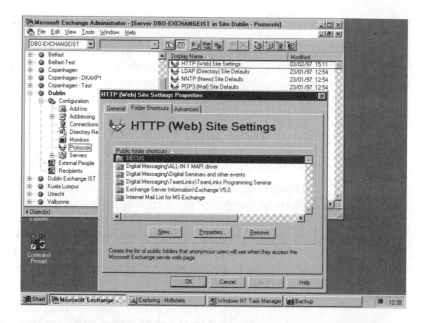

Figure 2.20
*Configuring
Public Folders
for anonymous
access*

Figure 2.21
*A browser
accessing Public
Folders*

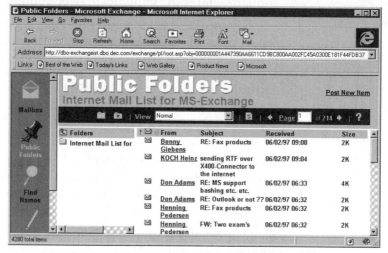

If you examine the URL in Figure 2.21 it's obvious that it doesn't provide a very obvious route to a public folder, nor is it something that the average human will remember. Exchange understands how to use the link to navigate through the Public Information Store to the right folder, but that's as far as it goes. However, you can certainly capture the URL and insert it into a HTML page to build a hot link to a public folder. For example, the Exchange server I use has a public folder that holds all the messages posted to the Internet mailing list for Exchange (ms-exchange@insite.co.uk). To create a link on a web page to this public folder I did the following.

1. Changed the client permissions for the folder to permit "read access" for anonymous log-ons.

2. Used the administration program to modify the site HTTP object and create a short-cut to the public folder.

3. Logged on with anonymous access to the server and checked that I could access the folder.

4. Clicked on the "update page address" button to retrieve the full and complete link for the folder. The information appears as a URL at the top of the browser, and I pasted it into the clipboard.

5. Opened the HTTP source of the page where I wanted to create the link and added the following text:

```
<a href="http://dbo-exchangeist.dbo.dec.com/exchange/anon/
root.asp?obj=000000001A447390AA6611CD9BC800AA002
FC45A0300E181F44FDB37D011A5480020AFF54A230000000331810000">
Internet Mailing List for Microsoft Exchange</a>
```

Note that this address is specific to a server. As you can see, the URL is pretty horrible but the important thing is that it works. With the new page in place I then tested the link, and the result is shown in Figure 2.22. Think of the possibilities this functionality allows. Marketing information can be easily published to the web or technical support hints and tips from your help desk made available to users through a link on your company's home page, and so on. Perhaps the potential for information dissemination will become more important to some enterprises than simple mailbox access.

Figure 2.22
*Accessing a
public folder via
an embedded
URL*

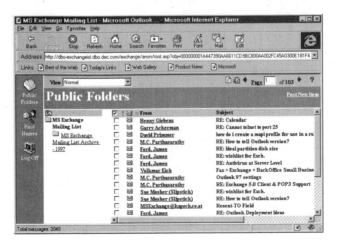

2.7   IMAIL: The Protocol Engine

All Exchange clients, including the lightweight variety, connect to the Information Store service. Up to V5.0 the only supported protocol was MAPI, with client communication performed via RPCs. IMAIL, a new software layer within the Information Store, was introduced in Exchange V5.0 together with the POP3 protocol stub that's necessary to allow POP3 clients to connect in. The layer is extended in Exchange V5.5 to support IMAP4. Browsers still connect via MAPI, but only indirectly, as the MAPI calls generated by OWA are created and dispatched on their behalf by Active Messaging, which also takes care of translating any results to HTML before dispatching it to the browser.

Three access protocols are supported by the Information Store: POP3, IMAP4 and MAPI. MAPI is tied more closely than the other two methods because it can talk directly to the store and supports the RTF format used to store content within the Information Store. Exchange is expanding the number of protocols supported by the server all the time. The world of applications is moving quickly towards HTML (or a more developed version of the current HTML protocol) as the de facto standard for platform-independent content storage. These two influences mean that changes must be made to allow support for new protocols to be incorporated seamlessly, and to support the introduction of HTML as the native content format used by Exchange. IMAIL, the protocol engine provides the foundation for support of other protocols in the future.

Figure 2.23
The role of the IMAIL protocol engine

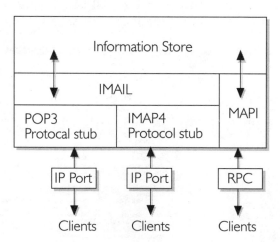

As illustrated in Figure 2.23, the task of the IMAIL software layer is relatively simple. It sits between the Information Store, where messages, attachments, header information, and other items of data are stored, and the different protocol stubs supported by Exchange. As data is moved between the store and the different protocols the IMAIL engine is able to convert the data from the format used by the store to the format most acceptable to the calling protocol. Thus, when a POP3 client retrieves messages from the store, the IMAIL engine takes care of extracting the RTF message content and packaging it up into whatever the requesting client can accept. The information in message headers is likewise extracted from the Information Store and sent down to the client.

IMAIL is already used to perform RTF to HTML content conversion for OWA. RTF will remain a valid native content for the Information Store, but the announced direction for Exchange is to move towards a situation where HTML becomes the preferred native format. This move shouldn't be surprising because we are already seeing evidence of the same switch in other Microsoft products (the Office 97 application suite is an obvious example), and it will happen gradually, as the opportunity and need arises. The next major version of Exchange is likely to be the time when HTML supplants RTF as the server's native format, unless other development priorities rule this step out. In any case, when the time comes the IMAIL protocol engine will be there and ready to handle the RTF to HTML and HTML to RTF format conversions that will be required.

2.8   Selecting the desktop environment

Windows NT is the only operating system option for an Exchange server, but as we've just reviewed, there is a reasonably wide choice of DOS or Windows-based clients. Given that all of the Windows-based clients offer roughly comparable functionality, which desktop operating system offers the best option for large-scale deployment of Exchange clients?

Most large customers I have worked with in the last year or so have reduced the choice for client desktop operating system to two: Windows NT V4.0 (workstation) or Windows 95. DOS is seen as a solution only for the rapidly-reducing population of 80386-powered PCs (in corporate computing environments), while Windows V3.1 and Windows for WorkGroups are crippled by the flaws in the old Windows architecture that are so readily exposed if a user attempts to run more than two large applications together at the one time. Moving to Windows NT or Windows 95 on the desktop will cost money for application upgrades and extra hardware, but the costs are somewhat offset by reduced help desk calls generated by frustrated users complaining of depleted system resources.

Windows 95 arrived in a blaze of publicity in August 1995, easily winning the all-time award for hyped-up software. Despite all the talk about the evolution to 32-bit desktop computing, Windows 95 hasn't quite achieved the full status of a 32-bit operating system because its' kernel remains a hybrid mixture of 16- and 32-bit code. Microsoft probably would have liked to have more 32-bit code in Windows 95 but time and the need for backwards compatibility for applications dictated that some 16-bit code survived. The resulting mix works well, most of the time. Windows 95 is far more reliable than Windows V3.*x*, and users can plan for a complete day's work without factoring in the need to reboot to recover leaked system resources. While more memory is needed, far more applications can be run together and Windows 95 will cope with the load. Using Windows 95 as my day-to-day workhorse platform I typically run Word, PowerPoint, Excel, and multiple mail clients together at the same time without problems.

Windows NT had a slow start but has greatly improved since its early days. The workstation edition of Windows NT V4.0, suitably equipped with the Windows 95 user interface shell, is the top of the range user desktop environment available today. While Windows 95 increased reliability and robustness over the previous version by a user-perceived factor of 10 or more (based on my own personal experience), Windows NT is even more reliable, secure, and network-aware. In addition, Windows NT is hardware-independent and not tied to the Intel *x*86 architecture, allowing screamingly fast desktop systems to be built around high-end RISC CPUs such as the DIGITAL Alpha chip.

Interestingly, although Windows NT sales are higher than ever before and continue to set new records each reporting period, Windows NT workstation still can't compete with Windows 95. According to International Data Corporation, approximately 2.2 million copies of Windows NT workstation were shipped in 1996, against 60 million copies of Windows 95 (shipped since its release in August 1995). This data backs up my own experience that the majority of major corporate enterprises have standardized on Windows 95 on the desktop. The main reasons being because Windows 95 requires less hardware resources, offers better support for plug and play, and under the terms of many support contracts, doesn't carry an upgrade fee to move from Windows V3. Windows NT, on the other hand, has better security and is more robust, but it carries an upgrade fee (the standard price is $95). When all the costs are put together Windows 95 looks much more attractive.

Which desktop operating system should you use? Certainly I would not recommend Windows V3.*x*. Apart from the restrictions imposed by Windows in its 16-bit implementation Microsoft are not developing Windows V3.*x* any further. The old saying that "when the horse is dead, it's time to get off" comes to mind here. Windows 95 or Windows NT represents the best options for the future, but both require a considerable investment to install across all desktops in any medium to large enterprise. Because it is priced for the home/small office market Windows 95 is the cheaper of the two options. As noted above, Windows 95 still scores over NT in terms of Plug and Play and power management, meaning that if you're interested in using notebook computers Windows 95 is the best choice. Windows NT V5.0 includes many of the features to support notebook computers that are missing in V4.0, but this version is unlikely to see widespread deployment until mid to late 1999.

Windows 98 certainly deserves some consideration, but perhaps after it has had some months to settle down. Most corporate deployment teams are reluctant to use a new operating system until they've had a chance to compare notes with other companies, and I don't imagine that they'll make an exception for Windows 98.

In desktop environments Windows NT is a little more expensive, but it is built on a firm 32-bit code base and is a more robust and secure operating system. Microsoft's direction towards a Windows NT desktop environment is also pretty clear, so if you can afford the extra cost then Windows NT workstation is the option I would go for. You are paying more now, but it's probably a better long-term bet for the future.

Selecting the desktop operating system is only the start. Apart from a potential requirement to upgrade hardware with additional memory and faster CPUs, if you install a new desktop it's likely that you'll also want to review the application software in use too. Migrating everyone from Microsoft Office V4 to Office 95 or Office 97 costs money, and then all the terminal emulators, databases, programming languages, and other applications might require new versions too if real advantage is to be taken of your new 32-bit desktop. Putting all the costs together that might be incurred in evolving towards a 32-bit desktop it's easy to see how a $60 product[7] could become a major push factor behind a decision to invest between $500 and $2,000 per desktop.

One way to keep costs down is to adopt a "one-upgrade" approach. In other words, when you change the messaging system to Exchange

---

7.   Exchange clients are priced differently depending on the number of clients purchased and the country they are purchased in. I've taken $60 as an average price for the purpose of illustration only. Contact your local Microsoft office to get current price information about Exchange servers and clients.

you do so as part of an ordered, co-ordinated upgrade for the entire desktop environment. The move may involve the following operations:

- Hardware upgrade or replacement for existing PCs. Adding new memory to accommodate the demands of Windows 95 or Windows NT, or just switching out old PCs for new.

- Installation of the new desktop operating system.

- Configuration of network protocols. For example, you may wish to switch over to TCP/IP as a universal network protocol. If so, the PCs need to be configured correctly in terms of an IP address, connection to WINS, DNS and DHCP servers, and so on. You may need to configure the PCs to run multiple network stacks—TCP/IP for client to server connectivity and Novell IPX for file and print services are a pretty common combination.

- Installation of desktop applications. Configuring client software for Exchange is obvious, but you'll probably need to upgrade the office application suite, terminal emulators, and so on. After everything is upgraded the applications may need to be configured to connect to the right printers, etc.

- Training of users to deal with the new environment.

People generally find it easier to move in one operation rather than to be constantly bothered by a series of upgrades spread over an extended period. Change disrupts users, but the cumulative disruption caused by a series of upgrades is generally more than experienced in a single upgrade operation that deals with everything at one time. Apart from the effect on users, it is also cheaper to concentrate the efforts of technical and support staff on a set of "one-time" upgrades. Every time a technical person touches a desktop to upgrade an application or the hardware it costs money. Minimizing these interventions will save money in the long run.

Selecting the right platform for client deployment is an important part of your overall computing infrastructure for the next few years. But clients are only a small, low-cost part of the overall equation around Exchange. The question therefore needs to be asked whether a $60 client can drive the whole desktop in terms of its evolution and technical environment? Only you can answer that question.

2.8.1   Hardware resources for clients

The rich functionality contained in Outlook clients is implemented in millions of lines of complex code. Large programs that offer extensive functionality fight a constant battle between the constant demands from users for increased functionality and the need to up the minimum hardware threshold. Complex code, no matter how optimized, has to be loaded into memory sometime, the modules, executables and other data files representing the program must be stored, and all the machine instructions generated by the code will be executed on processors. If there isn't enough memory, disk space, or processing power available to handle the demand generated by the program it will either not be able to execute or will run slowly. Everyone wants programs to run fast, but users, no matter how hard they lobbied for the new features frown on any slow-down produced through the introduction of new functionality. This is the conundrum for all engineering groups.

The minimum specified hardware base for Outlook is different from the minimum practical base. The difference is, of course, in that Microsoft certify that Outlook will run with a certain hardware configuration, but they don't specify the level of performance, perceived or otherwise, a user will experience with the configuration. This tactic isn't unique to Microsoft as all software vendors seek to qualify products against low hardware configurations in order to increase the total potential user base for their product. While Outlook will run on a basic 80486-powered PC with 8MB of memory under Windows 95 the performance will be slow and unacceptable.

If you're coming from a Microsoft Mail background expect to have to take a long hard look at current hardware resources on user desktops before migrating to Exchange. Microsoft Mail is a very much simpler product in terms of architecture and implementation and is therefore able to comfortably perform on a PC with a far lower specification. Expect to have to add extra memory to the majority of your PCs and eliminate any low-end PCs that are in use. Don't expect to be able to use 80386-powered systems for anything else but DOS systems, or perhaps to connect via a POP3 client or web browser.

The situation can be further complicated in terms of overall client hardware configurations if you want to upgrade applications and desktop operating system at the same time, for example to move to a Windows 95/Office 97/Outlook desktop environment. It seems that every desktop application is gently expanding in size and complexity as features are added in each new release, and each addition has to be paid for somewhere. Consider the complex interconnections underpinning a message composed by a user with Outlook when Word for Windows is used as the cover note editor. Now drag an Excel worksheet from the Windows Explorer and drop it into the memo. Then double-click on the newly embedded icon to start Excel so that the figures in the worksheet can be verified before being sent. Three highly functional applications working smoothly together in a relatively seamless manner under Windows 95. Is it any wonder that PCs need to have faster CPUs today than the largest minicomputers had at the start of the 1990s?

Table 2.6 suggests some sample configurations for desktop computing environments that must support Exchange client as well as a mix of commonly-used personal productivity applications (Word, Excel, and so on). These configurations are not the minimum specified by Microsoft for any of the operating systems. Instead, they are the minimum configurations I recommend to people who come to me for advice. The central ideas driving the recommendations are to create a system that works well (all the time) and has scope to grow and accommodate increased demands generated by users, or new versions of operating systems or applications. The recent history of computing tells us that any system that appears to be slightly over-configured today will be the smallest usable system in the very near future, and that future comes closer every day.

Table 2.6   *Sample configurations for desktop clients*

Desktop Operating System	CPU	Memory	Basic Hard Disk requirements
DOS (V5 or above)	Intel 80386 upwards	8 MB upwards	200 MB upwards
Microsoft Windows V3.1 or Windows for WorkGroups	Intel 80486 25 MHz upwards	12 MB upwards	300 MB upwards
Microsoft Windows 95 or Windows 98	Pentium 166 MHz	16 MB upwards	1GB upwards
Microsoft Windows NT 4.0 workstation	Pentium 166 MHz upwards, or any DIGITAL Alpha CPU	32 MB (Intel); 48 MB (Alpha)	2GB upwards
Apple Macintosh System 7.5 or 8.0	PowerPC	8–12 MB	300 MB upwards

2.8.2   Seeking a replacement of the Video Terminal

Video terminals are cheap and easy to maintain, but no-one ever alleged that they provide an interesting and graphical place to work. Companies running email systems like IBM PROFS or DIGITAL ALL-IN-1 operate large communities of video terminals and are aware that these devices are much easier to manage than a PC. The initial hardware cost is usually a big factor in a decision to move from a video-terminal based email system, but the total cost of PC ownership is receiving more and more attention from market analysts today. Purchasing a PC is just the start of the bills that accumulate from a PC deployment. In the 1996–97 period Microsoft came under increasing pressure from both customers and competitors to justify all the costs associated with PCs, and many different efforts are under way to arrive at an answer to the problem. Potential answers include:

- The Network Computer (NC)
- The NetPC
- Hydra (officially called Windows Terminal Server, or WTS)

The NC, supported by companies like Oracle, Sun, and Netscape, has little or no local disk storage and downloads all the application software it requires from large servers situated around the network. Despite Microsoft's antipathy towards the NC, OWA is a great NC application, better (because it's here now) than some of the other applications the proponents of the NC constantly refer to.

Microsoft announced the NetPC in mid-1997. The NetPC is designed to be a simpler, easy to support PC for corporate deployments. At announcement, the NetPC was based on a minimum configuration of a Pentium 133 MHz CPU with 16MB RAM installed into a sealed case. These details are prone to change, so check:

```
www.microsoft.com/windows/netpc
```

for the latest information. From an Exchange perspective, the important thing is that the NetPC is designed to be 100% compatible with Windows applications like the Outlook client, and comes with remote management features to make it easier to deploy and monitor client software.

Hydra is an add-on to Windows NT Server V4.0 (and V5.0) that enables Win32 and Java applications to run on a server and incorporates technologies from Citrix Winframe that have been in use since 1995. The Hydra client runs a "super-thin" protocol to upload keystrokes and mouse clicks to the server, and accept screen output for display in return. The client can run on existing PCs and is a reasonable solution for low-end 80486 or even 80386 CPUs that frankly struggle to run the latest Microsoft Office applications. Citrix client plug-ins are available for the Hydra server to support DOS and UNIX clients. A Hydra server can certainly support a community of Outlook clients, but be prepared to pay for extra server resources to handle client demands. The network will also experience a significant increase in load as it transports all the graphical data between server and client. Testing continues to discover the optimum server hardware required to support different numbers of clients, and I expect that this area will quickly evolve in the near future.

Any of these solutions could take the place of a lot of unintelligent video terminals in use today. They could also replace a large number of PCs, especially those used by people who never really exploit the power of the PC but remain connected to the LAN all day long.

2.9   Windows CE

Windows CE (previously codenamed "Pegasus"), a cut-down version of Windows for Hand-Held PCs (or H/PC) was first released in November 1996, and V2.0 appeared in late 1997. Windows CE is based on a stripped down sub-set of the Win32 APIs. Some reports place the amount at roughly 30% of the code base in Windows 95, but this shouldn't be taken to imply that Windows CE is based on Windows 95. In fact, Windows CE is more like Windows NT in many respects. For example, all characters used in Windows CE are 16-bit UNICODE, totally unlike the mix of 8- and 16-bit characters used by Windows 95. Out of the box, Windows CE includes a number of applications, including Pocket Word, Pocket Excel, and a messaging client. Some of the more advanced features of the full-sized applications, such as grammar checking, are removed to reduce the demand on system resources.

Despite its cut-down nature, Windows CE is an elegant 32-bit pre-emptive multitasking operating system with a built in database. Interestingly, like Windows NT, Windows CE is designed to be cross-platform and is currently able to run on Hitachi SH3, NEC, and MIPS processors. Much of the code is execute-in-place, meaning that it can run directly from ROM and doesn't need to occupy valuable RAM. Everything has to fit into 2MB of memory, the minimum configuration for a H/PC. Anyone who is really interested in using these devices for more than a few casual notes should invest the extra money to equip their H/PC with at least 8MB. Computers at the upper end of the H/PC spectrum can accommodate up to 32MB.

The functionality of all the pocket applications is minimal when compared to their grown-up equivalents. Such a comparison misses the point—who really cares that Pocket Word isn't able to exert the same page formatting control as Word for Windows, or that Pocket Excel doesn't have all the modelling functions built into the regular version. I don't think I shall ever be tempted to do any heavy-duty writing on a H/PC if only because their small keyboards represent a large challenge to my uncoordinated fingers! Peering at a (small and dim) monochrome 640 × 480 LCD dot panel, even with the ever-improving clarity that LCD panels achieve, is also not something that I'd care to do for an extended period. It's hard enough to deal with the screens on notebook PCs. The second generation H/PCs now available provide larger and clearer screens, and the high-end H/PCs support color. Even such relative luxury is still possibly not enough to consider writing for more than a page or two.

H/PCs are intended to complete with pocket organizers, the classic example being the Psion range of hand-held computers. The applications included in H/PCs must be able to pass information to and from PCs and allow their users to work on a document, spreadsheet or other item away from the office. Based on the success of other hand-held computers, H/PCs are likely to be attractive to people who spend a lot of time shuttling between meetings and other appointments. These folks want to jot down a few ideas as they occur, or to use these tiny computers for a form of "emergency e-mail". You won't do very much more than make a few notes, as the tiny keyboard is not conducive to any major writing endeavor. However, it's certainly more than possible to write up meetings and other events with the intention of polishing up the text with a desktop PC later on.

Attempting to craft something like a book on a H/PC misses the point of the device however. The major advantage of combining Windows CE with a HPC is its compatibility with common desktop applications, plus the excellent synchronization features that allow users to upload and download files from PCs. Similar in concept to the Windows 95 briefcase, you can easily set up a H/PC to synchronize its contents with a desktop PC. Microsoft provides a H/PC Explorer application (for Windows NT and Windows 95) to allow you to browse thorough the H/PC's contents when it is connected to a desktop system.

A POP3 messaging client is bundled with Windows CE, so it can connect straight into Exchange. Windows CE also supports PPP networking, which provides the foundation for its communication with desktop PCs. A version of OWA for Windows CE (which doesn't use frames) is available from the Microsoft application farm, and some vendors such as Ruksun Software[8] have an IMAP4 client that works with any Windows CE device equipped with a MIPS or SH3 CPU. The IMAP4 client is fully compliant with the IMAP4 server incorporated into Exchange V5.5. Ruksun can also provide an LDAP client for Windows CE. H/PC messaging clients typically connect to servers using dial-up connections.

Windows CE supports many standard PCMCIA modem cards, so dial-up is as easy as in Windows 95. However, standard AA batteries

---

8.   http://www.ruksun.com/wince

power HPCs, and these are rapidly exhausted once modem activity starts, understandable because PCMCIA cards are designed for the power supplies in "real" notebook PCs. An AC adapter is an essential tool for anyone who wants to use one of these devices on the road. Some H/PCs, such as the Philips "Velo" incorporate a built-in modem, but you'll still need a good power supply when you connect to the network. Multitasking is another way to drain power. Switching between Pocket Word, Pocket Excel, and the mail client is possible, but the computer has to manage all the context switches and does so in memory, creating a drain on the battery.

Palmtop PCs, similar to the H/PC concept, have incorporated editions of electronic mail clients before, so this isn't a new concept. Hewlett-Packard palmtops, for instance, are provided with a cutdown version of Lotus cc:Mail. You can't compare the functionality to that of Outlook running under Windows 95 or Windows NT, but it does a reasonable job of reading messages, and creating and sending mail. Those who are really serious e-mail users will probably not be satisfied by a Windows CE PC, and opt instead to use a high-spec notebook.

2.10   Using the crystal ball

Lots of people like making predictions, and some make predictions about subjects they know little or nothing about. Trying hard to avoid that trap, let's look into the crystal ball to see how client technology might evolve in the next few years. My own view is that:

- The old (Exchange) client will not be developed any further past its current version (5.0). If already deployed, continue to use this client until the next opportunity presents itself to move to Outlook. The same comment applies to Schedule+, which you should migrate towards the Outlook calendaring application.

- Outlook is the focus for all future client development within Microsoft and will remain the premier client for Exchange.

- Newer versions of Outlook will incorporate even more support for Internet standards. Expect HTML to become the default content format instead of RTF. In addition, protocols such as LDAP, IMAP4, POP3, and SMTP will be exploited to allow Outlook to be a highly functional client for other servers. It's interesting to speculate on what the combination of an Outlook client and a Netscape mail server might accomplish!

- The Outlook Express client will continue to access Exchange via POP3 or IMAP4, but will not approach the degree of integration and functionality of the MAPI-based Outlook client until the Internet messaging protocols evolve to incorporate support for features like cross-platform calendaring. MAPI is still important, but its role is likely to be taken on by IMAP4 (or a future development of this protocol) over time. One view is that MAPI is now a mature interface that doesn't need any further development as all the functions required by Outlook are already present. If this view is accurate then IMAP4 will rapidly evolve to become the most important client protocol across the Outlook family.

- Expect all clients shipped by Microsoft (Outlook, Outlook Express, Outlook Web Access) to eventually share the same user interface so that training costs can be reduced and users are more easily able to move between clients. The common user interface will be very close to the Outlook interface we see today.

- The incorporation of Web browsers into the range of possible Exchange clients expands the potential audience for Exchange considerably, but should you use a browser and drop specialized e-mail clients? Remember that Exchange is Microsoft's mail server for the Internet, and that Microsoft, as a company, is very heavily focused on the Internet. Web access and browsing will appear as a basic part of Windows clients over the next year or so, and if this is accepted, we can then project the evolution of Outlook to incorporate some degree of Web capabilities. However, the Web client will remain as the platform-independent option and will never have the same array of features that can be built into a "full" Outlook client.

- Windows CE and HPCs are interesting devices, but only for a small section of the user community. But keep an eye on this stuff—you never know what might happen!

Some of this stuff is happening already. The important thing is to keep your eyes open and realize what's going on, then interpret the data as it arises and decide whether it is important for you. There's certainly no reason not to continue to deploy the Outlook V8.03 client delivered with Exchange V5.5 rather than stopping an implementation project to wait until your company is ready to install Outlook 98.

The same argument holds with respect to browsers. Yes, you could decide to concentrate primarily on browsers today and start using Netscape Navigator or Internet Explorer to work with Exchange e-mail, public folders, and scheduling functionality as well as continuing "normal" access to Web resources. But perhaps the degree of functionality available to browsers is a touch immature in comparison to the full-blown Outlook client. Given today's technology and the degree of development reached by the Web/Exchange components, in most cases the most pragmatic and functional approach is to use an Outlook client to process e-mail, schedule meetings, or work with public folders, no matter how much the Web paradigm appeals. The day when the browser is as functional in all respects to purpose-designed programs may come, but it's just not here yet. The development environment for Web tools has to become far richer before it is able to deliver code that matches today's Visual C++ programs. I have no doubt that Microsoft is working hard to bring Web development tools up to speed (the appearance of tools like Visual Java is evidence of this), and in the next two years I expect Outlook Web Access to grow more and more in terms of features.

Every additional client variant deployed increases the pressure on support resources. Every additional client makes it harder to plan software upgrades to ensure that people are using relatively up to date software. Every additional client requires extra training, and perhaps a new set of training or support material, if your company produces these items. In short, each new client means extra cost, even if the client software is free. For these reasons it is unwise to get too carried away with all the different clients. Select one, focus on it, and deploy it successfully. Then see if you really need another client and have the resources necessary to deploy, support, and maintain the new client in production. It's nice to have freedom of choice, but maybe it's even nicer to have a supportable client environment.

It's always good to attempt to remain pragmatic and focused when technology is changing so rapidly. It's bad to fall too deeply in love with the latest and greatest technology. Select what seems right for you today and deploy a client environment with a plan to keep it stabilized for the next two years. At the end of that period the fog will have cleared and you'll be in a good position to go through a similar exercise to plan for the following two years. One thing's for sure: expect change in the client area. We will be using different client technology in the future; the only question is when that future will arrive.

3

Establishing the Infrastructure for Exchange

3.1   Introduction

Every computer system or application is built on a set of basic concepts that must be mastered before an implementation can be considered. This chapter is my attempt to explain what I believe are the most important concepts relating to an Exchange implementation. We'll look at Windows NT, the basic organization of the Exchange messaging infrastructure, how to connect servers together, and the impact of Exchange on a network.

More detailed discussions about some of the points raised in this chapter, such as how to select and deploy the different connectors to link sites and other messaging systems together, are described in detail in Chapter 7.

Exchange and Outlook are packaged and sold as shrink-wrapped software that you can purchase at many retail computer outlets. Unwrapping the packaging and taking out the CDs is done in a blink of an eye, but it's unwise to continue to rush forward and run the SETUP utility to install the new server. Successful Exchange implementations require a lot of detailed up-front planning and system preparation, especially if you plan to operate a multi-server, multi-site, distributed organization. The process of planning begins by understanding how an Exchange environment is developed on top of Windows NT.

3.2   Organizations, Sites, and Servers

Anyone considering the implementation of a messaging infrastructure built around Exchange needs to understand what the terms "organizations", "sites", and "servers" mean within the context of the overall system.

Figure 3.1
Organization,
sites, and servers

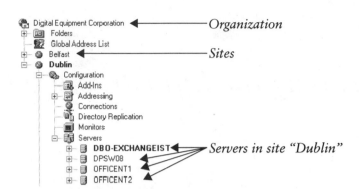

The organization created to implement Exchange represents the total messaging enterprise and is layered on top of the Windows NT security model. The organization can be described as the full messaging infrastructure, and is composed of one or more Exchange sites.

A server is a computer running the Windows NT Server operating system, with Exchange Server software installed on top of the Windows NT operating system. Note that there is a differentiation between Windows NT Server and Windows NT workstation, the two variants of the operating system. A computer running Windows NT workstation can be an Exchange client, but is not able to act as an Exchange server.

A site is often a single physical or geographical location where one or more Exchange servers are situated. Communications between the different Exchange servers forming a site are carried out with synchronous RPCs so the network links between the servers must be capable of supporting the load generated by client-generated calls in a very responsive manner. It is also important that the network connections within a site are reliable and predictable, and not prone to failure, as this will affect the replication of data between the different servers in the site.

Knowing how users communicate with each other is good information to have when planning where to locate servers or how they might be formed into sites. Keeping messages on a single server provides the fastest possible delivery service for users, so it's a good idea to locate users who need to communicate on a frequent basis on the same server. Building a site from a collection of user groups who pass information between the groups is a logical progression of the same idea. Clearly it's easiest to build up message patterns when you already operate a mail system, but even if you don't have an existing system to monitor it pays to spend some time on the subject to try and develop some educated guesses. Any data based on reality will result in a much better initial implementation of Exchange server than would otherwise occur if users are allocated to servers in an unstructured manner.

If you do have an existing system look for opportunities to improve the current message flow. It's a sad fact of life that many systems have evolved through passive management and there is no guarantee that users are allocated in an optimum fashion today. Don't be afraid to move users from server to server (within a site) after the implementation begins, if that seems to make sense.

Network connections are an important influence on the decision whether a location will be a discrete site or join other servers in (usually) close physical proximity to form a site. An office serving many people might, for instance, be deemed to be a site in its own right because its network connections to the rest of the organization cannot sustain the predicted traffic generated by the flow of messages in and out of the server. Unlike other messaging systems, Exchange server uses a type of specially encoded message to replicate data, so items like directory updates must be taken into account when predicting network traffic. It is also a reasonable argument for a single server to become a site because of the number of supported users. However, in situations where many users are to be supported multiple servers will always provide better system availability, as you'll eliminate a potential single point of failure.

Once a site is established all of the Exchange servers that collectively form the site share a single collection of data relating to connections (to external systems), and recipients and other directory information. All of the servers in a site can be administered from a single central location. General wisdom is that it's better to limit the total number of sites within an organization if at all possible because this makes everything easier to manage. While there are no practical limit to the total number of servers that can form a site, you should restrain yourself to no more than 50 servers in a site. The logic behind this recommendation is simply based on the fact that it's easier to manage fewer servers than more. Also, a certain amount of network traffic is generated between the servers in a site. The more servers, the more network traffic is created. It is impossible to operate a very large site unless you can base it on a high-speed network.

3.2.1   Network connections between Exchange system components

Perhaps it makes things easier to associate the network links that tie things together with the terms that have just been introduced. A range of different types of links is normally used to create the network infrastructure that ties an organization together. Consider a multi-national enterprise with offices in Europe, Asia, and the United States. Three separate geographical areas are involved in this scenario, and each is likely to have different characteristics in terms of the connections that are available. Within the United States it is generally easier and cheaper to establish high-speed, high-bandwidth connections between locations than in Europe or Asia. Within the organization therefore you might find satellite inter-continental links, 64 Kbps land-line links between offices in an individual country, and fiber-optic FDDI extended LANs connecting locations in a single metropolitan area.

Within a site the range of network links is much simpler. Exchange servers in a site share a common repository of information, but this is impossible unless the connections between the servers are fast enough to accommodate the data that passes around. Consider directory replication. In a site directories are replicated automatically in the form of messages generated, sent, and processed as background operations. An automatically updated directory ensures that messages are not addressed incorrectly and permits users to send messages to new recipients as soon as they are added to the system. Substantial networks are required to carry all the information between servers, so much so that you'd be forgiven in thinking that network vendors sponsor Microsoft!

Exchange clients are normally connected to their servers via a LAN so the connection is fast and only limited to the speed of the LAN (10 or 100 MBit/second for Ethernet). You shouldn't ever encounter problems transferring data between servers and clients unless message contents are huge or the LAN itself is saturated. Abnormal conditions will sometimes occur to interfere with the perceived transfer speed (for users), such as when many users at one time access very large messages, but in general LAN throughput shouldn't be an issue.

3.2.2   Two or more organizations

As we've seen, the model used by Exchange attempts to encapsulate a complete enterprise in terms of a single self-contained unit called an organization, breaking the enterprise down into sites and eventually servers. The model works well for smaller enterprises where co-operation is easier to achieve but poses some challenges for larger corporations. If the corporate operating model stresses decentralization with each department taking charge of their own computing destiny, then multiple Exchange organizations can easily evolve, perhaps one for each country or one for each operating unit. What can be said about these situations?

Apart from its messaging connectors Exchange is equipped with no mechanisms to facilitate the transfer of information from one organization to another. Aside from setting up replication through NNTP, no form of public folder sharing is possible; message encryption might be prohibited between one organization and another another, and direc-

tory entries cannot be replicated automatically. The problem of message encryption is largely addressed with the advent of S/MIME and
the new advanced security features built into Exchange V5.5 SP1.
Workarounds must be found to transfer information, either via the
messaging service or with some home-grown manual processes.

A little lateral thinking reveals that a certain level of inter-organization data exchange can be accomplished as follows:

- Messaging between the two organizations shouldn't be a problem. If both organizations use TCP/IP networks and can connect
  to the Internet the easiest way to establish a messaging connection is via the Internet Mail Service. Using TCP/IP as the base
  protocol for an X.400 connector is also more than feasible.

- It is possible to create rules for public folders so that when new
  information is posted it is automatically sent to a recipient,
  which could be a public folder in the other organization. Deletions cannot be handled by rules, so manual notifications of
  deletions are necessary if the different sets of public folders are
  not to become very much out of step with each other. Also, conflicts that occur when multiple users change public folder contents at the same time cannot be detected, as would be the case
  within a single organization. As mentioned earlier, NNTP can be
  used to replicate the contents of public folders between organizations.

- Directory information can be exported from each participating
  organization and imported into whatever other organization is
  interested in it. Directory exports are in the form of CSV (Comma
  Separated Value) files that can be mailed to an appropriate recipient. The contents of the export file need to be edited before they
  are imported as the mailbox recipients from the exporting organization are custom recipients for the importing organization. Editing can be done with a variety of tools, including a spreadsheet,
  but as it's a repetitive operation following well-defined rules it's
  best to write a program to do the job. Alternatively, the Exchange
  Resource Kit includes an inter-organization directory sychronization connector, but many system administrators are loathe to
  deploy the utility simply because it is not part of the shrink-
  wrapped product.

As Exchange grows in popularity I'm pretty sure that either ISVs
will create a toolkit to make inter-organization transfers easier. Tools
like this are essential to help solve some design problems posed by
companies such as distributed conglomerates. After all, not every enterprise has the luxury of being so well co-ordinated to fit into a single self-
contained unit.

3.3   Windows NT, domains, and security

Apart from mail encryption and digital signatures, Exchange provides no special security features of its own. Instead, Exchange relies on all of the security facilities built into the Windows NT operating system. For instance, a user must be able to authenticate their identity to Windows NT before they can ever connect a client to an Exchange server. Providing a valid account name and password during the initial log-on from a client to a Windows NT server authenticates a user. The Windows NT NetLogon service validates the account name and password against the Security Account Manager (SAM) database, and if the authentication check is successful a user process is created on the client. After it is created, the process is granted the set of rights allocated to the user account in the form of a security access token. The access token contains information about the user. It can be used to check whether a user is entitled to access a file or other object such as a mailbox.

Because Exchange is so tightly integrated with Windows NT you must take account of the Windows NT domain and trust models that are already in place, or design a model that will accommodate the needs of the messaging system. No implementation of Exchange will succeed if the underlying Windows NT structure is unstable. It is important to note at this point that restructuring a domain is not a matter of setting a few switches or parameters following by a reboot of all the systems in the domain. In most cases, changing anything fundamental in the domain structure requires a complete re-installation of Windows NT on each system in the domain. Given the potential workload generated by reinstallations as well as the impact on users and an organization, this is clearly not something that any reasonable system administrator wants to even consider.

Just to get a formal definition in place, a Windows NT domain is a logical set of workstations and servers that are managed as a single unit. The domain shares a common security policy and user account database, as encapsulated in the SAM. The SAM is stored as part of the Windows NT registry and contains information about global and user accounts, including the user name, password, groups which the account is a member of, any restrictions that might be in place, and the account's SID (Security Identifier). All of this data is doubly encrypted.

The minimum requirement for a domain is one system running Windows NT server software, which acts as the Primary Domain Controller (PDC) and holds the copy of the domain's SAM. A domain can also contain many other servers and workstations distributed across a wide area. Because all servers in a domain share a common SAM it is only necessary to create a user account once for each domain. Once equipped with a valid account name and password a user is able to connect to their resources by logging on to any of the server computers within the domain. A domain can contain one or more Windows NT servers and manage a wide array of clients including Windows NT workstations, Windows 95 and Windows 98 systems, and 16-bit Windows for WorkGroups.

3.3.1   Domain controllers

Within each domain, at least one server will be allocated the task of authenticating all the log-on requests from clients. This server stores and maintains the security database for the domain and implements all the changes made by applications throughout the domain. For example, if a user is granted the necessary access rights to be able to manage someone else's mailbox, the fact that the access rights have been granted will be registered in the security database. A small domain will have one server, referred to as the Primary Domain Controller, and there can be only one PDC per domain. However, large domains typically implement one or more backup domain controllers to enable operations to continue should anything happen to the PDC. These servers are called Backup Domain Controllers (BDCs) and they hold copies of the security database. Changes to the security database are automatically replicated between the PDC and the BDCs, normally every five minutes (the update interval is controlled by a setting in the system registry). The copies of the security database therefore should never normally be more than 5 minutes out of date, although it is possible for some small inconsistencies to arise if replication has not been completed.

PDCs are computers and all computers, no matter how reliable the operating system and reliable the environment, are prone to operating problems. If the PDC experiences a problem such as a system crash or becomes unavailable due to a network outage, one of the BDCs can be promoted to become the PDC on a temporary basis until normal service is resumed. This switchover arrangement allows the domain to continue to operate while the original PDC is off-line. When the original PDC is available again any changes the backup controller has made to the security database are automatically replicated back and synchronized.

Apart from the possibility of taking over from the PDC in case of failure, BDCs can also be used to balance the load generated by user authentication requests and so provide a degree of fault tolerance in this respect. When this happens the authentication requests are channeled to the BDC for verification in a totally transparent manner. Users are certainly not aware which server is responsible for handling their log-on. In large installations it's wise to avoid PDC saturation at peak times such as the start of the business day by sharing the authentication load across BDCs. The general recommendation is to have a BDC for each physical LAN or site running Exchange, although in the light of experience over the past two years I have now concluded that every Exchange server that hosts user mailboxes should be a BDC (but never a PDC).

The logic in making every Exchange server a BDC is simple. When a server is booted the set of NT services that collectively form Exchange start up. During this process the Exchange service account is used to authenticate each service to NT. Authentication needs the presence of a domain controller to check the credentials for the service account. If the network link to the nearest domain controller is unavailable for any reason the attempt to authenticate will fail and the Exchange services cannot start. Users will therefore be unable to access their mailboxes, even if the network failure does not affect their ability to connect clients to the server. The essence of Murphy's law states that what can go wrong will go wrong, so it therefore makes sense to avoid potential authentication issues by making each mailbox server a PDC. Of course, servers that host Exchange connectors or public folders are also important, but the effect of a network failure on these systems is of less impact to users than the inability to access mailboxes. Also, if a network failure has occurred it is likely to have wider impacts such as the inability for a connector to send and receive messages with other systems.

The usual argument against making each mailbox server a PDC is that this approach results in too many controllers within a domain. Domain controllers certainly need to communicate with each other to synchronize security information and inside an account domain there may be many separate transactions on user accounts during a day that need to be replicated to all controllers. However, I recommend that all the Exchange servers in an organization are placed inside a separate resource domain. In this case the number of accounts is minimal (chiefly machine accounts and Exchange service accounts) and the number of changes to those accounts tiny. Keeping all Exchange servers inside their own resource domain eliminates a great deal of other worries that come into play when multiple domains are involved and I hate using more trust relationships than are actually required.

In any relatively medium to large Windows NT installation the PDC will have to satisfy a reasonable workload of authentication requests and updates to the security database. Whatever about the speed in which updates are applied to the security database, it is critical that authentication requests are serviced quickly and users can complete the log-on process quickly. For this reason it is unwise to install Exchange on the same Windows NT computer that acts as the PDC. A more practical consideration is the fact that if Exchange is running on the same computer as the PDC it is difficult to restore the Exchange databases from backups to an operational state should a problem occurs. We'll discuss this particular issue in chapter 5 (see page 339).

3.3.2   Trust relationships

Windows NT uses trust relationships to link domains in terms of the actions a user can take. If domain A trusts domain B it means that a user from domain B will be able to log onto a server in domain A, and then access resources controlled by domain A. Access is permitted because the trust relationship between the domains attributes rights and permissions for objects controlled by domain A to any registered user from domain B. Of course, there are some limitations to what a user from a trusted domain is allowed to do or the data they can access, but this simplified explanation will serve for now.

Message tracking provides a good example of the domain trust mechanism in action. As discussed in chapter 11, Exchange can log details of messages into a log that is changed every day. The logs are held in a directory that is shared out, enabling a message to be tracked from server to server through the logs held on each server. Trust relationships must be in place to allow messages to be tracked across servers if the servers are installed into different domains.

3.3.3   Windows NT domain models

Understanding an existing Windows NT domain and security model or designing an appropriate domain model (if you are starting to use Windows NT) are critical pieces of an Exchange implementation plan. In fact, getting the domain model right or understanding how best to leverage off an existing domain model is probably the single most critical item on the path to a successful implementation.

There are four distinct Windows NT domain models that can be implemented within an organization. These are:

- Single domain model
- Single master domain model
- Multiple master domain model
- Complete trust domain model

Obviously if you don't have a Windows NT infrastructure already in place you have total freedom over the type of domain model you select. Lots of enterprises have experimented with Windows NT since it was first released in 1993 but may not be using Windows NT for anything other than a desktop operating system or to provide shared file and print services to other Windows clients.

Although proponents of Novell NetWare will disagree, Windows NT is probably the finest desktop operating system available today and it certainly does an excellent job of providing shared file and print services. But many implementations to provide file and print sharing tend to be carried out in a local or departmental manner and do not pay special heed to the needs of the organization as a whole. In other words, you can very quickly install Windows NT servers and connect clients in to form your own domain, but if everyone does this for their own department the resulting Windows NT infrastructure is fragmented. It's also highly likely that no comprehensive set of trust relationships exist. We'll return to the question of what tactic to take in this instance, but first let's review the options open for domain models.

3.3.4   Single domain model

The single domain model (see Figure 3.2) is by far the simplest domain model that can be implemented for Windows NT. It is also the most common model selected for departmental-style implementations, especially where Windows NT has replaced another network operating system such as Novell NetWare as the base for shared file and print services.

Figure 3.2
Windows NT
single domain
model

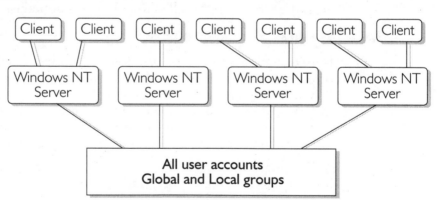

Within the single domain model all users are registered in a single security database, but there are practical and technical points that need to be borne in mind. Windows NT V3.5 increased the upper limit for the number of user accounts that can be registered in a domain from 10,000 to a theoretical limit of 40,000. That limit remains today although it is likely to be increased in Windows NT V5.0. However, the logistics involved in managing such a large number of user accounts almost always means that another model is considered well before the "old" limit of 10,000 is attained, unless there are lots of system administrators waiting around for work to be done.

The technical limitation of 40,000 is not actually a simple matter of Windows NT reaching a magic number and then refusing to register any more users. Instead, the upper limit is determined by the size of the SAM database file in conjunction with the amount of physical memory available on the PDC. Microsoft recommends that the size of the SAM is kept below 40MB. Databases larger than 40MB have been tested in software laboratories and work, but it's wise to pay attention to the firm recommendations from Microsoft. A quick calculation of 40MB for 40,000 users appears to indicate that the details of each user account occupies 1K in the database and indeed it is possible to create a situation like this, as long as no global groups or machine accounts[1] are not created.

Within any large user population the normal situation is to operate with a selection of global groups, if only to reduce the level of system administration overhead required controlling access to shared resources, so it's highly unlikely that no groups will be active. Group details occupy varying amounts of space, depending on the number of members within the group. Microsoft suggests using 4K as an average for each group, driving down the space available within the SAM for individual user accounts and decreasing the theoretical maximum from 40,000.

Within a single domain model no trust relationships are required because no other domains are known. If you are a small, single-site enterprise with a small number of users (well below 10,000) then the single domain model is a natural choice. This model allows fairly simple and straightforward centralized management of all user accounts and global resources, including those used by Exchange.

The major drawback is that the PDC can become overloaded and slow down other computers if it is not capable of handling the authentication demand created by the user community. Each authentication request or log-on is processed by the PDC, so it must be able to process those requests at peak time. Clearly slow network links to servers and clients located in different parts of the domain can contribute to the problem. The authentication workload can be somewhat off-loaded to BDCs, but the PDC still has a lot of work to do in circulating security information updates to its backup controllers. Concentrating the security workload in a single PDC is the major reason why the single domain model is not recommended for large numbers of users or an enterprise that is distributed across many sites.

---

1. Machine accounts are automatically created by Windows NT to allow workstations or servers to participate in the security model

A lot of goodness can be gained by simplifying the domain structure to create a seamless environment for everyone to work in. We've just discussed some technical limitations that might get in your way and force the deployment of multiple domains, but there are some practical issues too. The management tools in NT are primarily designed for small to medium domains and have some problems dealing with very large domains. For example, User Manager for Domains caches SAM data before displaying it to system administrators. If you attempt to change details of a user account in a large domain, like the password, it can take a long time before the data is displayed and you're able to work with it. The problem is exacerbated if slow network links are used. One of the domains in DIGITAL has a SAM that's 28MB today (32,000 user accounts), and it can take over half an hour for User Manager for Domains to display on a server in a location with slow links. Third-party management tools are available for Windows NT, but it can be quite expensive to deploy these in large companies as they are typically priced on a per seat basis. As discussed in chapter 8, the Active Directory in Windows NT V5.0 is designed to address many of scalability and management issues encountered in large domains today.

3.3.5   Single master domain model

Once a number of different sites are present within an organization you might start to consider expanding away from the single domain model. The natural evolutionary step is the single master domain model, named because a single central domain is established as a point of unification for subsidiary Windows NT servers. User accounts and global groups are registered in the central domain but local resources can be managed from the subsidiary servers. Because of the reliance on the central domain it's essential that systems to act as BDCs are maintained.

Figure 3.3 illustrates a single master domain created for a company called World-Wide Systems Incorporated. It is possible to create a model where authentication is carried out in one place for log-ons and other security requests originating in Asia, the U.S., Europe, and Australia, but this would only be practical if extremely fast and dedicated network links are available all the time. Possibly a better and more realistic example would be a single master domain established to serve all users within a large metropolitan area like London or New York, with the individual subsidiary servers distributed to different locations within the area.

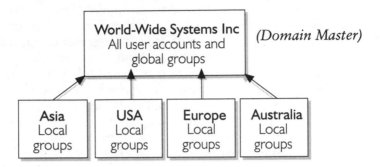

Figure 3.3
*Single master
domain model*

3.3.6 Complete trust domain model

Once an organization grows past approximately 10,000 user accounts a single domain often becomes unwieldy. Two options exist, one usually regarded as fairly difficult to set up and administer while the other is fairly simple, albeit less structured. The simple option is the complete trust domain model, a way of distributing the management of all resources to different domains located throughout an enterprise. Each domain creates and manages its own user accounts and groups, for instance. No attempt is made to unify the domains together, but each domain trusts the others so resources such as Exchange public folders can be shared. The model is very flexible because new domains can join at any time, but it can also be somewhat chaotic because no strong central co-ordination is achieved.

Figure 3.4
*Complete trust
domain model*

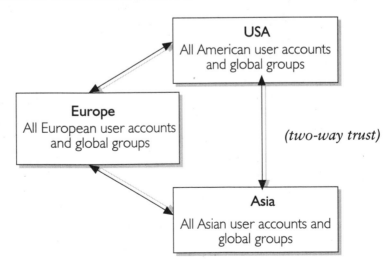

The complete trust domain model (Figure 3.4) removes the upper limit of 10,000 users and can therefore be considered to be scaleable. Connecting two or three domains together in this manner to allow people to share information certainly does the job. If you are not worried about having a complete trust relationship with the other domains the simplicity of the model has much to recommend it, especially if Exchange is the major Windows NT application in use. However, if you require better co-ordination, centralized management, or the ability to partition your Windows NT infrastructure in a more controlled manner the complete trust domain model may not be appropriate.

3.3.7   Multiple master domain model

The two-tier domain model (Figure 3.5) is the most scaleable model. The first tier contains a set of master domains that maintain two-way trust relationships between each other. User accounts are registered in one or other of the master domains. The trust relationships between the domains mean that all user accounts are known throughout the enterprise.

Figure 3.5
Multiple master domain model

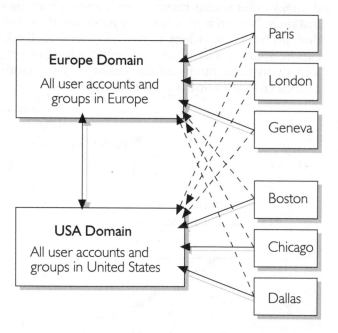

The second tier is composed of domains serving discrete sections of the overall organization. These sections might be created along departmental, organizational, or, as shown in the figure, geographical divisions. The responsibility for managing resources resides at the second tier. Note that the second-tier domains all maintain one-way trust relationships with the first-tier domains. This means that the second-tier domains trust any information provided by the first-tier whereas the opposite is not true.

Each new domain added at either tier increases the number of trust relationships that must be managed so it's wise not to become too enthusiastic when creating first-tier domains. Try and establish a fairly high-level picture of the overall enterprise at the first-tier, using convenient divisions such as the continental sections as illustrated. Enterprises broken down into operational divisions such as Manufacturing, Sales, Marketing, and so on can consider using these divisions but geographical lines are probably more practical because network links are normally organized like this, with very fast connections within a physical location and slower connections maintained between countries. Once again it's important to have BDCs deployed within each second-tier domain, just in case.

Because of its relative ease of management that scales well over thousands of user accounts, most large distributed enterprises, including the internal networks operating by Microsoft and DIGITAL, use either the master domain model or multiple master domain model. DIGITAL, for example, has three master domains called DIGITAL1, DIGITAL2, and DIGITAL3, respectively serving North America, Europe and the Asia/Pacific regions. The largest account domain holds well over 30,000 accounts. Apart from the issue of approaching the design limits, the major problem with such large domains is that the management tools supplied with Windows NT are designed to deal with domains containing less than 10,000 accounts.

The examples of the master domain model presented here are based on a geographic separation of resources. Even if you're not very widely distributed in a geographical sense there is still a case for adopting the master domain model. In this instance you'd create a resource domain for Exchange (and perhaps other applications). Figure 3.6 illustrates the type of domain structure chosen and implemented in the majority of the large Exchange implementations I have been associated with over the past 2 years. A number of account domains are linked together through two-way trust relationships. The value here is that a user can be authenticated anywhere. If the account domains are broken up on a geographic basis it's a good idea to distribute BDCs so that authentication can take place even if WAN links are temporarily broken. For example, Figure 3.6 shows two account domains for the Americas and Europe. If a BDC for the Europe domain was not installed close (in a physical sense) to the Americas domain then requests for authentication from users from the Europe domain could not be honoured if the network link was broken between the two domains.

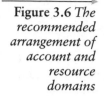

Figure 3.6 The recommended arrangement of account and resource domains

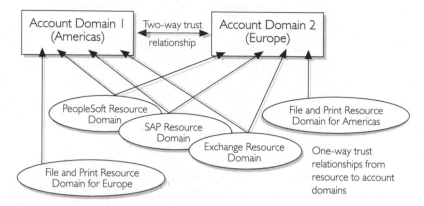

It's best to limit the number of account domains if at all possible. DIG-ITAL has three for roughly 60,000 accounts. The approach suggested above of operating BDCs in all geographic areas is used, so that BDCs for the DIGITAL2 domain (Europe) are installed in both the US and Asia/Pacific, the geographies served by the DIGITAL1 and DIGITAL3 account domains. The net effect is to allow people like me, who travel extensively, to log-on and connect to network resources around the world. In the past year I have done so in places as far apart as San Francisco, Sydney, Kuala Lumpur, and Tokyo using a mixture of RAS and local LAN connections. All have worked, and usually flawlessly—a tribute to both the domain design and the people who operate it.

Figure 3.6 breaks applications into separate resource domains. There's a mix between local applications, like those providing file and print services, and distributed applications that have users everywhere such as Exchange, PeopleSoft (a popular human resources application), and SAP/3 (a financial application). Distributed applications have one-way trust relationships to all master account domains to allow users to access the applications from any account. Local applications provide services to a subset of users, so their trust relationships can be limited to the set of account domains (often only one) where those user accounts are located.

The Exchange resource domain will have no user accounts—they'll all be in the master domain, so the only accounts that operate within the domain will be the service accounts required for Exchange administration and inter-service communications. It is important to note that there is no need for anyone to ever log into the service accounts to perform administrative operations. Everything can be done from accounts in the account domain that have been granted the appropriate permissions over objects in the Exchange directory hierarchy. The service account is typically only ever logged into to perform installations.

Placing Exchange and the other applications into their own discrete resource domain is a great way of cutting down the administrative workload by creating an integrated Windows NT environment that can be managed totally separately from other applications and user accounts.

In summary, if you are considering a large-scale implementation of Windows NT (initially) leading to a deployment of Exchange, the master domain model and the multiple master variants are both leading contenders.

3.3.8   Making a decision about the domain model

The domain option selected by any other company is not necessarily a recommendation that a particular domain model is best for your situation. However, my experience of working with many large companies to create a suitable Windows NT infrastructure for the implementation of Exchange has been that almost all of these companies have selected a variant of the master domain model. In some cases this decision has required those companies to discard their existing Windows NT implementation, mostly because it was either fragmented or deployed without any regard to the requirements of an application like Exchange which is so tightly integrated with Windows NT. We'll discuss the topic of working with existing Windows NT domains in more detail in just a few pages.

Making the decision about the Windows NT domain model to use is possibly the most critical of all the decisions you'll have to make as you approach an Exchange deployment. It's certainly the first decision to take, and the one that influences many of the other deployment options down the line. I have one major recommendation to make at this point in time. Make sure that the people who are making the decisions have enough knowledge about Windows NT and Exchange before the decisions are taken. This means that whoever's involved in the decision should get some training (attending a one-day overview seminar or a similar event is not enough—go and get some proper training) so that they fully understand the implications of selecting one domain model over another. Making decisions based on what someone thinks they know rarely, if ever, leads to success.

3.3.9   Don't forget WINS and the rest of the Windows NT infrastructure

The decision about the domain model is important but it's not the only item on the Windows NT agenda. The point has already been made that Exchange is inextricably linked with Windows NT and depends on that infrastructure. Bitter experience over a large number of deployments reveals that the most common problems are not due to Exchange but rather flaws in the Windows NT infrastructure.

WINS (Windows Internet Naming Service) is an important part of the Windows NT infrastructure for any distributed organization. WINS tracks the association between TCP/IP addresses and computer names, and in a distributed environment it's likely that there will be several WINS servers to manage the set of TCP/IP addresses and computer names used by a company. The history of WINS implementations has not been smooth. Originally, general wisdom held that WINS servers should be distributed around a network to keep them close to concentrations of computers, but this opinion has moderated through experience so that implementers typically have smaller numbers of WINS servers than before. The WINS software suffered from some bugs too, most if not all of which have now been addressed. Certainly, Windows NT V4.0 does a much better job of managing the WINS database than NT V3.51.

Exchange servers should all have fixed TCP/IP addresses. There is nothing dynamic about a server computer! Once an entry is made into WINS for an Exchange server that's the address it should use all the time. If this is the case, does a dependency exist between WINS and Exchange? The answer is that it all depends on your network and how the WINS servers are distributed.

For example, there have been instances where public folders were re-homed onto a server because the original home server couldn't be found due to a WINS problem. In one case a whole collection of public folders were re-homed to a server in Australia because the original owning server (in the United States) couldn't be contacted for a few days by the Australian server. It seems that Exchange assumed that the home server had been removed from the network and decided to adjust the public folder hierarchy to take account of the new situation! When the WINS problem was fixed and the Australian server could contact the original home server, all of the folders had been rehomed, an unfortunate side effect of public folder backfill. See the discussion on the DS/IS consistency adjuster (see page 326) for more background on why Exchange might rehome folders and the steps that can be taken to prevent this happening. Because of the risk of rehoming exists, reason many experienced system managers keep entries for all Exchange servers in each server's LMHOSTS file. Hopefully the future unification of Exchange and Windows NT directories will go a long way to eliminate problems like this.

WINS is important, but so is DHCP (for client address allocation), SMS (for software updates and client inventories), and file and print sharing. The impact and deployment of other BackOffice applications like the Internet Web Server also need to be considered. Everything needs to be brought together into a comprehensive and sensible plan for Windows NT. Third party products also need to be factored into the plan, especially if they are used to help manage the Windows NT environment. Unfortunately people implement on a fractured, unco-ordinated manner and fall into the black holes that lurk in bad deployments. The blame is then often attributed to Exchange because it's the most obvious application in the hands of users.

3.3.10   WINS, large domains, and client authentication

Exchange uses Windows NT to authenticate client connections. Whenever a client attempts to connect to the Information or Directory Stores via the standard NT Challenge/Response mechanism, Exchange must locate a domain controller to authenticate the client's credentials against those for the primary NT account for the mailbox. You might assume that Exchange will know where the nearest domain controller is, and will always attempt to connect to it to perform authentication, but this is not the case. Instead, Exchange will attempt to establish a secure channel to the first domain controller to respond to a logon request. The local domain controller may be busy when the request is made, so it is quite possible for a response to arrive from another controller first.

This behaviour is not a problem in small domains, as all of the servers tend to be in close proximity. In large or distributed domains, it is usual to deploy backup domain controllers to each location to ensure that clients can continue to be authenticated even if connection is lost to the rest of the network. For example, DIGITAL uses a single account domain for European employees. The domain holds 26,000 accounts and 45 BDCs are deployed. Most locations have a BDC, but some have two or three (one for each major network segment). To complete the picture, 18 WINS servers are deployed. With so many domain controllers in use, it's obvious that the potential exists for multiple responses to logon requests.

Inside large NT infrastructures, a set of WINS servers are usually deployed to allow servers to find each other. WINS delivers significant benefits to an NT infrastructure, but the combination of multiple domain controllers communicating with WINS can result in slow client authentication. Because the problem is linked to the number of domain controllers in use, this is a problem that will not be seen in pilot deployment. It will become apparent as the infrastructure expands and is a great example of how NT, WINS, and Exchange have to be treated as an intermeshed combination during the design phase of projects.

If WINS is enabled on an Exchange server (as it should be), the first step Exchange takes to check client credentials is to ask WINS for a list of controllers. WINS returns a list of up to 25 controllers, composed of the PDC plus the last 24 BDCs that made themselves known to WINS.

Clearly, in small domains the list can be much smaller. Exchange uses the list to broadcast a request for authentication, and a secure channel is established with the first controller to respond. The secure channel remains in place and is used to authenticate subsequent client connections until two consecutive errors occur on the channel. At this point Exchange attempts to find another controller and establishes a new channel.

Many factors contribute to the speed in which a controller responds to a request. A controller might be unusually busy, under load, temporarily unavailable, or the network link between the Exchange server and the controller might be saturated. It is possible for Exchange to end up communicating with the most unlikely domain controller, usually the one that's furthest away. When secure channels are established in this manner, client logons will be slower than normal and people will begin to complain that it takes a long time for Exchange to respond and let them into their mailbox. It's not Exchange that's slow, but Exchange takes the blame for one of the little quirks in Windows NT networking. So, when large domains are deployed, it's a good idea to think about how to direct Exchange to the "right" domain controllers.

It is possible to specify the IP address of the preferred domain controller in the LMHOSTS file for each server. For this to work the Enable LMHOSTS Lookup property must be enabled for the TCP/IP protocol in the Control Panel Network applet. An entry for the preferred controller can then be placed into the LMHOSTS file. For example:

```
16.240.80.144 "EXDOMAIN \0x1C" #PRE
```

This entry specifies that the preferred domain controller for the EXDOMAIN domain is found at IP address 16.240.80.144. The #PRE suffix means that the address should be loaded into the NetBIOS cache. Note that the text within the quotation marks should be exactly 15 characters long, so spaces are inserted to pad out to the desired length. When complete, the NBTSTAT utility can be used to reload the NetBIOS cache with the new data that's just been inserted into LMHOSTS.

Making an entry in LMHOSTS in this matter will not affect the current secure channel. It merely instructs NT where to look the next time it wants to establish a channel. NLTEST, a utility included in the Windows NT Resource Kit, can be used to determine what controller is being used for a secure channel at any point in time. For example, the command:

```
NLTEST /SC_QUERY:EXDOMAIN
```

instructs NLTEST to check the controller for the domain EXDOMAIN. NLTEST can also be used to force a server to re-establish a secure channel. If NLTEST is used to establish a new secure channel it will use the contents of the NetBIOS cache to determine whether a preferred domain controller is specified, so NLTEST can be used in conjunction with an updated LMHOSTS file to force NT to establish a new secure channel to a specified controller.

While effective, the combination of LMHOSTS and NLTEST is relatively labor-intensive and needs to be set up on each server. It is preferable to employ a mechanism that can be manipulated programmatically as the need arises. SETPRFDC, a utility available from Microsoft Technical Support, can be used for this purpose.

SETPRFDC stands for "Set Preferred Domain Controller". Its function is to provide Windows NT with a list of the preferred controllers to look for when a secure channel is required. The syntax is simple:

```
SETPRFDC <domain name> <list of controllers in preferred order>
```

For example:

```
SETPRFDC EXDOMAIN EXBDC1 EXBDC2 EXBDC3
```

In this instance, SETPRFDC is used to instruct Windows NT that any time a secure channel is needed for the domain EXDOMAIN, a connection should be made to the controller called EXBDC1. If EXBDC1 is unavailable, an attempt should be made to contact EXBDC2, and so on. Separate calls to SETPRFDC are required if mailboxes are allocated to accounts in several different NT domains.

The necessary commands can be included into a batch file and scheduled for execution at regular intervals. Inside DIGITAL, where SETPRFDC is used as a matter of course, the batch job normally executes once an hour. Running SETPRFDC has no impact on either the network or NT, so it can be run as often as you like. A more sophisticated version of the batch file might consult a data file to determine the correct domain controllers for any particular server, which allows for changes in the NT infrastructure as more servers and controllers are added.

3.3.11 Using Novell NDS instead of NT authentication

Using standard Windows NT authentication services is the default option, but it's not the only one. Novell Directory Services (NDS) for Windows NT can also be used for this purpose, and is often considered when companies have already deployed NetWare (or InternetWare).

Access to the Windows NT SAM is controlled by functions in two dynamic link libraries—SAMLIB.DLL and SAMSRV.DLL. Any application that needs authentication dispatches calls to SAMLIB.DLL, which in turn communicates with SAMSRV.DLL over RPCs. NDS provides a substitute SAMSRV.DLL, which effectively redirects any attempt to access the SAM to a NetWare server running NDS. The substitute SAM-DRV.DLL is installed on the PDC and all BDCs in a domain. Novell has announced their intention to ship a version of NDS that can run on a Windows NT server by mid-1998, so everything could be done within NT at that stage.

The advantage of the approach taken by NDS for Windows NT is obvious: applications, including Exchange, remain unaware that they are communicating with anything other than the SAM. The substitute SAMDRV.DLL appears to be just like the original provided with Windows NT, only that the information it deals with comes from NDS, not the SAM. Functions in the substitute SAMDRV.DLL mask the different formats used by NDS and the SAM, so an application requesting data receives it from NDS in exactly the same manner as it would had the data come from the SAM.

SAMDRV.DLL is a standard part of Windows NT. Replacing it carries some risks. Microsoft is well within its rights to make changes to SAMDRV.DLL at any time for its own reasons, including enhancing security or administrative functions or even just to fix bugs. It's quite possible that a future service pack for Windows NT will replace SAM-DRV.DLL, so each service pack needs to be carefully examined and verified before it goes anywhere near a production environment.

Experience with some small deployments has revealed no great problems using NDS instead of the SAM. Utilities are provided to import data from the SAM into NDS before the switchover occurs, and afterwards you can continue to use programs like User Manager for Domains to manage users and groups as before. Performance didn't seem to be an issue, despite the extra step required to transfer data to and from NDS. However, it must be emphasized that NDS for Windows NT must be tested in your own environment before a decision can be made as to whether it is a feasible solution. Companies attempting to deploy Exchange across many different NT domains won't find that NDS solves all problems magically, and it's not a solution either if you're still using NetWare V3.*x*.

3.3.12 The Exchange Service Account

A privileged Windows NT account is required for the installation and operation of Exchange. The standard Windows NT Administrator account can be used for this purpose, but it's a good idea to create a special account in each domain to use for all aspects of Exchange administration, including installations. Apart from anything else, using a different account creates a clear separation between Windows NT and Exchange administration. Often the same people will take care of everything, but in large installations it is quite common to have different teams looking after general system administration and messaging. In these situations it's best to allocate each team their own working environment so that they don't interfere with each other. Never make the mistake of assuming that Windows NT administrators need to exercise some control over Exchange as they don't. Administrators enjoy open access to user mailboxes (if they care to use this privilege) so it's clearly important to restrict the number of people who have privileged access to Exchange.

Select an account name such as EXADMIN or EXCHANGEADMIN for the service account. It is normal practice to use the same name for all Exchange servers in an organization as this makes administration easier. Indeed, the same service account must be used for all servers within a site. Obviously, if all Exchange servers are installed into a dedicated resource domain it is very easy for all servers to use the same service account. On the other hand, if the servers span multiple domains you cannot use the same service account. The service account should have the same privileges as the standard Windows NT Administrator account. You may need to include the service account into any administration groups that are used to manage Windows NT.

Some consultants recommend that different service accounts should be used for each site as this minimizes the obvious problems that might arise if the service account was deleted accidentally. Such a deletion won't be noticed until the next time a server is started or an attempt is made to start one of the Exchange services, in which case the attempted log-on to the service account will fail. If you use separate accounts for each site it's a good idea to prefix each account with some indicator of the site. For example, "DUBLINADMIN" and "LONDONADMIN" could be used for sites in Dublin and London respectively.

Some administrators, especially those who wish to run the most secure environment possible, don't like using names that convey any idea of the purpose that an account is used for. In these situations the usual approach is to use an account name like ZZYYYXX, the logic being that no hacker is going to guess that such an account is privileged. The same logic dictates that the normal Windows NT administrator account should be disabled and another account created for administrative purposes.

The Exchange installation procedure grants special rights and permissions over Exchange objects to the account used to perform the installation (usually the service account). If you want to use other accounts to manage Exchange afterwards you'll have to grant those accounts the necessary permissions to deal with whatever objects they are interested in. Tracking down all the places where permissions have been granted is a little tricky, so it's best to leave the original account used for installation alone if at all possible.

As noted earlier, administrators do not need to log in to the service account to work with Exchange. In fact, there is no need for anyone to ever log in to the service account except to perform software upgrades. Grant the necessary permissions to the administrators' own accounts or to a special account or set of accounts created for this purpose and use these accounts for administration.

3.3.13   Getting help—automated tools

Two software tools can help to collect information about the essential characteristics of the Windows NT and Exchange organizational structures. These tools are:

1.   The Windows NT Domain Planner

2.   The Exchange Server Modeling Tool

Both tools also included in the Exchange V5.0 and V5.5 Resource Kits. The basis of the tools is simple. A question and answer session is conducted using "wizard" technology. In the case of the Domain Planner you answer questions such as the total number of users, whether you want to administer all servers centrally, and so on. After all questions are answered you can generate a report containing the recommendations arrived at by the wizard. If you don't like the recommendations you can go back and modify earlier answers and see if the recommendations change.

Everything you enter into the domain planner is captured into a configuration file. In turn, the domain information held in the configuration can be fed into the Exchange modeling tool. This reflects the close and intimate relationship between a solid implementation of a Windows NT domain structure and eventual success with Exchange being deployed on top of that structure.

The Exchange modeling tool offers similar opportunity to input details about the type of Exchange organization you want to build. The questions cover points such as the different network connections available to link sites, which sites will host public folders, whether messages can flow constantly or if they'll follow a schedule, and so on. The design is arrived at through a process of constant refinement, and the graphical nature of the tool allows you to quickly see the current situation at any time. It's possible to experiment with different scenarios to analyze how a change will affect the overall situation. At the end of the exercise the modelling tool creates an organizational diagram.

I've used quite a number of automated system design tools in my time. Those available for Windows NT and Exchange provide an excellent starting point for the design exercise. Apart from anything else, using tools like this forces you to collect information together in a logical fashion, something that's extremely valuable in itself. If you feel that you lack knowledge or experience with Windows NT or Exchange you can engage in the data collection exercise yourself and then bring the data along for analysis and review by an expert.

Treat the recommendations issued by the tools as an input to the design process, not the final and absolute decision. Automated tools are all very well, but human knowledge and experience often produce insights that have critical influence on the shape of the best possible design.

3.3.14 Installing Exchange on top of an existing Windows NT infrastructure

As discussed previously there are going to be a large number of situations where Windows NT domains are already operational within enterprises. The question now arises of how to incorporate or leverage an existing infrastructure for use with Exchange.

If the enterprise is small and a single domain is in use then introducing Exchange is a straightforward process, providing the network in place is able to handle the volume of additional traffic introduced through Exchange messaging and replication activities.

Planning is more complicated where several different domains are already in use. Many companies started to use Windows NT as a direct replacement for shared file and print services that had previously run in a Windows for WorkGroups or Novell NetWare environment, a situation I refer to as "legacy NT implementations". These implementations operate as fragmented islands of NT, and are not a suitable foundation for the deployment of an enterprise-wide application like Exchange.

It's easy to fall into the trap of implementing Windows NT in line with a workgroup rather than a corporate model. In other words, the server is installed to fulfill a specific purpose, to provide file and print services to a small client workgroup. Each workgroup is a separate domain. No real attempt is made to consider inter-working with other domains outside the immediate physical location, so the servers in London don't know about the servers in Paris, or New York, or anywhere else. Why should they, if all that's being provided is local file and print services?

Look at the set of Windows NT domains illustrated in Figure 3.7, the result of browsing the internal DIGITAL network. Having 939 domains visible to the network (and there are probably a lot more lurking under the surface) is a classic example of domains gone wild, almost to a point where it is impossible to know what each domain has been set up to do. Networking is taken for granted within DIGITAL. DIGITAL operates the largest commercial network in the world. At one time there were over 40,000 computers attached to the internal network, so it's not altogether surprising or frightening to discover so many Windows NT domains in use. DIGITAL has used Windows NT since the operating system became first available as a beta test. There are many technical people inside DIGITAL, and many of those who are quite capable and happy to set up and maintain a new domain. These two influences, along with no centralized control being exercised on domain creation, lead to hundreds of domains. Is it a problem? Probably not, as long as the people who created the domains in the first place remain happy to manage them, and there are no fights about domain names. It is desirable? Absolutely not—flexibility is important, but anarchy is unwanted.

At this point it is worth noting that the project teams who implemented Windows NT and Exchange as corporate services within DIGITAL ignored what had gone before and did not attempt to use any existing domains. This was a very wise decision because it removed any of the convoluted interconnections, like trust relationships, that would otherwise have been required.

Figure 3.7
Browsing a very large Windows network

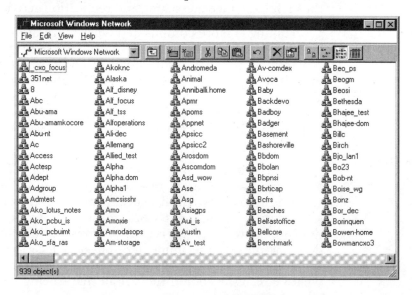

Enterprises distributed across large distances where LAN connections are not possible can use the complete trust domain model to unify domains that are already operational, as long as there aren't too many domains. The complete trust model requires trust relationships to be set up between all the different domains. The bulk of the work to establish the trusts is a one-time operation. Maintaining the trust relationships isn't too difficult if new domains are not added. Bringing new domains into a set of trusted domains requires a new and separate relationship to be created between the new domain and each one of the existing domains. This can rapidly get nasty because the number of trust relationships expands to a point where there are just too many to easily manage. For example, in a situation where 20 domains are involved in a complete trust relationship, a total of 380 (19 × 20) trusts must be set up between the different domains. Creating 380 trusts is one thing; managing 380 trusts over an extended period of time is quite another.

Trust relationships (Figure 3.8) come into play if sites are to span domain boundaries. When a new server is installed the installation program requests details of an existing server in the site and then attempts to retrieve information about the site from that server. A Windows NT trust relationship is enough to allow the two domains to see each other, and this permits the installation program to make the request to the remote server for site information. However, if the account being used to perform the installation does not possess permissions to administer the organization, site, and configuration objects on the target server it won't be able to update the remote server's configuration. Failures to possess the necessary permissions will cause the RPC queries to be rejected by the target server and the installation procedure will not be able to proceed.

It's altogether too easy to forget to set up a trust relationship, in turn leading to problems with Exchange features such as public folder affinity, single seat administration, and message tracking. Administrators sometimes make mistakes and remove trusts, leading to similar problems for Exchange. Worse again, if a site connector is in use to connect sites across two domains the removal of the trust relationship will instantly stop messages flowing between the sites. For all these reasons it is best to avoid trust relationships if at all possible, lending weight to the argument that a complete Windows NT redesign should be undertaken before any Exchange deployment begins.

In situations where you're faced with a large number of independent domains steps should be taken to rationalize the situation and form a more unified Windows NT infrastructure before any deployment of Exchange is begun. Normally this means that you have to design and implement a new Windows NT infrastructure from scratch. If the existing domains have only been used to provide shared file and print services it shouldn't be too hard to connect the desired services to the new domain and then move or even recreate user accounts. Some user accounts may need to be renamed if the same account name has been used in multiple domains.

Figure 3.8 *Trust relationships*

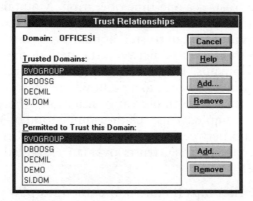

Clearly creating a new Windows NT infrastructure is not a task to be undertaken lightly. It is an exercise that won't be cheap in terms of time and effort, and few people will understand why anyone would want to redesign an infrastructure that's successfully providing users with good service today. Of course, these people (some of whom are likely to occupy senior roles within your company) are looking at the situation at a pretty superficial level and don't understand the issues involved. Good communication of all the reasons why it's important to have a solid, integrated, and scaleable Windows NT infrastructure as a base for Exchange will therefore be important.

Remember that Exchange sites can map domain models in different ways. Sketching out the basic shape of the Exchange organization to illustrate where sites and servers will be located and the names each site and server will have is a very fundamental and important step in the planning of any Exchange implementation. A site can map a domain on a one-to-one basis and this is the most probable implementation where domains and sites are created to serve different geographical locations (London, Paris, Geneva, and so on). And as we've seen, sites can also be built from servers spanning different Windows NT domains as long as the necessary trust relationships exist.

3.3.15   Pirate Exchange organizations

Computer professionals love new technology (a complete generalization I know, but useful for the purpose of illustration). As such, they like to deploy new applications. Sometimes the desire to deploy new applications, like Exchange, conflicts with the need to plan the implementation to the necessary level of detail that's required by corporate deployments of Windows NT and Exchange. I've been in a number of projects where some departments in a company are started to operate Exchange servers that have been installed with little or no co-ordination with other departments. There might be one Exchange organization in production, but then again, there might be several different Exchange organizations up and running. The latter scenario is very difficult to manage because each additional organization will eventually need to be integrated into a whole.

Suddenly being given the job to create a unified messaging environment from an already-installed loose collection of Exchange organizations, sites, or individual servers is a variant of the problem created by an existing Windows NT infrastructure. One of the joys of Exchange is the ease with which the server software is installed. Forty minutes or so after the shrink-wrap is removed the server can be up and running with clients happily sending messages to each other. Once you have a Windows NT server you can install Exchange and unfortunately sometimes people get carried away and Exchange servers can proliferate within an organization, perhaps as a result of different organizational units carrying out their own pilot deployments. I refer to unauthorized or uncoordinated Exchange implementations as "pirates". People running Exchange like this may think they're delivering a valuable service to their users, but the long-term implications of early and unplanned deployment carries a heavy price to pay. I see four major issues with pirate deployments:

1.   Pilot implementations should be treated as early deployments of the corporate model. If they are not they're not very valuable (what do they prove?) and will have to be redone. We'll return to this topic later in chapter 9.

2.   If early implementations are not in line with the Windows NT domain model and the Exchange organizational model that are eventually used for the corporate deployment, there is a very high percentage chance that the software (NT, Exchange, or both) will have to be re-installed. Adjusting domains, site names, or server names after a server goes into production is difficult, if not impossible.

3.   No utilities exist today to incorporate an external Exchange server into an organization. You cannot merge Exchange organizations together. Microsoft has been working on a tool that is able to change the complete naming context of a server by altering every directory entry relating to the server to change the name of the site or organization it belongs to. Such drastic surgery on the directory is not a task that can be undertaken lightly. At the time of writing it is not clear whether the tool will achieve the necessary level of quality to allow it to be

included in Exchange V5.5 SP1, but it is a hopeful sign that Microsoft will provide such tools in the future. In passing I'll note that no utilities exist to split out an Exchange server from a site either. However, the manual tasks to perform such a split are fairly straightforward.

4.   Pirate implementations may not comply with other standards under consideration for the corporate deployment. For example, items like public folder creation and permissions, document retention policies, operational policies such as backup software and hardware, server platforms, and so on. It's certainly easier to bring these inconsistencies back in line with corporate requirements than it is to fix problems with Windows NT or the Exchange organization, but why should you have to do the work?

Pilot implementations need to be planned. There is no point in going through all the effort and incurring all the expense involved in a pilot if the work must eventually be discarded. Yet pilot implementations will have to be discarded, software re-installed and re-configured, and users may lose data if every system administration does their own thing, creates their own NT domain structure or defines their own Exchange organization model. The need imposed by the Exchange directory to define naming conventions for the organization, sites, servers, and mailboxes means that it is very difficult to take a server that's being operated by one department or another and incorporate the server into a corporate Exchange organization. As noted above, no tools or utilities exist today to merge Exchange organizations, or import a complete organization into another. If a "pirate" server does not match the organizational model created for the corporate implementation then Exchange will have to be installed on that server.

The close relationship between Windows NT, Exchange, and the individual servers that collectively form a corporate-wide implementation makes re-installation inevitable. The question therefore needs to be asked of anyone who considers deploying Exchange early, before everything is planned and ready to go: "Are you ready to accept that the work you're doing will be discarded once the corporate deployment starts?" In most cases, the enthusiasm of the potential pirates is tempered when the realization that their work will have to be redone.

So what can you do to integrate standalone systems into an Exchange infrastructure which spans the enterprise? There are two basic approaches.

1.   Leave the existing servers in place and integrate everyone with a unified messaging backbone to connect all the different servers together. In this scenario each location that oper-

ates an Exchange server retains its existing user accounts, server names, and other attributes and is treated as a separate and distinct Exchange organization (rather than site).

2. Start over by designing the Exchange infrastructure from the base up so that all the servers are connected together into sites within a logical Exchange organization. In this scenario all the existing servers will eventually be assimilated into the new infrastructure. Because of the dependence on Windows NT domains, security, and networking this process will inevitably be more painful for some user communities than others.

3. Merge the two organizations by moving servers from one organization into the other. Hopefully this can be done with the "Move Server" tool scheduled for Exchange V5.5 SP1.

Clearly the first approach is faster and easier to implement. It devolves the responsibility for operation away from a central co-ordinating body to the system managers in individual locations, and this may make the approach attractive to managers of central MIS groups who struggle with shrinking budgets. All that the central group has to provide is the messaging backbone and this can be based on SMTP or X.400. A centrally co-ordinated corporate directory is an optional extra.

Requiring servers which are already up and running to basically stop operations and change to come into line with standards determined for a corporate Exchange infrastructure will clearly impact system managers and users alike. Software will probably need to be re-installed to change organization, site, or server names, meaning that users will have to save the contents of their mailboxes to personal stores (PST files), or discard whatever they had stored in their mailboxes and start over again. Servers may have to join different Windows NT domains to allow public folder affinity. Connectors may have to be re-installed and communications re-established with other messaging systems. User accounts may need to be renamed to come into line with whatever corporate standard is felt best. If you've just been running pilot systems the best idea may well be to stop and start from scratch again, but clearly this approach is more difficult for all concerned if the system has been operational for any length of time. This is another good reason to pay attention to the overall design for Windows NT and Exchange before attempting a corporate implementation.

3.3.16   Franchised sites

Sometimes you want to be able to allow people to deploy Exchange on their own, taking responsibility for delivering service to a particular user community while remaining a full participant in a company's deployment. These deployments are based on a concept known as franchised sites.

The main characteristics of the franchised sites concept include:

- Each site serves a distinct user community. It may be a physical location such as the London site. On the other hand, it may be an organizational entity, such as the Human Resources department.

- The site takes full responsibility for the deployment of whatever servers they wish within the site. Hardware configurations and designs remain totally under the control of the people managing the site, although they may well take advice from a central group.

- The site connects into the central core organization via an agreed type of site connector. Typically the X.400 connector is used because it allows the greatest degree of control over network traffic. The connection is made to a nominated server within the core organization.

- The site does not install other connectors unless on an agreed basis. No one wants sites to introduce connectors without consultation as an unplanned growth in the number of connectors merely complicates the organizational routing table for everyone.

- The site shares a common address space with the rest of the organization, including other franchised sites. Because of this the site must agree to follow naming conventions, especially for user display names.

- The site establishes a directory replication connector to the core organization and participates in the organization GAL.

Franchised sites allow distributed management. Many corporations already have distributed administration already and are interested in the concept. If you've been running a local Microsoft Mail or cc:Mail Post Office you're already well aware of local administration!

Franchising has many advantages. However, it can't work without a strong core implementation in place to link all the franchised sites together. It also can't work if everyone does not have the discipline to comply with the practices that allow everyone to work together. Finally, local administration cannot be done if local administrators are not trained to the same level of professionalism and knowledge as the people who plan, design, and carry out the central deployment. The last point is possibly the most important.

3.3.17   **The consequences of not getting Windows NT 100% right**

Exchange is a messaging system so it's not altogether 100% correct to say that its servers must share the same Windows NT security context before successful operation is possible. Putting all the Exchange servers in a separate resource domain or establishing a reliable set of trust relationships between a set of domains will make things easier to set up and manage. Connections between servers and sites, for example, flow much more easily if their underlying connections are underpinned by a well-planned, solid Windows NT design. But if you're in a position where it's impossible to bring all the servers together into a single domain or trust relationships prove unreliable for one reason or another it is still possible to create a messaging infrastructure, albeit at the expense of lesser functionality.

The most important point to recognize is that all communications between Exchange servers, including replication, can be accomplished through the interchange of messages. As long as a network capable of supporting the TCP/IP protocol is in place and the servers can "see" each other across the network, messages can be exchanged and data replicated. So what functionality does not work? Here are the most important issues:

- Public folder affinity is not possible.
- Single seat administration cannot be performed.
- Message tracking doesn't work.
- Server monitors don't work.

Public folder affinity (see discussion beginning on page 294) will not work unless a client is able to authenticate itself to the server controlling the public folder. If I have a client connected to a server located in Domain A, and the public folder is stored on a server located in Domain B, then the client must be able to authenticate itself in Domain A and B before the servers will allow affinity to proceed and the client to access the contents of the public folder. If all the servers are located in the same domain or appropriate trust relationships are defined between the different domains then authentication is achieved during the initial client log-on.

Most companies like the idea of being able to manage a complete network of Exchange servers from a central server (or workstation). But again, the administration program must be able to authenticate itself to a server before the server is happy to accept administrative instructions. If the administration program is used to browse an Exchange organization and then selects a computer in another domain, an attempt is made to log-on to that computer, which is of course impossible if the appropriate rights are unavailable.

Message tracking (see discussion in chapter 11) is based on the availability of message tracking logs, held in a network share called "tracking.log" on each Exchange server. Message tracking can only follow the path of a message from one computer to another as long as the trail can be established through examination of the message tracking logs, so the network share on each server in the path must be available to make full tracking feasible[2]. If the servers reside in different domains and trust relationships are not in place the network shares cannot be accessed and tracking halts at the stage when the message exited the domain.

Server monitors (also discussed in chapter 11) can be used to establish whether important Exchange services, such as the Store, System Attendant, or MTA are up and running on one or more target servers. RPCs are sent to the target servers to glean information about the services the monitor is interested in, but the RPCs will not be responded to if they come from an un-authenticated source.

Over time it may be the case that other functionality is unavailable when a unified security context cannot be established across all Exchange servers in an organization. We simply don't know the minds of the Exchange engineers on this topic. As such, I believe the best thing to do is to attempt to create the most solid Windows NT infrastructure that's possible, and then execute the Exchange implementation on top of that solid foundation.

3.4   Layering the site design on top of the network

When designing the Exchange organization for your implementation will you:

- Create a small number of large sites?
- Create a large number of small sites?
- Create a mixture of large and small sites?

The automated tools mentioned earlier in this chapter (page 138) can help to clarify the best solution to your requirements. Sometimes the decision will be made for you. If you don't have fast network links between servers that are capable of handling the RPC load generated to synchronize site-wide shared data structures such as the directory then you won't be able to combine the servers together into a site. Anything less than a dedicated high-quality 64 Kbps link (the recom-

---

2.   Tracking must also be turned on for the different components (connectors and the MTA) that handle messages if tracking logs are to be filled with valuable information.

mendation generally given by Microsoft) provides too little bandwidth for the RPC-based site connectors to operate in a satisfactory manner. It's often difficult for companies, especially outside the United States, to justify the operation of such high-speed links just to connect some mail servers together. In these situations careful attention must be paid to the location of servers and how servers are combined together into sites. Everything is layered directly on the network and if the network can't carry the load the Exchange organization cannot function.

Be wary of assuming that just because a network connection is there its total available bandwidth is available for use by Exchange. In most instances other applications will want their own slice of the bandwidth, leaving Exchange with whatever is left over. Another issues to consider is that a line rated at a certain speed may not deliver the maximum bandwidth all the time, perhaps because of some low-quality links that occur at places along the line. Indeed, in many cases there is a significant difference between a line's maximum theoretical bandwidth and its committed information rate (CIR).

The CIR is a much more reliable indication of how much information a line can transmit because it represents the information transfer rate which the network (or network provider) is committed to transfer under normal conditions. The CIR is always averaged over a period of time before it is determined, and this takes account of any retransmissions required because of low line quality. RPCs in particular are sensitive to low line quality, so a line that apparently provides 64 Kbps bandwidth might only achieve an information transfer rate of 32 Kbps or less due to RPC time outs and other errors. Aside from a line's CIR, bandwidth tends to be absorbed in many different ways. For these reasons it's wise to begin planning on the basis that 128 Kbps links are used for RPC-based site connectors with 256 Kbps links deployed to connect servers together within a site. You can reduce network capacity you like, but always with detailed knowledge of exactly what's passing across the network.

Now that I've stated a rule let's acknowledge that exceptions will always be found. Large network pipes are best for Exchange, but reliable data transmission depends on the capacity and quality of the network link. There are instances where people have experienced difficulties transmitting RPCs between sites over 128 Kbps links, and other examples where the RPCs were happy to travel over much lower rated links. Line quality dictates whether data flows easily, so the 128 Kbps link was obviously very low quality while the 9.6 Kbps link was high quality. The short-term solution to the problem experienced across the 128 Kbps link might be to increase capacity to 256 Kbps or greater, on the basis that increasing the size of the pipe will let more data through. The solution will probably work, but it doesn't address the underlying problem that provoked the issue in the first place.

If you're moving from an older text based mail system you may need to consider how the characteristics of these systems differ from Exchange, especially when considering whether or not you want to connect clients across WAN links. Text-based systems normally transmit much lower quantities of data when messages are processed. Delivering the first page of a text message to a terminal might transmit between 2 and 4K across a link. Only the first 24 lines or so must be sent, together with some primitive formatting directives such as bold, reverse video, or underlining. The data is transferred in a file-like manner. When Outlook reads a message content to fill the current view is fetched from the server using RPCs. The data is more complex and contains attribute information (TO, CC, BCC, and so on) as well as text. A simple message might take require 10K to transfer, and if a large distribution list is included, maybe more than 50K. The nature of the network is important too. Many companies have networks designed to transfer complete files around. In such a network it's not really important if latency and retransmissions slow the arrival of a file by ten or twenty seconds, but the same is not true in a client/server environment. Clients will be affected if RPCs timeout or don't complete, and users will notice a real difference in performance. For this reason it is wise to look at a network in its entirety—original design, current throughput and capacity, and future plans, during the design phase of any Exchange implementation project.

When you look at any anecdotal evidence of an Exchange implementation and examine the network connections in use, consider how much data flows between sites, and between servers within sites. The amount of data to be carried is an important influence on the network that we need, but it's often an issue overlooked during the planning phase. Take the example quoted as using 9.6 Kbps links. If only a small number of messages were sent between users in the different sites, and there wasn't a lot of public folder replication, and not many changes were ever made in the directory, then it's entirely possible that the small pipe is more than able to handle the load. However, if people make energetic use of e-mail, use e-forms, replicate public folders that contain large Word documents, PowerPoint presentations, and other files, and regular directory synchronizations are performed with directory data taken from other messaging systems, then the network load between the sites is going to be much heavier. Attempting to link heavily trafficked sites together across 9.6 Kbps connections may work, but only at the expense of slow message delivery and potential message queues building up in the MTAs on all sites. In addition, the resilience of the network will be quite low, and if network outages occur, it will take a considerable amount of time before message back-logs can be cleared. Large network links really come into their own when it's time to clear a lot of work.

No example is enough evidence for anyone to make a firm recommendation that you should have 9.6, 56, 64, 128, or 256-Kbps links installed in your company. The starting point is to base the core site design on the way data flows through the transmission network, taking special note of places where the network designers have attempted to segment traffic through the installation of network routers and bridges. As a first principle, do not attempt to connect servers into sites across extended network segments, as this is not normally good use of network resources. After all the information is gathered, use local experience of network conditions, measurements of data transmission rates, errors, and evidence of any time-outs known to occur to help decide how much bandwidth you need, but above all concentrate on achieving line quality as without quality the RPCs will find it difficult to get through.

3.4.1   The mistake of depending on the examples of other companies

Many companies start planning on the basis that there should be as few sites as possible in the organization, and concentrate on building very large sites even over widely distributed geographic areas. The experiences of the Exchange implementations in Microsoft and DIGITAL are often quoted as examples of how to build and operate very large sites. Microsoft's North America site, for instance, has over 160 servers in it. DIGITAL also has a very large site spanning North America, the difference between the two implementations largely being the size of the servers. The early deployments used different hardware. Microsoft deployed relatively small servers, so there are a lot of them. DIGITAL preferred large servers (a graphic illustration of the power of Alpha technology), so deployed 20 or so to serve all of North America. Simple figures conceal a lot of details about both implementations. Microsoft has a lot of servers concentrated in a small area (the campus at Redmond, Washington). DIGITAL also has a large number of users concentrated in a small part of America, in this case in the New England area. Both implementations depend on high-quality, high-bandwidth networks (including satellite links) because both companies have invested heavily in an extremely capable network for internal communications over the years. Both companies also depend on electronic mail and other forms of communications, like internal Web or electronic forums, to share information.

Not all companies have the luxury of such extensive and capable networks, at least, not the scale deployed within Microsoft or DIGITAL. So is it reasonable to select the same implementation model if the underlying foundation is radically different? The answer, of course, is "No". A little additional probing past the headline points of both implementations reveals that:

- Microsoft has a number of small sites in South America. When they began their deployment in 1995–96 those sites were not connected by permanent high-speed links, so RAS dial-up connectors were used to link servers in the sites into the rest of Microsoft. Dial-up connections are limited by modem speed (often 28.8 Kbps) and the quality of the telephone line. Synchronizing a very large directory over such a connection can take several days.

- DIGITAL has more users located in Europe and the Asia-Pacific regions than Microsoft. In many instances the network link back to a hub site is 64 Kbps, but that link is not solely available for Exchange and must carry traffic from many other sources. Because Europe is spread across multiple international boundaries and many telecommunications providers it is both harder and more expensive to put high-speed network links in place. Thus, DIGITAL has found that it is impossible to run a single site across Europe (see next section). The sites are linked together with X.400 connectors because they are more reliable and robust across low-speed links than site connectors.

- Communications in Asia-Pacific are also expensive and the people are widely dispersed. Creating a single site is impossible when there are several thousand people to serve.

With these points in mind I think it reasonable to look at the Microsoft and DIGITAL implementations in order to learn, but not to assume that just because these companies have deployed Exchange in large sites within America that this is the only and best way to proceed. There is no reason why any company's culture and implementation should directly influence your implementation, unless you want this to happen and understand the consequences. The network places the most immediate and important constraint on the way Exchange sites are built and linked together, and this point must always be paramount in the minds of those who architect an Exchange solution.

3.4.2   Learning never stops

All products go through different stages in their lifecycle. Exchange is still in the early stages of its lifecycle and it follows that many people are still learning a lot about effective ways of deploying Exchange, and the trade-offs and decisions that must be taken as an implementation plan or design is arrived at. Much of the experience we have today comes from early adopters (the companies who were brave enough to agree to put Exchange into production very early on—their nickname is the "brave-hearts"); Microsoft's own implementation of Exchange; and books, conference papers, and other consulting studies. Much of this information is valuable and should be carefully considered when building new organizations, but to date it has necessarily been created from a reasonably narrow base and can't be considered as the absolutely best way to do everything.

Judging by experience of the lifecycle of other messaging products, the really ingenuous and clever deployment techniques only come about after some years, really after people have had time to see the product in action and think through how they could improve matters. Unless you pay attention to all available sources of information and ideas some of the new techniques will pass you by and you'll never be able to take the kernel of the new learning and apply your local knowledge to put the techniques into practice for your company.

The experience of DIGITAL illustrates how an Exchange deployment evolves under the joint influences of increased experience and maturity in the capabilities of the product. The original design called for three sites (one each for the Americas, Europe, and Asia-Pacific). That design worked fine for pilot deployments, but suffered increased strain as the number of mailboxes grew. Network resources in parts of Europe and Asia/Pacific forced the number of sites to begin growing very soon after the deployment began to reach these areas.

Today (early 1998), DIGITAL has split its original three sites into 31 both to take control of network traffic and to facilitate some degree of freedom for specific groups to run their own Exchange sites under the franchise model. America, with its rich network infrastructure, remains largely unchanged, but the original Europe and Asia/Pacific sites have been decomposed into multiple sites. The number of Exchange servers has gone past 200 to support 62,000 mailboxes. DIGITAL operates over 2,000 servers for enterprise applications like Exchange plus local applications like file and print services in its complete NT infrastructure. An average DIGITAL mailbox sends 10 messages a day and receives 20. The volume grows all the time. Over 1 million messages are sent daily.

The average number of users per server is approximately 310, which is smaller than you might expect and lower than originally predicted. Many large servers are operated, but as the deployment progressed out to cater for all of the locations DIGITAL operates in (more than a hundred around the world), individual systems were installed in many places to serve small user communities, reducing the average. Now that Exchange V5.5 has removed many of the barriers to scalability, a study is underway to see how some of the 200 servers can be consolidated into a much smaller number, which will reduce the scope, expense and difficulty involved in managing large number of servers.

3.4.3 Inter-site communications

Every server in a site communicates with its peers on a regular and unregulated manner. In other words, you can't prevent a server talking to its peers when it wants to rather than when you'd prefer it to. Servers exchange details about configuration changes, they update each other with directory information, and messages are routed between servers without regard to the network or any schedule. Sometimes, when I try and illustrate this point in seminars, I compare Exchange servers in a site as insecure human beings with a constant requirement to reassure each other that everything's OK. At the end of the day all you can say is that each server will connect to its peers on a regular basis to establish a full-mesh network. Nothing can be said about the amount of data that will travel across the links, because that amount is highly dependent on the way Exchange is used within a company. Another interesting point is raised by the RPC mechanism used by servers to communicate together. RPCs are sensitive to network quality, and if that is not high enough RPCs will time out or otherwise fail to get through, leading to a large number of retransmissions.

Firm and quantitative data can only be gathered as a result of a data collection exercise, watching the data flow between servers and measuring how much is sent out and received. The bottom line here is that you shouldn't introduce servers into a site unless permanent, robust, and highly capable network links exist between the server and every other server already in the site. In short, you need a high-speed, high-capacity network. If the network links between servers are incapable of offering a solid, reliable, and generous supply of bandwidth to satisfy the sometimes seemingly insatiable demands of the servers, then you are better to create separate sites and connect them together with site or X.400 connectors.

In general the recommendation is to limit the number of sites within an organization. While moving objects within a site is easy, moving users and servers between sites is a difficult, manual process. Putting effort into the organization/site design is important. Ask yourself questions like "How can we expand without breaking the organization if a large number of new users needs to be added" or "What happens if our company sells a building, de-centralizes, or otherwise physically changes the shape of the company?" A design should be flexible and able to expand (or contract) as business requirements dictate.

An organization with more than fifty sites is going to be moderately difficult to manage. A site with more than twenty servers in it will also be difficult to manage. Try to restrict the number of points of management, at least at the beginning. It is very easy to add a site or server to your Exchange organization afterwards, if required, but organizations that start off sprawled and scattered don't tend to regain any coherent shape without great effort on the part of system administrators.

3.4.4 The strong hub site approach

It's fascinating to observe how different approaches to the problems posed for Exchange site design in different circumstances has evolved since 1996. DIGITAL consultants have had an opportunity to develop over 200 enterprise-level designs in that time, but even so, new techniques appear all the time. Some are created by people who really don't know what they are doing, but others are interesting and deliver real value.

Figure 3.9 *The Hub Site approach*

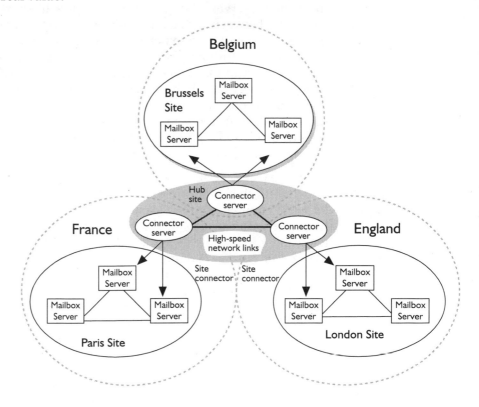

Figure 3.9 illustrates an approach I'll call the "strong hub", a design that has a lot of support amongst colleagues in Microsoft Consulting Services. The design is characterized by the establishment of a set of servers in a hub site. No mailboxes are hosted on these servers. Instead, the servers act as message switches to connect all the other sites together. High-speed network links that are capable of transporting large quantities of data (usually rated at 512 Kbps or better) connect the servers in the hub site. Site connectors are used between the hub and mailbox sites.

Nothing too strange so far. The interesting aspect is the location of the servers in the hub site. Instead of being brought together into a central place, the servers are distributed out into the different geographic regions, close to large user communities. Consider the site design outlined in Figure 3.9. There are four sites, the strong hub and sites containing mailbox servers in Paris, London, and Brussels. One server from the hub site is co-located alongside each of the mailbox sites. The intention is to build a great deal of resilience into the overall messaging system by keeping a server in the hub site physically close to the mailbox servers. For example, it is less likely that the local network link between the nearby hub server and the mailbox servers in the Paris site will ever experience a lengthy outage. Therefore, messages will flow smoothly between the mailbox servers and the hub site without interruption. Once in the hub site the messages can be swiftly routed between the hub servers. Even if a network outage occurs between the hub server in France and its English counterpart, messages for users in the London site will be automatically rerouted via the hub server in Belgium. The hub site also hosts connectors to external mail systems and the Internet.

The classical design for a network spanning three countries might create the hub site in one of the countries (often the place where the largest computer centre is located) and use X.400 connectors to communicate with the sites in the other countries. This type of design is tried and tested and will work effectively. However, if network problems occur fast manual intervention is often required to prevent large message queues from building up. On the other hand, the classic design is cheaper to implement as it is able to function across network links that are lower quality or offer less capacity than the links required to build a strong hub site. Once again, available network resources dictate the type of Exchange organizational designs you can even begin to consider. Given large network pipes anything is possible.

3.4.5   Serving locations with small number of users

Sometimes you won't want to put a server into a location. Perhaps the network doesn't extend there or maybe there aren't enough people to justify the expense and effort required to bring an additional system into production. Local sales offices that host two or three people are a common example of such a location. What can you do to connect these people in with the rest of the organization? Two choices exist:

1.   Run an extended WAN connection to the location

2.   Use telephone connections

The number of clients that can be connected over a WAN link depends on the bandwidth delivered (the more bandwidth, the more clients) plus the type of work that the clients do. A 64 Kbps link might be able to support more than 20 users if they are just going to read and send a few messages on a sporadic basis. On the other hand, the same link will be hard pressed by a relatively small number of users who insist on working with large documents that are stored in public folders. Sending large attachments (greater than a few hundred kilobytes) across an extended WAN link will degrade performance for everyone else, and there's always the temptation to use the bandwidth for other activities, such as surfing the web, terminal connections to mainframe or mini-computers, and so on.

Table 3.1   *Calculating whether a local server is required*

Link speed	Number of users	Is a local server required?	Is the available bandwidth enough?
< 64 Kbps	< 10	No	Yes
< 64 Kbps	10–30	Usually not	Dependent on client usage
< 64 Kbps	> 30	Yes	N/A—Local Server
128 Kbps	< 10	No	Yes
128 Kbps	10–50	Usually not	Dependent on client usage
128 Kbps	> 50	Yes	N/A—Local Server

Table 3.1 provides a rough guidelines for deciding whether a local server should be installed in a location where a WAN link of 64 Kbps or 128 Kbps is available. The table is based on "medium" users, people who don't create or send a large volume of messages. Based on some tests, an Outlook client occupies between 1.5 Kbps (medium) to 4 Kbps (heavy) of a WAN link after the initial log-on process is complete. Log-on is particularly heavy on network resources and can occupy up to 25

Kbps for a single client. You can expect surges in demand during peak hours, and users will experience significantly degraded response when a number of other clients are logging on. Outlook does some compression of message content (the figure is around 40%), and attempts to use some intelligence by only fetching enough data to fill the view (the area of the screen where message content is displayed). Attachments are not fetched until a user double-clicks on their icon. A separate connection is established to the public folder server, and data is fetched to display the hierarchy. Data is also retrieved for each public folder favourite because the client must display the count of new items in each folder.

New versions of client software may affect the capability of any link to support a certain number of users. For example, Outlook 98 introduces background synchronization, a feature that allows users to work while their off-line folders are synchronized with server folders. This may not seem important, but background synchronization controlled by software can impose a constant demand on the network in place of the intermittent demand generated as humans read and answer messages.

You might assume that clients based on simpler protocols will use less network. This is sometimes true and sometimes not. For example, a POP3 client must conduct a log-on sequence each time it connects to a mailbox. Also, the POP3 protocol does not feature bodypart compression, so the complete content of messages are fetched. The extra load imposed in these ways is offset by the overall reduced level of functionality available in the client. POP3, after all, has no concept of public folders, so no need exists to fetch information about the hierarchy or new item counts for favorites. Web browser access is usually pretty lean, but there are instances where OWA is heavier than Outlook. Because connections are routed through the IIS the log-on process for OWA is more complex. Message content is provided in HTML, but it is not compressed, and so on. Again, the reduced level of functionality available to OWA clients is usually enough to offset the increased traffic generated by some functions. And, as I have noted earlier on, OWA is able to connect over really bad links when the RPCs used by Outlook just can't complete.

Educated use of network resources increases the number of users that any link is able to support. For example, if users are coached to make connections to the server every couple of hours or so, synchronize their folders, and then work off-line until the next connection time, most of their work will be done off-line and the network will only have to handle bursts of activity. It's not easy to convince people to be so disciplined. Most individuals will fall into the habit of assuming that the network link is available all the time for their exclusive benefit and proceed to work on that basis.

Telephone connections are best used when the number of users in a location is very small, possibly between 1 and 5. In this instance users must be disciplined because each connection is going to be charged for, and the longer people spend on line the higher the charges. I have known of cases where a senior manager became distracted when working over a telephone link, and left the PC connected to the line overnight. That connection was from a hotel, and the call had been placed to a server in another country. The end result was a bill well into the thousands of dollars, an extreme example perhaps, but a useful war story to tell to users when you're trying to encourage good habits.

Telephone connections require a RAS infrastructure to be in place too. You'll also need the fastest possible modems at both ends of the connection. I have been able to connect in over a Nokia 2110 GSM modem that delivered a 9.6 Kbps link, but progress was slow and folder synchronization seemed to take forever. On the other hand, my current modem connects at a range of 24 Kbps to 33 Kbps, a more than adequate level of performance.

People often rule out telephone connections as an option if the remote locations are in another country. The thoughts of international phone call charges mounting up on a regular basis is enough to push network planners to try and secure dedicated network connections to foreign offices. The logic here is that it's better to pay network charges up front and deal with a known figure that can be factored into a budget rather than live with the unpredictable nature of telephone bills. I can't fault the logic, but sometimes a little lateral thinking can result in another solution for international calls.

The Internet is everywhere and it's easy to make cheap, even free telephone calls to local "points of presence" serviced by an Internet Service Provider (ISP). If this is the case, then why not use the Internet to channel network traffic from remote clients back to an Exchange server? The normal answer is "security". No one wants their mail to be read by hackers who might intercept messages as they move across the Internet. But technology exists today to allow encrypted tunnels to be built between clients and servers across the Internet, and so transfer messages and other data in a very safe and reliable manner. One such technology is DIGITAL's AltaVista Tunnel.

AltaVista Tunnel encrypts IP packets as they leave clients, and decrypts the packets as they arrive into a private network. The result is a Virtual Private Network (VPN) built between the client and the private network. The tunnel is built through PC client software, which is responsible for initiating and managing the tunnel across the Internet, and an AltaVista Tunnel Server, which is located inside the firewall that guards a company network. The AltaVista Tunnel Server decrypts the data sent across the VPN, and routes it to the end destination, in our case, an Exchange server. No change has to be made by the local ISP, who remains blissfully unaware that their services are being used to build a VPN. If the ISP were to monitor the transmissions between an AltaVista Tunnel client and the Internet, all they'd see is perfectly normal IP packets.

You may think that using an encrypted tunnel across the Internet still represents a risk, probably because you need more information than can be presented here to help you become more comfortable with the concept and technologies used to implement the tunnel. Encrypted tunneling does work, and has been used in a number of projects to facilitate people in remote locations or users who move from place to place and need to connect in when a RAS environment isn't available. Perhaps the biggest benefit is the way that costs are reduced by eliminating expensive international telephone calls in favor of cheap local calls to an ISP. The downside is speed. Although more than acceptable for most of the time, the Internet is congested, and there's no doubt that messages sometimes take longer to transmit and receive than would be the case if you had made a dial-up RAS connection. However, given the cost benefits, tunneling is still an interesting option for anyone who needs to connect in small offices cheaply.

3.5   Connecting up an Exchange organization

Once you have an Exchange server up and running and some clients happily connected and sending mail to each other the next natural step is to consider how you can connect your server to others. Connecting a new server into an existing site isn't an issue because connectivity is largely transparent and is automatically accomplished when the new server joins the site.

The major options for connecting Exchange sites together are:

- Direct RPC connections between Exchange sites (AKA Site Connectors)
- Using the Internet Mail Service to connect Exchange sites together
- Using the X.400 connector to link Exchange sites together
- Using an SMTP-based backbone

- Using an existing X.400 backbone (in other words, a non-Exchange MTA)

These methods are listed in order of convenience. In other words, making a direct connection between two Exchange sites over an RPC-based connector is a quick and easy way to get things going. It is also the lowest cost option and probably the way that most people will use when they start to connect sites together. However, it is an Exchange-specific solution and only suitable where a low to medium volume of messages need to be transported within the boundaries of a single physical LAN or WAN. The basic and most fundamental thing to understand here is that if the network cannot support and reliably deliver the RPCs between servers in the different sites you shouldn't even begin to think about using site connectors. The X.400 or SMTP connectors are able to function over lower-quality and less capable networks, and are the pragmatic choice when the network is not able to deliver permanent, high-speed, robust connections.

3.5.1   Selecting a corporate messaging backbone

Once the requirement arises to connect to other messaging systems, inside or outside your organization, another approach must be taken. At this stage a fundamental decision about the corporate messaging structure may have to be taken. Are you going to use SMTP or X.400 as the basic messaging backbone? This decision is one of the most important that messaging system implementers must make.

X.400 is an internationally agreed standard designed to enable interoperability between different messaging systems. The standard describes the structure and format of messages, and how they can be exchanged between different systems. It is issued in the form of a set of recommendations that can be used by vendors when they build messaging systems. Exchange complies with the set of recommendations issued in 1988 and is able to connect to systems that support either the 1984 or 1988 recommendations.

SMTP is the messaging protocol generally used to send messages throughout the Internet and is designed to operate over TCP/IP networks. Initially drafted in 1982, SMTP is an old protocol now, even older than the first set of X.400 recommendations. Originally designed to facilitate the transmission of simple text messages between systems, SMTP has evolved (not always gracefully) through the add-on of different extensions to the protocol. The extensions have allowed SMTP to compete on an almost equal basis with the underlying richness promised by the more comprehensive nature of the X.400 recommendations. Continual evolution through add-ons rather than a complete redesign of a protocol is not always the best way to bring a protocol forward. Some industry observers have asked whether it's not time to carry out a full review of SMTP so that it can survive and prosper past the year 2000. An exercise like the effort carried out for the IP protocol that resulted in IP V6.0 would be good for SMTP at this point in its life-cycle, but no such project is in view at present.

Exchange uses the Internet Mail Service to allow connections to SMTP-based mail systems. You can use the Internet Mail Service to send messages to other messaging systems, as long as you can connect to the other system via TCP/IP and it is able to accept SMTP-type messages either directly or via an SMTP gateway. Alternatively, you can use the Internet Mail Service to tie Exchange sites together over a TCP/IP network.

Debates about the best messaging backbone have raged over the years. Over the last decade X.400 has traditionally proved to be more popular in Europe than in the U.S., possibly because of the high level of support the majority, if not all, of the public telecommunications carriers in Europe have given to establishing X.400-based messaging services. Indeed, in the United States, there is at times almost visceral antipathy towards X.400 and any messaging system associated with the set of standards. Even the mention that an X.400 connector might be used to connect some Exchange sites together is enough to provoke a strong reaction, with people rushing to deploy site or SMTP connectors instead, just in case they might be infected with the X.400 "disease". This is a silly reaction. Just because a particular technology is built on a set of standards that you might not particularly appreciate is no reason to ignore X.400 connectors. The current implementation of Exchange is, after all, largely modeled on the broad outlines of the X.400 and X.500 recommendations, yet it is totally possible to deploy Exchange without realizing that X.400 is playing a part. In the same way, it is possible for X.400 connectors to be deployed without anyone outside the administration community knowing about it.

The Internet was slower to spread in Europe and the number of Internet connection points and choice of public providers is still far lower in Europe (the number grows all the time). A purely cynical view of the X.400/SMTP debate is that X.400 was designed by a committee so it's bound to be overly complex and bureaucratic whereas SMTP has evolved through practical implementation so it's more down-to-earth. The truth lies somewhere in between.

Table 3.2 looks at X.400 and SMTP backbones from a number of perspectives important to system administrators. These are personal opinions and you're quite welcome to agree or disagree. X.400 offers more inherent security features than standard SMTP, but these are largely offset by Exchange's ability to encrypt and apply digital signatures to messages before they are transmitted over either backbone (within a single Exchange organization).

Table 3.2 *Comparing X.400 and SMTP*

	X.400	SMTP
Security	✓	
Reliability	✓	
Target population		✓
Cost		✓
Technical complexity	Difficult	Easy
Ease of interoperability		✓
Ease of operation/administration	Difficult	Easy
Ease of use (addressing)		✓

In some respects an X.400 backbone tends to be more reliable than a SMTP equivalent, if only because of the superior notification options supported by X.400, including non-repudiation of messages. It should be noted that a draft specification intended to allow SMTP to support delivery and read notifications is currently under active consideration, and this may well erode the current advantage held by X.400. At the end of the day SMTP scores heavily in terms of its target population (the number of people reachable through SMTP), the cost of deployment, and the ease of use when it comes to addressing.

Using the Exchange directory to mask the complexities of addresses necessary to reach remote correspondents makes the point about addressing somewhat academic. However, if an SMTP type address is exposed to a user it's obvious that:

```
Tony.Redmond@digital.com
```

is a little friendlier and more understandable than:

```
/C=IE/A=EIRMAIL400/P=DIGITAL/O=DIGITAL/OU=DBO/G=TONY/S=REDMOND
```

Addresses can change as they move from network to network so an address that starts off being stated in a fairly simple form (as shown above) can become very cluttered and hard to decipher, even for people who are very au fait with messaging standards.

Possibly the most important difference from a user perspective is the way that an SMTP backbone enables easy interoperability for compound messages. These are messages composed of both cover memos and attachments or embedded objects. Clients that connect to SMTP backbones use the MIME protocol to encode compound messages, and almost every messaging system available today is able to understand and interpret MIME. The SMTP and MIME combination make it very much easier for people to send each other messages containing Word documents or Excel spreadsheets than through the sometimes extreme contortions necessary with X.400. The pragmatic approach of user-driven standards as seen in the Internet beats the conformance-driven approach of X.400. Making things easier for users has a bonus for system administrators too because less time has to be spent setting up the connections between servers and the backbone, tuning parameters to enable complex messages to travel from one system to another, and responding to user queries when problems arise.

Ease of use and administration also makes SMTP a more attractive option from the point of cost. Time is money, so the less time spent setting up and managing the backbone the better for all concerned. Compare the time taken to configure the Internet Mail Service and the X.400 Connector to see how more configuration effort X.400 requires. The extra effort also requires more knowledge of X.400 and OSI that implies training and experience on the part of the system administrator, or an additional cost to buy in expertise from external consultants.

Lest it be assumed that I overly favor SMTP over X.400 let me review some of the arguments often used in rebuttal by the proponents of the X.400 recommendations.

The establishment of the X.400 recommendations has enabled bridges to be built between vastly different messaging systems. The recommendations are well understood and supported by many public electronic mail carriers and PTTs (public telephone authorities) throughout the world. Because X.400 is supported by so many organizations it's easy to make connections between different companies. Finally, the construct of X.400 messages follows an agreed scheme that preserves content as messages move from one system to another. All are valid assertions, but the value of the arguments is being eroded all the time by the sheer weight of the SMTP/MIME combination driven forward by the Internet juggernaut.

Those interested in reading more on this topic before making a decision should look at John Rhoton's book "X.400 and SMTP: The Battle of the E-mail protocols" (ISBN 1-55558-165-X, Digital Press, 1997).

3.5.2   **Factors governing the choice**

Both X.400 and SMTP allow you to build and maintain connections between Exchange sites. The decision as to which to use depends on a number of factors including whether an X.400 or SMTP infrastructure is already in place and type of connections you want to make with other people outside your company.

For example, if you are migrating from a situation where a well-established X.400 backbone is in place (to link different messaging systems together and to provide connections to external companies), then it might well be best to leave the existing backbone alone and concentrate on integrating Exchange in with the other messaging systems using the X.400 connector. Remember that Exchange isn't limited to just one X.400 connector (within an organization) and two or more might be used; some to connect Exchange sites together and another to link Exchange to the corporate backbone.

If your organization only uses X.400 for external connections or another OSI application, such as Electronic Data Interchange (EDI) transactions with trading partners, the best idea is probably to leave the X.400 backbone in place for its present purposes and establish a single X.400 connector between a bridgehead Exchange server and the backbone. In circumstances where sites are upgrading from Microsoft Mail or Lotus cc:Mail to Exchange and no messaging backbone exists the easiest option is to go with SMTP, but only because there are less steps to take to connect sites together with the Internet Mail Service than there is using X.400 connectors.

My personal preference is to use X.400 connectors to link sites whenever available network bandwidth will not support the deployment of the RPC-based site connector. The preference is driven by a simple fact—the X.400 connector is the only one that supports scheduled connections, enabling a far greater degree of control to be exerted on data transmitted across the network. This simple fact is enough to always recommend X.400 over Internet Mail connectors in large corporate messaging environments. SMTP messaging systems do not incorporate the concept of scheduled connections, although there is nothing to stop the Internet Mail Service including such functionality in the future.

Despite a preference to use X.400 connectors, my prediction is that 75–80% of all Exchange implementations that need a messaging backbone will use SMTP, and the rest will use X.400. Some people will select SMTP because it's simpler; others because they regard X.400 as being some sort of European standard that's being fostered on the rest of the world; and a few more because Internet protocols in general, including SMTP is where all the action appears to be at present. In most large networks some sort of gateway will connect the two backbones, mostly because the messaging world is still so diverse. At this point it's important to emphasize that the selection of SMTP as a corporate messaging backbone does not rule out the selective deployment of X.400 technologies within Exchange. In fact, because the original design of Exchange was closely aligned to the X.400 recommendations in many places you don't get much choice in the matter and will end up using X.400 even if you don't really want to.

Some system administrators propose to use SMTP to connect Exchange servers together using the Internet as the glue in between. Again, I think this is a reasonable plan to get systems connected quickly, but some of the attributes of the Internet, such as its openness and availability to all, are not conducive to the creation of a reliable, dependable and secure messaging system. For example, do you know what route messages will travel along as they proceed through the Internet? Can you be certain that other people aren't going to be able to intercept your messages and gain access to commercially sensitive information which could potentially damage your company? Also, what guarantee have you that messages will move across the Internet in any guaranteed time, and will the operations of your company be compromised if the message flow is interrupted by network problems within the Internet? A lot of the same issues arise within internal networks, but at least the network is under your control and can be managed as such. The advent of technologies like PPTP (Point to Point Tunnel Protocol), included in Windows NT V4.0 onwards, certainly delivers an answer to the problem of data protection as it passes across the Internet, but the other points still need to be considered as there's no easy answer immediately obvious today.

Knowledge of your existing messaging environment, the systems involved, how they are connected, the external connections in place or required and how you want the overall messaging environment to evolve are important inputs to the SMTP/X.400 backbone decision. Because this decision is so critical and its effects pervade all parts of the messaging infrastructure it's critical that the decision is right, so if you don't have the right level of knowledge and experience it's a good idea to seek help. The details of how to go about connecting into SMTP and X.400 backbones are covered in a later chapter. You may want to read these sections before considering your options.

3.5.3   Using Exchange connectors or X.400 backbones to connect sites

It is possible to create an organization of Exchange sites, each of which uses an X.400 connector to link to a corporate X.400 backbone. In this scenario messages are routed out of Exchange via the X.400 connector to the backbone, over the backbone and then delivered to the X.400 connector of the recipient's site. Sometimes this is the only option to take because a direct connection cannot be made between the Exchange sites, but if a direct connection is possible the question must be asked as to why the backbone is involved at all? Wouldn't it be simpler to keep all the messages within the Exchange organization and only involve the backbone if a message were being sent to a non-Exchange recipient?

The answer is that the backbone does introduce another step, one that is strictly speaking, unnecessary. There can be good reasons for routing messages across the backbone. Many X.400 backbones allow messages to be logged and tracked, enabling messaging administrators to verify the well-being of the overall messaging environment by checking that the flow of messages is never halted. The logging data can also be used for charging purposes, or to analyze the performance of the backbone, identify bottlenecks and plan for growth.

The benefits of routing across a backbone have a downside too. Some administrators do not understand that Exchange uses messages for everything—replication of data for the directory, public folder hierarchy, and public folder content; configuration data; and then the normal interpersonal messages that are expected. Transmitting all of the data sent between Exchange sites across a backbone may introduce new strain on the backbone, possibly one that the backbone is not configured to support. Extra network resources will be consumed to send messages to and from the backbone. Finally, routing messages across the backbone will probably be slower than over a direct site to site connection, so the quality of the messaging service is not as good as it could be. The quality represented by consistently fast message delivery is subjective. If users are migrating from a LAN-based system like Microsoft Mail where message delivery times across an extended network are usually slower than mainframe or mini-computer based systems then routing across a backbone is not a problem.

Keeping messages inside an Exchange organization as far as possible reduces network demand, speeds message delivery, and is easier to set up and administer. Therefore, the rule of thumb when planning systems is to use native Exchange connectors whenever possible, and only use a backbone to connect Exchange to other messaging systems. Note that this rule holds for connections to Microsoft Mail and Lotus cc:Mail systems because native Exchange connectors are available. The old adage is that exceptions prove the rule, but if you make an exception be sure that you understand the consequences of the decision in terms of the issues discussed above.

3.6   Naming systems

The name given to a Windows NT system is not only the name that the computer is known as within your network, it's also the name that Exchange will use when the software is installed. With this fact in mind it is clearly important to define a well-structured and easily understood naming convention for Windows NT systems intended to run Exchange.

A good naming convention allows system administrators to gain an immediate snapshot of a computer's role in the overall scheme with a quick look. This requirement immediately rules out any name that might be defined as "cute". For example, it's a bad idea to name all computers after cartoon characters because there's a reasonably small pool of names to choose from. There's no indication of what a computer might do or where it might be located if it is given a name like "Goofy", "Happy", "Sneezy", and so on.

Exchange is designed to be an organization-wide system so the naming convention must reflect this aim. Any organization is likely to include a number of geographical sites, and each site may have one or more computers that act as mail servers. This three-tier structure can be expressed in the naming convention. For example, let's assume that the XYZ Corporation is located in three sites in Asia, Europe, and the United States. The initial servers in the three sites might be named as follows:

```
XYZASIA001
XYZEUROPE001
XYZUSA001
```

As servers are added in the three sites it's easy to see that the numeric value at the end of the name is incremented by one to create a name for the new computer that's unique and conveys some idea of the overall organizational structure.

You can take this idea further and incorporate as many different levels as you like. Larger organizations that operate many Windows NT domains might like to include the domain name as the second element in server names. As an example, if the XYZ Corporation operated with manufacturing and sales divisions, each of which was represented by a different Windows NT domain, the names for the computers might look like this:

```
XYZMANASIA1
XYZSALESASIA1
```

Note that this scheme implies that the divisions operate different Exchange sites in addition to the two Windows NT domains. You also have to make sure that the server names don't exceed the 15-character limit imposed by Windows NT. Just to complicate matters, some versions of SMS (V1.0 through V1.2) cannot perform remote control of systems with 15-character NetBIOS (computer) names.

There may be situations, especially with smaller offices, where multiple organizational units are represented in the same place, perhaps a location that has a slow network link back to the rest of the organization. Clearly it would be silly in this situation for the users from each unit to have different Exchange servers, so the server naming scheme might need to have some flexibility built in to allow for such circumstances.

Creating an arbitrary naming convention is an activity that system managers may enjoy, but users sometimes find confusing. Sometimes the need for a structured naming convention is obvious, but in situations where sites span single geographical locations such as Dublin, London, and Paris, the naming scheme for Windows NT domains and Exchange sites could be based on city names or other geographical terms. A naming scheme based on Australian cities is used for illustration purposes in many places in the Exchange administration documentation.

Geographically based schemes provide the immediate and obvious advantage of creating a very familiar naming convention that is totally obvious to all. Given that sites are named on a geographical location, for example "Dublin", the servers within a site might be named DUBLIN001, DUBLIN002, or DUBLINSALES, DUBLINORDERS, and so on.

If you plan to connect to other X.400 messaging systems it is not recommended to use the underscore character in any name associated with Exchange (server, site, or organization). Exchange passes information about itself to the receiving X.400 systems and some can't handle underscores in system names, leading to undeliverable messages. To avoid problems in the future use hyphens instead of underscores to separate parts of server and site names as shown above[3].

3.6.1   Naming the organization and sites

We've just discussed the rather esoteric topic of how to name Windows NT servers. Applying a well-designed naming convention to Windows

---

3.   The advice on using hyphens as separators holds as long as other products don't have problems with server names that include hyphens. For example, SQL Server (for all versions up to and including V6.5) cannot perform replication if system names include hyphens! The lesson here is to check all angles before settling on a naming scheme.

NT servers makes it easier for system administrators to instantly recognize a server's location and purpose, but it's only going to be possible if you're able to install and commission the servers from scratch. Any installation that's been operating Windows NT for some time won't have this luxury and will have to do with the server names that are in place. In the case of the installation illustrated in Figure 3.10 where existing servers called DBO-EXCHANGEIST, DPSW08, OFFICENT1 and OFFICENT2 form the "Dublin" Exchange site. This is a practical real-life example of where Exchange has been installed on four existing Windows NT servers that have been combined to form a site. It would be wonderful if you always had the chance to create and implement a logical naming scheme throughout an organization, but this won't always be possible.

You may not be able to do anything about the names given to Windows NT server, but you do need to plan out names for the Exchange organization and the sites that will comprise it. These are important decisions that shouldn't be taken on the spur of the moment because these names are used as the basis of the unique entries created for objects held within the directory as well as messaging addresses. Directory information is propagated to many places within the Exchange environment so it's impossible to change the name of the organization or a site in a single place. If you need to change the name of the organization you need to re-install Exchange on every server within the organization while a change to the site name implies a re-installation for every server in the site. In effect, you will be rebuilding the organization or site from scratch.

Figure 3.10
Different servers in site "Dublin"

Cryptic, heavily coded, or artificially short names are not necessary for site names. All system administration is carried out through the rich graphical interface provided by the Exchange administration program. Use fully spelt out names that make sense and look good. In general it is best to avoid commas and hyphens in organizational and site names if at all possible. While there is not a general prohibition on these characters, past experience with many different applications demonstrates that curious problems often arise when they are used. For example, the Key Management Server component wouldn't work in Exchange V4.0 if the organization or site name contains a comma. The problem is fixed in Exchange V5.0 (and 5.5).

3.6.2   Does the organization name really matter?

The organization name matters because the software must be reinstalled if a decision is made to change the name. All directory objects use the organization name as part of the distinguished name used to identify an object within the Exchange directory, and there is no way to move down through the directory and change all the distinguished names.

The name of an organization shouldn't change too often, but it has been known to happen. Companies that operate as part of a large conglomerate, those involved in mergers, or those that grow through the acquisition of other companies, can often encounter situations where the organization name needs to be changed. For example, when the Sandoz and Ciba pharmaceutical companies merged to form Novartis, what options were available to them (if they both had Exchange organizations)? They could continue running two separate organizations, select one organization and merge in all the users from the other, or begin over from scratch and install Exchange again. None of these options are especially attractive and all come with a cost.

The question has to be asked whether we should therefore worry about the name given to the Exchange organization. The name is important, but only because it forms the root of all the distinguished names. Users never see the organization name, and it doesn't have to feature in any email address published outside the organization, as the format for these addresses can be set through Site Addressing defaults. In fact, only the administrators ever see or otherwise know about the organization name.

A number of companies have considered the issue and come to the same conclusion: the Exchange organization should be given a neutral name that can survive merges, acquisitions, or the management desire to rename a company. Suitable organization names in use today include "EMAIL", "MESSAGING", and even just plain "EXCHANGE". All work quite happily and users are unaware that anything has been done in the background.

The vast majority of Exchange organizations will continue to be named after the operating company. After all, it's the natural thing to do. But if you're involved in a company that might change its characteristics over the next 5 years or so, maybe some additional consideration should be given to a neutral organization name?

3.7   Permissions

A number of separate Exchange permissions are used to manage and control access to Exchange resources. Exchange permissions are totally different and separate to Windows NT permissions. This fact often causes confusion when people can't understand why they aren't able to "make" Exchange do something despite having all known Windows NT permissions granted to their account.

3.7.1   Naming contexts

Exchange holds its configuration data within containers arranged in a hierarchical structure. Four naming contexts are established within the container hierarchy. Windows NT accounts can be allocated permissions within each of these naming contexts. Once a Windows NT account has been granted a set of permissions for a particular naming context within the hierarchy it also automatically inherits the same permissions down through objects arranged beneath the naming context.

The four naming contexts are:

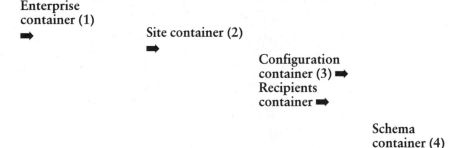

Thus if a Windows NT account is granted a set of permissions over the site container it also inherits the same permissions over the configuration and schema containers. The recipients container is an exception. Permissions for this container are inherited from the site container, but not from the enterprise (organization) container. Permissions are modified or granted by double clicking on an object and then selecting the permissions property page. It can take several seconds for Exchange to display the permissions property page within large organizations that span several domains. This is because contact must be made with all the different service accounts in the different domains before their details are listed amongst the properties.

Many of the problems seen in replicating directory or other information between sites lie in the fact that the Exchange site service accounts do not possess the necessary permissions for containers in remote sites. In summary, to avoid replication difficulties, the site service accounts should be granted the Exchange Admin role (or a role with equal or greater rights) on both the configuration and site containers in both sites.

3.7.2   Defining permissions for Exchange

Windows NT accounts assume permissions for Exchange through a collection of rights and privileges collectively referred to as a "role". A role defines the exact type of access a user has to objects held within a container. A set of default roles is provided with Exchange. These are:

- Admin
- Permissions Admin
- Service Account Admin
- View Only Admin
- User
- Send As

The account used to install Exchange is automatically allocated the Permissions Admin role. The site service account is granted the Service Account Admin role. The difference between these roles are that the Service Account Admin role holds all available rights whereas the Permissions Admin role lacks the replication, mailbox owner, and send as rights (see Table 3.3). The site service account is also granted the Windows NT Logon as a Service and Restore Files and Directories permissions for the local computer. These permissions allow the site service account to start the various Exchange services and to perform essential system backup and restore operations.

If you don't like these roles or believe you need additional roles you can proceed to define a new role by deciding which rights or permissions should be incorporated into the role. An Exchange right defines a specific action that a Windows NT account can perform within an Exchange context. The available rights are listed in Table 3.3.

Table 3.3   *Rights used to define roles*

Right	Meaning
Add Child	Gives the account the ability to create a new object underneath this object. For example, to add a new custom recipient to the recipients container.
Modify User Attributes	Modify the user attributes associated with an object.
Modify Admin Attributes	Modify the administrative attributes associated with an object.
Delete	Delete an object.
Send As	Send messages from a mailbox. This permission allows a user to send messages from a mailbox as if the owner of the mailbox had connected to it. It is different to the "Send on Behalf" option because the messages appear to have come from the mailbox's owner and are not marked as having been sent by another user on behalf of the mailbox's owner.
Mailbox Owner	Able to log on to a mailbox and use it to send and receive messages.
Logon Rights	Log on to any server within a site using ADMIN.EXE (the administrator program).
Replication	Replicate directory information with other servers
Modify permissions	Modify permission for the object.

Bringing everything together, the different Exchange permissions allocated to the set of pre-defined roles are listed in Table 3.4.

The question of exactly who should be allocated permissions for Exchange objects should be addressed in all implementation plans. Send As permission is especially interesting because it allows someone to send a message which appears as if it's been sent from someone else. There is absolutely no indication to show that someone who has no connection to the apparent sender originated the message. Most senior managers or auditors find this a slightly difficult concept to appreciate.

People who have been granted the Permissions Admin permission are able to grant themselves the Send As permission, so the general advice is to restrict Permissions Admin as far as possible. There is no reason for first-level administrators to have Permissions Admin. All the permissions necessary to manage mailboxes or perform day to day maintenance on an Exchange server are encapsulated in the Admin permission, so that's what an administrator should normally be allocated. Only the very highest level support personnel, those who already occupy positions of trust within an organization, should have Permissions Admin, and it's probable that only two or three people in a small organization, or one or two people in each location in a large organization, will need Permissions Admin. Regular audits should be conducted to assess who possesses different levels of permissions and make adjustments as required.

Table 3.4 *Roles and Permissions*

Roles ➡ Permissions ⬇	Admin	Permissions Admin	Service Account Admin	View Only Admin	User	Send As
Add Child	✓	✓	✓			
Modify User Attributes	✓	✓	✓		✓	
Modify Admin Attributes	✓	✓	✓			
Delete	✓	✓	✓			
Logon	✓	✓	✓	✓		
Modify Permissions		✓	✓			
Replication			✓			
Mailbox Owner			✓		✓	
Send As			✓		✓	✓

You should also ask yourself whether all Windows NT administrators should also hold administrative permissions for Exchange. My view is that there is no logic to dictate that every Windows NT administrator should be an Exchange administrator. Should someone who deals with file and print services be able to manage Exchange, possibly messing around with settings on an X.400 or directory replication connector? Of course this shouldn't be the default case, and the ability to manage Exchange should only be given to people who really need it. Again, make a list of the Exchange administrators and don't distribute the right too widely as otherwise it will be impossible to keep track of who's making changes to system configurations.

3.8   Third Party Products

Microsoft is a very aggressive software company and its products never stay still for very long. The list of features in Microsoft products grows at a rate that its competitors find difficult to keep up with. With such activity, is there any role for third party products to play in an Exchange deployment? The answer is "Yes", and largely so because Microsoft concentrate on building the base messaging functionality and providing a framework that third party developers can leverage off.

Microsoft Mail had a large and committed community of third party developers that busily produced all manners of extensions that could be added to a Microsoft Mail system. These developers are slowly but surely moving their products across to pursue new revenue streams with Exchange, and the number of third party products grows all the time. The more success Exchange enjoys, it is inevitable the more add-on products will be available. The trick then is to identify which areas of functionality are likely to be most useful, and then focus on buying products in those areas that are well integrated with Exchange and exhibit a high level of quality.

Experience gained over 15 years of corporate messaging projects indicates that the major areas of interest for third party products are likely to be:

- Backup software (see section beginning on page 356)
- Virus checkers (see section beginning on page 292)
- Full text retrieval packages
- Workflow
- Document management
- System monitoring
- FAX connectors
- Connectors and gateways for external messaging systems like MHS
- Directory synchronization tools to help build, populate, and maintain a corporate directory
- Extensions to the Universal Mailbox concept. For example, products that integrate SMS and voice mail technologies with Exchange.

Some of these areas are not going to be useful to everyone. Small installations will probably be happy to use the standard backup software provided with Windows NT. Installations dedicated to messaging are unlikely to be too interested in full text retrieval systems, and those who don't have to communicate with legacy mail systems won't need connectors for those systems.

FAX connectors are a special case. Unlike the majority of the areas listed above, the selection of FAX connectors is heavily influenced by the availability of local expertise and support in addition to approval from the local telecommunications authority or PTT. Many countries insist that FAX connection software is certified before it can be used, largely to prevent the introduction of automated systems that might introduce an uncontrolled stream of faxes into the public network. There are many, many FAX connectors available for Exchange and a healthy discussion about FAX connectors takes place in the Internet mailing list dedicated to Exchange. After you've researched who the local suppliers are, what level of expertise they possess, and what software is available, it is a good idea to review the comments about the different connectors in the mailing list. At least you'll get relatively unbiased opinions there, unlike the propaganda issued by the more disreputable software vendors.

Paging and voice mail technology integrated with Exchange is available today. Like FAX connectors these technologies can require local regulatory authorization, so they are not yet available everywhere. The basic idea is simple. Software and hardware extensions are created to direct paging and voice mail messages from sources like a PABX to user mailboxes. Outgoing messages to pagers are also supported. The technology works, but the resulting messages (for voice mail) are relatively large and great user discipline is required if the Information Store is not going to be filled with voice mail.

Integrated full text retrieval systems like Fulcrum Find! or Verity's Search 97 help with any medium to large public folder deployment. Public folders have a habit of growing to a stage where it becomes difficult for users to navigate within the hierarchy. If navigation is difficult, finding the right information becomes impossible and people stop using public folders. You might even find that people revert to using NT file shares instead! Indexing won't solve the problem of a badly designed public folder hierarchy, but it does help people to find information fast. I don't suggest that you index all folders (unless you really want to), but certainly select the folders you think will be most popular and index those.

Workflow and document management products provide natural evolutionary steps for email systems. If you've deployed a complete email infrastructure you want to maximize the advantage gained from it. Workflow is often characterized as a form of structured, intelligent or automated messaging, and certainly the best products in the space enable business processes to be incorporated into day-to-day messaging. Document management products take up where public folders leave off, and add essential features like tracking changes, versions, audit controls, a more granular set of permissions, and perhaps even integration with workflow functionality to complete the picture. DIGITAL Work Expeditor is a good example of a combined workflow/document management integration for Exchange.

Whatever third party products you are interested in, it is essential that they are incorporated into a pilot or other pre-production environment to ensure that the components really work. The products need to be tested against different combinations of Windows NT, Exchange, and their service packs so that you know which combination works and which will not. You need to know how quickly the products will support a new version of Exchange (client and server extensions may be involved), as well as any dependency a product may have with another software or hardware component. The help desk need to know the support chain for the product, who to call, how issues can be escalated if required, and what degree of local expertise is available. Finally, licensing needs to be negotiated. It's easy to fix a price for a single server or group of users, but what happens when the use of a product expands within a company? Do you want to negotiate a price based on the initial user group or one that allows for easy and cost-effective expansion should the product be successful?

Exchange and the Outlook clients work well together in international deployments. Regretfully, the same cannot be said for every piece of software you might want to deploy alongside Exchange. In particular, some third party products might have difficulty dealing with multi-byte character sets used in countries like Japan. For this reason it's important to fully test any third party product in the operational environment you want to deploy before making a decision to buy.

The complexity of integrating all the different pieces into an overall implementation rises as the number of components increase. Make sure that you make the right choice, have a clear view of the value added by the products you introduce, and know how the products will evolve in step with Windows NT and Exchange over the next few years. With these precautions in place you shouldn't have too many problems with third party products.

4

Selecting Hardware for Exchange

4.1   Introduction

Hardware resources are an emotive topic. Software engineers want their software to work well and not encounter difficulties imposed by what they see as insufficient system configurations. System administrators want to run with correct configurations too, but are often restricted by operational or financial constraints.

In general, Exchange servers require more hardware resources than the computers used for LAN Post Offices. This reflects the demands of the Windows NT operating system as well as the expensive functionality available within the server, especially in the system management subsystem. Installations upgrading from Microsoft Mail need to reconsider the system configurations they use today to see whether the computers can be used with Exchange. Anyone else beginning to use Exchange needs to go through the same process of analysis and determination of the right configuration for their needs.

It's foolish to begin any project with "just enough resources". Always plan to be successful and expect growth to happen. Electronic mail systems are characterized by rapid growth in user interaction with the system. As people become more familiar with electronic mail they'll send and receive an increasing volume of messages and provoke more demand on the system, and if the system can't handle the demand users will perceive a reduced level of service.

The important elements of any computer configured to run Exchange are:

- The power of the CPU
- The amount of memory (RAM)
- The number and capacity of the hard disks
- The speed and capability of the connection to the network

These elements need to be combined together in proportion to each other to form an effective recipe for good performance. Too much of a resource can be as bad as too little. A little extra memory may, for example, help to compensate for a lack of sheer CPU processing power, but it can also disguise the underlying problem. In this case you might overcompensate totally and throw lots of memory where the real problem is the slow CPU. In general it's fairly safe to say that systems configured to run Exchange need to have a fast CPU, lots of memory, a fast network connection, and lots of disk space. In terms of disk space remember that it's the number of spindles (physical devices) rather than the sheer amount of storage space that's important.

I am always a little suspicious of vendor-provided system sizing tables. Vendors, through no fault of their own, are forced to measure system performance and throughout in artificial circumstances. No one can predict how your local user community will interact with the computer on a daily basis, so the workload used in system tests is created to represent the work that "average" users produce. Now show me an average user!

Sizing data and recommendations derived from that data will inevitably improve in accuracy as Exchange is implemented in different situations. The reasons for this statement are simple:

- Customers will provide realistic data taken from real-life situations back to Microsoft, and this data will be reflected in the testing scenarios used to produce sizing tables.

- Consultants, Microsoft, and customers will all gain experience from operating Exchange and will be better able to size systems based on that experience. The way people use the system and the load produced by users are especially important factors in this experience.

- New versions of Exchange will become available, and the performance characteristics of the new releases should reflect the experience gained from real-life operation.

Nevertheless, if you want to get a server up and running today what can you do to adjust vendor-provided sizing information?

4.2   Sizing an operational system

A good first step is to gather information from your current system, if you have one. Clearly an operational electronic mail system can provide a wealth of valuable and up-to-date data about user workload, and this will enable you to create a set of parameters to measure against the vendor tables. For example, you should know how many registered users are allowed to use the system, and also how many of those registered users actually connect at any one time. Some installations have a high ratio of registered to active users, sometimes as high as 10:1. However, in my experience the most common ratio is around 2:1. In other words, if there are 100 registered users, 50 are connected at any one time.

After you know how many users you have to cater for you can proceed to estimate the demand created by that population. Electronic mail is not like transaction processing. The same volume of work is not seen during the entire day. Most installations I have worked with over the years experience a number of "hot points" during the day when the demand for system resources is at its highest. Typical hot points include just after the start of the working day, usually around 9 a.m. each morning, around lunchtime, and again towards the end of day. At these times users want to send or receive mail, perhaps to complete tasks to meet deadlines. Heavy message traffic has the potential to cause bottlenecks as the system struggles to process message queues, so clearly it's important to size the system so that it can cope with the maximum predicted traffic plus a comfortable margin for error.

Tracking the flow of messages in and out of an existing messaging system and understanding where those message originate from and go to is invaluable data when sizing a new system. If some sort of message log is available, you should be able to determine figures for:

- The total number of messages processed each day. It is useful to determine the average number of messages processed each day over a reasonable period of time, for instance a month. Try to analyze the highs and lows in the traffic pattern so that you can see the peak demand.

- The number of messages sent each day by users in your organization. Users can be categorized in terms of the message traffic they produce, and it is helpful if you know how many of your users fall into each category. I use categories like "Light", "Medium" and "Heavy". We'll discuss various numbers that could be used to categorize users later on in this chapter.

Again, expect demand to grow over time. Users will generate more messages as their experience grows. You mightn't like some of the messages that are generated, especially those that don't have a direct connection to any particular item of business, but I think it's a sign of success when users become so accustomed to electronic mail that they use mail for just about everything!

4.2.1   Knowing what the system will do

Electronic mail is only one potential source of load for a computer system. All the other applications that will run on the system generate load and remove resources from the pool available to Exchange. Thus, to create an accurate prediction of the resources required to provide good service quality to users, you must be aware of the load likely to be produced by other applications and Windows NT system services.

All computers that run Exchange server within a site can offer the same set of core functions to users. These functions are:

- The Information Store.
- The Directory Store.
- Mail Transfer to other servers.

The other Exchange components that can be distributed across different servers within a site are:

- Connectors to other electronic mail systems.
- Public folders.
- Exchange administration.
- Site to site connections.

All of the other components are optional and can be distributed across different Exchange servers within a site. For example, in a small site (up to perhaps 100 users) it makes sense to have a single client installation point. If you already have a server acting as a shared application area, perhaps for the other Microsoft Office applications, it would be logical to make that server the place where clients access the Outlook installation kit. Depending on the speed and saturation of the network a larger site might determine two or more client installation points. After the initial burst of installations an installation point does not normally generate a great deal of day-to-day network traffic, so its overall impact on the network and host computer will probably not be heavy. However, this is not a reason to place an installation point on a server that is already stressed.

A "standard" Exchange server with one performance profile can quickly change. Consider the addition of Web, POP3, and IMAP4 clients to a server configured to deal with the demands of MAPI clients? Will any impact be seen? The answer depends on the type of work done by the clients. The system performance profile changes as the Internet Information Server is activated to accommodate Web clients, although this might be compensated for as the Web and POP3 clients generally make less demand on the system than Exchange or Outlook clients. The performance profile might also be altered through the addition of new applications such as a FAX connector or full-text retrieval package.

Administration is the only constant across all Exchange sites. The load generated by all the other optional components is highly site-dependent. Sites migrating from another mail system are likely to generate a high volume of message traffic through a gateway to the original mail system until all users are migrated over to Exchange. If you don't use public folders at all, or only use them to distribute small files then the replication load is not going to be heavy. But if electronic forms are used or large documents are stored in public folders, or there is a high and consistent level of remote access to the public folders then a substantial load can be generated for the server.

When facing the first implementation of Exchange within an organization it is difficult to predict what load will be generated by any of the Exchange services. This fact isn't at all surprising because the same is probably true of any moderately complex application. A great deal of intelligent guesswork is needed to come up with a configuration that will last in terms of adequate performance for more than a few months.

To complicate the entire sizing equation, the Windows NT systems you might want to use for Exchange server may already be providing other applications to users. One of the attractive points about Windows NT is its ability to construct a logical domain composed of many different server computers all connected by network links. Building a complete Windows NT environment to create the foundation for Exchange will inevitably use more applications than just messaging. People considering Exchange who focus in on Exchange and ignore the needs and requirements of all the other applications often miss this fact of computing life. Of course, vendors add fuel to the fire of confusion by publishing benchmark results for a particular application, and then detailing the exact hardware specifications of the systems under test. These results are accurate, but often must be adjusted to factor in the demands of more normal application mixes, as well as the load placed by network communications.

4.2.2 Putting everything on a single server

You can opt to try and put all your applications on one server. This is an acceptable course of action as long as you don't have many users to support. Even one of the low-end servers available today can certainly accommodate 30 people accessing Exchange when the system is also used as a domain controller, WINS server, and file and print server. Just make sure that the system is equipped with enough memory and disk space to allow all the applications to run without getting in each other's way. Microsoft's new Small Business Server allows BackOffice applications to be set up and run together in a reasonably flexible manner, albeit at the expense of some limited functionality from the Exchange point of view.

In large deployments these circumstances don't arise very often and the more common course of events is to distribute applications across servers. This approach allows system administrators to match available hardware configurations to application demands, so you end up with a situation where hardware is optimally used rather than perhaps being discarded as being of little use. For instance, a computer can be allocated the task of acting as the Primary Domain Controller and nothing else. A low-end 80486-class system could easily act as the Primary Domain Controller for a domain supporting a relatively small user community. The same system might also be used for shared file and print services. Making use of older systems in this way allows newer hardware to be reserved for new applications, like Exchange.

The need to distribute the various components of Exchange across servers differs from organization to organization. For instance, if you run an Exchange-pure messaging system then there may be no need for SMTP or X.400 connectors to other messaging backbones, so apart from the network connection overhead you remove the need to translate messages from internal Exchange format to the formats supported by the backbones in question. Because of all the different factors in the equation it is difficult for anyone to give hard guidelines for system sizing and load distribution without a detailed examination of current configurations in conjunction with some fairly accurate estimates of future demand.

The worst situation to be in is where Exchange and another application constantly contend for system resources. It is easy to see where some areas of contention might arise. A system acting as a Primary Domain Controller, or even as a Backup Domain Controller, for a large domain needs to provide fast responses back to authentication requests generated across the domain, so operating an X.400 connector to a heavily-traveled public X.400 service on the same system is not wise. In the same way, a system acting as an SQL database server is hardly likely to be a good Exchange host.

In these situations it is usually wise to leave the existing system alone and install a new computer for Exchange. This stops any prospect of application contention and creates a degree of resilience because applications are better distributed. You'll also be able to configure one or more systems especially for Exchange and won't have to compromise because of existing hardware. The configuration you install is also more likely to last longer, require less administration, and provide better service to users. Overall, initially it's a more expensive approach but better over the long term.

4.2.3 Dynamic buffer allocation

The Information Store is a multi-threaded process implemented as a single executable (STORE.EXE), which runs as a Windows NT service. As more users connect to the Information Store, the number of threads grows and memory demands increase. Before Exchange V5.5, the normal approach to tuning involved using the Performance Optimizer (see Chapter 11) to analyze a server and adjust system parameters, the values of which are usually stored in the system registry. In particular, the number of buffers used by the Information Store could be adjusted to reflect the expected demand generated by a defined number of users. Performance Wizard suffers a drawback in that it makes adjustments to system parameters based on a static snapshot of system load allied to some historical information. If load increases or decreases dramatically after the Optimizer has finished, the system is left to cope on its own. As load increases, additional memory requests will be made to Windows NT and result in excessive paging, while if load decreases memory reserved by Exchange will not be released to accommodate other applications, which results in more paging. Because Performance Optimizer deals with many other aspects of Exchange performance, it is still a useful tool for system tuning. The advent of the Dynamic Buffer Allocation (DBA) feature in the Information Store moves database tuning to a more automatic level.

DBA is designed to provide a self-tuning capability for the Information Store and is implemented as an algorithm to controls the amount of memory used by the Information Store database caches. DBA is analogous to the way that Windows NT controls the amount of memory used by the file cache and the working set for each process. To see the analogy, think of I/O to the Information Store databases as equivalent to paging to the system page file.

DBA is designed to ensure that STORE.EXE uses the appropriate amount of memory at all times, taking into account the relative need for memory for other active processes in the system. The goal of DBA is to help maximize system performance through more effective use of memory, largely by not taking memory that's not required and being able to free memory quickly back to the system to meet the demands of other applications.

DBA continually measures user load against system load. As load increases, more memory is requested from Windows NT, and when load diminishes memory is released and made available to other applications. If you monitor the system you'll see the memory allocated to

STORE.EXE grow and diminish over time. If Exchange is the only application active on the server, DBA won't have much work to do and the amount of memory will usually remain stable after it is first allocated.

In general, the more memory that's available, STORE.EXE will increase the amount of memory it uses more quickly on the basis that if memory is available it should be used. If system load increases as more applications begin working, or the demand on the other applications increase, the memory used by STORE.EXE decreases. However, memory is not released to other applications unless the DBA algorithm determines that releasing the memory will benefit overall system performance.

A number of Performance Monitor counters for the "Database" object can be used to analyze memory usage. Instances are available for both the Information and the Directory Stores. The "Cache Page Faults/sec" counter indicates the rate at which the database cache is consuming new pages of memory. "Cache Size" indicates the amount of memory used by each cache. In the case of the Information Store, the cache is used for buffers to hold recently accessed pages.

There's no doubt that DBA makes STORE.EXE behave differently in terms of memory consumption than Exchange V4.0 or V5.0. On dedicated servers it's likely that STORE.EXE will grow to a fairly large size pretty quickly and remain at that size unless the application mix changes. This is normal, expected behaviour, but it has led to many people assuming that a problem exists and that a massive memory leak has suddenly sprung in STORE.EXE. Watching the memory allocated to STORE.EXE change over time is an obvious indication that DBA is working. Heavily loaded servers exhibit a more subtle sign when DBA causes Windows NT to page out parts of the GUI subsystem to free up memory. This causes the server to appear to be unresponsive the next time the GUI is accessed because Windows NT must page the interface back into memory before it can be displayed.

This symptom is most obvious when the Information Store databases or transaction logs are located on the same disks as the page file. In this case you're trading a slight slowdown in the user interface for better memory utilization, leading hopefully to better overall system performance. A GUI slowdown is a good indication that a server is under severe load and is a candidate for hardware upgrade or replacement.

Servers that are dedicated to Exchange are probably not going to benefit as much as those that manage multiple high-demand applications. Dedicated e-mail servers are more common in corporate computing environments. The effect of dynamic buffer allocation is going to be more positive in the low to medium enterprise market, where servers run Exchange, SQL/Server, SMS, and many other applications together. Dynamic buffer allocation is not a fix for servers that are under-configured in terms of memory—these boxes will continue to run slowly, but any attempt to reduce paging is a welcome development and should benefit many servers.

4.2.4   Where system load comes from

So far we have discussed the load created by Exchange services and some additional Windows NT applications. However, the system load generated by Exchange and Windows NT represent only two parts of the overall equation as so far we haven't discussed the load imposed by user activities, such as reading and sending messages.

Even supposedly skilled and experienced people can generate user load unwittingly. For example, people connected to a server I manage complained bitterly about its performance, yet everything worked smoothly whenever I looked at the system performance monitor, or was working with the system itself. The answer lay in an OpenGL screen saver that I had turned on for the server in a fit of security consciousness. The screen saver worked, but whenever it was active it generated a huge load on the server (taking up to 100% of the CPU) to create all the pretty and intricate graphic images displayed on screen. This was a small, but telling point! Table 4.1 attempts to summarize the different loads that might be placed on a server. All potential loads are not listed here and the load will differ from environment to environment. Use the table to create an idea of the work you expect your servers to handle.

Table 4.1   *Different loads placed on a server*

Users	Exchange Services	Windows NT applications
Reading messages	MTA activity	Primary or Backup domain controller
Creating and sending messages	Connectors	DNS/WINS/DHCP
Searching folders	Replication	Internet Information Server (web)
Updating the contents of public folders	Executing rules	SQL Server
	Monitoring links and servers	System Management Server
	Key Management Server	SNA Server

The total load imposed by user activity tends to increase proportionally as the user population grows. However, unlike other elements in the load that maintain a consistent and constant demand on system resources, the user load arrives in peaks and furrows and is not distributed evenly over time. The classic view of messaging systems is that three peaks occur during a working day—first thing in the morning as users arrive and want to read mail; at mid-day as users send a couple of messages before lunch; and at the end of the day when users strive to clear their desks.

At first glance, Exchange is hardly likely to be different to other messaging systems in this respect. People will still want to read and send mail throughout the day and hot spots will occur. As long as real human beings create the workload the same type of demand is created. However, Exchange facilitates off-line working and servers that support large populations of mobile users often experience radically different peak loads than those supporting office-based workers. Consider the load generated by five hundred users who come into an office, connect their notebook computers to the LAN, start Exchange, and synchronize folders. All of a sudden, the server is swamped with requests to send messages or download copies of items into off-line folders. At this time the Information Store becomes extremely busy as it attempts to satisfy client demands, and the LAN also experiences a heavier-than-normal load. The demand is artificial because it is driven by client computers talking to the server at a speed that's comfortable to computers, but would never be generated by humans. After all the synchronization operations finish the load on the server declines to a more acceptable state.

Given that peaks will occur it is wise to configure systems that can accommodate peak demands without too much stress. Any system that runs at 90% load (for memory, disk, or CPU) is unlikely to be able to deal with sudden increases in demands. In reflecting on this point it should be understood that the additional demand will not come from Exchange or Windows NT services. Rather, users will generate it, and users will experience bad service times from the system if it cannot react or respond to the demand as quickly as it should. Systems also tend to degrade in performance over time, reflecting the eternal struggle between fragmenting disks, user demands, and system tuning and maintenance activities and the efforts of the system administrator to keep things running. With all these factors in mind it is clear that an attempt to operate an under-configured system close to the edge of its performance envelope generates a high potential for horrible performance.

4.2.5   **Categorizing users**

Should you attempt to categorize users? In other words, should you attempt to analyze the demands made on Exchange by the different people who use the system? I think it's always good to know what's happening on the servers you're responsible for. Each user is different, but it is possible to place users in a number of broad categories, and then use that information to predict the likely demand those users will place on system and application resources. Going through this exercise before system implementation is good, but repeating the exercise on a regular basis is even better as the information gained will allow you to more accurately predict the time when additional system resources need to be introduced. Proactive system management is harder than reactive system management, but it provides a much higher degree of service to users because system performance and response will be more predictable and less prone to sudden interruptions.

Table 4.2   *Categorizing user types*

	Type of user				
	Very heavy messaging	*Heavy messaging*	*Medium messaging*	*Light messaging*	*Intermittent access*
Number of items in private folders	2,500–5,000+	1,000–2,500	500–1,500	200–750	Under 100
Number of private folders	50–300+	50–200	40–100	20–50	5–10
Total size of data held in the Private Information Store	100–300+ MB	50–150 MB	25–50 MB	10–25 MB	5–10 MB
Number of outbound messages generated daily	50–100	35–75	10–40	3–10	1–2
Number of inbound messages received daily	75–200	25–50	15–40	5–20	2–5
Number of public folders owned/ maintained	0	0	0	0	0
Load factor	10	6	3	2	1

Table 4.2 suggests one set of categories that could be used to analyze users. The decision process used to determine the boundaries for each category wasn't very scientific, but the categories serve as a starting point for the discussion. For instance, if you follow the categories precisely no user who sends messages would ever be responsible for managing a public folder. This isn't likely to happen in reality, so you should try and adjust the criteria laid down for each category to match

your own view of the situation. User communities vary greatly, and it is a mistake to look at a simple number and base every decision on that. Look at the type of people you want to serve (traveling, office-bound, other), the type of work that they do, and the applications they want to run to adjust the gross picture to a more refined value.

The table assumes that everyone uses MAPI clients. Lightweight clients exhibit different characteristics, normally making lesser demands on a server. For example, POP3 clients make intermittent connections to the server to download and send messages. The concept of browsing through stores, defining rules, or many other advanced features are simply not implemented. Thus, given any server configuration, many more lightweight clients can be supported by a server. Because everything depends on user work habits it's impossible to quantify the difference except in gross terms, but it should be possible to support at least twice as many lightweight clients on a server than Exchange or Outlook clients.

In the model described in Table 4.2, a user in a category is defined as capable of placing a certain load on a server. This is expressed as a multiple of the load generated by a user who makes intermittent access, or someone who reads a couple of new messages every day. Thus, a user in the very heavy messaging category generates roughly ten times as much load as an intermittent user. Think of a user in the heavy messaging category as someone that is logged on all day long and seems, at times, to do little else but create, send, and read messages.

Clearly a system supporting users in the first two categories will exhibit significantly different characteristics than a system in the last two categories. One obvious difference is the amount of disk space that will be required to support the volume of message traffic generated by the users, and in turn probably lead to further requirements to optimize disk performance.

4.2.6 Calculating the size of the Information Store

Obviously, when you size hardware for an Exchange server it's important to know how large the databases will grow to. Disks have to be bought and configured, and enough room left for growth. The size of the Information Store also determines the time required for backups, so it's a pretty important calculation. Predicting the size of the Private Information Store gives rise to one of the great urban myths of Exchange. For years, people have used the simple calculation:

$$\text{Size of Private Information Store} = \text{Mailbox Quota} \times \text{Number of Mailboxes}$$

For example, if 50MB is allocated to every mailbox and a server is designed to support 1,000 mailboxes, the Private Information Store should grow to:

$$\text{Private Information Store} = 50\text{MB} \times 1,000$$
$$= 50\text{GB}$$

Exchange couldn't support databases larger than 16GB prior to V5.5. System designers used the store size calculation to work out how many users could be supported by a server given a specific mailbox quota.

Unfortunately, the calculation is very simplistic and doesn't take account of two important factors that influence the overall size of an Information Store. These factors are:

- The Single Instance Storage Model, or message commonality (see page 256)
- The Deleted Items Cache

A single instance storage model means that a single copy of a message's content plus any attachments is held in a central repository, in this case, the Private Information Store, and users access the content via pointers and a system of reference counts. The reference counts track the number of users who maintain a pointer to the content. Counts are reduced as people delete their pointers to messages, and when a count reaches zero, content is removed from the repository.

A Performance Monitor counter (MSExchangeIS Private\Single Instance Ratio) provides a snapshot of how effective the single instance storage model is on a server. My own observations show that the ratio will vary from close to 1 (very bad) up to around 3 or better (good). The ratio on my own server, which hosts a small group of consultants, usually hovers around the 1.8 point. The variation in ratio is explained by the size and work habits of different user communities. For example, a higher ratio will be attained on a server that hosts large user communities because there is a greater chance that any message will be delivered to a local mailbox, which means that sharing can occur. Servers that host small user communities or where people typically send a high percentage of messages to external recipients (on other servers or mail systems) will see low ratios.

Exchange "charges" the quota of each recipient with the size of a message. Thus, if a 10KB message is sent to 9 recipients on a server, Exchange charges 10KB against 10 mailboxes (the sender plus each recipient). The sharing ratio is very high immediately after a message is sent, and begins to decrease as soon as recipients start to delete their copies. We are interested in the fact that Exchange charges everyone with the full size of the message, rather than making any attempt to divide the message size by the number of recipients and charging each mailbox on a pro-rata basis.

Taking the sharing ratio and the way Exchange manages mailbox quotas together, it's clear that the simple (quota × number of users) calculation is only valid if the sharing ratio is 1. As the majority of servers will enjoy a ratio that's considerably higher it follows that Exchange can make much more logical space available within the Information Store than is physically available in terms of disk space.

Now that we've created some extra space, let's take some off. Exchange V5.5 allows servers to maintain a deleted items cache where deleted messages are retained for a defined number of days after they've been deleted from a mailbox. The idea is to allow users to quickly recover from situations where they've deleted a message in error, and in practice it works very well. However, the deleted items cache takes up some room in the Information Store, and this must be taken into account when we consider the disk space requirements for systems as well.

The size of the deleted items cache depends on the number of days messages are retained after deletion. Generally, the period is set to between 7 and 10 days on the basis that people normally realize they've made an error pretty quickly. Two Performance Monitor counters (MSExchangeIS Private\Total Size of Recoverable Items and Total Count of Recoverable Items) allow you to monitor the size of the deleted items cache and the number of items held. Similar counters are available for the Public Information Store, but have no relevance in a discussion on mailbox quotas. For planning purposes it's wise to assume that the cache will occupy between 5 and 10% of the Information Store, but this figure varies greatly from installation to installation.

So, the correct method of predicting the size of the Private Information Store is:

$$\frac{\text{Mailbox Quota} \times \text{Number of Mailboxes}}{\text{Sharing Ratio}} + \% \begin{array}{l} \text{(Allocated to} \\ \text{Deleted Cache} \\ \text{Items)} \end{array}$$

If we take our earlier calculation, apply a sharing ratio of 1.8, and allow 7% for the Deleted Items Cache, the predicted size of the Private Information Store is:

$$\text{Private Information Store} \quad = \frac{50\text{MB} \times 1000 \text{ mailboxes}}{1.8} + 7\%$$

$$= 29.7\text{GB (rounded)}$$

Some contingency should be applied to arrive at a final size. The contingency allows for internal database structures, a worse sharing ratio, or a surge in the deleted items cache. I normally allow 20% for contingency, so the predicted size is 35.1GB. The contingency allows for some inefficiency in the database, which is only 100% efficient immediately after it is rebuilt using the ESEUTIL utility (or EDBUTIL, for Exchange V4.0 and V5.0).

Two further adjustments must be made before we can decide on the physical disks required to hold the store. First, a decision has to be made on the level of RAID protection to be used. RAID5 requires a disk for parity checking, while RAID0+1 (striping and mirroring) requires disk capacity to be doubled. Both configurations protect the data in the Information Store and either can be used in a production environment. RAID0+1 provides better I/O throughput at the expense of additional disks. Finally, it is bad practice to plan to fill disks completely, so you should estimate on the basis that only 80% of a disk will be used for storage.

Of course, as we try and hone in on a more exact calculation many imprecise details come into view. For this reason many system administrators continue to use the original simplistic calculation. There is some value in this as too much disk capacity is normally calculated, and it is always better to have too much disk than too little.

When calculating the amount of users that can be supported by any one system it's unwise to allocate up to the limit. Users of messaging systems tend to fill any space they're allowed and leave you with no room for manoeuvre. Keep the view you've formed about your own user community in mind when the Information Store is discussed in order to arrive at a conclusion about the size of store (and hence disk space on the server) you'll need to operate. Note that determining limits in this way is artificial. Other factors, such as data migrated from legacy systems, the use of personal Information Stores, and the effects of commonality across the store influence the amount of space available to users. The answers determined at this stage are just for the purposes of initial sizing, and will need to be adjusted further once you understand if and how data is going to be migrated to Exchange, and how users are to be allocated across servers.

4.2.7   Selecting the right hardware platform

Unlike its lower-end desktop cousins, Windows NT is designed to be hardware independent. The Hardware Abstraction Layer (HAL) masks the complexities of different computer hardware architectures (the original set of architectures was Intel, Alpha, RISC and PowerPC[1]) from Windows NT system software and the applications built on top of Windows NT, including Exchange.

Simply put the function of HAL is to intercept instructions issued by applications or the operating system and translate them into the hardware-dependent code required by whatever specific processor type is in use at the time. HAL supplies the magic that allows Windows NT to work across different platforms, but its existence does not assure availability of any particular application. Just because an application is available for the Intel platform does not imply that the application can run on the PowerPC. An application must be compiled for each target platform to create a suitable binary executable, and this is the reason why the Exchange CD-ROM includes separate installation kits for each of the supported platforms—at the time of writing computers built around the Intel $x86$ and Alpha architectures.

With so much freedom of choice in mind the important thing is not to become focused on one particular platform unless absolutely necessary, perhaps because a strategic buying decision has been made to go with one platform or another. Use the flexibility of the Windows NT HAL implementation to select the right computer for the task in hand.

4.2.8   Typical hardware configurations

The content of any publication ages over time. Whether or not the value of the content decreases with age is another matter, but one thing's for sure—the pace of hardware development makes it impossible to offer guidelines for configuring systems that last for any length of time.

CPU speeds increase all the time. The speed of the latest processors is a little awesome for those of us with fond (or less fond) memories of early mainframes. Alpha processors have moved from 150 MHz to

---

1.   The power of HAL has certainly been illustrated by the implementations of the operating system across the different platforms. However, NEC, the major manufacturer of MIPS processors discontinued sales of MIPS-powered NT servers and workstations in late 1996. Microsoft and NEC committed to continue support for customers who operate MIPS systems, and Windows NT V4.0 is available for MIPS. The bad news was followed by the news that IBM and Motorola had discontinued support for Windows NT on the PowerPC platform, considerably weakening the HAL story. However, future versions of Windows NT and its applications will only be available for Intel and Alpha processors. 64-bit Windows NT will be supported on the Alpha platform (first) and then the new generation of Intel processors.

600+ MHz in the 1993–98 timeframe, with future processors predicted to go near the 1,000 MHz level well before the end of the century. The first Alpha Windows NT system (the AXP150) is now rated well down the power scale. The same is true of Intel-powered systems where the Pentium chip has been cranked up to 333 MHz. The race to develop faster and faster CPUs goes on, and I know that the speeds quoted here will look slow in just a few years.

While processors get faster, memory gets cheaper (at least in relative terms). There is no reason why servers should be under-configured with memory today. Tests at DIGITAL indicate that you should allow at least 64MB for Windows NT and then 100KB of memory for each client, equivalent to 164MB for a system supporting 1,000 clients. This is just a rule of thumb and some intelligence has to be applied to size a system in context. In reality, the amount of memory needed is closely related to the performance of the I/O subsystem. Exchange uses a lot of memory to buffer information from the Information Store. If you have a good I/O subsystem the system will be able to handle an increased I/O load, which will reduce the demand from Exchange for memory buffers. The same performance is often seen from systems with 256 MB memory and a low-end I/O subsystem, and one with 128 MB memory and a high-end I/O subsystem, proving that the I/O subsystem is something that you should be prepared to spend money on.

Always round up from the roughly calculated requirement to the next step in memory sizes to allow for growth in demand. For example, round up from 100MB to 128MB, from 200MB to 256MB, and so on. For example, the impact of connectors, full text retrieval products, virus checkers, workflow and document management applications, and web access must be taken into consideration. Nevertheless, it's good to have a basic rule to begin with.

Disk storage has reached the stage where the Mbyte/$1 plateau has been achieved in many world markets. The combination of increasing processor power, affordable memory and cheap large disks means that even very large and powerful Windows NT systems are well within the reach of restrained budgets. If falling prices help free money from your budget and a little extra to spend it's probably best to put it into peripherals that make systems easier to manage such as uninterruptible power supplies (UPS), automated tape loaders and RAID-5 disk arrays.

Vendors commonly publish suggested configurations for systems to support specified workloads. For example, you'll need a Pentium-powered system equipped with 128 MB of memory and at least 8 GB of disk to support a 200-strong Exchange user community. This is a very basic configuration, one that will have to be upgraded as users become more proficient with the system and demand more of it. Guidelines like these are a useful starting point, but they should not be treated as the sum of all knowledge. The problem is that each operating environment is different, so the results obtained in your installation will be different to those seen by Microsoft when they measure the performance and throughput of Exchange. Users behave differently and some will do very strange things that are never factored into simulated system workloads. Network overhead is also different across installations, and of course, system performance tends to degrade over time due to factors such as disk fragmentation. All of these things contribute to differences between performance results achieved in software laboratory conditions and those seen in real life.

Table 4.3 summarizes the hardware situation at the time of writing. As I've said above, the situation is likely to change over time.

Table 4.3   *Comparing processors for Exchange*

Hardware family	Pros	Cons	Suitable for
Intel 80486	Cheap!	Old	Dedicated servers such as Primary Domain Controllers, File and Print servers, or small Exchange servers
Intel Pentium	Performance at lowest cost	Obsoleted by the Pentium Pro	Smaller servers
Intel Pentium Pro	Optimized for 32-bit Windows NT and applications	Relatively expensive	Most production-class Exchange servers
Alpha systems	Sheer power	Requires more memory than Intel-based systems	High end servers and messaging connectors

To try and put a more practical slant on the matter let's take each of the categories outlined in Table 4.3 and build a system configuration to meet a set of requirements. With the high pace of change in CPU performance a chart like this is only able to offer some generic recommendations, so no attempt has been made to list all possible combinations. Base hardware configurations will change over time as particular chips come down in price or new processors are introduced. Take these suggestions as a base point to start from and adjust for the latest developments on the market.

Table 4.4   *Sample server configurations*

Requirement	CPU	Memory	Disk	Extras
Primary Domain Controller or File and Print server	Intel Pentium 100 MHz or above	32 MB	4GB	
Exchange messaging server for testing or to serve small (up to 100) user communities	Intel Pentium Pro 200 MHz	128 MB	8-12 GB	RAID-5
Exchange messaging/ public folders server for a small user community	Intel Pentium Pro 200-300 MHz	128 MB	12-16 GB	RAID-5
Exchange messaging/ public folders server for a medium (100–500) user community	Intel Pentium Pro 200-300 MHz or medium Alpha	256 MB/ 512MB (Alpha)	20-24 GB	RAID-5 array, UPS
Exchange messaging/ public folders server for a large (500-1500) user community	Dual Intel Pentium Pro 200-300 MHz or high-end Alpha	512 MB	30-40 GB	RAID-5 array, UPS
Computer dedicated to the Internet Mail Service	Intel Pentium Pro 200 MHz or mid-range Alpha	128 MB	4 GB	UPS

Note the configuration for the system dedicated to the Internet Mail Service, an example of how to deploy an Exchange server that does nothing else except concentrate on a single task. The growing volume of corporate connections to the Internet and the amount of messages flowing through those links means that many organizations need to consider a scenario that includes a system dedicated to the Internet Mail Service. Depending on traffic patterns you may need one system dedicated to outgoing messages and another dedicated to incoming.

The ideal situation is to build dedicated servers. Budget constraints may limit your capability in this area, but if you are given the budget try and split the different type of work across separate physical systems. In order of desirability try to:

■   Keep connectors separate from systems serving user mailboxes.

- Keep directory replication connectors and servers used for directory synchronization with other e-mail systems away from connectors.

- Keep public folder servers away from user mailboxes, especially if heavy use is made of public folders and contents are frequently replicated.

Performance tests carried out by Microsoft reveal that Exchange is sensitive to disk throughput at the high end of the performance spectrum. This means that if you want to build large servers you must be prepared to add lots of disk capacity. Large disks provide lots of capacity, but having multiple spindles available to spread the load and support disk striping is better still. If in doubt, use the Performance Optimizer utility to check your current configuration and make suggestions to possibly improve the distribution of files across the available spindles.

Remember that the Performance Optimizer cannot distinguish the difference between partitioned drives created on a single physical disk. Each drive on a system is measured in exactly the same way, so the suggestions made to redistribute files across partitioned drives may not be optimum and require reassessment once the Performance Optimizer offers its suggestions. As referred to above, more physical disk spindles are generally always better from a performance perspective than a single large disk. In other words, given the choice between two 9GB disks or four 4.3GB disks, you'll usually get better performance from the latter option. The difference made by tweaking at this level can be small and it's best to concentrate on the capabilities of the RAID controller and features like write back cache first.

The way the Performance Optimizer analyzes disks proves that you should never place too much trust in automated utilities. They're a great starting point and a guide towards better performance, but they are not infallible.

Pentium-powered servers have been the general workhorse system chosen for deployments in the 1996–98 period. New processors tend to fall in price after they have been available for a while and competitors have started to appear. The Pentium Pro is a good example. It was originally more expensive than the Pentium II processor when it was launched, but rapidly became the baseline system for Exchange from mid 1997. If the pace of development seen over the last three years is maintained the Alpha processor will maintain its lead in terms of sheer speed. Unlike its competitors Alpha is a 64-bit processor and the net effect of this is an increase in the amount of memory required on Alpha-powered systems in comparison to others.

A heavily loaded Exchange server demands a lot of a CPU. The sheer speed of the Alpha processor makes it an excellent choice for systems supporting large user populations or those that handle a high message interchange workload. Systems that act as X.400 or Internet connectors must translate messages from internal Exchange format to the formats used within X.400 or SMTP backbones, and this work can generate a lot of processing especially with large messages or those addressed to big distribution lists. Similar workloads are generated by incoming messages arriving from the X.400 or SMTP worlds.

If you're unsure about the potential of any particular configuration to support Exchange, perhaps that of a system which you have on hand ready to go, you can run the Exchange Load Simulator (LoadSim). The load simulator program creates a workload for the system and measures how it responds. A full description of the program can be found in chapter 11.

4.2.9 Preparing for success

My personal approach is to over-configure a system rather than attempt to get it just right. In order words, to expect the system to be successful and grow over time. The "just right" state lasts about one week after a system goes into operation and after that it's a constant battle between system administrators (who want to preserve as much resources as possible) and users (who have quite the opposite viewpoint). Apart from the general contest between users and administrators a number of other factors may have an impact on system performance after they go into production. Common factors include:

- New applications are added. For example, a web-based application using the capabilities of the Microsoft Internet Information Server is put into production. Some of these applications may have the capability to be "mail-enabled" through MAPI, and if enabled will use Exchange to create and send messages.

- The characteristics of user workloads change, as people become more familiar with the system. Instead of small, simple messages large complex, multi-attachment messages are generated and sent. Heavier use is made of calendaring. Larger distribution lists are generated and used. Workflow applications are created and put into use, perhaps using the Event service and CDO technology, or perhaps based on a different technology that's only loosely associated with Exchange. Users begin to move away from using messages to share information to the more powerful, but also more demanding, paradigm enabled by public folders.

- Heavier use is made of Internet or X.400 connectors. For instance, because the Internet Mail Service provides very easy access to Internet messaging resources users start subscribing to news groups and other mailing list, resulting in a new source of external messages arriving into the system.

- New connectors, such as the Lotus Notes connector, are added to the system.

- New features are incorporated into the overall messaging service. For example, workflow or document management functionality is added, you implement message journaling, integrate voice mail, or incorporate a FAX gateway or a paging service, and so on.

For these reasons, it's better to fight the battle to get the necessary budget to build a well-configured system from the start. Apart from anything else, deploying a high-end system will enable you to use the same system for a number of years from the point of initial deployment, avoiding the need to interfere with hardware configurations. Altering hardware configurations means taking a system off-line and interrupting service to users. Change brings its own benefits in that you can upgrade hardware, but it also delivers a potential for something going wrong during the upgrade and extending the time when the system is unavailable. Building redundancy and growth into systems from the start avoids the situation of having to continually patch in new hardware or other resources and play catch-up with user demands. Having additional memory, disk space, and CPU power from day one gives an element of assurance that the system will last a reasonable amount of time before it begins to creak at the edges.

4.2.10 Adjusting simulation results to achieve realism

Most hardware vendors are quite happy to provide a chart of suggested configurations for Exchange. Figure 4.1 is a good example of the type and lists the results achieved by Exchange V5.5 on different server configurations sold by Digital Equipment Corporation in February 1998[2].

The charts usually describe one or more hardware configurations and the number of users each supports. Apart from showing the steady increase in hardware and software performance through the ever-increasing number of theoretical users that can be connected to a single server, the charts act as a useful starting point to build a realistic configuration. Normally all of the components have been tested and verified to work together and some simulation tests have determined the likely client population the servers can support. However, the results gained in the vendor's laboratories will probably not match the

---

2.   See http://www.digital.com for up to date configurations and performance results.

real-life situation you need to design for, so some adjustments are necessary to arrive at a truly realistic configuration.

The hardware configuration is the first item to check. It is possible that the Exchange databases and other files were distributed across the disks in a manner that doesn't comply with your own practice. For instance, what RAID level was used to protect the disks holding the Information Store? Disks configured with RAID-0 will transfer data faster than those in a RAID-5 array, but RAID-5 delivers a higher degree of resilience. Enabling the write-back cache will up the performance for RAID-5, but the controller has to be capable of handling the write-back cache in a manner that protects the data. Where are the transaction logs located? What size of page file is configured for Windows NT? Were the tests performed for Exchange V5.0 or V5.5? Is there enough disk and hardware to enable the server to last for its intended lifetime? Many suggested configurations provide totally adequate platforms for running Exchange over a short term, but will need upgrades—maybe some disk, perhaps an extra CPU—if they are to last two or three years in production.

Figure 4.1 *The sizing chart for DIGITAL NT servers*

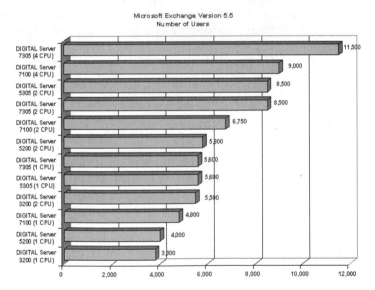

After hardware, some adjustments may have to be made for the software configuration. Benchmarks are often taken in an "application-pure" configuration. In other words, only the application under test is active on the server. Yet the fact is that hardly any production server is application-pure as all run much more than Exchange. Think of the influences that might grab valuable CPU cycles:

Network activity

All systems connected into a network experience some degree of network traffic. For example, the synchronization of security information between Windows NT domain controllers or the directory updates within servers in an Exchange site. Once a site has more than two servers there will be traffic for messages sent between the MTAs within the site. Once you join sites together another level of traffic is generated through replication of public folders and directory information. If you're connected to the Internet there might be some impact arising from the traffic generated by user access to the web and transfers from remote servers.

Exchange connectors

All of the connectors used to link sites together drain system resources. This is not a criticism. The valuable work done by the connectors must be paid for in the form of CPU and memory and, to a lesser degree, disk. The reason is simple. All connectors must perform some degree of processing to prepare and transmit messages. Some must also perform a format conversion before messages can be sent (the Internet connector is a good example, as it must translate messages between the internal format used by Exchange to SMTP/MIME). A very rough assessment of the impact of each connector is as follows:

- Reduce the number of users supported by a system by 15% if the server hosts the standard RPC-based site connector.
- Reduce the number of users by 25% if the server hosts the X.400 connector.
- Reduce the number of users by 30% if the server hosts the Internet Mail Service.
- Reduce the number of users by 30% if the server hosts the Internet News Service.
- Reduce the number of users by 40% if the server hosts the Lotus Notes connector.
- Reduce the number of users by 20% if the server hosts either the Lotus cc:Mail or Microsoft Mail connector.
- Reduce the number of users by 30% if the server hosts either the IBM SNADS or PROFS connectors.

The reductions are not cumulative and the net reduction in the number of supported users is greatly dependent on the volume of messages passing through the connector.

Different client mix

Most simulations are performed using MAPI as the base client protocol. A server that must support a mixture of MAPI, POP3, IMAP4, and web clients does a lot more work to deal with the different protocols.

Other applications

If you've taken the advice outlined in this book the systems running Exchange will be dedicated messaging servers. However, other applications will creep in and steal resources. The Internet Information Server (IIS) is one example, as are applications that distribute and update software, like SMS. Remember that the IIS may consume quite a lot of system resources if it is expected to service the demands of a large community of web clients.

Add-ons for Exchange

Third party connectors (FAX is the most common example) are the most obvious drain on system resources. Server-based virus checkers often work on the basis that a logon is made to each mailbox in order to check messages as they arrive. Because the additional logons are not creating work all the time this doesn't double the workload on the server, but depending on the amount of message traffic and the number of attachments (viruses are transmitted in the attachments, not the messages), an active virus checker can take another 10% of server resources. Other popular add-ons like server and messaging monitors, workflow or document management applications will impose their own demands.

Configuring a server with the hardware and software combination you intend to run in production and then running a simulation is the only way of determining the realistic workload that can be supported.

4.2.11   Two small servers is not equal to one large server

If one server can support 250 users will two servers similarly configured support 500 users? The answer is "No". Once multiple systems are connected together, within a site or between sites, the processing required to synchronize the systems together absorbs a certain amount of performance. In addition, the benefit of the single message storage model is eliminated, as messages must now be transported between users on the different servers.

How much system performance is absorbed by the connectivity overhead? There's no good or clear answer to that question because it all depends on the number of servers within a site and what type of work users do. Each server within a site periodically updates the other servers, forming a full-mesh network. The servers pass directory updates and other data to each other, similar to the way that all domain controllers communicate together within a Windows NT domain. Because the servers in a site form a full-mesh network it follows that the addition of a new server into a site exponentially increases the number of RPC connections made between servers and the amount of data transmitted on the network. After the requirement to keep servers synchronized is met the systems are then able to deal with interpersonal messages sent between users.

If messages can be kept on the same server they are processed in the same way as on standalone systems. For many years the usual rule of thumb applied when estimating the percentage of messages that will be sent off the system has been 80/20. In other words, 80% of all messages will be delivered to a local recipient, but 20% will have to be processed by a connector. The ratio will vary dramatically in different geographic and network environments. For example, if you operate a centralized site of very large servers, each of which serves 3,000 clients, then the percentage of local deliveries is likely to be higher than 80%, especially if you have taken care to place workgroups and departments on the same server. A different design that split users across many distributed servers, each supporting a few hundred clients, will generate a lot more network traffic as the number of remote deliveries climbs. The 80/20 ratio is a good starting point that is proven over time, but you must take account of the actual design before making any firm assumptions.

There is a difference in the way connectors process messages that must be taken into account too. If the message is destined to go to another server it the site it can be sent directly. The same is true of messages that pass over a site connector, but any message that travels across an X.400 or Internet connector must first be translated into the connector's native format. Servers that act as bridgeheads for connectors or directory replication will also have more work to do, and this will affect performance further.

Clearly not all systems will obey the 80/20 rule. It is important to try and keep people who communicate together on the same server and this is the reason why workgroups or departments are usually allocated to the same server. If this isn't possible and a department ends up being split across multiple servers it is inevitable that a higher percentage of messages will end up traveling off-system.

For planning purposes it is better to over-estimate the reduction of users. Based on experience gained over a number of projects, my view is that the user population supported by any server should be reduced by 30% once systems are connected. Therefore, if benchmark testing reveals that a certain system configuration is capable of supporting 1,000 users, then two systems connected together will only support $(1,000 \times 2) \times 0.7$, or 1,400 users. It is unfortunate that hardware vendors only publish figures for the number of Exchange users supported on a single server. Conducting benchmarks for a distributed network is much more difficult because all networks are different, so it's always going to be up to the people with most knowledge of the network to determine the overhead and how this impacts the number of users that can be supported.

It is very much easier to configure systems if they are dedicated to a single purpose, so this advice only holds for servers that only support mailboxes. Your mileage will vary, a good reason to run your own set of load simulation tests.

4.2.12 Large versus small servers

As far as I am aware no prize has yet been made available for building the largest Exchange server in the world. DIGITAL continues to hold this particular blue riband, operating a dual-CPU AlphaServer with over 2,700 mailboxes (the server is dedicated to messaging, no connectors or other activity takes place on the system). With Exchange V5.0 the design model tended to be around communities of between 500 to 1,000 users, with some going as high as 1,500. Very few large servers were designed to support more than 2,000 users. The changes made in Exchange V5.5 have moved the design model forward, and the upper practical limit for servers is now well over 3,000 users, as long as all aspects of the server are designed to operate with such a load in a production environment. Creating and operating servers of this magnitude is an art in its own right.

It can still be unwise to put too many users on a single server. The added resilience afforded by features like clustering is good, and the advent of the unlimited store in Exchange Enterprise Edition removes the infamous 16GB limit that so many people worried about. However, we now have different things to worry about. The disk subsystem is still a single potential point of failure, albeit one that can be largely guarded against by deployment of the right type of hardware. Backup (and restore) times are a prime concern. If a database grows to 100GB or larger, how long will backups take each day? Even with online backup, I think I would be concerned if the backup took longer than 4 hours to perform (25GB/hour for a 100GB store).

The LoadSim utility allows you to conduct automated tests on selected hardware configurations. Microsoft and hardware vendors use LoadSim to determine how many users can be supported on different CPUs. The results of these tests indicate that many computers are capable of supporting over 1,000 users. The upper limit (as tested) is set by 4-CPU Alpha systems tested at up to 12,000 users. Treat such figures cautiously. They are fine in theory but not in practice, not least because there's no point in configuring a system to support 12,000 users if you can't back it up each day. And if a problem happens, calls from 12,000 angry users can fully occupy a help desk!

Many experienced administrators of high-end messaging systems advocate mixing different types of users on each server so as to spread the workload generated by user activities evenly across all servers in a site. Spreading users across a set of smaller servers avoids a single point of failure and increases the amount of disk space that you can allocate to each user. Smaller systems are cheaper to buy and you have a wider range of hardware to choose from. You may even be able to use existing hardware after applying disk and memory upgrades rather than buying expensive new high-end computers.

If you decide to use low-end rather than high-end servers take care about how the user population is distributed. For instance, there is no point in grouping all the really heavy messaging users together on a single server unless you want to equip that server with the resources needed to handle their demands. Another tactic worth bearing in mind is to try and have as high a degree of message locality on each server. In other words, try and allocate users who need to send messages to each other on the same server so that the processing by Exchange's various connectors is reduced to a minimum. The same tactic can be taken with public folders, placing them close to the users who need to access the data held in the folders most often.

While low-end servers are cheap and easy to set up they come with some disadvantages. More servers in a site increases the overall complexity of the installation and drives up the time required to accomplish day-to-day housekeeping tasks, such as backups. System monitoring is more difficult as there are more data points to check. You may have to spend time moving user mailboxes from server to server in an attempt to balance the load, and the range of hardware installed within a site may make maintenance harder, especially for older hardware. Finally, when the time comes to upgrade to a new version (of Exchange or Windows NT) the task will increase in terms of complexity and effort in line with the number of servers.

The difficulties of upgrading large numbers of servers to new software versions has made some companies consider whether they should consolidate many small servers into a reduced set of large servers. The advantages that can be gained from consolidation include:

- Reduced system administration costs

- Less replication activity in the network
- Less duplication of information
- Reduced software licensing for Windows NT, Exchange, and any third-party software (such as monitoring or backup tools that run on each server)
- Reducing effort to upgrade software in the future

Given some of the limitations in Exchange V4.0 and V5.0 it was inevitable that companies would end up deploying too many servers. After its initial roll-out of Exchange, DIGITAL had over 160 servers deployed in offices around the world. The effort required to upgrade 160 servers in a controlled manner is staggering, and has increased as the number of servers has grown to over 200. Reducing the number of servers down to a more manageable number is something that is under consideration today. DIGITAL is only one company in this situation. There are a number of other companies who face the same challenge of monitoring and maintaining hundreds of servers.

4.2.13   Protection through fault tolerance

Most high-end Windows NT servers have multiple disk drives and applications are carefully distributed across all available drives in order to maximize the disk I/O capability of the system as well as minimize the effect of a failure. I believe that the majority of systems used to run Exchange in a production mode will automatically have configurations that mark them as high-end systems. In circumstances where reasonable hardware configurations are available keeping everything on a single drive is similar to keeping all your eggs in one basket: tidy, but prone to leave an awful mess should anything go wrong.

RAID, or Redundant Array of Inexpensive Disks, is a method of combining several inexpensive disks into what appears to be a single large physical device, largely replacing older methods implemented mainly for mini- or mainframe computers. The fault tolerant features enabled by RAID technology makes it an item to consider when configuring medium to large systems for use by Exchange.

It is possible to implement RAID in hardware or software, and indeed Windows NT facilitates both approaches. Hardware implementations are normally preferred, largely because the hardware can be optimized to provide a much higher level of overall disk performance than is possible with a software implementation. RAID comes in different levels, from 0 to 5. Generally speaking, each level offers an increased degree of fault tolerance at higher expense. Windows NT servers support RAID levels 0, 1, and 5 in software, but all six levels can be supported by hardware implementations. Apart from fault tolerance RAID can also achieve higher disk throughput through disk striping, a technique that creates a logical disk from a set of physical disks.

Disk striping increase performance by spreading I/O reads and writes across the physical disks in the set. In the case of a server that has databases concurrently accessed by many clients, far better performance will be seen if the stores are placed on a striped disk rather than large physical devices. A simple step towards better performance is to place databases on separate physical disks.

Any server deemed to be critical, such as those supplying messaging services to large user communities, should be equipped with some degree of fault-tolerance for disks that store essential information. The choice for Windows NT servers are mirrored disks, duplexed disks, or stripe sets with parity. When a disk is mirrored it means that a perfect duplicate copy of the contents of a disk partition is kept on a second partition, so that when a write operation is made to the primary partition the same data is written to the mirrored partition at the same time. Disk mirroring (basically RAID-1) provides a reasonable degree of protection against faults as long as errors are confined to a single partition and do not afflict the physical disk where the partitions are located or the disk controller that the disk is attached to.

Disk duplexing expands the concept of disk mirroring by removing the mirrored partition to a second disk controller. The technique used to assure data protection is similar to mirroring. Extra protection and resilience is afforded by spreading the two write operations across two separate disk controllers. A further advantage is achieved because the I/O load generated by the write operations is split, so there is less danger that an individual drive will become saturated by the I/O operations generated by applications or even Windows NT itself. Windows NT always attempts to read from the drive that it regards as the fastest path to the required data, so a slight potential increase in read access to data can also be considered an advantage gained by splitting activity across two controllers.

Striped disks with parity checking are the basis for RAID-5 fault tolerance. In a RAID-5 array the equivalent of one disk is dedicated to the storage of backup information, but the actual backup data is spread across the entire array[3]. RAID-5 permits multiple read and write operations to proceed simultaneously. Today, it is accepted best practice for production servers to protect the Exchange databases (Public, Private, and Directory Stores) by placing them on a disk volume protected by RAID-5.

---

3.   Striped disks with parity demands a minimum of three disks in the array.

In terms of database protection, RAID0+1 is a suitable alternative to RAID-5. This solution delivers much better I/O throughput and performance, albeit at the expense of requiring additional disks (all disks in the array are both striped and mirrored). Roughly speaking, a RAID0+1 array delivers 40% less capacity than an equivalent RAID-5 configuration. Servers that are I/O bound can often solve their problem by placing the Exchange databases on a RAID0+1 array. As the price of disks fall and capacity grows it's likely that more servers will begin to use RAID0+1 to take advantage of the increased I/O performance.

If RAID is operational and a drive fails the array should continue to operate. In these situations the array will mark the failed drive as bad (the correct term is orphaned drive) and continue to use the good drives that remain. However, at this point in time fault tolerance disappears and the bad drive must be replaced as soon as possible.

In a RAID-1 (disk mirroring) environment it is normally sufficient to replace the faulty disk with a new one and then take steps to break up the mirror set and then introduce the new volume to the set. All of this is done with the Windows NT Disk Administrator utility, and when the new volume has been successfully added Windows NT will copy the data from the other volume in the set. After the copy is completed and both drives mirror each other fault tolerance is resumed.

Roughly the same concept applies with striped arrays, the difference being that a new physical disk is added to the set. At this stage the backup data from the rest of the array is restored to the new drive and the full array becomes active again.

Hardware implementations of RAID use "hot-swapping" when drives become faulty. This means that as soon as a fault is detected in a disk it can be removed from the array and substituted with a new disk while the system is active. High-end controllers, such as DIGITAL StorageWorks RA-series or Compaq SMART-2 series also support hot spares, or a disk that remains inactive until a problem occurs at which time the controller automatically switches the faulty disk out of the array and brings in the hot spare.

Fault-tolerant disk technology evolves all the time and you should pay attention to new developments as they arise. The detail provided here is hopefully enough to inform you about some of the options available to help create a high-availability Windows NT system and form a solid base for Exchange. A messaging system that continually breaks down is good to no one and it's normally very visible within an organization. For that reason alone (job preservation for system managers), make sure that all important systems in your installation are satisfactorily protected against disk faults.

4.2.14 The importance of the I/O subsystem

Why pay so much attention to the I/O subsystem? The reason is simple. On low-end systems you don't have to worry so much about the speed disks transfer information. There won't be too many users to stress the system and an investment in extra memory will probably pay a higher dividend than installing a high-speed disk controller. Also, with only a few users to support you probably don't want to spend a lot of money to protect the disks because the extra hardware drives up the overall cost per seat. Good backup practices (and good luck) will protect the system against accidents.

On high-end systems the situation is different. These systems may support hundreds or thousands of users and are well configured in terms of CPU (or multiple CPUs) and memory. All the work done by the users generates a great deal of I/O and a bottleneck is immediately created if the I/O subsystem cannot handle the load. In addition to the work generated by users the operating system must run faster to manage all the different processes and threads, resulting in an increased demand for system paging and even more pressure on the I/O subsystem. Tests performed by DIGITAL engineering groups indicate that an Exchange server can generate up to 1 I/O operation per second at peak demand for each active client. However, the average I/O load is typically between 0.2 and 0.3 I/O operations per second per active client. The I/O subsystem for a server supporting 1,000 active users must therefore be able to sustain a constant I/O workload of 300 I/O operations per second.

Disk throughput is a critical factor in achieving high performance for Exchange servers, and if attention is not paid to the I/O subsystem a bottleneck is quickly evident. The system is unlikely to exhaust CPU or memory resources because everything must wait for the disks to catch up. Disks should be monitored regularly to observe queues. The desired queue length is less than 0.5 per disk.

There's a temptation to assume that the full size of a disk is available for storage. Strictly speaking this assertion is true. You can fill a disk with data if you wish. However, if a disk is filled the application that depends on the disk will normally stop, a disastrous thing to happen for a mission-critical application like Exchange. It is therefore important to plan on only using between 80 and 90% of the available disk space, and use the remainder as a buffer into which application files like the Information Store can grow while you're making the necessary arrangements to increase the available space. This is a much more preferable situation to allowing Exchange to fill the disk and have either the MTA or the Information Store stop. Of course, the

Windows NT performance monitor utility can be used to monitor the available free space on disks and signal alerts to an administrator after a defined threshold is exceeded. Setting up monitors for situations like this is good system management practice.

The importance of the I/O subsystem can be seen from a real-life example. As noted earlier, the largest server in production world-wide (at the time of writing) operated by DIGITAL is an Alpha supporting over 2,700 mailboxes. During the day the CPU is seldom very taxed, operating at between 40% to 60% load. However, this is only possible because the I/O subsystem has been configured with a high-end RAID controller and the fastest possible disks. Such an example is not unusual and is true for Pentium or Pentium Pro systems as well as Alphas. It's also true for other operating systems such as OpenVMS and UNIX. The lesson is if you don't treat high-end systems as a whole and ignore parts of the configuration the best possible system performance will never be achieved.

4.2.15 Compression—not for Exchange

Never fall into the temptation to compress the Exchange database and transaction logs. On the surface this seems like an attractive option that will save some disk space, but the overhead imposed to achieve the result is too much to consider for a production system. Each write to a compressed file requires the system to uncompress the data, make the write, and then compress the file again. Compressing the Exchange databases and logs will drive up the number of write operations on a system by up to three times, something that is totally unacceptable in a production environment.

On the other hand, there is no problem compressing the Exchange binaries and other files that are read and not written.

4.2.16 The question posed by write back caching

Many high-end disk controllers and disks support write back caches. A write back cache increases I/O performance by holding data in memory until the controller is able to write it to disk. Applications shouldn't realize that a write back cache is in use because the combination of controller hardware and device drivers effectively disguises its existence. As far as the application is concerned once the controller tells it that data has been committed, the data has been written to disk. This is a very simple explanation of write back caching, but it is sufficient to prove the point.

Database applications like Exchange are sensitive to I/O performance so anything that increases throughput is normally good news. Enabling the write-back cache on a RAID-5 controller can increase throughput by 300%. However, caching represents another hardware component that must function perfectly to ensure database integrity. Unhappily, write back caching doesn't always work as well as you'd hope and can contribute to database corruption, and this is especially the case with caching on hard drives. Most prudent OEMs like Compaq, DIGITAL, HP, and IBM recognize this fact by disabling write back caching on disks at the factory. I never recommend enabling write back caching for hard disks used by Exchange.

In the past Microsoft has advised against any use of write back caching. A knowledge base article (Q151789, written in 1996 and then updated in mid-1997) clearly outlines their view on the matter. Microsoft's advice is sensible provided it is taken in context. You play with fire if you enable write back caching and then don't bother to protect the system with good battery backup to ensure that cached data is always written to disk even if power is lost. High-end controllers equipped with technologies like ECC, mirrored cache, and battery backup increases system resilience rather than detracts from it. Ideally, the battery backup should cater for power outages lasting at least a couple of days and the cache and battery should be mounted on a "daughtercard" that can be removed (with cached data still intact) should the controller itself fail. Some controllers also allow the cache to be tuned for different percentages of read/write activity. In these cases it's best to set the cache for 100% writes to gain maximum performance.

In summary, if your server is equipped with a full-featured controller it is OK to enable write back caching and take advantage of the extra performance. On the other hand, always disable the write back cache on cheaper controllers that do not protect the cache against system failure of component breakdown.

4.2.17 Symmetric multi-processing

Symmetric multi-processing (SMP) is the ability for multiple CPUs installed in a single computer to share work. Because SMP removes a dependency on the power delivered by a single CPU it is a major contributor to server scalability.

The multiprocessor performance of Exchange V4.0 and V5.0 is poor on both Intel and Alpha platforms. For example, tests performed by DIGITAL showed that Exchange V5.0 scaled from 3,100 simulated users on a single-processor AlphaServer 4100 to 3,250 users with two processors and 3,600 users with 4 processors. SMP performance improved in Exchange V5.0, but it was still not very impressive. In reality the 16GB limit on the size of the Information Store imposed a restriction that stopped SMP performance becoming too much of an issue. It's not surprising that time is required to enable complex applications support SMP well. After all, several releases of SQL/Server were needed before good use of multiple processors was attained. With the limit removed in Exchange V5.5 the need to improve SMP performance became a much bigger issue.

The Information Store is the heart of Exchange. It is a multi-threaded program that handles all client connection. A lot of work was done to isolate potential sections of the code within the Information Store that could represent a bottleneck. Much of that work focused on critical sections within the code.

In the Windows NT environment, a critical section is a small piece of code that allows a single thread to gain exclusive access to a region of shared data. The Exchange code base has thousands of critical sections. Contention occurs when multiple threads attempt to access the critical section at the same time, blocking the ability of the code to execute. As load increases the amount of contention rises to a point where no further workload can be handled. This point marks the upper limit for SMP scalability because no further increase in CPU resources can work around the contention.

Figure 4.2 *SMP performance in Exchange V5.5*

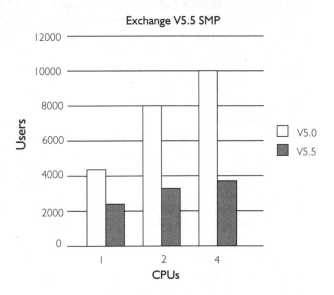

Some smart detective work found that a particular critical section relating to MAPI sessions was experiencing a huge amount of contention. The effect of the fix was spectacular. Not only was SMP performance dramatically increased for both Alpha and Intel platforms, but the uniprocessor performance also increased. Tests showed that the number of users supported on a single CPU AlphaServer 4100 improved from 2,600 to 4,500 (73% better). The number of users supported by the uniprocessor system under Exchange V5.5 was 1,400 more than V5.0. The dual-CPU system increased 146% from 3,250 users to 8,000, while quad-CPU performance was 178% better, increasing from 3,600 users to 10,000. For comparison, an Intel-powered system (quad-CPU 200 MHz Pentium Pro) achieved an improvement of 93% (3,500 to 6,750 users) under the same test. The increase in scalability is very obvious from the chart in Figure 4.2.

The tests I've referred to are only one set. Because the tests compare the same hardware configuration reacting to the same client workload working with two different versions of Exchange the results are accurate enough to demonstrate that Exchange V5.5 has much better scalability than V5.0.

Every test configuration is capable of producing different results and it's often difficult to compare apples with apples when you browse through press releases from hardware vendors. For example, shortly after Exchange V5.5 was released in November 1997, Compaq announced that they had managed to support 9,000 clients on a quad-CPU 200 MHz Pentium Pro system. On the surface, the difference between the results achieved by Compaq and DIGITAL is difficult to explain, but unless tests are performed in controlled laboratory conditions you are never comparing apples with apples. The truth of this assertion can be seen from the results achieved on the server range launched by DIGITAL in February 1998 (Figure 4.2), when a quad-CPU Intel-based server (DIGITAL 7100 Server) also supported 9,000 clients. A quad-CPU Alpha (DIGITAL 7305 Server) achieved 11,500 clients in the same tests.

HP then came along the following month and announced that they had achieved 14,000 simulated users on a NetServer LXr Pro8. The difference here is that the HP system was equipped with 8 200 MHz Pentium Pro processors and a 1MB Level 2 cache. There's no way that Exchange V5.0 could have coped with 8 processors, so this test again proved the degree of additional scalability achieved in V5.5.

All vendors seek headline numbers to prove that their hardware is better than anyone else's, an increasingly difficult task given that so many components are commodity items. Spectacular numbers are achieved, and it is true that a single Alpha-powered Exchange server, as demonstrated by Microsoft during the "scalability day" in New York in May 1997 can support 50,000 simulated POP3 clients. But such numbers are nonsensical in reality. No one in their right mind would suggest that you should connect so many clients to a single server in real life. Headline numbers are important in terms of tracking the progress of hardware/software combinations in probing the edge of the performance envelope, but that's about the extent of their importance.

To really investigate the results gained by two different configurations you'd need to have both configurations side by side in laboratory conditions. Each configuration would be built from exactly the same hardware, linked by the same type of network, with Windows NT set up in the same manner, and with the same simulated client workload. There are too many variables to be able to accurately compare one test against another. This is the reason why I advise anyone who's interested in running a very large server to test the configuration, or a number of variations on a basic configuration, in their own operating environment before making the final decision.

4.3   Exchange and clusters

In simplistic terms clustering is the ability for a group of computers to transparently share common information while allowing computers to join or leave the group without interfering with the service provided to users. People who use a clustered computer system see a single identity (often called a namespace) for the cluster and are not normally aware of the complex interaction that takes place behind the scenes to make all the component systems work together.

Clustering is important for messaging systems because it allows you to build highly available resilient systems. For many enterprises messaging rapidly becomes a mission-critical application, and whenever a problem occurs to interrupt the messaging service, howls of pain can be heard throughout the organization. For example, it's easy to see why a marketing department would be annoyed if the server hosting the public folder where all the latest pricing information is located goes down. Or how people who communicate with external organizations might have their plans interfered with if the server where the X.400 or SMTP connector is located goes off the air. A personal observation of mine is that there is less tolerance for interruptions the higher up users are within an organizational structure, leading to situations where it is imperative that the messaging system is available for as close to 100% as possible.

One way of looking at clustering is to draw an analogy between it and the way Exchange allows a site to seamlessly expand itself across a number of individual servers, all of which share common data structures. When you want to add users from a new department all you need to do is to install a new Exchange server and have it join the existing site. Once data has been replicated the new server is up and running as full and participating member of the site. A clustered system works at a lower level, but also allows you to expand the overall power and resources available to users by allowing you to introduce new hardware when required without affecting the hardware that's already installed.

4.3.1   Early clusters

The first production-quality clustered systems were delivered in the middle 1980s when Digital Equipment Corporation developed VAX-clusters. VAXclusters originally required a very tight hardware-based connection between the individual systems within the cluster, but were evolved to allow looser coupling over network-based connections. A later development expanded clustering to accommodate different computer families and allowed the 32-bit VAX family of systems to be clustered with 64-bit Alpha systems, all using the single Open-VMS operating system (VMSclusters).

DIGITAL was one of the forerunners in clustering Windows NT servers. Several other vendors, including Compaq and NCR, brought their own clustering solutions to market. All of the clustering solutions featured two server computers connected to a SCSI-based disk array. Most relied on some form of data replication, essentially making sure that data was written to two places at one time so that, if a problem occurred, the unaffected server could continue working. Complex scripts and other techniques are used to control application failover, the process of moving work from one server to another. No clustering solution before Microsoft Cluster Services (MSCS, formerly known as "Wolfpack") supported Exchange. Other messaging systems on NT, notably the Lotus Domino server, supported clusters before Exchange. However, support is attained through vendor-specific mechanisms and not the generic cluster services provided by MSCS.

4.3.2   Microsoft Cluster Services

The full functionality of MSCS will be provided over multiple releases. Today (1998) we have MSCS Phase 1, which requires Windows NT V4.0 SP3 plus a number of bug fixes[4]. MSCS Phase 2 is scheduled as part of Windows NT V5.0. The major features of MSCS Phase 1 are:

- Clusters are composed from a group of independent systems that appear to (applications and the network) as a single system.

- Clusters are managed as single systems.

- Clusters share a common namespace.

- Services are "cluster-wide" and can be accessed from any of the servers.

- Existing client connectivity is not affected by clustered applications.

---

4.   ftp://ftp.microsoft.com/bussys/winnt/winnt-public/fixes/usa/nt40/hotfixes-postsp3/roll-up/

- Clusters are built on the "shared nothing" principle. In other words, the shared disks and other cluster resources are under the exclusive control of the active member of the cluster and cannot be concurrently accessed by the other server.

The last point deserves further comment. Building a cluster as "shared nothing" has its good and bad points. Its goodness derives from the fact that the cluster is much simpler to engineer and is therefore cheaper for customers to buy. But a shared nothing cluster is weakened by not being able to allow all servers to do as much useful work as they are capable of on a concurrent basis. Each must wait its turn until it becomes the active server. Compare this scenario to a "shared everything" approach as in VMSclusters. Here all member servers can work and share information in real time.

MSCS Phase 1 is therefore not the final answer to NT clustering. Features will be added as clustering technology matures (hardware and software) matures. For the moment the major value delivered by MSCS is the achievement of an added level of server resilience. We have to wait for true load balancing and increased scalability.

4.3.3 Evolving Exchange to understand clusters

Apart from the obvious requirement to provide redundancy through hardware, several challenges exist for engineers who wish to support Exchange in clusters. One of these is how to handle the stores, or databases used by Exchange. Another is to work around the problem of associating user mailboxes to particular Exchange servers. Exchange configuration data relating to items such as bridgehead servers for messaging and directory replication connectors can also be server-specific.

The Exchange Information and Directory Stores use quite a complex transaction model and the full stores are represented by databases, transaction logs, and queues held in memory. Any failover needs to be able to seamlessly switch the stores back into the state they were in when a problem occurs. With its capability to roll outstanding transactions forward into the database from the transaction logs Exchange can handle this requirement. The transaction logs also satisfy the MSCS requirement for data to be persistent. In other words, data should always be written somewhere that it can be accessed even if the cluster goes through a transition.

When any server suffers an unexpected failure (such as a power outage), transactions are recovered automatically the next time the Information Store service restarts. This is known as a soft recovery. When the active server fails in a two-node cluster much the same type of recovery is performed, with the newly activated server taking responsibility for committing any outstanding transactions to the database before allowing users to reconnect. Conceptually therefore the Exchange Information Store was always reasonably well prepared for the advent of clustering.

Breaking the association between user mailboxes and configuration data and specific servers is trickier. Within sites, servers can be assigned certain work. Some servers might only handle public folders, some deal with connections, while others act as hosts for user mailboxes. Exchange knows the work performed by each server through information held in the Directory. In this situation the name of a physical server represents the namespace used by services to access data.

Figure 4.3 *An MSCS cluster for Exchange*

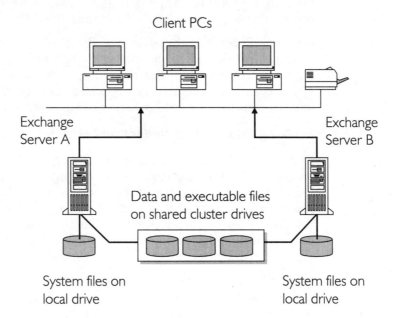

Clusters deliver resilience by ensuring that each server in the cluster is able to perform the work of its peers, if called upon to do so. A method must therefore be built to allocate work to the cluster as a whole, rather than an individual server, and then the software must be modified to permit individual cluster members to assume tasks as required as the cluster state changes. A cluster alias provides the answer for the first requirement because an alias allows us to address the cluster as a named entity. In short, the namespace represented by a physical server is altered to accommodate the concept of a virtual server whose workload can be represented by any server in the cluster. In cluster terms the virtual server is defined as part of a cluster resource group, a term we'll come back to slightly later on.

Figure 4.3 illustrates a typical cluster configuration for Exchange. Two physical servers, called "Exchange Server A" and "Exchange Server B", are connected around a set of shared drives. A separate name is given to the cluster, for instance "Messaging". Any reference to the services provided by Exchange (the application) when it is running on the cluster is therefore via "Messaging" rather than "Exchange Server A" or "Exchange Server B". It is the function of the cluster management software to amend the namespace as circumstances change so that references to the virtual "Messaging" server are directed to whatever physical server is currently providing the service.

Figure 4.4
*Exchange
detects that
MSCS is active
during SETUP*

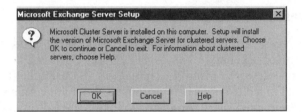

A set of other changes is made throughout Exchange to complete support for clustering. Most of these are at the application level (the Exchange services—MTA, Information Store, Connectors, and so on) on top of underlying APIs provided by MSCS. For example, each Exchange service is treated as a separate resource, so an administrator can "fail" a single service such as the Internet Mail Service without stopping the Information Store. However, you can't fail a single service and have it restart on the passive member of the cluster. All Exchange services must run on the active member of the cluster

The code base in Exchange V5.5 supports clustering in the following ways:

- The SETUP utility understands clusters. If MSCS is installed SETUP will prompt you to install the cluster-aware version of Exchange (Figure 4.4). In fact, you cannot install the standalone version of Exchange onto a server where MSCS is active.

- Support for the concept of a cluster resource group. When Exchange is installed onto a cluster a new resource group is created to hold details of the cluster-wide resources used for Exchange. These include the disks used to store the application files and binaries as well as a network name. The network name functions as the name of the virtual server that runs Exchange in the cluster and appears as the server name when you view the cluster through the Exchange administration program. It's also used to specify the name of the cluster when defining a bridgehead server for a messaging or directory replication connector.

- Support for cluster state transitions. When the active server fails the cluster goes through a state transition. In other words, responsibility for running applications passes to the passive member, which now becomes active. Exchange V5.5 includes the modifications to allow its services to gracefully failover to the other server.

- The Exchange administration program is changed to allow server monitors work with virtual servers. However, you can only stop and restart services using the MSCS administration program.

4.3.4   Installing Exchange into a cluster

The MSCS administration program must be used to create a cluster group for Exchange before beginning the installation. Different processing occurs to install Exchange on the primary (first) and secondary servers in a cluster. When you install Exchange on a server where MSCS is present the SETUP program performs the following processing:

- Creates the Exchange Server directory structure (normally \EXCHSRVR) on a shared cluster drive. You cannot select a drive destination that isn't a shared cluster drive. All of the Exchange executables and data files are copied to the selected drive. The executables used on a cluster are different to those used on a standalone system.

- Creates and registers the Exchange services.

- Copies system shared files into the local %ROOT\SYSTEM32 directory.

- Creates resource dependencies within MSCS. For example, the Exchange MTA depends on the Information Store. If the store isn't running the MTA can't start.

After all of this is done you'll be given the chance to run PerfWiz. Note that PerfWiz will only analyze disks that are defined in the Exchange resource group, meaning that disks local to a server are ignored. In a cluster environment you can't locate files like the transaction logs on any disk that isn't available to the cluster as a whole. If you place files like the transaction logs or Exchange MTA work files on local disks cluster failovers wouldn't work because the data necessary to complete the transition won't be available. While clustering does deliver resilience, it's important to note that the shared disks still represent a potential single point of failure. Good backup discipline remains critical in a clustered environment!

A cluster can begin operating once Exchange is installed on the primary node, so you can leave a gap between the primary and secondary installations. The installation on the secondary server is simpler because the majority of the files used by Exchange are already located on the shared cluster drive. The following processing is performed:

- System shared files are copied into the local %ROOT\SYSTEM32 directory.

- Resource dependencies are created.

- Exchange services are created and registered.

Exchange uses wizards to configure the Internet Mail Service (IMS) and Internet News Service (INS). These wizards have been altered to deal with clusters and should only be run on the primary node. An "update node" option is available to update the registry on the secondary node.

4.3.5   Administering a cluster

After the secondary installation is complete the cluster administrator should be able to view a similar situation as illustrated in Figure 4.5. In this case the two servers are called CSSNT1 and CSSNT2, whereas the cluster itself is called "EXCHANGE" (see the top of the tree in the left-hand pane).

Figure 4.5
Exchange running on a cluster

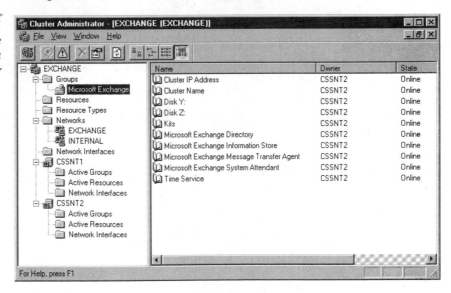

Expanding the contents of the cluster group (called "Microsoft Exchange") clearly shows that CSSNT2 is the currently active server, or owner of the service, and all of the normal Exchange services are running. The cluster group also includes a number of other resources that are used by Exchange in a cluster: the static IP address that will be used to route to the virtual server and the shared disks where the Exchange databases, binaries, and other files are located.

Figure 4.6 illustrates the cluster as viewed from the Exchange administration program. The site name is Copenhagen and only one server is shown, called "EXCHANGE". Anyone familiar with the Load-Sim utility will notice from the mailbox names that the cluster is being used for a simulation run.

Figure 4.6 *The Exchange administration program running on a cluster*

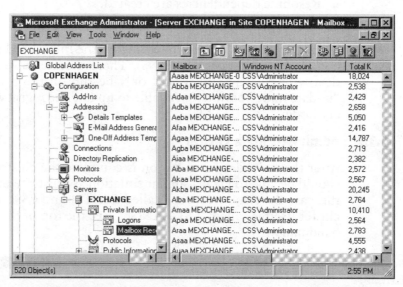

Figure 4.7 *The network interfaces used inside the cluster*

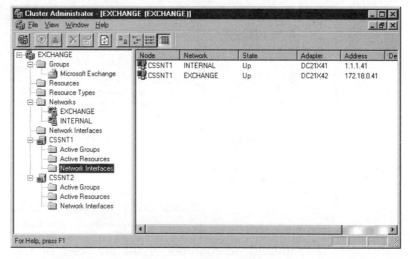

If you refer back to Figure 4.5 you'll see that two network names are defined within the cluster, EXCHANGE and INTERNAL. In this case, EXCHANGE is the name of the virtual server and is used to associate user mailboxes with a server or to define the name for a bridge-head server. INTERNAL is the name of the "heartbeat" connection between the two servers. The heartbeat is the device used by the servers to monitor the existence of each other. If the heartbeat fails (no response is detected from the other server), the cluster manager begins a failover. Figure 4.7 shows the view of the network interfaces as seen from node CSSNT1. Note that each interface has a separate IP address.

4.3.6 Failover for Core Services

In clustered environments Exchange is divided into "core" and "non-core" services. Core services represent the kernel functionality of the server and are automatically restarted when a failure occurs. Non-core services require manual intervention and will not restart until the system administrator has made the necessary changes to the configuration of a service. The core services are:

- System Attendant
- Directory Service
- Information Store
- MTA (including the X.400 connector)
- Internet Mail Service
- Event Service

Figure 4.8
*Exchange
services coming
back online after
a transition*

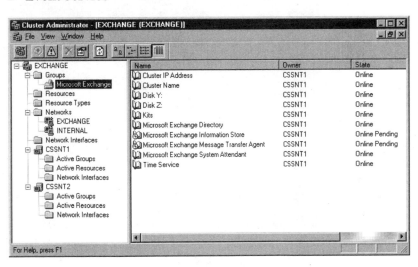

Figure 4.8 shows the view of a cluster administrator as the set of core services is restarted following a failover. If you compare this illustration to Figure 4.5 you can see that the cluster has transitioned responsibility for running the set of Exchange services to node CCSNT1. Before any core services are restarted the system registry is updated from the primary to the secondary node. The registry check-

points defined for MSCS instructs the cluster which portions of the registry are kept in sync by the cluster service between the two nodes. This ensures that any configuration changes made to Exchange (such as the path to the disk holding the transaction logs) on the original primary node will be respected when the services are restarted. There are some known issues with the X.400 connector running in a cluster. See article Q169113 in the Microsoft Knowledge Base.

4.3.7   Cluster dependencies

Following the normal start-up order used by Exchange, the System Attendant and Directory services are the first to start, followed by the Information Store and then the MTA. A dependency tree defines the order that services are started. The tree records the needs of each service and is checked by the cluster whenever a service is restarted. Anyone who has experience of Exchange will understand the concept of dependencies because these exist even outside a cluster. The MTA cannot start before the Information Store is available because the MTA interacts with the store when sending messages.

Figure 4.9 *The dependencies for the Information Store service*

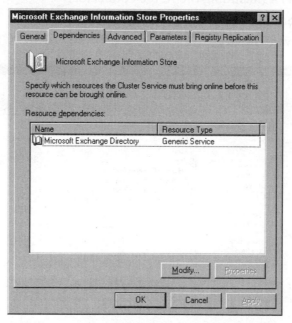

Similarly, the Exchange administration program is of little use if the Directory service has not been started because it will have nowhere to fetch configuration data from. The matrix of Exchange dependencies is extended in a cluster. The cluster name and IP address must be available before anything can start, and then the shared disks must be brought on-line. When these conditions exist, the Exchange services are started. Dependencies are defined as properties of each service. Figure 4.9 shows that the Information Store service can only start after the Directory is available

4.3.8 Failover for non-core services

The non-core services are:

- Microsoft Mail Connector
- Lotus cc:Mail Connector
- Key Management Server
- Internet News Service (INS)

In most cases the manual intervention is pretty straightforward. For example, the cc:Mail connector needs to be reconfigured using the name of the active node as its post office name. The default for the Key Management Server is not to start on failover because it relies on a password being provided when the service starts. Normally the password is fetched from a diskette, but the diskette would have to be always available for automatic failover to be possible. In addition to the above you'll need to configure IIS as a separate cluster group in order to be able to support OWA connections after cluster transitions. Although the Internet News Service is not considered to be a core service, it does not require any manual configuration to occur before it is restarted. If you want the INS can therefore be reconfigured to restart automatically.

The new connectors in Exchange V5.5 (Lotus Notes, IBM PROFS and SNADS) are not currently supported as part of a clustered environment. MSCS also does not yet support the Dynamic RAS connector, the IMS or INS over dial-up connections, the X.400 connector when run over an X.25 link and asynchronous connections to Microsoft Mail. I expect that most, if not all, of these restrictions will be lifted over time.

4.3.9 How long do cluster transitions take?

Conceptually clusters offer the promise of transparent failover. In real life obstacles tend to get in the way. When the cluster transitions Exchange might be only one of the applications that need to transfer from the passive to the active server, so it may take several minutes before the transition is complete and clients are able to access mailboxes as before.

Don't expect the transition to occur in seconds even in situations where Exchange is the only application on the cluster. The MSCS resource libraries are used to monitor the correct operation of the

Exchange services. Probes inserted in the cluster-aware versions of the services and are monitored by MSCS at regular intervals, providing feedback to show that a service is functioning as expected. However, not all of the Exchange software is yet capable of providing feedback to the cluster (the engineers just didn't have the time to go completely through a massive code base).

When a failover is performed all services are moved, so some might have to be shut down. Even on a standalone server it can take some time for a service to close down properly, especially when the Information Store is large. After the cluster transition is complete transactions may have to be rolled forward into the Information Store or Directory. Network connections have to be re-established to link to other Exchange servers, sites, and external messaging systems. The exact time required for a cluster state transition will vary greatly depending on workload, time of day, and hardware configuration (faster CPUs and I/O subsystems will complete transitions more quickly). Testing will establish initial baseline figures for your own configurations and environment. As we are still very much in the early days of clusters it's reasonable to expect that experience of how to determine optimum configurations will help speed matters up.

4.3.10 Client communication with clusters

Clients are largely unaffected by clusters. Point the client at the cluster name rather than an individual node and everything works. If user mailboxes are transferred from a non-clustered server to a cluster within the same site MAPI clients will automatically adjust their profile to point to the cluster. POP3 and IMAP4 clients point to a host name that's bound to a TCP/IP address. The cluster transition will take care of rebinding the TCP/IP address to the new virtual server so the switchover should be invisible to these clients as well. Providing that IIS is configured to run on both nodes and start automatically on failover web browsers should be able to continue to use Outlook Web Access.

The administration program can be regarded as a form of client. Like Outlook, it uses RPCs to communicate with the Exchange services. However, ADMIN.EXE is one of the binaries stored on the shared disk resources, and this makes it a little difficult to run the administration program on the passive node. It is possibly better to perform administration from another system such as an NT workstation as this will not be affected by a cluster transition.

4.3.11 Upgrading Exchange into a cluster

As noted earlier, Microsoft does not officially support the upgrade of existing servers to form clusters. This is a restriction specific to

Exchange and does not arise from any limitation in MSCS. Greenfield installations are always simpler than upgrades and the expectation is that new hardware will be used for clusters. The requirement to use symmetric hardware chosen from the cluster compatibility list is enough to stop most people even thinking about upgrading existing hardware. Given that you buy some suitable hardware what can you do to introduce a cluster into an existing Exchange environment? Two approaches can be taken.

First, you can introduce the cluster as a new server within an existing site. This is the easiest option as all you need to do is make sure the cluster joins the right site when Exchange is installed. Afterwards you can move mailboxes, public folders, and connectors over to the cluster from older servers. When everything is settled down you can think about removing the older servers from the site.

The other option is a forklift upgrade, which is only feasible in a multi-server site. Exchange services are stopped on the old server, a backup is taken of its Directory and Information Stores, and the server is then removed from the network. Exchange is then installed with the SETUP/R option, meaning that files will be moved onto the shared disks but the Exchange services are not started afterwards. After the installation is complete on the primary node you restore the Directory and Information Stores into the appropriate directories on the cluster and then start the Exchange services. At this time the cluster is effectively swapped into your organization and takes the place of the old server. The installation onto the secondary cluster node can take place some time afterwards. These steps aren't particularly difficult. They just take care in planning. A forklift upgrade can take up to one day to perform, assuming that everything goes to plan. Forklift upgrades involving large stores (over 8GB or so) will take even longer. The big problem here is the potential for downtime. If the cluster can't be made operational over a weekend there's probably no point in even attempting an upgrade. Also, don't expect too much help from Microsoft PSS if things go wrong!

I don't honestly foresee many attempts to upgrade. If you are going to the expense of buying hardware off the compatibility list and investing in the necessary copies of Windows NT and Exchange, it seems logical to introduce the cluster as a new server into an existing site. After the cluster has settled down into the site user mailboxes can be migrated over. The older servers can then either be withdrawn from service or continue as dedicated connector or public folder servers.

4.3.12   Hardware and software requirements for clustering

The hardware and software requirements for an Exchange cluster different significantly from a single server environment. The following requirements must be met.

- Windows NT V4.0 Enterprise Edition (NTS/E). MSCS must be configured and running before the Exchange installation starts. NTS/E is much more expensive than the standard edition of NT, so this is an added cost that should be taken into account.

- Exchange Server V5.5 Enterprise Edition. The standard edition of Exchange does not support clustering. You'll also need the Enterprise Edition if you want to use the unlimited store, the other essential component required to build very large servers. Most corporate installations will use the Enterprise Edition anyway, so this is not a difficult requirement to satisfy.

- The hardware used to build the cluster must be registered on the hardware compatibility list maintained by Microsoft.

There are two ways for a configuration to get on the list. Either the manufacturer submits a complete configuration to Microsoft for their verification or they can conduct their own tests using a Self-Certification kit provided by Microsoft. The configuration consists of the server itself, the storage controller, the expansion storage, and the network controller. For example, DIGITAL originally certified two configurations through Microsoft, as shown in Table 4.5. Given the speed at which servers change today these configurations are supplied for illustration only[5].

Table 4.5   *Valid cluster configurations*

Server	Storage controller	Expansion storage	Network controller
AlphaServer 4100	KZPSA-BB	StorageWorks RA450	DE500-AA
Intel Prioris ZX6200	Adaptec 2944W	StorageWorks RA310	DEC450-CA

Because clusters can only be built from specific hardware you'll need to review existing configurations before you know whether the hardware you have today can be reused in clusters. Indeed, Microsoft does not support upgrades for existing standalone servers to form clusters even if you have assembled the necessary hardware. The insis-

---

5.   Consult http://www.microsoft.com/ntserver/info/hwcompatibility.htm to get the up-to-date list.

tence that cluster hardware comes from a controlled compatibility list may be relaxed as more experience is gained with clusters.

Microsoft requires both of the servers in the cluster to run symmetric configurations (CPU speed, number of CPUs, amount of memory). Why must this be so? Well, the Performance Wizard (PerfWiz) only runs on the primary node in the cluster. It cannot run on the secondary node because it won't be able to access the shared disks where the Exchange data is held. PerfWiz attempts to determine optimum performance settings for Exchange including initial memory buffer allocations and the best (hopefully fastest) location for important Exchange files, like the Information Store. All of this information is written into the registry. If the hardware is asymmetric the performance settings for the primary node may not match the characteristics of the secondary node after a failover occurs, and performance will inevitably suffer. However, if the two servers are relatively close to each other in memory and CPU speed it's probably OK to accept that the performance settings aren't going to be 100% optimum after a failover.

Exchange V5.5 introduces dynamic buffer allocation, code to constantly monitor and adjust the memory utilization of Exchange with respect to the other demands for memory made to Windows NT (see page 185). Dynamic buffer allocation will negate some of the impact of failing over to asymmetric hardware but possibly not all. For best results you should follow Microsoft's recommendations and use identical hardware for both nodes.

4.3.13 Does clustering buy me anything extra?

Do you need to cluster the systems you use for Exchange? Clustering helps high-end Windows NT servers to attain a higher degree of overall system availability in terms of very robust servers. Challenges still remain. Many people will ignore clusters for now because they don't want to pay the extra money for copies of Windows NT Enterprise or the hardware mandated by the compatibility list. The disk I/O subsystem remains an obvious potential for a single point of failure that can knock a cluster out. It is possible to generate almost the same degree of resilience by splitting a user community across two separate servers as long as those servers are equipped with high-end configurations, especially in the disk I/O subsystem.

MSCS and Exchange V5.5 are the initial point of the cluster journey. Things will improve and I expect clusters to be a very popular technology over the company years. For now they're a little expensive for most. Above all, clusters are not an excuse for system administrators to pay any less attention to the fundamental techniques of system management—excellent system monitoring, good backup practices, diligent capacity planning, and proactive maintenance. Failure to pay attention to these points will render the most resilient of hardware useless once a problem occurs.

4.4   Designing a luxury hardware configuration for Exchange

Given that the system configurations discussed so far are pretty basic and that I have expressed a view that you should build well-equipped servers from the start, what type of configurations should be considered if budget is not a limiting factor? Here are some suggestions for you to consider.

CPU

Get the fastest possible CPU you can get your hand on—you'll use it! I like to configure all Exchange servers with dual CPUs. Installing a second CPU when the system is first built is a very cheap upgrade, and it will mean that the system will easily be able to handle any peaks or unexpected surges in user demand. The added CPU should also extend the lifetime of the system. Systems to handle over 2,000 users should consider quad-CPUs. The better SMP support in Exchange V5.5 will make sure that the extra CPUs are used. A dual-CPU 200 MHz Pentium Pro system is a good choice for a server, as is a dual-CPU Alpha processor.

Pentium Pro systems come with built-in secondary (L2) cache memory, so I don't need to worry too much about this aspect of system sizing if this CPU is selected as the system processor. However, if offered the chance to use a (cheaper) high-end Pentium CPU, make sure that it is equipped with as much L2 cache as you can afford. Upping the L2 cache reduces bus contention and normally delivers more beneficial effect on system performance than a simple CPU upgrade, which may not be altogether effective if other system components, like the motherboard, are unable to fully handle the speed of the upgraded CPU.

Disk

Apart from Windows NT (the executables) and other applications, we have three main sources of I/O on an Exchange system, each of which needs to be isolated from the others. The three sources of I/O are the Information Store, transaction logs, and MTA work directory. Systems experiencing heavy traffic through the Internet Mail Service should also look at a separate disk for the IMS work directory (\IMCDATA). Isolation across separate physical disk devices delivers the highest possible performance while also allowing us to build a high degree of resilience to software or hardware failure.

The I/O generated by the MTA work directory and transaction logs is very different to that produced by the Information Store. In addition, the degree of resilience required by the Information Store is much higher than the other two. The Information Store (and Directory Store) on any Exchange server used in production environments must always be protected. RAID-5 is the most common approach taken today, and our luxury configuration is no different. Make sure that the array contains some hot spare disks, ready to be inserted into the array if a problem occurs. Hot spares ensure that the array can be kept operational all the time, even if a disk fails. Remember the comments about the write-back cache earlier on in this chapter. The extra money spent to upgrade the controller to support features like the write back cache will return great benefits in terms of performance.

To achieve the optimum balance between protection and performance the system should be equipped with a hardware-based RAID-5 controller with a bus adapter. Hardware-based RAID systems are always faster and more flexible than software-based equivalents. For example, if a disk fails in a hardware-based array, you can plug in a "hot spare" and proceed. The array will take care of any required adjustments automatically. Software-controlled arrays, on the other hand, need to be reconfigured before new drives can be added. RAID0+1 (striping and mirroring) will deliver better I/O performance, but you'll need more disks. If you need sheer performance and believe that you'll want to dynamically increase the amount of disk space available for Information Stores, then RAID0+1 (with mirroring performed at the host, and striping at the controller) is a better choice than RAID-5. Aside from the difference in performance, you should also remember that any expansion of a RAID-5 array requires you take a backup, reconfigure the array, and then restore the databases from a backup, not a task that you'll want to take on very often.

If money is no object then you can consider using a combination of striping with parity (RAID-5) and mirroring (RAID-0). This is a RAID-6 (sometimes called RAID-10) solution, commonly implemented in server configurations designed to support many hundreds of users for intensive applications. RAID-6 delivers great robustness and reliability at the expense of additional cost for all the extra disks required to mirror the RAID-5 striped set.

You can get RAID controllers that are integrated in the system backplane, but these controllers are slower than those that are separate from the backplane. You'll appreciate the extra speed if things go wrong, a disk fails, and the array needs to synchronize itself. Read-ahead caching on the controller should be disabled because it slows down I/O performance for databases like the Information Store.

Don't just focus on just the physical space available on a disk when considering the question of equipping the system with drives. Systems can avoid I/O bottlenecks (indicated by large I/O queues that are present on a constant basis) by increasing the number of physical disks rather than focusing on very large disks.

Data written to transaction logs is always written to the end of file. Optimum performance is gained by placing the transaction logs on their own separate disk. Head movement is restricted to slight movement to add transactions to the end of file or when new logs are created. Our luxury system has a separate 2GB disk for transaction logs. Apart from speed we gain another advantage in that it is highly unlikely that the system will ever stop because there is no available space to create a new transaction log! Strictly speaking the transaction logs don't need a whole pile of resilience because the Information Store is well protected by the RAID-5 array, but as we're building a luxury system we should add a level of protection by mirroring the disk holding the transaction logs. Some people protect logs by copying them across the network to another system at a regular interval. Copying transaction logs may seem a touch excessive, but it might be very valuable if a catastrophic situation occurs and the server is physically destroyed. The combination of transaction logs and a full backup of the Information and Directory Stores is enough to recover a server.

The amount of I/O generated by the MTA depends greatly on the type of work done by Exchange. Systems that are dedicated messaging or public folder servers (or both) probably won't need a separate disk for the MTA work directory. Any system that acts as the focal point for a lot of other systems (bridgehead server, or server in a site that connects together lots of other sites) may experience a lot of messages passing through the MTA. In these situations it is advantageous to place the MTA work directory on its own separate disk. Select the fastest possible disk for this task, because you want to switch the messages through the MTA as quickly as they'll go. No great degree of mirroring or other protection is required.

Memory

Our luxury system should have lots of memory, at least 256 MB. Early versions of Exchange didn't make good use of more memory than this, but the latest versions are quite happy to use 1GB or more. However, you shouldn't need to equip the system with quite so much memory. 256MB provides a good starting point and it's sufficient for all but the largest systems designed for over 1,500 users. These systems will want 512MB. Do pay attention to the system page files, and attempt to reduce system paging as much as possible by deploying a number of page files across the different disks on the system. Do not put a page file on the dedicated disk allocated to transaction logs.

Tape Drive

A system is only as good as its weakest point. There is plenty of resilience built in for the disks, but that's no reason to avoid taking backups on a regular basis. Buy the fastest tape drive you can so that you can take a full backup of the Information Store and Directory, if possible, every night. The size of today's Exchange databases are only constrained by available disk space, so you need to make sure that the backup technology deployed is able to handle very large files. Any increase in backup speed is very useful if you have a 100GB database to deal with. Digital Linear Technology (DLT) tape drives are the fastest available today, so they should be your starting point. Drives that compress data as it is streamed out to tape are preferable. In production environments, it's possible to achieve rates of up to 32.5GB/hour for backups with quad-DLT devices arranged in a RAID array (Compaq DLT 7000s were used in this case). The same array can restore data at over 18GB/hour.

Don't forget to back up all the other information on the system, like Windows NT and application executables and the system registry, at regular intervals too. Full backups of the Exchange databases will make it much easier to get a system back on line and working should a problem ever occur that necessitates a restore. Combine the fast tape drive with backup software that can take advantage of the drive's speed. Windows NT backup is OK, but it's slow, so spend some time looking for a good third party backup utility.

UPS

All production Exchange servers need to be reviewed to decide whether or not a UPS is required, and the default should be to establish a source of uninteruptable supply. In many parts of the world, where electricity supplies are known to fluctuate, the decision is easy, and a UPS is added to system configurations without a moment's thought. In other places, where a reliable electricity supply is assured the decision is less clear. Accidents happen, even in the most reliable of circumstances, so adding a UPS to our luxury configuration is not a hard decision. Look for a device that has a long battery life as this will enable a system to continue working during all but the most severe power outages.

Futures

Given the ever-changing world of computers it is impossible to say what new features will be added over the years. CD-ROMs were new a few years ago, now an 8× CD-ROM is deemed to be slow. It's important to continually review developments in both the hardware and software markets so that you're able to take advantage of new technology when it becomes available. Clustering is of particular interest to those who want to build very resilient servers. Our luxury system isn't clustered, but it could easily be.

In general all parts of the configuration should be bought with an eye on robustness, performance, and expandability. Components (including disks, controllers, and power supplies) that are hot swappable are especially valuable. CPU boards that can be upgraded with new CPUs or by installing additional CPUs provide a useful mid-life kicker to systems.

Finally, our system should be equipped with the capability for remote management and monitoring. If something goes wrong, like a controller or disk error, we want to know about the problem as soon as possible. The system should be capable of sending messages to an engineer when problems occur so that any downtime is minimized.

4.4.1   Example configurations

Some real-life examples are always useful benchmarks when you begin to consider what type of hardware to use. Here are a couple of high-end examples from major Exchange projects rolling out in early 1998. The first configuration is for one of the earliest Exchange clusters to go into production. The cluster is sized to support 3,000 users and has been tested to deliver good response to Outlook clients when loaded. Only 1,000 users are connected in production. Remember that only a single server is active in an MSCS cluster.

Component	Description
Server	Two DIGITAL ZX6200 Prioris (Quad-CPU 200 MHz Pentium Pro with 512K level 2 cache)
Memory	512 MB (each server)
Disk configuration	■ Mirrored (RAID-1) 9 GB disks for system files ■ StorageWorks 7000 controller for Ultra-SCSI RAID arrays (3 arrays) ■ 9 × 9GB RAID-5 for Exchange stores ■ 2 × 9GB RAID-1 for transaction logs ■ 2 × 9GB RAID-1 for other applications ■ Controller cache (128MB) mirrored to prevent loss of data
Backup device	Mirrored DLT
Network interface	100MB FDDI

The second configuration is sized to support 2,000 users in an unclustered environment. Again, the configuration is quite able to support more users and the decision to restrict numbers to 2,000 reflects the desire not to affect too many users if a system fails.

Component	Description
Server type	Compaq Proliant 6500 (Quad-CPU 200 MHz Pentium Pro with 512 MB level 2 cache)
Memory	512MB

continued▸

Disks	■ SMART-2P array controller ■ Mirrored (RAID-1) 4.3GB disks for system files ■ Mirrored (RAID-1) 4.3GB disks for Exchange transaction logs ■ Second SMART-2P controller ■ 14 × 9GB RAID-5 array for Exchange stores
Network Interface	100Mb FDDI
Backup device	Compaq Tape Array II (4 DLT7000s), driven via 2 Fast Wide SCSI controllers (tapes configured in a RAID array)

Both configurations operated with write-back cache enabled for optimum performance on the RAID-5 arrays hosting the Exchange databases. Note that the arrays are equipped with top of the range controllers, in line with the assertion that you should spend extra money on the I/O subsystem. These configurations are designed to last for between two and three years without any need for hardware upgrades during that time.

4.5   A growing strain on existing network resources?

Does your LAN and WAN operate in a satisfactory manner today? Of course you'll say "yes" and why wouldn't you? But the facts are that many LANs are tied together with so much string and good wishes and just about manage to limp along on a wing and a prayer. If you're in this type of situation then you need to consider whether you can even attempt to implement Exchange in such a flimsy network environment.

Even if your network is in good shape Exchange is going to impose some extra demands. If you replace several LAN Post Offices with one or more Exchange servers you may find that people will start to use the system more because message delivery is more reliable. They'll also like the additional functionality that Exchange provides. Clearly with such a range of network capabilities it is important to plan how information is exchanged between the different systems.

All Exchange servers should be equipped with the best and most capable network adapter you can afford. Don't try and limp by with an old or low-throughput adapter because its flaws will be revealed once the pressure goes on. Given that client-server systems place a huge emphasis on network stability and throughput it's important that you provide a solid base for your clients to connect to servers and for the servers to service the clients. Servers designed to support large numbers of clients should be equipped with multiple LAN adapters and caching controllers on disks to ensure that network and disk I/O demands generated by clients can be met. Equipping the servers with fast CPUs, fast disks, and lots of memory will be wasted investments if the server can't pump data down to clients as quickly as it would like to because of an old or underpowered network adapter.

4.5.1   Sources of network demand

What are the potential sources of additional network demand? First, there is a general increase in the average message size being seen within messaging networks. In the old text-based environments an average one-page message, complete with all its header information and whatever other data was necessary to transmit the message from originator to recipient could comfortably fit into the 4K–6K range. The advent of rich text messages complete with all the huge attachments regularly generated by the current suites of desktop office products has driven the average message size up dramatically. As we've already discussed in chapter 1, some installations report an average message size of 40K, some see higher, and all expect the average message size to grow. The features and functionality of desktop applications encourage users to incorporate highly graphical items in their documents, and all the glitz must be paid for in size.

Users gain in confidence all the time. Electronic mail was once an application to be approached with care, but not any more. The electronic age makes e-mail just another way to communicate and users create more and more messages all the time. Added to the increased comfort zone there are more ways to create messages through mail-enabled applications. Almost every application today can add a "Send Message" option to its menus. External message feeds from other organizations and the Internet drive up the number of messages within the system. If just a few users subscribe to some Internet news groups you can expect to see many hundreds of messages coming in from that source on a daily basis.

You can help users to work with Exchange in an intelligent manner and restrict their use of system resources. Most of this is done through good habits instilled into individuals through training (a good reason not to skimp on user training during any implementation). An example of a good habit is using public folders to share documents rather than mailing large documents around to multiple recipients during a review cycle. Training allows you to divert people away from using neat client features that, although attractive, impose a real strain on the network.

Figure 4.10 *A really bad user habit—including a graphic into an autosignature file*

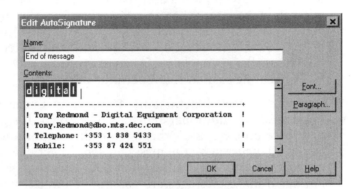

Including a bitmap image of the corporate logo in an Auto Signature is a good example of how a feature can be misused, the reason being that several kilobytes of bitmap data will be appended to every outgoing message. Figure 4.10 illustrates how easy it is to include a logo into the auto-signature feature. In this case the overhead is relatively low at 2K per message, but only because the bitmap was available in 16-color format. It is entirely possible for users to insert a complicated graphic that's only available in 256 colors! As long as you can use the standard Windows cut and paste facility to move a graphic around it can be slotted neatly into an Exchange auto signature. And of course, users aren't necessarily going to insert the corporate logo. All manner of smiling faces, cute cats, or other icons can be pasted into an auto-signature. The worst example I know of (to date) involved a senior manager who became a proud father for the first time. He promptly scanned a photo of his new offspring to create a digital image, which was then inserted into his autosignature file. Everyone who received a message from this individual over the next few days was very happy to know that he was a father, but less happy about the 1MB of digital imagery that accompanied the message.

Those interested in discovering where the contents of your auto-signature are held should look for a file called AUTOTEXT.SIG in the Windows directory, or, if you're using Outlook 98, in:

```
\Windows\Application Data\Microsoft\Shared\Signatures
```

Clients prior to Outlook 98 store signature files in Rich Text Format and can be edited with NotePad or WordPad (if you want to see the native RTF formatting commands), or Word for Windows to see the auto-signature in all its glory. Outlook 98 stores signature files in all the formats supported by the client (ASCII, Rich Text Format, and HTML).

You can also help to enforce good user habits by placing restrictions on some of the available gateways or connectors. Not allowing users to send messages larger than 1 MB seems like an intelligent step in the right direction. If a user really has a good business need to transmit a message larger than this they should really find out if there's a better (faster or more functional) method to accomplish the same task before possibly clogging up a vital e-mail link. Directives (or "Tips on how to use the system better") can easily be brought to users' attention by distributing easy-to-reference hint sheets.

The enhanced functionality available in Exchange and its clients imposes some additional demands of its own. It's great to be able to distribute public folders throughout the organization, but there's an overhead incurred by the messages sent to get data from one place to another. The automatically synchronized Exchange directory is great, but again more messages are generated and exchanged between systems to keep the directory synchronized. And if you turn on advanced security (see chapter 6) there'll be authentication requests generated too.

Finally, just to make the situation even more complicated network planners must take account of the impact of the Web, whether it's used in an Intranet or out on the Internet. Users love being able to browse remote locations to discover new information and that information is generally presented in a very graphical and attractive manner. But again, the network must be able to handle the load generated by shipping all the data from one place to another. System administrators and network planners in quite a few corporations that I work with are now discovering that Web traffic is taking more and more network capacity. I think this trend will continue over the next few years, and the net effect will be a continuing and growing demand for more and more network bandwidth.

These are just some of the potential sources for growth in network demand. Implementing a new messaging system often focuses minds on the infrastructure required by the new system, so this is a good time to perform a health check on the underlying network and take steps to ensure it is able to cope. Without a good network you have little chance of a good implementation of Exchange.

4.6   Tuning Windows NT for Exchange

Exchange is an application that runs on the Windows NT operating system. This simple statement implies that Windows NT must be kept in good health if Exchange can ever deliver any reasonable quality of service. New hardware can be installed to address performance degradation but if the system isn't properly tuned then the degradation will inevitably return. Few can afford to get into the very expensive cycle of constant hardware upgrades. It's much cheaper to install a reasonable configuration from the start and then make sure that the system is tuned on a consistent basis.

Normal tuning rules apply. If the system is paging heavily you either need to add more memory, increase the page file size, introduce additional page files on lightly loaded disks, or redistribute the file I/O generated by applications across all available disks. If one disk is a bottleneck it may be possible to redistribute applications to other disks, and so on. Just because a server is running Exchange there is no reason to approach it in any other manner other than normal.

Figure 4.11
Using the system applet to minimize the boost given to foreground applications

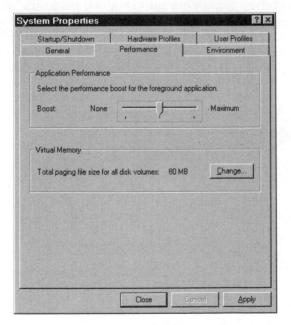

There are a few minor points relating to Windows NT that should be born in mind for Exchange. These are addressed by instructing the system to behave in a manner most appropriate to the service-oriented workload generated by Exchange. Use the control panel to make the changes.

- The system applet (Figure 4.11) is used to tell Windows NT how to divide its attention between background (services) and foreground (interactive) demands. A typical Exchange server runs a lot of services so you should elect to give background applications more of a boost than foreground. Running an interactive application will be a little slower, but messages will be processed faster.

- The network applet is used to tell Windows NT how to deal with the network. The setting we're interested in here is "Maximize Throughput for Network Applications" (Figure 4.12), in effect saying that the system should devote more of its time to handling the demands of applications that generate network requests, like the RPCs used to communicate with other servers in a site.

- The system applet can also be used to resize the system page file. An Exchange server tends to use a large amount of virtual memory, so the system page file needs to be large enough to handle the demand without resorting to an excessive amount of paging. The workload generated by the system will determine the correct size for the file, but it's difficult to know what this will be until the system goes into production. In the meantime a good rule of thumb is to set the page file size to be the amount of physical memory plus 125 MB. Thus, a system with 96 MB physical memory should start with a page file of $96 + 125 = 221$ MB. Paging should be carefully monitored after the system goes into production and adjustments made if necessary afterwards.

Figure 4.12
Optimization for network applications

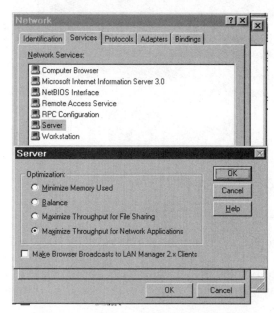

Figure 4.12 shows Windows NT system properties being set. I took this screen capture from my notebook PC, which is configured to run Windows NT and Exchange. The notebook boasts a high specification (150 MHz Pentium and 56 MB memory) but its primary use is as a notebook computer, not a server. The settings made reflect its use and shouldn't be taken as a guide for a production computer.

5

The Joy of Managing Exchange

5.1   Introduction

Exchange won't manage itself. Time, commitment, and energy are all required to keep a server operational. Much of the internal workings of Exchange remain hidden from the eye, and at times it is downright difficult to know exactly what a server is doing, let alone influence the server to do what you'd like it to do. Messages pass between servers without let or hindrance, network bandwidth is absorbed without permission, replication takes place in the background, and disk space is silently filled up. The GUI administration interface hides all of this in a mass of property pages, drop-down lists, and check boxes. The administration program is nice to look at, but sometimes it would be nicer to have some more information coming out of the server. System usage statistics and reports are generally a weak area for Exchange.

When things go well Exchange is a joy to administer, but when things start to go wrong and the system falls down around your ears you'll need to have some idea about how Exchange works from a management perspective. Good system management practices for Windows NT and Exchange reduce the chances that something will go wrong as well as helping people get out of trouble when problems appear.

This chapter reviews some of the day to day issues that system administrators have to deal with, and discusses how the issues might be approached. There is never only one good way to deal with a problem, so be prepared to look at the solutions outlined here and then make your own mind up as to how you'll do things.

5.2   Exchange Services

Exchange is not engineered as a single monolithic server process. It is broken down into a number of separate processes, each of which runs as a Windows NT service. The collective group of these services make up the application we call Exchange. The table below lists the most important of these services together with the name of the executable that you'll see in the list of active processes. All the executables are stored in the \EXCHSRVR\BIN directory.

Table 5.1   *Major Exchange services*

Name of Service	Executable
System Attendant	MAD.EXE
Directory	DSAMAIN.EXE
Information Store	STORE.EXE
Message Transfer Agent	EMSMTA.EXE
Internet Mail Service	MSEXCIMC.EXE
Internet News Service	EXCHINS.EXE
Directory Synchronizer (MS-Mail)	DXA.EXE
Key Management Service	KMSERVER.EXE

Figure 5.1
Exchange services

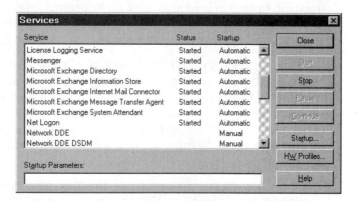

The Services applet of the Windows NT control panel controls how services are run. Figure 5.1 lists the services running on a computer, and shows that a number of Exchange services are active. Note the start-up state for each service. All of the Exchange services are "automatic", meaning that they will be started up without manual intervention each time the computer is booted. This is the preferred state, as anything else will force the system administrator to select each service and start it up after a system reboot. Not only is this boring work, but it's impossible to be there each time a computer is restarted.

Selecting the service and then clicking on the start-up button can change the start-up type for a service.

Figure 5.2
*Changing the
start-up state*

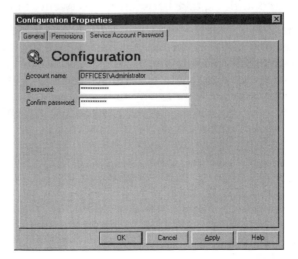

Apart from the start-up type, the dialog (Figure 5.2) reveals the account name used to run the service. When the service starts up Windows NT uses the account name and password information furnished here to conduct a log-on and establish security credentials. If the password information is incorrect credentials will not be issued and the service will fail to start. The account name used is the Exchange service account (see page 130). Exchange is slightly special in this respect because password information is held in two places: in the SAM (accessed and managed via the control applet) and in the Exchange directory, where the password information is held as a property of the site.

Figure 5.3
*Changing the
service account
password*

When an Exchange service is started a check is performed to make sure that the password provided matches the password held in the directory, and if they don't match the service will terminate abruptly on the basis that a potential security breech has occurred. Never use the Windows NT User Manager for Domains utility to change the password for the Exchange Service account. Always set the password for the Exchange service account by amending the properties of the site object, as shown in Figure 5.3.

5.2.1   Shutting things down

Exchange does a lot of work in the background. Part of the reason for this is the attitude taken to user-initiated work, which Exchange always gives priority to over system work. For example, if a user request to send a message is detected, Exchange will stop what it's doing to accept the message. Working like this means that users get best response from the server, but it does mean that even where there doesn't seem to be too much obvious activity, the server is probably busily dealing with work like flushing transactions out of memory and committing them to the database.

Shutting down a busy Windows NT server can take a few minutes from the time you instruct the server to begin the shutdown process to the time when the server has finally ceased operation. Shutting down a busy server takes even longer. There are a number of background processes that must be halted, and before those services can be stopped they may have operations to complete or data to save. Connectors finish dealing with new messages, the Information Store must commit any outstanding transactions to its databases, the message queue must be flushed, and so on. All of this activity means that a busy server can, in some conditions, take between ten to twenty minutes to shut down.

There is, of course, the temptation to lose control and hit the "power-off" button. After all, Exchange has a great transactional database that is able to automatically roll-forward any outstanding transactions when the Information Store service starts up. It is correct that Exchange will take care of any outstanding transactions that had not been committed to the database when the system starts up. That's what the checkpoint file is for (discussed later in this chapter). However, the brutal power-off approach to life brings other dangers—like a corruption of the MTA queues. If Exchange is shut down abnormally then checks must be performed when the server is restarted. Some minutes might be gained by powering a computer down quickly, but all those minutes will be paid for when the server restarts because a number of internal checks must be performed to ensure that everything is OK. Checking the MTA queue files on a large server can take quite a time!

Apart from the amount of work to do to close all the services down properly, it seems that the amount of inter-process chat that goes on during the close down procedure contributes to the overall slowness. Many experienced system administrators recommend that you manually terminate the Exchange System Attendant[1] process before commencing a general system shutdown. There's no obvious logic to this assertion, but closing down the System Attendant forces all other Exchange services to shut down gracefully, one after the other. It is perhaps the graceful and co-ordinated way that the Exchange services shut down before a general shut down commences that contributes most to faster elapsed times. The only reason I can come up with is that Windows NT can give the Exchange services the chance to close themselves down efficiently without any contention with other applications and services. As always, your mileage may vary, but it's something to try if you get frustrated with long system close down times.

5.2.2   What do I connect to?

Exchange is a messaging system built in the client/server paradigm. This mouthful, so beloved of the marketing fraternity and the computing purists, means in reality that we have clients making network connections to server computers in order to use the services offered by the servers. But in an Exchange context, where are those connections made to?

MAPI clients connect to Exchange server using RPCs. The connection is made between the client application (e.g., EXCHNG32.EXE or OUTLOOK.EXE) and the Information Store service (STORE.EXE). Each connection results in one or more threads being created within the Information Store process. The store allows access to user mailboxes, public folders, and directory information.

Exchange uses Windows NT for security purposes. Each connection must be authenticated, or possess security credentials trusted by the domain where the server is located. The default mechanism is to use network credentials that are already established, those created as a result of a client logging on to a domain. If those credentials are not available, or the server is located in a different domain to the one that the client logged onto, a log-on dialog will be presented to allow the user to enter the account name and password. This information is then used to create security credentials (if valid) and allow the client to connect to the server.

---

1.   From the purely trivial perspective, I can't help wondering why the System Attendant executable was given the name "MAD.EXE". Is this service the mad dog of the Exchange world?

Passwords entered into log-on dialogs are never sent to the server, as this would create a potential danger that password information might be intercepted and decrypted en route. The server and client both share a common secret—each knows the password, so the password can be used as the basis for a challenge/response sequence that establishes whether the client is authorized to use the account that they have nominated. The server encrypts a random string with the account's password and sends it down to the client. The client is now challenged to decrypt the string and return it (the response) to the server. If the string can be decrypted successfully the server accepts that the client really must be who they say they are, and will issue the necessary credentials. This is a simplified version of the steps in the challenge/response sequence, enough to establish that a client must either possess credentials or be able to establish bona fides by responding correctly to server demands.

Figure 5.4
Setting up encrypted client connections

An optional client setting determines whether the RPCs are encrypted using a 40-bit algorithm when connected over either a LAN-type connection or via dial-up networking. The degree of protection is increased to 128-bit encryption for Windows NT clients connected to Windows NT V4.0 servers, but only if both are running the American edition of NT V4.0 SP2 or later. Figure 5.4 shows the advanced properties of the connection to Exchange are set to use encrypted RPCs. Electing to use encrypted RPCs certainly protects against any possibility that an intercepted RPC can be read without a great deal of effort on the part of the eavesdropper, but at the expense of some additional overhead. The overhead isn't enormous and probably won't be noticed by users when connected by a LAN. The extra overhead may affect performance over a slow dial-in link when encryption is more desirable.

5.3   Inside the Information Store

In Exchange V4.0 and V5.0 a restriction imposed by the design of the database prevents an Information Store database growing past 16GB. When the limit was first designed 16GB was possibly a limit that seemed to be well in advance of anything that people would need to use. As we've seen, the ever-expanding size of messages and attachments has driven the requirement to support larger stores much faster than people might have expected. A server in DIGITAL reached a 15.5GB Private Information Store in early 1997, after roughly 6 months of production activity. Spirited use of the EDBUTIL utility to compact the store and judicious transfer of user mailboxes to other servers managed to keep the server from hitting the magic 16GB limit, but there's no doubt that production servers hit the design limits sooner than many expected.

Exchange V5.5 silenced all the discussions about the size limitation for an individual database. The theoretical limit is now 16TB, a size that is so far in advance of the largest disk volume supported by Windows NT now and in the foreseeable future that Microsoft is quite correct to refer to this as the "unlimited store." In early 1998 the expectation was that the largest store that would be put into production in this millennium would be less than 125GB. Given the operational challenges involved in maintaining very large files I doubt that anyone will rush to be the first to have a store larger than 100GB, but someone will claim the prize!

By default, each server has two stores—the Private and Public Information Stores, so a single server can manage huge amount of data, providing that the necessary hardware is provided. There can be many servers within a single Exchange site. The number of servers operated within any individual site therefore dictates the maximum available storage for a site. Users store messages in the Private Information Store of their host server. You can balance disk space usage across the servers in a site by moving user mailboxes from server to server. As this can be a tiresome activity that must be accomplished when people are not using their mailboxes it pays to carefully plan the allocation of users across available servers.

An Exchange server does not necessarily require the presence of both Public and Private Information Stores. It is possible to configure a server to be "messaging-only" in which case only a Private Information Store is operated. The converse case is to have a server dedicated to public folder access only, in which case no user mailboxes are allocated to the server. Smaller sites are not likely to operate dedicated servers, but in larger sites a good case can be made to exploit

Exchange's flexibility in this manner by deploying servers configured for particular tasks. For example, one large server with a fast CPU and large disk arrays might manage all the public folders for the site, leaving general messaging activity to a set of smaller servers.

Figure 5.5
The general properties of the Private Information Store

When you create a site it is important to consider whether all servers will host both types of store or if different servers will take on different tasks. The "General" property page for the Private Information Store (see Figure 5.5) is used to define the server location for the associated Public Information Store. When a user creates a new public folder it is normally created on the same server that hosts the user's mailbox, but if the location of the Public Information Store is redefined the new folder is created on the other server.

Exchange V4.0 allows servers to be operated without Private Information Stores. This policy was stopped in V5.0 after the mechanism for inter-site directory replication was changed. The Private Information Store is now used to hold the messages generated for directory replication, so it is no longer possible to delete the Private Information Store from a server.

5.3.1   The type of database used by Exchange server

Relational database technology forms the heart of Exchange server. The data contained in user mailboxes, public folders, and the Exchange directory are held in three databases called PRIV.EDB, PUB.EDB, and DIR.EDB; the stores that contain all the important information used by an Exchange server. Understanding the technology and knowing how to keep these databases healthy is clearly important if you want to avoid problems with Exchange.

Exchange V4.0 and V5.0 used a variant of Microsoft's "Jet"[2] database technology called "Jet Blue", an object store which is roughly similar to a traditional relational database. Exchange V5.5 has an upgraded database engine called ESE (Extensible Storage Engine) or ESE97. Both engines are provided as dynamic link libraries called EDB.DLL or ESE.DLL and are integrated into STORE.EXE. Note that this single multithreaded process is responsible for access to both the Private and Public Information Stores. Be aware that some problems were seen with the new engine after V5.5 shipped, some of which caused STORE.EXE to take 100% of the CPU on a regular basis. A hot fix[3] was issued for the problem and incorporated into Exchange V5.5 SP1.

A lot of myths and rumors have built up around the database used by Exchange server. One popular story alleges that Exchange uses SQL/Server for all database access, while another says that Exchange uses the same database engine as the popular desktop Access product, probably because Access is also based on Jet database technology (but not the same technology as Exchange). As mentioned above, there are some similarities to a relational database such as those implemented in SQL/Server and Access, but the two implementations are very different beasts. Both SQL/Server and Access deal in rows, tables, and joins like other database applications while Exchange is very much focused on the definition of a MAPI message store.

The Exchange developers have designed the Information Store to be optimized for the type of activity produced by users creating and sending messages, or the traffic generated by directory and public folder replication. Remember that a large amount of messages are generated, sent, and deleted to carry out behind the scenes database synchronization. Public folder replication, system attendant updates for configurations, and directory updates are all examples of messages that go through the database without too much notice being taken (unless things go wrong). When added to interpersonal messages the traffic generated by background messages was enough to require the Exchange architects to pay special attention to database efficiency in terms of message throughput, leading in turn to the decision reached to use a specialized database engine.

---

2.   JET stands for "Joint Engine Technology", an internal Microsoft database project.

3.   The hot fix is available at:
      ftp://ftp.microsoft.com/bussys/exchange/exchange-public/fixes/Eng/Exchg5.5/PostRTM/ESE-FIX/

Apart from its high-volume message processing capacity the chosen database confers other advantages. In addition to having a smaller "footprint" (amount of memory that the code occupies) than an SQL-based equivalent the ESE technology allows for a number of unique features such as record level locking and "on the fly" indexing. "On the fly" indexing means that Exchange automatically indexes the values contained in object properties as objects are added to the database. Good indexes are a critical factor in allowing users to execute very fast searches despite specifying complex criteria. For instance, looking through a large Information Store for all instances of documents authored by "Tony Redmond" which mention "Exchange server" in the title would take a long time unless the author and title attributes (or rather, MAPI properties) are indexed in some way.

The closest thing a MAPI message store has to the concept of a join across tables is a "multi-valued property". If a document stored in a public folder has multiple authors (properties) there is no need to create separate tables for document and author and join them just to see who the different authors are. This is another example of a major difference between Exchange server and other Microsoft database implementations.

Even if Exchange does not use a relational database that's no good reason not to learn from the lessons learnt from many years of relational database use in high-availability production environments. The best example of this in practice is the transaction rollback and roll-forward capabilities built into the Exchange Information Store, plus the elimination of the requirement to halt the server to perform backup operations. Using the correct tools (those that know about the capabilities of the Information Store) backups can be taken while users are accessing the Information Store, a characteristic of high-end transaction systems.

Over the long term the plan of record for Exchange is to move from its own database to Microsoft's strategic object store, or OFS, a common storage model supported by Windows NT and applications. Microsoft people are careful to emphasize that the transition to OFS will follow a conservative approach and should be seamless to end users and administrators alike.

5.3.2 Exchange databases

The two most important data structures requiring regular and consistent backups are the Information Store and the Directory Store. The Information Store, containing public and private folders and other system-wide objects, is split between two separate database files called PRIV.EDB and PUB.EDB whose default location is the \MDBDATA directory. The Directory Store, holding information about recipients, other servers, and connectors, is held in the DIR.EDB file located in the \DSADATA directory. The table below summarizes the major databases and associated files used by the Information and Directory Stores.

Table 5.2 *Exchange databases*

Database/File	Purpose	Default location
PRIV.EDB	Private Information Store. Location for all private folders.	\EXCHSRVR\MDBDATA
PUB.EDB	Public Information Store. Location for all public folders.	\EXCHSRVR\MDBDATA
DIR.EDB	Directory Store	\EXCHSRVR\DSADATA
EDB.LOG	The current transaction log file for the Information Store. A separate EBD.LOG is maintained for Directory Store transactions.	\EXCHSRVR\MDBDATA
EDBn.LOG	Backup transaction log file	\EXCHSRVR\MDBDATA
EDB.CHK	Database checkpoint file	\EXCHSRVR\MDBDATA
RES1.LOG	Reservation log file used to hold transactions if disk space is exhausted.	\EXCHSRVR\MDBDATA
RES2.LOG	Reservation log file used to hold transactions if disk space is exhausted.	\EXCHSRVR\MDBDATA

While the \MDBDATA directory is the default location for the Information Stores there is no requirement for you to keep the stores together in the one directory. Keeping everything together is neat and tidy but it concentrates disk activity to a single place, a situation that will eventually lead to the disk being swamped with I/O requests generated by database activity. If you want to optimize disk performance it's best to keep the two stores apart on separate drives, and also to move the log files (more on log files shortly) to another drive.

On all but the smallest or disk-starved servers the Performance Optimizer will recommend that the various files used by the Information Stores and Directory are spread across all available disks. It is logical to spread the I/O load generated by any application across all available disk spindles, and the approach taken by the Performance Optimizer is in line with well-established system management practices. Keeping everything on one or two disks will deliver satisfactory performance for small user populations, but performance will steadily degenerate as the number of users grow or the demands created by the users increase. You can amend the location of any of the files through the "Database Paths" property page (see Figure 5.6). Note that Exchange does not support the placing of its database files on a networked drive. All databases must stored on local disks. There is no support to place the databases on DFS-serviced drives.

Figure 5.6
Amending
database paths

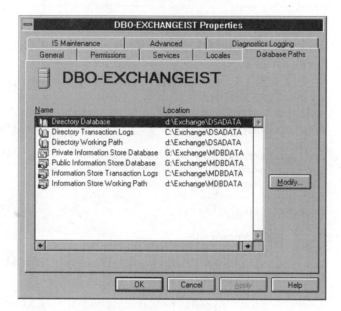

5.3.3   Upgrading to the unlimited store

Essentially the same file format and database schema is used for the store in Exchange V5.0 and V5.5. As we'll discuss later on, the database engine is different, but the change here did not affect the ability of the store to become larger than before. Internally, an Exchange database is constructed in a set of pages, each of which is 4096 bytes. Each page has a unique number that is stored in the high 3 bytes in the page. In Exchange V4.0 and V5.0 22 of the 24 bits in these 3 bytes were used for the page number, limiting the number of pages to 2^{22} pages. Multiplying 4,194,304 pages by 4,096 bytes comes to 17,179,869,184 bytes and sets the previous (and infamous) 16GB limit. The Exchange engineers changed the size of the page pointer to increase the size of the store, which is now only limited by the amount of disk space a server's I/O subsystem can handle (the theoretical limit is around 16TB). Microsoft has already tested stores of up to 300GB, a size that is frightening because it's still one single large file. The 16GB limit remains for the standard edition of Exchange. You must install the Enterprise edition to utilize the unlimited store. The Information Store service writes an entry into the application event to indicate whether the unlimited store is available whenever the service is started.

Available disk space is now the obvious limitation for the store. The ability to back up massive stores and, in the case of necessity, to perform a restore, is less obvious but still represents a very real limit. If a database grows to 100GB and the backup device is only able to write data out at 4GB/hour backup times become an unrealistic 25 hours! Restore times are normally longer than backups, and contemplating a 25-hour plus restore operation is enough to convince even the most macho system administrator that they need to invest money in the fastest backup device they can lay their hands on. Exchange V5.5 is faster at backup and restore operations than any other version, but its speed cannot be revealed if backup devices are slow.

Some people have questioned the wisdom of using a single large database to hold the contents of all mailboxes on a server and wonder why Exchange doesn't split its store across multiple physical files. After all, the Information Store is already logically divided across two databases, PRIV.EDB and PUB.EDB, so couldn't a store be split itself? The quoted advantages of such an approach include easier and faster backup and restore operations plus the ability to divide the I/O load generated by the store across multiple disk spindles or controllers. However, these advantages must be weighed against the almost inevitable loss of single instance storage. It's easy to see how single instance storage works when rows are updated in a single database as new messages arrive. Now think how a message must be delivered if mailboxes are divided across multiple databases. Is the loss of single instance storage enough to convince the engineers to rethink their storage mechanism? It'll certainly be interesting to monitor how this debate develops as very large stores are built over the next couple of years.

5.3.4   Major characteristics of the Exchange database model

Exchange is designed to meet the ACID (Atomicity, Consistency, Isolation, and Durability) test for database transaction integrity. Exchange uses transaction logs to achieve atomicity. In other words, if a system interruption occurs the Information Store will attempt to apply any outstanding transactions when the Information Store service is restarted. Outstanding transactions are those that are held in logs but have not been committed to the database. Incomplete transactions, which may be found at the end of a log, are ignored. They are normally the result of transactions that are in progress when the system outage occurred.

The process of transaction log checking and committal occurs automatically every time the Exchange databases are started, and because all transactions are applied to the database in a controlled manner a great degree of consistency is achieved. The multithreaded nature of the Exchange Information Store service allows database operations to proceed as if each transaction was the only one currently active. Although many different user-initiated operations may be proceeding simultaneously, each is isolated and dealt with on an individual basis. Finally, the separation of transactions into logs and database, and the ability to conduct automatic transaction recoveries after system outages gives Exchange a high degree of durability.

Moving away from the requirements ACID test, let's focus on some of the major characteristics of the Exchange databases. These are:

- Single-instance storage
- Atomic transaction model
- High throughput
- Designed for on-line $7 \times 24 \times 365$ operation

5.3.5   The single instance storage model

Unlike PC LAN-based electronic mail systems, which typically create copies of messages for each recipient, Exchange server uses a single instance or shared message storage model. In other words, a single copy of a message is stored on a server and all of the users who have access to the message hold a database pointer to the single copy within their folders. The shared message model is well tried and tested and has been in use with other messaging systems, such as DIGITAL's ALL-IN-1 server, since the early 1980s. There are a number of obvious advantages in a shared message model. For instance:

- Disk activity is reduced because the system doesn't have to create, delete and otherwise manage multiple physical copies of messages. This is especially important when message content is large and the average size of messages is increasing. Think of the disk activity required to create 100 copies of a 100K message. Now scale it up for 250 copies of a message (perhaps one circulated to everyone in a site) that has a very large attachment.

- Disk space required for message data is much reduced because no redundant copies are created.

- Because of the two previous points the shared message model is the most scaleable type of electronic file cabinet or message container.

Apart from making effective use of storage, the single instance model also effectively increases the maximum size of the Information

Store from the physical limit imposed by available disk space upwards towards a higher logical plateau. Charging the size of a message (and its attachments) against the quota of each recipient does this. If a 10K message is sent to three recipients, then 10K is physically occupied in the store but 30K is logically occupied (10K for each recipient). Depending on how many users share messages and how long users retain those messages (in a single instance model the number of sharers inevitably decreases over time), the commonality factor allows the logical limit of the store to expand many times.

The effectiveness of the single instance storage model is highly dependent on the way users interact with the system. For example, if users keep the majority of messages a higher storage ratio will be attained than in a situation where users tend to delete messages shortly after they are read.

While it is very scaleable and uses least disk space a shared message model imposes some additional load on the mechanism used to register messages. The database engine used in the Information Store is responsible for tracking user access to messages through pointers, and must make sure that "hanging" pointers, or pointers belonging to messages no longer wanted by any user on the system, are removed. The actual message contents are removed from the system once all the relevant users have deleted their pointers, in effect reducing the count of interested parties to zero. The database must also track the movement of messages from location to location within the overall filing system, and all this must be done quickly and without being obvious to users.

Note that the single message model only extends to the confines of a single server and does not span a site. A message sent to several users in the same site will be delivered to the Private Information Store on each server connected to by the recipients of the message. It is therefore possible to have several copies of a message within a single site, albeit only on the servers whose users have an interest in the message.

The unlimited space available in the Private Information Store is enough to allocate huge mailboxes to large user populations. The amount of available disk space imposes a physical limit, but this is misleading in one sense because the total logical total size of messages is increased by the commonality imposed by the single message model. As explained earlier, if ten users access a single 100K message, a megabyte is logically allocated and shared between the users. The physical increase in the database is just 100K, give or take the additional bytes uscd to store message attributes. Thus, on a system with a high degree of message commonality the Information Store can apparently hold more than you might think.

Practically speaking, the size of the disk array where the Information Store is located restrains the number of clients that can be supported by an individual server. Administrators have to decide whether they want to support hundreds of clients with small space allocations, or to install the necessary disks to provide a larger allocation to a smaller number of clients. The very practical nature of this trade-off makes some of the claims for massive numbers of supported clients for specific server configurations only valuable in a theoretical sense. There's no point in being able to connect 10,000 clients to a quad-CPU server if they're only allowed to store 50 messages each, unless of course this is precisely the type of system you really want to operate!

Another way of looking at the number of clients that can be supported by a system is to consider the assertion that the majority of computers running Windows NT today have far less than 20GB of disk storage in total, let alone 20GB to dedicate to the Information Store. If this is true, and I have seen no evidence to the contrary, then available hardware resources will be the first limit to overcome. Another factor that must be considered is that after a server has been in use for some time a set of power users might each occupy a gigabyte or more of disk space, considerably limiting the user population that can be supported by that server. There's two answer to all these issues: either install another server into the site (and transfer some of the users to the new server), or upgrade the disk subsystem on the existing server.

It's been interesting to see just how quickly people can fill a store and approach the limit. Servers that support communities migrating from other mail systems are more affected than those used by people who start from scratch. The reason for this is simple. When you migrate data (old messages) it is loaded and stored in user mailboxes in the Private Information Store. Afterwards the migrated data is like a stone around the neck of the store. It seldom reduces in size quickly (how many users do you know to clean out old messages on a regular basis?) and reduces the space available for new messages, forcing the store to fill available disk space much faster than if the store held no migrated data. Compacting the store with the ESEUTIL utility (see the discussion from page 364 onwards) makes little difference because the old information is so static, so all the system administrator can do is look at a store racing to fill disks up.

An orderly shutdown of the Information Store service is conducted if an Exchange V4.0 or V5.0 server reaches the 16GB limit (or, indeed, a V5.5 standard edition server). Orderly means that outstanding transactions are committed before the service halts. After the shutdown users will discover that their connections to the store are disconnected. The store will have to be shrunk before the service can restart, so the immediate course of action is to run EDBUTIL. Before this can happen you have to find enough disk space to create the temporary database created during the compaction process. Finding a spare 10 or 20GB of disks is not always easy!

As soon as EDBUTIL is finished a smaller store should be available. At this stage the Information Store service can be restarted and any outstanding transactions will be committed. Users can access their mailboxes, but before this happens you should transfer a number of users (a hundred or so for a start) to another server in the site to reduce the chances that the store will hit the limit again in the near future. If possible, transfer the mailboxes to a brand new server, otherwise select the server in the site with the largest amount of free space to grow into. Better still, upgrade at least one server in the site to Exchange V5.5 and transfer the mailboxes to that server. Then, over time, upgrade all of the other servers to V5.5. The Information Store can still exhaust available disk space, but after V5.5 is installed you only have to worry about physical limits and not those imposed by the software.

5.3.6   Measuring the effect of single instance storage

A Performance Monitor counter (MSExchangeIS Single Instance Ratio) can be used to report the average number of references to each message. This figure gives some idea of how effective single instance storage is for a particular server. The higher the figure the more effective single instance storage is.

A low ratio (anything below 2) invariably means that a lot of messages are delivered off-server. Low ratios are also commonly seen inside widely distributed organizations with many sites and servers. For example, inside DIGITAL I have seen ratios ranging from 1.6 to 2.1, and I have been told of servers used inside Microsoft whose ratio hovers around 1.1!

Measuring servers that are newly commissioned will produce different results to servers that have been in use for a year or more, where the contents of the Information Store have had time to settle down and mature. Messages enjoy the highest possible single instance ratio immediately they are delivered. To see what I mean, use Performance Monitor to capture figures for the number of messages delivered per second and the number of message recipients per second. Divide the recipients by the number of messages to determine the ratio for newly delivered messages. Soon after delivery, the ratio begins to reduce as recipients delete the pointers to their copies, but after a while the ratio stabilizes as messages are filed away into folders for long term storage. On some systems, users are very good at keeping messages and there is far too much long term storage.

Ensuring that all members of a workgroup or department have mailboxes on the same server will maximize single instance storage. Once people are distributed across multiple servers some amount of data duplication is incurred in addition to the extra network traffic required transporting messages between servers. Moving users between servers usually reduces the ratio as messages are transferred from one server to another.

Another way of measuring the single instance storage ratio is to total the sizes of mailboxes reported by the Exchange administration program and then compare that figure to the physical size of the private store. The "Save Window Contents" feature in the Exchange administration program allows data to be captured in CSV format, which can then be analyzed using a spreadsheet like Excel (see the discussion on Save Windows Content feature later on in this chapter).

Even if servers don't make effective use of the single instance storage model it's important to realize that the model brings additional benefits outside storage. The most obvious benefit is the decrease in the I/O operations required when messages are delivered to mailboxes, or when users delete messages. In the first instance a single message is added to the store followed by updates to multiple tables, in the second a pointer is removed from a table. In both cases the amount of I/O generated is much less than if separate copies were maintained per mailbox.

5.3.7   Tables inside the Private Information Store

The internal structure (or database schema) of the Private Information Store is very similar to a classic relational database and is built from a set of tables, the most important being:

- The mailbox table. One row is used to hold properties for each mailbox on a server.

- The folders table. One row is used for each folder in every mailbox.

- The message table. One row is used to hold content for every message.

- The attachments table. One row is used to hold content for every attachment.

- A set of message/folder tables. A separate table is built for every folder.

The Public and Directory Stores are also organized in tables. However, because everyone uses e-mail the private store deserves a higher level of attention.

Pointers link one table to another within the store. This interaction forms the basis of single instance storage and delivers a unified view of store contents to clients. The processing that takes place when a mailbox is opened and a message selected for reading illustrates how pointers tie the tables together. Let's examine what happens when an Outlook client opens a mailbox. Sample data is used to illustrate the explanation, and the data has been simplified for clarity.

Table 5.3   *Sample contents of the Folders table*

Folder ID	Folder name	Folder owner	Count of items	Count of new items	Parent Folder ID
10445872	Inbox	TonyR	195	10	0
10427756	Magazine	TonyR	15	0	0
10427558	Articles	TonyR	29	1	10427756
10475586	Newsflash	TonyR	5	0	10427756
10479514	Deleted Items	TonyR	85	0	0
10475866	Inbox	BillR	100	15	0
10557660	Deleted Items	BillR	16	0	0

Exchange supports nested folders. In other words, folders can contain sub-folders. Clients construct a tree view of folders by reading data from the Folders table. Each folder is allocated a unique identifier (a GUID), and sub-folders are recognized by having a parent folder ID. The sample data in Table 5.3 shows that the "Articles" and "Newsflash" folders are both sub-folders of the "Magazine" folder. The count of new items is used by clients to bold folder names and provides a visual sign to users that they should review the contents of the folder.

A separate table is used to hold header information (all of which are MAPI properties) for each folder. Maintaining header information in a separate table allows each folder to have its own sort order. The alternative is to request data from a much larger table, albeit sorted and indexed. The scheme used by Exchange minimizes the data transmitted between client and server when clients wish to display information about a folder. For example, when an Outlook client builds the folder list it proceeds to display header information from the currently selected folder (usually the inbox) in the right hand pane in its main window. Fetching data similar to that shown in Table 5.4 from the appropriate message/folder table performs this operation.

Table 5.4   *Contents of a Message/Folder table*

From	Subject	Received	Size	Priority	Attachment Flag	Message ID
Don Vickers	Florida holidays	01-Sep-1997	4KB	Normal	No	42955955
Elaine Sharp	Clustering Exchange	29-Sep-1997	3KB	High	Yes	48538505
Ken Ewert	Exchange V5.5	30-Sep-1997	948 bytes	Low	No	42552902
Kieran McCorry	Customer trip report	30-Sep-1997	22KB	Normal	No	49919495
Administration	New cafeteria	01-Oct-1997	2KB	Normal	No	41848910

The message ID (another GUID) links a row in a message/folder table to message content. When a user selects an item and double-clicks to read it, the message ID is used to fetch content from the message table and the combination of header and content information is used to populate the form used to display the complete message.

Table 5.5   *Contents of the message table*

Message ID	To	Message Body Content	Usage Count	Attachment Pointer
48538505	Tony Redmond	Exchange V5.5 now supports *clusters*...	4	
49919495	Tony Redmond	On my recent trip I visited...	25	66456776
52195995	Kieran McCorry	Has anyone tried the new fish dish in...	1	

Table 5.5 illustrates the type of data we might find in the message table. The message body content is stored in Rich Text Format (RTF). If attachments exist for the message a pointer will be found in the attachment pointer field and the client can use this to retrieve the attachment(s). The usage count field is very important. It contains the count of folders that contain a reference to a message. The count decrements over time as users delete their references to messages. When the usage count reaches zero the row is removed from the table.

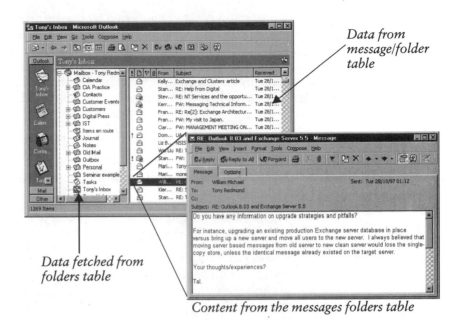

Figure 5.7
How the user interface accesses database tables

Data from message/folder table

Data fetched from folders table

Content from the messages folders table

From reading this brief description of some of the tables held inside the private store it's obvious that clients retrieve data from a number of tables when a message is read. Clients are not aware of all the work because the store masks the entire interaction through the appropriate service provider. Thus, the MAPI service provider assumes the responsibility of fetching the necessary information whenever Outlook reads a message, as illustrated in Figure 5.7.

5.3.8   Atomic transactions

The atomic transaction model used by Exchange means that any messaging operation (add, change, delete) is composed of a set of clearly defined steps which collectively form a transaction. Exchange will never commit a transaction to the database unless all steps have been followed, meaning that theoretically it is impossible to write invalid information, for example a corrupt message structure, into the database. All transactions are actually written twice; first into a transaction log, and then into the database. The write-ahead logging scheme is a common implementation in high-end database systems (for example, SQL/Server or Oracle) and helps Exchange achieve its goal of high transactional throughput. The Exchange database is capable of handling a very heavy transaction load and is not going to be the limiting factor in scaling systems. Other items such as the physical size of the store or the lack of clustering are more likely to throttle back the number of users you'll connect to a server.

No transaction is ever committed by the Information Store unless it is complete. All transactions are comprised of a series of multiple operations against different tables. Now that you understand the basic structure of the tables in the Private Information Store an outline of just what happens in a complete transaction can be built. Let's review what happens when a new message is delivered to four users on a server.

1.   The mailbox table is read to verify that mailboxes exist for the users.

2.   The folders table is read to locate the rows for the inboxes for each user.

3.   The message table is updated with a new row containing the body for the new message.

4.   The message/folder table for each of the four inbox folders is updated with header information for the new message. Pointers link the message/folder tables with the row in the message table.

5.   If attachments exist rows are written into the attachments table.

6.   The inbox row in the folders table for each user is updated with the count of new messages and the total count of items in the folder.

7.   The transaction is complete and is written into the current transaction log (EDB.LOG).

Client notification occurs after the transaction. MAPI clients receive an RPC notification. Other clients, like those using Outlook Web Access or POP3, need to check the inbox at intervals to find new messages.

Exchange is designed for 7 × 24-hour use, 365 days a year. There is no requirement to stop the server to perform maintenance. The database is defragmented on-line and backups can proceed with users connected and working with the server. Much of Exchange's capabilities in this area come from the transaction model that's used, as we'll see below.

5.3.9   Interaction between transaction log files and the Information Store

Each transaction (a new message, for example) for the Information Store is recorded into a transaction log file called EDB.LOG as well as an area in memory. This avoids the need to constantly write information directly into the databases, which would generate large amounts of I/O for the system to process. Updates are deferred, gathered together into efficient "chunks", and then committed from memory to the databases when time and system demand allows. Read operations are handled differently to writes. Instead of log files, Exchange uses a series of buffers (the Information Store buffer pool, or IS buffers) maintained in memory to hold details of recent transactions. When a client requests information from the store, the database engine first checks its buffers and attempts to find the data there. If the data cannot be found in the buffers, an I/O is generated to retrieve it from the database.

When a user sends a message a transaction is begun. For example, to write a new message into the store we have to:

- Begin the transaction
- Insert the message content into the Messages table
- Insert any attachments into the Attachments table
- Insert the header information into the Inbox folder table for each recipient
- Update the Folders table to increment the number of messages and unread count for the Inbox folder for each recipient
- End the transaction
- Commit the transaction to the database

When complete the transaction is written into a queue in memory and also into the current transaction log.

Figure 5.8
Transactions for the Information Store

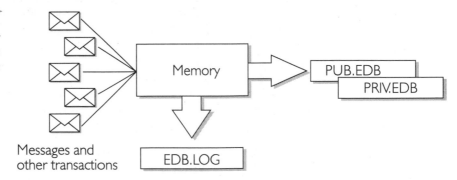

When system load allows, the database engine reviews transaction logs to discover items that have not yet been committed to the store. As items are committed, the database checkpoint (maintained in a file called EDB.CHK) is moved forward, so that it always indicates the last successfully-committed transaction. Checksums are used to ensure that the data read from the transaction log is the same as that written into the database. The system of dual-writes means that the database can never be considered to be totally up to date until the transactions in the log file are taken into consideration. If no users are using the system for more than five minutes it is fairly safe to assume that all the transactions in memory will have been written into the database. You can "force" transactions to be written in two ways. First, by using a backup utility to take a full online backup of the Information Store. We'll discuss this operation in more detail later on. The second way is to close down the Information Store service. In both cases it's important to check the system event log to ensure that no error messages have been recorded to indicate problems occurred when the database was updated.

Because transactions are preserved in log files a physical record of the processing that has been performed for the database is always available. The transaction log files can be used in the event of a problem with the Information Store when transactions can be rolled back from the logs into a recovered copy of the Information Store to bring it up to date. For this reason it is dangerous to delete transaction logs without first knowing that their contents will no longer be required.

EDB.LOG is the name of the current or active log file. In other words, EDB.LOG is the file that details of new message transactions are written into. A new log file is created after approximately 5 megabytes of transactions (message operations) have been recorded. When the current transaction log is filled up EDB.LOG is renamed and a new file is created. A single message with one or multiple large attachments can span log files. For example, a message with a 6MB PowerPoint attachment might have the message content and first 2MB of the attachment in one log file, and the last 4MB of the attachment in the next. On a very busy server many thousand transactions flow through the log files daily and it's not uncommon to see hundreds of log files created during the working day. Apart from normal messaging activity, log file creation also comes about when large amounts of data are imported into the Information Store, notably when the migration wizard is running.

Each log file is allocated 5MB immediately it is created[4]. This step ensures that all transactions can be written without running the risk of suddenly exhausting disk space. If File Manager reports that a transaction log is anything other than 5MB (5,242,880 bytes) it is likely that the log is corrupt. In this case you should check the event log for errors, stop Exchange, take a backup, and then restart Exchange services. All the log files should have been erased and the database brought fully up to date. Check too that the disk where the log files are stored hasn't encountered any hardware problems.

4.　Early base levels of Exchange used 1MB log files. The 5MB size is used in all versions since Exchange V4.0. The ever increasing size of messages once prompted me to ask some Exchange engineers why the log file size had not increased further, so that more messages could be stored in each log. The answer was that the overhead incurred to create a new log file was so small that it wasn't worthwhile changing the size now.

Figure 5.9
*Files in the
MDBDATA
directory*

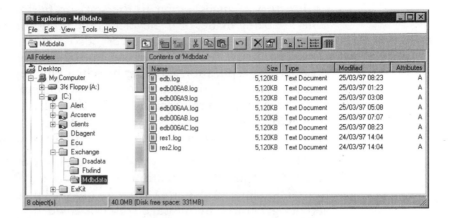

Transaction logs are "tied" to their database in two ways. First, a unique identifier is written into each log file as it is created. The identifier (sometimes referred to as a signature) in a log must match that in a database before the log can be used to recover transactions. The Information Store service checks log files when the service starts up, and if the identifiers do not match the service terminates with error 530 or 531. Second, the path to the directory where the databases are located is hardcoded in the log file, so logs "know" where its targets are when the time comes for recovery. Interestingly, databases do not know where their transaction logs are, but Exchange can fetch this information from the system registry. Identifiers and other interesting information can be found by running the ESEUTIL utility with the /ML (SP1 onwards) switch to dump the header information from EDB.LOG.

Log files are numbered sequentially using a file-naming scheme of EDBxxxxx.LOG, where xxxxx is a hexadecimal number from 0 to f). After a couple of days of moderate messaging activity on a small server you end up with EDB00001.LOG, EDB00002.LOG, and so on (Figure 5.9). Depending on the number of messages generated on your system and the frequency that backups are taken it's common to find that the \MDBDATA directory stores ten or more log files.

Systems that engage in heavy replication activity turn over transaction log files quickly, as can those that handle large incoming NNTP news feeds. Replication (see page 294) is the process by which servers update each other about the contents of public folders or directory information. Servers can be very "chatty" if allowed to do so. For example, servers will send each other frequent snapshots of the public folder hierarchy, just to make sure that everyone knows where all the different public folders are located. The snapshot information is circulated in the form of messages, and these must be logged in exactly the same manner as interpersonal mail. Systems handling large numbers of directory changes, either in the start-up period when many additions are being made, or if they act as the point for directory information dissemination to other servers also generate lots of work for transaction logs. You can cut down on the number of messages being produced by replication activities by scheduling replication to occur at particular times of the day rather than whenever Exchange feels the need. Scheduling in this manner also reduces traffic through whatever connectors you use to link sites together, thus preventing any potential delays for interpersonal mail that might otherwise creep in.

The \MDBDATA directory is the default location for both the transaction logs and the Information Store. It's more efficient to move the transaction logs away onto a separate physical disk so that the disk I/O activity generated by message traffic is divided across multiple spindles. From a performance perspective some anecdotal evidence exists that transaction logs should be placed on a FAT-formatted drive. The assertion normally being that:

1.   Fewer overheads are incurred by the system when writing files to FAT drives than NTFS.

2.   Transactions are written in a sequential manner to the end of the logs. Thus, no sophisticated indexing or file structure management is required.

Your mileage may vary! In all cases, FAT or NTFS, make sure that the disk where the transaction logs are created has plenty of disk space. The very best thing is to allocate transaction logs to their own disk as it is very embarrassing for a system administrator if the Information Store suddenly shuts down because no more space exists to create a new log.

The EDB.CHK file acts as a database checkpoint. Its function is to track the transaction log files and make sure that they are synchronized with the databases. When the Exchange database engine starts up it checks EDB.CHK to determine the current status of the database and takes whatever action is required to enable the database to commence operations in a stable state. At this stage any transactions in the log file that have not been recorded are applied. If you are ever unfortunate enough to suffer a major corruption of the database you may be able to get up and running fast by restoring a recent backup and starting the server. If possible, all of the transactions that occurred since the backup was taken will be applied and the database restored to full working order. Of course, this type of restoration depends on good quality backups being taken at regular intervals.

When backups are taken the transaction log files are automatically purged by the backup utility. The process of purging basically zeroizes

EDB.LOG, to ready the log to accept new transactions. All other log files (EDB00001.LOG and so on) are deleted and the disk space returned to the system. Cleaning up log files in this manner is logical because the database has been written to backup media in a consistent state with all outstanding transactions applied before the backup is allowed to begin, so there is no longer any need for the log files to be retained. As the log files can take up quite a bit of disk space the automatic deletion is welcome, but if you want to be cautious you can always back the log files up before commencing the database backup.

Two special log files, called RES1.LOG and RES2.LOG (the reservation logs) are used by the system to ensure that there's enough disk space available for Exchange to complete operations in a controlled manner should the computer run out of disk space. In other words, if disk space is exhausted, Exchange can use the space allocated to RES1.LOG and RES2.LOG to complete whatever it needs to do before halting.

In any case where Exchange discovers that there isn't enough space available on a disk to create a new transaction log an error condition is generated which causes the Information Store to shut down, hopefully in a graceful manner. When a shutdown occurs it is possible that transactions are waiting in memory to be written to a transaction log and of course this isn't possible because there's no disk space. The current log files are also full, which is the reason why the error condition has occurred in the first place. Exchange resolves the immediate problem, what to do with the in-memory transactions, by writing them first to RES1.LOG and then, if necessary, to continue writing on into RES2.LOG. It's not altogether clear to me what happens if there is more than 10MB of transactions waiting in memory, but it's perhaps fair to assume that such a volume and quantity of transaction data would never be held in memory. After all transactions are flushed into the reservation logs Exchange will shut down.

5.3.10 Source of transactions

Interpersonal messages are the most obvious source of transactions, but in an Exchange environment many other types of messages are generated on a daily basis. Remember that public folder and directory information is replicated over the mail system, and these messages contribute to the overall message volume experienced by a system. If you look at the various sources that typically generate messages you'll find:

- Interpersonal messages
- Directory replication

- Public folder hierarchy replication
- Public folder contents replication
- System attendant messages
- The migration wizard
- The Move Mailbox option

A busy system that supports hundreds of active users can easily generate 40 log files each day (200MB). Large systems that support thousands of users generate even more log files, and I have known systems that generate 2GB of logs daily. This is an excellent reason to place the transaction logs on a disk where space is unlikely to be exhausted. It's a good idea to throttle back the replication schedule for public folders and the directory to wider intervals than the defaults (every 15 minutes) just to reduce the message load on a system. Extending replication intervals also relieves some of the demand for disk space for transaction logs (unless you use circular logging) and helps to prevent any embarrassing episodes such as the Exchange services being shut down prematurely because there's no more disk space available to create any more transaction logs.

5.3.11   Circular logging

Circular logging is the default transaction logging behaviour implemented when Exchange is installed. Circular logging is a scheme where transaction logs are "re-used" after the transactions that they contain have been committed into the database.

Circular logging is supported for both the Directory and Information Store (the same setting applies to both the Private and Public Information Stores). Exchange is instructed to use or ignore circular logging through the advanced property page for a server (Figure 5.10). The affected services (Directory and Information Store) need to be stopped and restarted before a new setting becomes active.

Systems running circular logging normally use between one to four transaction logs, but under times of heavy messaging activity it is possible to see a few more logs created. If you experience this situation, for example during a period when you use the migration wizard to import lots of user data onto a server, be assured that the logging scheme will return to its normal situation the next time the Exchange services are started (normally following a system reboot).

Using circular logging means that Exchange is less likely to run out of disk space, but you will lose the capability to replay transactions from a log should it be necessary to recover a database after a hard disk crash. All you can do is restore the last available backup tape and go forward from that point.

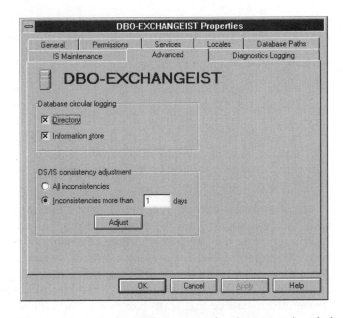

Figure 5.10
*Enabling
circular logging*

The logic behind making circular logging the default is simple. A lot of Exchange servers will be low-end systems designed to support small populations, and there may not be a skilled system administrator around to look after disk space. Getting rid of administrative tasks in this environment makes a lot of sense, but if you expect to run a high-end server that supports hundreds or even thousands of users it's madness to consider using circular logging. Circular logging is really only useful for test servers or those that only host connectors. Any situation where mailboxes or public folders are hosted on a server should immediately end any interest in circular logging.

If you implement circular logging it's important to note that incremental and differential backups of the Exchange databases are not possible. When circular logging is enabled full backups must always be taken. Because circular logging negates the additional protection afforded through the logging mechanism you may want to take file-level backups of the Exchange databases as well as online backups. File-level backups are only possible when all the Exchange services are halted.

The Information Store is designed for use in a situation where regular and frequent backups are taken. Good system management practices dictate that any system supporting important data should be backed up, and in view of these points it is hard to make a case to use circular logging instead of the system of creating and erasing multiple log files. After all, provided you take backups you shouldn't run into situations where the disk space occupied by the transaction log files is excessive and causes problems for the system.

5.3.12 Checkpoint files

During normal operation transactions in the in-memory queue are written into the Private or Public Information Store when the system is a little quieter and messaging activity is not so intense. The database checkpoint file (EDB.CHK) keeps track of the buffers that have been written out of memory and into the database, so Exchange knows at any time what transactions remain in the logs and are waiting to be written into the database.

As mentioned earlier, you can "force" Exchange to flush transactions out of memory and write them to the database by stopping the Exchange Information Store service. This happens when a system is shut down gracefully. If a system is forced to stop abruptly, for example when a power outage occurs, it is more than likely that some transactions will not have been written into the database. However, the transactions will be in a transaction log and can be replayed when the Information Store service is restarted after the system is powered up again.

During a recovery operation, the data in the checkpoint file determines which transactions are replayed, basically by comparing a time-stamp in the checkpoint file against the transactions in the log files. If the transactions in the logs are newer than the time-stamp in the checkpoint file they will be replayed and written into the Information Store. Note that replayed transactions don't just include new messages and attachments; they can also include deletions and updates. If many transactions remain to be replayed when a system powers up then the Information Store update can take a few minutes to complete.

Whereas it is convenient to have EDB.CHK available before beginning a recovery operation it is not a pre-requisite. If Exchange finds that the checkpoint file is not available it will read the transaction logs to determine the point at which transactions had been committed to the database.

5.3.13 Soft and hard database recoveries

Replaying transactions after a power outage or similar failure is referred to as a "soft recovery". The database is available and just needs to be updated from the transaction logs. Each time the Information Store service is started the checkpoint stored in EDB.CHK is consulted to see whether any transactions remain outstanding. If EDB.CHK is not present the store reviews the contents of the current transaction log, EDB.LOG, to verify that everything's normal. Outstanding transactions are replayed and committed to the store before clients are allowed to connect. The time taken to recover a log depends on the speed of the CPU and disk I/O subsystem, but even the smallest system should be able to recover logs at better than 1 log/minute.

Figure 5.11 A soft recovery is recorded in the Event Log

	Date	Time	Source	Category	Event	User	Computer
	12/02/98	11:52:50	MSExchange Pop3	Configuration	11507	N/A	DBO-EXCHANGEIST
	12/02/98	11:52:48	MSExchangeIS Priv	General	1000	N/A	DBO-EXCHANGEIST
	12/02/98	11:52:48	MSExchange IMAP	Configuration	11500	N/A	DBO-EXCHANGEIST
	12/02/98	11:52:48	MSExchange NNTF	Configuration	11500	N/A	DBO-EXCHANGEIST
	12/02/98	11:52:47	MSExchange Pop3	Configuration	11502	N/A	DBO-EXCHANGEIST
	12/02/98	11:52:43	MSExchangeIS Pub	General	1217	N/A	DBO-EXCHANGEIST
	12/02/98	11:52:43	MSExchangeIS Priv	General	1217	N/A	DBO-EXCHANGEIST
	12/02/98	11:52:40	ESE97	Logging/Recover	110	N/A	DBO-EXCHANGEIST
	12/02/98	11:52:37	ESE97	Logging/Recover	109	N/A	DBO-EXCHANGEIST
	12/02/98	11:52:24	ESE97	Logging/Recover	109	N/A	DBO-EXCHANGEIST
	12/02/98	11:52:07	ESE97	Logging/Recover	109	N/A	DBO-EXCHANGEIST
	12/02/98	11:51:44	ESE97	Logging/Recover	109	N/A	DBO-EXCHANGEIST
	12/02/98	11:51:24	MSExchangeMTA	Resource	9156	N/A	DBO-EXCHANGEIST
	12/02/98	11:51:24	MSExchangeMTA	X.400 Service	4282	N/A	DBO-EXCHANGEIST
	12/02/98	11:51:13	ESE97	Logging/Recover	109	N/A	DBO-EXCHANGEIST
	12/02/98	11:51:11	ESE97	Logging/Recover	108	N/A	DBO-EXCHANGEIST
	12/02/98	11:51:08	ESE97	General	100	N/A	DBO-EXCHANGEIST
	12/02/98	11:51:08	ESE97	System Paramete	191	N/A	DBO-EXCHANGEIST
	12/02/98	11:49:37	ScanMail Exchange	None	4	N/A	DBO-EXCHANGEIST
	12/02/98	11:49:31	MSExchange NNTF	Internet News Ser	13001	N/A	DBO-EXCHANGEIST
	12/02/98	11:48:52	MSExchange NNTF	Internet News Ser	13036	N/A	DBO-EXCHANGEIST
	12/02/98	11:45:57	MSExchangeSA	General	5000	N/A	DBO-EXCHANGEIST
	12/02/98	11:43:42	MSExchangeMTA	Resource	9156	N/A	DBO-EXCHANGEIST

Figure 5.11 illustrates a complete cycle of events in a soft recovery caused when the Information Store process halted after the disk where its transaction logs exhausted available space. The events to look for are 108 (the recovery process is initialized), 109 (a log file is replayed), and 110 (the recovery process successfully completes). Five separate log files are replayed to recover transactions, something that indicates that the server was under a certain degree of load when the information store service terminated. Because the number of log files replayed reflects the number of outstanding transactions that had not been committed when the information store service halted, the general rule is that the more log files replayed, the higher load the server was under. Note that the data in the outstanding log files might have been generated through the arrival of several large messages in quick succession, so it's entirely possible that a number of logs represent a period of peak activity in an otherwise quiet day.

Figure 5.12 illustrates the detail of the 109 event that records the replaying of a specific transaction log.

Figure 5.12
*Detail from the
event log*

Soft recovery is an automatic process that requires no human intervention. Many system administrators are probably unaware that it has
happened, although evidence exists if you care to look for it in the
application event log. Note that exactly the same approach is taken to
replay logs for the Directory Store.

Hard recoveries need human intervention. Exchange cannot deal
with a hard disk failure on its own. After the disk is replaced you need
to restore the last full backup plus any incremental backups that have
occurred since, which contain the transaction logs generated since the
last backup. I normally recommend that installations take a full
backup each night to avoid the requirement for multiple restore operations. When the store and all transaction logs have been restored you
can restart the Information Store service, which then begins to replay
the transactions in the logs.

Logs are replayed sequentially so it's essential to restore all of the
logs. Missing logs terminate the replay procedure and not all transactions will be recovered. If restoring from an offline backup (one taken
with the Information Store service stopped), the ISINTEG utility should
be run with the -PATCH switch to adjust the GUIDs used inside the store.
This step is performed before the Information Store service is started.
There is no need to run ISINTEG if a restore is performed from an
online backup. After all the transactions are replayed the Information
Store should be in the state when the failure occurred, or as close as can
be achieved given the availability of data in the transaction logs. Take a
full backup after all the logs have replayed so that you have a backup

containing all the transactions. All of this can take several hours so clearly you should protect yourself by putting the Information Store on a RAID-5 array, preferably one that supports hot-swappable disks.

When dealing with hard recovery situations you'll have to restore all the last full backup of the database that you have available plus all the transaction logs that have been created since. When the Information Store service starts up it will recognize that the database is out of date and proceed to replay transactions from the logs. Because hard recoveries rely on the availability of log files it is obvious that if the log files are on the same drive as the database you run the risk that corruption will affect both database and log files and so make any recovery exercise impossible. This is a pretty fundamental reason for you to separate the database and transaction logs on any Exchange server intended for production work. Indeed, most large production systems place transaction logs on their own separate disk.

The use of a relational database and the way folders, messages, headers, and attachments are stored within the database makes backup and restore operations a very interesting exercise, even if you never considered the way that transactions are stored in memory, log files, and the database.

5.3.14   Exhausting available disk space

As a general rule for all messaging servers you can never have too much disk space, just in case. I have seen instances where the Information Store exhausts the space available on a disk. In most cases the problem occurred on systems that have been on the threshold of available disk space for some time, meaning that it was always a struggle to find available disk space for any application let alone one that has to manage shared files on behalf of many users. Failure to pay attention to system administration compounds this particular problem as all systems tend to accumulate files over time, albeit perhaps files that should be automatically cleaned up by the application that produced them. The reality of mail systems is that the amount of disk space used for messages can quickly mount up, so it's important that all system configurations are sized with a reasonable degree of seemingly excess disk space to allow for unplanned growth.

The most common cause for space exhaustion is when one or more users create and send messages with multiple large attachments. When messages are sent content is moved from the client to the server and Exchange attempts to add it to PRIV.EDB. If space is unavailable or becomes exhausted at this point the database will not be able to extend itself to store the new message and signal an error condition. In turn, the error causes the Information Store service to automatically shut itself down, as manual intervention is required from the system administrator. The Information Store service will also shut down if disk space is exhausted on the disk where the transaction logs are stored. The Internet Mail Service will also stop at this stage because it is dependent on the Information Store. Naturally, because the Directory Store uses the same database engine as the Information Store, a lack of disk space is equally effective at halting its operations.

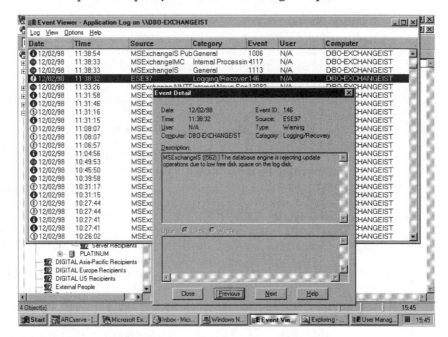

Figure 5.13 The Information Store service terminates because the transaction logs disks is full

A warning message is always sent to the Windows NT system log (see Figure 5.13) whenever the Information Store service terminates abnormally. Event 1003 indicates that the disk where the database is located is full, while Event 1113 means that the disk where the transaction logs are stored is full. Users will immediately know that a problem exists because clients will be unable to log-on to the server, in essence because the server will not be able to send details of the folders in the user's mailbox to the client due to the unavailability of the Information Store service. Possible solutions to the problem are:

- Increasing the available space on the disk where the databases are located by deleting unwanted or unnecessary files.

- Moving the databases to another disk. Other files used by Exchange (such as the transaction logs) or other applications might also be moved at the same time.

- Replacing the original disk with a larger disk. You'll need to restore a full backup of the original disk to the new disk before operations can begin again.

- Using circular logging for the Information and Directory Stores. This is not recommended on any production-level server.

In most instances the first solution is both the most immediate and pragmatic, although I would take immediate steps to consider the other two solutions over the long term. If the disk holding the Information Store runs out of space on one occasion it is likely to do so again in the future.

Some administrators like to keep a large but empty file with an appropriate name like JUNK.DAT on the disk that holds the Information Store. Typically, the file is between 200 and 500MB in size. If the disk starts to run out of space it's a simple matter of deleting the empty file to free space immediately, which keeps the service up and running. Later on, when you have time to consider what the best course of action might be, you can start to swap disks or files around out of hours. The Information Store and Directory services aren't the only services that will shut down gracefully when disk space is exhausted. The Exchange MTA will stop working if it detects that there is less than 10MB available on the disk where its working directory (\MTA-DATA) is located. The MTA working directory is prone to accumulate many small (and some not so small) files on systems that are under heavy load, and it may take the MTA a lot of time to clear those files. The performance characteristics of Exchange give most weight to user response. In other words, any request for service from a user will be attended to first before Exchange will proceed to process any outstanding background work.

Large MTA queues are often observed on heavily loaded systems, and those queues translate into files in the \MTADATA directory. The solution to the problem is simple—clear out some files on the same disk as the \MTADATA directory and restart the MTA service. Do not delete files in the \MTADATA directory without knowing what you are doing as this will inevitably result in a loss of messages.

A small bug in Exchange V5.5 means that the size of a database (Private, Public, or Directory) is not reported accurately by the Windows NT Explorer. In fact, the only way to be absolutely certain of the size of a database is to stop Exchange and look at the file sizes. The bug is scheduled to be fixed in SP1, but until then system administrators need to ignore the file size reported by the Explorer and concentrate instead on the actual free space available on the disk volumes where the databases are located.

5.3.15   Limiting user disk space

You can limit the amount of space a user can occupy within a store, and if you have the opportunity to set limits and so encourage good habits within users by forcing respect for disk space from the start, you should seize your chance quickly. Users who are allowed free range will run rampant and occupy as much space as they can, a good proportion of which is unlikely to store messages and other data of great strategic importance.

Limits (defined in kilobytes) are set on an individual user mailbox (Figure 5.14) or on the Private Information Store as a whole, in which case the same limits are set for all user mailboxes. Three different limits can be specified. The limit set by checking the first box determines the point at which a user will start to receive warning messages generated by the system attendant. The second check box determines the point at which a user is stopped from sending or saving any more messages.

Figure 5.14
Mailbox storage limits

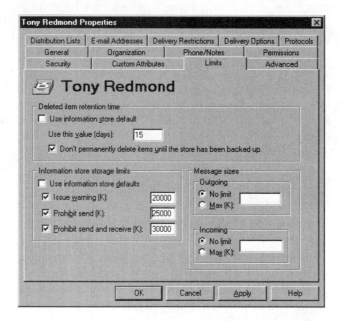

Up to Exchange V5.5, users who exceeded their quota are not able to create new messages, but they'll still be able to receive incoming messages. It was therefore possible for a user to grow the space they occupy within the Private Information Store after restrictions have been placed on them. Conceivably, it is quite possible for a mailbox to continue receiving new messages until the Information Store exhausts all available disk space and stops, something that wouldn't be easy to explain to managers.

Exchange V5.5 addresses the problem by introducing a new "Prohibit send and receive" checkbox. Messages that arrive at mailboxes that exceed this limit are rejected by the Information Store and a non-delivery notification is dispatched to the sender.

Interestingly, if a user exceeds their quota in the Private Information Store, Exchange will also stop them putting anything into a public folder. No doubt this restriction is in place to stop "smart" users getting around quotas by moving messages and other objects out of their private space into the public area. The only way a user can resolve the problem of an exceeded quota is to delete messages (and make sure that the Deleted Items folder is emptied) until they go under their quota or to have the system administrator give them a temporary increase in quota. Temporary increases in user quotas usually become permanent unless the system administrator is vigilant! Note that items in the deleted items cache do not count against a user's quota.

While I encourage you to impose limitations on the space allocated to individual users, make sure that reasonable amounts are allocated. There is nothing so boring or time-consuming for a system administrator as having to answer a continuous stream of requests for increases in allocations. Apart from taking up time to respond to each request, the requirement to ask for more space just to send a few more messages (for this is what it will appear in the mind of users) will cause irritation and reduce overall satisfaction levels with the system.

Figure 5.15
Listing who's
using what in
the store

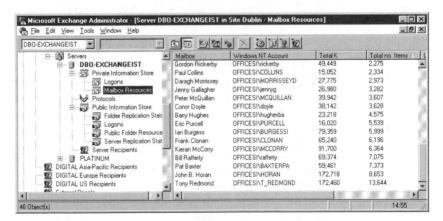

A proactive approach to system management dictates that every step should be taken to ensure that unpleasant surprises don't occur. Running out of disk space counts as one of the surprises no system manager wants to have, so you should perform manual or automated checks each morning to ensure that:

- The disk(s) where the Information Stores are located have sufficient free disk space. Start to get worried when less than 250MB is available on a system serving less than 100 users, and increase the free space threshold by 1MB for each user thereafter. Systems serving very heavy mail users may want to increase the warning threshold for free disk space. Remember that a single large message can chew up several megabytes very easily.

- Backups have been taken and that old transaction logs for the Information Store have been deleted.

- No user has exceeded their disk space allocation. If someone has they may be unaware of the fact so take steps to contact them and then help the user free up some space. It's a good idea to review mailbox quotas against usage on a regular basis, perhaps once a week. Figure 5.15 shows how the administration program can be used to quickly focus on the users who occupy most space. In one respect, because they occupy so many resources, these people are enemies of system administrators. On the other hand, people who use a lot of space might be the administrators themselves or senior managers, who always seem to have more information to store than anyone else.

Every night the System Attendant checks for people who have exceeded mailbox quotas. If someone is discovered to be approaching their quota a message is sent inform them that they may not be able to send any more messages. You can instruct the System Attendant to perform checks and send warning messages many times each day, if you think this is necessary (or you want to really bug the users).

Once the System Attendant determines that someone has actually exceeded their quota a stop is placed on any further send operations. People will be able to create new messages, and save them to their local disk, but they won't be able to send them until they free some of their allocated quota.

Figure 5.16 is a sample message sent by the System Attendant to a user who has exceeded their mailbox quota. There are two problems here. First, the message comes from an anonymous "System Administrator". Most users don't know who their system administrator is, so the end result is a call to the Help Desk. It would be nice to be able to customize the originator and short-circuit the process. In the same way, it is not possible to customize the text of the message to provide more information or give different instructions. For example, some installations never want people to use Personal Folders (PST files), yet the advice to do so is solemnly delivered in the message. I guess it's another opportunity for the Help Desk to have a heart-to-heart discussion with users.

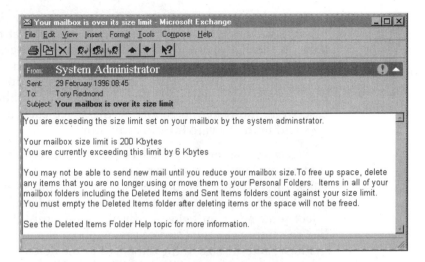

Figure 5.16 *A nice message from the System Attendant*

5.3.16 Freeing space inside the Information Store

There is no automatic way for a system administrator to free space by deleting obsolete messages from the Public or Private Information Store. Space is freed within the Information Store when messages are deleted. However, as we'll discuss later on, the space is returned to the Information Store and not to the Windows NT file system. Recovering file space from the Information Store requires additional steps, discussed on page 369.

Deletion is a two-stage process as the messages are first moved into the "Deleted Items" folder, and then only permanently removed from the store when the contents of this folder are purged. Users can set their working conditions from Exchange clients to purge the contents of the "Deleted Items" folder automatically when they exit. This is one of the choices available from the dialog displayed from the Options entry on the Tools menu. Purging the "Deleted Items" folder is not default behavior for the client, so users must change the setting manually. As pointed out before, setting default values for options like this is a very good reason to use the Exchange Setup Editor utility before client installations start.

It's somewhat surprising to find that there are no formal system housekeeping facilities to produce reports of the number of messages each user has in their mailbox and the amount of space these messages occupy. This is a pity, because reports of space utilization taken on a regular basis (for example, every month) provide invaluable data for use when planning the growth of a messaging system. You can, of course, use the Administration program to view the contents of the Private Information Store, and note the data presented there (Figure 5.15).

An undocumented feature of Exchange V5.5 makes the collection of statistics much easier than before. If you look at the options available on the File menu of the administration program you'll see the new "Save Window Contents" option. The option is active whenever the right hand pane contains data that can be reported. Good examples include information about mailboxes or public folders. In this case we're interested in reporting the space each user mailbox occupies within the Private Information Store.

Select a server and expand its contents to reveal the Private Information Store. Mailbox resources are one of the properties you can view. Click on "Mailbox Resources" and the administration program will now list data for all mailboxes in the right hand pane. You may need to select some addition fields for display to capture the data you want. I like to capture the total size of the mailbox, the number of items in the mailbox, and the size of the data held in the deleted items cache. When you're ready, select the File.Save Windows Contents option. A file save dialog will then be displayed, as shown in Figure 5.17.

Figure 5.17
Using the Save Windows Contents option to capture data about mailboxes

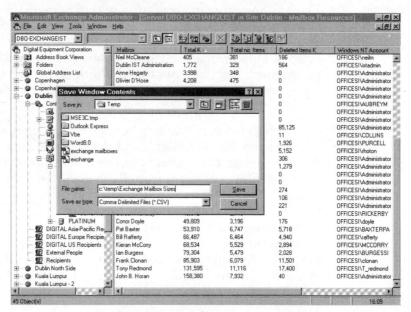

The data is saved in CSV (comma separated value) format. Many office applications, including Microsoft Excel and Access, are capable of importing a CSV file and manipulating its contents to create reports. Excel does an excellent job for quick reports, while Access is better if you want to do anything very complex. Figure 5.18 shows Excel being used to manipulate the data captured in Figure 5.17.

Figure 5.18
*Manipulating
user data with
Excel*

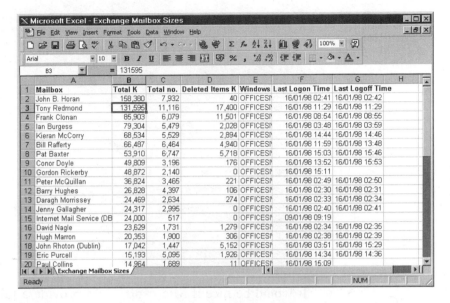

Reports on various aspects of Exchange can be obtained if you buy third-party add-on products. The best reporting utility for Exchange server I have seen to date being Crystal Reports for Exchange. A copy of Crystal Reports for Exchange is included in the Exchange Resource Kit.

5.3.17 Cleaning up mailboxes

Unlike the Public Information Store, where administrators can set expiry limits on folders, messages held in the Private Information Store never expire (they remain in the mailbox as long as the user wishes to keep them there).

Administrators can intervene and clean up a user's mailbox without their permission by using the "Clean Mailbox" option on the Tools menu (see Figure 5.19), but the sudden disappearance of a whole pile of messages from their mailbox is not likely to make a user very happy. It's probably better to reserve the clean mailbox option for the most intransigent users and restrain yourself to warnings for the others, unless of course you follow the "I know best" school of thought for system administration. It's not immediately obvious from the user interface or documentation, but you can select multiple mailboxes for the "Clean Mailbox" option to process with the CTRL/Click and SHIFT/Click key combinations to either select a range of mailboxes or a set of individually chosen mailboxes.

Figure 5.19 *The Clean Mailbox option*

It would be nice if Microsoft could provide a fully supported and integrated system housekeeping procedure to clean up user mailboxes on a regular basis. For example, a useful procedure would remove all messages over 30 days old from specified folders such as "Sent Items" as well as deleting the messages waiting to be removed from the "Deleted Items" folder.

A mailbox cleanup agent is part of the Exchange Resource Kit (see the section in chapter 11), and this add-on provides the missing functionality. The utility has evolved over a number of versions. All the known issues have been ironed out now and V1.9 or later of the Mailbox Cleanup Agent provides an effective way to exercise some control over user mailboxes. Unfortunately, the fact that the program is not part of the official kit is enough to make most system administrators think twice about running the utility.

If limits are not in place and mailboxes are left to take care of themselves it is quite a normal state of affairs to find that the Private Information Store grows gradually over time as messages accumulate. When people hit storage limits they are forced to exercise a form of triage over the contents of their mailbox, deciding what should be kept and what can go. Once they've cleaned up their mailbox users can proceed to create and send some more messages.

5.3.18 The space used to store messages

How much space within the Information Store is required for each message? The answer depends on the size of the cover note, the number of message attributes (addressees and so on), and the attachments.

I conducted some very unscientific experiments with a selection of sample messages to see what type of storage requirements was reported for each message type. The results of my experiments are shown in Table 5.6. Be aware that your mileage will vary depending on the types of sample messages you create and the size of attachments you include with messages, but the basic results should be pretty well the same.

Aside from the actual content of messages, the overall size is greatly affected by the number of people messages are addressed to. Inside DIGITAL it is common to receive messages (some generated automatically) dispatched to hundreds of people. These messages are usually 50K or greater in size, and it's disappointing to open such a message to find that the actual content is no more than a couple of lines of text.

Table 5.6   *Storage requirements for different types of messages*

Message type and contents	Size of message reported by client
Simple text message containing 65 words sent to 1 mailbox	610 bytes
Simple text message with 1 page cover note sent to 8 mailboxes	3K
Compound message sent to 5 mailboxes with 1 page cover note, 79 KB Word attachment, and 18 KB Excel attachment	100K
Compound message sent to 10 mailboxes composed of 5 page cover note and 1.004 MB PowerPoint attachment	1,104K

The shared message model used by Exchange means that all mailboxes on a server share a common copy of a message and its contents. The mailbox resources data reported by Exchange only indicate how much space within the Information Store is occupied by messages that individual users have a pointer to within their mailbox. This is quite a different figure to the amount of space within the Information Store that the messages for an individual user solely occupy. In other words, if a user sends a 1MB message to 10 other users, the next time you look at mailbox resources you will see that all of the users associated with the message, including the originator, have had an apparent increase of 1MB in the resources they occupy within the store. This isn't actually the case as just a single 1MB chunk is used to store the message. The commonality within the store achieved by sharing the single 1MB message with 10 other users just contributes to a form of optical illusion.

Any individual user will have a mixture of these message types within their mailbox, and it's probable that the average user will have more small messages than large. If you assume that the space reported by a client provides the more accurate of the two sets of figures, we can use them to create a rough forecast of the space likely to be occupied by any particular type of user.

For example, let's take a user with a mixed set of messages:

Number and type of message	Average size	Total space required
300 simple messages	600 bytes	180K
100 multi-addressee 1 page messages	3K	300K
75 compound messages	100K	7,500K
25 large messages	1000K	25,000K

In this instance the total requirement is calculated as 34,980K or almost 35 megabytes. This figure contains a considerable safety margin as a good proportion of the messages are likely to be shared with other users on the same server, unless the predominant communications pattern is off-server to other sites or messaging systems. Even the simplest messages described in our model (those sent to a single addressee) start off by being shared, so the 35 megabytes of apparent storage might well be less than 20 or 25 in reality. This figure is in line with other shared-model messaging systems that support PC clients where reasonable planning rates for "average" users dictate 20-30 megabytes for personal messages. People who send lots of mail, of course, are quite another matter and I have known some capable of easily occupying entire disks (over an extended period of one or two years) with the volume of messages they generate.

5.4   Managing the Public Information Store

Users who have been granted permission to create, write to or edit information held in public folders control the contents of the Public Information Store, the repository for all public folders on a server. Public folders are always created in the Public Information Store on the home server of the user mailbox who creates the new folder.

5.4.1   Issues to consider in planning public folders

Amongst the issues to consider when planning the implementation of the Public Information Store you should:

- Pay attention to the information that's being placed into public folders. Public folders should not be used as a dumping ground for all and sundry.

- Restrict the permission to create top level folders in the public folder hierarchy to a limited group of users. It's a recipe for confused storage if everyone is allowed to create folders at the top of the hierarchy. Top level folders represent the entry point to the public folder hierarchy so it's essential that a well-designed structure be instituted at this point. Users who have the permission to create top level folders are able to allocate permissions on the folders they create. In this respect, users with permissions to create top level folders can be regarded as guardians or administrators of the Public Information Store.

- Ensure that data is removed from public folders as soon as it is no longer valuable. You can arrange for data in public folders to expire after a set period, and this is a convenient feature where data held in certain folders has a regular and predictable life. However, it would be difficult to impose expiration times on public folders used by people as a point of reference. For instance, it is inappropriate to store documents describing a company's personnel policies and procedures in a public folder with a 60-day expiry. It is very appropriate to set a 60 day expiration limit on a public folder that stores bulletins relating to training courses or other events with a readily determinable life-span.

If you have lots of information that must be made available in public folders you might consider:

- Establishing a server to use as host for a set of "archive" public folders. Data can be transferred from the "live" set of folders to the archive server after a set period, for instance, every month, perhaps using some automated rules. The traffic to a set of archive public folders should be lighter than its live counterpart so you can factor this into network traffic planning.

- Splitting public folders over a set of servers rather than one specific server. Remember to ensure that everyone who needs access to the public folders has good network links. If you are moving public folders from one server to another you should also make sure that any affinities are transferred as well.

5.4.2   Public folder favorites

From a user perspective having hundreds, perhaps thousands, of public folders to choose from represents a rich vein of knowledge whose contents may hold the answers to many questions. But so much data is hard to track and it's easy to miss important items that are added to a public folder used for particular purposes, such as a folder used for project reports or new sales opportunities. As systems age the public folder hierarchy tends to become less structured and organized unless great attention is paid to the elimination of folders no longer required and careful control on the creation of new folders for possibly unneeded purposes. Duplication and wholesale proliferation of folders always happens if control is not applied, leading to a situation where public folder anarchy exists and information becomes impossible to find. The fact that the public folder hierarchy is automatically replicated to all servers within an organization means that control must only lapse on one server before unwanted folders are created and shown to users. It's hard to stop the system administrator of any individual server losing control, but the designers of Exchange have helped to get around the potential information overload by establishing the concept of "Favorite" public folders.

Each user maintains a unique list of favorite public folders. A public folder is included in a user's list by marking it with the clients "File.Add to Favorites" option. When a public folder is marked in this way Exchange knows that it must monitor the contents of the public folder for any new items that are added. New items are indicated by the maintenance of a folder unread count displayed in the same way as the presence of new messages are indicated for the Inbox folder (see Figure 5.20) A quick visual scan of the Favorites section shows any folder where something new is stored.

Figure 5.20
Public folder favorites

Public folder favorites are a very useful concept. The more folders are added, the more valuable the concept becomes, so users should be encouraged to use favorites to organize their own hierarchy of selected folders from the time they begin using Exchange.

5.4.3   Setting time expiration limits

Public folders experience different usage characteristics to private folders, and even within the range of public folders different usage patterns are seen. Consider the following points:

- Folders are often created for a specific purpose and receive considerable activity for a period of time. For example, a folder might be created to hold documents relating to a particular project. While the project is active the folder is in daily use, but once the project finishes a danger exists that the folder loses relevance but remains in situ, clogging the store up with unwanted material.

- Larger items tend to be stored in public folders. Messages flow in and out of private folders, and messages are usually quite small in comparison to the documents and other items placed in public folders. Thus, a small number of items can occupy a considerable amount of space within the store.

- Public folders may be maintained by a number of different people. Not all of the maintainers will be efficient when it comes to controlling the content of "their" folders. Some folders will be dynamic and only contain up-to-date information. Others will be stagnant and hold data that was valuable some time ago but is totally unnecessary today.

- Some public folders participate in NNTP news feeds. Items in newsgroups tend to expire quickly, usually after 7 days or so. It makes sense to apply the same age limits to the equivalent public folders, as shown in Figure 5.21.

Apart from a steadily growing demand for disk space, the larger the Public Information Store, the slower maintenance operations like backups will be. You should therefore consider whether age limits should be placed on any or every public folder. Age limits dictate how long material will be retained in a public folder. Once an item exceeds the age limit the system attendant process automatically removes it, normally once a day.

By default no age limit is applied for public folders. You can specify an age limit that applies to all folders created in a Public Information Store or set specific age limits on certain folders. For example, if you have a public folder used to distribute training announcements it's probable that you won't want to keep announcements that are more than sixty days old. Age limits can also be set on replicas of foreign public folders maintained in a store. The precedence rule is as follows:

1.   If set, the limit on a folder is complied with.

2.   If a general age limit is set for all public folders in a Public Information Store it is applied to remaining folders.

3.   If no limits are in place within a Public Information Store but an age limit applies for all replicas of a public folder, that limit will be applied but only for the folder in question.

Figure 5.21 *Age limits for Public Folders*

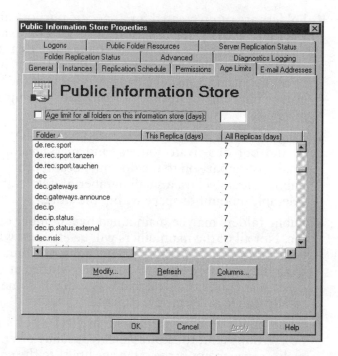

Setting a general age limit for new public folders is a good idea. Try 90 or 120 days as a starting point. If no one complains then this limit can remain as a default value. It will take some time before the default limit can take effect so in the interim you can analyze the public folders that are actually in use to try and determine what content is actually stored and how long it needs to be kept. The next stage is then to decide whether specific age limits need to be set on certain folders. Before you set any limits you should consult with the folder's owner as they may understand the effect of the limit on the folder's contents better than you.

5.4.4 Displaying the space used by public folders

A quick glance at the EXCHSRVR\MDBDATA directory reveals the physical size of the Public Information Store, but knowing what's actually occupying the space is more important. For this reason it's a good idea to review what public folders are located on a server and how much space they occupy on a regular basis.

In Exchange V4.0 the only way to check public folder resources was to display the properties of the Public Information Store and then look at the data through a small scroll box. This is OK when you have a small number of folders, but less so after the hierarchy expands with use. Exchange V5.0 allows the properties of the Public Information

Store to be expanded using the tree view in the administration program (Figure 5.22). In this instance, the resources are shown in the right hand pane. Exchange V5.5 improves matters through the "Save Window Contents" option, which can capture the contents of the right hand pane into a CSV file for later analysis.

Figure 5.22
*Displaying
Public Folder
resources*

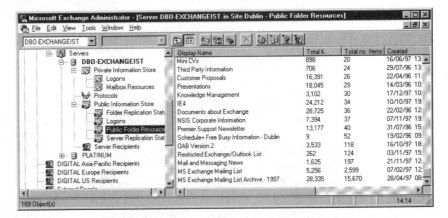

If you've set time expiration limits on some or all public folders the resources used will change all the time. The folders you need to pay attention to are those that consistently increase in terms of number of items and the space occupied. You should try and determine why the folder keeps on growing and see whether you can restrict the growth in any way. Sometimes the answer is simple. For example, the folder is used as a repository for documentation belonging to an ongoing project. You'd expect that this folder would grow as the project progresses and then can be cleaned out after the project finishes. Folders assigned to hold information about products can be expected to occupy a lot of space (graphics occupy much more space than plain text), but perhaps only hold a relatively few items.

It is good system management practice to know what's going on in a server. Reviewing the number of items in public folders and the space they occupy gives you essential system management data and helps you tune your system more effectively. Once you know more about the contents of public folders than indicated by just the raw size of the Information Store you can make decisions at the folder level. For instance, public folders experiencing lots of activity should be located on servers capable of handling the traffic whereas folders storing very large items should be allocated to servers with lots of free disk space.

5.4.5   Virus checking

Any Exchange message can include an embedded object. Embedded executables are an obvious source of potential contamination from viruses, whether included in messages received from outside the organization or those perhaps unwittingly passed on by people working inside. Most users are now aware of the problems posed by executable-based viruses and system administrators have taken steps to address the problem. For example, some sites disable floppy drives while most have implemented some sort of automatic virus checking for system memory and .EXE and .DLL files whenever PCs are booted.

The first document-transmitted virus appeared in the Word for Windows "Prank" macro in 1995. Recognizable by the presence of the "Payload" macro, the virus worked by inserting itself into NORMAL.DOT, the default Word for Windows document template. The virus is activated and infects a PC whenever a document containing its macros was opened. The virus is irritating but harmless, and easy to clean up. All it ever did was display a dialog box, but so much more damage could have been wreaked if the virus's author had included some more malevolent instructions. Word for Windows' macro language, WordBasic, is capable of including calls to Windows API functions and file operations which can, in turn, inflict grave damage on user files. For instance, it's easy to write a macro that will automatically delete all sorts of important system files whenever the macro is invoked.

Many Windows products have their own macro language, and the majority of these languages are already pretty capable of making the same type of damaging system calls. Exactly the same effect as the "Prank" macro could be created with an Excel macro written in Visual Basic for Applications, or in a WordPerfect for Windows macro. Macro languages are being improved all the time. They're also being made easier so vicious macros can be written without too much programming expertise. These developments make system administrators nervous because users don't seem to exercise the same level of care and attention when they deal with documents or spreadsheets. The lack of care when opening documents is perhaps natural because so many documents flow around a messaging system, but it means that viruses created as document macros spread rapidly once they've been introduced into an installation. As such document viruses are a major challenge for messaging system administrators, especially so in the case of systems like Exchange, which place a high degree of importance in information sharing through distributed document repositories such as public folders.

What can you do to defeat the best efforts of document virus creators? There are three basic approaches:

1.   *PC-centric*. Most of the commercial virus checking packages now available have been updated to include checks for known document viruses. In general, checking is performed whenever a document is opened. This approach is effective providing the virus checker is installed and used on every PC. It's essential that the virus checker is kept up to date to ensure that new viruses can be detected soon after they are generally encountered, and arrangements must be made to distribute new releases of the virus checker to all PCs, including notebooks. Traditional PC-based virus checkers focus on DOS files, so they're not much good in catching infected files stored in a PST, OST, or Exchange mailbox, although the virus checkers will be able to deal with infected files if a scan is made before files are imported into an Exchange container. The best option is to select a virus checker that is able to deal with Exchange data structures as well as traditional DOS devices and file shares. One such example is Thunderbyte for Exchange[5].

2.   *Server-centric*. Some virus checkers can be run on a server to scan all the documents held in a file system or electronic file cabinet. In the case of Exchange server you need a virus checker that understands the internals of the public and Private Information Stores, as otherwise it won't be able to check documents stored therein. Checking documents held in user directories is fine, but the real danger exists from documents that are stored and distributed via the messaging system. The first commercial server-based virus checker to support Exchange (Cheyenne Anti-Virus Agent[6] for Microsoft Exchange Server) appeared in October 1996. The Anti-Virus agent works with Cheyenne's InocuLAN 4 for Windows NT to detect and cure viruses in documents attached to Exchange messages. The Agent is implemented as a Windows NT service and works in real-time to detect and cure infected files attached to messages as they enter an Exchange server (from all sources). ScanMail[7] for Microsoft Exchange is another interesting product (from Trend Micro Inc.) which takes much the same approach to solving the problem by scanning for viruses as they arrive on an Exchange server. Other products similar in concept and implementation that I have not used include McAfee Group-

shield[8] and Dr. Solomon's Anti-Virus Toolkit[9] for Exchange. All store-based virus checkers incur a performance penalty for the system. Your mileage will vary, but expect to use between 5 and 10% of the CPU to check messages as they arrive in mailboxes.

3.   *Firewall-centric.* This approach uses a virus checker to check the contents of SMTP messages as they arrive into a messaging environment. MIMESweeper from Content Technologies Limited[10] is a good example of the type. While it's true that the majority of viruses will arise from external sources, especially the Internet, only scanning SMTP messages will ignore messages arriving from other sources. For example, messages delivered from other X.400 MTAs, or even messages generated by internal Exchange users who have (unwittingly) attached a document containing a virus.

Using a combination of the approaches described above provides a more resilient solution. The combination of server- and firewall-based checking is a good team, and should catch the vast majority of any viruses that come into view. There's lots of activity in this area and I expect other products to appear. Before making any choice you should take the time to search the Web to see if you can find better options to pursue.

One mistake with a virus can be very expensive. Disinfecting a system, especially a large networked system, will take a lot of time and effort and it's probable that the system will be unavailable to users while the viruses are being eliminated. Be proactive and ensure that your system is protected!

5.5   Public Folder Replication

Most system administrators who work with messaging systems are familiar with the concept of individual interpersonal arriving at and being dispatched from the system. This is the basic currency of any messaging system and there is nothing particularly new in the way that Exchange deals with interpersonal messages. Replication, on the other hand, is a somewhat more uncommon technique when applied to messaging systems. The major proponent of replication to this point in time has been Lotus Notes, where replication is used as the basic method to distribute information to servers throughout a network.

---

8.   See http://www.nai.com
9.   See http://www.drsolomon.com
10.   See http://www.integralis.com

Replication means that data is copied from an originating computer to other computers according to some predefined rules. In an Exchange environment replication occurs in two main areas:

1.   Directory entries are replicated to servers that share a common directory. Entries are made, amended or deleted by the server responsible for user accounts or other entries held in the directory. Once the entry is made, the "owning" server communicates with the other servers in the network to update them with the new information. Replication is performed with a special type of encoded messages, and it can take anything from five minutes to several hours before the process of replicating an update to all servers in an Exchange network is accomplished. Latency in data updates is an inherent fact when replication is concerned. The speed that replication takes place depends on how many servers are in the network, the connections between those computers, and the other traffic that flows between the servers. Directory entries do not impose a great strain on the network because the size of the messages containing replication data is quite small.

2.   Objects placed in public folders can be replicated to copies of the folders held on other Exchange servers so that users connecting to those servers can access the information held in the folders as quickly as possible. Like directory entries, public folders are associated with an originating server, the location where objects contained in the folder are managed. When a decision is made to share the contents of a public folder with another server, a replica of the public folder is created on the "foreign" server. Thereafter, whenever a change is made to the original public folder the amendments will be automatically replicated to the replica folders on all the servers that maintain an interest in the folder. Replication is performed by a background process and does not happen immediately.

Updates can also be applied to objects via replica folders. In this case, the changed data is replicated back to the original source folder and the update applied there. However, the distributed nature of Exchange which underpins the ability for updates to be applied in this manner opens up the question of what happens when updates arrive concurrently for the same object from two different replicas. We'll discuss what actually happens when multiple users make changes to a replicated document later in this chapter.

Directory entries are all similar in size, so the traffic pattern and network load generated by directory replication is predictable and should not change dramatically over time. Occasionally there may be major changes in the directory, for example, when a large group of people using a new server joins the network, but in most organizations the volume of directory changes is low, ranging from 1% to 5% of the user population per week.

Replication of public folders and directory entries is only possible when servers are connected together; thus, each system participating in replication must be licensed to run one of the available connectors.

5.5.1   Replication philosophy

The design philosophy behind public folders means that everyone's view of a public folder is the same no matter where the folder is physically located. No one instance of a public folder is the master copy. All instances of a public folder enjoy the same standing within the organization. Users are automatically directed to the replica with the lowest connection cost. Even within a site it can make sense to distribute replicas of heavily used folders to each server so that user requests don't have to travel off the local server.

Locating data close to users is the major advantage delivered by a system of distributed, replicated public folders. However, there are some disadvantages. For example, it is possible to put a copy of a public folder on a laptop's hard disk for use in off-line mode. Changes in folder contents are replicated down to the copy on the PC when it is connected to the network using the normal folder synchronization process. Exchange's logical behavior in treating every copy of a folder in exactly the same peer-to-peer manner can lead to an interesting side-effect if the laptop's owner deletes objects from the folder, thinking of course that the copy of the folder on their PC is totally under their control. Eventually the deletions made in a copy of a public folder are enforced in every location where the folder has been replicated to, potentially becoming a rather unpleasant surprise for the other readers of the folder. The lesson here is to be careful in allocating delete permission to public folders. Unless people really need to have delete permission they shouldn't receive it, just in case, following the old system administration principle that sometimes users need to be protected from themselves.

The way you must approach balancing public folders across servers is another interesting side effect of how public folders have been implemented. It's common to find that public folders begin life on one server just because the folder's owner happens to have their mailbox on that server. An assessment of whether that server is the most appropriate location for the folder is not performed, so you can end up with an array of popular, high-traffic folders on a server that's already struggling to keep up with the demands of normal messaging or other applications.

To move a public folder from a server you must first create a new folder replica on the target server and then wait until the contents of the folder are replicated to the target server. Replication may take some time to complete, especially over slow links or when the folder contains many megabytes of information. Once replication is complete you can remove the original public folder by removing it from local Public Information Store. Use the "Instances" property page for the Public Information Store to remove a public folder from a store. You will not be able to remove a folder in this manner if only one instance of the folder is available. Use an appropriately permissioned client to delete a single instance of a public folder.

After an instance is marked for removal Exchange will delete the contents of the folder from the Information Store and direct any future client connect requests for the folder to whatever replica is currently available at the lowest (network) cost.

5.5.2 Network traffic generated by public folder replication

Objects stored in public folders are highly unpredictable in terms of size and content and no assessment can be given as to the traffic and network load generated by the replication of a public folder until its content and usage pattern are analyzed within a specific production environment. Instead, some broad guidelines can be given and taken into account when designating the owning server for public folders. For example:

- Public folders used as document repositories may not have many updates, but the size of the objects held in the repository can span an enormous range. PowerPoint presentations equipped with highly graphic pictures, OLE-enabled worksheets and documents, and perhaps even a set of speaker notes can quickly occupy 10 megabytes. Word for Windows files, such as those used to hold the content for this book, are normally smaller, unless screen captures and other bitmap images are featured. Excel worksheets tend to be smaller again but swiftly grow when some graphs are included. Remember too that the basic unit of replication is the item or document, and not a page, section or field where a change was made. For these reasons it's a good idea to make smaller subsets of objects available whenever possible. Store chapters of a document rather than putting everything into a single file.

- Replicating a large object can saturate a network link for several minutes and hold up more urgent message traffic. With this in mind I think that it's important not to make too many changes to documents if you want to use a public folder as a point for revision control.

- Public folders used as points for interactive information dissemination, such as electronic conferences or bulletin boards have a higher volume of changes made to folder contents but the data involved in the changes is typically smaller. Public folders that use electronic forms produce similar network loads.

- Exchange treats all replicas equally (see discussion later on in this chapter). Thus, no difference is perceived (by the Exchange replication technology) between a replica created on a server running on a low-end 80486 CPU connected by a 56 Kbps circuit and another running on a high-end server equipped with 4 Alpha CPUs that's on an ATM circuit. Look at the network link to a server before deciding to place a replica there.

- Rules defining when replication occurs can be defined for each server. If the information contained in a public folder is not especially time critical, you can place the folder on a server which only performs replication outside normal business hours. Of course, business hours are different throughout the world because of work conventions and time zones, so don't assume that replicating large documents at 6 p.m. each evening will not interfere with other, more important network traffic.

The status of the replication activity on a server can be viewed in a number of different ways. A quick way to check that everything's in order is to look at the replication status via the properties of the Public Information Store (Figure 5.23). As you can see, each folder is listed with its current synchronization status. Another easy way to check is to look at the MTA queues. If there are large numbers of messages generated from the Public Information Store queued for transfer to the bridgehead server[11] in any other site there may be a problem with the connector to that site. Using a continually active server or link monitor (see chapter 11) to check the connections to the bridgehead server in each site is a good proactive way to avoid unpleasant surprises.

---

11.   See the discussion on bridgehead servers in chapter 7.

Figure 5.23
Displaying the replication status

5.5.3 Public folder hierarchy and contents

Exchange divides public folders into the folder hierarchy and the contents of each folder. Both are maintained in PUB.EDB, the Public Information Store. Each folder is also a directory object whose properties are maintained just like any other object in the Exchange Directory. Directory entries for public folders are replicated along with the rest of the directory. Common properties include the access control list, replication schedule, and e-mail addresses for a folder. The e-mail address is often used when a public folder is subscribed to an Internet mailing list, such as msexchange@insite.co.uk, the independent mailing list used to discuss issues about Exchange. Figure 5.24 shows the e-mail addresses of the public folder used for this purpose in the Exchange organization I use.

A set of global properties for the Public Information Store is also managed by the directory. The default replication schedule and the size of replication messages are amongst the most important properties.

The public folder hierarchy is automatically replicated between every server in an organization. When a new folder is created its details are entered into the directory and sent to every other server. When clients scan the hierarchy, they may see folders that are unavailable to them. There are two reasons for this: the folder has not yet been replicated to a server they can access or a restrictive Access Control List (ACL) exists on the folder.

Figure 5.24
*Directory
attributes for a
public folder*

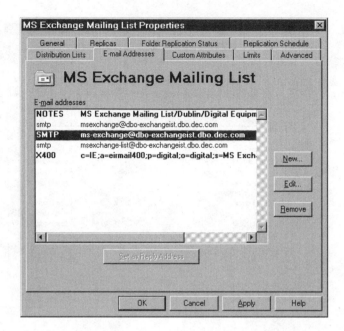

Every user mailbox is associated with a "home" Public Information Store where clients fetch information about the public folder hierarchy. In smaller servers, it is common to find that the public store is located on the same server as a user's mailbox. In larger installations dedicated public folder servers may be operated, normally to simplify the administration of public folders and to minimize the potential for replication traffic.

MAPI clients establish RPC sessions to both the private and public store at logon. Information about the hierarchy is fetched from the home server and is used to build the folder tree displayed when a client first accesses public folders. An attempt to access public folder content may result in a connection to another server. The initial attempt is made to fetch content from the home server. If a folder replica is not available, Exchange attempts to locate a replica on another server in the site. Exchange V5.0 and V5.5 support the concept of "sub-sites" where servers can be associated with geographic locations such as "New York" or "London". Figure 5.25 shows how the location is set as a property of a server. Locations are also used for routing purposes by the MTA, as explained on page 499.

If sub-sites are used, Exchange will attempt to fetch content from a server in the same location. Otherwise, another server within the site is selected at random using an algorithm called "connector modulus" (a random number), without regard to the underlying network topology. It therefore makes sense to establish sub-sites within large, distributed sites.

Figure 5.25
*Server
locations*

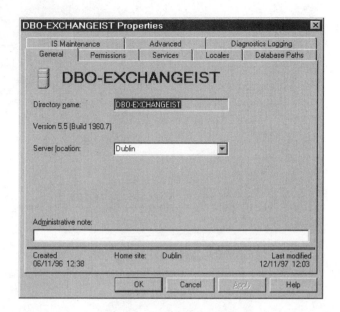

If a public folder replica is not found within the local site Exchange looks to remote sites. Affinity, a mechanism to attribute different costs to remote sites, is used to tell Exchange where to look. For example, the New York site might have an affinity cost of 10 for San Francisco and 20 for London. In this case, a client in New York will always attempt to access a public folder in San Francisco first if it cannot find content in its home site.

5.5.4   Replicas and affinities

There are two ways to distribute information in a networked environment—as shown in Figure 5.26.

The first approach is to place multiple copies of the information at different points throughout the network, basically in an effort to keep information close to users in terms of the network resources required to gain access to information. The second approach is to establish a single point of reference to hold the definitive copy of the information, perhaps supplementing the definitive copy with a number of distributed read-only copies. Exchange supports both models. Support for multiple distributed copies of information is gained through public folder replicas. Support for a single definitive point of contact is achieved through public folder affinity. In essence, public folder affinities allow local pointers to be maintained to remote folders held elsewhere on the network.

Figure 5.26 *The two methods of distributing information in public folders*

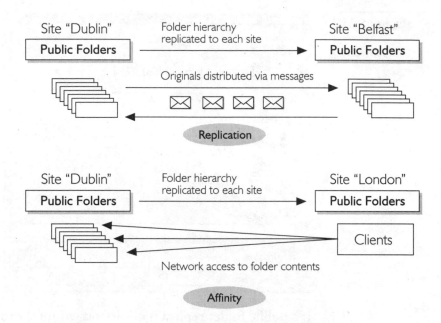

Figure 5.27 *Selecting Public Folders for replication*

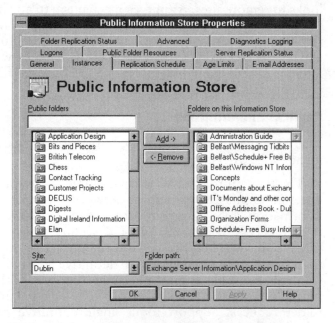

5.5.5   Key points to understand about replication

The replication mechanism is clearly an essential feature of the Public Information Store. The following events cause replication to occur:

- A new public folder is created and inserted into the hierarchy
- A new replica of an existing folder is created
- Content is added to a public folder
- Status requests
- Backfill requests

We'll get down to the details of what happens when replication occurs, but here are some key points to bear in mind:

- All replication activity is performed across the messaging infrastructure. Directory and messaging connectors must be in place before public folder replication can be successful.
- Replication happens at the item level. If a 2MB document is updated in a public folder, the whole document is replicated afterwards to all servers that hold replicas. This scheme is different to field level replication, where only the actual changed data is replicated.
- Replication activity is logged in the NT Event Log.

Replication is managed by a part of the Information Store service called the Public Folder Replication Agent (PFRA). The PFRA is composed of a number of background threads activated when the store is started. The following work is performed:

- Folder replica lists are maintained.
- Replication schedules are monitored and replication messages dispatched as determined by the schedule.
- Status messages are sent to other servers to ensure that no data is missed.
- Backfill requests are generated if data is missed.
- Backfill requests are responded to as required by other servers.

Status messages and backfill are discussed later in this chapter.

Replication is, by far, the mechanism that receives most attention in documentation and marketing material. Some of the reason for its high profile can be assigned to competitive pressure, but perhaps replication is viewed as a more high-tech option.

All the servers in a site automatically share the same directory and set of public folders. The contents of the directory are automatically replicated between servers in a site, and you only need to create replicas of public folders if you want to store them on multiple servers within a site. However, replication must always be configured when you want to share information between multiple sites.

5.5.6   Maximizing Exchange replication

Every design has its own set of advantages and disadvantages. The approach Exchange takes to replication seeks to:

- Bring data close to users by allowing them to connect to a local replica.

- Make data more available and resilient by keeping multiple copies around the organization

- Avoid excessive network traffic that would otherwise be required to pull information from single points in the network.

The last point is interesting, because the single point of contact is the model adopted by web-based information repositories. The most obvious disadvantages are:

- Maintaining several copies of information increases the data storage requirements of the system.

- Replication traffic can swamp a network if it is allowed to grow unchecked.

The art of system design is to maximize advantages and minimize disadvantages. In this respect we can take steps to ensure that each server that hosts a Public Information Store is configured with the appropriate storage, and then make sure that replication takes place at the right intervals. Folders, such as those that host interactive discussions or are used to track projects, that hold essential, time-critical information should be replicated at short intervals. On the other hand, folders that store data that doesn't change very often are replicated at long intervals. Folders that hold reference information, such as design documents, usually don't need to be replicated more than once or twice a week.

5.5.7   Affinity

The concept of public folder affinity (see the bottom part of Figure 5.26) establishes a mechanism where a single copy of a public folder is maintained in a set network location. The content of the folder is accessed there from all points of the network. Public folder affinity offers a number of potential advantages over replication that are attractive in concept:

- No network overhead is incurred to replicate new objects and changes to different sites throughout the organization

- No latency is experienced between the time when changes are made and the same data is available to everyone throughout the network

There is no need for conflict handling, and finally, information is not duplicated in different locations.

Public folder affinity does not happen automatically. It must be configured as a property of each site so that servers know what other sites are available to handle user requests to access information contained in public folders where replicas are unavailable in their "home" site. Affinity is defined by allocating costs to other sites (Figure 5.28). The lower the cost (the range is from 1 to 100) the more a site is favored by clients seeking information. Clearly, the site with the lowest cost is always going to be accessed first.

Affinity is useful if you want to maintain a single definitive set of data rather than replicating it to several or all sites. However, client access to remote data is usually slower than when a replica is maintained locally. Affinity connections are made using RPCs. It therefore makes no sense to declare affinity to a site that's linked via an extended X.400 or SMTP connection.

Figure 5.28
*Defining
affinity values
for a site*

The argument for folder replicas, or multiple synchronized copies of folders established at different locations distributed around a network is based on three points.

- Synchronized copies of public folders distribute the processing load generated by user access to folder contents. This improves response time for users because they will generally be accessing content from a location close to them rather than from some remote network location.

- Synchronized copies of public folders established at strategic locations within a network can dramatically reduce the amount of long-distance or WAN network traffic generated by users attempting to access folder contents.

- Synchronized copies of folders maintained on multiple servers mean that users will always be able to have access to the information, often mission-critical, held in replicated public folders. If one server becomes inoperative, users are automatically and transparently switched to another server to access a different replica.

Users are completely unaware that public folder replication occurs because Exchange hides everything from them. As far as users are concerned, they are able to see a public folder and access its content. They remain blissfully unaware that substantial programming and network magic has been performed to enable them to view a document, form, or other object with such ease. Because users usually retrieve information from a replica held on their own server, access to information is as fast as it can possibly be. With such strong arguments for replication why would anyone choose to incur the potentially long delays in accessing a single definitive copy of information held on a remote server?

Affinity can only work if a network connection can be made to the server that hosts the public folder. Two different requirements must be fulfilled if the affinity approach is to succeed. Clearly, a network path must be available on a consistent basis. There is no point in deciding to use affinity if your network is unreliable. Users will just be unhappy because they won't be able to get to information when they want to. Secondly, users must be authenticated or possess the necessary security credentials to access the information on the server that it's stored on. The security credentials gained through a user's original network logon are usually sufficient to navigate to other servers via affinity. However, the credentials will only be acceptable if all the Exchange servers are located in the same Windows NT domain or are able to mutually authenticate each other's users through a set of trust relationships. If you're unable to assure organization-wide authentication then affinity is not the best choice and you'd be better to use replication as the mechanism for public folder content distribution.

In all instances, whether public folders are distributed via replication or accessed via affinity, a copy of the public folder hierarchy from each site is always sent to all the other sites in the organization. This is a logical step to take as otherwise the system administrators in remote sites wouldn't know about the existence of any of the interesting folders they might otherwise connect to. There is no requirement to replicate any or all folders to all sites. System administrators have a great deal of control over folder replication and are able to select particular folders to be replicated to their server from any other server in the organization (see Figure 5.29).

Figure 5.29
Pulling a new replica

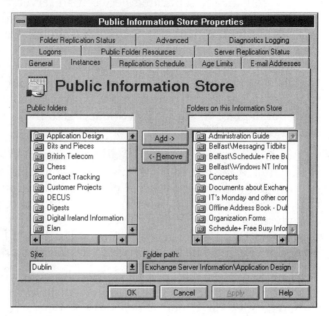

All of these points are valid and should be considered before taking the replication option. In the example illustrated in the bottom part of Figure 5.26, whenever a user in the London site wishes to access an item in a public folder on a system in the Dublin site, Exchange makes a transparent network connection between the two sites to retrieve the object's content. When an item is fetched a copy of its content is moved into the Windows temporary directory and is operated upon there.

The case for affinity is harder to argue in terms of user convenience. The most obvious advantage is the fact that a single network-wide copy represents definitive data. This can't be said of a replicated folder because the possibility always exists that a change to the content has been made somewhere in the network and hasn't yet arrived on the local server. Many organizations will be attracted by the concept of a single definitive source of information, especially when that information is critical corporate information. You have to make a decision whether your network is able to facilitate fast (or at least acceptable) access times to the information. If there are many slow links in the network replication is possibly a better solution.

5.5.8   The replication of public folder content and hierarchy

Replication of public folders occurs in two distinct steps—hierarchy and content. As mentioned in the last section, the public folder hierarchy is automatically replicated between all servers within an organization (see also page 311). Every server knows about all the public folders that are available on any other server within the organization. Replication of the hierarchy allows every user to see a full list of public folders when they click to expand the public folder portion of the overall folder hierarchy. A user's next step may be to double-click on a folder to access its content. If a local replica is unavailable or affinity has not been put in place to allow network access to the content an error message is displayed.

Because it happens automatically, you can't do anything about the replication of the public folder hierarchy. The challenge is therefore to determine the tactics to control content replication and how to avoid users becoming frustrated when they cannot access content. As I've already mentioned, keeping all your Exchange servers in a single Windows NT domain is the best way to enable affinity. If this isn't possible, arrangements must be put in place to implement a replication strategy.

New folder replicas can be created by either pushing or pulling. Pushing means that the administrator of the system hosting a public folder decides on which other servers a new replica of the folder should be created. The system administrator of any server that already holds a replica can push out new replicas of folders to other servers. This is done by expanding the set of public folders (at the top of the organization configuration shown in the left hand pane of the administration program), selecting the desired folder, selecting its properties, and then nominating the new target server in various sites to send the new replicas off to. For example, in Figure 5.30, the system administrator of the server called RUCKS[12] has just chosen the DBO-EXCHANGEIST server in the Dublin site and instructed Exchange to replica the contents of the folder "RUCKS Test Folder" to DBO-EXCHANGEIST. It's as simple as select and click, and contents can be replicated around the world without too much effort on the part of an administrator. All the work is done later by the messaging system, which must transport possibly many megabytes of data across the network to create the new replica.

---

12.   RUCKS is a word with special meaning to rugby fans where it refers to a particular game situation. I've had a server called RUCKS in my personal network for many years!

Figure 5.30
*Pushing a new
replica to a
remote server*

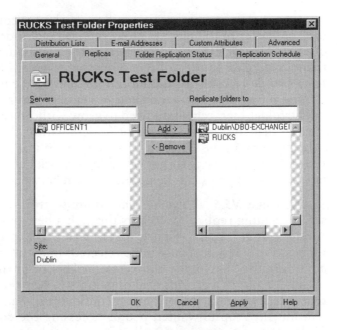

Figure 5.30
*Pushing a new
replica to a
remote server*

The administrator of the target server is not aware of this action. Any administrator can decide to push a replica towards another server, and because replication is performed using the messaging system, as long as there's a valid messaging path between the servers the content will be sent off to its new home. The only indications that a new replica has been established is an increase in the count of replicas and a growth in the disk space occupied by the Public Information Store on the target server. Most administrators will not be even aware that a new replica has arrived!

Whereas the "push" model is controlled from a server that already hosts a replica (remember that all replicas are treated as equivalent masters), servers that don't already have a copy use the "pull" model. In this case the system administrator of the server that wants to create a new replica browses through the public folder hierarchy until the desired folder is located. At this stage we can select the folder and click the "add" button, as shown in Figure 5.30. Immediately the change is applied, Exchange will proceed to request the host Public Information Store to begin transmitting the folder contents to the requesting server. Content is always transmitted in a series of messages, so it may take some time before the local replica is available for user access. Again, the owner of the original public folder has no idea that a new replica has been created.

Does it matter whether you pull or push? Of course it doesn't, as long as you want to create the new replica, and understand the consequences of your action. In most cases the consequences are no more than an increase in the volume of messages generated within the system. The more replicas, the more messages are required to ship data around for all changes—additions, deletions, and amendments. If the public folder hierarchy is allowed to grow without restraint a danger is created that the sheer number of folders within the hierarchy cloaks valuable data. In the same way, if multiple replicas are created without restraint, a danger exists that valuable network bandwidth is absorbed by unnecessary messages being transmitted between Exchange servers.

Exchange V5.5 allows system administrators to prevent remote servers pulling replicas of folders through a new property called local administrative access (Figure 5.31). When the property is set any request for a new replica will be rejected, much to the chagrin of the administrator that made the request. This is an important change because it allows a greater deal of control to be exercised over folders that might contain important or confidential material. While ACLs will initially stop unwanted people accessing the content of a public folder even if they take a replica, it is possible to work around these restrictions by creating a new site, replicating the desired folder to the site and then breaking the directory replication connector. If you run the DS/IS consistency adjuster (see page 326) afterwards the replica will be rehomed to your site and you'll gain administrative control. Stopping the folder replicating from the start is much more secure.

It's interesting to reflect on the philosophy inherent in a system that allows uncontrolled distribution of replicas to occur. There is no way that a system administrator can prevent an administrator of another system deciding that a folder created on their system should be pushed over the network, or indeed to create a local replica and pull content from your system. The reverse is true too. There is no method to prevent a remote system administrator rejecting an attempt to create a replica on their server. The replica may arrive, but as soon as its presence is noticed the local administrator can remove it, sending the folder back to where it came from.

When replicas are created, the folder access control list may prevent people seeing the actual content when it arrives. However, because the public folder hierarchy is automatically replicated everywhere and the facilities exist for replicas to be created outside some type of central control, a danger clearly exists that unwanted replicas might be created.

Figure 5.31
*Resticting a
public folder to
local adminis-
trative access*

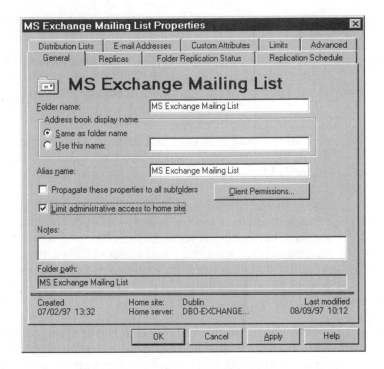

Implementation plans should address this issue by stating clear guidelines for the creation of replicas. In other words, who can create replicas and the conditions replicas should be created under. Regular checks should also be performed to see how many replicas exist for each folder, especially those that might contain sensitive information, and where those replicas reside. Finally, statistics should be kept to track the growth of the number of public folders and what use is actually being made of their contents. It is also useful to know who is creating the public folders and have a procedure to allow people to inherit control of folders when the original owners move on to other responsibilities.

5.5.9   How replication occurs

Replication between servers is controlled by the Public Folder Replication Agent (PFRA), part of the Public Information Store. The PFRA takes care of monitoring changes made to public folders, but only for folders where replicas exist. The list of servers that hold replicas, or instances, of the folder is maintained as a property of the folder. After changes are made the PFRA takes care of dispatching details of the changes to all of the other servers that hold replicas. Updated content, commands to delete items, and details of new items posted into a folder are sent through a special form of messages sent by the Public

Information Store on one server to the Public Information Store on another.

In addition to the relatively simple task of sending updates to other Public Information Stores, the PFRA maintains historical information about the state of each message in each replicated folder. A mechanism called Change Number Sets (CNS) is used for this purpose. Each folder has a unique set of change numbers, based on a GUID (global unique identifier, based on 64-bit hex strings). Conceptually you can think of the number set being incremented by 1 as each change is made to a folder (addition, modification, deletion). Thus, the first item added to a folder becomes change number 1, the second number 2, and so on. The CNS for the folder is now 1-2 (the actual values are much more complicated). If a replica is now created, the CNS is sent in a status message to inform the store on the receiving server that it must backfill its new replica with the content represented by CNS 1-2. The server name is added to make the CNS unique. Thus, you could think of the CNS as being something like:

```
DBO-EXCHANGEIST\PUBIS\0174345
```

The change number shows that this is change number 174,345 generated by the Public Information Store on the DBO-EXCHANGEIST server. Of course, real change numbers are created in an encoded fashion that makes sense to computers, not humans, so this example is purely to illustrate the point. The PFRA maintains a list of all predecessor change numbers for a store, meaning that the agent is able to recognize the most recent or current message.

A status message containing the current CNS is generated for each replicated folder every day and sent to all servers that hold replicas. This message serves to prime the replication system and ensure that servers are prompted to check the folder replication status and request backfills for any missing data. The CNS is also included in every message that contains replicated content, a step that ensures that backfill will occur even if status messages are missed for any reason.

The simplest replication task involves new items. When a new item is added to a public folder the PFRA creates a new change order and sends it along with the content of the new item to all of the other servers that hold instances of the folder. The receiving stores insert the content into their copy of the folder. Deletions are similar operations, except that content is not sent. In this case the message to the servers holding instances to instruct them that the item should be removed from their replica.

If permissions allow, all servers are entitled to modify items. Modifications are always applied to local instances, so the local PFRA takes responsibility for informing the other servers that a change has occurred. When a modification message arrives to a Public Information Store it replaces the original content, but only if the modification is more current than the existing message. The store uses the change number on the message and the predecessor change list to determine whether the message should be applied. If the store discovers that it has content than is more up to date than the content in the replication message it realizes that a potential conflict exists, and a conflict resolution process begins. That process is more fully explored on page 334.

5.5.10   Public folder hierarchy replication

Servers automatically exchange details of the folders that they host so that each server is able to build a complete picture of all public folders in the organization, and the place each folder occupies within the public folder hierarchy. A background thread checks the Information Store at a regular interval to detect whether new folders have been added, the properties of existing folders have been changed, or folders have been deleted. If any changes are discovered the details are bundled together into a message that is sent to all other servers in the organization. A single message is used, addressed to a virtual distribution list.

In large organizations, or when you know that the public folder hierarchy doesn't change very often, it is a good idea to lengthen the interval for the background thread. The interval is set by the "Replicate Always Interval" property for the Public Information Store. The background thread will notice any change made the next time it executes and adjust its schedule thereafter. An interval of 120 or even 240 minutes is usually sufficient in most cases. Apart from anything else, this will mean that the number of hierarchy replication messages will be reduced from 96 per day (4 per hour) to 12 or even just 6 daily.

Each Exchange server that hosts a Public Information Store also creates a "daily folder status report" message once a day that is sent to all other servers in the organization. The message is produced by another background thread that checks whether the server has reported its status in the last 24 hours. If not, the message is generated and sent otherwise the thread exits. The message contains a list of all the public folders in the hierarchy, not just the ones maintained on the server and is intended to allow servers to compare their lists with each other, and generate backfill requests for any data that's missing. The thread runs at 12:15 a.m. and 12:15 p.m. each day within the GMT time zone. In other words, it is not dependent on the time zone set for Windows NT.

Parameters can be set in the registry to control the time before a status report is sent, the wait period for the background thread, and the "skew", or delta between the preset GMT times and the actual time you'd like the thread to run. These parameters are:

```
HKEY_LOCAL_MACHINE\System\CurrentControlSet\Services\
MSExchangeIS\Parameters
```

Replication Send Status TimeOut	(default value 84,600 seconds—24 hours)
Replication Send Status Alignment	(default value 42,300 seconds—12 hours)
Replication Send Status Alignment Skew	(default value 0 seconds, meaning run at 12:15 a.m. and 12:15 p.m.)

There's no great reason to rush and modify these parameters unless you are concerned about the amount of replication traffic in your network and see evidence of large message queues accumulating at server MTAs.

5.5.11 Creating and managing folders

Public folders can only be created by MAPI clients. There is no facility to create public folders with POP3 or IMAP4 clients, or web browsers. Clients are able to administer folder security, but cannot perform other management operations such as creating a new replica, establishing a replication schedule, or defining which server is the "home" for a public folder. These operations must be performed through the Exchange administration program.

Individual folders can be administered by expanding the set of public folders shown towards the top of the organizational hierarchy and selecting the desired folder. Properties can only be altered on the folder's home server, but any server can view folder properties.

The administration program can also be used to manage folders for a specific server. Select the server and expand the properties of the Public Information Store. Figure 5.32 shows the folder replication status for a complete server being displayed. The columns list the names of the replicas in the Public Information Store for the selected server, the date and time an update to the folder was last received, the number of replicas within the organization, and the current replication status. Most of the folders have a status of "Local Modified", indicating that a modification has been made to the local replica that has not yet been replicated to all of the other servers. One replica reports "In Sync", meaning that all of the replicas throughout the organization contain the same data. You might also see "Remote Modified", which means that the server knows that a remote server has some updates for its replica, but that data has not yet been replicated.

Figure 5.32
*Monitoring
public folder
replication
status*

Managing a small set of public folders shouldn't cause anyone's hair to turn grey. Tracking down all the folders scattered across a distributed organization is quite another matter. Looking at folder properties through the administration program quickly becomes boring. Fortunately, the PFINFO program[13] from the Exchange Resource Kit (Figure 5.33) is able to scan the public folder hierarchy in a matter of minutes and create summary data for later analysis. For example, PFINFO is able to retrieve data for 350 public folders on the server I use in under a minute.

Figure 5.33
*Using PFINFO
to generate a
summary of the
public folder
hierarchy*

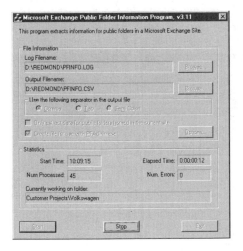

PFINFO generates a CSV file containing the following information:

- Folder name

---

13. Use PFINFO V3.1 or later.

- Folder path in the hierarchy (for example, Exchange Information\Tips and Techniques)
- Permissions
- List of replicas
- Number of replicas
- Number of items in the folder
- Size (in Kb) of the contents of the folder
- Age Limits
- Replication message priority
- Replication schedule
- Alias
- Storage limit (Kb)
- Date created
- Date last modified
- Home site
- Home server
- e-mail addresses

The CSV file is easily loaded for reporting purposes into a spreadsheet like Excel (Figure 5.34).

Figure 5.34
*Reviewing
PFINFO output
via Excel*

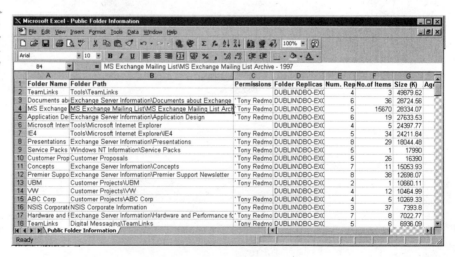

Aside from its obvious use in keeping track of the number and use of public folders, PFINFO is able to capture the administrative properties from each folder and store the data in a file. PFADMIN, another program from the Exchange Resource Kit, is able to use the file to reset the properties on public folders should the need arise, possibly after permissions and other information have been lost after the Public Information Store has been restored in a server. The PFINFO and PFADMIN utilities should be included in any Exchange administrator's toolkit.

5.5.12   The size of public folder replication messages

Public folder replication is accomplished by servers sending messages to each other. The MTA can be instructed to reject messages over a specified size. For example, you probably want to stop people sending 10MB PowerPoint presentations to each other, preferring instead to use public folders to share large documents like this. Public folder replication messages are different to interpersonal messages so they don't respect the same limitation. If you inspect the properties of the Public Information Store, you'll see that a size limit can be set. The limit only influences the size of messages that the store builds when it wants to replicate several items at one time. Let's assume that the limit is 100 kilobytes. If six 30-kilobyte items are placed into a folder, the store will not create six separate replication messages to send the content to other servers. Instead, two messages are created. Each is approximately 90 kilobyte in size and contains the data for three items. Compression is not used to reduce the size of messages. Replication traffic is minimized by this scheme.

If a large document is placed in a public folder, it is not broken up into several individual messages to comply with a size limit. Instead, the document is sent in one complete chunk and the MTA will allow the large message to pass.

5.5.13   Replication frequency

Data is normally replicated according to a global schedule defined for the entire Public Information Store. Figure 5.35 shows how a specific replication schedule can be created for a public folder. The time grid is set at hourly intervals, and replication activity will begin at the start of each hour. You can also set the grid to 15 minute intervals.

Individual folders, usually those that contain time-critical information, can have their own schedules. In either case, you can specify three intervals:

- *Always:* Messages will be created and sent according to the "Replicate Always Interval", a property of the store. The default value is 15 minutes, meaning that data is replicated every 15 minutes. This value is too short for most folders. Setting it to 60 or 120 minutes to restrict the amount of network traffic is a better idea.

- *Never:* No replication messages will ever be produced. If you know that network links are going to be unavailable for a period, it's a good idea to set the interval to "Never". This will stop the store producing messages that will only end up being queued by the MTA.

- *According to schedule:* Messages will be produced according to a schedule defined in the normal time grid used for Exchange management operations. Use this type of schedule to restrict replication operations to hours when interpersonal mail volume is low. This serves to prevent replication messages interfering with the flow of mail between users.

Figure 5.35
Setting a replication schedule for a public folder

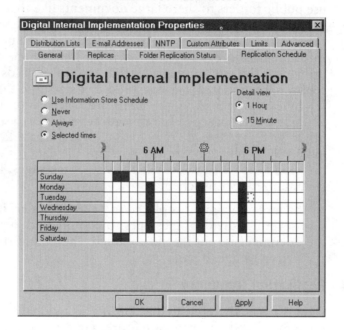

The normal approach for a new Exchange organization is to begin by setting a global replication schedule to restrict activity to off-peak hours. As the public folder hierarchy begins to be assembled the purpose of each folder and the type of information it holds can be reviewed to decide on the most appropriate replication frequency. Above all, make sure that a schedule that has the potential to swamp a network with replication messages is never implemented. Always err on the side of caution to ensure that interpersonal messages are accorded priority.

Following the same logic, it's a good idea to restrict the number of replicas within an organization. The attitude should be that each replica generates network traffic that must be justified. Don't allow administrators to create replicas just because it seems like a good idea. Computer systems managed by whim rather than through good planning are never successful.

5.5.14   Backfilling public folders

Backfilling describes the process by which a server updates an instance of a public folder when information is lost due to system outages. Backfilling also occurs when a new instance of a folder is created.

System outages include hardware crashes, which may lead to the Public Information Store being restored on a server. A restored store is out of date and lacks the content replicated since the backup was taken. When a server is restarted after the restore replication messages will begin to arrive again. At this stage the Public Information Store will look at the change numbers on the incoming replication messages and update its predecessor change list. Gaps will exist in the predecessor change list, forcing the store to look to fill the gaps, or backfill.

The server begins the process by generating a backfill entry, literally a placeholder inserted into the store to indicate that some data is missing. It then proceeds to dispatch requests for assistance to two other servers (chosen at random), that also hold replicas of the folders that are missing information. The request specifies the missing content and requests the receiving server to generate a message containing the content and send it back to the Public Information Store.

Backfill requests are never immediately activated. They are kept in a queue for up to 2 hours to await the arrival of messages containing the missing content for a replica. If the waiting period elapses a message containing the backfill request is sent to the store on the folder's home server. When the backfill request is received it is examined by the store to determine what content is required, as defined by the CNS. The store then generates one or more messages with the missing data and sends it off. A status message that contains details of the current CNS from the home server is also sent to inform the replica what the current situation is. Backfill requests continue to be made until the CNS of the replica is the same as the CNS on the home folder

5.5.15   Monitoring the flow of replication

Replication should flow smoothly as long as messages can flow between Exchange sites. User access is the most common problem, and the reason for this is usually one of the following:

- A local replica has not been set up
- Affinity has not been defined or can't work because servers lie in different, untrusted NT domains

- The user doesn't hold the necessary permission to access a folder.

If the problem is not due to one of these reasons replication might not be working. The easiest check is to see whether you can send a message to a mailbox on the server that hosts the folder being replicated. Set a delivery and read receipt on the message so you're notified when the message actually reaches the server and then again when it's read. You can use the Message Tracking Center feature in the Administration Program to follow the path of the message, providing that message tracking logs are enabled on all servers along the message's path.

Turning up diagnostics for the Public Information Store and examining the data that's collected is another approach. The normal setting is "None", meaning that only errors are recorded in the NT Application Event Log. Use "Medium" or "Maximum" to gain an insight into the level of replication activity on a server. Be warned that a large volume of events will accumulate quickly on servers that host busy public folders, or servers that replicate at short intervals. Figure 5.36 shows how to turn on the diagnostics setting for the Public Information Store so that replication events are written to the Event Log.

Figure 5.36
*Turning up
diagnostics for
the Public
Information
Store*

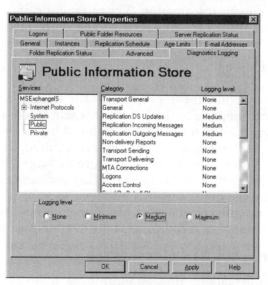

Adding content to a replica will cause replication to occur. This fact can be exploited to allow you to observe replication in action. Set diagnostics to Medium or Maximum. Select a folder that you know has a replica on the site you are having difficulty replicating to. Set its replication interval to Always. Add some content to the folder (create a new item, or drag and drop a small file into the folder). You should then see events appearing in the Event Log.

Figure 5.37 illustrates the type of information captured in the Event Log. The event is for an outgoing replication message for a folder called Exchange Server Information\Premier Support Newsletter (Premier Support Newsletter is a sub-folder of the top-level Exchange Server Information folder). The CNS is clearly identified, although the numbers don't mean a lot to humans. The message type is 4, meaning that this message contains new content being replicated from this server to another server.

Figure 5.37 *An outgoing replication message is logged in the NT Application Event Log*

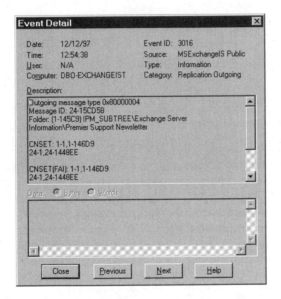

Other valid message type codes are:

Code	Meaning	Comment
2	Folder tree changes	A new folder has been added to the hierarchy or a folder has been deleted.
8	Backfill requests	A server is requesting some backfill data to complete its replica.
10	Status message	The server is reporting the CNS for one or more folders to other servers.
20	Status Request	The server is looking for a replica of a folder to retrieve information, or is reporting that it is still active.

Matching the diagnostic information that is reported with the knowledge you have of the public folder hierarchy and replication intervals provides invaluable background knowledge of how the PFRA works. This is a subject that is often ignored by system administrators, only to become a hot topic when things go wrong and everyone's wondering why replication isn't working, or why too much replication activity is going on.

5.5.16 Special Public Folders

A number of special folders are created in the Public Information Store in the first server in a site. These folders are hidden from user view but can be managed from the Exchange administration program, as shown in Figure 5.38. The folders include:

- The Offline Address Book (OAB—see page 621)
- A folder to publish Schedule+ Free and Busy information
- A folder to hold permissions for the Event Service
- The electronic forms registry. This is a repository for the electronic forms accessed by all users.

The system folders may all contain sub-folders. For example, the Events Root folder contains a sub folder to control access to the Events Service in each server in the organization. Replicas of these folders can be created on other servers. It is quite common to replicate the free and busy information across an organization to prevent clients having to make an extended network connection when they set up meetings.

Figure 5.38
*System
Folders*

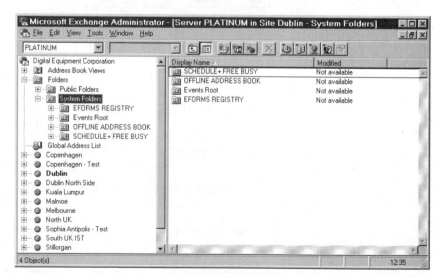

5.5.17   Public folder ownership and access control lists

All public folders have nominated owners. Or rather, all public folders should have at least one nominated owner. Owners are user mailboxes that have complete control over a public folder, typically used to manage the access control list for the folder (defining, in turn, the people who can access the folder and the degree of control they exercise over the folder's contents).

Roles, a collection of permissions defining the actions a user may perform on a folder and its contents, are used to control personal access to a public folder. Apart from "Owner", the role automatically given to the user who actually creates a new public folder, the default role is called "Author". A user holding the "Author" role is allowed to place new items in the public folder and edit items that they have put into the folder.

Exchange comes with a number of predefined roles to enable you to get up and running with minimum effort and not worry about having to sit down and define out roles and what each role can and cannot do. The default roles are shown in Table 5.7. If you don't like the rights defined in the default roles you can create your own.

Roles are changed or allocated to users by selecting a public folder and viewing its properties. The Permissions tab allows you to add or remove users to the list of people who have rights over the folder (see Figure 5.39). Roles can be allocated to individual mailboxes or distribution lists. Using a distribution list is a convenient way of allocating the same role to a large group of people in a single operation. It's important to understand that roles allocated to individuals supersede roles gained through membership of a distribution list. The same dialog allows you to define a new role, should the need exist.

Table 5.7   *Default Roles for Public Folders*

Role Name	Allocated to	Rights
Owner	User who creates a public folder.	All, including control over permissions allocated to other users.
Author	Default role allocated to other users.	Add new items to the folder and edit items they have provided.
Publishing Author	People who will provide information to the folder and use the folder as a work area.	Able to process own work and create sub folders.

Table 5.7   *Default Roles for Public Folders (continued)*

Role Name	Allocated to	Rights
Editor	User who will work on information posted into the folder by others.	Edit, read, and delete all information.
Non-editing editor	User who will review work posted into the folder by others.	Read and delete all contributions.
Publishing Editor	Second highest level (after user) of control over the folder.	Edit, read, and delete all contributions. Able to create sub folders.
Reviewer	People who you want to read but not interact with folder contents.	Read only access.
Contributor	People who you want to provide content to folders and forget about it afterwards. On the surface, a rather strange role.	Write only access.

Owners of public folders assume certain responsibilities. Apart from being able to control the access and permissions other users enjoy on a public folder owners are the only people who are entitled to create rules via the Folder Assistant. Just like the Inbox Assistant, the Folder Assistant is a rules-based agent that monitors objects placed in folders. If the objects meet the criteria stated in a rule the Folder Assistant will swing into action and execute whatever action is required. For instance, a public folder is created to accept a feed from an Internet Newsgroup. A rule might be created to monitor new objects as they arrive and reject anything that does not originate from the Newsgroup.

Sometimes folders lose owners. This isn't careless on the part of the folder, or a bug. It's just a by-product of normal system maintenance. The access control list (ACL) for a folder is composed of distinguished directory names that must point to a valid entry in the directory. If a user mailbox is removed from the directory, the entry in the folder's access control list that pointed to the mailbox is null and void and is therefore removed. We end up with a folder that has no owner. This isn't a disaster. You can use the administration program to manipulate the properties of a public folder, including client access and permissions. So all you need to do to amend folder ownership is to select the folder and then add one or more mailboxes from the GAL to the access control list, marking them as "owners".

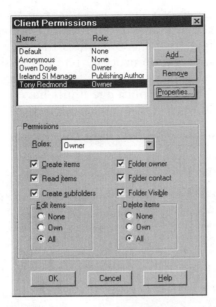

Figure 5.39
*Client permis-
sions for a public
folder*

Because access control lists are composed of directory entries it therefore follows that any type of valid directory entry can be inserted into the ACL. Individual mailbox entries are the obvious default option for ACLs, but custom recipient entries don't make much sense because you must be able to use Exchange before access can be gained to public folders. Distribution lists, on the other hand, are very useful because they reduce the amount of system administration overhead required to maintain ACLs. Figure 5.39 shows a typical ACL being manipulated. Two mailboxes have been nominated as the owners of the folder while a distribution list (Ireland SI Management) is used to establish a more general level of access. No access is permitted by default, or to anonymous (Web) users.

Using distribution lists to control access to folders creates a situation where a single entity, or group of entities (lists), are managed in place of a lot of individual mailbox entries. As mailboxes are added to or removed from the distribution list users gain or lose access to public folders, and all done through simple maintenance of a distribution list. Remember too that system administrators don't have to maintain distribution lists as this task can be allocated to users.

Each folder has a unique ACL. When a new sub-folder is created it inherits an initial ACL from its parent. However, in Exchange V4.0 when a change is made to a parent folder it is not automatically reflected in any sub-folders, so any change such as a new user being granted permission to access the parent folder needs to be made to any sub-folder as well.

A welcome change was made in Exchange V5.0 where additional properties are made available to control how changes are propagated to sub-folders. Figure 5.40 demonstrates the degree of control available during the propagation process. The most used of these properties is likely to be client permissions, but it's good to see that other major properties such as replica age limits have not been overlooked in the implementation.

Figure 5.40
Propagating properties to sub-folders

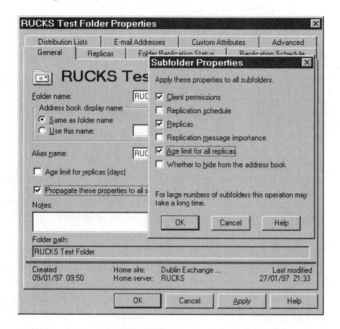

Deleting a directory replication connector can have the unfortunate side effect of affecting folder ownership. When a directory replication connector is deleted, all the entries associated with the connector are removed from the directory. An immediate disconnect can therefore arise between folder ACLs and the directory. If a substitute directory replication connector is established and the remote site has not changed the format of its directory entries (for example, by changing its site name), then no damage should arise. However, if the format of the directory entries have changed then they will no longer match the folder ACL and users will no longer be able to access folder contents.

5.5.18   The infamous DS/IS consistency adjuster

An option to run the DS/IS consistency adjuster is available through the advanced properties of a server. The adjuster is designed to verify that every object in the store has a matching entry in the directory, and fix minor inconsistencies that arise over time in the directory. An inconsistency is defined as a situation where a mailbox or public folder exists in the information store but a matching entry cannot be found in the directory, or vice versa. Deleting a directory replication connector is the most common way to create inconsistencies.

Essentially the adjuster works by comparing the contents of the directory with that of the private and public stores, and then applying whatever fixes are deemed appropriate. The intention is laudable, but for most of its early existence the work done by the DS/IS consistency adjuster was performed under a veil of secrecy, and no-one was quite sure what it did or what problems it fixed. Inevitably, problems arose when people, for one reason or another, attempted to use the tool only to discover later on that the tool had fixed some inconsistencies that weren't altogether obvious. Problems arose and people screamed when they discovered what the adjuster had done. Some of these problems were caused by administrators not knowing what they were doing. Others by the total lack of user interface to protect the innocent.

Figure 5.41
*The solemn
warning
about the
consequences
of running
the DS/IS
consistency
checker*

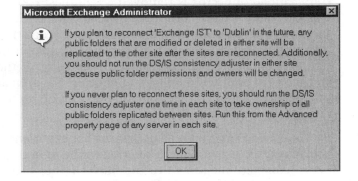

The Exchange developers didn't have the time to create an appropriate user interface for the DS/IS consistency checker during the Exchange V5.0 development cycle. Something had to be done to protect unwary system administrators, so a fix was inserted (from V4.0 SP3 on) to flag a warning about running the DS/IS consistency adjuster after a directory replication connector is removed. The actual warning is shown in Figure 5.41. Obviously, after a directory replication connector has been removed and all its associated entries eliminated from the directory the potential exists for a large number of inconsistencies to exist. For example, the access control lists for public folders may now contain entries for mailboxes in the site or sites whose directory entries were obtained through the now-disconnected directory replication connector. If the DS/IS consistency adjuster is invoked at this stage the entries for mailboxes in the disconnected sites will be removed from the access control list for public folders. This is not a problem if you never intend to replicate directory information with those sites again, but if you do, then you'll have to edit the access control list for all the public folders to add mailboxes in those sites after the directory replication connector is re-established.

Adjusting the access control lists on folders is one thing. Taking control over a public folder is quite another. Each public folder has a home server property. Administration (setting properties and permission) for a public folder can only be done from its home site, so it's obvious that maintaining the correct home site is an important thing to do. If the DS/IS consistency checker finds public folders whose home site is no longer available (because the directory replication connector for that site is gone), it rehomes the public folder into the site where the consistency adjuster is being run.

Rehoming a public folder certainly fixes the inconsistency between the Information and Directory Stores. However, in real-life situations, if the DS/IS consistency checker is run immediately after a directory replication connector is removed a real mess can occur. Rehoming a set of public folders off their original site is quite another matter because folders can only be administered from their home site. For example, you can only change the access control list for a folder if you connect to a server in the folder's home site. If the folder has been rehomed to another site that's in another NT domain or only accessible through a RAS connection you may not be even able to connect to a server in that site.

One major international company that experienced the effects of an unwanted consistency check referred to the re-homing of public folders as a "complete meltdown of the public folder hierarchy", after being forced to spend hours of administration effort to move folders back to their proper home server. Another company spent many days to rehome public folders from Australia back to New York after a novice system administrator had practiced administration techniques one day.

Exchange V5.5 fixes the problem with a combination of new features:

- The DS/IS consistency adjuster has a new user interface (Figure 5.42), which makes it clear what the tool is going to do. Also, you can now determine exactly what steps the adjuster will take to fix any inconsistencies it finds.

- The home server property for a public folder is now revealed and can be changed through the Exchange administration program. Thus, even if a public folder is homed to another server, the folder can be rehomed to its original server by setting the home server property to its correct value. Note that the server that you want to rehome the folder to must be on the replica list before rehoming can occur.

- As discussed earlier, it is now possible to limit administrative access for a public folder to its home site. If administrative access is limited properties can only originate in the home site. Any attempt to execute an administrative operation from a remote server (such as rehoming or even creating a new replica) will be rejected. This feature is only 100% effective after the complete organization is upgraded to Exchange V5.5. Exchange V4.0 and V5.0 servers have no knowledge of restricted administrative access and will continue to send changes to the home server through normal public folder and directory replication channels.

Figure 5.42
The new user interface for the DS/IS consistency adjuster

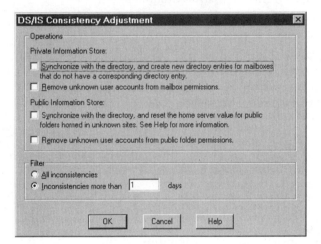

Even with all the changes great care should still be taken with the DS/IS consistency adjuster. It's important that all system administrators are aware of the link between the Directory and Information Stores and how the consistency adjuster works. Care should also always be taken when deleting directory replication connectors in a production environment.

If you do get into the situation where some public folders have been rehomed to places you'd really prefer them not to be, they can be rehomed using the PFADMIN utility (Version 1.1.2 or greater) from the Exchange Resource Kit. See Knowledge Base article Q178928 for details.

5.5.19 Fixing orphan public folders

If you unwittingly run the DS/IS consistency adjuster and find that some folder rehoming has occurred, you may have a number of orphaned public folders to deal with. An orphaned public folder is one with no owner and is the direct result of the consistency adjuster being unable to resolve any entry in the folder's ACL against the directory.

Thus, the ACL is empty, or possibly contains just the default "anony-mous" access (which should be at the level of "none") introduced in Exchange V5.0.

Orphaned folders originate somewhere. As we've discussed, orphans are normally created when a site connector is removed. If the disconnected site is ever to rejoin the organization you can leave the orphan folders alone. You'll still have to adjust their ownership when the site rejoins, but you should not rush to do anything else because any action you take against an orphaned folder will be replicated to other copies once connections are available again.

However, if the original site is never going to rejoin the organization the orphans represent some debris that must be cleaned up in the public folder hierarchy. Failure to reset ownership and delete the folders will leave erroneous entries in the hierarchy that only ever results in confusion for users. For example, if a user attempts to access an orphan folder they'll be told:

```
The folder could not be opened. The contents of this public
folder are currently unavailable. Either the Exchange server
computer servicing this public folder is down or the public
folder has not been replicated to this site.
```

Attempts to access the properties of orphan folders from the administration program also fail. The message in this case also complains that replication is not complete. These errors occur because the attempts to access the content of the orphan folder result in zero data. Alternatively, from a client perspective, the access attempt is rejected because the user has been denied access. In either case the solution is the same. You must add an instance of the orphaned folders to the local Public Information Store, then reset permissions so that a local user takes ownership (normally the administrator), and then delete the orphans. Cleaning up a set of orphaned folders is easier in Exchange V5.0 because permissions can now be propagated down through subfolders of a parent folder, but the work still needs to be done and will occupy valuable system administration time.

The bottom line is that the DS/IS consistency adjuster should only be run if a site is being permanently removed from an organization. Properly run, the adjuster creates any necessary directory objects for all folders in the public folder hierarchy, maintaining permissions for the users (within the remaining sites) on the folders.

5.5.20 Hiding public folders

The public folder hierarchy is replicated automatically from site to site within an organization. This is a nice feature if you want to publish the names of your site's public folders to everyone else, but sometimes it's nice to be a little more private.

Let's assume that you want to set up a public folder for use by a restricted group of users. You can, of course, protect the folder's contents through suitable permissions, but let's assume that you don't even want people to see the folder's name within the folder hierarchy. In short, you want to create a hidden public folder.

Hidden public folders cannot be created in the top level of the folder hierarchy. There is no mechanism to indicate that a top-level folder should be hidden. But sub-folders can be hidden and protected as follows:

- Create a top-level folder and give it a suitable name. For example, "Executive Information".

- Set the default permission on the new folder to "None".

- Create a sub-folder under "Executive Information". For example, "Secret Information".

- Set permissions on the "Secret Information" sub-folder to allow the users you want to have access to its content. If you are granting access to more than a couple of users you may want to create a distribution list and grant permissions to it. Users in the distribution list will then inherit the access permissions for the folder.

Users without the necessary permissions will be able to see the top-level folder, but any attempt to open the folder will display nothing. Only users with permissions will be able to see the sub-folders and other objects placed into the "Executive Information" folder.

5.5.21 Using public folders to reduce messaging activity

People will always have the temptation to circulate large files by attaching them to messages. Good examples of what I mean are documents under review by a committee, when a document might go through several review cycles before eventually being approved. Attaching the file to a message is quick and easy and makes sure that everyone the sender wants to see the particular file receives a copy. Whether or not the recipient ever looks at their copy is quite another matter.

While undeniably easy to use, sending large files as attachments does not make the most effective use of the functionality available to users. It is much more efficient and reduces the chance of redundant information being stored in many places throughout the network to place a copy of whatever file needs to be circulated in a public folder.

A short message can then be sent to act as a reminder to the circulation list that the file awaits their attention.

Public folders are an obvious source of shared information, but they're not the only one. If your Windows NT environment is designed in such a way as to allow general access to files no matter where they are located within the network you can even include a shortcut to a file, or even a program or installation kit within a message. And of course, Exchange supports embedded URLs to allow speedy access to specific Web pages.

After receiving messages containing pointers to public folders, shortcuts or web pages people can then go and retrieve the information as they wish. In the case of public folders if the folder allows write access they can even make their contributions by directly annotating the document in place so that everyone can see the comments as they are made. Beware of clashes occurring if two or more users attempt to update the document in the shared folder at the same time.

Using a public folder to replace large attachments won't always be possible, and it requires people to make decisions about the method to be used to distribute information to others. Users coming from other mail systems where public folders or similar mechanisms weren't available may not take kindly to the idea at all. But even if you can convince some groups within the user community to pay attention to the way they distribute and share information it will be a contribution towards increased system effectiveness. Users learn from each other (perhaps by a process of osmosis), and if one group sees that there's a better way to do something the new method will spread, slowly at first, but soon to become common practice.

5.5.22 Using public folder for collaborative authoring

Public folders make it easy to distribute any type of information amongst servers. Collaborative authoring, the collective creation of objects, chiefly documents, depends on easy access to the item being created by all contributing authors. Systems designed to facilitate and control the steps involved in the collaborative authoring process are sold under the label "Document Management Systems". Can Exchange fill this role?

The answer is a qualified "yes". Exchange certainly scores highly on its abilities to

- Organize information in a structured manner within the public folder hierarchy.

- Control access to information held in public folders through permissions, and to allow different people fulfil different roles during the creation and editing of documents.

- Distribute initial documents and changes applied thereafter to interested parties in a seamless manner through folder replication.

Problems lie in the way Exchange allows multiple users with write or edit permission to concurrently change documents stored in public folders. The underlying reason why the problem exists is that Exchange has not implemented any system of document check-in or check-out. In other words, a user cannot reserve a document for exclusive write access while they make changes to the content, and then automatically release or cancel their reservation once the edit is complete.

Consider the following scenario:

1.   User1 selects a document in a public folder and begins an edit session.

2.   User2, logged into the same server, selects the same document and also starts an edit session.

3.   User1 completes the changes they wish to make and exits the editor. Exchange saves the changes back into the public folder.

4.   User2 completes their changes and exits the editor. Exchange flags that the document was changed since User2 began working with it and so cannot be changed again (see Figure 5.43). User2's changes are then discarded and cannot be applied to the item. The work is not actually removed from the system as User2 can save the item as a file and then import it back into the public folder. However, this is a two stage manual process.

Clearly no user will be happy with such a situation. Three separate problems have been encountered. First, no warning was given to User2 that User1 was already working on the same document. Second, no indication is ever given as to which user actually has a document open or was responsible for making the last changes applied to the document. The original author's name is always shown and manipulating the document's properties cannot change it.

Given that these problems exist is there any way that they can be avoided to enable Exchange to be used as a collaborative document authoring system? The answer again is a qualified "yes", but achieving a satisfactory status requires users to be disciplined about how changes are applied to documents in public folders because a manual system for change control needs to be established and implemented. Two methods come to mind:

1.   All changes to documents are made after a copy is made through a drag and drop operation to a DOS directory. Changed documents are inserted as new objects when they are ready. The advantages of this method are that the last author name can be seen and that changes are never discarded.

2.   All changes to documents are made after they are moved to a special "Work" sub-folder. The same properties will be retained for documents, but it's immediately obvious that someone is working on a document if it is in the "Work" folder.

Given a little thought many variations on these themes can be constructed. As no document change history is made available by Exchange you might like to consider creating a note in each folder that could be updated by users as they make changes.

5.5.23 Conflicts arising from distributed updates

All manners of conflicts can potentially arise when multiple users scattered around a network attempt to change a document. The only real way to avoid conflicts is to lock documents against changes by not allowing anyone except a specified group of users to have permission to edit objects held in a public folder. Others can read and comment, but nothing can be changed. This enforces a simple rule that the author (or their nominees) is the only person permitted to make changes to a document. In this scenario people who want to suggest changes have to mail them back to the author who then takes charge of assessing the proposed change and eventually integrating it into the document. This is a reasonable way of working in many cases, but not always.

Exchange recognizes that instances will occur when multiple concurrent changes are made to objects distributed across multiple instances of folders. As we've seen, a mechanism is in place to intercept changes made to objects held in public folders before changes are finally applied.

Let's go through a fairly common scenario. Two users located in two different sites begin an edit on a document stored in a public folder. It doesn't matter which user starts first, just that both are engaged in edits at the same time. When both are finished they exit from the editor, and all appears to be successful as the edited object is applied to the local copy of the public folder. Thus, if each user were to immediately start another edit they'd see the changes they made last time around. Problems only appear once the replication engine has had time to kick into gear and communicate with the home server for the folder.

Changes to objects stored in public folders are posted back to the home server according to the replication schedule for the folder. In most instances replication occurs every fifteen minutes, although the actual elapsed time before the effect of replication is seen can be longer than this if the home server is unavailable for some reason or a long message queue needs to be serviced before the replication message is processed.

Figure 5.44
Message
notifying that a
conflict exists

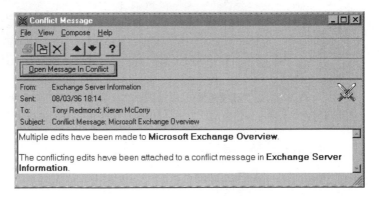

As soon as the home folder server detects that multiple changes have been made it begins a consultation process with the contributing authors to attempt to resolve the conflict. In effect the computer is throwing up its hands at the illogical behavior of humans and sending the problem back to the humans to have them sort it out. Computers, of course, are extremely logical and would never be guilty of attempting to make multiple concurrent updates to a single object. At least, not to something like a Word for Windows document which was never designed to support multiple concurrent updates!

Special messages are generated and dispatched to all of the users who have attempted to make a change to the object, plus anyone who is registered as having "Owner" permission on the folder. Figure 5.44 illustrates an example message sent to two users (Tony Redmond and Kieran McCorry) who attempted to make a change to a document called "Microsoft Exchange Overview" in the "Exchange Server Information" folder. The crossed-swords icon is used to provide a visual indicator for conflict messages when viewed in the Inbox folder.

When a user receives a conflict message the natural reaction is to go to the relevant public folder and see what's happened. If the user double-clicks on the object in conflict Exchange displays a dialog giving details of the conflicting changes and offering the user a choice of what to do next (Figure 5.45).

Figure 5.45
Instructions given to resolve a conflict

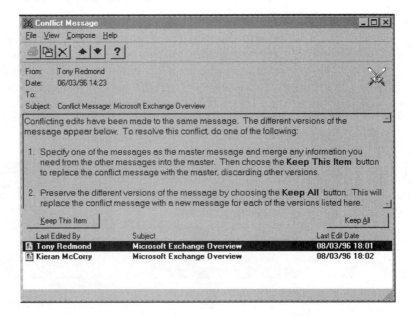

The options are:

- *Keep this item.* This means that the user has selected one of the changed objects that have provoked the conflict and now wishes to treat this object as the definitive version. All other changes are discarded. The authors who contributed the other versions should be contacted and their changes, if available, merged manually into the new definitive version.

- *Keep all items.* This is the more author-friendly version. It means that all of the versions offered for consideration are kept each as a separate object stored in the public folder. Later on, if desired, the separate items can be reviewed and their content drawn together into a single version.

If you allow distributed users to contribute to documents in a replicated environment you must set ground rules to cater for instances when conflicts occur, or better still, establish a method for working which avoids conflicts. Computers can resolve problems that are stated in a logical sense, but they have no chance in the resolution of different thoughts and ideas arriving in from multiple users.

5.5.24 Using Exchange as a document management system

Given the issues around conflicts and the problems associated with multiple concurrent edits can Exchange be used as a document management system?

The characteristics of a document management system include:

- A structured document repository
- Access controls to define who can do what with the objects stored in the repository
- Object check-in and check-out facilities
- Object audit trails
- A flexible high-speed search engine capable of scanning large quantities of information to identify objects meeting user-specified criteria.

Exchange exhibits the first two characteristics in a very positive manner. The last three points are not currently met by the standard Exchange software, although a combination of third party offerings may be enough to establish the basis for a document management system.

As we've discussed, an object check-in and check-out facility can be emulated through permissions and user discipline. It's harder to implement audit controls, something to track who did what to a document, for what reason, and when. You could implement a log in each folder and require users to complete it, but this depends on users complying with the request.

What is sure is that Exchange public folders can act as a more than adequate replacement for the shared directories on file servers that are used by many companies as document repositories. Ever since the first NetWare file servers arrived on the market people have used file services to allow users to share documents together. It's not just NetWare now. Companies use Windows NT, DIGITAL PATHWORKS, and other products too. All these systems allow people to share information, but they are more restrictive than public folders.

High end document management or text retrieval features can be incorporated into Exchange through third party products such as Fulcrum Find!, KeyFile, PC DOCS, or Verity's Search97 product[14]. In

---

14.   Check the latest third party product list as new products are added all the time.

terms of text retrieval the usual approach is not to ever search through the physical contents of public folders. Instead, background processes periodically scan public folders and construct an index that can then be searched against. Much greater flexibility and power is gained when searching, but at a cost of an additional load on the server (to build the indexes and run the search engine). There is also a danger that a relevant object might not be located because it has not been indexed since it was added to the Public Information Store.

5.6 System Backups

A very wise person once said that an important difference between an electronic mail and word processing applications was that when a word processor stopped working its effect was normally confined to a single user and perhaps a small quantity of documents. But when an electronic mail system collapses everyone is affected and normally it's the people at the top who notice fastest (and complain quickest).

Electronic mail systems depend on many different hardware and software components to keep everything going. If any element fails to operate in the required manner data corruption can occur. If the hardware suffers a catastrophic failure, or the site where the computers are located is afflicted by some disaster, you'll need to know the steps necessary to get your users back on-line as quickly as possible. In all these instances system backups are a prerequisite.

Backups, in their purest sense, are snapshots of a system's state at a certain point in time. All of the data available to the system should exist in the backup and should be restorable to exactly the same state if required. Backups can be written out to many different forms of magnetic or other media, although the most common type is some form of high-density magnetic tape.

The standard backup utility (NTBACKUP.EXE) provided with Windows NT V3.51 or V4.0 is not suitable for taking backups of an Exchange server due to the nature of the complex connections between the Information Stores and the transaction logs (see the discussion starting on page 249). When Exchange is installed the standard Windows NT backup utility is replaced with an enhanced version. The enhancements made to NTBACKUP.EXE are:

- Support for the transactional nature of the Exchange databases. In particular, the capacity to deal with the fact that the total content of the databases are represented by .EDB files, transaction logs, and transactions that might still be queued in memory.

- Ability to perform on-line backups. In other words, to copy the Information and Directory Stores to tape without having to shut down Exchange services. Users continue to work during backups.

- Extension of the NTBACKUP.EXE user interface to allow system administrators to select which sites and servers they wish to backup or restore.

Figure 5.46
*Using
NTBACKUP to
select a server
from an
organization
before backing
it up*

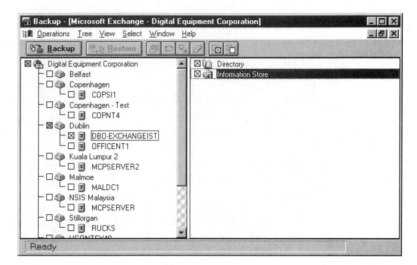

Figure 5.46 shows an Exchange organization displayed in the main window of NTBACKUP. The system administrator can select the server or servers they wish to backup, and whether or not the Directory or Information Store, or both, should be processed. The concept of single seat administration means that it is possible to conduct all backups and restore operations from a single server. However, the practical network limitations encountered when shipping many gigabytes of information over the network to a single server during backup operations means that you'll probably want to run backup from a server in each site, or even on each server.

Don't make the mistake of introducing a third-party extension to your system that conflicts with the requirements of Exchange. And don't fall into the trap of retro-fitting older software, such as a Windows NT service pack, which might over-write the change to enable NTBACKUP to support on-line backups of the Exchange Information and Directory Stores.

5.6.1   Creating a backup strategy

Although Exchange server does an excellent and almost automatic job of keeping its databases in shape, contributing to a high system availability level for users, hardware failures can and will occur. And when it's your turn to experience a hardware failure on the server you'll be glad that backups exist.

System failures come in two broad categories.

- Disk failure.

- Other non-critical system component failure. For example, the video monitor for the server develops a fault.

- Critical system component failure. For example, the mother-board or other associated component experiences a fault that cannot be quickly rectified.

Any failure situation requires some fast but calm thinking in order to make the correct decisions to get everything up on line again. If the system cannot be brought back up, can you substitute another similar system and restore application data? If it's a particular system component can it be replaced or can the system configuration be altered to work around the problem? Having backups around won't replace making the right decision, but they're a great safety net.

The MTBF (Mean Time Between Failure) rate for hard disks is improving all the time. This doesn't mean that you will never experience a hard disk failure, but it does mean that you are less likely to have one over any particular period of time. A high MTBF is no guarantee that the disk won't fail tomorrow, so the challenge for system administrators is to have a plan to handle the problem when it arises.

Without a RAID array, if something does go wrong with a disk you'll have to stop operations and fix the problem or swap in a new drive. Once the hardware problem is fixed you'll have to restore the data, and of course this simple statement assumes that you have copies of all the application files that were stored on the faulty drive, and possess the capability to move the data onto the new drive. Backups come into their own here!

Having the capability to take on-line backups is one thing. Making the backups is quite another and there is a temptation to leave backups to the side and concentrate on more interesting work. This is a short-term and dangerous attitude. Nightly backups of the Information and Directory Stores taken in tandem with full weekly backups of the server taken as a whole (in other words, including Windows NT, all the other applications, as well as the Exchange server files) must be taken if any guarantee as to the integrity of the messaging system is to be given to users.

The database-centric nature of Exchange poses a particular challenge for restore operations. There is no getting away from the fact that if a restore is necessary it's going to take much longer than you may realize. The length of time required to backup or restore databases from a production Exchange server may come as a surprise to some. It's easy to forget just how long it takes to move data to backup media. The Private and Public Information Stores both have the capacity to expand quickly, so your backup times will grow in proportion. After a server has been in production for a number of months you might find that it's time to consider looking for faster or higher capacity media to help reduce backup times. Remember too that it's not just Exchange data that must be backed up. Windows NT, user files, and other application data all contribute to the amount of data and length of backup operations.

Figure 5.47
*A successful
backup*

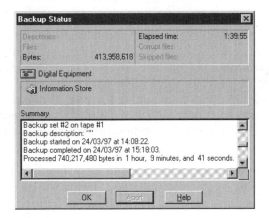

It is also important that the correct levels of service packs are applied to Windows NT and Exchange before commencing any restore operation. The database structure has changed a number of times as Exchange evolved from V4.0 through a series of service packs to Exchange V5.0 and then to V5.5. Generally speaking, you cannot restore a database from a backup taken with a higher software revision level. In other words, don't expect to be able to restore a backup taken with Exchange V5.5 to a server running Exchange V5.0. This rule does not hold true for all combinations of service packs and versions, but there's enough truth in it to make a strong recommendation that backups should be restored to servers running identical software versions.

All of the factors discussed here must be accounted for in the operational procedures you employ at your installation. Consider this question: how long will it take to restore one gigabyte of data from your backup media using the backup software you employ? Now, how long will it take to restore 3GB, or maybe 10GB, or how about a full-blown 100GB Private Information Store? And what about the Public Information Store? And the Directory Store? And all the other applications you may want to run?

In most circumstances, even when suitable hardware is waiting to be hot-swapped into your production environment the answer is counted in hours. Even when the restore is complete you may have other work to do before Exchange is available for use again. For instance, messages and other items waiting in the transaction logs may have to be written into the Private and Public Information Stores. Exchange does this automatically, but applying masses of transactions at one time delays the start-up operation (90 logs might take between 20 and 30 minutes to process). Users will be yelling at you to get the system back on-line as quickly as possible, so it's going to be a time when stress levels are rising, which just adds to the piquant nature of the task.

I'm not trying to scare you about restores. Instead, I'm trying to point out an essential fact of system management life. You must be prepared and able to conduct a well-planned restore of essential data in order to be successful. No one wants to explain to a CIO why the messaging system was unavailable for one or two days while staff fumbled their way through a restore. We'll discuss restores a little more later on in this chapter, but remember to secure your job continuation program by being prepared ahead of time.

Knowing how to properly use and safeguard backup media is an important part of a backup strategy. Think of the following questions: After the backups are performed how will the media be moved to a secure location? Is the secure location somewhere local or remote? When will the tapes or other media be used for backup purposes again? How can the backups be recovered quickly if needed?

5.6.2   Taking backups

The simplest way to perform a backup is to double-click on the NTBACKUP icon and start things off, as illustrated in figure 5.46. Easy as this is to do it's often inconvenient to take backups interactively. Backups should be taken on a regular basis and you're not always going to be around to start things off.

WINAT.EXE (see Figure 5.48) is one of the utilities available on the Windows NT Resource Kit. WINAT provides a GUI for the standard Windows NT AT.EXE (command line scheduler) utility and allows you to schedule tasks for execution in the background without human intervention. WINAT is similar to many other third-party scheduling programs that are available. These programs often have extended feature sets that ease the scheduling process, but WINAT provides enough functionality to get the job done in many cases. However, as we'll see later on, third party backup utilities come with significantly better scheduling capabilities that become very important for corporate installations.

Figure 5.48
Scheduling a daily backup with the WINAT utility

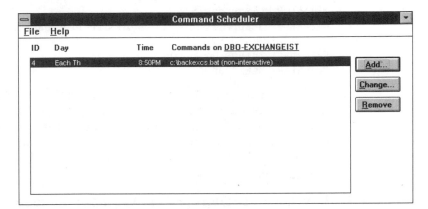

WINAT schedules batch files (.BAT files) to execute at specified times. Before you can use WINAT you'll need to write a simple batch file and create the commands to tell NTBACKUP.EXE what components should be backed up. You can take both on-line and off-line backups. On-line backups are those taken with all Exchange services active. Off-line backups are taken after all Exchange services have been stopped. Exchange has been designed to fully support on-line backups, so there's no reason why you shouldn't plan to take on-line backups all the time. Off-line backups permit system registry data relating to the Exchange configuration to be included in the backup. As such, an off-line backup is a more accurate and complete picture of the contents of an Exchange server, albeit one taken at the expense of stopping all services beforehand.

The complete set of parameters for NTBACKUP is described in chapter 15 of the Exchange Administrator's Guide. A two-line batch file to take a backup of the Information and Directory Stores on the DBO-EXCHANGEIST server is shown below:

```
NTBACKUP backup DS \\DBO-EXCHANGEIST IS \\DBO-EXCHANGEIST /v /d
"On-line backup of DBO-EXCHANGEIST" /t normal /l

Exit
```

Coding up the commands to stop and start Exchange services before and after an off-line backup is easy. You need to include a NET STOP command for each Exchange service before NTBACKUP is invoked, and a matching NET START command for each service afterwards. For example:

```
REM Stop the Internet Mail Service
NET STOP MsExchangeIMC
REM Stop the Information Store
NET STOP MsExchangeIS
NTBACKUP backup C:\ D:\ E:\ /v/d "Off-line backup for
DBO-EXCHANGEIST" /b
REM Start things up again
NET START MsExchangeIS
```

As you can see, there are differences in the NTBACKUP commands used for on-line and off-line backups. On-line backups specify whether the Information or Directory Store, or both, should be backed up whereas off-line backups ignore the stores and concentrate on backing up the files contained on specified disks (C:, D:, and E: in the example shown above).

5.6.3 How online backups process Exchange databases

The database engine used by Exchange allows on-line backup with users connected and actively using the databases. It follows therefore that transactions can take place during the backup process, for example when users create and send messages. During on-line backup processes a number of special-purpose files known as patch files are used by Exchange to track these transactions.

A separate patch file can be created for each store. The files are called:

- PRIV.PAT—Private Information Store Patch File
- PUB.PAT—Public Information Store Patch File
- DIR.PAT—Directory Store Patch File

The process of backing up an Exchange database follows these steps:

1. A patch file is created for the database. For example, PUB.PAT.

2. The current transaction log is disabled and prevented from accepting new transactions (this only happens with the Private and Public Information Stores).

3. The database and log files are written to the backup media. During this time any transactions written from memory are directed to the patch file.

4. The block on the current transaction log is removed to allow

it to accept transactions from memory again.

5.   The contents of the patch file are written to the current transaction log.

6.   The backup continues to stream data from the store to the backup tape. During this time transactions are recorded in the patch file.

7.   When the store is backed up, the patch file is written to the backup save set.

8.   The patch file is deleted.

9.   The next database to be backed up is selected.

10.   After all databases have been backed up all the transaction logs containing data now fully written and checkpointed in the database are deleted.

Patch files are created in the \MDBDATA directory. You will only be able to see them during a backup process. If you find the files after a backup has seemingly finished it's a good indication that you need to check the backup log to ensure that everything completed OK.

5.6.4   Restoring data to an Exchange server

Having backup tapes taken on a regular basis and then carefully stored away is clearly a great step towards assuring data security, but having the ability to restore data from the backup tapes is an equally important part of the overall equation.

Some sort of hardware failure is the most common reason why a restore is required. It's also possible for the Information or Directory Stores to be corrupted in some manner, perhaps as a side effect of an intermittent hardware fault. In this case the ISINTEG or ESEUTIL utilities (see page 360) may be able to rectify the problem and allow normal processing to continue. If not, a restore is required. In all cases where database corruption has occurred it's a good idea to have the hardware checked out to eliminate it as a potential underlying cause. There is no point in restoring a backup onto a server where a problem lurks deep in the hardware.

Let's assume that a hardware failure has happened. You can't use the server where the failure occurred. What steps need to be taken to get a substitute server up and running? Here's an outline checklist:

1.   Create a new server with a hardware configuration as close as possible to the original computer. This includes disks, tape drive, memory, and any special devices.

2.   Make sure that the correct version of Windows NT (complete with any required service packs) is installed.

3.   Connect the new server into the domain structure. The substitute system should have the same name as the failed system. The substitute should assume the same role in the domain structure. In other words, if the failed system was a Backup Domain Controller (BDC) the substitute should become a BDC. If it was a simple server with no role in user authentication that's fine too. The most complex situation is where the failed system was the PDC (see below).

4.   Install Exchange on the substitute. Use the same site and organization name as the failed system. Use the same Exchange service account. If joining an existing site use SETUP /R to install Exchange. The /R switch tells Exchange that configuration information for the newly installed server should not be replicated to the rest of the organization. Make sure that you reinstall any service packs before attempting to restart the Exchange services.

5.   You should also install the Exchange client software so that you can test the effectiveness of the restore once it's completed.

6.   Run NTBACKUP.EXE and restore the Directory and Information Stores from the backup.

7.   If the restore was performed from an off-line backup, run ISINTEG -PATCH to update the GUIDs (Globally Unique Identifiers) in the Information Store. ISINTEG does not have to be run if the restore is performed from a backup taken when Exchange was on-line.

8.   Use the Exchange client to check accounts and make sure that messages can be sent and read. Use the administration program to check that the correct correlation exists between Exchange mailboxes and Windows NT accounts.

9.   Make sure that all connectors are operating properly. Check directory replication connections if the system being restored should act as a directory replication bridgehead for the site.

10.   If you can only restore the Information Store and are unable to restore the directory, use the Directory Consistency checker to scan the Information Store and create a new directory object to match each Information Store object.

11.   Run the Exchange Performance Optimizer utility (see chapter 11) to optimize the Exchange configuration.

A strong recommendation has already been made not to run Exchange on the same Windows NT computer that acts as the Primary Domain Controller, or PDC (see page 121). The link between the Windows NT security database (SAM) and how authentication for access to directory objects is performed is the major reason behind the recommendation. When you only have one server to do everything it's impossible to avoid having Exchange and the PDC on the same system, but in all cases where multiple servers are in use you should definitely separate the two.

If you rebuild a system that acts as a PDC a new SAM is created. When the time comes to restore the Exchange directory any attempt to authenticate against the new SAM will fail, the net effect being that no Exchange service will be able to start and you won't even be able to log onto the Administration program. The Information Store can be restored and you can use a brand new directory to create mailboxes to access data in the store, but it's obvious that a lot of work is needed to recreate mailboxes and other directory information, and then propagate it to the rest of the organization. Apart from anything else there's lots of potential for error and confusion.

On the other hand, if the system being restored is a BDC a copy SAM will be retrieved from the PDC when the system is rebuilt. Note that you'll need to use the Windows NT Server Manager to demote the system from BDC status and then promote it again after Windows NT has been reinstalled on the computer. This step is necessary to ensure that the SAM data is copied correctly from the PDC to the new BDC.

The simplest case to handle is where the Exchange server being rebuilt takes no part in user authentication. In these cases it is sufficient to rebuild Windows NT and Exchange on the server as outlined above. User authentication will be accomplished by reference to the PDC and/or BDC in the domain that the server joins during the rebuilding process.

5.6.5 The challenge of bricked restores

Bricked backups (and restores) are much more complex than you might expect. The data for a mailbox is arranged across a series of different tables in the Private Information Store, yet during a backup it is streamed out to tape without any context. In other words, a mailbox does not exist in any one place or section of a tape. Instead, its components are spread out across the entire backup set on the tape. Streaming data out in this manner is the key to achieving fast backup and restore times, but it does impose a penalty when the time comes to restore a single mailbox.

Retrieving a complete mailbox requires a program to reassemble all the folders, items, and attachments. At the time of writing, I am aware of only one third party backup utility that can even attempt this feat (ArcServe[15]), which essentially connects to the database as if it was a MAPI client and reads information from mailboxes in the order it finds them. This is much slower than streaming the data out of the store directly to a tape, but it does mean that the mailbox can be recovered afterwards.

Restoring data brings its own challenges. The tables that comprise the store use pointers to link each other, and usage counts to track the number of references to specific items and attachments from other tables. When a mailbox is restored it is more than likely that a number of the pointers and usage counts have changed since the backup was taken. The net effect is that:

- Message attribute information (TO:, CC:, BCC: FROM:) is often missing.

- Restored messages are treated as newly created items. Each restored mailbox receives its own copy of an item.

- Format instructions in message content (bold, bullets, underline, and so on) may be missing because RTF (and HTML) are not supported.

- Links to attachments and other objects (like web pages) may be missing.

In addition, because of the processing required to reassemble a mailbox, bricked restores are slow. The exact speed depends on the hardware environment, but a bricked restore is likely to be several times slower than a regular restore. The slower speed is offset by the fact that only data for a single mailbox needs to be restored. Even with all these drawbacks the fact remains that the mailbox will be recovered and the user will have access to the majority of the information it once contained, which is probably all they're concerned with.

The majority of backup software packages, including NTBACKUP, do not support the ability to save or restore a single mailbox. NTBACKUP operates on the Information or Directory Stores at the database level, so if you want to restore a single user's mailbox you have to restore the entire Private Information Store.

Restoring a user's mailbox is a task that system administrators probably won't welcome with open arms. Experience with other messaging systems indicates that over the course of a server's productive life there is more than a 50% chance that you'll encounter a situation where a user

---

15.   Seagate is apparently working on similar functionality for their Backup Exec product.

mailbox is deleted in error, or a user deletes some important files in error and only realizes their mistake some time later. Given the human capacity to err, the latter situation is more likely to arise. It's difficult to restore the complete Information Store onto a production server. You could do this, but only through a set of complicated steps involving:

1.   Shut down the production server

2.   Take a backup of the Information Store

3.   Restore the backup of the Information Store that contains the mailbox you wish to restore or otherwise recover.

4.   Start up the Exchange Information Store, but don't allow users to log on and make sure that no external connectors are active.

5.   Log onto the mailbox and move all the messages you wish to recover from the mailbox to a personal Information Store (PST file). You can drag and drop individual messages or select all the messages in the mailbox and copy them in one operation to the PST.

6.   Shut down Exchange.

7.   Restore the backup taken in step 2.

8.   Restart the Exchange services and allow users to resume work. Make sure all connectors and directory replicators are restarted successfully.

9.   Provide the user with the PST and instruct them how to access the recovered messages from the PST.

Executing this complicated set of actions will take at least four hours on any reasonably sized server. Shutting down a production system for four hours and depriving users of their e-mail is not a recipe for generating popularity, so another tactic needs to be considered.

The obvious solution is to restore the Information Store onto another Windows NT computer and use that as the basis to retrieve the necessary messages. To do this you'll need:

- A Windows NT server with the same version of Windows NT and Exchange installed as on the production server. We'll call this system the "recovery host".

- A tape drive on the recovery host capable of reading the backups created on the production server.

- Exchange (on the recovery host) must be configured with the same organization and site name as the production server where the backup originates. If the organization and site name do not match you won't be able to restore the backup taken from the production server.

Equipped with a suitable recovery host you can proceed to restore the backup tape, log into the user's mailbox and extract the necessary messages to a PST. The pressure to do all of this is much less than when you've had to take a production server off-line, so you can take your time and make sure that everything's done correctly.

5.6.6   Restoring single documents

Restoring a complete mailbox is something that shouldn't happen often. Administrators, after all, don't normally delete mailboxes without good reason. Many installations make it a practice not to delete user accounts immediately after someone leaves the company or otherwise ceases to use a server on the basis that they might return. Instead, the account is disabled and kept for a period of weeks.

On the other hand, users delete documents and messages that they really want to keep all the time. It's easy to hit the delete key when an important message is highlighted, sending the message off to the Deleted Items folder. If you realize the error in time the message can be retrieved from Deleted Items, but it's a different matter if the user logs off from Exchange and the Deleted Items folder is emptied.

Unlike other messaging systems the messages managed by the Exchange Information Store never exist as individual files. Messages, documents, and other objects added to the Information Store reside in the database as binary objects, or BLOBS in database terminology. In other words, within the database messages are stored as collections of binary information which make little sense to anything else except the Information Store. As we've seen there are many advantages in this scheme, but there's a dark side too.

Prior to Exchange V5.5, documents or messages deleted in error can only be recovered by restoring a user's entire mailbox. The restore is only going to be possible if the document or message existed in the mailbox at the time when the backup was taken. Nothing can be done to recover the missing item if it was created and deleted since the last backup. The introduction of the deleted items cache in Exchange V5.5 dramatically changes the situation.

5.6.7   Deleted items recovery

When an item is "deleted" it is first moved into the Deleted Items folder. Eventually, any items in the Deleted Items folder are removed from the database when the folder is emptied. Items deleted from public folders are removed immediately. Removing an item from the database is referred to as a hard delete as any reference to the item is permanently removed.

The Exchange V5.5 Information Store includes a new flag (a MAPI property) to enable "soft" or two-phase deletes. After a soft delete the item is merely hidden from user view by setting the delete flag. Items that have been soft deleted are collectively referred to as the "deleted items cache". However, the cache does not exist in any physical sense and is merely a term to refer to items that are waiting to be removed from the store. Items are maintained in the store until their retention period elapses, after which they are removed from the store by the background IS maintenance tasks that are usually performed each night.

Figure 5.49
Setting the default item retention period

The default retention period for new or upgrade installations is zero days. In other words, delete behavior should proceed as before. This is understandable for upgrade installations because it's in line with the Microsoft philosophy that, wherever possible, an upgrade should never affect a system's configuration. You therefore have to configure both the Private and Public Information Stores to activate the deleted items cache, and this has to be done on each server within a site. Selecting a store and altering its properties to set an item retention period (Figure 5.49) activates the cache. Note the "Don't permanently delete items until the store has been backed up" checkbox. This tells Exchange that the contents of the cache should be kept until a backup is taken, even if that backup occurs many days after the item retention period is exceeded. The logic is simple. If an accident happens you'll always be able to recover an item from a backup tape!

It's possible that you will decide that the deleted items cache is inappropriate for some or all servers in your organization. Keeping electronic mail around worries corporate lawyers, who view the existence of e-mail as yet another source of data for potential discovery actions to uncover. Strict limits are sometimes imposed on users and the Mailbox Cleanup Agent from the Exchange Resource Kit is often used to enforce the length of time messages can be retained in mailboxes. However, even when limits are in place exceptions are possible. Just like storage limits for mailboxes, Exchange allows administrators to set special deleted items retention period on selected mailboxes. For example, you might decide that all members of the executive staff use a 30-day rather than a 7-day retention period. In this instance, you need to select each mailbox and set the deleted items retention period, as shown in Figure 5.50.

Figure 5.50
Setting a specific deletion period for a mailbox

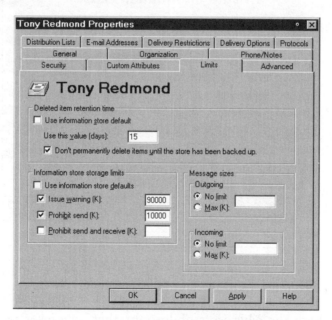

5.6.8 Recovering a deleted item

Pushing all the work to recover deleted items down to users is a great boon for administrators. Appeals to the help desk to recover an important message can now be bounced back to the user, but only if they are running the right client. Without the appropriate user interface, you'll never be able to recover an item, and not all clients support the concept. In fact, Outlook V8.03, the version distributed with Exchange V5.5

(or any later client such as Outlook 98) is the only client that includes such an option in its user interface (see Tools.Recover Deleted Items).

Earlier versions of Outlook, the Exchange client, POP3, IMAP4, and web browser clients are all left at the starting gate. An administrator can log on to a user's mailbox with Outlook V8.03 and recover items on their behalf, and this is certainly a strategy that can work for a limited period of time when clients have not yet been upgraded. It's also a viable strategy that can work if you have a large population of POP3, IMAP4, or web clients, but in this case it's probably a task that's best handled by the help desk rather than system administrators.

By default the Deleted Items folder is the only folder enabled for item recovery. Non-MAPI clients are able to delete items in place, without moving them through the Deleted Items folder. Outlook clients can also delete in place, by using SHIFT/Delete to delete an item. It's important to note that the deleted items cache is always active for all folders but the Outlook user interface is only activated to allow recovery from the Deleted Items folder. If non-MAPI clients are used or people have the habit of deleting items in place you may want to change this behavior and allow Outlook to recover items in all folders. The change can be made through a registry setting:

```
HKEY_LOCAL_MACHINE\Software\Microsoft\Exchange\Client\Options\
DumpsterAlwaysOn=1
```

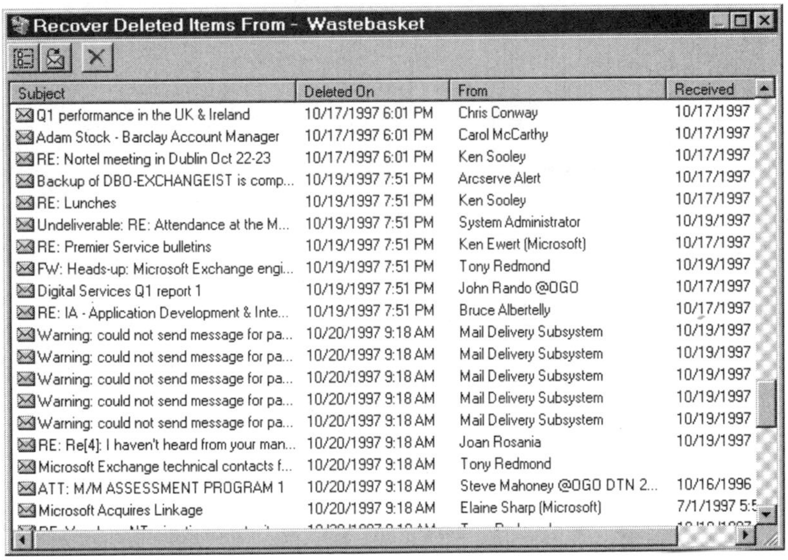

Figure 5.51
Viewing items in
the deleted items
cache

Items are recovered from the cache into the folder from where they were originally deleted. This statement sounds obvious but its implementation may catch some people. Private items are recovered into the Deleted Items folder while items for a public folder can be recovered directly into the folder. It's possible that some users might recover an item successfully only to find that it's deleted again when the Deleted Items folder is emptied the next time they exit Outlook.

Select either the Deleted Items folder or a public folder and then click on the Tools.Recover Deleted Items option. A list of items in the cache is revealed (Figure 5.51). Note that you can't use a public folder "favorite" to recover items. The base public folder must be selected before recovery can work. Select one or more items from the list and then click on the recover icon to instruct Outlook to fetch the item back from the cache.

5.6.9 The size of the Deleted Items cache

The deleted items cache forms part of the public and Private Information Stores so its implementation has an effect on the size of databases. There is no way to set the cache to a certain size. It's difficult to predict how much extra disk space is required for the cache because this depends on factors specific to each installation such as the volume of mail and the length of the deleted items retention period. Note that items in the cache are not counted against mailbox storage quotas.

Figure 5.52
Viewing the amount each mailbox has in the deleted items cache

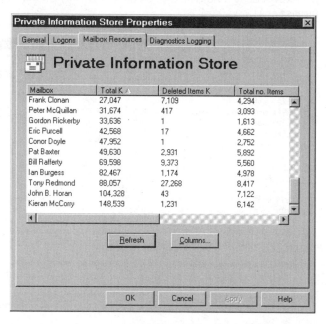

Clearly if the cache holds messages for 14 days rather than 7 it will be larger. Seven days seems like a reasonable retention period. After all, if someone hasn't recognized that a deleted message is required after 7 days maybe it's not so essential after all. Here are some ways you can monitor the size of the cache:

1. View the "Mailbox Resources" properties of the Private Information Store (Figure 5.52).

2. Alternatively, resources taken up by mailboxes can be seen by expanding "Private Information Store\Mailbox Resources" section of the tree view in the left-hand pane of the Exchange administration program.

3. Use Performance Monitor to monitor the size and number of items in the cache. The following counters can be used:

MSExchange IS Private	Total Count of Recoverable Items
MSExchange IS Private	Total Size of Recoverable Items
MSExchange IS Public	Total Count of Recoverable Items
MSExchange IS Public	Total Size of Recoverable Items

For options 1 and 2 you'll have to add the "Deleted Items K" field to the set of data that's shown. Using the Exchange administration program allows you to capture the data into a CSV file that can be later manipulated and reported on with Excel or Access.

Figure 5.53
*Using Perfor-
mance Monitor
to check the size
of the deleted
items cache*

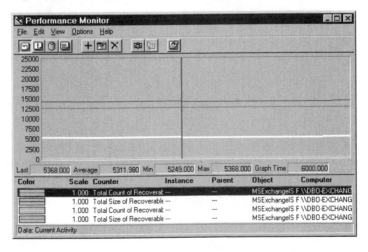

Figure 5.53 shows Performance Monitor being used to discover the size of the deleted items cache. The four counters are active and the highlighted counter shows that 5,368 items are in the cache (Private Information Store). The size of the cache is not immediately obvious from the screen shot but is in fact 1435 kilobytes (1.4MB). The cache

will take a little time to establish a consistent size. After a month, I expect that the number of items and size of the cache will be settled and will not vary dramatically thereafter.

5.6.10 Restoring the contents of public folders

Accidents can happen to user mailboxes, and users are more than capable of deleting objects from their mailboxes in error, and much the same type of accidents can happen to the contents of public folders. What can be done to recover an important document that's been deleted from a public folder?

The first thing to do is to check whether a copy of the document exists in a replica folder elsewhere in the organization. Changes, including deletions, have to be replicated before they are effective throughout an organization. It is therefore possible to go to a public folder replica on another server and recover a copy of the desired document before the deletion command is replicated. However, it must be acknowledged that such a recovery depends on realizing that the document shouldn't have been deleted as soon as the action is performed, quick access to a remote server hosting a replica (directly via the network or perhaps through a phone call to the local system administrator), and a large slice of luck.

If your luck runs out and you don't manage to get to a replica in time there is no alternative but to refer back to a backup. Much the same problems exist for the restore. You don't want to stop the production server to recover the document if at all possible, so using a separate recovery host is the best approach. After the document is recovered to a PST you can move the document from the PST back into the public folder.

5.6.11 Third party backup utilities

NTBACKUP is all very well, but as we've seen it's a pretty basic backup engine. The job gets done, and the Exchange databases will be written safely to tape (or another backup medium), but the interface and features available in NTBACKUP leave a lot to be desired, especially when you're dealing with high-end servers. The same situation existed for Windows NT before Exchange came along, and for that reason there are many highly functional and feature-rich backup third-party backup utilities available for Windows NT today. Most of these products have created add-on modules or new version releases to support Exchange, so NTBACKUP is not the only option. Table 5.8 lists some of the major third-party backup products that support Exchange. Use the web address to get information about the latest product features to help decide which is best for you.

Table 5.8 *Third party backup utilities*

Company	Product	Web address
Cheyenne Software (a division of Computer Associates)	ArcServe (Figure 5.54)	http://www.cheyenne.com
Seagate Corporation	Backup Exec	http://www.seagate.com
Barratt Edwards International Corporation	Ultrabac	http://www.ultrabac.com
Legato Systems, Inc.	Networker for Windows NT	http://www.legato.com http://www.storage.digital.com

It's always difficult to justify the additional expense of buying in a package to replace a standard utility, especially when there is a standard utility that appears to do the job in an adequate manner and there's a need to install the new software on many different servers. Backups are a system manager's parachute and if they don't work when they are needed then anyone involved may soon be looking for a new job, so it is reasonable to regard backup software as a very important part of the management armoury.

Figure 5.54
Viewing the ArcServe log to see details of a backup operation for Exchange

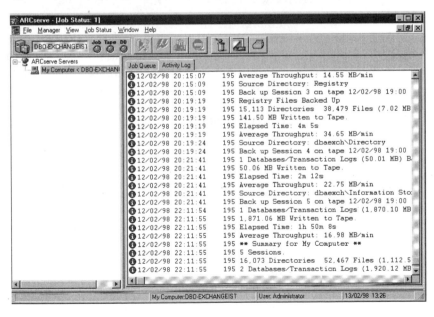

A specialized package often provides very useful features that are missing in the standard utility. In practice there are three major enhancements that a third party backup utility might provide over the standard NTBACKUP program:

1.   Scheduling

2.   Speed

3.   Control

Specialized backup products tend to support high-end features such as unattended backups, automated loading and unloading via tape libraries, and network backup to very large storage silos (CD-equipped juke boxes or similar). Such features are not critical to small or medium servers, but they need to be considered for any server that hosts large databases.

We've already reviewed how the AT and WINAT utilities can be used in association with NTBACKUP to schedule backups (see section beginning on page 342). However, the scheduling capabilities that are possible with this combination are rudimentary, to say the least. Third party backup utilities usually include a complete scheduling engine that allows any type of backup to be processed at whatever interval (daily, weekly, or monthly) that's desired. In addition, these scheduling engines tend to be very much easier to use, and make it possible to select different parts of Exchange for backup at different times. It is also possible to include important files and even the system registry when backing up a server.

Exchange permits on-line backups to be taken. In other words, there is no requirement to stop the different services (Information Store, directory, system attendant, and so on) while the backup is proceeding. It might therefore appear that speed is of little concern. After all, you can start a backup off each morning and have it running alongside users as the day proceeds. This is true, but it's only a partial picture. Backups can proceed on-line, but restores can only be done with a "silent" server. If backup software processes data quickly it's normal that restores are quick too. However, restores normally proceed at half the speed of a backup. Best practice is to plan for backups to take four hours or less to keep any restore operation to less than the length of a working day.

Significant performance improvements are made in the backup API in Exchange V5.5. It is now possible to pump data out to devices faster than they can accept it. The Exchange developers reported that their tests showed that they could stream data out of the store at the rate of 60GB/hour to a null device. Hardware slows things down, but even so, equipped with a dual-striped tape they were able to achieve real backup rates of up to 30GB/hour. This figure has been exceeded in production environments with quad-DLT devices working in a RAID array, which can process nearly 35GB/hour.

Increased speed and reduced backup times make it more feasible to take full backups every day rather than a more normal cycle of full backups every week with incremental backups taken on the days in between. The advantage gained here will only accrue if you have to restore the server. You'll be very happy to find that it's much easier and faster to restore from a single full backup than to go through the hoops and loops of restoring from the last full backup followed by all the incremental backups since. With large servers that have stores greater than 50GB for a single database the backup times may be a touch too long to take full backups every day, but with smaller servers it's certainly a tactic you should consider.

Better control over backup operations is the final advantage provided by third party utilities. NTBACKUP is quite content to overwrite the same tape with a new backup every day if the tape is left in the tape drive, as some people have discovered to their loss. Commands such as "eject tape after backup is complete" prevent accidents happening and contribute to data security. This type of problem is unlikely to occur in data centers where skilled operations staff work, but it's entirely possible in places where people only know how to insert tapes into drives. Effective tape handling is critically important for installations dealing with large stores that span more than one tape. You don't want to get into a situation where a backup never actually completes because someone forgot to take out the first tape and insert a new tape at the appropriate time.

A number of the third party backup utilities also allow you to backup the system registry, disks, and the Exchange databases in a single operation, much easier than having to make (and restore) three separate backup tapes. At the time of writing, ArcServe V6.5 is unique in its ability to allow bricked backups and restores.

If you decide not to use NTBACKUP, make sure that the same backup software is used everywhere. Don't allow yourself to get into the situation where some sites (or even worse, some servers within a site) use different backup software or different backup devices. With backups it pays dividends to keep things simple and that means creating the same backup environment everywhere—the same software, tapes, and drives. Due to the different ways that software can stream data out to tapes, it is highly unlikely that one backup software package will be able to read a tape created by another. Once you allow diversity the potential is created that a backup tape, for one reason or another, cannot be restored onto a system. And Murphy's Law dictates that this situation will occur just after a server hosting 500 users has crashed and cannot be got back on-line.

OFM (Open File Manager) from St. Bernard Software[16] has recently begun to attract the attention of administrators searching for the best backup solution. As indicated by its name, OFM allows backups to be taken of open files by using a cache to store data that is modified during a backup. OFM works with the majority of NT backup products, but doesn't require specific modules to deal with files like Exchange or SQL/Server databases, which means that OFM is a much cheaper solution than something like ArcServe or Backup Exec when complete with different modules. I have not used this product and cannot comment on its effectiveness, but it has received some good reviews within the NT community. No real experience of how well OFM has coped when the time came to restore Exchange databases after a catastrophic failure has yet been reported, and this will be the acid test of whether OFM can be used with Exchange. However, I must say that I have deep doubts about how well a cache is able to cope with very large databases that may take several hours to backup. Will the cache be able to hold all the data that changes during the backup? And what happens if it doesn't? As always, thorough testing, including recovery of databases to a different server, is recommended before deployment.

It's important to understand that while third party backup software can provide some valuable advantages, it's another piece to be fitted into the system configuration matrix. New releases of the backup software must be qualified against existing versions of Exchange, and then against new versions of Exchange. The backup software should also be checked against service packs of both Exchange and Windows NT. The Exchange development team cannot check their product against every third party extensions, so it's entirely possible that the installation of a service pack will introduce a problem that only comes to light when a backup operation is attempted[17]. Or, even worse, during a restore. The complex interaction between Exchange, Windows NT, and any third party product adds weight to the argument that all combinations of software products (including patches) should be well tested before being introduced to production servers.

5.7   Maintaining the Information Store

Since Exchange V5.0 was released, I have never encountered a situation where the Information Store has been corrupted through a proven soft-

---

16.   www.stbernard.com

17.   While it may seem inconceivable that an Exchange service pack will cause problems for backup software it did happen with Exchange V4.0 SP3. A minor bug in the service pack prevented products like ArcServe connecting to the Information Store, so backups could not be taken. The problem was quickly fixed and an updated module posted on the Microsoft Web site, but the fact that the situation happened is a cautionary tale for all of us.

ware bug. This isn't to say that the software is perfect (it is, however, getting better all the time). It does reflect personal experience and the fact that the vast bulk of known database corruptions are due to hardware problems. The most common problems that can cause corruption within a database are:

- Hard disk failures
- Bugs in controller software
- Controller failures

Installing the best possible I/O subsystem and then maintaining it properly is vital to success with Exchange. The situation is simple: either you think the Exchange databases are important and take every possible step to protect them or you don't. It is amusing to see so many people worrying about the speed or number of their CPUs while never spending any time or money on disks and controllers. In particular, the decision to spend a few thousand extra dollars to install a high-end disk controller to protect data and increase performance seems like a no-brainer.

Systems that are well configured and managed experience less outages than those who limp along hoping that problems (and bugs) won't happen. You can take the following steps to protect your data:

1.   Perform a backup every day. If possible, take a full backup (it makes restores easier).

2.   Isolate the transaction logs from the databases. Never put the transaction logs on the same physical device as the databases. If possible, use separate controllers. In some respects the logs are as important as the database.

3.   Protect the databases by placing them on a RAID-5 volume with a controller that supports hot swappable disks, battery backup-up and mirroring for the write ahead cache, and is protected by a UPS.

4.   Review event logs for database problems every day. Check for disk outages too.

5.   Know the capability of the Exchange maintenance tools and schedule time for maintenance.

6.   Never power down a server without shutting the Information Store service down cleanly. The power off button is only for emergencies and not the quickest way to shut a server down.

All of this is just common sense. Nevertheless, isn't it amazing how often common sense is discarded in the headlong rush to deploy new technology?

Exchange performs maintenance operations against the Information Store in two distinct ways:

1.   On-line maintenance performed as the server is operating.

2.   Off-line maintenance procedures activated when something goes wrong.

5.7.1   On-line maintenance

Like most databases, the internal structures within the Information Store become less efficient over time. Data is not stored in an effective manner and becomes fragmented throughout the database. Taking Exchange off-line to compact the databases stops people using the server, so an on-line maintenance facility is included to keep things in order and defragment or re-order data within the Private and Public Information Stores.

Exchange is designed for continuous operation. There is no requirement to take the Information Store off-line for maintenance. It can be kept running all the time with both backups and maintenance operations being performed while users remain connected. The time when online maintenance is performed is a property of a server. Normally, as shown in Figure 5.55, online maintenance occurs when the load on a server is relatively quiet, such as in the early hours of the morning. You can make changes to the schedule by selecting a server, expanding its properties, and then accessing the schedule through the "IS Maintenance property page". It is possible to have online maintenance active all the time, but this will occupy some system resources that could otherwise be devoted to users. On-line maintenance is also performed for the directory, in which case it's controlled by setting the "Garbage collection interval" on the general property page of the DS Site Configuration object.

During online maintenance a number of background threads begin to walk through the leaf nodes of the binary tree within the store, comparing adjacent pages in an attempt to fill data pages more completely. Messaging is an unusual database application. Messages arrive and are often quickly deleted. Messages come in all shapes and sizes, with and without attachments, with large and small distribution lists. Compared to the predictable world of the traditional financial database application the Information Store is a most unpredictable place.

Figure 5.55
Defining a main-tenance schedule for the Informa-tion Store

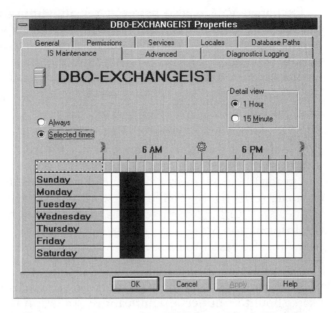

Online maintenance shuffles data around from one page to another. The table that contains message headers is a prime candidate for mainte-nance. Each message header takes about 400 bytes, so about 10 headers are stored per page. Because most folders are viewed in chronological order for best performance, it's important that headers are stored close to each other in that order. As new messages arrive into the data-base, their headers are inserted at the end of the binary tree, but dele-tions take place throughout the tree. Over time pages become less and less full, and if this situation is left unchecked performance will steadily degrade. Online maintenance therefore moves headers between adjacent pages to pack them more closely together. If two pages contain less than the content of a full page they are merged together, so a 30% full page will be merged with a 60% full page to form one 90% full page. The other page is left empty. After a while there is going to be a reasonable number of empty pages in the data-base, or "white space".

Exchange V4.0 and V5.0 are both able to perform page merging. Exchange V5.5 takes page processing a little further by shuffling indi-vidual records from adjacent pages to form pages that are 100% full, clearly the most efficient form of storage. Because their content varies greatly from message to message, pages that contain message and attachment content cannot be defragmented in the same manner. Deletions cause these pages to remain empty and become candidates for reuse.

Exchange V5.5 is also better at reusing empty pages and doesn't expand the database size quite as readily as V4.0 or V5.0 is prone to do. No attempt is made to restructure the database to arrange pages containing associated information (for example, to group all the headers for messages in a large folder) in a contiguous manner.

Given the database technology in use today, Exchange cannot eliminate the white space and shrink the size of the database to return space to the NT file system. Microsoft is working on how to solve that problem and a solution may appear in a future version of Exchange. You therefore have a choice. The store can be kept online all the time and gradually grow in size, or you can take it offline to run a utility to compact (effectively rebuild) the store with ESEUTIL to eliminate all white space. Offline compaction is the only way to reduce the size of the Information Store. Apart from regaining disk space, smaller databases are also faster to backup.

The effect of on-line maintenance is slight on most servers. Unless you are running close to the limits of your hardware's capabilities users shouldn't notice a significant degradation of server responsiveness as the Information Store is verified and any internal inconsistencies corrected. You can avoid any potential conflicts between the demands of users and the system maintenance processes by scheduling the maintenance to occur when a reduced number of users are active. As you can see from the maintenance times set in Figure 5.35, I like maintenance to occur when everyone is safely tucked up in bed or otherwise engaged in activities that don't require electronic mail.

5.8   Off-line maintenance

Two off-line maintenance utilities for the Information Store are provided with Exchange. These are:

- ISINTEG: the Information Store Integrity Checker
- ESEUTIL: the Exchange database utility

The executables for ISINTEG and ESEUTIL can be found in the EXCHSRVR\BIN directory. Both are command line utilities run in a DOS (command) box, with an extremely minimal interface. The Information Store service (and any associated services such as the Internet Mail service) must be stopped before either program is run. Further details of how to employ ESEUTIL and ISINTEG can be found in chapter 17 of the Exchange Administrator's Guide. Documentation for both utilities can be also be found in the \server\support\utils directory on the Exchange Server CD.

5.8.1 ISINTEG—The integrity checker

ISINTEG is designed to find and remove errors from the databases used for the Public and Private Information Stores. ISINTEG can test and fix a database, or just patch its contents.

In test mode a database is scanned carefully to determine whether any errors exist. Potential errors include incorrect reference counts for an object, table errors, or the discovery of objects that are not referenced anywhere within the store. The errors found in test mode can be fixed by ISINTEG as they are discovered. All errors are reported to a log file. ISINTEG is used in patch mode to repair an Information Store if it will not start up after being restored, for example, after a disk failure. Patch mode rectifies any inconsistencies that exist in an Information Store to ensure that data is not overwritten and that all data within the store is available to users.

Exchange uses a set of GUIDs held in the Information Store, the Windows NT system registry, and the Directory Store to verify that the contents of the Information Store are consistent. During normal operations the same value is maintained for the GUIDs in the three locations. If an off-line backup is used to restore the databases, perhaps after a disk crash, the possibility exists that the GUID in the restored database does not match the GUID in the system registry or that held in the Directory Store. Such an inconsistency will prevent the Information Store service from starting.

ISINTEG is able to adjust the GUIDs and allow the Information Store to start. This is done by running ISINTEG in patch mode, as shown below. The Directory Store service must be running before ISINTEG is started as otherwise ISINTEG will not be able to fetch the GUID information from the directory to adjust the Information Store.

```
C:\EXCHSRVR\BIN\ISINTEG -PATCH
```

All databases have some form of index used to catalog information. Exchange uses indexes based on GUIDs. In this instance, the GUIDs are partially based on the date and time when the identifier is created. Each Store (Directory or Information) has some base GUIDs that are created when the store is first established, and all of the objects created in the store from that time are allocated a GUID derived from the a base GUID. If a database is restored you are basically rolling back time, so you affect the date and time portion of the algorithm that creates new identifiers. Therefore, the potential now exists that the store might create a GUID that over-writes an identifier that's already allocated to another object within the store, with all the resulting confusion that would ensue. After an off-line backup is used to restore a database ISINTEG can validate the base GUID and update the store so that all new GUIDs are created correctly.

Restores performed from on-line backups do not require the store to be patched separately afterwards, mostly because the base GUIDs are checked and adjusted during the restore process. This is a good reason to always use the Windows NT Backup utility or a third party replacement utility that supports on-line backups of Exchange.

The structure of the Exchange databases is moderately complex. When ISINTEG is run in test/fix mode it validates the internal integrity of the structures by examining all the references and links between the different tables in the database. Reference counts, used by the single instance storage model, are also validated. Test/fix mode is run separately against the Public and Private Information Stores.

By default, ISINTEG produces a log file detailing what it has done. The log file should be checked afterwards so that you know exactly what's gone on. The default file names are ISINTEG.PRI for a run against the Private Information Store, or ISINTEG.PUB for the Public Information Store. I immediately rename these files to ISINTEG_PUB.TXT and ISINTEG_PRI.TXT to allow me use a text editor to view their contents. It's a pity that the Exchange engineers created yet another file type for what is purely a simple text file.

```
Microsoft Exchange Information Store Integrity Checker v4.993.3
Copyright (c) 1986-1996 Microsoft Corp. All rights reserved.

Started: 11/06/96 13:30:23

Store path: g:\Exchange\MDBDATA\PRIV.EDB
Store size: 147333120 bytes
Output log: isinteg.pri
Check mode: check and fix

Starting test 1 of 24, 'Categorization Tables'
Finished Categorization Tables. Time: 0h:0m:0s
Starting test 22 of 24, 'reference count verification'
Fix: Message[0001-0000001EBABD].RefCt: Deleted message table row
Fix: Attachment[0001-0000001EBABA].RefCt: Bad count - prop(1)<>calc(0) .. Fixed
Fix: Attachment[0001-0000001EBABC].RefCt: Bad count - prop(1)<>calc(0) .. Fixed
Finished reference count verification. Time: 0h:0m:17s, number of fixes = 3

Starting test 24 of 24, 'Row Count'
Warning: table DeliveredTo row count: Calc(1) <> Prop(0)
Warning: table Folders row count: Calc(600) <> Prop(0)
Warning: table Mailbox row count: Calc(28) <> Prop(0)
Warning: table ACLList row count: Calc(10) <> Prop(0)
Warning: table PerUserRead row count: Calc(505) <> Prop(0)
Warning: table ReplidMap row count: Calc(38) <> Prop(0)
```

```
Warning: table NamedProps row count: Calc(360) <> Prop(0)
Warning: table DeletedAttachments row count: Calc(2) <> Prop(0)
Fix: The performance monitor counters are set to the correct values
Finished Row Count. Time: 0h:0m:0s, number of warnings = 8, number of fixes = 1

. . . . . SUMMARY . . . . .

Total number of tests : 24
Total number of warnings : 8
Total number of errors : 1
Total number of fixes : 4
Total time : 0h:4m:5s
```

Figure 5.56
Extract (above)
from ISINTEG
log file

Edited highlights of an ISINTEG log file from a run against a Private Information Store are shown in Figure 5.56. Two of the tests performed by ISINTEG encountered errors. Test 22 validates reference counts for messages and attachments are correct. If the reference count is too low it is increased, avoiding the potential of the item being removed prematurely, and if the reference count is too high it is decreased so that it will be deleted at the right time. The final test validates the count of rows in each of the tables in the database and makes changes as required.

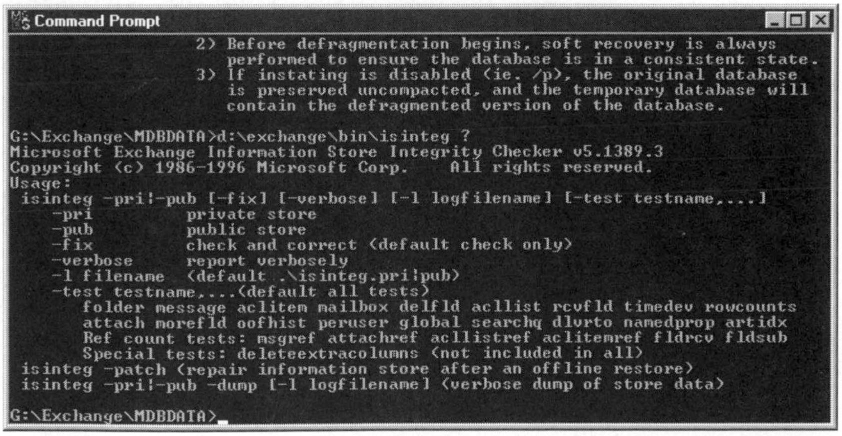

Figure 5.57
ISINTEG
options

The tests performed by ISINTEG and the way the utility operates in test/fix mode has evolved over time. Exchange V4.0 performed 24 tests, while Exchange V5.0 believed it sufficient to perform only 21 (for Private Information Stores). If you look at the bottom of the ISINTEG command-line options illustrated in Figure 5.57, you can see that a large number of switches for various tests are available. The screen shot is from V5.0, but serves to illustrate the point. Exchange V5.5 forces administrators to think about the tests they wish to perform and doesn't allow you to say "test and fix everything" anymore. In Exchange V5.0 it was sufficient to input:

```
C:\EXCHSRVR\BIN\ISINTEG -PRI -FIX
```

to have all available tests performed (and any errors fixed) for the Private Information Store. The utility will merely blink back at you if you input the same command in Exchange V5.5 (a good reason to check all batch files that use command line utilities after a new release of a product like Exchange). ISINTEG now requires a more focused and targeted set of tests to perform. For example.

```
C:\EXCHSRVR\BIN\ISINTEG —PRI —FIX allfoldertests, message, delfld
```

This command line will invoke the "allfoldertests" test (a combination of three other tests), and the tests for the message table and that for deleted folders. The requirement to know the tests to specify is one way to ensure that administrators read the documentation, but it does make life a little harder. Apart from the change in operation, ISINTEG now supports tests for the deleted items cache. Note that an environmental variable called _CLUSTER_NETWORK_NAME_ must be set to the network name of the cluster before ISINTEG can function. If this does not happen, ISINTEG will exit with an error indicating that a duplicate key was detected. In all cases, including the —VERBOSE switch in the command line forces ISINTEG to output details of everything it does, perhaps far more information than you care to view.

Should you run ISINTEG to check the contents of the Information Store on a regular basis? The answer is that it all depends. If you're a cautious person (or paranoid, depending on your point of view) and really want to know that the store is functioning at 100% then you can take the time to run ISINTEG at regular intervals. Except on servers with very large databases, it usually doesn't take very long to run ISINTEG to validate the structures in the store and fix any problems that it comes across. The time taken to run ISINTEG depends on the number of tests performed, size of the store, the speed of the CPU, and the speed of the I/O subsystem. Expect a full test of the Private or Public Information Store to run at approximately 2GB/hour. Running ISINTEG in patch mode is much quicker.

Testing a store with ISINTEG can reveal problems that you never even contemplated. Systems that have run beta software in the past have suffered from inconsistencies, but as the database engine in Exchange has matured the number of inconsistencies has reduced. Indeed, we have now reached the stage where ISINTEG is seldom required to fix errors, so there is really no great need to run ISINTEG unless you want to know what's happening or begin to experience database errors that cannot be explained by events you know about (like a problem with a disk).

In all instances, if you use ISINTEG to fix or patch a store, make sure that you take a backup afterwards.

5.8.2   ESEUTIL—off-line maintenance for Exchange databases

EDBUTIL (Exchange V4.0 and V5.0) and ESEUTIL (its V5.5 equivalent) perform the equivalent of open-heart surgery on Exchange databases. ESEUTIL is an improved version that's able to deal with the unlimited store. Both EDBUTIL and ESEUTIL are multithreaded programs, but ESEUTIL appears to make more effective use of threading than its predecessor, and processes data faster than EDBUTIL. You can't run EDBUTIL against a V5.5 database (warning messages are signalled and the utility terminates) and shouldn't attempt to run ESEUTIL against an earlier database because the schema and internal structures are different.

On the surface, open-heart surgery seems an extreme analogy to choose. Some of the Microsoft engineers told me that rearranging groceries on the shelves in a store is a better comparison, but I just don't agree. It's justified on the basis that, like surgery, ESEUTIL can perform a great deal of good yet is also often called for when radical action is needed to rescue data. ESEUTIL can only be run when the Information Store or directory services are stopped to allow exclusive access to the respective stores. ESEUTIL is not a utility for idle experiment. Never run ESEUTIL without good reason and always ensure that you are familiar with its command switches.

Like ISINTEG, ESEUTIL runs in a DOS command box. Don't expect fancy graphics accompanying such serious work! ESEUTIL is often associated with ISINTEG, but the link does not hold true. One comparison between the two utilities is that ISINTEG knows about the contents of the store whereas ESEUTIL operates much lower, dealing with raw data.

Microsoft has a simple position on the use of ESEUTIL and EDBUTIL. They believe that the Information Store is essentially a self-maintaining entity and that the online maintenance performed in the background is enough to maintain the internal structures. Exchange is designed to be online all the time and never needs to be taken down for maintenance. This is true—but only if you are content for the Information Store to gently swell over time to fill as much disk space as it desires.

Microsoft therefore recommends that these utilities are only ever used when recommended by their support organization (PSS), normally after a problem has occurred with a database and the utility is deployed in an attempt to fix the problem through a rebuild or repair. Indeed, Microsoft got so concerned about over-enthusiastic use of

EDBUTIL in customer installations that they seriously considered leaving ESEUTIL off the Exchange V5.5 kit. This would have been a pity as the program is useful when correctly used, but I understand the logic that would drive them to such drastic action. Perhaps EDBUTIL was overused in the past, and I know of situations where people tried to rebuild a corrupt database, lost data, and then panicked, took the wrong actions, and ended up by having to reinstall Exchange from scratch. I still believe that ESEUTIL can be used to rebuild databases when the right conditions exist. My stance has led to some spirited discussions with the Exchange engineering group who have attempted to convince me that the changes made in the Exchange V5.5 database engine have rendered any rebuilds totally unnecessary. I remain somewhat sceptical, but am willing to be proven wrong over time.

For the moment my recommendation is that you should consider using ESEUTIL to rebuild databases at appropriate intervals to recover disk space and reduce backup times. The exact interval is highly dependent on your operating environment and it is fair to say that the changes made in Exchange V5.5 have lengthened the interval. This is another situation where it's important to understand what a utility does so that you can make your own mind up whether you want to use it or not.

5.8.3   Compacting the Information Store

Off-line compaction is the most common use for ESEUTIL. Both EDBUTIL and ESEUTIL use a temporary database called TEMPDFRG.EDB during the rebuild. EDBUTIL reads pages from the source database and writes them into TEMPDFRG.EDB. When all the pages have been processed TEMPDFRG.EDB is renamed to become the new active database. ESEUTIL does a lot more work in place, and uses TEMPDFRG.EDB to maintain working information about the database as it is rebuilt.

The new database is usually smaller than the old, but conceivably, it could be the same size. You'll need to have enough free disk space to allow the new database to be built. Typically, a rebuilt database is up to 20% smaller than the original, although the percentage of space recovered greatly depends on how long it has been since the database was last rebuilt and the type of workload. As we'll see when we look at some actual results, a larger percentage is returned on Exchange V4.0 and V5.0 systems because the database engine is less efficient than the V5.5 model. Remember that the database will begin to grow again after it is rebuilt. The disk space that's recovered is only on a temporary loan to the server and it will eventually be reclaimed by the Information Store.

Rebuilding the private store will usually return more space than the public store, probably because items tend to be transient and shorter lived in user mailboxes than public folders. New messages arrive, are read, and then hopefully deleted or filed away. All this activity results in separate database transactions, potentially leading to a database that can become fragmented very quickly. The exact time when an unacceptable level of fragmentation occurs depends on how many people use the system and how many messages they send and receive. The private store will continue to grow even on servers where new messages are delivered to user PSTs. The reason is simple—messages have to transfer through the store en route to a PST, something that may not happen immediately unless clients are connected to Exchange. After messages are transferred to the PSTs they are deleted from the store, but the space the messages occupied during their stay in the store may not be recovered and until the store is compacted.

Public folders do not usually get the same volume or quantity of traffic as mailboxes. Larger items, like documents, spreadsheets, and presentations are often stored in public folders. When these are deleted they leave a large hole that's easy to fill. A large single item has only one set of attributes and occupies only one row in several tables in the database. The same physical space might be occupied by dozens of mail messages which, when deleted, leave lots of little holes that contribute to fragmentation. The exception is when NNTP feeds are directed to public folders. NNTP feeds can generate massive amounts of data through large volumes of relatively small messages, similar in many respects to interpersonal messages. NNTP messages tend to age quickly, and it is common practice to have them automatically removed after a relatively short period of between 7 and 28 days. Public Information Stores that host feeds are candidates for regular monitoring to track the rate of growth of the store and eventual compaction.

For Exchange V4.0 and V5.0 servers, you should consider rebuilding the Information Store every three months. The task can be performed less frequently with Exchange V5.5. The Directory Store should not need to be rebuilt as frequently, so only consider a rebuild if a large number of directory updates are made. For instance, if you regularly delete large number of custom recipients before importing new entries from an external directory. This advice conflicts with the Microsoft position that Exchange is designed for 100% availability. I have no argument with this assertion and you can certainly keep Exchange up and running all the time, providing that you are happy to see the database grow and are content to provide the necessary disk space. I just believe that it's wise to rebuild important files from time to time, if only to ensure that the system never runs the risk of running out of disk space.

Always take a backup before proceeding, and take a backup afterwards too. The backup afterwards is needed because rebuilding a database renders transaction logs null and void. Transactions in the logs cannot be read and committed into the new database because its internal structures are changed as they are rebuilt. This advice cannot be over-emphasized enough. If you proceed to play with ESEUTIL without taking backups before and afterwards you won't receive an iota of sympathy from Microsoft support if you have problems afterwards.

Table 5.9   *EDBUTIL results with different stores*

Store	Size before EDBUTIL	Size after EDBUTIL	Elapsed time for EDBUTIL run
Private Information Store	774 MB	472 MB	24 minutes
Public Information Store	340 MB	220 MB	14 minutes
Directory Store	7.5 MB	6.5 MB	42 seconds

Table 5.9 lists some representative results taken from running EDBUTIL against the different stores on a small Exchange server (a Pentium 100) equipped with a RAID-5 array holding the public and Private Information Stores.

Table 5.10   *ESEUTIL results*

Store	Size before ESEUTIL	Size after ESEUTIL	Elapsed time for ESEUTIL run
Private Information Store	1.28GB	1.12GB	40 minutes
Public Information Store	672MB	607MB	21 minutes

Table 5.10 details results for ESEUTIL when run on exactly the same server some months later. In both cases the stores had been running interrupted for approximately two months, so the same degree of defragmentation could be expected. Apart from the obvious difference in the amount of data processed, which is easily explained because the stores grew through user activity in the period between the two tests, the most obvious difference is the percentage of disk space recovered by the two utilities. EDBUTIL managed to recover nearly 40% of the disk space occupied by the Private Information Store, but ESEUTIL "only" recovered 13%. EDBUTIL recovered 35% of

the Public Information Store, whereas ESEUTIL recovered less than 10%. The length of the runs was linear in respect of the amount of data processed. Both EDBUTIL and ESEUTIL processed data between 32-34MB/minute. No other applications were active, apart from the Exchange MTA. These are experiments conducted in a very unscientific manner, but provide satisfactory evidence that database engine in Exchange V5.5 is better at online defragmentation and reusing deleted pages in the store. You can therefore expect to recover a lower percentage of the disk space for any run of ESEUTIL.

Logically, the larger the server the more space will be recovered. However, it must be acknowledged that larger servers have the most difficulty in arranging the necessary time to rebuild databases. Large servers host large user communities and have large Information Stores. Rebuilding large stores, even on fast servers, takes a lot of time, and during that time Exchange is unavailable to users.

In general, it's fair to assume that all systems will be taken off-line, even in the most demanding production environment. Software upgrades and patches have to be applied, and hardware maintenance performed. These interruptions in normal service provide opportunities to run ESEUTIL and recover some disk space. The improvements inside the database have almost removed the argument that the stores should be regularly rebuilt to improve internal efficiency, so the only real reason that remains for a rebuild is a desire to reduce time for backup and restore operations. ESEUTIL might be also used after a large number of mailboxes have been moved from one server to another within a site. The space originally occupied by the moved mailboxes can be recovered to the file system by running ESEUTIL to compact the Private Information Store.

5.8.4 Rebuilding a store

To rebuild a database, shut down the appropriate service and invoke ESEUTIL in a DOS command box. For example, to compact the private store:

```
C:> \EXCHSRVR\BIN\ESEUTIL /D /N /ISPRIV
```

The /D switch instructs ESEUTIL to rebuild the store and the target store is indicated by the /ISPRIV switch. /ISPUB targets the public store and /DS the directory. You can substitute a file name instead, like C:\EXCHSRVR\MDBDATA\PRIV.EDB, although in this case you must specify the /L qualifier to tell ESEUTIL where the transaction logs are stored. The /N switch instructs ESEUTIL to output details of what it's done to a file called DFRGINFO.TXT. If you don't want to rebuild a database you can use the /G switch to scan for logical or physical corruptions.

Rebuilding a database is CPU intensive and considerable demands are also made on the disk I/O subsystem. Systems with multiple CPUs are impacted less (one CPU is occupied by ESEUTIL, the others are available for different work), but even on the fastest systems don't expect to process data at rates faster than 3-4GB/hour. Small Pentiums, such as the one used for the sample runs (see Figure 5.58), should certainly be able to process data at more than 1GB/hour, assuming that no other heavy application is active. The requirement to rebuild a new database allied with the time necessary to complete the task means that compaction is not something that you do on a whim. Good planning is required to minimize the deprivation of service to users.

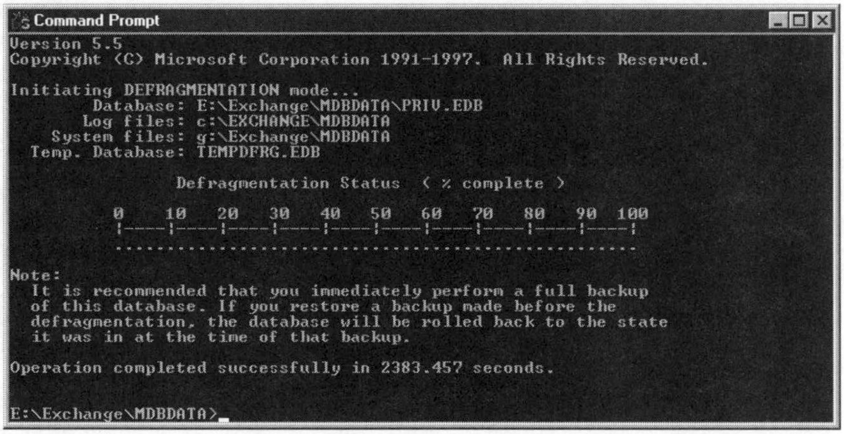

Figure 5.58 *A successful run of ESEUTIL*

```
Command Prompt                                                        _ □ ×
Version 5.5
Copyright (C) Microsoft Corporation 1991-1997.  All Rights Reserved.

Initiating DEFRAGMENTATION mode...
        Database: E:\Exchange\MDBDATA\PRIV.EDB
       Log files: c:\EXCHANGE\MDBDATA
    System files: g:\Exchange\MDBDATA
   Temp. Database: TEMPDFRG.EDB

              Defragmentation Status  ( % complete )

         0    10   20   30   40   50   60   70   80   90  100
         !----!----!----!----!----!----!----!----!----!----!

         .................................................

Note:
   It is recommended that you immediately perform a full backup
   of this database. If you restore a backup made before the
   defragmentation, the database will be rolled back to the state
   it was in at the time of that backup.

Operation completed successfully in 2383.457 seconds.

E:\Exchange\MDBDATA>_
```

ESEUTIL uses a lot of disk space to rebuild a database, potentially up to the same amount as the database currently occupies. It can be difficult to find enough disk space to hold the temporary database, especially with the unlimited store. By default, the temporary database (TEMPDFRG.EDB) is created in the same directory as the store being processed, but the /P switch allows you to select another file name or directory. It's not always easy to find enough space on the same drive, but you can direct the output to any drive available to the server, including network drive. Make sure that no other application can grab space on the target drive while the database is being rebuilt. It is all to easy to miss errors and assume that everything proceeded as planned and the potential exists to end up with an incomplete database being brought online.

Always take a full backup after a database is rebuilt. The internal structure is changed because the pages are rearranged in order, so it is not possible to roll forward any transactions in transaction logs held in backup sets. Thus, it is not possible to fully recover the database from backups taken prior to the compaction should a problem occur. Unfortunately there is no mechanism to scan a database to discover how much "white space" (space that will be recovered when the database is compacted) is within a database at any time. The constant movement of messages in and out of the store creates little spaces in the database, and the on-line defragmentation performed nightly merely rearranges space in the database to pack information in more tightly. The end result of defragmentation is an area of unused space at the end of the database. Exchange will use this space to store new messages, but space will never be returned to the file system until ESEUTIL is run. It would be nice to be able to make a quick check, preferably with the database on-line, to discover how efficient the internal structures are and how much disk space would be recovered if ESEUTIL was run. Perhaps these features will appear in a future version.

After compacting and database repair the last use of ESEUTIL is to upgrade a database's internal structures or provide information about those structures. This option is only ever taken upon advice from Microsoft. Why might this happen? Who knows—the internal structures in the store have changed as Exchange has evolved. Such changes are expected when a product is being developed, but internal changes were also made during the upgrade from V4.0 to V5.0, and then more changes to go to V5.5. The need to conduct separate upgrades for a store outside the boundaries of a product version change can be envisaged, but it shouldn't happen often. The only reason I can think of is where a problem in the store requires a special software patch, normally provided by Microsoft product support. Before or after the patch is applied one or more of the stores might need to be updated.

5.8.5   Life on the dark side—repairing a database

Compacting a database is a pretty simple affair. Read a page from the source database and write it out to the target, continuing until all of the input pages have been read. No attempt is made to determine whether the input pages contain valid data and can be used after they are written into the newly rebuilt database. ESEUTIL can also be used to repair a database. This is not a mode that you should seek to use the utility in. Repair mode should only be invoked when you are sure that a corruption exists and you cannot rescue any other way. Always attempt to restore a database and roll transactions forward from the transaction logs before resorting to a repair. Careful checking of system event logs to pick up warnings issued by Exchange can often prevent a repair becoming necessary. But sometimes hardware corruption can bring a database to its knees and force you into repair mode.

In repair mode pages are read from a target database and checked. ESEUTIL performs this process in place and uses REPAIR.EDB as a temporary work area. In comparison, EDBUTIL reads from the source database and writes to TEMPDFRG.EDB. However, unlike a rebuild operation, the pages are now subjected to an examination to ensure that they do not contain any corrupt data. Note that repairing a database cannot fix fundamental corruptions. Fixing a corrupt index is certainly possible, but ESEUTIL will terminate if the data in the pages cannot be read due to corruption.

A checksum is calculated for each page and compared with the stored checksum. If the checksums match the page is accepted and either retained in the store (ESEUTIL) or written to TEMPDFRG.EBD (EDBUTIL). Any pages that fail the checksum test are ignored. After all pages are processed a new, clean database is available, but the failed pages contained data, and this data is now lost.

ESEUTIL is a valuable weapon to have. I would hate not to be able to restrain the ever-expanding size of a database and I'd hate not to be able to rescue data if circumstances warranted. But it is like surgery, something that can restore health but dangerous in untrained hands.

Discarding pages results in data loss. Quite what data is lost depends on whatever is stored in the page. Pages can store many different types of information relating to the various tables held in the database. Consider the following scenarios:

- Pages containing data for the folders table results in the loss of potentially many different folders.
- Pages containing data for the messages table results in the loss of content for a number of messages.
- Pages containing data for a folder table results in the loss of header information for messages in specific folders.

The most catastrophic loss is the first. If folder information disappears then all the content and attachments held in those folders are no longer accessible.

With potential losses like this it follows that ESEUTIL's repair mode is very much a last resort. It is much preferable to restore the database from the most recent full backup plus all the intervening transaction logs, and then let Exchange perform a soft recovery (roll-back of all outstanding transactions) when the Information Store service is restarted. Of course, reverting to a recent backup is only possible if good backup disciplines have been followed and the backup sets are available.

In summary, the message about ESEUTIL is simple. It is a valuable utility for system administrators because it's the only way to recover disk space from a store. It is recommended that a database rebuild with ESEUTIL is factored into maintenance plans on a reasonably regular basis, especially the Private Information Store. However, avoid using its repair mode unless absolute necessary—backups are important!

5.8.6   Limiting user logons to the Information Store

After performing off-line maintenance operations it is likely that you'll want to check the server out before allowing users to logon. This poses a small problem for Exchange, because its normal behavior is to start its services and begin to immediately accept client connections to the Information Store. A block must be inserted if you want to prevent total access or (more likely) restrict access to a nominated set of individuals.

Microsoft Knowledge Base article Q146764 describes a registry setting that can be used to control user logons, and so create the type of block we need. It's a hidden feature of Exchange. The basic idea is to provide Exchange with a list of distinguished names of mailboxes (users) that it will allow clients to access via the Information Store. A client that presents a distinguished name that isn't on the list will be refused access.

Thus,

`/o=Digital Equipment Corporation/ou=Dublin/cn=recipients/cn=TonyR`

`/o=Digital Equipment Corporation/ou=Dublin/cn=recipients/cn=BillR`

Means that only the users with these distinguished names are allowed log on to the Information Store. How can you find out the right format and content to pass for distinguished names? Select a mailbox and examine its raw properties, something that requires you to run the Exchange administration utility in raw mode. See Chapter 8 for more details on distinguished names and raw mode administration.

The magic registry key is:

`HKEY_LOCAL_MACHINE\SYSTEM\CurrentControlSet\Services\`
`MSExchangeIS\Logon Only As`

You shouldn't find this value in the registry on any active server. If it's there, someone has attempted to insert a roadblock and, for one reason or another, has left the value around. The idea is to provide Exchange with a set of distinguished names (each on a separate line) of mailboxes that are allowed to gain access. If the registry parameter is left blank it means that all users should be prevented from gaining access!

The correct way to use this feature is as follows:

1.   Stop the Information Service.

2.   Take a copy of the system registry.

3.   Run REGEDT32.EXE.

4.   Add the new value to the registry, typing the value as described above and illustrated in Figure 5.59. The parameter data type is REG_MULTI_SZ (multiple string values).

5.   The registry editor displays a data box to collect information for the new value. Type the distinguished names of the mailboxes you will allow access to. Put each mailbox on a separate line.

6.   After all names are added, click on OK.

7.   Exit REGEDT32.EXE.

8.   Restart the Information Store service.

9.   Test that the specified mailboxes are able to access the store, and that those that aren't on the list cannot. Mailboxes not on the list should be told that the set of server folders couldn't be opened.

After you are finished working with the server and are ready to allow general access, use the registry editor to delete the key. Do not forget this step as leaving undocumented and unsupported registry settings floating around is not good system management practice.

Figure 5.59 *A hidden feature! How to allow just your friends to log-on*

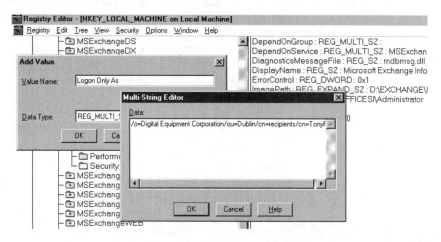

6

Managing Exchange Users

6.1   Recipients, Mailboxes, and People

Users are the most important part of any system, and perhaps especially so in the case of systems that automate common office tasks and enable better human interaction. Without users there's simply no point to an electronic messaging server. In this chapter we'll look at the challenges involved in day to day operation of an Exchange server, covering topics like setting up and managing the user community, distribution lists and so on.

Anyone who has ever been faced with the task of managing a mail server knows that people have to be registered before they can use the system. Exchange server is no different in this respect. Users have to be registered and allocated space to hold their messages, but Exchange is a little different because a wide range of valid mail destinations, including people, are registered together in a single directory. Some or all of the recipient types are supported by other servers, but possibly not in as complete a fashion as Exchange. Valid recipient types are:

- *Mailboxes*. This is the most common type of recipient. Everyone who wants to use Exchange to send and receive interpersonal messages must be able to access a mailbox. Several users can share a mailbox, and it is possible for someone to delegate access to their mailbox to other users (see section on mailbox surrogacy later on in this chapter).

- *Distribution lists*. A distribution list is a collection of recipients of any valid types. When messages are sent to distribution lists copies are dispatched to every recipient that appears in the list.

- *Custom recipient*. Someone who uses any other messaging system. For example, an Internet user who receives mail via SMTP, or someone who receives messages sent via an X.400 link between Exchange and another X.400-compliant messaging system such as AT&T Mail.

- *Public folders*. A folder is a sub-section of the Information Store, used to arrange information in a logical order. Unlike folders in the personal message store, information placed in public folders becomes available to anyone who has access to the folder.

By default, details of user mailboxes and distribution lists are stored in the Recipients container in the Exchange directory. Two interesting aspects of mailbox entries in the Exchange directory are:

- You don't have to reveal all mailboxes by adding them to the Global Address List. The "Hide from Address Book" checkbox on a mailbox's Advanced property page controls whether a mailbox is included in the Global Address List. Senior management or other individuals occupying sensitive posts are often excluded from directory listings, the e-mail equivalent of an ex-directory telephone number.

- The Directory Restrictions property page controls the addresses a mailbox can send messages to as well as the people the mailbox will accept messages from. You can use these properties to restrict users to a subset of total possible recipients, or to stop messages arriving into a mailbox from people you'd rather not receive mail from. Contract workers who join an organization for a short time and need e-mail connectivity are candidates for restricted send options. Senior management might also like to be protected from a flood of messages, so they are candidates for restricted delivery options. Controlling a large exclusion list for send or delivery restrictions can be quite time-consuming, but you can cut down on the work by using distribution lists instead of specifying individual mailboxes, as shown in Figure 6.1.

Figure 6.1 Using a distribution list to prevent a mailbox accepting messages

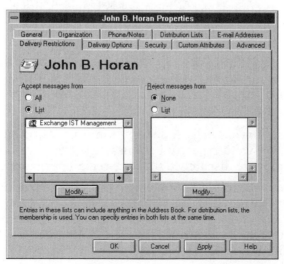

6.1.1 **Breaking up the directory**

Multiple containers can be defined to hold recipients, allowing you to break up large user communities into more manageable chunks. Apart from anything else, dividing recipients up into different containers makes it easier for users to select from a set of particular addresses when they add recipients to mail messages.

Figure 6.2 *Using a container to hold detail of external recipients*

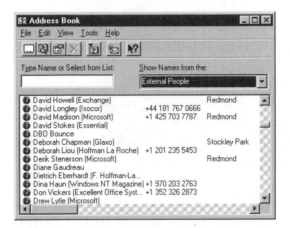

Figure 6.2 shows addresses for a new message being selected from special container called "External People". This container holds all the custom recipients defined system-wide. It's easier for someone to look through a small container holding all the addresses of a specific type, in this case, everyone external to the company, than it is to wade through a potentially very large global address list. It is also very much faster to conduct a search for a specific name in a smaller segment of the overall directory than to scan through the complete global address list.

Before you enthusiastically break up your GAL into dozens of separate recipient containers please read the discussion on address book views in chapter 8 (see page 627). While splitting users across multiple containers might make them easier to find when searching the GAL, there are some side effects to consider. Also, if you create entries for lots of custom recipients outside your company it's a good idea to clearly identify such recipients in a way that makes it clearly obvious to users that they have addressed or received a message from an external correspondent. The simplest way to do this is to include the name of the recipient's organization in the display name for their directory entry. This provides a very effective visual indication, as obvious in Figure 6.2. You can make things even easier for users by combining this approach with an address book view sorted by company name.

Figure 6.3
*Reading
messages from
two external
recipients. Note
the company
information in
the display name
in the bottom
example*

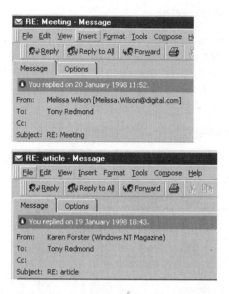

Inserting an external recipient's company name into their display name brings another benefit. Each time Exchange receives a message through a connector, the sender's email address is checked against the directory. If a match is found the display name found in the directory is used whenever the message content is read. Figure 6.3 illustrates the difference between the display information shown for a recipient that cannot be found in the directory (top screen capture) and one that can (bottom). The company information is, of course, also included in the message header when a new message is addressed to an external recipient. Apart from anything else, visual indications like this may stop someone sending some confidential information outside the company.

Public folders are fairly special entities. As such they deserve a separate discussion removed from the topic of how to set up and name the accounts used by people to access Exchange.

6.1.2   Distribution lists

Exchange can currently store a maximum of 5,000 objects in a distribution list. At least, the user interface will prevent you adding more than 5,000 objects to a list. There is no restriction on adding more than this number programmatically.

Note the word "objects". An object can be an Exchange mailbox or a custom recipient, but it can also be another distribution list, leading to a situation where distribution lists can contain nested distribution lists, greatly expanding the total possible user population that can be addressed through a single list. However, while it's nice to know that it's technically possible to create a mega-distribution list to address thousands of users at a single keystroke, once a list contains more than 100 users or so perhaps public folders offer a much better way of distributing information to wide interest groups?

Distribution lists are expanded by the MTA when each recipient is checked against the directory. The default is to expand lists on the server where a message originates. Large lists, or those that contain nested lists, impose a considerable demand on resources during expansion, so you may need to consider expanding lists on specific servers, perhaps those that usually serve public folders.

Nested distribution lists are useful, but they pose a special challenge to the people who maintain the lists. That challenge is to ensure that recipients only get one copy of a message. For example, assume that you have distribution lists for the following groups within a company:

- Management
- Sales
- Engineering

A company-wide list is also maintained and is formed by nesting the three other lists. Managers work in all departments and, as such, feature in the Management list and the list for their specific department. If a message is sent to the company wide list each manager will receive two messages: one sent when the management distribution list is expanded; the other when their department's list is expanded. It's very difficult to arrive at a situation where duplicate messages are avoided, but it is annoying for users to receive lots of duplicate messages.

Because Exchange treats them like any other recipient, distribution lists are useful when setting permissions on folders, much along the same lines as delivery restrictions. When permission is given to a distribution list all members of the list inherit the permission. The advantage lies in the fact that it's very much easier to grant permission to a single entity, the list, than it is to manage separate permissions for each individual on the list. And better still, when people join a distribution list they'll inherit permissions granted to the list, and when they are removed from the list the permissions are revoked.

6.2   Managing user mailboxes

We've already discussed the topic of well-designed server names. If you've been running an electronic mail system, including PC LAN-based systems, you're also aware that each user must be uniquely identified to allow proper control of access to the system and also, possibly more important from the user perspective, to make sure that messages are delivered correctly. To accomplish this each person wishing to use the Exchange messaging system is allocated a unique identifier, otherwise known as an account or user name.

Successful operation of Exchange requires management of user accounts and mailbox names. Plunging forward to create accounts and mailboxes without considering the long term ramifications of what you're doing may work for a 20-user operation. But you're bound to run into problems when the system expands and has to accommodate more accounts or mailboxes, so it pays to consider your options before starting.

All messaging systems impose their own requirements in terms of the number of characters that can be used in an account name, and which characters may legally appear in the name. Some installations have well-defined guidelines as to how account names are made up, although some of these ideas are a little obscure. For example, if your organization allocates numbers to staff members it may seem sensible to use the same staff numbers as the basis for allocating e-mail account names. In reality however such a scheme falls down badly as the resulting addressing scheme is very unuser-friendly. I hold badge number 150847 in DIGITAL's personnel system, but I'd hate to be thought of as a mere number, or to have other people forced to address messages to me as 150847. National social security numbers are unique and are sometimes proposed as the basis for an even more unuser-friendly account naming convention. Thankfully it's illegal to use social security numbers in this way in many countries. But, strange as it may seem, there are organizations who think it's a good idea to use cryptic, esoteric naming schemes.

The most sensible principles to remember when considering what type of account naming scheme is appropriate for your organization are:

- *Logical*. Users shouldn't have to go through mental contortions to remember the account name for the people they want to send mail to.
- *Friendly*. Some logical schemes are well, too logical. Look for a compromise between logic and user-friendliness.
- *Straightforward*. Avoid complexity at all costs.

Surnames are often considered to be the first and most obvious basis for planning a naming scheme, and it's often possible to use surnames in small e-mail systems. However, the statistical fact is that the more users a system supports the more chance there'll be that common surnames exist. In a small system supporting 50 users you might only have one "SMITH" (or the equivalent most common name in a country or language), but I'll guarantee that in a system supporting more than a hundred or so users there'll be more than one surname clash to contend with. Surnames are also a western convention that doesn't always apply well in international deployments. There are places in the world (Malaysia, Iceland, parts of India) where the concept of a surname is not universally observed, and others (China) where the surname is the primary name.

6.2.1 Accessing your mailbox

Everyone who wishes to use an Exchange server to send and receive messages must have access to a Windows NT account. Normally, a Windows NT account is associated with a single Exchange mailbox, although a privileged account is able to use its elevated permissions to access a mailbox apparently reserved for another account. You could, for instance, log into the computer's privileged Administrator account, run the Exchange client program, and define a profile to connect to a mailbox allocated to another account. This is quite legal and understandable, if not altogether desirable from a user perspective. All that's happening is that standard permissions are being used to override the protections on a mailbox. Being able to log-into a user's account in this way is a useful feature for an administrator, but it can be disconcerting for users to discover that their mailbox can be accessed in this manner, especially as no permanent trace or audit record is left that a mailbox has been accessed from a different account[1].

Exchange is little different from many other messaging systems that permit privileged administrators to "take over" user mailboxes for debugging or maintenance purposes. System administrators (and sometimes operators) basically have access to any data held on a computer unless special steps are taken to restrict their access to specific information. This fact is something to think about when appointing people to fill positions with access to such a range of sensitive information. The advanced security features of Exchange (discussed later on in this

---

1.   The log-ons property page for the Private Information Store lists the mailboxes which access the Private Information Store together with the Windows NT account last used to access each mailbox. This information provides the only obvious sign of instances where a privileged account was used to access a user mailbox. However, the information is transient and is over-written each time a mailbox is logged on to. It is possible to log the use of privileges to access user mailboxes by turning diagnostic logging on for the logon category for the MSExchangeIS Private service through the Diagnostics Logging property page for a selected server. When logon diagnostics are enabled privileged access to user mailboxes is recorded in the Windows NT event log. You can see these events by viewing the log (look for events 1011, 1016, or 1009).

chapter) help by preventing unauthorized access to encrypted messages. Even if someone else is privileged enough on the Windows NT level to be able to access your mailbox they shouldn't be able to read encrypted messages unless you hand over your security password.

The implications of privileged user access to electronic mail should be factored into your security policy and the consequences of unauthorized access to messages clearly spelt out. A wide variety of views are present in the computer industry on the nature of information held in electronic messages. I believe the majority of companies treat the contents electronic messages as private to the sender and recipients and take steps to ensure that no unauthorized access is tolerated. However, the increased incidence of "discovery" actions taken by lawyers in attempts to uncover potentially damaging revelations about incidents or business dealings is causing companies to review the data contained in electronic mail systems with an aim of protecting themselves if the time comes to defend such an action.

How would you deal with a request to search your system to identify and recover all messages relating to a specific topic? Would it make things harder if the request focused in on a particular range of dates? I've been involved in a couple of discovery cases where lawyers requested copies of all messages sent by a particular group of users over the period of a month two years back from the time of asking. Fulfilling such a request is an expensive and time-consuming exercise. Exchange does not offer any text search and retrieval functionality capable of meeting such a request, so the only option in this case is to check the mailbox of each user on the list to see what it contained during the particular period.

Note that the "search subfolders" option is disabled automatically whenever a search involved folders that may span multiple servers. While it is reasonable to expect a search to be able to conduct a fast scan through all the folders in a specific folder tree when the folders are stored locally, it's quite another matter to attempt to do the same thing when the folders may be scattered throughout the network. Executing live, distributed queries would take a long time to complete. It's a problem that database vendors have been looking at for quite a time, but so far no good answers have arrived. In the interim, full text retrieval products like Fulcrum Find or Verity's Search 97 for Exchange can be used to index and search large folders very quickly.

In a discovery situation before any check can be made the system must be restored back to the exact state it was at the time in question. This point raises the question of just how long you need to keep system backups around in today's legally-charged atmosphere. Is two years enough? Probably not. If you take full system backups at regular intervals you should plan to keep the backup tapes around for at least five years, just in case.

6.2.2 Mailboxes and Windows NT accounts

Mailboxes can be created when new Windows NT user accounts are set up or by using the Exchange Administrator program to create a new mailbox for an existing Windows NT account. In most situations there will be a one-to-one mapping between users and mailboxes, but it is also possible for several users to have access to a shared mailbox, such as in the case where a group of users need to monitor messages arriving at a mailbox set up as a generic recipient. For example, a mailbox created to receive requests to register for training events, or a mailbox that people can send messages to report problems to the help desk.

Windows NT account names tend to be rather terse and pretty unuser-friendly, and are limited to 20 characters. For instance, my account names on the two servers I connect to regularly are T_REDMOND and TONYR. Exchange treats everything associated with the server as an object in one form or another, and the Windows NT account name is an attribute of a user object, albeit one that's pretty important. However, you're not limited to account names as Exchange also allows for a more complete name as another user attribute, so I can be referred to as "Tony Redmond". A complete user name is sometimes referred to by users as a "pretty name", probably because it's nicer to look at on-screen or in printed format than the shorter computer account names. While it's by no means essential to have two names for an account, from the human interface point of view it's also possibly true that people feel better addressing messages to "Tony Redmond" than "TONYR".

Using surnames as the basis for Windows NT account names meets the criteria of being logical, friendly, and straightforward. So it makes sense to persist and try and use a variation of pure surnames as the basis for a naming scheme. How about adding an initial to the surname so that I, for instance, become "TREDMOND". This is more unique but incurs the disadvantage of throwing all our account names out of synchronization, mostly because it's easier and more logical to view a user directory when it is ordered in the same way as the telephone directory—in surname order.

It's therefore better to use initials as a suffix rather than a prefix, giving us "REDMONDT". Now all the names are sorted according to the same order you'd expect, making it easier for users to follow. If Tony Redmond and Tom Redmond are on the same system we can add another initial to create a difference. For example, "REDMONDTY" and "REDMONDTO".

Some installations separate the surname from the initials with a character such as "," (comma), or "." (period). Underscores ("_") should be avoided in electronic mail addresses because some mail systems are unable to deal with addresses that contain underscores. My preference is to use a period as a separator, but only because this has been successfully used within DIGITAL for many years and has therefore withstood the test of time. Thus, the preferred Windows NT account name is a choice between "REDMOND.T" or "REDMOND.TONY". Remember that 20-character restriction. It may limit your options in situations where you have to cater for very long names, so be prepared to be flexible.

6.2.3 Exchange user names

After you've successfully managed to log onto your Windows NT system you can proceed to connect to Exchange. Mailboxes have a number of user name attributes that link Windows NT accounts with the correct Exchange mailboxes. These are:

- *Display Name.* The name that appears in the Administrator window (and used to select mailboxes when their details are changed or otherwise worked with by an administrator). This name can be up to 256 characters long, so even the longest name in the universe should fit. The display name is sometimes referred to as the "pretty name" because it is seen when addressing messages, as part of a distribution list, or in the header information when a message is viewed or printed. Because the information from Global Address List cannot be customized when recipient information is viewed by users large organizations often include some additional data in recipients' display names to allow users to distinguish between common names. For example:

  John Smith (Sales)

  John Smith (Training)

  If department names aren't enough consider using locations or other hints. For example:

  John Smith (Sales—London)

  John Smith (Training—Geneva)

  The display name is also shown when the contents of a recipients container is viewed using the administration program.

- *Alias Name.* An alias can be up to 64 characters and is used to associate other mail addresses with an Exchange mailbox. As such, the mailbox alias must be unique on a server. Exchange will stop you if you attempt to allocate an existing alias to a mailbox.

Apart from its use within the directory the alias is used as the "account name" portion of an SMTP address. Many experienced system administrators like to set the Exchange mailbox alias to be the same as the Windows NT account name. The Alias name is also used when logging on to a POP3, IMAP4, or LDAP client.

- *First Name*, *Initials*, and *Last Name* are all optional naming attributes that can be up to 32, 2, and 64 characters long respectively. While you don't have to enter this information it is useful to do so, especially in an X.400 environment where these attributes form part of fully qualified X.400 originator/recipient addresses.

Figure 6.4
Automatic name generation options

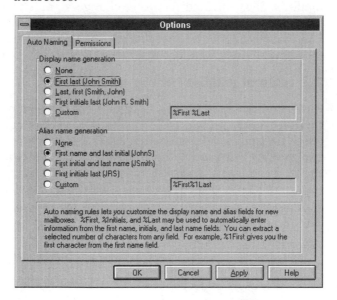

The auto-name generation feature of Exchange, as shown in Figure 6.4, is able to generate a display and alias name for a new recipient when you enter details of the first name, initials, and last name. If you don't like the names generated by Exchange feel free to override the defaults and create your own versions. For example, you might decide to generate aliases based on the new recipient's surname and the first letter from their first name. To do this, select the Options menu from the Administration utility, select the "Custom" radio button for Alias name generation, and type %Last%1First into the provided field. If you change the scheme used for automatic name generation midway through adding mailboxes or custom recipients some newly-generated aliases may clash with entries already in the directory when you attempt to add them. Fixing this problem is easy—all you need to do is create a custom alias for the affected recipient or mailbox.

When addressing messages Exchange clients allow you to enter the full display name, a mailbox's alias, or a user's surname in the TO:, CC:, or BCC: controls. Names are always checked before messages are sent from the client to the server. Names that are successfully validated against the global address list (server or off-line) or the personal address book are underlined in the control to show that Exchange has recognized the address and knows how to route the message to it. Names that are not underlined have not been validated but Exchange will validate the names when the message is sent and before it is actually passed on to the MTA for onward dispatch. If a name cannot be found in the global address list by reference to the full display name, a mailbox alias, or a surname, Exchange signals this to the client and refuses to accept the message. At this stage the user must "fix" the address, possibly by perusing the global address list to select the address they actually want, before resubmitting the message to the server.

6.2.4   The value of mailbox naming conventions

If the value of a discussion about mailbox naming conventions appears small to you I think you're probably running a small organization, one with less than 1,000 mailboxes. The challenges involved in managing and dealing with multi-thousand mailbox deployments escalate after the first thousand, and past this point it is essential to pay close attention to details. Consider two questions:

1.   How long will it take to display a GAL containing five, ten, or twenty thousand when a user attempts to browse through the GAL before addressing a message?

2.   What's the most logical way to organize a large GAL? How will users expect to have the information presented to them? In surname order (like most telephone directories) or in first name order (the default used by Exchange)?

You can't do much about the time necessary to browse a large GAL. Indeed, the problem of a large GAL is much less severe for MAPI clients (like Outlook) than for Web and POP3 clients that use LDAP to access the directory. The sole problem is time. How long will people wait for the client to retrieve and then display information from the directory? With MAPI clients the delay is measured in seconds, but LDAP clients can take much longer than this.

Given that browsing a large GAL can take some time it clearly pays to use an efficient approach to browsing, and that's where a good mailbox naming convention is valuable. If mailbox display names are generated using the standard First Name Last Name syntax the GAL is displayed sorted by first name. But people have largely accumulated the habit of consulting directories sorted by surname, so it is more effective to use the same sort order in the GAL? Compare the following two GAL orders:

```
Jane Doe              Archer, Julian
John Jones            Doe, Jane
John L. Robb          Jones, John
John Rogers           Robb, John L.
John Smith            Rogers, John
Julia Sommerville     Smith, John
Julian Archer         Sommerville, Julia
```

Which seems more logical to you?

6.2.5 Maintaining mailbox details

Exchange allows system administrators to enter lots of information about user mailboxes, possibly more details than you would ever want to know about users, including who their manager is and who their direct reports are (if they have any).

One possible flaw in the implementation is the fact that only system administrators, or rather people who hold the privilege to run the Exchange administration program, are able to amend user mailbox details. The logic behind this stance is easy to understand. User mailbox details are used as the basis of the directory and are replicated to other sites within the organization. It is therefore important to have a certain level of quality control and consistency imposed on the information entered into the directory.

To achieve quality in the directory users are not able to change even the most non-sensitive fields, such as their telephone numbers. Everything has to be done by system administrators, and I can foresee many help desk requests from users to change small details about the information that's been entered into the directory.

It's hard to review the contents of the directory as a whole. The administration program focuses on small groups or single objects. Sometimes it is easier to export the entire contents of a container to a CSV file and review the data with a product like Access or Excel. You don't have to export every field, just the ones that you want to be consistent across, so it's a good idea to build a header file that specifies the fields you're interested in. Amendments made to the CSV file can later be imported back into the directory as updates.

Other implementations of corporate messaging systems allow users to update their own details in the directory, so is this a competitive disadvantage for Exchange? Not really, those same implementations have discovered to their pain that user-initiated directory updates produce a lot of potentially unnecessary network traffic to propagate user-initiated changes throughout the organization. Restricting users from endless fiddling with their own details stops this traffic and helps to maintain the quality of directory information. A lot depends on corporate culture and previous expectations. If people expect to be able to amend personal information, like telephone numbers and office details, only to find they can't with Exchange then you can expect a certain level of grievance. In these situations it's best to address the grievance head-on by explaining to users the reasons why they can't update the directory. But be prepared to seek another solution in the event of major push-back, possibly by writing a client extension that permits a certain degree of access to the directory.

6.2.6   Keeping the mailbox cache refreshed

The Information Store needs to know about mailboxes. In Exchange V4.0 and V5.0 the Information Store reads the directory to retrieve updated information each time a directory object is changed. This is an activity that goes on in the background and no-one, apart from the Exchange engineers, was aware that it was going on. Many performance enhancements are made in Exchange V5.5. One of these is to instruct the Information Store to refresh mailbox data from the Directory every 120 minutes. From an engineering perspective the change makes perfect sense, as it reduces the level of communication between the Information Store and Directory. However, there are some side-effects.

Let's assume that you change the primary Windows NT account for a mailbox. In earlier versions you'd be able to use the account that the mailbox is now associated with to log-on immediately, but the new caching behavior forces a user to wait until the Information Store has refreshed its cache. It's not acceptable to keep people waiting for two hours, so you can add a new parameter value to the registry to force more frequent updates.

The new registry value is:

```
HKEY_LOCAL_MACHINE\SYSTEM\CurrentControlSet\Services\
MSExchangeIS
```

```
\ParametersSystem\Mailbox Cache Age Limit
```

It is a DWORD value. Enter 1 (hex value) and exit the registry editor. The next time the Information Store service restarts it will refresh the mailbox cache once every minute.

6.3   Mailbox surrogacy

Mail surrogacy or delegation is where users are authorized to take control of other users' mailboxes for specific purposes. The classical example of this functionality in action is where a secretary or administrative assistant controls a senior manager's mailbox. Even today, a minority of very senior executives actually process their own electronic mail and some are still at the stage where they demand that their messages are printed down each day for their perusal. They then mark the printed copies of the messages with their comments or replies and leave the marked-up messages with their secretary who takes care of generating an appropriate response.

In the early days of electronic mail systems tended to be unsophisticated when compared to the systems in use today. Delegation was accomplished in an easy to work but totally insecure manner when users would give their system password to whoever was going to process messages on their behalf. System administrators hated this method because it totally compromised system security, but users find it easy to understand, especially when passwords were handed over on scraps of paper that could be conveniently posted on their pinboard or securely stored in their desk drawer!

As electronic mail systems evolved attention was paid to eliminating the security hole caused by such a general interchange of passwords. Facilities to allow other users to connect to all or specific parts of mailboxes began to appear in the early 1990s, but even so many users persist in their old habits and continue to exchange passwords today. Exchange takes a comprehensive approach to the problem by:

- Not restricting users to only allowing one other account to access their mailbox. Any number of users can be granted the permission to send on behalf of a particular mailbox.

- Allowing system administrators to control the permission centrally by using the Administration utility (see Figure 6.5) to edit details of user mailboxes while also permitting users to issue their own permission using the client Tools.Options menu choice (Figure 6.6). Outlook 98 has greatly expanded the degree of control a person can exert over access to the different types of information held in their mailbox, as is obvious from the screenshot.

A newly delegated mailbox does not automatically appear after permission has been granted. Users must reconfigure their profiles to access additional mailboxes and then reconnect to the server after permission is received. Exchange does not break any new ground in mail delegation. However, it does build on the lessons learnt in other messaging systems and has made the whole process a little easier.

Figure 6.5
*Granting Send
on behalf
permission to a
user mailbox*

Figure 6.6
*Giving
delegate access
to another user
in Outlook 98*

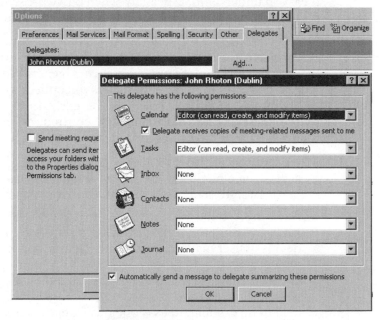

6.4   Client installations and settings

The Windows registry holds MAPI user profiles on all 32-bit platforms. A MAPI user profile consists of information about a user's
working environment including the mailbox and server they connect

to as well as the services they have configured. The normal set of services include Exchange and the Personal Address Book, and traveling users will probably configure Personal Folders as well. Optional services such as Microsoft Mail or Internet Mail can be configured as required, and all the details written into the registry.

Figure 6.7
*Details of a
MAPI profile*

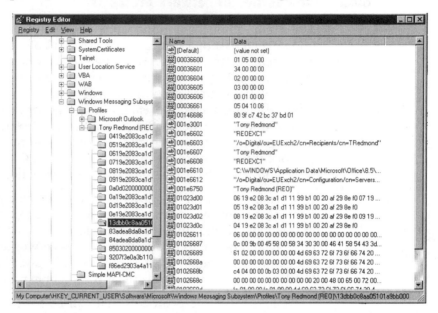

Figure 6.7 shows the Windows registry editor, REGEDIT.EXE, being used to view details of a mailbox profile on a Windows 95 client. The registry key that points to all of the MAPI profiles on a PC is:

```
HKEY_CURRENT_USER\Software\Microsoft\Windows Messaging
Subsystem\Profiles
```

Like the vast majority of registry entries made for Microsoft products the contents are somewhat esoteric. There is good reason for this. If the meanings of the values were immediately obvious, it might encourage people to make changes without really understanding the effects.

The system registry is also used to store user-specific settings for Exchange on Windows NT. On a Windows V3.*x* the settings are held in a standard application initialization file in the Windows directory. For example C:\WINDOWS\EXCHANGE.INI or OUTLOOK.INI.

Application initialization files group settings into a series of sections, each of which holds values applicable to a specific part of the application. An initialization file can be edited with any ASCII editor, such as the Windows Notepad editor, but care should be taken when editing as it's all too easy to slip and make an inadvertent change that doesn't quite have the intended effect. Always make a copy of an initialization file before making changes. Just to be complete let me note that the settings for DOS clients are stored in a file called EXCHANGE.PRO.

6.4.1 The question of network protocols

Establishing good communications between clients and servers is a fundamental part of a successful deployment of a client/server messaging system. In the case of Exchange, clients communicate with the server using RPCs, which are able to use a range of network protocols. Each protocol is attempted in the order stated in the protocol binding order, a setting specific to each PC. If a network infrastructure is in place and working then clients should be able to fit in and connect to the server without any difficulty. Problems occur when parts of the network infrastructure are unreliable or the PC attempts to connect using a protocol that isn't supported within the network.

It's common to hear Windows 95 users complaining that the Exchange client takes many minutes to start up. Lots of people have written entries on this topic to the Internet mailing list for Exchange, and they can't understand how their PC is so slow when a co-worker is able to start up and get working within a few seconds. The answer lies in the bowels of Windows 95 networking and afflicts this client in particular.

Table 6.1 lists the protocols that can be used by a MAPI client to connect to a server. The protocols are listed in the default order that the installation procedure writes them into the system registry. This is important, because if your site doesn't support a protocol or wants to use a particular protocol you have to adjust the contents of the registry to force Exchange to do the right thing. Time-outs occur when the client attempts to make a connection to the server using an unsupported protocol, or when an attempt is made to resolve the server name via a mechanism (like WINS) that isn't totally reliable. Network time-outs are the reason why some users can't start up Exchange quickly and others can. Those who start up quickly use PCs where the network protocol binding order is stated in an optimum manner, while those who start slowly are attempting to connect over many and varied protocols that just can't be used for one reason or another. It's really that simple.

Of course, if you can't connect at all then there is a fundamental network problem that has to be resolved. Something like making sure that TCP/IP is correctly configured on the PC with a valid IP address allocated, and so on. No manner of adjustments made to the network protocol binding order in the registry can compensate for issues such as a badly defined or missing IP address.

Table 6.1 *Network protocols for Windows 95 clients*

Protocol as set in registry	Meaning
NCALRPC	Local RPC calls (client and server on the same system).
NCACN_IP_TCP	TCP/IP transmitted over Windows Sockets. The server is located using DNS, a local hosts files, or a raw IP address. NetBIOS is not used.
NCACN_SPX	Novell SPX using the NetWare Bindery to locate the server. NetBIOS is not used.
NCACN_SP	Named pipes. The server is located using a NetBIOS computer name, WINS, or LMHOSTS.
NetBIOS	The default NetBIOS protocol.
NCACN_VNS_SPP	Banyan Vines.

As already noted, the problem of badly stated protocol binding orders is specific to Windows 95 clients. The protocol binding order can be changed by editing the appropriate value in the system registry, as shown in Figure 6.8. The setting is specific to Exchange, so the registry key is under the Exchange root within the registry. You can help solve the problem by making sure that the correct binding order is used on each PC.

Figure 6.8
Modifying the Windows 95 network protocol binding order

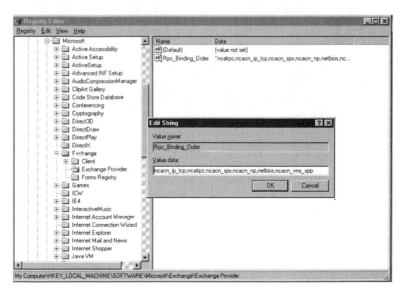

For example, in a Novell NetWare environment you should move NCACN_SPX to the top of the protocol binding order, whereas if you want to use TCP/IP it's clear that NCACN_IP_TCP should be at the top of the list. You can remove protocols that are never used. Also, in TCP/IP environments make sure that DNS is operational and can be accessed by each client.

6.4.2 "Hot" PCs and roaming users

A hot PC is one that isn't always used by the same person. It might be a PC used in a multi-user shift environment, or just one that's available for visitors to use when they arrive at an office.

User mailboxes, public folders and directory information are all maintained in separate databases on an Exchange server, so users can connect to the information held in these containers from all PCs. There are some files and other information that can cause concern to those who move around. These include:

- MAPI user profiles
- Personal Information Stores
- Off-line folders
- Advanced Security Encrypted Password Files
- Personal Address Book (PAB)
- Autosignature file
- Profile Information

Most of these sources of data are discussed in separate sections in this or other chapters. For the moment we'll concentrate on their involvement in the act of roaming from PC to PC.

Personal Information Stores can be located on any disk. In the normal course of events users create personal stores on local hard drives, although I know of some cases where stores have been successfully used on floppy diskettes. If a store is held on a floppy it's easy to move from PC to PC, but there are some disadvantages including the high potential for media corruption (in comparison to hard drives) and the relative lack of space. Floppy diskettes are really only suitable for moving stores containing simple messages, not large amounts of complex documents. In most cases it's more realistic and useable to place personal Information Stores in personal directories on a networked file server. The only problem then occurs when people want to work in a location where they can't access the file server.

Off-line folders are snapshots of server-based folders that allow users to work with the folder contents when they are disconnected from the server. People who move from PC to PC and are able to connect to their server won't need off-line folders. Problems only occur when server connections aren't possible and off-line folder files aren't available. Exchange requires users to make an initial connection to the server before they can use off-line folder files, probably to ensure that the folder hierarchy is correctly synchronized between the server and client. This means that you can't just take an off-line folder file from one PC and move it to another and expect it to work. First you'll have to create a profile (or update an existing profile) and indicate that off-line working is required, and then make a connection. Catch-22 if the network's unavailable!

Encrypted password files are only necessary when advanced security is enabled. Someone who wishes to encrypt or decrypt messages, or apply digital signatures to messages must be able to access their password file. It's easy to move the password file from PC to PC, but it's embarrassing and frustrating to find yourself in a remote location after forgetting to copy your password file before you left home base.

The PAB is typically stored in a location such as:

`\EXCHANGE\MAILBOX.PAB`

Losing access to your PAB becomes a minor annoyance if you wish to use another PC, especially if the PAB contains the addresses for many external correspondents who don't have an Exchange mailbox. The "Briefcase" feature of Windows 95 can be used to move a PAB from one PC to another (along with many other files), and then synchronize any changes that may have occurred when you return to the original PC. However, using the briefcase in this manner requires a discipline that lots of people just don't have so some frustration is likely. It's also important that you don't overwrite a PAB belonging to someone else when you move your PAB onto a PC, so it's good to recommend to users that they give a more appropriate name to their PAB, such as REDMOND.PAB.

It would be nice if PAB data could be stored in a folder in the Private Information Store rather than a DOS file. Using an OST, the PAB could still be made available for off-line working. Unfortunately this is not the case and we are left to deal with the issue of PAB mobility. The Outlook client stores "Contacts" information in a folder in the store, so hopefully this is a pointer for the future. It's not quite a final solution because the Contacts folder is only able to hold information about individual people, including their e-mail addresses whereas the PAB is also able to store personal distribution lists. In the meantime the best idea is to place the PAB on a network drive and direct the client to go there. A client locks the PAB when it is in use so you'll need to edu-cate users to always log out when they leave a PC. Otherwise you'll end up in the situation where someone moves to a new PC, attempts to log on, and can't connect to his or her PAB.

Figure 6.9
Extract from an
AutoSignature
file

```
\rtf1\ansi\ansicpg1252\deff0\deftab720{\fonttbl{\f0\fswiss MS
Sans Serif;}{\f1\froman\fcharset2 Symbol;}{\f2\fswiss\fprq2
Tahoma;}{\f3\fswiss\fprq2 Arial;}}
{\colortbl\red0\green0\blue0;\red0\green0\blue255;}
\deflang6153\pard\plain\f0\fs17\i Tony Redmond, Technical
Director, Mail and Messaging Consulting Practice
\par Digital Equipment Corporation
\par
\par \plain\f0\fs17
\par \pard\plain\f2\fs17\i \plain\lang2057\f3\fs20\cf1\ul
mailto:Tony.Redmond@digital.com\plain\f0\fs17
\par }
```

Sending a couple of messages without your normal signature isn't a great disaster. Most people will accept this as a side effect of moving away from their normal PC. The challenge is greater for users who roam as a matter of practice.

Exchange clients keep autosignature information in a file called AUTOTEXT.SIG. Unhappily the file is stored in the Windows default directory, so it poses a particular challenge for users who move between computers. The file contains the RTF source code for one or more sections of text. The normal situation is for the file to contain just one section, the default signature applied to new messages when they are sent. Optionally, the signature file can be appended to replies and forwarded messages. For example, an extract of the RTF code in my signature file is shown in Figure 6.9. If you're still using Exchange clients you need to store autosignature files on a file server and arrange for them to be copied into the local Windows directory when a user logs-on.

Outlook clients prior to Outlook 98 use a file called <profile>.rtf, where <profile> is the name of the MAPI profile used to log-on. Using the profile as part of the file name is a step forward, because it means that multiple people can use a PC without interfering with each other's autosignature. Unhappily, the default location remains the Windows directory. However, you can configure the registry to instruct Outlook to access an autosignature file through a UNC path. For further information, see articles Q175047 and Q167397 in the Microsoft Knowledge Base. Outlook 98 clients can select from multiple signature files, all of which are stored in the directory:

```
\Windows\Application Data\Microsoft\Shared\Signatures
```

MAPI profiles contain details of user working environments. On a shared PC it's quite possible to find many different profiles set up, one for each person who's passed by and used the PC. When you move to a PC you've never used before you'll need to either create a new profile or change an existing one to reflect items like:

- The name of the server you want to connect to
- The name of your mailbox
- The network protocol binding order
- Whether you want to work with off-line folders
- The name of your PAB

Manually configuring a new MAPI profile or changing an existing profile to suit your tastes are not tasks that every user will enjoy. The steps necessary to move a complete working environment from one PC to another are reasonably complex and full of potential error, but it's important to say that roaming users who use shared PCs normally only want to access a basic messaging service. They want to quickly use a PC to see whether any important messages have arrived, or have the chance to send a few messages of their own. Given that this is the case system administrators can accommodate the requirement of roaming users by ensuring that it's possible to connect PCs to all the servers in an organization. Users who require more advanced facilities, such as security or access to a personal Information Store, can be coached or instructed how to make their own arrangements, or you can go the whole way and use the Exchange profile generator to automatically create profiles for roving users.

6.4.3   The profile generator

The profile generator is a program called PROFGEN.EXE, an unsupported utility provided via TechNet or available from the Microsoft Web site. It works in conjunction with NEWPROF.EXE, the program that users see when they manually create a new MAPI profile. Together the two programs work to automatically generate a profile for a user when they first log-on to a client computer. PROFGEN can be used with Windows V3, Windows 95, and Windows NT clients, although Windows 95 and Windows NT clients are easiest to set up.

To achieve full roving capability, users should store PST and PAB files on personal network shares. The network shares should use a consistent drive letter for all users. Many sites use H: (for home drive). In addition, user profiles need to be configured so that they follow the user from PC to PC. Windows NT and Windows 95 have slightly different mechanisms to achieve the "follow me to the next PC" effect, but the basic idea is the same. Once the user authenticates himself or herself within a domain their registry settings can be downloaded from the domain controller to the PC. MAPI profile details are amongst the data that can be downloaded. Full details of PROFGEN can be found in the BackOffice Resource Kit, but there are a few important points that should be made here. You should also read the Knowledge Base article Q148595 for details of roving Windows profiles.

Figure 6.10
Extract from
DEFAULT.PRF

```
[Service List]
Service3=Personal Address Book
Service4=Personal Folders
[Service3]
PathToPersonalAddressBook=H:\EXCHANGE\MAILBOX.PAB
ViewOrder=1
[Service4]
PathToPersonalFolders=H:\EXCHANGE\PERSONAL.PST
```

The Exchange setup editor should be used to create a new default client preferences file (DEFAULT.PRF) so that the pointers to PAB and PST files are directed to the user's home drive. The client preferences file is in simple text format and can be edited with Notepad or a similar editor afterwards. The setup editor won't make the changes to point user files to a networked drive, so after all the other default settings are made, exit the setup editor and open the preferences file with Notepad. Make changes similar to those shown in the extract in Figure 6.10.

Once a properly configured preferences file is available you can add a line in users' Windows NT log-in scripts to call PROFGEN. The idea is simple. If a MAPI profile for the user already exists on the PC then exit, else call PROFGEN to generate a new profile based on the information held in DEFAULT.PRF. You'll know if this step works because the file is renamed to DEFAULT.PR~ afterwards. PROFGEN is called like this:

```
\\servername\share name\PROFGEN C:\EXCHANGE\NEWPROF -p
H:\EXCHANGE\DEFAULT.PRF
```

PROFGEN starts up and calls NEWPROF to generate the new profile, instructing it to use the preferences file pointed to with the –p switch. If you like, the –l (create log file) and –s (use the GUI interface from NEWPROF) switches can also be specified. It's a good idea to create a log file the first time out!

The Outlook Deployment Kit contains the latest utilities to assist in automatic profile generation. It can be ordered from Microsoft or downloaded from the Microsoft web site. Another interesting web site at www.slipstick.com holds copies of utilities that can be used to configure clients during deployments. Clearly none of this can work unless you configure the server and client environments to support home directories and log-in scripts. By default this isn't done, so it needs to be incorporated into the Windows NT deployment and implementation plan.

6.5   Transferring users

It's hard to achieve perfection when the time comes to allocate users to servers, unless of course you only have a single server to work with. In any large system the time will come when you have to redistribute user accounts across servers, to balance the user-generated messaging load on each server or perhaps to keep users who communicate together on the same server in order to reduce off-server message traffic.

Figure 6.11
Moving a user's mailbox

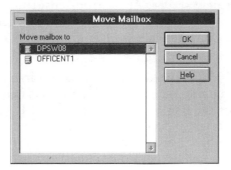

Moving a user's mailbox from one server to another within a site is child's play. Select the "Move mailbox" option from the Tools menu in the Administration program (Figure 6.11) select the user to move and the server they are to be moved to, and leave Exchange to do the work. The contents of the user mailbox are moved by sending messages from the source server to the target, emulating what would happen if someone forwarded each message in a mailbox to a mailbox at a new address. However, Exchange is intelligent enough to check whether messages in a user mailbox are already in the Information Store on the target server. Each message has a unique identifier, so it is possible to query the store to discover whether a message is present. If a message is found its reference count is updated and the content is not physically moved. A certain amount of work is still required to create the necessary entries in folder tables and so on, but the amount of data transferred is reduced. This approach helps to preserve the essence of the single instance storage model and makes everything happen faster than otherwise possible.

Because messages are moved around, one or more transaction logs will probably be created during the move, depending on the size of the mailbox being moved. It is usual that the physical space occupied by a mailbox is increased after a move, largely because all the messages in the mailbox are not shared when they arrive on the target server.

Because servers in the same site share the same directory and configuration information and are normally connected by high-speed links it's feasible to allow the software to take total control of:

- Lock the user's mailbox so that no new messages are delivered while the move is in progress. Messages are queued and delivered to the relocated mailbox once the move is complete.

- Move all the folders and messages from the Private Information Store on one server to the Private Information Store on another.

- Updating the directory to indicate that the user's mailbox is now hosted on a new server. Apart from ensuring correct delivery from external sources this step ensures that other servers within the same site copy new messages to the correct Private Information Store.

The process of moving all the information in a user's mailbox may take time to complete, especially if the user has managed to build up a large mailbox or the servers involved are busy. It's best to perform all moves during off-peak server times and after the user has been "encouraged" to delete any unwanted messages from their mailbox. If the user won't cooperate with the request to clean their mailbox out, you may have to convince them by threatening to use the "Clean Mailbox" option (see discussion starting on page 281). Because of the obvious potential difficulties that might occur it makes sense not to attempt to move a mailbox when the user is logged in. This is yet another good reason to move mailboxes when everyone's gone home and the systems are quiet.

Moving someone from one site to another or from one organization to another is not so straightforward. No options exist to do the job for you, so it's pretty much a manual task that requires co-ordination between the system administrators for the source and target systems.

Indeed, the relative complexity of the steps required in moving a user from one site to another has been enough to convince some very large enterprises to combine several physical locations into one very large site. The logic behind such a step, which on the face seems pretty surprising, is that if you've got very high speed private networks already in place you might as well go ahead and build a big logical site from the distributed physical locations. For example, one large company has built a site from five locations within the United Kingdom. With the site in place the administration workload is simplified and reduced, but I believe it is too early today to determine whether easier system administration can be justified by throwing expensive network links at the problem. Given that servers are pretty "chatty" within a site and network bandwidth is in constant demand by any and all applications it's possible that all the extra bandwidth might be taken up without any great benefit being accrued. Another factor is that Exchange system administration should mature to accommodate trans-site operations. In the meantime, the people who made these courageous design decisions will see whether or not their logic is flawed. You might like to ask the same questions when considering the design for your Exchange organization. But unless you expect to have to administer a highly mobile workforce I wouldn't generally recommend such a radical solution.

Moving back to the subject in hand, the basic steps to move a user from one site to another are:

1.   Have the system administrator on the target site create a new mailbox for the user. After this is done, hide the user's original mailbox from the global address list using the "Hide from Address Book" option when editing mailbox details. This prevents two mailboxes for the one user appearing in the global address list. You should also modify any distribution lists that the user's old mailbox featured in by changing each list to include the new mailbox.

2.   Set a redirect address for the old mailbox on the source server to transfer all newly arriving messages to the new mailbox on the target system. All new messages arriving on the old server should now be forwarded to the new mailbox.

3.   To speed up the transfer process ask the user to delete all unwanted messages held on the server or do the job for them with the "Clean Mailbox" option.

4.   Create an auto-reply message stating that the user has moved to a new server. This step is optional and is really only important if the user is physically transferring location and won't be able to answer messages for a few days.

5.   Move the contents of the user's server-based mailbox to a personal Information Store (.PST file). This is a manual process that requires the user (or the administrator) to log on and move the messages with drag and drop operations.

6.   For any reasonably sized mailbox, the PST file will be quite large. You will need to arrange to transfer the PST file to the target system, possibly through a simple FTP copy.

7. Disable the Windows NT account for the user on the source server to prevent them logging on once the transfer process is complete.

8. On the host system, the user can import their messages from the PST file into their new mailbox. Alternatively, better still, they can use the PST file as an archive for messages processed before their move.

9. After you are happy that the new mailbox is operational you can delete the old mailbox, erase the directory entry, and generally clean up any trace of the user on the source system. This will also remove the redirect address and the auto-reply message, if set.

These steps take no account of items like distribution lists where the old mailbox is included. Distribution list memberships must be updated manually.

If you're using advanced security no special steps have to be taken for intra-site transfers. However, moving users with secure messages from one site to another requires care if they are to be able to access their messages afterwards. The Exchange Resource Kit includes a tool (EXMERGE) to automate the movement of users across sites. The tool seeks to automate many of the manual steps described above. As always, check that this tool does what you need before deploying it into production.

6.6   Remote mail

Roaming users want to be able to get to their mail anytime, anyplace, anywhere. There are two basic approaches that can be taken to retrieve messages from an Exchange server when you're working off-site. These are:

1. Use the Remote Mail facility (see the Tools menu on the client). This option is only available if you connect in off-line mode.

2. Make a dial-up connection to the server computer and work on-line as if you were connected via the office LAN.

Each approach comes with its own set of advantages and disadvantages. You'll probably want to experiment with both to see which approach is best in your own environment.

6.6.1   Using the Remote Mail facility

The basic idea behind the Remote mail facility is to make a quick telephone connection to the server, send any messages that are queued and waiting to go, and grab details of messages that are waiting in your inbox. The connection can then be broken, leaving you to browse through header information for the messages in the inbox. You can mark which messages you'd like to retrieve, leave the others alone, or even decide that you want to delete some without reading. Another dial-up connection is then made to grab the full content of the marked messages. This type of interaction is pretty typical of the way you'd want to do things when you're concentrating on just processing new mail or want to keep phone bills to an absolute minimum. One major disadvantage about the remote mail facility is that you can't work with folders other than the inbox (and the outbox folder indirectly when sending messages).

Some method of communicating between your PC and the server must be established before you can use remote mail. The easiest way I know is the combination of the dial-up networking feature in Windows 95 and Windows NT RAS. Dial-up networking is one of the reasons why Windows 95 is so good to use on notebook PCs. Windows NT V4.0 workstation edition is also OK in this respect, but for now I think Windows 95 remains the easier option for notebook users who represent the bulk of the people interested in remote mail. You are not compelled to use Windows 95 and dial-up networking if you don't want to. The sole criterion is the ability to make a reliable connection between the PC (client) and the server computer. Likewise, while RAS is very convenient because it's a standard part of Windows NT, you can use one of the other approved network modem managers you want on the server, such as Shiva LanRover.

Figure 6.12
*Configuring a
dial-up
connection*

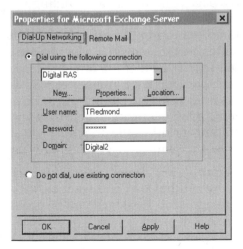

Dial-up networking allows you to configure all the details of how a network link is established to a server computer over a telephone link. As you can see from Figure 6.12, all of the important information such as telephone number to dial, the modem type to use, and the server capabilities are easily accessible. Advanced options, for instance the ability to use a text box to input commands directly to the modem (sometimes useful when dealing with strange and wonderful telephone systems occasionally encountered around the world) are also available.

Figure 6.13
*Properties of the
Remote Mail
connection*

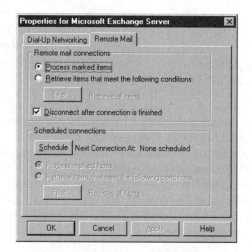

After testing to ensure that your dial-up connection actually works and contact can be made with the server, you can proceed to use remote mail. The properties option ties things together by allowing you to associate the dial-up networking connection you want to use with the remote mail option. Dial-up networking is located on one tab of the property page. The other tab, holding the options that affect how the interaction between the client and server are conducted during the telephone connection, is a little more interesting. For example, you can set a filter on the items that the remote connection will process. I use a filter specifying that I'm only interested in messages of 20K or less, to ensure that I am not bothered by very large messages. More importantly this filter stops me attempting to download messages with large attachments over a slow or expensive connection. Large documents, presentations or other file attachments can always wait until I get back into the office and connect to the LAN.

Remote mail properties also allow you to set up a schedule for connections. If you're on the road and want to make a connection each night to pick up and send messages you're probably not going to be too interested in a scheduled connection. Instead, the connection will be made when you're good and ready, perhaps when you're relaxed and ready to face whatever's in the mail after a good dinner. Scheduled connections are of most use to people who are located in offices that don't have permanent links back to the server. In most cases these are locations that don't have enough users to justify the expense of installing and operating a permanent network connection, so people have to dial-in and collect their mail at regular intervals if they're to stay in touch. Scheduled connections enable messages to be sent and fetched automatically, according to the schedule that's created. You might, for example, decide to connect four times a day, or every hour, or maybe only at 5 o'clock every evening. Scheduled connections are one major advantage of the remote mail facility.

Once all the properties are set a telephone connection can be made. Once the connection is made user credentials are examined (domain, account name, and password) and, if OK, you'll be logged on to the domain. At this stage a link exists between the server and client. Remote mail always checks first to see whether any new messages are waiting to be sent. Exchange is quite happy for you to work in off-line mode.

Any messages you create and send when working off-line are held in a special folder (you can rename the folder if you like—I call mine "Items en Route") that is checked whenever a connection is made to the server. Any messages waiting in the "en route" folder are immediately dispatched by being transmitted from the client to the Information Store for onward delivery.

After any waiting messages have been sent remote mail turns to retrieve header information for messages in the inbox that meet the criteria stated in the filter. Headers provide a snapshot of the messages waiting in the inbox, including details of the originators, date and time sent, subject, and size. The size is important because it determines the time it will take to download the complete message, if that's what you decide to do later on. Exchange predicts the time required to download a message by comparing the speed achieved with the modem connection against the size of the message. Anyone who has ever downloaded a file from an on-line service like CompuServe, America OnLine or a Web site knows that predicting download times is, at best, an inexact science because there's nothing to prevent a connection degrading or something like a server hiccup interrupting data transfer. However, it's useful to have an idea as to how long it is likely for an operation to take and the remote mail facility does a fair job in this respect.

If no filter is specified header information is retrieved for all messages. When available, the header information is presented in the remote mail window, allowing you to browse through and mark the messages you're interested in. In Figure 6.14 you can see that several messages have been marked. Different icons indicate the action that will be taken for each message. The first message is marked to be downloaded, the second to be deleted, and so on. Two separate download actions are available. You can opt to download messages from the inbox on the server and leave copies of the messages on the server, or chose to download messages and delete them from the server. Leaving messages on the server is a good idea if you're not the only person to access a mailbox, but otherwise I recommend cleaning up after a download by deleting the messages from the server. Remember, you can always use the synchronize option later on to make sure that the server inbox matches the content of the off-line inbox. As a matter of practice, I usually synchronize all folders before I go away on a road trip and after I return to the office. This ensures that I have up to date material at my fingertips wherever I am.

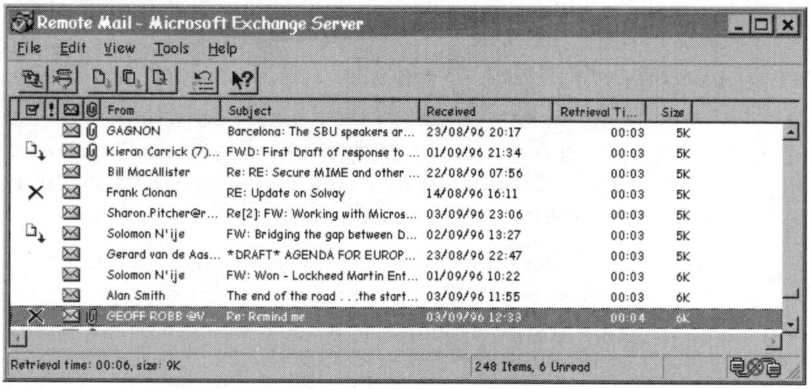

Figure 6.14
*Browsing
through details
of messages in
the Inbox*

Retrieving the actual content of messages is done by making another telephone connection and instructing the client to pick up the messages you've marked. At the cost of a little extra time on-line you can do everything over a single connection. That is, make the connection, send any waiting messages, download headers, browse and mark, and then retrieve the messages you've marked. Telling remote mail not to disconnect the link after headers are retrieved allows everything to be done while maintaining a single connection. Once the headers are available you can make a quick review, select the ones you want, and proceed to download. The telephone link can be broken at any time with the disconnect menu option or command button.

There's a reasonable amount of functionality in the remote mail facility. It's certainly superior (and faster) to the equivalent functionality offered by other PC mail clients such as Microsoft Mail. Indeed, users extensively criticized the remote mail capabilities of Microsoft Mail in the past because of its relative unreliability and slow throughput, so anyone upgrading from Microsoft Mail to Exchange will notice an immediate and significant improvement. However, I've got to say that working in such a disconnected manner is not my favored approach. Seeking to minimize costs through bursts of communication between client and server seems to be the best method for people working with slow modems, unreliable telephone lines and low-spec computers. Given the speed of today's modems and a desire to use telephone connections to access more than just e-mail, the fact that you can only work with Exchange and a restricted set of folders is the final nail in this feature's coffin. At least, it is from my point of view!

6.6.2 Working with Dial-Up Networking

Fortunately there is an alternative way to work remotely. As we've seen, Exchange is quite happy for a client to talk to a server across a wide range of network protocols. Point to point protocol (PPP) is a variant of the TCP/IP protocol specially developed to efficiently handle remote connections over a telephone line. Once again, the combination of Windows 95 dial-up networking and Windows NT RAS scores heavily in the ease-of-use stakes.

My preferred approach is to establish a PPP connection to my server and connect the client across that link. The following advantages are accrued:

- As soon as the connection is made, the client performs automatic synchronization of folders whose contents have been changed since the last on-line connection. Messages created and sent are dispatched to their final destination. Other actions such as deletions or modification of objects in folders are also synchronized with folders on the server. Outlook 98 clients behave in a different matter and use background synchronization to reconcile the contents of off-line and server folders.

- All folders are available in both the Private and Public Information Stores. I can therefore refile messages from the inbox into other, more appropriate folders, as they are read.

- E-form applications are available and can be used.

- New message notification works. Not a big advantage, I know, but it is sometimes very useful to know that a new message has arrived, especially if you're in the midst of a series of messages flying between a group of people.

- All rules work.
- The same network link can be used for other applications. For example, I use the same PPP connection to browse the Web at the same time it's being used to connect me to Exchange. Basically you can work as if you were in the office, albeit at a reduced pace.

Working across a PPP link is my preferred way of connecting when I'm on the road, but it may not be the most cost-effective. Once connected there is always a tendency to stay connected for just a little too long. However, the higher communication bills are being offset somewhat by the use of faster modems and I believe that the extra flexibility and power delivered by this way of remote working makes me more productive.

It's worth noting that the way Outlook clients talk to the server contributes to a great deal of robustness for dial-up communications. Clients do not have a continuous connection with the server. Instead, they communicate via RPCs on an as-needed basis. In other words, if a client wants some information it asks the server and then receives whatever the server cares to provide. Otherwise the chatty discourse that other clients and servers engage in is not present. The advantage here is that the telephone connection can be dropped (hopefully you'll notice) and re-established without forcing you to stop working, apart of course from the necessity to use whatever software you have to reconnect. In certain parts of the world it's quite common for lines to disconnect at frequent intervals, and if you were forced to restart sessions all the time the opportunity to process e-mail would rapidly lose its charm.

Data sent between the client and server is compressed to minimize the amount of connect time. You can see this for yourself by monitoring the number of bytes sent by a modem when sending messages, or moving a document into a public folder. My own observations lead me to believe that a compression ratio of approximately 2:1 is achieved, although this clearly varies with the type of information being sent.

The human tendency to stay connected too long can be moderated by disciplined habits. One habit I try to adopt is to make a connection (which immediately sends any messages that I had previously created and sent), immediately synchronize my inbox folder, and then disconnect. The effect is to populate the inbox folder in my off-line store with an exact replica of anything that's on the server, reducing the length of the telephone connection and thus the cost (very important when you look at the outlandish surcharges applied to telephone calls by many hotels). I can then begin to work off-line and process these messages, generating whatever responses I wish.

Two problems with working on-line trip me up from time to time. First, downloading a full inbox (more than 100 messages) can take a long time, especially if you don't first carefully review the messages to ensure that none contains a large attachment. Second, once disconnected and working off-line you won't be able to refile messages and stay organized. There are partial solutions to these problems. In the first case, it's important to make a quick browse through the inbox and refile any messages with large attachments into another folder (I use one called "To Do"). You can refile messages into other folders, but only if you've marked them to be available when working on-line and off-line. Once this is done you can cheerfully refile to your heart's content, but you must remember to synchronize all the folders once you get back into the office as otherwise all your refiling will be for nothing.

In passing, let me also note that you should turn off the journaling feature of Outlook unless you really want to note any access to a Microsoft Office document. If you don't, an entry is created in the Journal folder every time a Word, Excel, Access, or PowerPoint document is worked on, including entries for attachments sent with messages. It is annoying to find a folder full of references to documents that you might have only ever worked with once, and all those entries have to be replicated up and down between the client and the server.

6.6.3   Rules and dial-up connections

Unfortunately there's a small side effect of the way rules work that can slow down working on a dial-up connection. The majority of rules can be processed when a client is not connected to the server. This is different to the rules services implemented by other e-mail clients, which require a server connection before any rules are processed. A rule requiring messages to be moved to a folder that's not in your mailbox is a notable exception. People commonly use rules like this to move incoming messages from specific individuals to different folders (some of which may be public or others in a personal Information Store), but these rules are only processed when a server connection is made.

If, like me, you subscribe to a number of Internet mailing lists that generate a fair amount of message traffic daily you can arrive at a situation where you log on, find that the Inbox is cluttered up with messages from all the different mailing lists, and then find that the Inbox Assistant busily goes to work to move messages out of the Inbox to their predetermined locations. The only problem is that while the Inbox Assistant is busy a great deal of traffic is generated on the asynchronous telephone link and you won't be able to do much work while all this is going on. Even with a 28.8 modem processing 50 or so messages can take a few moments, so prepare by having a good cup of coffee to hand. I'm pretty sure Microsoft will do something about this in the future but for now the way the Inbox Assistant processes "move to other folder" requests leaves a little to be desired.

6.7   How rules work

For the most part, the Exchange clients are pretty straightforward. Messaging functions work like you'd expect them to, but rules seem to cause people a lot of problems. At least, that's been my experience over a number of deployment projects.

There are a number of reasons why people possibly can't use rules as effectively as they might. First, user training tends to skip over rules, tending instead to concentrate on basic functionality such as how to send and receive mail. Second, as we've just discussed, some rules only work when clients are connected to the server. Third, there's no really good explanation of rules and how they work in any documentation.

I can sympathize with the difficulties that people have applying rules to electronic mail. In 1988 I contributed to a project to implement rules processing for one of DIGITAL's electronic mail systems. That effort eventually resulted in a patent being granted, but no one could ever get to grip with rules. They were difficult to explain in concept, and hard to put into practice. Since Exchange first appeared, a lot of work has been devoted to making the creation of rules as simple as possible, and the new Rules Wizard in Outlook 98 is a great step forward. Figure 6.15 shows the final step in creating a rule to automatically move some messages (in this case, notifications that my expenses have been paid) to a specific folder. The Rules Wizard is able to convert rules previously created with the Inbox Assistant.

So how do rules work with Exchange? In a sense, rules can be divided into those that can operate on a folder under all circumstances and those that are "profile-dependent". In other words, rules that can only be executed if a client is connected to server through a specific profile that's associated with the rule.

Rules are composed of a set of actions, properties defining the criteria that must be met for the rule to be triggered, and some other assorted properties, chiefly flags, but also a sequence number that determines the order in which rules are assessed. Rules are stored in a table in the folder they are associated with. Rules are held in a table in the folder that they are active for. The table used to hold rules is invisible, and can never be seen by a client.

When a new message is delivered to a folder (private or public), the rules table is opened by the server. Each rule is then evaluated according to the sequence number property. When a rule is evaluated its stated criteria are checked against the properties of the newly-delivered message. If the evaluation determines that the criteria are met, the actions associated with the rule are applied. For example, a message containing "FYI" (For Your Information) in the title might be automatically moved into the Deleted Items folder!

Some actions cannot always be applied. For example, if the action states that a copy of the message should be moved to a PST the action cannot be performed if a client is not connected to the server. The same is true of movement to public folders. In this instance the public folder may be available on the same server that the rule is being applied, but access to the folder may require authentication in the form of a log-on to a Windows NT account. These rules can be regarded as being profile-specific. Exchange notes rules that are profile-specific by examining the actions associated with a rule when each rule is created. If the server determines that an action cannot be performed a special stamp is placed on the rule to indicate that it requires client intervention. The stamp also indicates the user profile that created the rule.

Figure 6.15
The Outlook 98
Rules Wizard

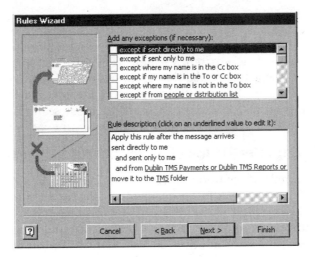

Actions that a server cannot perform are stored away until a suitable client connection is next available. The actions are stored in items called Deferred Action Messages (DAM) in a special hidden folder called the Deferred Action Folder (DAF). DAMs contain any data required to fulfill the rule that could not be executed by the server and also a reference to the message that triggered the decision to create the DAM. Each time a client connects to the server it interrogates the DAF to discover whether there are any DAMs available for it to process. Each DAM is examined to see whether its properties match the current profile. If a match is made, the action is then performed.

All this sounds quite complicated, but it's pretty simple once you understand how rules are resolved by the server and how the rules are linked to user profiles. Unfortunately explaining this type of implementation to users often isn't easy!

One final point to consider about rules. There is a 32K "packed data" limit for the rules created for any folder. The maximum number of rules fitted into the 32K depends on the size of the rules defined and the amount of data required for a rule. For example, a rule to move messages into a folder, for a single recipient, takes about 660 bytes. Hence there is no defined limit for the maximum number of rules that can be assigned to a folder. On average it is between 40 and 50 rules per folder. The following error will be displayed when the number of rules exhaust the 32K memory limit:

```
Changes to the rule could not be saved. There is not enough
memory or the rules are too complex. Try deleting some rules.
```

6.8   Using Personal stores

Exchange is built around the Information Store as the repository for messages and other items created by users. The Information Store has many notable attributes—high performance, single message instance storage model, availability from any client, and so on. However, the Information Store also suffers from a number of drawbacks. Personal Information Stores can be used to offset some of the disadvantages, while off-line stores supplement the usefulness of server-based storage.

6.8.1   Making effective use of personal Information Stores

Personal Information Stores are files that reside on users' local drives, either those on a PC or space allocated to users on a network device. You can even create a personal Information Store on a floppy disk, a feature that allows stores and their contents to be quickly transferred from one PC to another. Personal Information Stores are commonly referred to as PST files and are used to hold personal folders, a term that differentiates the content from that held in private or public folders, both of which are server-based. Messages are stored in two formats within a PST—RTF and ASCII, because it is conceivable that some clients will be unable to read RTF-style messages.

Figure 6.16
*Entering a PST
password*

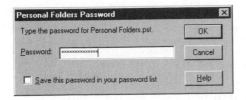

PSTs can be encrypted and compressed to enhance security and minimize disk space storage, and if a password is set on a PST users must provide it before a client will open the PST (Figure 6.16). The encryption depends on a user-supplied password, but there is no mechanism to recover data from an encrypted PST if a user forgets their password. Not even Microsoft can "break" into an encrypted PST. Unfortunately this fact is not normally realized until after the first incident of a user forgetting their password for a PST that contains some very important documents. However, some Internet citizens have figured out how to break into encrypted PSTs, and if the need arises you'll be able to find a program to crack a file open[2]. Use any programs that interfere with the internal structure of a file at your own risk. Microsoft will be very unsympathetic if things go wrong.

PST files allow users to create and manage their own private document archive. As we've seen it's obvious that any server is going to have some storage limitations in terms of either the total available physical disk space installed on drives connected to the server or the space allocated to individual users within the Private Information Store. It's easy to run out of space, especially if you're in the habit of creating or circulating messages with large document or worksheet attachments. In these situations space can be freed within the Private Information Store by moving files to a PST. Moving messages into PST files effectively "unshares" the message in Private Information Store the insofar as a separate copy of a message is created and moved to the PST.

Encouraging users to work with personal folders is fine as long as individuals use the same PC all the time. But if people move from one PC to another they'll leave information behind them. In these situations it's best to concentrate on server-based storage (which can be accessed from any PC) and leave personal folders to those who can use the same PC all the time. One way to accommodate roaming users (those who move from PC to PC) is to place their PST in their directory on a networked file server. If you do this remember to tell users to

---

2.   At the time of writing, the latest version of the PST decryption program is PS19UPG.EXE. An appeal to the msex-change mailing list usually produces a copy of the latest program.

always fully log-out from each PC they use, otherwise they won't be able to connect to their PST when they move to another PC.

If the same person uses the same PC all the time then personal folders can provide an additional advantage in that Exchange can be instructed to deliver messages to an inbox in a PST. Mail delivery to a PST is configured using the Delivery tab of the client Tools.Options menu option (see Figure 6.17). Don't rush to divert messages from the server to the PST because there are a few points that need to be considered before making what is, to some extent, a pretty radical change in a basic function of the messaging system.

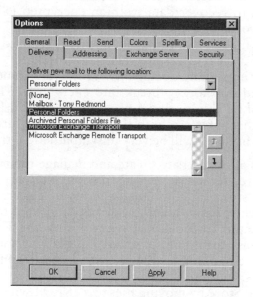

Figure 6.17
Configuring mail delivery to a PST

When messages are delivered to a PST they are held on the server until a user connects and then the messages are transferred down to an Inbox folder in the PST. If you decide to redirect mail the Exchange client automatically transfers all messages currently stored in the Inbox folder down to the PST, and then deletes them from the server.

Delivering mail to a PST is commonly used by installations wishing to build Exchange servers that support many hundreds or thousands of users. If server-based mailboxes are used the space available to each user is constrained by the physical disk available to the Private Information Store. If PSTs are used then the storage on the server is largely transient because messages are only held there until the PST is available. Users can therefore be allocated relatively small quotas within the store (10MB or less), allowing many more users to be supported on a single server.

Diverting message delivery from the Private Information Store to a PST eliminates the effect of the shared message model, removing a major benefit normally enjoyed by Exchange. Quite obviously, a message delivered to a PST cannot be shared. The storage model therefore moves from being database-centric to something similar to that used by Microsoft Mail (where messages are stored in MMF files). All of the disadvantages in the Microsoft Mail model, including the storage of multiple redundant copies of messages are inherited to achieve an advantage that doesn't really seem to be worth the price.

Another important factor to consider is that using a PST for mail delivery means that only users with physical access to the PST will ever be able to read messages sent to the mailbox's owner, eliminating the potential problem of unauthorized but privileged users reading other people's mail. Adopting this solution is a double-edged sword and a price is paid for privacy. In some cases, especially if a company believes that mail messages are of short-term use, responsibility for backing up and securing the messages in the PST passes from the system administrator to the user once messages are redirected into a PST. In most other cases where the PSTs used for mail delivery are held on networked file services, the responsibility for backing up the PSTs remains with the system administrators. Backing up individual PSTs is easier than backing up a very large Information Store, chiefly because there is a wider range of backup software available that is capable of processing individual files (the PSTs). Restoring an individual file from a backup tape is much easier than restoring a user mailbox from a backup of an Information Store, and this fact alone makes the use of PSTs an interesting item for consideration until the time comes that Exchange supports "bricked" restores and this fact alone makes the use of PSTs an interesting item for consideration if you don't run a backup program that supports bricked backups and restores (and indeed, use the facility).

While on this point it's interesting to note that Exchange clients automatically disconnect from a PST after 30 minutes of inactivity, allowing system administrators to plan to take file-level backups of PSTs stored on shared file services even if users insist on leaving their PCs logged on (hopefully protected by a password-enabled screen saver). The next time a client operation commences that uses an item in the PST Exchange will automatically re-establish the connection.

Many installations try and encourage users to view the Private Information Store on the server as a repository for working documents, or those that must be available no matter which PC is used to connect to the server. In this model users are supposed to move files to a PST once the files are no longer current or perhaps become less important. The model assumes a fair amount of discipline on the part of users, something that's not always easy to find, and also devolves responsibility for data security to users once files have been moved away from a server-based store. One of the undoubted advantages of server-based storage is the assurance that someone else will take care of backing up all your important data. People aren't so good when the time comes to create backups or copies of local data on a PC.

Figure 6.18
Changing the display name of a PST

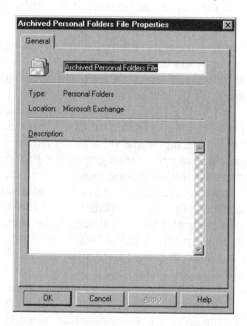

Exchange does not limit users to a single PST. It is entirely possible to configure multiple PSTs for use, perhaps having one file on a networked file service and another on the local DOS device, with maybe a third on a floppy disk. Putting a PST on a floppy disk may seem strange, but it's certainly a valid method to transfer files from one PC to another, or one user to another. Each PST is individually configured into a profile. By default, the display name of each PST is "Personal Folders", so things can get slightly confusing if you don't change the name afterwards to reflect the use that the PST will be put to. For example, "Network Personal Folders", "Archived Folders", "Mail Folders", and so on. The display name of a PST is easily changed by selecting the PST from the client and then bringing up its properties, as shown in Figure 6.18. It would be useful if the actual location (file name) of the PST was available through its properties, even in read-only mode, but if you want to find out where a PST is physically located this must be done through the client Tools.Services menu option (Figure 6.19). No aspect of Personal Folders can be configured or otherwise controlled by system administrators through the administration program. Remember—these are *personal* folders.

Figure 6.19
Personal Folders properties

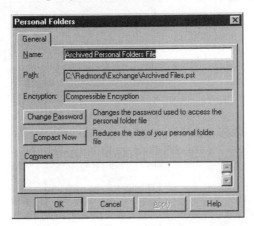

Users moving to Exchange from Microsoft Mail will find personal Information Stores a very natural extension of the mode of working they had become accustomed to. In a Microsoft Mail environment it is normal to pull messages from a post office server down to a mailbox file held on the PC. In an Exchange environment the situation is somewhat reversed, as the normal way of working is to leave messages on the server rather than moving them to the PC. Users can move messages down to a PST if they wish, albeit through a drag and drop operation rather than having the mail system do it automatically. Installations moving from Microsoft Mail should carefully consider whether they want to migrate the many megabytes of user messages into the private, server-based, Information Store. In my opinion it is best to leave messages where they are—on the PC by converting the Microsoft Mail format mailbox to a personal Information Store. Apart from reducing the demand for server resources, this approach means that users can be migrated to Exchange much more quickly than otherwise possible.

Training sessions clearly offer an opportunity to encourage good work habits such as the effective use of PSTs in people. Hint or cheat sheets can also be used to get your point across and so relieve some pressure on server-based resources. As with most features there are pros and cons that need to be understood before you can make the most effective use of them. Table 6.2 summarizes the most important issues to understand about PSTs. Make sure you understand the impact of these issues before you rush into using PSTs.

Table 6.2   *Pros and cons of using Personal Stores to supplement server storage*

Pros	Cons
A PST can be stored on any available device, including floppy disks.	A PST can't be shared between users. For example, you can't use a PST to share documents between a manager and a secretary. Users who leave a PC logged on can inadvertently block their own access to a PST if they move to another PC.
PSTs can be used to transfer files between users, including users in different Exchange organizations.	A PST can be encrypted to protect its content against other users, but if the password is lost there is no way to recover it.
A PST can expand to any size up to a theoretical 2GB limit, subject to available disk space. The largest PST in use is at least 400 MB (there is a limit of 64,000 items in a single folder). Thus, users can be allocated more space in the Information Store.	Delivering mail to a PST removes the benefit of single instance storage. Also, the space required to store a message is doubled because they are held in RTF and ASCII.
PSTs can be backed up with any file-level backup utility.	If people use PSTs they must make sure that the files are actually backed up. There is an increased chance of message corruption because there is no rollback/transaction log mechanism available for PSTs.
PSTs are easier to restore than the Exchange Information Store.	Deferred mail messages won't be sent unless the client is actually connected to the server.
The Auto-Archive feature in the Outlook client uses PSTs to store archived items.	Inbox Assistant rules won't be processed unless the client is connected to the server.
PSTs provide an easy way for Microsoft Mail users to move to Exchange because they can convert MMF files to PSTs.	There is a decreased ability for system administrators to monitor disk usage because messages and other items can be stored on the server and scattered across user PSTs.
	Extra network traffic is generated to move information to and from PSTs. Messages for delivery to a PST are held on the server until a client connects, and if a lot of mail is waiting the initial connect can take quite a long time.
	PSTs are not available to Web browsers, nor can they be accessed from POP3 or IMAP4 clients.
	The administration program "Move Mailbox" option does not move items stored in PSTs. These must be manually moved.
	PSTs may not be available to roving users. For example, people who want to work with the same data at home and in the office.

6.8.2   Off-line slave replicas (OSTs)

Off-line folders are replicas of server-based folders, stored in special files with .OST extensions. An off-line folder file is created automatically when you configure a user profile and indicate that you want to be able to work in off-line mode. Thereafter the off-line folders are made available when you elect to work in off-line mode rather than connecting to a server. Examining the advanced properties of the Exchange service reveals the file name of the OST.

MAPI clients can use off-line folders to store and access information without being connected to the server. In one way the concept behind off-line folders can be thought of as snapshots of server-based folders (the folders held in OSTs are, in fact, true slave replicas of server based folders). In another they can be thought of as a more intelligent version of personal folders, but only because facilities are provided to automatically synchronize an OST with the contents of server-based folders.

Aside from synchronization, the most fundamental difference between an OST and a PST is that an OST is tied to a specific MAPI profile. If you don't log in and authenticate using the profile originally used to create the OST then the client will refuse to open the OST. This is because the profile stores an encrypted "cookie" created from the mailbox's unique ID. The mailbox unique ID can only be accessed when connected to the server, so it follows that an initial connection must be made to create the cookie and store it into the MAPI profile. Every time you attempt to work in off-line mode afterwards the profile is read to determine whether the cookie exists. If the profile is unavailable the OST will refuse to load, issuing a warning that you must connect to the server (to recreate the cookie) before you can use the off-line folders. Not using the right profile is the most common reason for not being able to access an OST. Deleting and recreating the server mailbox is a more radical version of basically the same reason. In this instance the next time you connect to the server the master ID for the server mailbox will not match the data held in the profile and the OST will refuse to load.

An .OST file can be created anywhere, including network drives, but the usual location is somewhere like C:\WIN95\REDMOND.OST. I don't like storing anything in the Windows directory, so recommend that you create a separate directory to hold user-specific information. All my Exchange files (OST, PST, and PAB) are held in a directory called C:\REDMOND\EXCHANGE\, a name that instantly indicates that the files belong to me and are associated with the Exchange application. Placing an off-line folder on a network drive may seem pointless, but it does mean that off-line folders will be available if you log in and wish to work in off-line mode from different PCs.

The set of special mail folders—Inbox, Outbox, Sent Items, and Deleted Items are automatically added to off-line folders if off-line folder use has been configured in the user profile. These folders allow you to process messages while disconnected from the server. For example, you can create and send messages to anyone you want. In this case the client holds the messages in the Outbox folder and automatically sends them the next time you connect to the server. Sending messages in this way is done by synchronizing the contents of the Out-Box off-line folder with the Outbox folder on the server.

Figure 6.20
Folders marked for offline access

Folders are marked for off-line access by changing the synchronization property. By default, a folder is not marked for off-line access, so you must select each folder you want individually. Once marked, a slightly different icon is used to indicate that the folder will be available when working in off-line mode. Figure 6.20 shows the set of folders in my mailbox that have been marked for off-line access. The set includes folders such as "Tasks", "Tony's Inbox" and "Travel Info", and one public folder, the "MS Exchange Mailing List". Note that before a public folder can be marked for off-line access, it must first be included in your public folder favorites (see page 288).

Outlook 98 introduces off-line filtering. In other words, a filter can be applied to a folder so that only items that met the criteria set in the folder will be moved to the off-line replica. For example, you might decide to only move items that have been posted to a folder in the last month, or items that relate to the projects or customers you work with. A filter becomes active the next time you connect to a server and means that you will only ever see items that pass the filter. This means that is can be a big mistake to apply a filter to a folder like the Inbox as it's all too easy to filter out newly arrived messages that you might want to see.

Because OSTs contains slave replicas of server based folders they can be used to recover information from accidentally deleted mailboxes. Let's assume that a mailbox is removed by a system administrator, only for the administrator to then discover that the mailbox should have been retained. All the database rows and tables relating to messages in the mailbox are discarded by the Information Store immediately a mailbox is deleted, so there is no way to recover the mailbox on the server except by restoring a full backup of the store. If an OST is available, you can start the client and opt to work in off-line mode. All of the deleted messages are available in the OST and can be moved out of the OST to a PST. Once the movement is complete you can log out of the client, delete the OST file, and reconnect to the server. The old OST is invalid because the mailbox ID is changed when the mailbox is deleted and recreated so there's no point in attempting to use it. Anyway, the messages we're interested in are safely held in the PST and once we're connected back to the server the messages can be dragged from the folders in the PST to folders on the server. Following that, synchronizing with the newly populated server folders can rebuild a new OST.

Any profile can be used to open a PST because these files are profile-independent. If PSTs were not profile-independent they couldn't be used to transfer user files from one site to another, or from one user to another, or even (conceivably) for archiving. Table 6.3 contains a more exhaustive list of the basic differences between OSTs and PSTs.

The contents of folders marked for off-line access can be synchronized with the server using the client Tools.Synchronize option. You can elect to synchronize a single selected folder or all folders at one time. Of course, only the special mail folders plus any other folder marked for off-line access is synchronized when the "all folders" option is selected. Unless you really must have everything available to you when you work off-line it's a good idea to restrict the number of marked folders plus the number of items stored in these folders. Even when synchronizing a single folder the whole process can take several minutes to complete if there are several hundred messages to deal with. Inbox and Sent Items folders tend to accumulate messages so give these folders a good clean out every so often to save yourself some time.

Table 6.3   *Differences between PSTs and OSTs*

	Personal Information Store (PST)	**Off-Line Store (OST)**
Valid locations	Any DOS device.	Any DOS device.
Storage type	Permanent, persistent storage in its own right.	Transient storage that's inextricably linked to the contents of the master (server) folders.
Can be opened by	Any Exchange or Outlook client, using any MAPI user profile.	Any client, but only using the same MAPI profile that originally created the OST.
Synchronization	None—all movement between the PST and other stores is user-initiated and performed manually.	Automatic for server-based personal folders upon each connection to the server. Specific synchronization must be requested for replicas of public folders, or of any personal folder when connected to the server.
Encryption options	Optional encryption with a separate password (individually defined for each PST).	By default, OSTs are automatically encrypted. No password used (because of OST association with server mailbox).
Managed through	By configuring a Personal Folders information service (Tools.Service).	Off-line Folder File Settings tab from Advanced properties for Exchange information service (Tools.Services).
Multiple PST/ OST possible	Yes	No

Automatic synchronization of the Outbox folder is performed when a client connects to a server to make sure that any message generated by the user when working in off-line mode is sent to its final destination. If changes have been made to any other folder when working off-line, including replicas of public folders, those changes (additions, updates, and deletions) will also be synchronized back to the server-based folders. After all synchronization operations you can see exactly what happened during the synchronization process by viewing a log that ends up in the Deleted Items folder. As you can see from the sample log illustrated in Figure 6.21, the synchronization process updates new and deleted folders in the folder hierarchy as well as the actual folder contents. Synchronization logs are produced by the Exchange client and any version of the Outlook client prior to Outlook 98. The advent of background synchronization in Outlook 98 has consigned the synchronization log to the great byte bucket in the sky, largely because this client only produces a log if something goes wrong during synchronization (for example, a client does not possess the necessary permission to access a folder).

Figure 6.21 *A synchronization log*

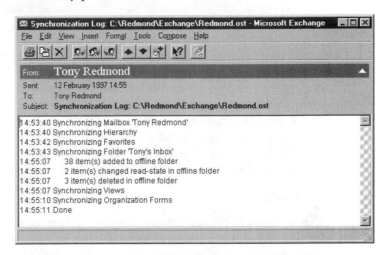

Accidents happen, and it is possible that an OST file becomes unavailable for one reason or another, the most common being that a PC's hard disk experiences a failure and no backup exists. Unlike a PST, it is easy to recreate the OST, albeit with some minor problems. After the disk is restored or replaced, remove any trace of the OST if necessary, then use the Tools.Services client option to access the properties of the Exchange service. The Advanced tab allows you to define the name of a new OST. Enter the name for the new OST and click on OK. Exchange checks whether the file exists, and when the OST cannot be found, offers to create a new file. Accept the offer. Log-off and log-on again, and the OST is now available. However, recreating the OST removes the folder properties controlling whether a folder is available on-line only or both on-line and off-line for all folders except the special folders (Inbox, Deleted Items, and so on). Before synchronizing the other folders (including public folder favorites) you must mark each folder you want to use in off-line mode.

Apart from their obvious use in processing messages off-line folders are very useful for anyone who travels. You might, for instance, want to take a copy of all documents relating to a particular project before going on a trip. During the trip changes might be made to some or all of the documents, and when you get back to base you can synchronize the changes back with the data held in the server-based folder. Conflicts can occur when synchronization is attempted. If this happens you'll have to resolve the conflicts manually as there are no intelligent agents available to help out.

I can live without PSTs, but my general day to day working life would be greatly affected by the loss of the off-line folder capability. My OST typically contains between 3,000 and 5,000 items in a variety of folders, and occupies up to 100MB of disk space. I am certainly not the record holder in this respect, as I know of people who keep hundreds of thousands of items off-line, using more than 1GB of space. Off-line stores compliment the excellent dial-up capability of the Outlook clients and make it much easier for road warriors to get their job done. Without the ability to browse and then reply to messages off-line I wouldn't have much chance of getting through the hundreds of messages I receive each week, and access to public folders such as the one that's subscribed to the msexchange mailing list make it much easier for me to keep up with developments in the world of Exchange.

6.8.3   Archiving

Users, despite the suspicions of some system administrators, are only human. As such they will accumulate mail messages and other items in their mailboxes in the same way as they collect anything else. Some people will be very neat and tidy, maintaining an efficient and effective folder structure. Others will let chaos exist with messages piling up in folders that were created for a purpose long forgotten. Most users exist between the two extremes. They do their best to keep their mailboxes reasonably clean, eliminating dead wood from time to time, but generally there's a lot of excess information kept hanging around, occupying valuable space in an Information Store on the server.

Archiving is an attempt to provide some automatic assistance to users. In the context of a messaging system, archiving means that messages that meet certain conditions are moved from the "live" store to a "passive" store. In the context of Exchange, the live store is a user's mailbox in the Private Information Store and the passive store is a PST file. Archiving also helps to increase performance by reducing the number of items in folders. The more items in a folder, the slower it is to access. This is especially so for folders like the Inbox, Journal, and Calendar.

The conditions for archiving are age-based. In other words, messages become candidates to be moved to the passive store once they exceed a certain age—28 days, 15 weeks, or maybe 6 months. The net effect of moving messages from the live store is to reduce the amount of information held on the server, although the actual physical size of the Private Information Store will not be reduced unless the store is rebuilt with the ESEUTIL program (see page 364). Reducing the space occupied in server-based stores is good from a system administrator's point of view. More space is created for new items, optimal use is made of disks, and backup times are reduced.

In Exchange, archiving is client-driven and the server plays no great role, apart from processing client requests during the archival process. Not all clients include archiving functionality. Outlook is the only client that offers archiving, either on an automatic basis or on an explicit basis according to criteria defined by the user.

Figure 6.22
*Setting up auto-
archive options*

A client can archive messages in two ways. First, the Outlook client has an "Archive" option on the File menu, producing the dialog shown in Figure 6.22. The default option presented by the dialog is to create an explicit instruction from the user to the client to review the contents of selected folders (and sub-folders) and archive any items contained within that are older than a specified date. Alternatively (by clicking the first radio button in the dialog), a scan can be performed against all folders that have an auto-archive property set, and all items that meet the criteria stated in the property will be processed. For instance, if the "News" and "Views" folders both have an auto-archive property of "archive after 3 months", then the scan will examine these folders to locate any message older than 3 months, and will then move any such messages to the passive store (the PST). PSTs can, of course, be located on any DOS device—even a floppy disk. Placing PSTs used for archiving in user directories on networked file services is probably the best approach because these directories are more easily backed up to tape than local hard disks. Both the Exchange and Outlook clients support the concurrent use of multiple PSTs, so it's possible to have a PST for the purpose of archiving on a network file service and another PST to use for personal documents on a local hard disk.

The second archiving method is called "auto-archiving", a two-step process. Before any automatic archiving can be performed the parameters for archival must be set by defining the auto-archive property for the mailbox. This is done via the auto-archive property page accessed from the Tools.Options menu choice, as shown in Figure 6.23.

Figure 6.23
*Setting general
auto-archive
options*

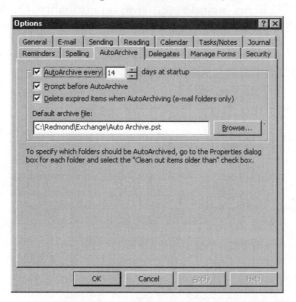

The initial implementation of archiving (in Outlook clients prior to Outlook 98) suffered because archiving items from server to local folders is a slow process, especially the first time items are moved. Users who hit the "OK" button when they were given the option to archive quickly learnt that the process could take up to 30 minutes to complete (depending on the folders and the number of items in each folder), and during that time they could do nothing else. Outlook 98 has a better solution. Archiving is now performed in a background thread, much like background synchronization. Users can continue to work while archiving proceeds, albeit with reduced response times.

6.8.4 SCANPST—First Aid for PSTs and OSTs

There are plenty of utilities available to maintain the contents of the server-based stores. There's also a need to ensure that the DOS-based stores are adequately protected against inconsistencies that can arise through normal operation. Over a period of time it can be expected that not every RPC sent between the client and server or vice versa will complete; that network interruptions will occur; there may be errors reading or writing data to the hard disk; and PCs might be powered off abruptly while a PST or OST is open by an Exchange or Outlook client. The files themselves might continue to work in an apparently normal manner, but sooner or later a problem will come to light.

With an OST you can opt to create the file from scratch, as described earlier. The sole drawback to this arrangement is the length of time taken to synchronize the contents of all the server folders down to the OST. Problems in a PST take on a different dimension because the folders in a PST are not replicas of anything else; they are the sole containers for the data they hold. A tool that is able to "fix" a PST to get around the problem is therefore a pretty important weapon in an implementation team's armoury. That tool is SCANPST.EXE, and it is found in the same directory as the Exchange client software.

Figure 6.24 *A successful run of SCANPST*

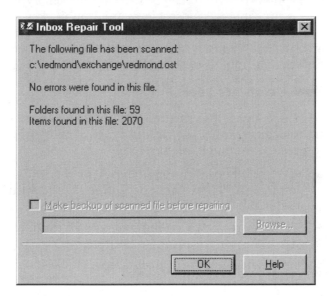

SCANPST can only be run if it can gain exclusive access to the PST or OST you want it to process. After the target file is opened a series of 8 tests is performed to establish whether any inconsistencies exist in the internal structure of the file and the links between folders and items stored within. If any inconsistencies are detected you'll be given the opportunity to repair the file, or, in the case of a successful run the program reports the number of items processed and will go no further (Figure 6.24). There is no need to run SCANPST unless a problem is encountered. There's no harm in running the program either, and it does provide a certain peace of mind for the more paranoid of the Exchange community.

6.9   Keeping secrets

No one likes to think that their messages might be read either en route to a recipient or by someone other than the recipient after messages have reached their final destination. The Advanced Security features in Exchange provide two major features to users.

1. Message encryption and decryption

2. Digital signatures

These features are based on software that Microsoft has licensed from both Entrust Technologies and RSA Data Security Inc., augmented with some code developed within Microsoft. RSA is a public-key encryption system that can be used for both encryption and certification and is probably the most widely used public-key encryption system in use today. RSA was originally developed in 1977 by Ron Rivest, Adi Shamir, and Leonard Adleman at the Massachusetts Institute of Technology. The initials of the authors' surnames make up RSA.

6.9.1 How secrets are kept

Before plunging into the details of how advanced security works, let's try to bring together the various types of encryption used by Exchange to protect communications.

- MAPI clients can optionally encrypt the RPCs to and from the server. RSA RC4 stream encryption is used with a 128-bit key is used in the US and Canada, and 40-bit elsewhere.

- All server to server communications within a site or across the site connector are automatically encrypted.

- Site to site communications across the X.400 connector are not encrypted.

- Site to site communications across the Internet Mail Service (SMTP connector) can be sent as encrypted RPCs. In this case, the servers authenticate themselves to each other using NTLM.

- Site to site communications across the Internet Mail Service can also use SSL session encryption. This means that the servers exchange X.509 certificates with each other during the early part of the SMTP connection, and all data sent afterwards is encrypted. Like RPCs, SSL encryption is performed using RSA RC4 stream encryption.

- Client connections to Exchange over the LDAP, POP3, HTTP, NNTP, and IMAP4 protocols can all be protected using SSL. None of these protocols use encryption by default.

Table 6.4 summarizes the different methods available to protect client to server and server to server communications.

Table 6.4   *Different methods of ensuring privacy*

	Basic (clear-text)	NTLM	Encrypted RPCs	SSL
Client to server				
Outlook (MAPI)		X	X	
POP3	X	X		X
IMAP4	X	X		X
Outlook Web Access	X	X		X
LDAP	X	X		X
SMTP	X			X
NNTP	X	X		X
Server to Server				
MAPI RPC		X	X	
SMTP	X		X	X
X.400	X			
NNTP	X	X		

6.9.2   Message encryption and digital signatures

Exchange divides the security workload between clients and server. All encryption and decryption is performed by clients, which also take care of applying digital signatures. The server keeps track of the users who are entitled to use advanced security as well as allowing management operations such as the allocation and revocation of security certificates, which are stored in the directory. More about these certificates and the part they play in advanced security later.

A scheme called asymmetric encryption is generally used to secure e-mail. Asymmetric encryption uses a pair of keys, one private and one public. The keys share a mathematical relationship but it is extremely difficult to derive one from the other. Thus, it is safe to distribute a user's public key to anyone who wishes to send them messages, safe in the knowledge that the user will be able to use their private key to view encrypted information after it arrives.

Message contents are encrypted with a single-use bulk key generated on demand, a symmetric encryption (the same key is used for encryption and decryption). The bulk key uses a 40-bit, 56-bit, or 64-bit algorithm depending on the country (the two strongest algorithms are only available within the US and Canada; France permits no encryption software at all).

Additionally, each recipient's public key is used to encrypt the encryption key for the message. In effect, this creates a lockbox or outer wrapper for the message. The algorithm used to build the lockbox is based on 512 bits and is therefore much stronger than the base encryption. Because of the computational power required, using such strong encryption is only realistically possible when only a small amount of data is to be encrypted. When someone receives their copy of the message they can use their private key to open the lockbox, retrieve the bulk key, and proceed to decrypt the message. In affect, a hybrid combination of symmetric and asymmetric encryption is applied to protect messages. The bulk encryption algorithm is either CAST (from Entrust) or DES, while the public-key algorithm is RSA. DES (Data Encryption Standard) is a complicated algorithm for the encryption of data designed by the U.S. National Bureau of Standards. The intention behind DES was to create an algorithm that is extremely difficult to break, certainly well beyond the capabilities of anyone equipped with copious time and anything else than a supercomputer or a networked array of workstations. Even with such powerful hardware resources the 56-bit key used by DES[3] to create a binary encryption key with 72 quadrillion possible combinations is enough to make any attempt to break the code a relatively fruitless activity.

In a practical sense the presence of different encryption algorithms in use within a single Exchange organization doesn't affect matters in the least because non-U.S. servers are able to decrypt messages originating from the U.S., and vice versa. The difference lies in how messages are encrypted in the first place rather in how they are eventually decrypted.

For comparison's sake it's interesting to note that Lotus Notes Release 4 also uses 64-bit keys in its international versions[4]. However, the last 24 bits of each key are registered in escrow with the U.S. government, reducing the amount of key-cracking to 40 bits. Of course, giving the U.S. government a head start when the time comes to crack a key is done just in case someone wants to officially read your mail at some point in the future.

---

3.   The specification for DES is contained in the Federal Information Processing Standard Publication 46 of January 15, 1977.

4.   Page 738, "Using Lotus Notes 4", Que Books 1996.

Governments generally like to know what people are up to, and steps are often taken to put obstacles in place to stop people protecting their privacy. The U.S. government, for example, was really upset when Phil Zimmerman, the author of the PGP (Pretty Good Privacy) encryption algorithm, placed his code into the public domain through the Internet. Following much the same line the French government do not permit the import of any encryption software into France[5], so any Exchange server used in France cannot include the encryption functionality. Even if a server located in France cannot generate encrypted messages people using the server will still be able to read encrypted messages originating from elsewhere. Microsoft cannot be criticized for shipping different encryption technology to different countries. As a U.S. company, Microsoft is limited by law to the software they can provide, and the implementation in Exchange is similar in many respects to the approach taken by other products, most notably the Lotus Notes server which supports a mixture of United States and "international" keys to encrypt messages.

I'm not sure that it really makes a lot of difference to the average user whether their messages are encrypted with 40, 56 or 64 bits. Huge amounts of computing horsepower are necessary to decrypt even a single message encrypted with a 40-bit key. The resources required are sizeable enough to prevent anyone but national security agencies and other government bodies from even attempting to browse or intercept the volume of messages generated on an average server. And anyway, the content of the majority of messages is hardly earth-shattering and is of little commercial or other importance. If you're really interested in probing the outer edges of message encryption perhaps you should investigate messaging systems that support the U.S. Defense Messaging System (DMS) standard. A variant of Exchange V5.0 that supports DMS is now available.

Digital signatures can be described as an electronic stamp or seal placed on a document. The seal affirms that a person with access to someone's private signing key has sent the message. By creating a "digest" of the message by feeding its contents through an algorithm and encrypting the result with a private key you can also create a checksum for the message. The checksum can be verified at any time by decrypting the digest with a user's public key. If anyone has changed the message content since it was sent the checksum will fail. Thus, digital signatures allow non-repudiation of messages, provide a level of confidence that a known individual sent the message, and give a guarantee that messages have arrived in exactly the same form sent

---

5. The prohibition against encryption software is described in Decree 92-1358, dated December 1992.

by the originator. Exchange uses the MD5 algorithm (from RSA) for digital signatures.

Recent examples of legal discovery actions throughout the world have awakened people to the danger of putting something in an e-mail message that they wouldn't like someone else to see in the future. It's difficult to explain to a lawyer that a remark about a competitor's product, or even someone else in your company, wasn't more than a throwaway thought on your part. Once committed to e-mail that thought becomes a fact that might be presented in court one day. In the United States, where the majority of discovery actions have occurred to date, the situation is complicated by a concept known as "negligent waiver of privilege", meaning that an insecure message sent between two people in the same company can constitute a waiver of the lawyer/client privilege. In this context, insecure means that the message is not encrypted and could be read by someone else, such as a system administrator.

Consider a situation where two managers are discussing the termination of an employee and one is unwise enough to send an e-mail saying "I never really liked him/her from the start". What would a trial lawyer do with such a statement in front of an employment tribunal? The moral of the story is clear. Encryption of business-sensitive messages provides added protection against potential legal difficulties in the future, at least in the United States. The question therefore is whether the advanced security features of Exchange have the correct balance of usability and features to protect your enterprise. I believe the features are certainly there; to a large degree the question of usability (and therefore compliance) depends on how advanced security is implemented.

With Exchange V4.0, advanced security was only possible within the confines of a single Exchange organization. The reason for this limitation was simple: there was no defined mechanism for organizations to share or synchronize directory information together, so the data used in the encryption/decryption process could not be exchanged between organizations. In Exchange V5.0 and V5.5 the situation is a little different. There still is no way for organizations to send each other their security data on an organizational level, but it is now possible for individual users to set up security arrangements between themselves and other people who may use a different Exchange organization. Figure 6.25 shows how someone (in this case, myself) can create a special type of message to send to another user. The special message contains the sender's public keys. When the message is received the public key information can be extracted and inserted into the recipient's PAB, much the same way as key information can be held in the OAB (see page 621). As you can see, the message can contain other information too, allowing a complete PAB entry to be created. This functionality is known as Person-to-Person Key Exchange (PPKE).

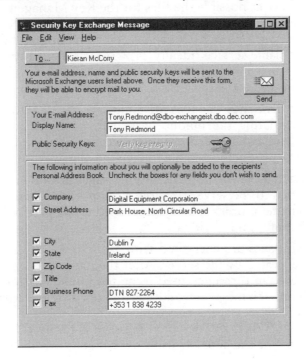

Welcome as this development is, the ability for users to exchange key information between each other is a short-term solution to the problem. It does nothing, for instance, to address the cases when a user changes their public key, or when keys are revoked or reissued. It is far more desirable to have the ability for Exchange organizations to be able to automatically share directory information between each other on a scheduled basis. That functionality is not yet with us, but it should be in the future.

6.9.3   Basic points about message encryption

Before plunging into the inner details of how advanced security works we need to create a broad sketch of the security implementation. The basic points regarding message encryption, or message sealing, as implemented in Exchange are as follows:

- Encryption is accomplished through a mixture of public and private keys allocated and controlled by a single nominated Exchange server within your organization. This server runs an optional component known as the Key Management Server. It is obvious that this computer must be located in a secure environment as if it is physically accessible or becomes unavailable the entire encryption scheme is compromised. Because of its need to be as secure as possible the files for the Key Management Server must be located on a disk using the Windows NT NTFS file system. The server must be capable of providing as high a degree of available service (ideally 24 × 365) as a hardware configuration can make possible.

■ 512-bit RSA public/private key pairs are used to verify a sender's authenticity. The RSA MD5 message digest algorithm is used for calculating the unique hash used to check message integrity. These techniques are similar to those employed by other encryption products available today.

■ Each user who will encrypt messages must be individually identified to the server to allow a temporary token to be generated. The temporary token is then used to allocate public and private keys for an individual.

■ Messages are encrypted with a one-time "bulk" encryption key generated by the server. After the message is encrypted the bulk key is in turn encrypted using the public key for each recipient. Thus, if a message is addressed to ten different users, the bulk key for the message is encrypted ten times using ten different public keys. When an encrypted message is received it is decrypted by fetching the bulk key using a recipient's private key, and then the retrieved bulk key is used in turn to decrypt the content of the message.

Because client software is used to encrypt messages it follows that it is eminently possible to export the technology on a laptop PC, or even import it into a country, no matter what the wishes of the respective governments are. Some countries, including the United States, require their citizens to keep records of the occasions when they exported (albeit unknowingly) the encryption software along with the rest of the client, and these records can be demanded for inspection by government officials. This requirement may change over time, but it's an interesting indication of the attitude that governments have to encryption technology when it's incorporated into (almost) consumer products.

6.9.4 Keys and Certificates

The concept of keys is clearly very important when attempting to understand how advanced security works. Signing and sealing of messages is controlled by a scheme of private and public keys in line with the ITU X.509 set of recommendations for authentication information. Each mailbox enabled for advanced security receives a key pair composed of a public and private key. Public keys are provided as fixed-length strings that are published and made known to any process that needs to encrypt information destined for that user. Two public keys are used, one to encrypt messages before they are sent, and one to read electronic signatures on received messages.

Private keys are also stored as fixed length strings. However, their values are kept private to the user and never revealed. The private keys are stored in an encrypted file (with an extension of .EPF) stored on the user's computer. As in the case of public keys, two separate private keys are used within the Exchange security scheme. One for message decryption and one to apply electronic signatures. Table 6.5 summarizes the key types and when they are used.

Table 6.5   *Private and Public Key usage*

	Encryption/Decryption	Electronic Signatures
Sending messages	Public key used to encrypt message contents	Private signing key used to apply signature
Reading messages	Private key used to decrypt message contents	Public signing key used to interpret applied signature

Perhaps it's easier to think of keys as follows:

	Encryption/Decryption	Electronic Signatures
When sending a message	Use Recipient's public key to encrypt content.	Use Sender's private key to sign message.
When reading a message	Use Recipient's private key to decrypt content.	Use Sender's public key to verify digital signature.

Like passwords, it's easy for human beings to forget their private keys. With Exchange advanced security losing a key isn't a total disaster so there's no need for users to write their keys down on a piece of paper that can be kept in a convenient location. If users forget their private key the key server can allocate a new key.

In all versions of Exchange up to and including V5.5, the public/private key pairs are based on X.509 V1 security certificates, which are created and managed by the Key Management Server. When fulfilling the role of certificate manager the Key Management Server is known as the Certification Authority or "CA" because it is responsible for creating and maintaining the security key pairs and special certificates. Certificates are an authentication mechanism used by many security schemes. Certificates are used by Exchange to maintain users' public keys, which are held and replicated via the Directory Service and contain:

- A unique serial number for each certificate which the Key Management Server generates.
- The encrypted password of the Certification Authority. This is sometimes known as the CA signature.
- The directory name of the Certification Authority. This allows clients to send messages back to the Certification Authority via the mail system.
- The directory name for the user who holds the certificate.
- The user's public keys for either signing or message encryption.
- The expiry date of the certificate, if set by the Certification Authority.

Two certificates are issued to each user who is enabled for advanced security. One certificate holds the public signing key, the other the public encryption key. A copy of the CA's own certificate is also distributed to each user. This certificate is stored in the user's .EPF file along with the user's personal certificates.

A wax blob impressed with the seal of office of a mayor or other public official and affixed to a formal document is a reasonable analogy for a special certificate, which fulfils the same role in attesting that the item it is associated with has been authorized by a specific individual (or public body).

6.9.5 Electronic signatures

Much of our discussion so far has been focused on message encryption. Exchange also allows messages to be "signed" by users to enable non-repudiation and message integrity. These features utilize additional keys, known as signing keys, which are quite separate from those used to encrypt and decrypt message content.

Non-repudiation means that a message can be associated with a specific individual who cannot deny that they sent a message (because it has been electronically signed by them). Of course, just like passwords, non-repudiation only works if individuals do not reveal their signing keys to others. It is also very unwise to keep copies of signing keys taped to the bottom of a keyboard.

Message integrity can be assured by creating a "hash" value, an algorithmically derived value calculated by passing the contents of a message through a complex set of computations. The end result of taking such an electronically mixed snapshot of a message's contents is a unique numeric value, the hash value. Before sending the message the hash value is encrypted with the sender's private signing key. When the message is received its contents can be verified by creating another hash of the contents using the same algorithm and comparing it against the original hash which is fetched from the message using the originator's public signing key. Any difference in the two hashed values indicates that the message has been changed since the originator signed it, and in fact that it was the named author who sent the message.

6.9.6   Installing advanced security

The installation of the Key Management Server is easy and accomplished by selecting the checkbox for Key Management from the menu of available options for Exchange Server. After the installation is complete the Key Management service starts up and functions in the same manner as any of the other Exchange services, such as the System Attendant.

The installation of the Key Management Server involves the creation of two passwords, both used to decrypt, or unlock, the "lockbox" which protects the Master Encryption Key for the Key Management Server. The master encryption key protects all keys held within the security database.

The first password is written to file called KMSPWD.INI on a floppy diskette that you'll be asked to provide during the installation. If you want to you can avoid writing the information to the floppy, but this decision can lead to future inconvenience because the password will then have to be manually input each time the Key Management Server is started. If the floppy disk containing the password is not available whenever the Key Management Server is started you'll be asked to insert it, and failing this, the server will not start up because the master encryption key cannot be accessed. Remember, without access to the master encryption key the server cannot even begin to process security requests, so make sure that the floppy containing the master encryption password is always available. Don't leave the floppy in the computer's floppy drive because the computer will attempt to use its contents to boot an operating system the next time it is restarted, and Windows NT doesn't boot too well from a key management server floppy disk!

Floppy disks are very prone to error, especially when they are used over a long period of time. It's therefore a good idea to copy the diskette containing the password and store the copy in a safe place.

The second password is created for use by the system administrator every time they attempt to carry out any management operation that involves the Key Management Server. For example, if you select a recipient and attempt to enable them for advanced security you'll be asked to enter the password. As it can get quite tiresome to continually be prompted for a password Exchange allows you to decide whether the password should be "remembered" for up to five minutes at a time. This allows you to get on with the task in hand such as enabling a whole group of users for advanced security.

A default value for the security administrator password is provided (the password, strangely enough, is set to "password") and you should change it as soon as possible after the installation is complete. Remember to share the password with anyone who will participate in any security management operations. At first glance it may seem that the management of the Key Management Server involves lots of passwords being demanded, it's logical when you think of the attitude that should really be adopted when you approach the implementation of a secure messaging system. Either you want to have a secure system or you don't. There really isn't a half-way point in this respect.

Exchange V5.5 adds additional protection by allowing you to define that administrators must possess an additional level of clearance to perform specific tasks by requiring additional passwords for each task (see Figure 6.26). These tasks include:

- Adding or deleting security administrators
- Key recovery
- Key revocation

As noted previously, a single central Key Management Server is allocated the role of creating and managing all security keys allocated to users within an Exchange organization. In all advanced security implementations the central Key Management Server is installed first. You can switch and change the Key Management Server across different systems, but only within the same site. This process is accomplished by simply copying the security database, security DLL, and service to the target server. If you make a mistake and want to move the Key Management Server to a system in another site you'll have to withdraw all the existing keys and issue new ones, adding up to a lot of work that's easily avoided by making the right decision in the first place.

The effect of the initial Key Management Server installation is to create the "CA" object in the site configuration container (Figure 6.27). Once created, details of the CA object are replicated to all the other servers in the organization in the same manner as other configuration data. Using the CA object as a marker prevents another server becoming the central Key Management Server for an organization, but only after replication has occurred. It is technically possible that two administrators install the Key Management Server component in different sites at the same time, something that will result in chaos after replication occurs and two certification authorities vie for primacy. Advanced security needs to be planned, not just dropped into an organization on an ad-hoc basis.

Figure 6.26
Stages in implementing advanced security for a user

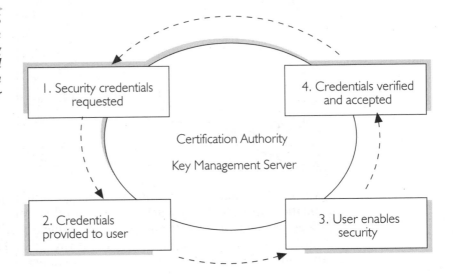

Figure 6.27 *The CA object inserted by the Key Management Server*

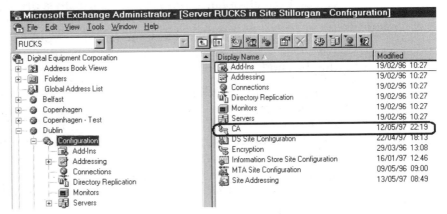

Although the central Key Management Server is the sole definitive source of security keys within an organization the Key Management Server software should be installed on a server in each site. These installations can be thought of as secondary Key Management Servers. They don't allocate or control security keys, but allow local recipients to be enabled for advanced security by routing any security-related messages back to the primary Key Management Server for processing.

Figure 6.28
*Adding
administrators
to the CA object*

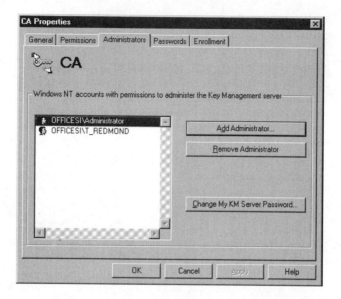

All security-related operations such as credential generation and verification are channelled back to the central system where the central Key Management Server is running, so clearly it's important to carefully select the right server to take on this role. The central Key Management Server should be located on a system that has good network links and is able to undertake the load generated by security processes. In small organizations it's not normally a problem to determine which server should be nominated to act as the host for the central Key Management Server, but larger organizations need to look at how advanced security is going to be used in the organization before making the choice.

Exchange V5.5 allows multiple administrators to be enabled for advanced security by adding them to properties of the CA object (Figure 6.28). The "Passwords" tab allows you to define the password policies for advanced security. For example, will you require two passwords (one from each administrator) before a new administrator is added? This concept is called "missile silo" passwords, from the dual-key arrangement used to prevent a single person firing a missile.

Once the decision is made to implement advanced security and a suitable server nominated you should take steps to ensure some level of physical security for the server. This implies that the server should not be easily accessible to users and that as few people as possible should be able to log-on to the system in a privileged mode.

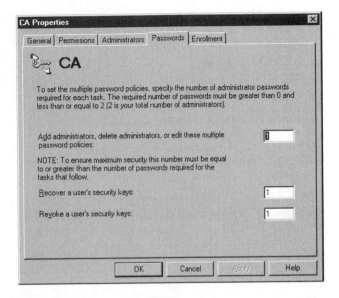

Figure 6.29
*Defining
password
policies for the
CA object*

6.9.7 Enabling advanced security

Before anyone can use the advanced security features of Exchange the system administrator must authorize or enable the user for these features. This process can be performed individually, or for a whole group of users at one time. Authorization can only be accomplished after the Key Management Server component is installed and running.

Before examining the details of the steps taken to enable a user for advanced security, it's important to know how all the different security components fit together. Security components are divided between Exchange clients and the Key Management Server and are shown in Table 6.6.

Once everything is installed you can begin to enable individuals or groups of users. As illustrated by Figure 6.26, enabling a user is a four-stage process.

1. Temporary security credentials are requested for the user.

2. The credentials are provided to the user.

3. The credentials are used to enable advanced security from a client.

4. The security server recognizes that the credentials have been properly used by a client and allows the user to begin using advanced security.

Table 6.6 *Security components*

Location	Component	Use	Filename
Client	Security DLL	Contains code to sign/verify or encrypt and decrypt messages.	ETEXCH.DLL (16 bit) ETEXCH32.DLL (32 bit)
Server	System Attendant	Interacts with clients when advanced security is enabled. The System Attendant works with the Security DLL to store and manage key pairs as required by the system.	
	Key Management Server	Allows the System Administrator to use the Security property page to enable advanced security for users.	SECADMIN.DLL
	Key Management service	Accepts and actions requests from the Administrator program and the functions contained in the Key Management Security DLL.	
	Key Management database	A collection of files managed by the Key Management service. These files contain security information about clients.	\EXCHSRVR\KMSDAT A directory.[a]
	Security DLL	Functions to enable the server to respond to security requests generated by clients.	SECKM.DLL

a. The most important file is KMSMDB.EDB. Unlike previous versions, Exchange V5.5 stores key information in an encrypted ESE97 database. You must make arrangements for this database to be backed up on a regular basis. Stop the Key Management Service before taking the backup.

Figure 6.30
*Temporary
security
credentials*

Temporary credentials (sometimes called a token) are generated by selecting the security property page for a recipient from the administrator program and clicking on the "Enable Advanced Security" button. The Key Management Server then proceeds to create temporary security credentials for the user and displays them to the system administrator (see Figure 6.30), who should note the credentials down exactly as they are displayed. The credentials can be thought of as a password for the user to identify themselves to the security server during the later phases of enabling. At the same time the public and private encryption keys are generated and stored in the security database on the server.

Figure 6.31 *The bulk enrollment option*

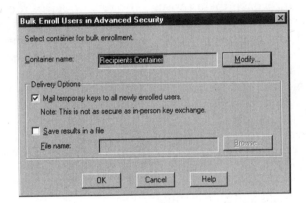

Exchange V5.5 provides a new "bulk enrolment" feature, illustrated in Figure 6.31. This allows an administrator to select a complete recipients container and have temporary security credentials generated to all mailboxes at one time. Optionally, the credentials can be mailed to each mailbox, or the administrator can capture the credentials for each mailbox in an output file. In the latter case, some arrangement must be made to provide the credentials to each user so that they can complete the authorization cycle. Writing down credentials on small pieces of sticky yellow paper is probably not the correct nor most secure method available. Yelling details of the credential across a crowded office is probably not the best way either.

Figure 6.32 is an extract from a sample of the file that can be generated during bulk enrollment. The top two entries are for users that already use advanced security, and the last three entries show the temporary credential generated for each recipient. Note that the alias rather than the display name is reported for a mailbox, so you may have to do some reconciliation between the alias and display names in order to understand who should receive which temporary credential.

Figure 6.32
*Sample output
from a bulk
enrollment
process*

```
o=digital equipment corporation/ou=dublin/cn=recipients/
cn=ericp, already enabled
/o=digital equipment corporation/ou=dublin/cn=recipients/
cn=tonyr, already enabled
/o=digital equipment corporation/ou=dublin/cn=recipients/
cn=billr,COQXEWDLKYSS
/o=digital equipment corporation/ou=dublin/cn=recipients/
cn=johnh,BJIOSHISPUMY
/o=digital equipment corporation/ou=dublin/cn=recipients/
cn=peterm,HHAJZNYMZFKO
```

In small sites it may be possible for the administrator to visit the user and coach them through the remainder of the process. This isn't practical for large installations where the issuing of keys and their provision to users might fully occupy a system administrator for quite some time. Assuming that it takes an average of fifteen minutes to create the temporary credentials, note them down, visit the user, and enable security from the user's client, only four users can be processed in an hour, or 32 in an eight hour day. Chasing users to enable security isn't a good use of a system administrator's time, so in this situation it is best for the administrator to concentrate on the task of generating the temporary credentials and noting them down before passing the credentials to one or more others, possibly users who have been nominated to help with this task, who will then visit users to pass on the credentials and help complete the whole process as quickly as possible.

It is possible to have the KMS generate and send a message to each user as their temporary credentials are generated. This feature is highly convenient, but some will worry that it is not secure. It's true that the message might be read by other people, or printed down and inspected by someone who shouldn't see it, but it must be remembered that temporary credentials are for one-time use with a specific mailbox. These credentials are no use to any other mailbox, nor can they be used to encrypt or decrypt messages, or add digital signatures. In short, I don't worry about mailing credentials. If you do worry, take advantage of the feature that allows an administrator to edit the text of the message sent with the credentials (Figure 6.33). Add some suitably terse and stringent warning of the dire consequences that will befall anyone who is rash enough to divulge details of their temporary credentials to anyone else, and advise the recipient that they should immediately print and eat the message after they read it.

Figure 6.33
*Editing the
enrollment
message*

After receiving their temporary credentials (by whatever means) each user then enables advanced security from a client by selecting the "Security" property page from the Tools.Options menu option (Figure 6.34). The user must now type in the temporary security credential and provide a password of their own (which must be at least six characters long). This step generates the public and private key pair to be used for electronic signatures.

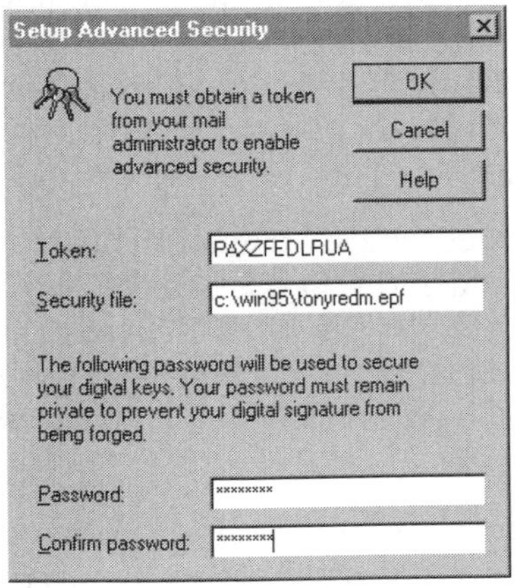

Figure 6.34 *A
user enables
advanced
security with
their temporary
security
credentials*

As mentioned earlier, the special security certificates generated for the user and the copy of the CA's own special certificate is written into a file with an .EPF[6] extension. This file is normally stored in the Windows directory, for example: C:\WIN95\TONYREDM.EPF. The security file is encrypted using a CAST-64 algorithm to prevent unauthorized access, and the contents don't mean much to human beings if the

6.   EPF = Encrypted Password File

file is edited using a utility like NotePad (Figure 6.35). The security file must be available before encrypted messages can be read or sent.

Figure 6.35 The contents of a user's EPF file

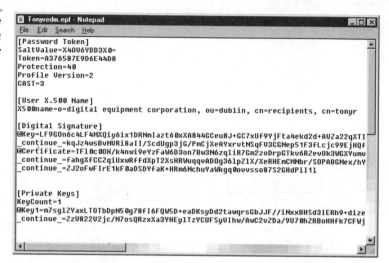

Local availability of the .EPF file has implications for users who roam from workstation to workstation to read their mail. It is possible to copy the .EPF file to a floppy and point the client to the floppy when it attempts any security operations, and this is possibly the best way for roaming users to cope. Indeed, keeping the .EPF file on a floppy disk guarantees maximum security at the expense of relying on relatively fragile media. If people opt to use floppy disks to hold EPF files make sure they know that they need to have a copy available just in case problems occur.

After the user enables security from a client an encrypted message is automatically generated and sent back to the Key Management Server to indicate that the user has provided their credentials and a satisfactory password and wishes to begin using advanced security. This message contains the public signing key, which is in turn stored by the Key Management Server.

The Key Management Server checks the credentials and, if they are satisfactory, generates a message back to the user to inform them that they can now begin to use advanced security. The user receives the message from the "Security Authority", the name that the Key Management Server represents itself by to users. This message includes some hidden data containing the encryption key pair that was earlier generated by the Key Management Server as well as the pair of X.509 certificates to use later on for signing and encrypting messages. A copy of the CA's X.509 certificate is also enclosed. Before the message can be read the user must provide the password they originally specified when they received the original enabling message. This step ensures that the same user is involved at all stages of the enabling procedure. If the password matches the encryption key pair is written into the .EPF file and once it is present the user can begin to encrypt and sign messages.

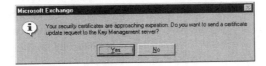

By default security certificates are valid for one year from the date of issue. As a user approaches the end of a certificate's validity the Key Management Server sends them a message to request whether the certificate should be updated for another year (Figure 6.36). This process continues from year to year unless the security administrator issues a certificate that is valid for a specific period.

Security keys can be recovered anytime after they have been issued. This would be in cases where a user loses (or forgets) their password or corrupts the security file on the PC. Another reason is because the user suspects, for one reason or another, that their password is compromised, possibly because they shared it with someone else on a temporary basis.

Along the same theme, the administrator can revoke security keys if any reason arises to believe that a user should not be able to use the features of advanced security. Revocation works by the server writing the number of a user's certificate into a revocation list maintained in the directory. Once a certificate has been added to the list no other user can encrypt a message for that user.

6.9.8 Using advanced security

After a user is enabled for advanced security they can proceed to encrypt messages and attachments and apply digital signatures. Users can select to encrypt or sign every message by default, or elect to encrypt or sign a specific message.

Encryption isn't much good if no-one else is able to decrypt the message. Code within the Outlook and Exchange clients dictates whether encryption is possible and which algorithm can be used. Everything depends on whether or not public keys for the recipient can be retrieved from the directory or the PAB. For example, if a message is addressed to someone outside your organization (like a custom recipient), the directory will not be able to provide a public key. The client will then know that it cannot encrypt the message and offer the option to send the message in clear text (Figure 6.37). This approach is reasonable as it's clearly folly to send an encrypted message out across an SMTP or X.400 link to a recipient who potentially uses another mail system that knows little or nothing about Exchange-style encryption. Intelligence is also applied when encrypting messages circulating within an organization. If a recipient is connected to a server located outside the United States or Canada their directory entry will notify the client that a 40-bit key and algorithm should be used.

Figure 6.37 *Non secure recipients*

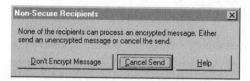

Because recipients are checked to ensure that they have been enabled for advanced security and will be able to decrypt messages you cannot encrypt messages when working off-line unless a copy of the OAB has been downloaded. Amongst the information about users extracted from the directory, the OAB contains copies of X.509 certificates, so public keys are available for encryption purposes. However, if the OAB has never been downloaded or is out of date then the keys will be unavailable, a record may not exist for a user that has been added to the directory since the OAB was last downloaded, or some of the public keys may be obsolete. For this reason, people who travel and need to generate encrypted messages on the road should always download an up-to-date copy of the OAB before they leave the office.

Common reasons why Exchange will determine a user cannot receive encrypted messages include:

- They have not been enabled for advanced security.
- The message must pass through a gateway before it can be delivered to the recipient. In general any attempt to get encrypted information through a gateway fails. As discussed earlier, Exchange and Outlook clients are able to send special messages containing public keys to users in other Exchange organizations that may be connected via X.400 or SMTP backbones. In these cases, when both parties at either side of the backbone possess the necessary key information to allow encryption/decryption to proceed, encrypted messages can pass through connectors. However, encrypted messages can never be sent to non-Exchange recipients such as an IBM PROFS or Lotus Notes user, even if the messages pass through an Exchange connector.

Encrypted messages or those bearing digital signatures are indicated by using a different icon when messages are shown in a folder.

The lock icon indicates that a message is encrypted, while the pen icon means that it has been digitally signed.

6.9.9 Location of security objects

We've been through a lot of fairly complicated and interlinked structures which work together to allow someone to encrypt or sign messages. Table 6.7 describes the location of each security object after advanced security has been enabled for a user. As you can see, there are four main locations.

Table 6.7 *Location of security objects*

	X.509 certificate	Key Management Security database	User's personal EPF file	Exchange Directory Store
User's directory name (mail address)	✓			
Signing certificate			✓	
Encryption certificate			✓	✓
Private encryption key		✓	✓	
Private signing key			✓	
Public encryption key	✓			
Public signing key	✓	✓		
Certificate expiration date	✓			
Unique certificate number	✓			
CA signature	✓			
CA directory name (mail address)	✓			

6.9.10 Making a decision about advanced security

Advanced security is one of those features that seem awfully attractive on the surface, so why won't it be immediately implemented in all organizations that operate Exchange? Table 6.8 lists some of the advantages and disadvantages of advanced security.

Table 6.8 *Advantages and disadvantages of advanced security*

Advantages	Disadvantages
Users can apply digital signatures to messages so that the messages cannot be repudiated.	A lot of work is imposed on system administrators to generate, distribute, and manage security credentials
Users can encrypt messages before they are sent, and decrypt messages received from other users.	Encrypted messages can only be sent to other recipients who are "security enabled".
Encrypted messages can only be accessed when a user's personal security password is provided, even if another user's mailbox is accessed by a privileged user.	The .EPF file must be physically available before messages can be decrypted.

System administration workload is the biggest issue influencing the decision whether to implement advanced security. Small organizations or those able to dedicate a person to fill the role of security administrator won't experience too many problems handling the work, but the same cannot be said for larger sites or organizations.

Before making a decision consider:

- Who is going to act as the security administrator?
- Who is going to be the back-up to the security administrator to handle their work when they are on vacation or sick?
- What is the maximum number for users in the organization that are going to be security enabled?
- Where are these users located? How and when are they going to be enabled for advanced security? How are the initial credentials going to be provided to users, especially users remote from the security administrator?
- How will roaming users access their .EPF files as they move from workstation to workstation?

- What server is best to act as the Key Management Server? Has it an appropriate hardware configuration to handle the expected load? Is it capable of providing a highly available service to users?

- How physically secure is the chosen Key Management Server? Where is it located and who has access to it?

- When will the security data used by Key Management Server be backed up? Is this operation included in regular system maintenance activities?

Do not attempt to enable advanced security unless you are happy with the answers to these questions. Cleaning up a bad security implementation and starting over again will require a lot of work and cooperation from users, especially when new credentials have to be issued or a new, different Key Management Server installed. In the latter case users won't be able to read any messages encrypted with credentials issued by the original Key Management Server, proving the point that it's very important to get your security implementation right first time.

If you decide that you can't implement advanced security it is still possible to protect sensitive information. For example, it is possible to use application-specific password protection for documents and spreadsheets. Users can set their own passwords to protect items stored in their private folders and shared passwords can be determined and used by groups who want an extra layer of protection for confidential information in public folders. I know of quite a number of installations that have opted to protect information in this manner. It's certainly not an infallible scheme, but it is simple to operate and is enough to stop casual unauthorized browsing through data.

6.9.11 Third Party security products for Exchange

The Advanced Security subsystem in Exchange provides all the protection required by the majority of users. However, in some situations people require even better security and that's where third party security extensions can help. Two basic areas of added values are normally proffered by third party extensions.

1. The availability of algorithms that are harder to break, especially outside the U.S.

2. The capability to exchange key information with people who don't use Exchange.

As noted earlier Exchange supports 40, 56, or 64-bit encryption algorithms. However, due to US Government restrictions the 40-bit algorithm is the only one available to someone like me, who isn't resident in the United States or Canada. I'd like my mail to be secure as anyone else's yet the fact remains that data encrypted with a 40-bit key can be decrypted with less effort than you imagine. The basic rule of encryption is that the longer a key is, the harder it is to break. Anyone outside the United States or Canada who is interested in highly secure mail must look further than Exchange advanced security.

Third party security products can be broken down into two camps. There are products that depend on a Certification Authority implementation similar to that used by Exchange, and there are those that also use public/private key pairs but rely on personal administration and distribution of the keys. The best known example of the latter approach is PGP (http://www.pgp.com, which is now owned by Network Associates). It's worth noting at this point that the Certification Authority style provides the basis for almost all SSL (Secure Sockets Layer) and other Web-based security today, clearly because it's much easier to manage security when you have a central point of reference. Personal distribution of keys is all very well, but it's difficult to manage in a large-scale or distributed enterprise and the system relies heavily on user co-operation and, to a certain degree, knowledge.

More and more products appear in this space all the time, and notable recent arrivals include:

- *MailSecure for Exchange* from Baltimore Technologies:
  - (http://www.baltimore.ie)
- *Secure Messenger for Microsoft Exchange* from Deming software:
  - (http://www.deming.com).

Both products are provided as plug-ins to the Exchange or Outlook clients and add their own security options to the client menus. Both products use the S/MIME (Secure MIME) protocol to send encrypted messages between Exchange users, or indeed users of any mail system that supports S/MIME, like Exchange V5.5 SP1. Of course, any public/ private key scheme can only work when users have made their public keys available to the people they wish to correspond with, so both MailSecure and Secure Messenger come with facilities to generate and distribute keys, much like the PPKE feature in Exchange. The combination of S/MIME support and the ability to distribute keys means that these systems can be used in a heterogeneous messaging environment or to implement advanced security between two Exchange organizations, even if they all haven't upgraded to V5.5 SP1. MailSecure is especially interesting for installations outside the United States because the encryption algorithms did not originate in the US and therefore cannot be restricted by the Government. Instead of the 40-bit algorithm offered by Exchange, MailSecure is able to use one based on 128 bits, a huge increase in the level of security. A certification authority is available for MailSecure (UniCERT), based on either an X.500 directory or the file system. As discussed earlier in this article, the certification authority is an important component of a secure mail system, so its availability is an important plus for MailSecure.

These products aren't the only offerings on the market. A browse through the archives of the Exchange mailing list will reveal a number of PGP extensions for Exchange. The majority of these are shareware or freeware, but some commercial products based on PGP have also appeared recently.

Third party security plug-ins cost money. Expect to pay between $50 to $100 per license depending on the quantity you buy. Inevitably some users will question the need to pay anything when Exchange provides advanced security facilities in the base product, so be ready to explain the reasoning behind your decision if you choose to upgrade security. Justification isn't hard, but it needs to be done. Client technology will evolve over the years so make sure that the selected vendor is able and willing to keep their software up to date. Some additional cost will probably be attached to upgrades, and this should also be factored into your decision.

6.9.12 The evolution towards S/MIME in Exchange V5.5 SP1

Originally, Microsoft planned to make major changes in the Advanced Security subsystem in Exchange V5.5. For many reasons, including the lack of S/MIME support in the Outlook 8.03 client, the changes were dropped from the final release, but are incorporated into SP1. Essentially, the major change in SP1 moves Exchange away from the earlier X.509 V1 type certificates, which can only be understood by other Exchange servers, towards a security infrastructure that facilitates interoperability with other messaging systems.

The S/MIME standard provides the cornerstone of interchangeable secure mail. Up to SP1, it could be argued that Exchange supports a well-known standard for its security certificates, but the format of a secure mail message is proprietary to Exchange. Instead of encoding secure content in a MIME body part, all the earlier versions of Exchange implemented secure mail through a set of MAPI properties that are highly specific to Exchange. When messages leave Exchange, the MAPI properties are stripped off, making interoperability impossible.

S/MIME is a standard that many different email vendors are building towards. As we've learnt with message content and calendar information, a common cross-vendor approach is vital if interoperability is to be achieved. Microsoft, Lotus, Novell, Netscape, and other messaging vendors have agreed to support the S/MIME standard and are working to include it into their products.

Three types of message are supported:

- Clear signed
- Opaque signed
- Encrypted

Opaque-signed and encrypted messages both result in a binary-encoded body part, or attachment, and are the two formats defined in the original S/MIME V1.0 specification. Exchange has always been able to transport S/MIME bodyparts. After all, S/MIME just adds another content type to MIME, so Exchange looks at S/MIME content as if it was an audio clip or PowerPoint presentation. The client takes care of translating the content of a message into an encrypted body part that looks like any other MIME-encoded content. When the message is received, the client decrypts the content from the S/MIME body part.

Sending encrypted messages as attachments allows transfer through gateways, which typically leave binary attachments alone. But a binary bodypart brings its own difficulties, such as when you want to post a signed message to an NNTP newsgroup. In this instance the bodypart could not be read unless an S/MIME client is used. The S/MIME V2.0 specification defines the clear signed format in an attempt to solve the problem. The difference between clear signed and opaque signed is that signature information is split out and kept in a separate file. Thus, the content of a message (or posting) can be seen, and the signature information kept apart for clients or people who are interested in viewing it. At worst, a client that doesn't support S/MIME will see a foreign attachment that they cannot open.

The Internet Mail Service handles all MIME conversions. A change is made in Exchange V5.5 to handle clear signed S/MIME messages to avoid any potential problems that might occur with the format translation from Exchange internal message format to MIME. Most of the time, the IMS is nearly 100% perfect in translating from internal format to MIME, and almost 100% is perfectly acceptable for everything except a digital signature, which must be passed through with perfect fidelity if it is to be accepted as valid by a recipient. A configuration option, which is not set by default, is therefore available to "preserve S/MIME clear signed signatures". If you turn on the option the IMS will not send the entire signed message as a binary attachment. In other words, the work that the IMS would otherwise do is left to the receiving client, which must be able to decipher the attachment. S/MIME clients are able to do this, but older MAPI clients like the original Exchange client or Outlook V8.03 can't. Older clients will receive an attachment they can't process, which is the reason why the configuration option is turned off by default, meaning that the IMS will strip off any signature information before sending messages out. It's actually better to remove the signature rather than send on a potentially invalid signature. In the latter case, users who receive an invalid signature will get an error message informing them that the message has an invalid signature any time they read it, leading to a spate of help desk calls. Once the majority of users are converted to Outlook 98 or some other S/MIME client it is safe to instruct the IMS to send the signatures on.

SP1 makes an important change in the format of security certificates, which are now issued in X.509 V3.0 format by the Microsoft Certificate Server (available as part of the Windows NT V4.0 Option Pack). The role of the Key Management Server changes too, as the Microsoft Certificate Server now becomes the preferred Certification Authority. X.509 V3 certificates comply with the latest industry standard. More importantly, this format is commonly accepted by many different vendors, so there is an excellent chance that Exchange will be able to interoperate and understand certificates used by the other messaging systems you want to communicate with.

All versions of Outlook Express since the release of Internet Explorer V4.0 have been able to both connect to Exchange (via IMAP4 or POP3) and send S/MIME encrypted messages via SMTP. However, Outlook Express must store and retrieve certificates locally, and is unable to query the Exchange directory in the same way as MAPI clients. Instead, Outlook Express and Outlook 98 store their keys in the Windows protected store, sometimes referred to as the "Microsoft Wallet". Outlook 98 is able to read and upgrade an existing .EPF file, and an .EPF file can also be used to import or export keys to or from another PC. Outlook 98 also supports the industry standard .PFX format (also know as PKCS#12) for import/export operations, so it's possible to export your private keys to a non-Microsoft client, like Netscape Communicator.

Key information continues to be stored in the Exchange directory. Outlook 98 is able to query and fetch the X.509 V3.0 certificates from the directory service (the PR_USER_X509_CERTIFICATE directory attribute is used for this) on an Exchange V5.5 SP1 server. As in the past, Outlook 98 is also able to store copies of certificates in the OAB and local Contacts folder. In fact, you can begin to use X.509 V3.0 certificates immediately and don't have to wait for everyone to be upgraded to use Outlook 98 clients. Remember, before an encrypted message is sent to a user, clients must check the directory to see whether the user has been enabled for advanced security. When Outlook 98 performs the check it discovers the type of certificate held by the addressee (X.509 V1 or V3) and selects the correct message format automatically. Older X.509 V1 certificates issued by previous versions of the KMS are still understood and managed. When these certificates expire, newer V3 certificates will replace them. V1 certificates can still be generated to allow backward compatibility with older Exchange and Outlook clients.

The PPKE concept continues to work with Exchange V5.5 SP1. However, a specific electronic form is not required to send someone a copy of your keys. All you need is to use Outlook 98 to send a signed S/MIME message to an external recipient, who can then capture a copy of your public keys from the message. In the same way, you can extract keys from signed messages you receive and store them in your Contacts folder. No mechanism exists yet for keys exchanged on a personal basis to be updated automatically if they are changed.

The Microsoft Certificate Server can act as the Certification Authority for an entire enterprise, not just for Exchange. In Exchange V5.5 SP1, the Microsoft Certificate Server takes over some of the functions of the KMS, such as:

- The issuing of new X.509 V3 certificates
- The issuing of X.509 V3 Certificate Revocation Lists (CRLs)

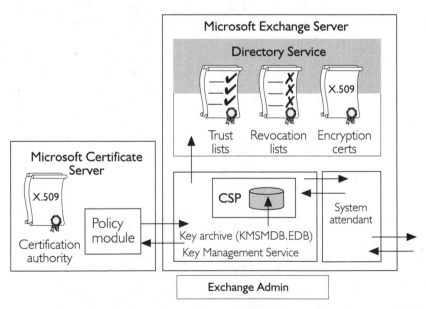

Figure 6.38
The advanced security architecture in Exchange V5.5 SP1

The X.509 certificates, revocation lists, and trust lists remain stored in the Exchange Directory. Think of the Microsoft Certificate Server as the Intranet authority, and the GAL (Exchange directory) as the Intranet directory service. In Internet terms the Certification Authority is a publicly agreed commercial company such as Verisign (http://www.verisign.com) that issues keys for different types of encryption such SSL, and the GAL might be a public LDAP server where certificates are stored along with directory entries. In all cases clients are provided with somewhere to retrieve public keys when they wish to encrypt a message. Outside the Intranet, other arrangements must be made to accomplish secure encryption across the Internet.

Exchange V5.5 SP1 supports the concept of Certification Trust Lists (CTL). A CTL does not mean that you go out and grab a copy of all the keys from another organization (and provide them with a copy of your own), and then insert the keys into the directory for local access. A CTL is a secure mechanism for an administrator to centrally publish a trust policy, which defines the set of external trusted organizations. Once your organization trusts another organization, clients will accept and trust signed messages coming from that organization. However, this doesn't mean that users will be able to send encrypted messages to people in a trusted organization. You still need to have someone's public key to be able to send them an encrypted message, and some arrangement must be made to acquire their keys. Personal acquisition through PPKE is easy, but there are other methods, including:

- Direct LDAP lookup to a certification authority across the Internet
- LDAP referral lookup across the Internet
- Inter-organization LDAP replication that includes key information
- Manual import/export into the Exchange directory via CSV files

Using the Microsoft Certificate Server, you continue to manage certificates through the Exchange administration program. In this instance the Key Management Server is used as the tool for secure key recovery in case users lose their keys, as well as taking care of key distribution and expiration. Keys can also be obtained from an external Certification Authority, but you'll have to import the keys into the Exchange directory. This can be done by creating a CSV file and using the administration program to import the data, or by writing bespoke code (through LDAP, MAPI, or ADSI) to add the certificates.

Some user interface changes are made for KMS administration in Exchange V5.5 SP1. However, the general approach to enabling a user for advanced security, including bulk enrolment, remains the same.

7

Connecting Exchange

A messaging system that's only able to communicate internally or with other systems of the same kind isn't much use in today's heterogeneous world. This chapter reviews the methods an Exchange server can use to connect to other electronic messaging systems.

7.1   The growing set of Exchange connectors

Connectors are the components that provide links between the Exchange MTA and other messaging systems, normally over an intermediate network connection. Two types of connectors exist—site connectors and external connectors. When Exchange V4.0 was first released Microsoft limited the number of connectors provided in the standard edition, forcing people who wanted to connect to almost any other system to a separate purchase of the necessary connector. The licensing philosophy has greatly changed since and the standard edition now comes fully equipped with connectors for sites, the Internet, Microsoft Mail, Lotus Notes, and Lotus cc:Mail. Separate purchases are only required if you want a connector for X.400, IBM PROFS, or IBM SNADS. All available connectors are bundled into the Exchange Enterprise edition.

7.1.1   Options to connect sites

As the name implies, site connectors are used to send messages between one Exchange site and another within a single organization. In fact, four different connectors can be used to link sites together:

- Direct site connector (also called the site connector)
- X.400 connector
- Internet Mail Service (called the Internet Mail Connector in Exchange V4.0, and often shortened to the IMC or IMS)
- Dynamic Remote Access Server (RAS) connector

Direct site connectors operate through Remote Procedure Calls (RPCs) between the connected servers. This is the preferred connection in a LAN environment or when a permanent high-speed connection exists between two sites. The dynamic connector depends on Windows NT Remote Access Server and it is used when a dial-up connection is made between two sites to send mail to each other. The connection between small branch offices where a single server is located for a small group of users and a larger central department is a good example of the type of situation where a RAS connector might be used. Naturally you'll need to ensure that RAS is configured on the servers involved in the transactions, and provide telephone lines and modems to make the physical connections.

In addition to standard asynchronous connections made over the telephone RAS can also be used over X.25 links. X.25 is a little more complex because you have to install an X.25 card and software in the computers that will talk together.

Apart from the options available to connect sites together, Exchange servers are able to send messages to each other over X.400 and Internet connectors, even when the systems are in the same Exchange organization. Conceptually the primary function for X.400 and Internet connectors can be viewed as to exchange messages with non-Exchange mail systems. In reality these connectors are going to get far more use in linking Exchange servers together. They are also a useful fall-back option for situations where it may be more convenient to piggy-back onto an existing corporate messaging infrastructure than to establish one especially for Exchange. For example, if an SMTP messaging backbone is already operational and used to tie together all the different systems used within an enterprise, the best course of action might be to use the Internet Mail Service to send messages across the SMTP backbone instead of site connectors.

7.1.2   Connecting other mail systems

Reaching outside the organization, the major external connectors provided with the enterprise edition of Exchange are:

- Microsoft Mail
- X.400
- Internet
- Lotus cc:Mail (available from Exchange V5.0)
- Lotus Notes (from Exchange V5.5)
- IBM PROFS (from Exchange V5.5)
- IBM SNADS (from Exchange V5.5)

The Microsoft Mail connector facilitates backwards connectivity with the Microsoft messaging system replaced by Exchange. This is important not only because the installed base of Microsoft Mail systems are a rich vein of opportunity for the initial deployments of Exchange, but also because the migration period from one messaging system to another often covers quite a long time, especially in larger organizations. The Microsoft Mail connector also allows installations to continue using Microsoft Mail gateways to other mail systems that they may have previously installed.

This connector is very important to Microsoft because it answers an immediate problem for the many thousands of Microsoft Mail installations—"how can I connect to Exchange". The answer is, of course, "Easily—through the Microsoft Mail connector". Thus, this connector is an intensely strategic weapon in the battle to get installations migrated to Exchange. There are other routes—you could certainly use either X.400 or SMTP to link Exchange to Microsoft Mail, but it just wouldn't be as straightforward, seamless, or easy, all arguments that carry enormous weight with system administrators.

We've already discussed how the X.400 and SMTP connectors can be used to connect sites in an Exchange organization together. Now we see them in a different light, facing externally rather than the purely internal view taken so far. The X.400 and SMTP connectors are very important to the overall success of the Exchange program, but in a different way to the Microsoft Mail connector. Unlike Microsoft Mail, whose development was totally under the control of Microsoft, X.400 and SMTP offer the promise of openness in the electronic messaging world, and most international or large-scale organizations will use one or the other, or even both methods to tie different organizational units or sites together. Without easy and out-of-the-box connectivity to X.400 and SMTP Exchange would face a much harder struggle for general acceptance in corporate environments. Equipped with the ability to connect over both X.400 and SMTP Exchange is in a much stronger position, if only because of the fact that many other messaging systems require you to purchase additional components or gateways before they can connect in a similar manner.

While SMTP and X.400 now represent the generally accepted methods for widespread electronic mail, this hasn't always been the case. Corporations have been deploying electronic mail since the start of the 1980s, and there's an often-bewildering array of systems in operation today. Whereas many of the older systems might be tagged with the "legacy" label and they might be scheduled for replacement by a newer system like Exchange in the long term a connectivity need still exists. A set of add-on connectors are therefore available and must be purchased and installed separately.

The Lotus cc:Mail connector first appeared with Exchange V5.0. This connector is a strategic weapon in the war of hearts and minds waged between Microsoft and Lotus. The aim is simple. If Lotus cc:Mail users find it easier to move to Exchange than Lotus Notes (the preferred option for IBM/Lotus) then that's what they'll do. "Easier" means easy to connect, more functionality, and ease of migration. The latter point is addressed by the cc:Mail migration tools provided with Exchange, and now the cc:Mail connector comes along to bridge the remaining gaps.

The Lotus cc:Mail connector works in roughly the same way as the Microsoft Mail connector. In other words, the connection to Exchange seems to be just another cc:Mail post office within the cc:Mail network. So good so far, but this isn't the real value to cc:Mail users. That value is delivered by the ability of Exchange to act as an SMTP or X.400 server for cc:Mail users. Remember that messages introduced into an Exchange organization by any connector can be routed by Exchange to any other connector, so messages sent by cc:Mail users can be routed by Exchange out to Internet (via the Internet Mail Service) or X.400 addressees (via the X.400 connector), or indeed to FAX, PROFS, or any other messaging service connected to Exchange. This functionality is certainly something that could be delivered by connecting cc:Mail to a Lotus Notes environment, but it's harder to configure and certainly doesn't work automatically, without a great deal of configuration. To me, this is the biggest win for cc:Mail users and it will be interesting to see if they agree, and a lot of cc:Mail installations migrate to Exchange. Microsoft certainly hope so.

7.1.3   New connectors in Exchange V5.5

LinkAge Software was a Canadian company specializing in interconnectivity between different messaging systems. Microsoft bought LinkAge in May 1997 to capture the expertise and some of the technology base within the company. The most obvious result of the purchase is the inclusion of connectors for Lotus Notes, IBM PROFS, and IBM SNADS in Exchange V5.5. Substantial engineering work was performed to integrate the Linkage connectors into the rest of the Exchange code base and remove dependencies like the need for SQL/ Server.

Some of the work didn't get done for the release of Exchange V5.5. The Linkage connectors remained bound to the Intel platform, a reflection of their previous history, and Alpha customers had to wait until Exchange V5.5 SP1 to be able to run native connectors. However, it must be noted that it is entirely possible to run one of these connectors, such as that for Lotus Notes, on an Intel server in an Exchange site and so provide a connection to any other server (in the site or throughout the organization). Address generators, required to allow addresses for the connectors to be generated when mailboxes and custom recipients are added to the directory, existed for both Intel and Alpha from V5.5 onwards.

Lotus Notes is obviously the major competitor for Exchange. Many major corporations have user populations of both Notes and Exchange and wish to bridge the gap between them. The Lotus Notes connector enables excellent interconnectivity between Notes and Exchange, including directory synchronization, and provides an in-the-box answer to the problem. Apart from bridging the gap between Notes and Exchange, the existence of a connector also provides a tool that can be used to migrate Notes users over to Exchange.

The IBM connectors can be used to link Exchange to many different variants of two basic systems (PROFS and SNADS) that run on IBM mainframe computers. The SNADS connector requires Microsoft SNA server (version 2.11 or V3.0) and can also be used to link to systems like Verimation MEMO, Fischer TAO, Soft*Switch Central, and Lotus Message Switch.

Both connectors provide excellent messaging interconnectivity, but neither connector supports directory synchronization in Exchange V5.5. Microsoft is working to fill this gap and expect to have shipped directory synchronization code for the SNADS connector by the time you read this book (but not as part of Exchange V5.5 SP1). The SNADS connector will then support synchronization between the Exchange directory and the:

- IBM Enterprise Personal Address Book (EAB)
- IBM Personal Services/CICS Shared Addess Book (PSAB)
- Verimation MEMO Directory

The IBM connectors serve a steadily-shrinking client base, albeit one that is important because of its deep roots in corporate computing circles. Microsoft can be expected to plug any gap that prevents a PROFS or SNADS community migrating to Exchange, but don't expect a vast enhancement in functionality in the IBM connectors otherwise.

The Lotus Notes connector is a different case. Lotus Notes is not only the major direct competitor to Exchange, it is also found in use by individual workgroups inside larger companies, who typically use a bespoke or off-the-shelf application developed on top of Notes. Sometimes users aren't even aware that they have a Notes client on their desktop. Notes applications can represent an enormous stumbling block to the deployment of Exchange, so it is clearly in Microsoft's best interest to keep the Lotus Notes connector up to date and as functional as possible.

7.2   Optional connectors

The Exchange MTA is responsible for delivering all messages sent to recipients who do not reside on the originating server. This task includes communication with other Exchange servers over all types of site connectors, other X.400 MTAs, and gateways to other messaging systems. As illustrated in Figure 7.1, the MTA does an excellent job as a single point of contact or message switch for messages arriving into the server from many different sources. The clearly defined nature of the connection engine allows third parties to build new connectors and then introduce them to the MTA in a very clean manner. Once installed a connector takes care of accepting messages from a particular source before providing them to the MTA for eventual delivery to user mailboxes. The process of acceptance may involve format translation before messages can be given to the MTA. For example, the Internet Mail Service converts newly arrived messages from SMTP/MIME format to the internal format used by Exchange. In much the same way outgoing messages may also require conversion by a connector before they are handed over to an external messaging system.

Figure 7.1 *The Exchange MTA acts as a connector engine*

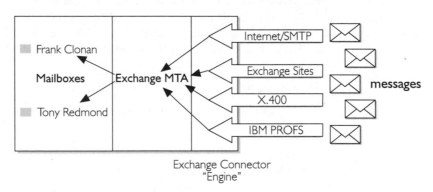

Despite the fact that Microsoft has now bundled most of the connectors required to link corporate messaging systems into Exchange, ISVs continue to develop connector technology. Microsoft has left some gaps, and the third party connectors aim to fill these. FAX is the most active area and a large number of FAX connectors are available, including products from Fenestrae (Faxination), Omtool (FAX Sr.), and FACsys. Voice mail connectors that link PABXs so that voice messages can be delivered directly to your inbox and read using PC loudspeakers are also active with several products available.

It's impossible to review all the third party connectors in a book like this. Great variations exist from country to country, so a certain amount of local research is required before you can find out what options exist for you. Fortunately the presence of so much information accessible from the web makes the search a little easier. Here are a number of questions I recommend you ask about any connector:

- How well integrated with Exchange is the connector? Can the connector be managed from the Exchange administration program or does it need a separate program?

- Are any client extensions required before the connector can be used? Do the extensions depend on any particular version of a client, such as Outlook 98? Are the client extensions available for all languages you are deploying Outlook in?

- What track record exists in terms of software releases that track new versions of Exchange? For example, did the connector require an update for Exchange V5.5 and, if so, how long after Exchange V5.5 was the update provided?

- What local support exists for the connector?

- Does the connector satisfy local legal requirements, such as those imposed by PTTs for FAX connections?

- For FAX connectors, how are inbound faxes handled? Can they be directed automatically to recipient mailboxes? What format are the faxes stored in? Can their content be read on all workstations? Are outbound faxes routed to the nearest fax machine? What status reports are provided to users to confirm that faxes have been successfully sent, and what reporting facilities are available to administrators to detail fax traffic in a specified period (how many faxes were sent, where did they go, who sent them, the costs incurred, what level of incoming traffic was handled, where it came from, and so on).

These are questions that any vendor should be able to answer.

7.2.1   Good connector books

The rapid evolution of Exchange as a message switch is one of the success stories of the product. Indeed, it has now become impossible for a book dedicated to best implementation practice to cover the connectors in sufficient detail without expanding the size of the book to well over 1,000 pages.

Details of these connectors can be found in the standard Exchange documentation kit or through many of the books covering Exchange administration. "Connecting Exchange Server"[1] provides good descriptions of most of the connectors, while "Microsoft Exchange Connectivity Guide"[2] is probably the best book if you're interested in migrating from Microsoft Mail.

7.3   The Message Transfer Agent (MTA)

Internally, the Exchange MTA is a true implementation of the X.400 messaging model. In other words, all of the recommendations described in the X.400 standards issued by the ITU in 1988 are complied with. The MTA processes data internally according to the X.400 model, and X.400-type messages are sent across the network when the MTA on one server communicates with the MTA on other Exchange servers. The same communication paths are used between MTAs in the same site, or the bridgehead server in another site connected via a site, X.400, or a dynamic RAS connector. The last point is not often understood, but it's very important. While the Windows NT RPC mechanism is used to transport messages across the network used to link a site or dynamic RAS connector, X.400 P1/P2 format messages pass "on the wire". Exchange may well use its own data format to transport content (MDBEF), but the fact remains that the messages being send are built according to the X.400 recommendations. And of course, messages sent across X.400 connectors naturally comply with the recommendations. It is only in the case of other connectors, such as the Internet, MS-Mail, or cc:Mail, that data conversion must occur and messages are transformed into the format demanded by the foreign connector.

X.400 messages are divided into envelopes (P1) and content (P2 or P22). Another interesting point is that the MTA usually only ever works on the P1 part of messages. The actual content is never touched unless the MTA is forced to open the message to effect data conversion, and that's only ever when the message is going to be transported across a foreign connector. Think about sending a message to a distribution list. When you read a copy of the message you see the name of the distribution list in the message header. No matter how many people the distribution list is eventually expanded to when the message is delivered you'll never see the names of the members of the list displayed in the header. This is because clients display the P2 part, or content, whereas the MTA has performed distribution list expansion when it processed the P1 part of the message.

---

1.   Author: Kieran McCorry, published by Digital Press (1998), ISBN 1-55558-204-4.
2.   Authors: Rodney Bliss and Rebecca Wynne, Microsoft Press (1996), ISBN 1-57231-230-3

7.3.I **The work done by the MTA**

We've mentioned in passing some of the work done by the MTA. A more complete list includes:

- *Message Routing and flow.* The most basic and important task of the MTA is to route messages according to the addresses placed in the envelopes. Remember that Exchange messages come from other sources than users, so the MTA takes care that messages are directed to the Public Information Store, other MTAs, the directory service, and so on. Messages sent to local recipients are directed to the Private Information Store. The MTA includes retry logic to make sure that messages are directed along different paths to their eventual destination if the premier or preferred path becomes blocked. The MTA also takes care of the creation and dispatch of non-delivery and delivery notifications.

- *Distribution list expansion.* Note that it is possible to expand distribution lists on the server that originates the message or on the server that hosts the distribution list. In the latter case messages must be routed via the home server before the list can be expanded. Each object in the list must be examined separately and checked against the directory. An object could be another distribution list that will, in turn, require expansion. Distribution lists that contain less than 100 or so entries can usually be expanded without causing a server too much strain.

- *Loop detection.* Obviously distribution lists can be nested inside other distribution lists. Unless loop detection code is implemented it would be possible to have distribution list "Team A" called by distribution list "Team B", and have the "Team B" list nested inside "Team A". Loop detection prevents the thread that expands the list getting very confused and makes sure that people on the list only ever receive one copy of the message.

- *Message Fan-Out.* A message might be sent to 100 recipients, but only 3 connectors might serve those recipients. The MTA applies intelligence to determine how many copies of the message have to be sent to the different connectors or other MTAs in order to effect the most efficient delivery.

- *Format content conversion.* Clearly the different connectors require different formats of messages routed their way. Some of this conversion occurs within the connector. For example, the Internet connector converts messages to SMTP/MIME format. The MTA must take care of any format conversion required before messages are dispatched. A good example of this is where a connection is made to a 1984-compliant X.400 MTA. In this case message content must be downgraded from the 1988/1992-type formats (P22) used by Exchange to the much simpler 1984-type formats (P2) used by the foreign MTA. Conversion between different character sets used by X.400 MTAs such as IA5 and ISO-Latin-1 is also performed by the MTA. The set of template files (.TPL) in the MTA work directory (\EXCHSRVR\MTADATA) define how the MTA deals with other X.400 systems. The template files include the ASN.1 rules for conversion between format types. Having template files allows encoding problems to be fixed through simple edits of one or more files and prevents the need for the MTA code itself to be recompiled or otherwise rebuilt.

Normally, the MTA does not participate in local message delivery as the Information Store is quite capable of moving a message between mailboxes as long as all the recipients are on the same server. The MTA only gets involved when messages need to be sent out to another server in the same site or via a connector to another site or mail system. Interestingly, the MTA service (EMSMTA.EXE) also incorporates the site connector.

Servers that run the messaging archive or journaling feature of Exchange V5.5 SP1 must route all messages, even those to local recipients, through the MTA to ensure that copies of messages can be captured. Moving local delivery away from the Information Store will impact performance. At this stage it's difficult to say how much the impact will be because everything depends on the ratio of local to remote deliveries. Some early assessments put the impact at around 30% reduction in the number of supported users. Time will tell.

While the Exchange MTA and its associated connectors are usually very reliable and self-maintaining it is necessary to keep a watchful eye to make sure that messages are flowing at a regular and predictable rate. Before looking for signs that everything's all right we have to know what to look for and what we might see.

7.3.2   Monitoring MTA queues

The easiest way to check message flow through the MTA is to select the queues property page for the Message Transfer Agent and then view the list of queues and the number of messages in each queue as shown in Figure 7.2.

Your own knowledge of a connector and its normal traffic pattern will tell you whether an abnormal number of messages are in the queue. Clearly the best case is to have zero or very few messages in each queue because this indicates that no delay is being experienced in transmission. If you see that a number of messages have built up for a connector consider whether any unusual activity has recently taken place on your server which might have generated a large number of messages. For example, these activities can generate many messages for a connector:

- Moving public folders from one server to another.

- Adding or amending a large amount of Information Stored in public folders.

- Modifying the contents of the directory by adding, changing, or deleting recipients.

- Importing or synchronizing directory entries from another messaging system.

- Unblocking a connection to another messaging system, which results in a large number of messages being delivered to a bridge-head server.

Figure 7.2
MTA queues

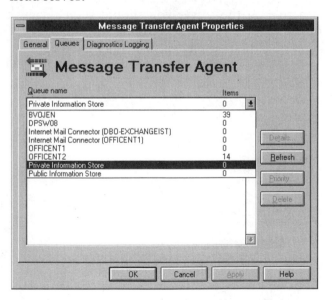

Taking the screen shot shown in Figure 7.2 as an example we can see that 39 messages are queued for BVOJEN and 14 for OFFICENT2. Both of these are servers, one located in a remote site (BVOJEN), whilst the other was a server in the local site (OFFICENT2). You should know what's happening with all local servers so it's the first and easiest problem to investigate. In this case the answer was easy—the server was off-line for hardware maintenance, but there can be more problematic situations to resolve such as a server failing due to hardware or power problems. Monitoring queues helps to identify these situations by forcing system administrators to ask questions as to why queues should be building up for a local server.

The BVOJEN situation is a little harder to resolve because the server is remote. First we must know the type of connector used to link our site with BVOJEN. Knowledge of the Exchange environment (sites and servers) should provide the answer. In this case BVOJEN acts as the bridgehead server for the Belfast site and it is connected with a site connector.

The next step is to determine whether the server is operational and whether the necessary Exchange services are running. Link and server monitors (see chapter 11) help by revealing whether a network connection can be made to a server (link monitor) as well as the Exchange and other Windows NT services that are currently running (server monitor). If you haven't already created and implemented some monitors you should do so now and review the results as soon as they are obtained. Assuming that the server in question is running and the MTA is active on the server you should then review the contents of the queue to see if you can determine why so many messages are there.

Figure 7.3
*Details of an
MTA queue*

Figure 7.3 shows the messages at the beginning of the BVOJEN queue. The contents are ordered in message priority (High/Medium/Low) sequence. Interpersonal messages are scattered among the messages generated by background system activities. You'll find messages from the Directory Service, the Public Information Store and the System Attendant, reflecting the messages sent to replicate information

between servers. The order of messages in the queue shown in Figure 7.3 looks a little strange at first glance. Why, for instance, is there a message generated by the Directory Service at 18:50 on April 1 (right at the bottom of the list) when messages generated by the same service throughout April 2 are at the top? The reason is simple: messages move up and down within the queue as attempts are made to send them. As problems have clearly occurred sending messages to the BVOJEN server over a period of days the messages from different days have become intermingled. You can manually intervene if you like by giving messages different priorities, but in most cases it is easier to let the Exchange MTA deal with the messages in the order they are presented.

I prefer to give interpersonal messages most importance, so the first step I take when dealing with a blocked queue is to immediately increase the priority of all interpersonal messages to "High". This action forces interpersonal messages to the top of the queue and makes sure that they will be sent first when the block is released. The logic behind this attitude is simple. Users complain when they receive non-delivery notifications, but the system components are much more patient and are content to wait for their messages to get through eventually.

The internal ordering of the queues also appears to give large messages a slightly higher priority than small messages. Once I've bumped all the interpersonal messages to the top of the queue I then like to move the small messages forward, the only reason being to clear the queue faster (at least on the surface). If the queue doesn't start to go down after all of this it's time to stop and restart the MTA on the target server, or perhaps restart the MTA on your server if lots of different queues are backing up. Restarting an MTA forces an internal reset and may clear out a problem that you can't see through the GUI.

In this instance the problem wasn't connected to Exchange at all. The network link between the two sites had become saturated because some large software kits were being copied from one computer to another. This goes to prove that all potential reasons must be considered when problem solving.

7.3.3   The MTA sliding window

A "sliding window" protocol is used by the MTA to transfer messages to other MTAs or gateways. This means that the MTA sends a certain amount of data, waits for an acknowledgement that the data has been received correctly, and then proceeds to send more data, continuing the process until the whole message is transferred. For comparison, many other messaging systems attempt to send complete messages as single entities, an approach that delivers satisfactory results with small to medium messages. Problems can occur when larger messages are sent, especially with network links that aren't very reliable. Given that the average message size continues to grow due to the influence of large and complex attachments the sliding window protocol is a reasonable solution for a messaging system that is designed to cope easily with large messages.

System administrators can influence the sliding window by setting a number of properties for the Site MTA (using the Advanced page). The important properties are:

- **Checkpoint size**—the amount of message data to send before the MTA inserts a checkpoint. The default is 30K.

- **Recovery time-out**—the amount of time after an error occurs before the MTA will wait for a reconnection. If the connection cannot be re-established the message fails and is returned to the queue. The default is 60 seconds.

- **Window size**—the number of checkpoints that can remain unacknowledged before the MTA will suspend data transfer. The default is 5.

In most instances the default values are appropriate and should only be changed if you suspect that the MTA is unable to process messages in a satisfactory manner. For example, if you suspect that the network is experiencing some problems that are causing messages to fail (evidence of this would be provided by a queue building up for a connector that doesn't normally have a queue of more than a few messages), then you might reduce the window size from 5 to 2. This step will force the MTA to send less data before an acknowledgement is received. Reducing the checkpoint size from 30K to 10K is another step that could be taken in a situation where network problems are being experienced.

7.3.4   MTA data files and the MTA work directory

If you browse through the MTA work directory you'll come across some data files named DB000001.DAT, DB000002.DAT, and so on. These files are used by the MTA for items such as message queues, internal indexes used by the MTA, and temporary storage of mail messages en route through the MTA. Collectively the set of DB*.DAT files is referred to as the MTA database. To assure performance, especially when problems cause large numbers of DB*.DAT files to accumulate, the MTA work directory should always be placed on an NTFS volume.

Of course, the MTA database isn't a database in the same sense as the JET databases used for the Information Store. But there's a very good reason to elect to use the NT file system to build a file-driven data store, which is in fact what we have here. Consider the work that the MTA is expected to do. There's no real sense of data retention because the MTA should be accepting messages and redirecting them to their proper direction all the time. The only reasons why files should remain around for any real length of time are because:

- The system is under heavy load and messages can't be processed by the MTA as quickly as they arrive. In this case files will build up in the MTA work directory, but they should be deleted fairly quickly as soon as the system load reduces and the MTA is able to get access to CPU and memory.

- There's a network or other problem (perhaps a connector is stopped or has terminated abnormally), causing messages to accumulate in the MTA work directory. In this case the solution is simple: get the network connection back in operation or investigate why a particular connector stopped and return it to normal operation.

The installation process creates an initial set of 35 data files which are required to initiate MTA processing. As processing proceeds the set of files changes with the demand placed on the MTA. The number of files is influenced by the number of messages in the queues or other work in progress, but on fast systems where there are no problems sending messages through any of the attached connectors you shouldn't ever see more than 250 files or so in the directory. However, this figure depends on the size and workload of a system. If you run the Performance Monitor and tune the system to handle a large user community, say 600 users, then the MTA will increase the number of files that it uses in an attempt to handle the predicated load generated by such a user community.

When messages arrive into the MTA they are written to disk. Messages are also written into a cache in memory (one of the reasons why EMSMTA.EXE appears sometimes to occupy more memory than you think it might). Processing data held in memory is always faster, so the MTA attempts to do as much as possible with the messages stored there. The MTA is multi-threaded, so multiple operations can be concurrently executed against single message objects. For example, a message sent to a large distribution list might be sent by one thread to an MTA on other server in the same site, to the Internet connector for transmission to an SMTP addressee, and to an MS-Mail connector to be sent to an MS-Mail addressee. A scheme of message roll-in and roll-out of the cache is implemented to accommodate heavy processing times when there mightn't be enough memory available to handle the number of messages arriving to the MTA.

In Exchange V5.0, two registry entries control the number of files that the MTA uses for transient message storage in its work directory and to state a threshold value for the maximum size for a transient file. The two entries we're interested are can be found in the

`Hkey_Local_Machine\System\Services\MSExchangeMTA\Parameters`

section of the registry and are:

`DB File Handles`	Determines the number of the file handles kept and using for caching.
`DB File Size Delete Threshold`	Defines the maximum size of a file to be kept. Any file exceeding the threshold is automatically deleted after it is finished with.

The Exchange V5.5 MTA is self-tuning and removes the requirement to mess with registry settings. Don't worry if you've put these parameters into the registry as the MTA now ignores them.

Even with the fastest and most efficient file system it would not be good for performance to have file creation and deletion going on all the time. On heavily loaded systems it is quite possible to fully occupy the disk I/O subsystem with the demands of file creation and deletion if a new file was created for each new message. The MTA therefore maintains a set of files that it attempts to reuse. A separate handle (literally an I/O channel) is kept for each file by the MTA, allowing it to flush the content of a file after a message has been dispatched and reuse the on-disk storage to capture the content of a newly arrived message. Thus the overhead of file creation and deletion is kept to a minimum. It is entirely possible that users will send ridiculously large messages over time. Messages containing video clips are a particular favorite of mine, and such messages occupy many kilobytes or even megabytes of storage. The threshold parameter controls whether the MTA retains large files within its set. For example, let's assume that the threshold is set to 300 KB. If a new 400 KB message comes in the MTA will create a new file to hold its content. Once the message has successfully passed through the MTA it will immediately delete the file and not retain the file for reuse.

7.3.5 When problems occur in the MTA work directory

Note the caveat in the last section—"where there are no problems … through any of the attached connectors." Once problems occur files start to accumulate in the \MTADATA directory, and you can get an unpleasant surprise at the rate that these files build up. For example, if a connection between one site and another is inoperative for a few days several thousand messages are queued by the MTA. A simple test I performed involved disconnecting a server from the network over a three-day period. The server was connected to the Exchange organization via a site connector to another site that served as a hub to five other sites, a factor that contributed to an increase in the messaging load. During the disconnected period over 3,500 messages built up in the MTA queue for the unavailable server, and when that server was reconnected to the network it took nearly two hours for the queue to be cleared. In this instance the two servers were connected over a LAN, so network bandwidth was not an issue and the messages cleared from the queue pretty rapidly. In another scenario, where the bandwidth between the two sites is not so copious, the queue will be reduced much more slowly.

Figure 7.4 *A large MTA queue*

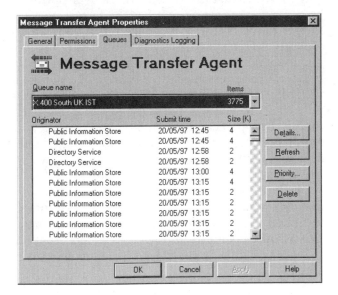

The problem of large MTA queues is not unique or confined to site, X.400, or Internet connectors. Exactly the same situation can arise if a server is disconnected from its partner servers within a site. If servers remain unavailable for any length of time a queue of messages will build within the MTA. The queue will only be cleared when the missing server is restored to action and restarts the Exchange MTA service. In fact, because you have no control whatsoever over the messaging activities that take place between servers in a site the number of messages in the queue build up very rapidly. On the other hand, because intra-site connections are normally LAN-based, the queue will be quickly reduced once all the servers are available again.

Apart from the obvious system workload that arose once the servers were able to resume normal operation across the site connector, another potential performance issue came into play because the 3,500 messages were also stored as .DAT files in the \MTADATA directory. Most systems are able to manage several thousand files in a directory, but significant strain is placed on system resources if more than 20,000 files are allowed to accumulate. If you doubt what I say test the theory by allowing some thousands of files to build up in a directory and then attempt to list the files with the Windows NT Explorer (or even just a simple DOS DIR command in a DOS command window). The system will take a little time to satisfy your request, so keeping the number of files in the \MTADATA directory down to a reasonable level is important in terms of system performance.

Putting the \MTADATA directory on its own physical disk is a good way to assure that the system will deliver optimal performance. You'll be assuring that the system has the fastest possible access to the work files required by the MTA. But even if you can afford the luxury of a separate \MTADATA disk, you should still pay close attention to MTA queues and never let them mount up to a situation where more than a few hundred messages are waiting to go across a connector. Placing the \MTADATA directory on a separate disk helps to avoid another potential problem by reducing the likelihood that the MTA will be forced to stop because it is unable to create new .DAT files in its work directory. During normal operation, with messages flowing freely, disk space exhaustion should not occur. As we've seen, messages and queues are represented by many individual files ranging in size from 8K right up to the size of the largest individual message. If message queues start building disk space will be consumed, eventually leading to exhaustion if action is not taken to start messages flowing again. The MTA will shut itself down if it detects that less than 10MB of disk space is available on the drive hosting its work directory.

It is a fact of system management life that servers will become unavailable during day to day operation. Wise system planners never base system designs on an assumption that computers and network connections will operate on a basis of 100% availability. Power outages or planned building, computer or network maintenance can all affect availability. If interruptions in service are not catered for you can end up with a situation where servers take many hours or even days to deal with the workload that has been accumulated when normal communications are unavailable.

We've already discussed how a simple site connector can build up a queue of over three thousand messages during a network outage. Hub sites, those that act as a central network point of contact for other sites, are especially sensitive to network problems. Consider a situation where a site acts as a hub for a number of the other sites. If network connections are lost to one or more of the "spoke" sites, the MTA queues in the hub site will start to grow. Messages arriving in from sites that are still connected must be held until they can be sent. The longer the network connections are unavailable, the bigger the queues will grow. In one case in my experience a hub site had a network problem for four days. At the end of that period there were queues of over four thousand messages for the three spoke sites the hub could not communicate with. Clearing the backlog took almost two days, and the system that acted as the central hub did not provide good performance to its own users while it cleared the backlog. The lesson from this is clear: if you operate hub sites, make sure that there is at least two servers in the hub site, and spread the connections to other sites across all available servers. This won't stop network problems arising, but at least it will divide the queues across a number of servers and help to get everything back working sooner once the network problem has been resolved.

Where can so many thousand queued messages come from? If you view the contents of any MTA queue you'll see that messages come from the system attendant, the Public Information Store, the directory, and interpersonal messages generated by users. The vast bulk of the messages are normally system-generated, that is, those generated to keep systems up to date with each other's configurations or to replicate data for the Directory or Public Information Store. The number of background messages generated by servers can be restrained by amending replication schedules for public folder replicas and directory connectors. If network bandwidth is an issue or no assurance exists that connections will be available at regular and predictable basis close attention should be paid to the schedules set for these items. Why, for instance, do you need to replicate directory information every 15 minutes when perhaps 1 hourly or even 2 hourly-intervals will suffice? See the discussion on page 598 for suggestions how to avoid mail storms brewing through excessive replication.

You might use some or all of the suggestions given below to avoid problems occurring with large MTA queues:

- Check MTA queues on a regular basis (at least twice a day) to ensure that no queue is building up for an unknown reason. If a large queue is present try and determine why the queue has accumulated and take action to rectify the situation.

- Consider the effect that system outages have on message queues and try to avoid breaking the connections between Exchange servers if at all possible. Review your Exchange organization to try and work out how various network failures might affect message flow between the different sites. Don't power down systems within a site unnecessarily as this will provoke large queues too.

- Put the MTA work directory (\MTADATA) on a disk that isn't heavily used (not the same disk as the database transaction logs). Check that space is available to create work files on the disk, especially at times when message queues begin to build up. The MTA-DATA directory can be moved away from its default location (the same disk as the Exchange executables) to a more appropriate location with the Performance Optimizer (see chapter 11).

- Throttle back the schedules for directory and public folder replication so that an unnecessarily high volume of messages isn't generated between servers.

- Spread the connector load across several systems in a site so that, if a network problem occurs, the queues accumulate on several servers and so can be processed more quickly once the problem is resolved.

The MTA creates additional data files for messages and queues as required. Because the files are all used for internal processing it is impossible to predict the exact contents or use of any particular data file. It is therefore very unwise and dangerous to take the chance of deleting any of the data files. You might be deleting a message, or a connector queue, or something else needed by the MTA. In much the same way as the Information Store transaction logs, leave these files alone and let Exchange take care of them.

7.3.6   Clearing MTA directories in case of problems

As we've discussed, sometimes very large MTA queues build up. You don't want to delete all the messages because you might delete important replication data or even interpersonal mail, and you don't want to run MTACHECK (see page 502) for much the same reason. On the other hand, you don't want the MTA to take huge amounts of system resources to clear the queue, resources that might be dedicated to connectors or mailboxes. In these situations you can move the accumulated backlog of messages to another server and have them processed there, leaving the original server to get on with other work. I must emphasize that such a step should only be taken after the cause of the backlog is determined and fixed. Because the MTA is capable of processing files much faster, moving to another server is required far less often in Exchange V5.5 than in earlier versions. However, it's a useful technique to have at hand.

A two-phase process is used. The first phase captures all the messages in the queue and gets the MTA service up and running with new files. The second phase moves the queue to another "replay" server (which must be in the same site) and processes them there. If you don't have another server immediately available you will have to find another server and bring it into the site before the queue can be processed.

The steps in the first phase are:

- Stop the MTA service, if it hasn't already been halted.
- Copy all of the DB*.DAT files from the \MTADATA directory to another directory.
- Delete the DB*.DAT files from the \MTADATA directory.
- Repopulate the \MTADATA directory with a set of "boot" data files (located in the SERVER\SETUP\<cputype>\BOOTENV directory on the Exchange Server CD). Make sure that the correct CPU type (i386 or Alpha) is selected.
- Remove the read-only attribute for the DB*.DAT files that you've copied from the CD.
- Run the MTACHECK utility.
- Restart the MTA service.
- At this point the MTA should begin functioning with a skeleton set of files. Send a message to another site, or one that loops back to your own mailbox via a connector to verify that the MTA is processing messages correctly. Request a delivery receipt on the message to create extra traffic.

Phase two begins after you are happy that messages are being processed correctly on the original server. The steps in this phase are:

- Make sure that the replay server has no queues outstanding. Also, replication traffic should be up to date. This step is important because you are going to remove any waiting messages from the replay server when the replay process begins. It is also wise to restrict replication traffic during the replay, if only to ensure that newly arriving messages don't complicate the process.
- Stop the MTA service on the replay server.
- Delete any DB*.DAT files from the \MTADATA directory on the replay server. This irrevocably removes any waiting messages.
- Move the DB*.DAT files for the queued messages from the directory where they were stored to the \MTADATA directory on the replay server.

- Add a new key to the registry:

```
HKEY_LOCAL_MACHINE\SYSTEM\CurrentControlSet\Services\
MSExchamgeMTA\Parameters\Dispatch remote MTA messages
```

The value is a DWORD. Set its value to 1.

- Start the MTA service on the replay server.

Monitor the queues to ensure that messages are being processed. If messages do not move it may be an indication that one of the DB*.DAT files that contain a message is corrupt. Alternatively, one of the core DB*.DAT files that the MTA uses for its internal queues and other purposes may be missing or corrupt.

When a new MTA is installed, 39 core files are created in the \MTADATA directory. The files are named DB000001.DAT through DB000020.DAT (a hex numbering scheme is used, so files like DB00001E.DAT are included in the set), plus DBBITMP.DAT. The core files must be present before the MTA service can start. If DBBITMP.DAT is not present, it is an indication that the MTA service did not shut down cleanly. Separate queue files are created the first time the MTA starts. The first of these is DB00002B.DAT, which holds the work queue file. A separate data file is created for each queue handled by the MTA. In Exchange V5.5, there is also a new file called DBREFS.DAT, which maintains inter-object reference counts. Like DDBITMP.DAT, DBREFS.DAT is not visible during normal operations. Both files are created after the MTACHECK is run or after each clean shutdown of the MTA service.

If there is a very large number of files to be replayed (over 10,000) you can conduct a series of incremental replays. This means that you will split the set of files into a number of sets. Each set contains the core MTA files plus a subset of the DB*.DAT message files. For example, if you had 10,000 messages to process, you might split this operation into 5 separate runs (and could, in fact, divide the processing across five separate servers). Each run will process 2,000 DB*.DAT messages files. The same steps as outlined above to replay a complete set are performed, except that only the necessary subset (2,000 message files plus core files) are copied to the \MTADATA directory of the replay server each time. If any set of files refuse to replay you know that a problem (probably a corrupt message file) exists in the set. You can then isolate the set and continue on to replay the next set, coming back to the problem set after all other sets are processed. The problem set can then be split into smaller sets and the replay procedure carried out until you've narrowed down the set of potential problem files. At this point you can decide to close off the replay procedure and pass the suspected corrupt files to Microsoft for further analysis and diagnosis.

Splitting up the MTA database (for this is what the DB*.DAT files are) is not something that you do lightly. Microsoft does not recommend any arbitrary division of the database because, apart from splitting the files into equal sets, no clear guideline can be applied to tell you where the dividing line should be. Only take the "divide and replay" route if a full replay cannot be performed, and make sure you involve Microsoft PSS in the exercise.

When the replay is complete and all the MTA queues are clear you should remove the "Dispatch remote MTA messages" entry from the system registry.

Clearing MTA queues in this manner is not a common activity. Clearly, an understanding of how the MTA works and what the various files do is key before attempting any operations of this nature. Finally, it must be emphasized again that you must rectify the problems that caused the build up in the first place before attempting to clear the queues.

7.3.7   Expanding distribution lists

Before we get to the details of how a message is routed by the MTA to its ultimate destination it's important to understand that the MTA must first expand the contents of any distribution lists in the message recipients. An Exchange distribution list may not be a simple object. It can contain addresses for mailboxes, custom recipients, public folders, and other distribution lists. The process of expansion must be performed recursively until all list, including those nested within any original distribution lists, are conclusively resolved.

Distribution lists are not immediately resolved (decomposed into the set of individual recipients) when a client first sends a message. At this stage the message is passed, without interference, from the client to the Private Information Store, and from there to the MTA. Distribution lists are always expanded by the MTA after the message has been delivered by the Private Information Store. The rule therefore is if a message contains a distribution list it is always sent to the MTA for resolution, even if the distribution list only contains local mailboxes. For this reason the MTA service must always be active, even on servers that aren't connected to anything else.

Distribution list expansion can be a CPU-intensive task, especially if the list contains very large or nested distribution lists. In Exchange V4.0 and V5.0 it was quite common to see CPU use shoot up to 100% when a server was given a list to expand. Microsoft experienced a famous problem with a huge distribution list called "Bedlam" that generated an internal mail storm. The problem focused attention on the resources required to expand large distribution lists, and everyone has now benefited.

Offloading expansion to dedicated servers is a solution that is always available, but it's not always possible to establish a dedicated distribution list expansion server. Exchange V5.5 improves matters dramatically through changes in the MTA, so this shouldn't be an issue now unless the lists are very large. Microsoft test the MTA with distribution lists that contain 30,000 entries, and the times required to expand such monster lists continue to fall. Further improvements are made in Exchange V5.5 SP1, much of which is due to the use of the less complex LDAP protocol to read from the directory instead of XDAPI.

The recommendation is now to establish a dedicated distribution list expansion server for every 100 active servers. From this ratio you'll see that not many implementations will ever need a dedicated server now.

7.3.8   Message routing algorithm

The following algorithm is used by the MTA to decide how a message can be delivered to an external recipient.

- *According to the contents of the GWART, what connectors are available?* Which of the active connectors on this system can handle the message?

- *The retry count should not have been exceeded for any connector being considered.* A check is performed to ensure that the maximum number of retries for a message has not been exceeded. This ensures that a message is returned with an "undeliverable" status to a user within a reasonable time after sending. Note that retry counts cannot be specified for site connectors, so it's possible for messages to stay in a site connector queue being retried constantly until they expire after a few days, at which time they'll be returned to the originator as undeliverable.

- *Scan for active connectors.* Which of the connectors that are able to process the message are active on the system right now? Dynamic RAS or X.400 connectors often operate only at specific times during the day. If two routes are available and only one is active (albeit even apparently at a higher cost), then it's logical to dispatch messages via the active route.

- *Lowest retry count.* Which of the active connectors have the lowest retry count? In other words, which connector is most likely to be able to dispatch the message first time around? The initial check was to ensure that the message retry count had not reached its maximum value, this check is to determine which connector has been attempted the least number of times.

- *Not currently trying*. A check is performed to ensure that an active connector isn't currently processing the message.
- *Lowest cost*. Given all else, if two or more connectors are available, which connector can transmit the message at lowest cost? We'll discuss how costs are allocated to connectors later on in this chapter.
- *Local over remote*. If a local connector is available to handle the message, send it locally rather than attempting to use a remote connector.

Any connectors that disallow the message due to other restrictions are excluded from this decision process. For example: content length, delivery restrictions, X.400 1984 links if downgrading has already failed locally.

Hopefully a suitable connector is determined at the conclusion of these steps and the message can be sent on its way. It may well be that several connectors present themselves as willing and able to dispatch the message, and if so, the MTA attempts to balance the connection load by making a random selection from the set of suitable connectors.

After all that, if a message is returned immediately or very soon after it is sent it's a good indication that the message is either badly addressed or the address space for the target connector is badly defined. The MTA always tries to reroute a message immediately if it encounters a failure on its first attempt. If the message cannot be rerouted it will remain in the MTA queue for the relevant connector and have its retry count incremented by one. The properties of the Site MTA object define the default retry interval (normally 600 seconds— 10 minutes), and the maximum number of retries. These properties are known as the "Open Interval" and "Max Open Retries" respectively. The amount of rerouting that occurs within an organization can be substantially reduced by configuring the MTA to use least cost routes, as discussed in the next section. This may be advisable in scenarios where the underlying physical network does not provide redundancy and multiple "routes" (possibly imported from a downstream site) exist in the MTA routing table to a particular recipient.

If the message exceeds the maximum number of retries it will be returned to its originator wrapped in a non-delivery notification. The user can then, if they wish, click on the "Send Again" command button to see whether the message can get through. It may well be, for instance, that a connector who depends on a specific network link is unavailable because of hardware or other problems. In this case lots of non-delivery notifications can be generated, causing considerable frustration to users and lots of calls for the help desk. The sole silver lining in this particular cloud is that the useful "Send Again" command button on the non delivery notification gives users a chance to send the message again with little difficulty.

7.3.9   The Gateway Routing Table (GWART)

When Exchange sees that a message has been sent to external recipients it passes the message to the MTA to begin a process called message routing, or the determination of how that message is going to be delivered to its recipients. Message routing requires the MTA to check what connectors are capable of getting the message to a recipient as well at what cost, no matter how many connectors the message must pass through en route to its final destination(s). The calculation of cost is based on figures entered by system administrators when connectors are added to an Exchange server. The final calculation is a cumulative figure composed of the cost required to navigate from connector to connector on different Exchange servers. The simplest cost to determine is, of course, when a direct connection is made from one site to another.

Connectors are configured using the Exchange Administration program. The two most important items specified when a connector is configured are:

- *Address Space:* literally, the types of mail addresses that can be handled by the connector. Directory replication ensures that all servers within an organization know about all the connectors installed on other servers. Thus, the MTA is able to consider all connectors for potential message dispatch. The process of reviewing all possible connectors for message delivery is known as selection.

- *Connected Sites:* the list of sites to which mail can be sent through the connector.

After a connector is configured the remote routing table for the server is rebuilt in order to make the new connector active. In effect this includes the new connector in the site address space so that the connector can be assessed and possibly used whenever the MTA reviews the addresses on an outgoing or incoming message. An address for the new connector is also added to each user record in the directory so that any message arriving via the connector is delivered correctly. For example, the SMTP type address is used to indicate user addresses that the Internet Mail Service should handle. The administrator can define the set of sites serviced by the connector when the connector is configured.

The information relating to connectors is stored in the configuration container and is replicated by the directory service to adjacent sites. The system attendant and MTA work together to create a routing table known as the Gateway Address Routing Table (GWART) to use when routing messages. Servers maintain their own GWART. You can think of the GWART as a set of address information relating to all possible routes that can be used to deliver messages.

The GWART is stored in the directory and can be viewed through the Routing property page of the Site Addressing object (see Figure 7.5). The routing table is also available as a simple text file in the \EXCHSRVR\MTADATA directory. Two copies are kept:

- GWART0.MTA—the current routing table
- GWART1.MTA—the routing table prior to the last change

The GWART is loaded in memory when the MTA service is started.

Figure 7.5 *Site Address Space*

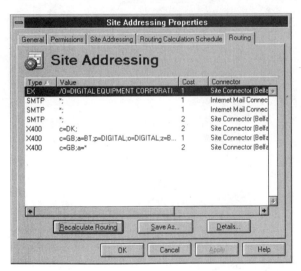

The text files used by the GWART are created each time a change is made to the routing table. You can force Exchange to recreate the routing table by pressing the "Recalculate Routing" command button (Figure 7.6); otherwise the routing table is rebuilt automatically at scheduled times. A "Recalulate Routing" command button is also available on the general property page of the MTA on each server.

Connectors arc installed on specific servers, but every server in a site needs to know how to route messages as a whole, rather than an individual case. Normally one server in each site takes care of the task of rebuilding the routing table. In large sites supporting multiple connectors a rebuild can be a fairly intensive exercise, certainly not one to allocate to a server supporting many hundreds of users, or one that's scheduled to occur at 9 a.m., just as all the users log-on and begin reading their mail. Rebuilding the routing table involves a scan through the address spaces from each server within the site and the connectors installed on all servers. The resulting routing table is then distributed throughout the site via the directory, the same mechanism used to update other sites within the organization. Depending on how directory entries are replicated throughout your organization it may take some time before all servers are made aware that a new connector has been added or a change (such as an update for the routing cost of a connector) been made.

Figure 7.6 *Least cost routing set on an MTA*

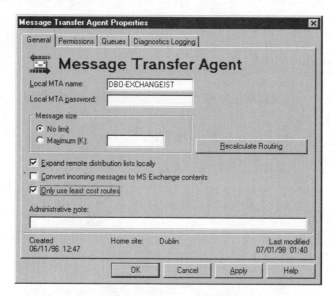

As you can see from the Site Address Space illustrated in Figure 7.5, the routing table contains a subset of complete addresses. In other words, the table contains only the necessary elements to identify the route that a message should take. The table is divided into three major types of addresses:

1. Type "EX": These entries refer to native format Exchange addresses (distinguished names) and relate to site connectors. The illustration shows a single "EX" entry corresponding to a single site connector.

2. Type "DDA" (Domain Defined Attribute): These entries refer to the gateways and connectors that are used to send messages to custom recipients. The most common examples are "MS" (Microsoft Mail Connector) and "SMTP" (Internet Mail Service).

3.   Type: "X400" (X.400 Originator/Recipient): These entries relate to X.400 connections to either other Exchange servers (site X.400 connectors) or to foreign X.400 MTAs. As you can see from the screen shot, three X.400 O/R addresses are specified for two different countries (DK = Denmark, GB = Great Britain).

Each line in the routing table corresponds to a route that the MTA can take to deliver a message. As illustrated the table is pretty simple and is similar to what you'll find in a small organization. The table gets much more complex after the organization begins to grow to more than a couple of sites and other connectors are added in. DDA address types might be defined for "LOTUS" (Lotus Notes), "FAX" (different FAX connectors), "SNADS" (IBM Distribution Services), "PROFS" (IBM PROFS), and so on. The only sure thing is that the table will often be a challenge to interpret and understand how messages are routed within an organization.

There is an understandable temptation for each site (or even multiple servers within a site) to install and configure their own set of connectors. This is a mistake. Not only will all the extra connections complicate the routing table it can also lead to messages being routed to places that you didn't really want them to go.

For example, take the situation where sites in Dublin and Denmark both install an Internet Mail connector, configuring each to be able to handle any SMTP type address (the address space for the connector is configured as SMTP:*) with a routing cost of 1. Connector information is part of the configuration data automatically replicated between sites, so shortly after the two connectors are installed and configured in the respective sites every other site in the organization will learn of their existence. The routing table in each site will also be recalculated, and the MTAs on every server will insert an entry in their GWART. Every time that the MTA meets a message addressed to an SMTP destination it consults the GWART to discover that two routes can be taken, each with a similar routing cost. Normally the MTA favors the home connector, but if it is unavailable for any reason the MTA seeks to use alternate routes to get the mail through. An arbitrary decision will be taken to determine which route each message should take. In this case the messages will be rerouted to Denmark to be sent via the Internet Mail Service in that site. The same situation pertains for messages generated in Denmark. Routing via foreign destinations is great for messages interested in tourism, but it's hardly efficient.

Up to Exchange V5.5, a simple technique must be practiced to control routing. Only install the connectors you absolutely need and make sure that the right routing costs are allocated to each connector so that the optimal route is always chosen by the MTA. This is not as easy as it seems, because everyone wants to give the local connector the lowest possible routing cost. You therefore end up with a set of connectors, all with a routing cost of 1. As we've seen above, as long as the connectors are active everything is OK and the messages will be routed via local connectors, but when things go wrong the messages can be routed in "interesting" directions.

Exchange V5.5 supports "least cost routing". This means that you can instruct the MTA to only use least-cost routes to get messages to their final destination. Let's assume that an X.400 connector with cost 1 is the normal route for messages sent between the New York and Chicago sites. Another X.400 connector (cost 1) is available between New York and San Francisco, and another connector (cost 1) between San Francisco and Chicago. If the connector fails for some reason between New York and Chicago the MTA will attempt to reroute messages via San Francisco, a route costed at 2 (1 + 1). If least-cost routing is enabled the MTA will wait until the connector between New York and Chicago is available before sending any queued messages. Least cost routing is enabled on a server by server basis (see Figure 7.6) and is not turned on by default. Further control over routing can be achieved through address scoping, as described on page 499.

7.3.10 Understanding the GWART

The GWART contains information about the paths available to route messages to their final destinations. Interpreting the GWART is by no means a graphic experience. Determining the route from one site to another through the GWART is easy for the MTA (after all, it is a computer program), but human beings tend to struggle with the somewhat esoteric detail available in GWART0.MTA, the text representation of the routing table. It would be nice if Microsoft could provide a graphical representation of routing paths that system administrators could use to discover just how messages flow between sites in their organization. Apart from anything else, the ability to view routing paths graphically would make it easier to identify likely problems, such as SMTP mail for a particular domain not being routed out through the optimal IMS connector. While giving some wishes to Microsoft, let me ask them to add the ability for an administrator to input network details (bandwidth and type of link) and have it shown with the routing paths. Such a tool would be an invaluable aid in planning the ebb and flow of data within an Exchange organization, especially for those of us who have to deal with large, complex networks with many sites and connectors.

GWART information is automatically replicated to all other servers in an organization, so every server knows about all the connectors on other servers. This makes life easy for administrators, except when you don't want people to use a connector. We'll discuss how to restrict access to connectors later on in this chapter.

GWART0.MTA and GWART1.MTA are both simple text files that can be opened and examined with the Notepad utility or any other text editor. Once you know the terms used by Exchange and can follow the X.500-style naming conventions for directory objects the contents can be interpreted, but at first look the routing table is a touch unapproachable.

The GWART is organized into sections. Each section tells Exchange how messages sent to a particular type of address can be routed. Native "Exchange"-style addresses are listed first, with a separate entry for each site in the organization. Figure 7.7 shows details of the addresses for six sites, with a seventh site appearing at the bottom.

The initial entry for each site shows the organization and site name. Note that the routing table stores directory names, which are not necessarily the same as the display names for objects shown in the administration program.

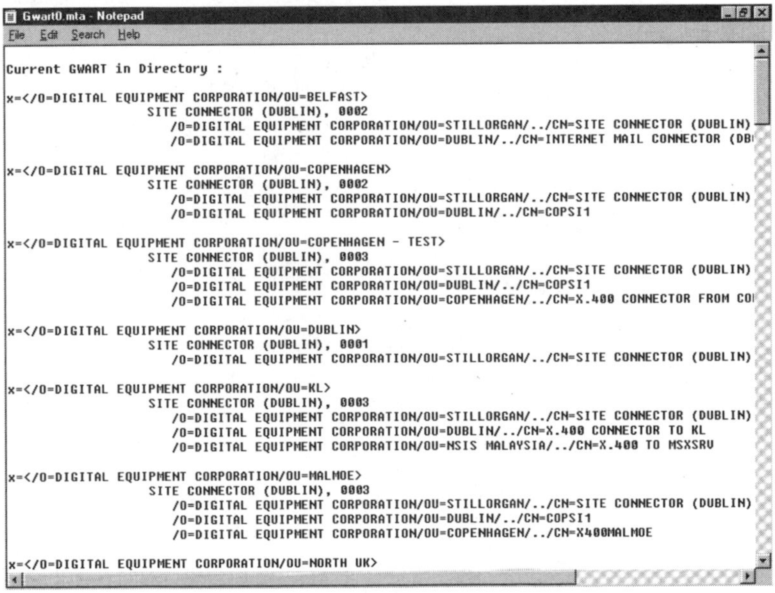

```
Gwart0.mta - Notepad
File Edit Search Help

Current GWART in Directory :

x=</O=DIGITAL EQUIPMENT CORPORATION/OU=BELFAST>
                    SITE CONNECTOR (DUBLIN), 0002
                       /O=DIGITAL EQUIPMENT CORPORATION/OU=STILLORGAN/../CN=SITE CONNECTOR (DUBLIN)
                       /O=DIGITAL EQUIPMENT CORPORATION/OU=DUBLIN/../CN=INTERNET MAIL CONNECTOR (DB

x=</O=DIGITAL EQUIPMENT CORPORATION/OU=COPENHAGEN>
                    SITE CONNECTOR (DUBLIN), 0002
                       /O=DIGITAL EQUIPMENT CORPORATION/OU=STILLORGAN/../CN=SITE CONNECTOR (DUBLIN)
                       /O=DIGITAL EQUIPMENT CORPORATION/OU=DUBLIN/../CN=COPSI1

x=</O=DIGITAL EQUIPMENT CORPORATION/OU=COPENHAGEN - TEST>
                    SITE CONNECTOR (DUBLIN), 0003
                       /O=DIGITAL EQUIPMENT CORPORATION/OU=STILLORGAN/../CN=SITE CONNECTOR (DUBLIN)
                       /O=DIGITAL EQUIPMENT CORPORATION/OU=DUBLIN/../CN=COPSI1
                       /O=DIGITAL EQUIPMENT CORPORATION/OU=COPENHAGEN/../CN=X.400 CONNECTOR FROM CO

x=</O=DIGITAL EQUIPMENT CORPORATION/OU=DUBLIN>
                    SITE CONNECTOR (DUBLIN), 0001
                       /O=DIGITAL EQUIPMENT CORPORATION/OU=STILLORGAN/../CN=SITE CONNECTOR (DUBLIN)

x=</O=DIGITAL EQUIPMENT CORPORATION/OU=KL>
                    SITE CONNECTOR (DUBLIN), 0003
                       /O=DIGITAL EQUIPMENT CORPORATION/OU=STILLORGAN/../CN=SITE CONNECTOR (DUBLIN)
                       /O=DIGITAL EQUIPMENT CORPORATION/OU=DUBLIN/../CN=X.400 CONNECTOR TO KL
                       /O=DIGITAL EQUIPMENT CORPORATION/OU=NSIS MALAYSIA/../CN=X.400 TO MSXSRV

x=</O=DIGITAL EQUIPMENT CORPORATION/OU=MALMOE>
                    SITE CONNECTOR (DUBLIN), 0003
                       /O=DIGITAL EQUIPMENT CORPORATION/OU=STILLORGAN/../CN=SITE CONNECTOR (DUBLIN)
                       /O=DIGITAL EQUIPMENT CORPORATION/OU=DUBLIN/../CN=COPSI1
                       /O=DIGITAL EQUIPMENT CORPORATION/OU=COPENHAGEN/../CN=X400MALMOE

x=</O=DIGITAL EQUIPMENT CORPORATION/OU=NORTH UK>
```

Figure 7.7 *Routing for Site Connectors*

The first entry shown in Figure 7.7 tells us how messages are routed to users in the "Belfast" site within the organization called "Digital Equipment Corporation". Two steps are required. First, messages must be routed across the site connector that links this site (called "Stillorgan") to the site called "Dublin". When messages reach Dublin they are routed across an Internet Mail Connector to Belfast. Fortunately the names allocated to the sites and connectors make this GWART reasonably easy to read. If you had fallen into the trap of allocating cryptic names for sites and other objects in the directory it would be a lot harder to read the GWART. This is another good reason to use meaningful terms when naming objects!

Moving down through Figure 7.7 we see a number of sites where messages must be routed through three steps. For example, messages to the site called "Malmoe" (a city in Sweden) are routed across the site connector to Dublin, then across a connector between Dublin and a server called COPSI1 (which I know is in the Copenhagen site), and then across another connector to Malmoe. More explicit details of the routing from Dublin to Copenhagen and Copenhagen to Malmoe can be discovered by examination of X.400 or SMTP connector information held later on in the routing table.

Figure 7.8
Routing across X.400 connectors

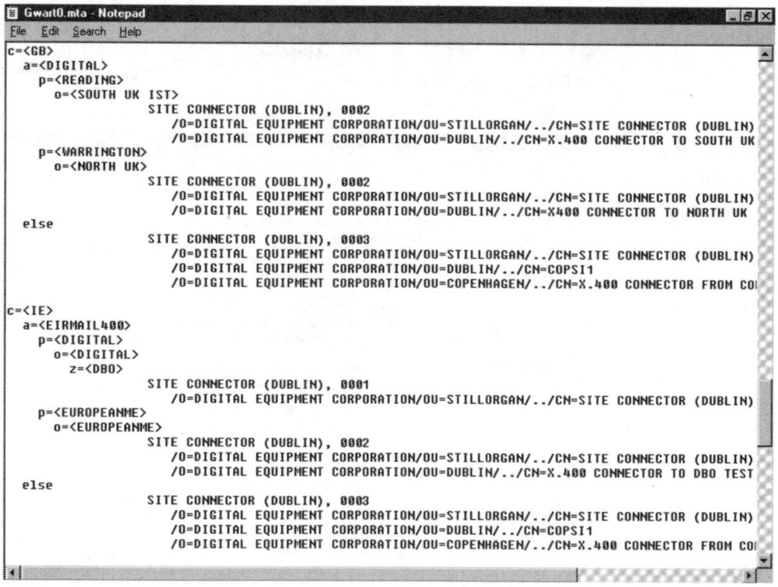

Figure 7.8 illustrates some of the routing instructions for X.400 addresses. Remember that multiple types of addresses are generated automatically when new recipients (mailboxes or custom recipients) are added to the directory. The typical set includes:

- A native, X.500-like Exchange address
- An X.400 style address

- An SMTP address
- An MS-Mail address
- (from Exchange V5.0 onwards), a Lotus cc:Mail address

You have control over this process and can decide not to generate different address types if you don't need them. For example, if you're never going to use the cc:Mail connector there is absolutely no need to generate cc:Mail addresses. Removing unwanted addresses is a good idea because it restricts the amount of directory data that must be replicated around the organization. On no account should you remove X.400 addresses because these are fundamental to the way Exchange routes messages within an organization. Note that some address types, such as SMTP, allow multiple addresses of the type to be maintained for a recipient. I use this facility to allow myself to be addressed in different ways (some of which aren't too complimentary).

An X.400 address is defined as a set of attribute pairs. When the MTA checks an address on a message it looks for just enough attributes to discover how to route the message. The scan begins at the left-hand side of the address and moves to the right until the MTA has built up enough of the address to be able to determine the route by reference to the routing table. The first attribute is the country code followed by the administrative domain, private domain, organization name, organization units, and on to an individual's given name and surname. Normally the first four or five attributes are enough to route a message. For example, if you examine the addresses shown in Figure 7.8 you can see that two routes are defined with a country code of "GB" (Great Britain) and two with "IE" (Ireland). Under each country code you can see the other attributes stated in descending order until uniqueness is achieved. Thus, the four attributes:

```
C=GB;A=DIGITAL;P=READING;O=SOUTH UK IST
```

is enough for the MTA to know that any address beginning with these attributes should be routed across the site connector to Dublin and then via the X.400 connector to the South UK site. Immediately underneath we see that the attributes:

```
C=GB;A=DIGITAL;P=WARRINGTON;O=NORTH UK
```

is enough to tell the MTA that messages beginning with these attributes should be routed across the site connector to Dublin and then via a different X.400 connector, in this case to the North UK site. To complete the picture, an "else" clause says that any other X.400-style address that begins with C=GB should be routed to Dublin, then to Copenhagen, and then on to another connector back to the UK. Anyone who knows European geography probably realizes that doesn't make much sense to route from Ireland to Denmark and then to the UK, so all I can conclude is that someone (probably in the Copenhagen site) has made an entry for this routing in their site routing table. As mentioned earlier, routing information is automatically replicated between all the servers in an organization so any "strange" routing instructions entered by one site will be provided to everyone else. It's a good idea to review the routing table occasionally to uncover anomalies like this.

Reading routing information must be a little like reading hieroglyphics. Once you know the rules of syntax everything becomes obvious! Now you know what to look for, try and use your knowledge to interpret the routing for the two Irish sites at the bottom of Figure 7.8.

Of course, while X.400 is the best connector to use to link sites across low-bandwidth connections, it's by no means the only connector you're going to find within an Exchange organization. Moving on down through the GWART we encounter instructions to tell the MTA how to process SMTP and SNADS addresses (Figure 7.9).

By now you're old hands at interpreting routing instructions so these entries are easy to understand, at least at first glance. The SMTP=* instruction tells the MTA to route any SMTP-style address sent from this site across the connector to Dublin and out via the Internet Mail Service there. But what are all the fully qualified domains specified here, like:

```
BVOJEN.BVO.DEC.COM
```

and

```
UTO-EXCHANGEIST.UTO.DEC.COM
```

The answer is simple but perhaps not very obvious. When you connect a new site using the Internet Mail Service you typically provide a routing address to tell the connector how to route mail to the site. At some point in time these addresses were used to connect sites together with the Internet Mail Service. The data will stay in the routing table unless it is explicitly removed. It is good practice to remove spurious routing information from the table, but as you can see from this example, it's all too easy for it to creep in, especially when different system administrators are responsible for each site. An entry for a solitary SNADS connector completes our tour through the routing table. Four steps are required to reach the connector, a not unusual state of affairs for connectors that link to mainframe messaging systems.

Figure 7.9 *SMTP and SNADS addresses in the GWART*

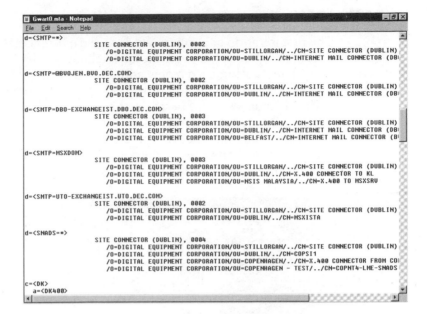

7.3.11   Taking control of routing

The situation where a connector in Copenhagen routes messages for Dublin is acceptable in some cases. In companies that have many different connections to the Internet it probably doesn't make a whole heap of difference if a message finds its way via a slightly torturous route to an eventual destination somewhere in the Internet. There's probably no great difference in the cost of an Internet message dispatched from Dublin to one sent from Copenhagen. And anyway, because routing favors local connectors until problems occur, the default mechanism that implements alternate routing offers significant benefits in terms of speeding the delivery of messages. It is only in situations where you positively want to route messages through a specific connector or wish to prevent messages from remote sites routing through local connectors that problems really arise.

Take the situation of connectors that have definite costs attached to each message. FAX connectors are a good example. You don't want to install a new FAX connector in a site in Australia to suddenly discover that users in sites throughout the world are sending faxes through the connector. Apart from anything else, the costs involved in someone sending a local fax via a remote connector are considerably higher than if they had used a connector in the local site.

7.3.12   **LOCAL address types in Exchange V5.0**

The first iteration at a solution to hide the existence of connectors from other sites was made available in Exchange V4.0 SP4 and Exchange V5.0. The solution used a new address type called "LOCAL" to inform the MTA that it should not inform other sites about any route specified with this type. Any connector associated with a LOCAL address type could still be used to route messages, but only within the "owning" site. The "cloaking" mechanism effectively stops routing information for connectors appearing in the routing table in the remote sites and so prevents users from sending messages where they shouldn't.

Figure 7.10
Adding a LOCAL address space to the Internet Mail Service

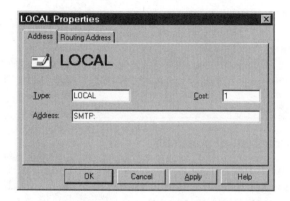

Marking an element in a site's address space for local use only stops it from being replicated outside the site. Local address space entries are unique to a connector, so a separate entry must be created for each connector you wish to restrict.

Let's suppose you want to stop other sites using the Internet Mail Service in your site. The default address space is probably something like "SMTP: ", meaning that any SMTP message can be handled by the Internet Mail Service. When you restrict access to the connector you replace the existing address space with one that looks like "LOCAL:SMTP". Amending the existing address space entry can't create the necessary routing instruction for the MTA. You will need to add a new "General" address space entry similar to that shown in Figure 7.10, and then delete the existing SMTP address entry. After these two steps have been taken you should end up with a connector address space similar to that shown in Figure 7.11.

The existence of the LOCAL address space allows the GWART generation code to include the connector in the local site routing table while instructing the mechanism that builds the GWART in other sites to ignore the connector. The other sites will continue to receive information about connectors that you'd like them to know of, such as the one and only SNADS connector in an organization. Only servers running the correct level of code obey the address space restriction. Servers running Exchange V4.0 (pre SP4) or beta versions of Exchange V5.0 will ignore the hurdles now being placed in their way.

Figure 7.11
The address space for the Internet Mail Service after adjustments have been made

It is possible for administrators to override local address space entries on other sites. This is useful where you are willing to allow another site in the same country to have access to something like a FAX connector, but you definitely don't want people in foreign sites sending their faxes through your connector.

7.3.13　Refining techniques with Address Scoping

It's obvious that the LOCAL address type, although effective, suffers because it is not provided with any specific user interface. This is an inevitable side-effect from including a feature late on in the Exchange V5.0 development cycle. The engineers had time to design a more complete solution for Exchange V5.5. Different scopes can be applied to address types to limit their availability to users. Three scopes are available.

- *Organization.* The address is available to any server within the organization.

- *Site.* The address is available to any server within the site.

- *Location.* The address is only available to servers in the same location.

Let's assume that we have installed the Lotus Notes connector for test purposes. We don't want to make the connector available everywhere within the organization. An address space is automatically created when the connector is installed. By default the address is allocated an organization-wide scope. To restrict it, we need to select the address space property page and edit the address space.

Figure 7.12
*Changing the
scope of an
address*

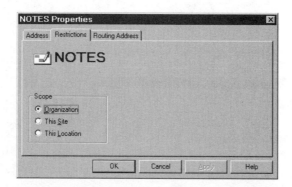

Figure 7.13
*Defining a
location for a
server*

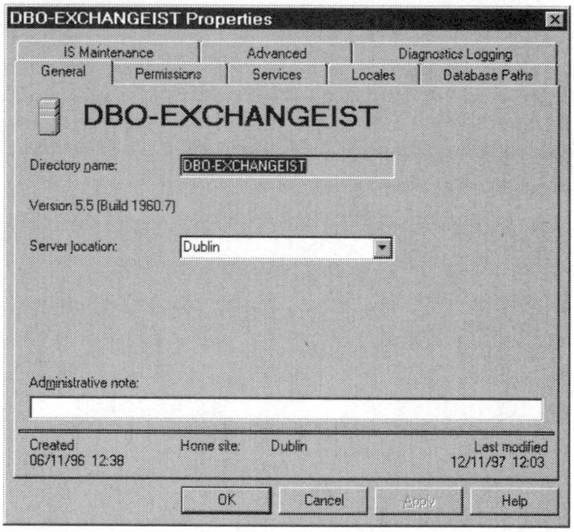

Figure 7.12 clearly shows how the scope can be changed from organization to site or location. The latter is a term that may be not well understood, largely because it has had little use up to now. A location is intended to help group together a set of servers within a site. Normally the grouping is done to reflect network constraints or identify servers in a particular geographic location or department. For example, all the servers in New York, or those belonging to the IT Department. A location name is allocated to a server by editing its properties, as shown in Figure 7.13.

After the scope of an address is reduced the MTA will comply with the stated restriction. Unfortunately only MTAs on Exchange V5.5 are intelligent enough to understand that they must obey the restriction. Table 7.1 lists the valid location types. Note that no validation is performed when a location name is created and it is entirely possible to have the same location name used in different sites. This really doesn't matter because a location has no meaning outside a site.

Table 7.1   *Address scope locations*

Value in Server Location	Meaning
<None>	The default setting, which serves as a catch-all location for every server in an organization. When a server is in the "<None>" location, it is not the same as if it had no location. All undefined servers belong to the "<None>" location.
Location name (for example, "Dublin", "New York", "London")	Any text string can be used to define a location. After the location has been created and replicated to other servers, it can be used by administrators.
* (asterisk)	Servers in the special asterisk location have access to all other locations as well as allowing all other locations to have access to the address spaces defined within the asterisk location.

It is possible to combine the scope for an address space with server locations to precisely control connector availability within an organization. The following points should be understood:

- Connectors homed on servers in the special "None" location cannot use the "Location" restriction. Instead, all connectors homed on servers in "None" treat "Location" as if it was a "Site" restriction. In other words, any message created by any server in the "None" location can be routed to any connector homed on a server within "None".

- Every server in a site is able to use connectors homed on servers in the special "*" (asterisk) location. Therefore, placing a "Location" restriction on one of these connectors is equivalent to setting its scope to "Site".

- All of the servers in the "*" location are considered part of all of the other locations defined in the site, so their messages can be routed to any connector, even if that connector appears to be restricted to a particular restriction.

Let's look at how this might operate in practice. Table 7.2 lists how different address scope restrictions would affect the ability of servers in a site called "Europe" to route messages via connectors. In this case, the only locations used in the site are the special "<None>" and "*" locations, and a defined location for servers in Dublin.

Table 7.2   *The effect of server locations and address space scoping*

Server location	Address scope	Real meaning of restriction
<None>	Organization	Organization
<None>	This Site	Any server in the "Europe" site.
<None>	This Location	Any server in the "<None>" location, plus any server in the "*" location.
Dublin	Organization	Organization
Dublin	This Site	Any server in the "Europe" site
Dublin	This Location	Any server in the "Dublin" location, plus any server in the "*" location.
*	Organization	Organization
*	This Site	Any server in the "Europe" site
*	This Location	Any server in the "Europe" site.

7.3.14   Message journaling

Rule 17A-4 of the US Securities and Exchange Commission (SEC) requires broker-dealers to retain physical records of documents relating to transactions. The retention period is either 3 or 6 years, depending on the category of record. The SEC issued a amendment in February 1997 to cover email, and stated that messages must be treated in the same way as paper correspondence. This requirement meant that any company working in the US financial community must retain all email messages in physical (printed down on paper) or electronic form.

Other government agencies in the US enforce similar requirements. For example, the FBI requires any company under investigation to retain messages for at least 6 months. The State of Florida's "Sunshine Law" requires that all government correspondence should be available to the public. This is similar to the situation in Sweden, where reporters are able to examine the Prime Minister's mail to see if anything interesting has arrived. Other countries are likely to follow the lead established by the US and Sweden, which poses an interesting problem for Microsoft and the other software vendors that build email systems.

As a concept, message journaling is not difficult to master. The major challenge is to determine the best place in the system to intercept messages so that copies can be taken. It's important that the selected place captures all mail—messages sent to local recipients as well as that sent to external recipients via a connector. A client-based solution is unacceptable because it would require code to be installed and maintained on every client. In the end, because the MTA handles all messages to external recipients, it is the most logical starting point, and that's what has happened.

Message journaling is part of the Exchange V5.5 SP1 release and is controlled by registry parameters. The new parameters force all local mail, which is otherwise handled by the Information Store, to be redirected via the MTA. Journaling is designed to capture all interpersonal messages and ignore system messages, such as replication messages for the directory or public folders. Messages posted directly to public folders are not captured. Logic is incorporated to ensure that a message is captured once within the boundary established for journaling. The boundary can be configured to be site-wide or organization-wide, and the default scope is organization-wide. Journaling is not effective site-wide or organization-wide until all relevant servers are upgraded to Exchange V5.5 SP1 and the registry parameters are set.

When the MTA captures a message it redirects a modified copy (to indicate that the copy is a journal copy) to the journal location. Journal copies have low priority, so normal message traffic will always be processed first. The location can be a mailbox or public folder, and the location can be organization-wide, site-wide, or server-specific. In other words, a single mailbox could receive copies of all messages generated across the entire organization. Administrators need to take care to monitor the contents of the journal location, so that storage limits aren't exceeded. Also, the journal location should be secured from normal user access (hidden from the GAL). Encrypted messages are delivered intact. There is no facility to decrypt message contents en route to the journal. In the future, if a regulatory authority wishes to read the message, the original recipient must provide their private key to decrypt the content.

The relevant registry settings used by the MTA to control message journaling are shown below. The parameters are found at:

```
HKEY_LOCAL_MACHINE\SYSTEM\CurrentControlSet\Services\
MSExchangeMTA\Parameters
```

Parameter	Type	Value	Example
Journal Recipient Name	REG_SZ	String containing the distinguished name of the recipient of the journal copy.	/o=Digital/ou=Dublin/cn=recipients/ cn=Archive
Per-Site Journal Required	DWORD	0 or 1	0 (or absence) means that journaling is done on an organization-wide basis, 1 means that the journal is kept on each site. This value is ignored if the Journal Recipient Name parameter is missing.

The Internet Mail Service must be instructed to reroute messages through the Information Store (and hence the MTA). This is done by setting the following parameter with a value of 1:

```
HKEY_LOCAL_MACHINE\SYSTEM\CurrentControlSet\Services\
MSExchangeIMC\RerouteViaStore
```

Finally, the Information Store is instructed to disable local delivery with the following parameter with a value of 1 (or any non-zero value):

```
HKEY_LOCAL_MACHINE\SYSTEM\CurrentControlSet\Services\
MSExchangeIS\ParametersSystem\No Local Delivery
```

From time to time the contents of the journal location can be moved to a more permanent location (such as a CD). This process is not automatic, and separate procedures must be established to export messages from the journal location.

Rerouting all messages through the MTA, eliminating the ability of the Information Store to handle local deliveries, and the extra message traffic generated by journal copies are steps that clearly impact overall system performance. No substantial body of performance data exists yet to help assess the likely impact, but the extra work is unlikely to go unnoticed by the system. My guess is that journalling will generate a similar load to a heavily-used connector, perhaps reducing the number of supported clients by between 20% and 25%. Your mileage will vary. Users are unlikely to notice any degradation in terms of the time taken to deliver messages unless the system is close to capacity, at which time the requirement to route local messages via the MTA will increase delivery times.

It's important to note that the server that hosts the mailbox or public folder used to accept copies of journaled messages must be equipped with enough disk space to hold the messages. Because a lot of messages are normally transient (they are received, read, then deleted) it's difficult to predict exactly how much disk space will be required to hold journaled messages, but you can be quite sure that it will be much more than you expect. To calculate the requirement to any accurate degree, observe the growth in storage over the first days or week that journaling is enabled and calculate what space is required for a year's storage, assuming that the same volume of messages is handled each day.

Message journaling controlled by registry parameters and to a mailbox or public folder delivers functionality, but it's not very approachable. I think it's a good example of how Microsoft builds enabling technology into Exchange and then leaves the stage for other software vendors to come along and improve matters with complete applications that use the technology. The DIGITAL Enterprise Archive is a good example of such a product. The DIGITAL Enterprise Archive provides all the user interface necessary to set up and control sophisticated message journaling, complete with an integration with HSM (Hierarchical Storage Management) products to move messages into a controllable archive.

7.3.15   The MTACHECK utility

Corrupt data files or messages can cause the MTA to stop processing, or simply refuse to start. The \EXCHSRVR\BIN\MTACHECK utility is provided to help rectify the situation by reviewing the internal structures used by the MTA and make any changes required.

The MTACHECK utility:

- Checks the consistency of the MTA queues.
- Checks the integrity of all of the objects used by the MTA.
- Removes any "orphan" files from the \MTADATA work directory that are no longer required by the MTA.
- Deletes any objects that the MTACHECK utility believes to be corrupt. Hopefully it is the removal of these objects that allows the MTA to restart.

The command switches that can be used with MTACHECK are described in Table 7.3.

Command line switches can be combined. Thus:

```
MTACHECK /V /F MTA.LOG /RP /RL /RD
```

Will produce verbose logging into the file MTA.LOG while removing any replication or link monitor messages from the queues.

Table 7.3   *Command line switches for the MTACHECK utility*

Command	Effect
MTACHECK	Utility run with minimal logging
MTACHECK /V	Set logging to verbose. Output information about each object as it is processed.
MTACHECK /F MTA.LOG	Log output to a file called MTA.LOG
MTACHECK /RD	Remove any directory replication messages found in the queues
MTACHECK /RP	Remove any public folder replication messages found in the queues
MTACHECK /RL	Remove any link monitor messages found in the queues

The time taken for an MTACHECK run is directly dependent on the number of messages in the queues. MTACHECK is able to process messages faster in Exchange V5.5, but it will still take some time to process several thousand messages. For example, a test on a system powered by a Pentium 100 took 20 minutes intense activity (CPU at 75–80% load throughout) to process 11,500 files in the \MTADATA directory. Only 200 files remained at the end of the run.

MTACHECK is normally only used in situations when known problems occur with the MTA. Those blessed with a curious nature can run MTACHECK at any time, just to see what it does. Before running MTACHECK remember to shut the MTA service down so as to prevent any possible contention between normal processing and the potential fixes made by MTACHECK. If the MTA closes down abnormally for any reason, it will invoke the MTACHECK function inline when it is next restarted. However, it is sometimes helpful to run MTACHECK offline to allow a more controlled recovery after a long system outage.

Occasionally you may want to clean out replication messages from the queues. For example, a mistake was made and the replication interval for public folders or the directory was cranked right up so that the servers are sending replication messages between themselves every couple of minutes. Or, a very large queue has built up due to a network outage and you want to remove all the replication messages so that any interpersonal messages are freed and will be sent as soon as the network link is restored. MTACHECK is certainly able to delete lots of messages for you and the queues will be freed up quite quickly, but there is a price to pay in the future if replication messages are removed.

Deleted replication messages may contain changes for public folders or the directory. The fact that the data is missing won't be noticed until the next time a replication message arrives at a remote server. At that time the server will examine the status information contained in the replication message and determines that its replica is missing some content. A backfill request is then generated and sent to be fulfilled. The backfill request is then responded to through the generation of a replication message that contains the missing data. The net effect of deleting replication messages is to put the workload off to another time. This is acceptable providing that the network is restored to good health when the backfill requests are issued.

Messages containing information about deleted objects are an exception as there is no mechanism to detect that backfill is required. Be careful with the /RD switch as its use will certainly clear out any directory replication messages, but it may also lead to orphaned objects in sites throughout the organization. See the discussion beginning on page 603.

If the MTA service is interrupted abnormally as in the case of a power failure or premature system power-down, the MTA queues may be in an inconsistent state. The next time the MTA service is restarted Exchange detects that a problem may exist and verifies the queues, making any repairs that are deemed necessary. This process usually doesn't take very long, except on systems that have many messages waiting in the MTA queues. Each queued message must be verified, and it is conceivable that the MTA service is unavailable for up to 15 minutes (any longer is a cause for real concern) after the system reboots. Exchange V5.5 has improved matters in this area through a complete rewrite of the MTA start-up code. Even with large queues the integrity check and fix completes much faster now.

Summary information about the actions performed during a MTA check after system restart is recorded in the system event log. Detailed information is available in the MTACHECK.TXT file in the \MTA-DATA\MTACHECK.OUT directory (see the edited text taken from an actual MTACHECK.TXT in Figure 7.14). Any corrupt files detected during this process are removed from the MTADATA directory to \MTACHECK.OUT.

Figure 7.14
Extract from
MTACHECK.TXT

```
Checking queue XAPIWRKQ (id 01000020)

Checking queue OOFINFOQ (id 01000025)

Checking queue REFDATQ (id 01000026)
```

```
Checking queue MTAWORKQ (id 0100002B)

Checking queue /O=DIGITAL EQUIPMENT CORPORATION/OU=DUBLIN/
CN=CONFIGURATION/CN=SERVERS/CN=DBO-EXCHANGEIST/CN=MICROSOFT
DXA (id 010000B8)

Checking queue /O=DIGITAL EQUIPMENT CORPORATION/OU=DUBLIN/
CN=CONFIGURATION/CN=CONNECTIONS/CN=INTERNET MAIL SERVICE (DBO-
EXCHANGEIST) (id 010000C8)

Checking queue /O=DIGITAL EQUIPMENT CORPORATION/OU=DUBLIN/
CN=CONFIGURATION/CN=CONNECTIONS/CN=INTERNET MAIL SERVICE
(OFFICENT1) (id 010000D9)

Checking queue /O=DIGITAL EQUIPMENT CORPORATION/OU=DUBLIN/
CN=CONFIGURATION/CN=CONNECTIONS/CN=MS MAIL CONNECTOR (DBO-
EXCHANGEIST) (id 0100003E)

Starting object integrity checks
  Checking object 03000002 - OK, on queue 01000026
  Checking object 0A000003 - OK, on queue 01000020
  Checking object 0B000004 - OK, on queue 01000020
  Checking object 0B000005 - OK, on queue 01000020

Object 000000C7 invalid
  - corrupted object file.
  - MTS-ID:           Unavailable

Object 000000D8 invalid
  - corrupted object file.
  - MTS-ID:           Unavailable

Starting removal of corrupt objects
Move of .\DB0000C7.DAT successful.
Move of .\DB0000D8.DAT successful.

Starting garbage collection of orphaned objects
Deleted D:\EXCHSRVR\mtadata\.\DB00002F.DAT successfully.
Deleted D:\EXCHSRVR\mtadata\.\DB000032.DAT successfully.
Deleted D:\EXCHSRVR\mtadata\.\DB000035.DAT successfully.

Database repaired, some data may have been lost.
  - 0 queue(s) required repair out of 8 detected (0%).
  - 2 object(s) damaged out of 1230 detected (0%).
```

During the time that the MTA queues are being verified people may still use Exchange to access their mailboxes and send and reply to messages. The unavailability of the MTA will not affect users in the short term as the Information Store service is enough for people to access mailboxes. Over a longer period the lack of the MTA affects the capability of the messaging service. Users will still be able to send messages to other users whose mailboxes are on the same server (all such messages are handled by the store and not by the MTA), but any messages for remote users will be queued and not processed until the MTA restarts. In the same way, message exchange with remote servers and other mail systems will not operate until the MTA is available.

7.4   General notes on Exchange connectors

With the exception of the X.400 connector and RPC-based site connector, which run as part of EMSMTA.EXE (the MTA executable), all of the other Exchange connectors run as distinct multi-threaded processes on a Windows NT server. You can decide to run all of the connectors on a single computer within your organization, but you must consider the fact that each connector imposes a certain processing load on the system and attempting to push too much work through a single place may create potential messaging bottlenecks. All of the connectors are registered as entries within the Exchange directory, so once a connector is installed and active it becomes available to any user within the organization. This poses some interesting questions, especially with systems distributed internationally.

Do you, for example, want to have everyone sending messages to external bodies world-wide through a single SMTP or X.400 connector? Given the volume of messages that might be sent to recipients in the Internet this mightn't be a smart idea. Allowing users based in England to send faxes generated by a connector in Germany may not be convenient and might generate higher telecommunications charges. On the other hand, you might decide to take advantage of lower telecommunications charges in a certain country and route all fax traffic out through that country, but would this be legal? Interesting questions, and of course you can configure the different connectors to take account of these issues, but it's amazing how many people never even pause to think.

An implementation plan will ideally clearly identify the set of external communications required by an organization and propose how Exchange can make those connections. If you are running an electronic mail system now you'll be able to extract much useful information from whatever connections are already operational, including the volume of messages that are sent and received over a set period. It's better if you have statistics for message traffic over an extended period, ideally taken at a regular interval such as weekly or monthly as these statistics will allow you to see whether volume is growing or declining, and the rate at which the increase or decrease is occurring.

Once you know what connections are needed and the volume that each connection will support (plus a suitable percentage increase to accommodate growth for the first year of operation) you can proceed to plan where the connectors will be installed. Remember to take the network overhead necessary to transport messages to connectors when you look for the correct system to host connectors. The connector software is relatively low-cost so don't try to save too much on expenditure if you're going to impact the service delivered to users.

7.4.1 The bridgehead concept

When you read the Exchange documentation you may come across the term "bridgehead" and wonder what it means. A bridgehead server is a system within a site that is nominated to operate as a point of connectivity between that site and either another site or a foreign mail system. The bridgehead server acts as a target for other sites or gateways to transmit messages to.

For example, if you had a site with three servers and wanted to establish a connection to the Internet it wouldn't make sense to install and configure the IMS on all three servers. Apart from anything else, extra system administration overhead is incurred for each operational IMC. In this situation the best idea is to nominate one of the servers to act as the bridgehead between the site and the Internet and install the IMS on that server. Because of the extra processing performed to send and receive messages to and from another system it is normal to select the system with the best configuration to act as the bridgehead.

7.4.2 Avoiding bottlenecks

Another fact to take into account that anywhere that connections or gateways exist between one system and another represents a potential bottleneck. Exchange is designed to handle many thousands of messages per hour, but achieving a high rate of throughput relies on optimal transmission paths and a low or nil requirement to convert messages from one format to another. No gateway between systems can be regarded as optimal because electronic mail systems can differ in so many ways, leading to a situation where it is inevitable that some "fix-up" processing has to be performed before a message can be transmitted from or to Exchange server. Even the Microsoft Mail connector has to convert messages from MS-Mail format to MAPI and vice versa.

If the network link used by a connector is slow and the message volume passing through the connector is large you run the risk that queues of messages will build up waiting to get through the connector.

Installing a heavily used connector on a server that has good network links but is overloaded by other processing is also a good recipe for bottlenecks. Even with properly configured systems fast connections can be overwhelmed by heavy message volume, and a particular danger time is during a migration from one system to another when connections are used to bridge the gap between the old electronic mail system and Exchange. During migration periods you may have to install and operate several different connectors until the bulk of users have moved over to Exchange, at which time the message volume should decrease.

7.5 Configuring and operating a site connector

Before engaging in the discussion as to how to select and configure a connector between two sites in the same Exchange organization it's important to know the type of data that will flow through the connector. It's also good to know which Exchange components are responsible for the generation and transmission of the data. Figure 7.15 illustrates how messages pass between servers over a site connection. As you can see, the MTA in the bridgehead server in each site communicates with its partner MTA to exchange data in the form of messages.

It's easy to see that interpersonal messages flow from the Private Information Store to the MTA for onward transmission. You might also recall that public folder and directory replication is accomplished via messages too. Table 7.4 lists the major types of messages that flow across a link between sites. If you use Directory Synchronization (DX) then messages will also be generated through this service.

Figure 7.15
Messages sent between Exchange sites

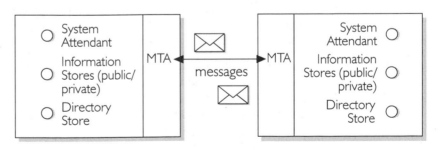

Note that within a single standalone site composed of a number of different servers the MTA does not handle messages for the Directory Store. The directory service processes its own messages in this case.

Table 7.4 *Messages exchanged between sites*

Type of data	Component generating the messages
Mail messages generated by users	Private Information Store
Replication of changes and additions to objects placed into public folders	Public Information Store
Replication of the public folder hierarchy	Public Information Store
Delivery and Non-Delivery Reports	MTA
Replication of changes and additions to the Exchange Directory Store	Exchange Directory Service
Directory Exchange (DirSync) updates	Directory Exchange Service
Link Monitor test messages	System Attendant (via the Private Information Store)

7.5.1   The options to connect sites

The full list of connectors capable of linking sites together has already been discussed. To recall, you can select from the site connector itself, the X400 connector, IMC, and dynamic RAS. Which of these should you use? Table 7.5 lists some common requirements along with an appropriate solution.

The standard site connector is generally the fastest in transmitting information, as long as the network link between the servers in each site is capable of handling RPCs in reliable manner. The connector is relatively simple in comparison to the X.400 connector, so there is less overhead when messages are processed, and the connector performs at anything up to 20% faster than an X.400 or SMTP equivalent, both of which requires messages to be converted into a different format before transmission.

The standard site connector is also able to transmit to several servers within a site whereas the X.400 connector is restricted to a single named server. On the other hand, the X.400 or IMS connectors are more resilient when it comes to dealing with network connections that are unreliable from time to time. The X.400 connector is unique in that it is the only connector that supports scheduled connections between sites. The Internet Mail Service is able to support scheduled RAS dial-up connections to services such as those provided by an ISP, and it is possible to backbone sites across the public Internet, but this is not as elegant or as straightforward as the scheduled connections of the X.400 connector. Apart from this aspect of scheduling, because the functionality of the two connectors is so close (apart from delivery and read receipt notifications) selecting the IMS or X.400 to act as connectors linking sites together often comes down to the question of which messaging standard do you prefer?

Table 7.5   *Selecting a connector to link sites*

Situation	Select
■ Very reliable and high bandwidth (128 Kbps or better) network links between the sites connected by networks capable of supporting RPCs (named pipes, NetBIOS, Windows Sockets)	Site connector
■ TCP/IP, TP4 or X.25 connectivity available between bridgehead servers ■ Requirement to schedule message exchange at particular times ■ Best ability to utilize low bandwidth ■ Requirement to restrict message size	X.400 connector (best option) or Internet Mail Service
■ Dial-up connectivity when no permanent LAN/WAN connection is available	Dynamic RAS, or (even better) X.400 over the Microsoft "Steelhead" multi-protocol service

In earlier versions of Exchange, the dynamic RAS connector was the only option available when a telephone connection connects a location to the network. This connector is deployed most often in cases such as small or distant offices, or when you don't want to invest in a bespoke network just for messaging. Another example when the RAS connector is valuable is when sophisticated network links are just not available. Microsoft, for example, connect four sites in South America through RAS connectors because they weren't able to install the type of dedicated network links required to support the X.400 or IMS. Available bandwidth is the biggest issue with RAS connectors. It's OK if a site supporting a few messaging users is at the other end of the connection, but problems come into focus if people try and replicate very large documents between public folder replicas. In all instances where RAS connectors are used it's a good idea to keep a constant eye on the queue for connector so that any problems are quickly detected before they result in a large backlog of queued messages.

The initial directory back-fill can also cause problems across a RAS connector. When the new site joins the organization the initial contact is fine, and messages start to flow across the connection. But joining a moderately complex organization can result in having to receive a great deal of directory information containing the GAL and configuration information for all the other sites. If you get in a position where you need to use RAS connectors, consider performing the initial installation at a location where a LAN connection is possible, wait for directory replication to complete the back-fill operation, and then dispatch the computer to its eventual destination.

Exchange V5.5 supports X.400 or Internet connectors that run using multi-protocol routing (also known as the Windows NT "Steelhead" technology). Messages can also be routed across the Internet and picked up through dial-in connections to local ISPs. Either option can provide higher capacity for distributed locations than the Dynamic RAS connector and should be reviewed before a final choice is made. In fact, the Dynamic RAS connector was broken by Exchange V5.5 and doesn't function at all. The problem is fixed in SP1, but maybe it's a hint from Microsoft that they'd really prefer you to use another option.

It is possible to configure multiple connectors for each site. A cost is allocated to each connector to tell Exchange which connector should be used as the default link. Let's assume that you have a site connector and an X.400 connector established to link the Dublin and Belfast sites. The site connector has a cost value of 1 whereas the X.400 connector has a cost of 50. In the normal course of events messages will always be sent via the site connector, but if any problems occur with the site connector messages can be rerouted via X.400. Messages are not rerouted automatically, and messages are not taken off one queue to be dispatched via the connector that is now taking up the load. Everything must be done manually by amending the relative costs attributed to each connector.

If you give the two connectors the same cost Exchange will attempt to balance the load of messages transmitted across each connector. Load balancing through multiple connectors enables a degree of fault tolerance within the messaging network. If one connector fails the other will continue transmitting messages until its companion resumes. A connector can be given a maximum cost of 100, but this has a special meaning in that Exchange will only use it as a very last resort when no other connector is available.

Remember that the replication of organizational information means that sites know about the connections existing between other sites. You may have no control over the connectors established by other system administrators or the cost allocated to these connectors. It's possible to get into strange situations with cost values because they are cumulative. In other words, if messages have to pass through one site to get to another the cost of each link is added to form a cost for the overall route. It may well be that a direct route between two sites is created with a cost of 10, but Exchange "discovers" that it is possible to route messages via an intermediate site using a connector with cost 5 and another (from the intermediate site to the target site) of cost 4, resulting in an overall cost of 9, lower than the direct and preferred route. Clearly this points to a need to understand the connections that exist within an organization and not to introduce new connections without being aware of the potential impact on other sites. Hopefully if you look after the interest of other sites, their administrators will look after yours!

It is possible to attribute different costs to different servers within a site when using the site connector. The normal course of event is to transmit messages to a bridgehead server in each site, but it's also possible to seek to balance the load across multiple servers in the same way that you'd try to balance the connectivity load across multiple connectors.

7.5.2 Making the connection

When a server transfers messages to a remote server in another site, the MTA must bind to the remote MTA using the Exchange service account. It is possible to use different service accounts in both sites, as long as the accounts in each site possesses the necessary permissions to bind to the remote MTA, but it's much easier and convenient to use the same the same service account in both sites.

As described in chapter 3, to use a site connector you must establish a Windows NT trust relationship between the communicating domains if the sites being connected reside in different Windows NT domains. The rule here is that the domain for the site being connected to must trust the site making the connection. If different accounts have been set up for Exchange in the two Windows NT domains it is necessary to use the property pages of the site connector to instruct Exchange that a specific service account should be used to connect to the remote site. You'll have to provide a password for the account in most cases.

In effect you're telling the Exchange MTA to connect to the remote site using a different account than that used for normal day to day administrative operations. Think of this as similar functionality to the Connect Network Drive (Connect As) option used by the File Manager when connecting to a file server.

Figure 7.16 illustrates the general properties of a standard RPC-based site connector. In this case we're configuring the connector in the Dublin site to talk to the Belfast site. Note that the server OFFICENT1 is specified as the server to act as a bridgehead for the local site. The Target Servers property page allows you to specify one or more servers to connect to in the remote site.

Configuring a site connector is a relatively straightforward operation that can be accomplished in a few minutes. Once the connector is established it will take a little while for the configuration information for the remote site to be replicated across the link and appear in the organizational tree displayed by the administration utility. As long as the data transmitted by the RPCs can pass without hindrance from one server to another you should see little problems with the site connector.

Figure 7.16
Configuring a site connector

7.6   Exchange, X.400 and X.500

Compliance with international messaging standards is a good thing. Without standards it is very difficult to communicate from one messaging system to another, a fact that all too many corporate telecommunications technicians are unpleasantly aware of. It is easy enough to send a text message from one system to another, but sending compound messages, those composed of several different body parts, requires a good deal of understanding on both sides before successful transmission is accomplished.

X.400 and X.500 are two important sets of recommendations for the exchange of electronic mail messages and directory services. The recommendations are defined through the efforts of the CCITT (the International Consultative Committee on Telephony and Telegraphy), a division of the United Nations now called the International Telegraph Union (ITU) and based in Geneva, Switzerland. The ITU bases its recommendations on the Open Systems Interconnection (OSI) model, taking into account the needs and requirements of many different bodies before the final shape of a standard is issued. Although X.400 and X.500 are sets of recommendations which are only mandatory when organizations decide to make them so, a set of recommendations is often referred to as a "standard".

The primary goal of any standard is to make things easy. Standard screw sizes make screwdrivers easier to manufacture and sell. The X.400 standard seeks to establish ground rules to allow users of different messaging systems, perhaps in the same organization, exchange messages with each other as easily as if they were connected to the same system. Three separate set of X.400 recommendations have been issued to date in 1984, 1988, and 1992. The recommendations continually evolve to better define the internal structure of an interpersonal message and its components (such as attachments), the basic structure of the message handling system, and how messages are transported from one point to another within the system.

7.6.1   Using X.400 with Exchange

The original version of Exchange was heavily influenced by the X.400 recommendations, and Exchange was always intended to be an excellent X.400 messaging system. That goal was fully realized in Exchange V4.0 and has only been improved on since. The tight connection between the X.400-based MTA and the X.400 connector is evidence of the solid X.400 base inside Exchange. The Internet protocols press their case to serve as the potential long-term replacement for X.400, but are still less functional in some respects. Given the rapid pace of change in everything connected to the Internet it would not be at all surprising to see Exchange evolve to a stage where the MTA is based on SMTP rather than X.400, but that time is not yet here.

The X.400 connector is the most generic of the range of connectors available to Exchange system designers. It can be used to connect Exchange sites together as well as connecting to any other X.400-compliant MTA. The generic nature of the X.400 connector means that it is a little slower to transport messages than the RPC-based site connector. However, the X.400 connector more than makes up for the slight reduction in speed with its capacity to transport messages over much slower links.

Apart from the range of systems it can connect to the X.400 connector delivers a number of significant features that may well be of interest to administrators when deciding what type of site connector should be used. Amongst these are:

- Message transmission can be set to occur at scheduled times. This optimizes the traffic that goes across potentially expensive network links by ensuring that data is passed in a long continuous stream rather than in small pieces throughout the day.

- A limit on the size of messages accepted by the connector can be set. This stops people sending very large messages and potentially blocking a slow connection to all other traffic.

- Limits can also be set on the set of users authorized to use the connector. Due largely to deployments in corporate messaging environments it is common practice in X.400 implementations not to let everyone communicate with external parties via X.400. Apart from the obvious risk that confidential information is transmitted to unauthorized individuals, restricting the set of users reduces the risk of virus-laden binary files arriving through the mail. Remember that for many years X.400 was the only way to transmit binary information through the mail with some assurance that files could be read by a suitable application when it reached its destination. SMTP/MIME offer this capability too, but MIME has only been readily available in the recent past.

Exchange is able to communicate with other X.400-based systems that comply with either the 1984 or 1988 recommendations using a multi-threaded Windows NT service called *MSExchangeMTA*. The first step in an X.400 implementation is to decide which transport stack is going to be used by the MTA to host the X.400 connector. Connections can be made simultaneously to a number of X.400 MTAs via three different transport stacks:

- TP0 (Transport class 0) over a TCP/IP connection via the RFC1006 specification. Exchange V5.5 SP1 allows multiple TCP/IP links to be configured between a given MTA-pair. This allows (for example) large message traffic to be scheduled while smaller messages flow at all hours on a separate (restricted) link.

- TP4/CLNP (Transport class 4/Connectionless Network Protocol) to provide a suitable OSI interface across a LAN.

- TP0 over a X.25 connection using an Eicon port adapter on a Windows NT computer.

- Exchange V5.5 SP1 adds supports for Cirel X.25 hardware (popular in Europe, particularly France). This interface using standard Windows Sockets (Winsock).

Configuring a new transport stack for the MTA is done with the File.New Other.MTA Transport Stack option from the Administrator program. Once a stack is installed (such as the TCP/IP stack shown being configured in Figure 7.17) we can proceed to get a new connector up and running. Before a connector can be created we need to know something about the capabilities of X.400-based messaging. We also need to understand the different terms used in the X.400 world.

Figure 7.17
*Configuring a
TCP/IP stack*

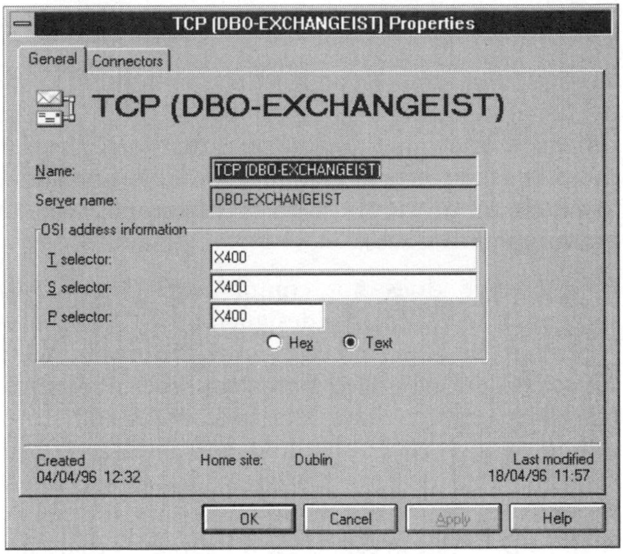

7.6.2 The different X.400 recommendations

Most other X.400-compliant mail systems available today communicate using the 1984 or 1988 recommendations. In general, complying with a later recommendation implies that a greater degree of communication is possible with less effort, especially when dealing with multiple bodyparts, or attachments. The 1984 recommendations, for instance, only distinguish between text and binary bodyparts whereas the 1988 recommendations allow each body part to be allocated its own tag, or indicator of which application should process the body part's content. We'll return to this point later on in this chapter.

Clearly it is best to pass as much explicit information as possible when communicating with other messaging systems, and the 1988 set of recommendations, at this point in time, represents the most complete and pragmatic guideline for inter-system message exchange available today. Before a connection is made to another messaging system it is important for you to know whether it supports the 1984 or 1988 recommendations.

7.6.3   Exchange and the X.500 standard

The X.500 standard sets rules by which mail user agents and other applications are able to inquire for directory information no matter where the directory is located or how it is accessed. In terms of implementation the most common use of a mail directory is to look for the correct mail address to use for a particular person. Validating the addresses for a message doesn't need an X.500 service the Global Address Book does an effective job for Microsoft Mail users. However, an X.500 directory is not restricted to just storing information about mail addresses; a directory can hold information about any type of data item that an application cares to store (and eventually retrieve). The value, of course, is that once the data is held in an X.500 directory the route to that data is well defined and the data is therefore available to any application that complies with the public X.500 programming interfaces.

Exchange does not comply with the X.500 recommendations. Instead, Microsoft have designed an "X.500-like directory schema" to represent the directory entries for people and routing between servers. This distinction between different types of entries is important. Unlike the classic model of a mail directory, X.500 stores information about people who receive mail and how messages can be routed to other systems. The directory used by Exchange is very similar in many respects to a standard X.500 model but it does not support interfaces such as DAP (Directory Access Protocol) that can be used by external agents to interact with the directory. In addition, Exchange server does not support the XDS (X.500 Directory Services) API, and given the focus on LDAP today it is doubtful that they ever will. Address synchronization between Exchange server and other directory sources, such as those maintained by other messaging systems, would be facilitated if Exchange supported the full gambit of interfaces described in the X.500 recommendations. Until the time arrives when Microsoft upgrade Exchange to comply with the full set of protocols defined in the X.500 recommendations it is inevitable that hand-crafted tools will be required to keep Exchange co-ordinated with other systems.

Exchange is often represented as a strong supporter of the ITU standards. This position is correct in relation to X.400, but the story is weaker for X.500. However, it is important to draw a clear line between the areas where Exchange fully complies with standards and the places where Microsoft have, for one reason or another, taken a stance that aligns a server component with the appropriate international standard but doesn't quite get there in terms of implementation or interfaces.

7.6.4 The X.400 messaging model

The X.400 standard is based on a store and forward messaging model. A store and forward model means that messages are transferred when links between servers and backbones are available, and when links are not present (for example, because of network failure) messages are held within the system ready to be released when the links are re-established. After a message is sent it flows long the backbone from link to link, much like a telephone connection is made across a series of switches. In both cases the user who originated the transmission is unaware of all the work and links made on their behalf. The system takes care of the internal management and, as far as the user is concerned, they don't have to do anything more after the message enters the system. The store and forward model is robust, proven, and well suited to heavy traffic between multiple distributed sites.

The X.400 recommendations describe a complete messaging system, referred to as a Message Handling System, or MHS. The components of a MHS include:

- The Message Transfer Agent (MTA). Literally, a method to route messages from their submission through user agents to the point of eventual delivery to recipients. A complete MTA is bundled in Exchange server, so a single server can act as an MTA. However, a more practical view of an Exchange implementation would create a single MTA composed of a number of Exchange sites with a number of optional gateways for communication outside the MTA.

- The Message Transfer System (MTS). The set of one or more MTAs that communicate with each other to send and receive messages. Think of a number of Exchange servers located in a set of distributed sites that send messages to each other.

- The Message Stores (MS). In many electronic mail systems the message store is referred to as a "file cabinet", a somewhat more human-friendly term to describe the location where messages are stored in transit between their creation and introduction to an MTA. In an Exchange environment the message store can be thought of as the set of folders used when people generate and send messages. Stores can hold messages and other objects, text or otherwise.

- The User Agents (UA). The client programs used to generate, send, and retrieve messages from an MTA. Think of the set of clients supported by Exchange server and you'll know what user agents are. Some user agents operate in a remote manner over dial-up connections.

- The Access Units (AU). Gateways or methods used to communicate with other messaging systems that do not comply with the X.400 recommendations. For example, the Microsoft Mail X.400 gateway.

Figure 7.18
*X.400 Reference
Model*

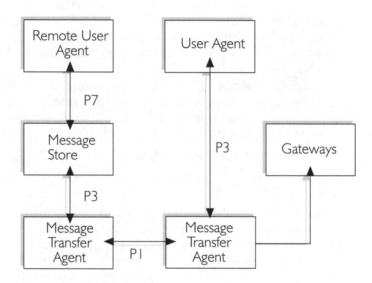

Figure 7.18 outlines the components of the X.400 model and the protocols (Pn) used to communicate between the different components. We'll return to a variation of this picture shortly to map Exchange on top of the model.

The fundamental principles of an X.400 Message Handling System embody the concept of a global messaging network or global MHS. In other words, nothing is done while implementing an MHS to prevent its expansion to accommodate growth to a stage where the MHS is capable of serving a global audience. The global MHS, while obviously an X.400 messaging network itself at a macro level is comprised of other, smaller X.400 messaging networks underneath.

X.400 is not a new standard that has suddenly descended onto the shoulders of electronic mail administrators. It is well known and understood and has formed part of the electronic mail strategy for many large corporations for the last ten years or so, especially in Europe. However, if you are moving from a PC LAN-based mail system you're probably not too familiar with X.400, as the standard didn't play a big part in LAN implementations, except when used as a connection from the PC mail system to other mail systems. The Microsoft Mail Gateway to X.400 is a good example of one such connection.

The first set of X.400 recommendations were defined in 1984 and a more functional set arrived in 1988. These dates are important when qualifying compliance. A system complying with the 1988 standard is capable of delivering more functionality than one that is 1984-compliant.

7.6.5 How can Exchange use X.400?

Exchange is able to use X.400 to interface with other mail systems in a number of different ways:

- **To communicate with other mail systems**: This is the most obvious use of X.400. Connections are made between Exchange servers and an X.400 backbone or MTA that acts as a message switch. The X.400 MTA might belong to a public carrier when communication is required with other organizations, or it might be an internal X.400 MTA used to provide a common messaging backbone for all of the mail systems in use within an organization.

- **To connect two or more Exchange sites together via an X.400 network**: Each Exchange site is a separate MTA and the two connect on a peer to peer basis over an X.400 backbone. Messages are sent by each Exchange site to the X.400 MTA that forms the "glue" in the middle. The X.400 MTA, probably provided by a public carrier such as a PTT, takes care of the routing and delivery of the messages to their destination where they are received by another Exchange server for eventual delivery to user mailboxes. This type of set-up could be used to connect lots of different Exchange servers together in a single country without having to go to the trouble of establishing connections from each server to the other. The solution is flexible because a new server can be introduced without affecting other servers.

- **To link to Microsoft Mail systems via the Microsoft Mail Gateway to X.400**: In this scenario an Exchange server and the Microsoft Mail gateway are two entry points to an X.400 MTA, again probably one provided by a public provider. Messages are sent by Exchange to the X.400 MTA and then fetched by the gateway for deliver to the Microsoft Mail users in the normal manner. This is an alternative to a direct connection from the Microsoft Mail clients to the Exchange server, possibly because the Microsoft Mail users are in a location that isn't served by a good or continuous network link.

As illustrated in Figure 7.19, from a purist's perspective Exchange does not implement the X.400 reference model, largely because of the use of MAPI as the internal protocol instead of the P3/P7 combination outlined in the model. Implementing the complete reference model would be an interesting exercise, but Exchange is designed to handle many more e-mail connections than X.400. The Exchange MTA and its X.400 connector form a practical and pragmatic real world X.400 implementation that fully interoperates with other X.400 MTAs.

Figure 7.19
*Exchange
and X.400*

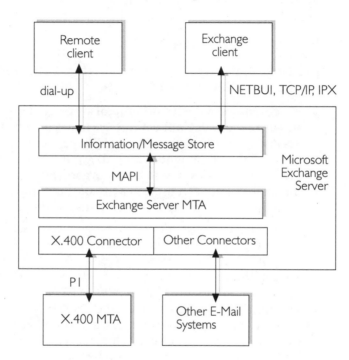

7.6.6 X.400 body parts

Obviously because X.400 is all about standards, an X.400 message is built according to a carefully defined formula. That formula incorporates the concept of header data, including information about the message originator and the recipients the message will eventually be delivered to, and the component body parts, literally the pieces that collectively form the content.

Simple messages have a single body part, sometimes known as the cover memo. Depending on the user agent, cover memos can be created with a simple text editor or a more comprehensive editor. The Windows 95 Exchange client can create cover memos with Word for Windows, for instance, an editor that's slightly more complicated than the Windows Notepad, a good example of a simple text editor.

Table 7.6 *X.400 File Tagging mechanisms*

X.400 recommendations	Body part type	File format information passed as
1984	Body Part 14 (BP14)	None. Mail user agents must decide how to process binary body parts which could contain any format type (apart from text).
1988	Body Part 15 (BP15)	X.400 Object Identifier (OID)
1992	File Transfer Body Part (FTBP)	Original file name encapsulated and passed in the attachment attributes.[a]

a. Exchange V5.5 adds support for the Latin-1, Latin-2 and Cyrillic character sets in messages.

Compound messages have a set of one or more body parts, or attachments, which follow the cover memo. Each body part is tagged to tell receiving mail systems how to deal with the attachment. For example, if the attachment is an Excel worksheet an indication is given that this is the case, although the tag that's placed on the attachment is up to the originating user agent and there is no general agreement between user agents from different vendors as to the tags that should be used for different types of attachments. Some of the more intelligent user agents available today are equipped with either format detection technology, which allows an attachment to be "sniffed" and identified, often by comparing the first couple of bytes from the attachment with a set of known electronic "signatures". Once the attachment is identified it can be processed by launching the appropriate application or, if an application isn't available, the normal backup method is to call a specialized viewer program that is able to display the content of a file but not edit it.

In addition to the body parts listed above Exchange also supports body part 9 (BP9) to handle embedded or forwarded messages within an X.400 messaging system.

The difference in tagging behavior defined by the various sets of X.400 recommendations (see Figure 7.20) is often a cause for confusion when the time comes to connect different systems together. The 1984 recommendations were defined at a stage when PC file formats were not generally used in electronic mail systems, so defining different types of attachments didn't receive much attention. All attachments in a 1984-compliant X.400 system are tagged as binary files, known as body part 14, or BP14. In this scenario it becomes the responsibility of a receiving user agent to interrogate the various binary attachments and decide what format they actually contain. An attachment could be a Word document, or an Excel worksheet, or even a simple text file. In all cases there is no external sign of what's inside. BP14 is also known as bilaterally defined since it assumes that sender and recipient both agreed on any data they are sending or that the sender has communicated the type to the recipient

The 1988 recommendations took note of the growing influence of PC systems and the wide variety of file formats in use and expanded the tagging scheme considerably to allow user agents to include format information to be sent along with each body part. 1988 X.400 systems use a tagging scheme referred to as body part 15, or BP15, where information about the file format of attachments is passed as an "object identifier", or X.400 OID.

Figure 7.20
*Simplified
X.400 message
structure*

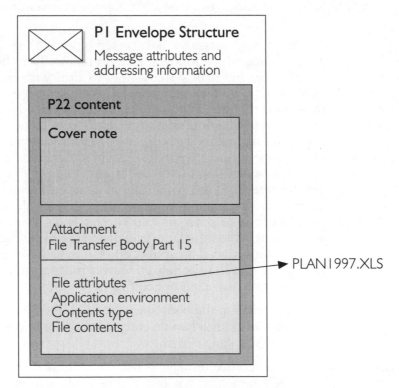

If a human being looks at an X.400 OID there is little information about file formats immediately obvious. Like many data structures associated with standards, an OID is carefully constructed to accommodate all possible circumstances. The eventual OID is therefore a string containing many different pieces of information, all useful in their own way, but the resulting combination is very un-human friendly. Of more concern to application developers, if applications are to be able to deal with message attachments code must be written to extract the information about format types from the OID. The extraction code is, in itself, not particularly difficult to write nor will it take long to execute when the time comes, but sometimes incorporating a requirement to decipher encoded strings to extract a file format tag seems a bit of an overkill.

The latest version of the X.400 recommendations was established in 1992 at which time another attempt was made to provide format information. Body part 15 encoding has been superseded (in some respects) by the File Transfer Body Part, or FTBP15. Instead of holding format information in an OID the original file name of an attachment is passed as an attribute. This scheme relies on user agents being able to use the file name to locate the correct application whenever the attachment's content needs to be processed and is by no means foolproof. For example, if I use Lotus Word Pro to create a document called FOO.DOC and attach it to a message, I rely on the mail user agents being used by recipients knowing that FOO.DOC should be processed by Word Pro. If, as in many cases, another application also creates documents with the .DOC file type much potential exists for confusion.

In defense of the FTBP scheme, creating associations between file types and applications is a well known and understood method, and one that has been in use for many years by Windows clients. The most common example is perhaps the Windows File Manager, which creates associations between file types and applications to be able to launch the correct application when a user double-clicks on a file. The direct association between a file type and an application is very simple, a quick and dirty method to get the job done, and as we've seen above, is prone to error. Later versions of Windows, including Windows V3.1 and Windows 95, use a Windows API function called *FindExecutable* to search the system registry to match files up with applications able to process their content. The use of the system registry in a Windows-dominant environment improves matters by largely ensuring that the correct application is located and then launched, provided of course that an appropriate application is installed on the PC.

Exchange was the first mainline messaging server to use FTBP15 as its baseline for communication with other 1988 X.400 MTAs, a fact that clearly causes some difficulty if any of the other MTAs you want to talk to don't support FTBP15. Encouraged by industry groups like the Electronic Mail Association (EMA), many X.400 vendors are retro-fitting FTBP15 support into their 1988 X.400 implementations, but the majority of MTAs have not yet been upgraded. It seems ridiculous to make such a remark about a standard, but until the time arrives where all X.400 MTAs can agree on a common interchange format for multi-bodypart messages, probably FTBP15 in the long term, some degree of confusion and negotiation between MTAs will be required before seamless message exchange is automatic. If possible, try and use FTBP15 as the basis for interpersonal message transmission between Exchange and other X.400 systems.

7.6.7   Encoding schemes

Before messages are introduced into an X.400 system they must be encoded. This is done to ensure that messages are sent in a common internal structure that can be processed globally. The internal structure of messages transmitted within an X.400 network differs according to the set of recommendations supported by the systems making up the network. The lowest common denominator for X.400 systems is a structure known as P2 established as part of the 1984 recommendations. X.400 1988 systems use a more developed internal structure referred to as P22.

The fact that encoding occurs at all and the differences between P2 and P22 are completely hidden from users so you don't normally have to worry about it, except to know that there is an overhead incurred by an Exchange server to encode messages for transmission via an X.400 link. The encoding translates messages from the internal MAPI structures (known as MBDEF, or Message Bodypart Encoding Format) used by Exchange into the format expected by other X.400-compliant systems. For instance, OLE objects inserted into Exchange messages are transformed into X.400-type body parts because there is no guarantee that the receiving system will be able to deal with an OLE object. If the translation wasn't done then objects would arrive as random collection of bytes that don't really make a lot of sense to recipients. Exchange server knows which encoding should be done because the content type is defined when an X.400 connection is defined to the system. Clearly it's important to get this right because the two types of X.400 encoding are very different.

As well as the communication load, any Exchange server where an X.400 connector is active incurs all the processing overhead involved in translating messages from Exchange to X.400 structures and vice versa. A heavy load of messages being sent or received to or from an X.400 connection can slow an entire system. Evidence that this is happening can be gained from user feedback or the fact that queues of messages waiting to be sent to X.400 build up. In these circumstances it is best to move the X.400 connector to a more powerful system or to install a dedicated server to take over the load. The same can be said of any Exchange connector, but perhaps the X.400 connector needs to have most attention and monitoring, This is especially true in circumstances where the X.400 connector is used to link Exchange to other legacy messaging systems together. In these situations you should monitor the connector regularly to preserve the quality of service delivered to users, especially during the period where users are migrating from the older system to Exchange.

The work required translating from MBDEF to the appropriate X.400 content type is only strictly necessary to communicate with other messaging systems. If you're in the situation where you want to use an X.400 network to link different Exchange servers you could instruct the connector to perform no conversion and send MBDEF content directly. This enables faster throughput and imposes lesser demands on the server, but you will run into problems if messages find their way to non-Exchange systems, or if the X.400 network performs format integrity checks as messages are transported across the network. Several public X.400 systems will fail messages containing MBDEF content if they consider the messages to be "invalid" because of their MBDEF content, so always perform some tests before making a final decision.

7.6.8   Interoperability with other X.400 messaging systems

Microsoft have validated the ability of Exchange server to exchange messages with other X.400-based systems using a suite of interoperability tests defined by the OSINET (USA) and EUROSINET (Europe) organizations. Table 7.7 lists some of the X.400 systems that Exchange server has been tested against

The test suites cover points such as

- P1 interoperability to test whether the information in message envelopes can be passed between Exchange and other MTAs. The most important information in this context is the MTA name, password (if required), and OSI addressing data.

- P2 and P22 interoperability. P2 defines the content of 1984-type messages and P22 defines the content for 1988-type messages. The test suites see whether Exchange server can successfully send and receive messages to and from other MTAs and that recipients (user agents) can successfully view the content of the messages after they arrive. The tests cover BP14, BP15, and FTBP15 as well as text-only body parts.

Table 7.7 *Interoperability with other X.400 MTAs*

Manufacturer	X.400 MTA	X.400 standard
Retix	Open Server	1984
Microsoft	Microsoft Mail X.400 Gateway	1984
Lotus (IBM)	Soft*Switch Central	1984
Digital Equipment Corporation	Message Router X.400 Gateway (MRX)	1984
Isocor	Isoplex 800 MTA	1988
Hewlett-Packard	OpenMail	1988
Lotus/IBM	Message Switch	1988
Control Data Corporation	MailHub	1988
Digital Equipment Corporation	MAILbus 400 MTA	1988
Novell	MAWG X.400 Gateway	1988

Further testing is performed to establish that communication can be achieved using TP0 over X.25 and TCP/IP connections, and TP4 over CLNP links. Finally, tests are performed to verify that Exchange can communicate with public administrative domains operated by PTTs and other public X.400 service providers world-wide. Amongst the ADMDs tested are:

- AT&T X.400 and X.25 services (USA)
- MCI X.400 and X.25 services (USA)
- SPRINT X.400 and X.25 services (USA)
- Infonet X.400 services (USA)
- Northern Telecom X.400 services (Europe)
- British Telecom X.400 and X.25 services
- NTT X.400 services (Japan)
- Australia Telecom X.400 and X.25 services (Telstra)
- Swedish Telecom (Televerket) X.400 and X.25 services

OSTC (Open Systems Testing Consortium) act as a single point of contact for many other European PTTs including France, Germany, and Switzerland.

The existence of such a broad range of test suites and results means that there's a good chance that Exchange server will be able to successfully interoperate with other X.400 MTAs which don't feature in the list above. After getting over the initial hurdle of getting the two systems to connect to each other the next most likely problem area is successful body part recognition as messages flow from one system to another. It's always likely that simple text messages will get through, but the fun only starts once multi-format attachments come into the picture. A process of trial and error is often required before a consistent and reliable message flow is established.

7.6.9   User Agent format handling

All systems should be able to exchange simple text messages without real difficulty, but the true interoperability test is when compound messages with multiple body parts flow between systems without hindrance and all body parts can be read without difficulty by any user agent. Even after all the issues with body parts are resolved much of the responsibility for interpreting format tags correctly to make sure that the correct applications or viewers are called to process message contents is still devolved to user agents. Some intelligence or auto-format detection functionality is often built into the more feature-rich user agents. Auto-detection is usually carried out by reading a few bytes from the start of a file to see if it matches a known "signature" attributed to a particular file format. Most user agents don't engage in this degree of sophistication and rely on the format tag itself to indicate which application should be called to process message content. This isn't usually a problem when a single integrated messaging system is used because the same format tag can be used everywhere. For example, a format tag of "XLS" always indicates an Excel attachment, while "WK3" might mean a Lotus 1-2-3 spreadsheet. However, it can often be a real issue when heterogeneous systems are operated.

How does the Exchange client handle format tags? The answer lies in the Windows system registry, the common repository on Windows-based systems where information is stored about applications. Details such as the OLE capabilities of an application, or the correct DDE commands to instruct an application to print a file are stored in the registration database, as well as a set of associations to link a format tag, such as XLS, with an application such as Excel. The majority of Windows applications capable of producing files in a specific format now provide details for the registration database and these details are loaded into the database during the installation procedure.

When the Exchange client encounters an attachment the format tag is compared against the registration database and if a match is found the associated application is launched to read or print the content. Problems can arise if the registration database is inaccurate or application details have not been loaded, but this is unlikely to occur. Greater potential for problems arises when multiple applications share the same file extension. Selecting a common set of applications to use across an organization and ensuring that a consistent set of format tags are used everywhere normally eliminates the source of the problem.

7.6.10 Message-encoding schemes used by Exchange

Several different message-encoding schemes have been mentioned to this point. Some belong to X.400 and some do not. Before going any further this is an appropriate point at which to attempt to consolidate our knowledge of where and when Exchange uses the different encoding schemes available to it, outlined in Table 7.8.

Table 7.8 *Message encoding schemes*

Encoding scheme	Where used
MAPI (Microsoft Messaging Application Programming Interface)	Native coding scheme for Exchange message properties such as TO: or CC: recipient lists.
MBDEF (Message Bodypart Encoding Format)	Native coding scheme used to encapsulate body parts as they pass from Exchange server to server.
MIME	Internet format used to encode multiple body parts for transmission across an SMTP messaging network.
TNEF (Transport Neutral Encapsulation Format)	Used to package a message's MAPI properties into a binary attachment when a message passes across a non-MAPI backbone en route to another Exchange server.
P2	X.400 coding scheme used for transmission of message contents to 1984-compliant X.400 MTAs.
P22	X.400 coding scheme used for transmission of message contents to 1988-compliant X.400 MTAs
P1	X.400 coding scheme used for transmission of message envelopes to foreign X.400 MTAs.

7.6.11 The meaning of TNEF

TNEF allows Exchange server to preserve extended features such as rich text message content and information about attached or embedded (OLE) objects when messages are sent between Exchange servers across a messaging backbone that doesn't support the transmission of such data.

For example, X.400 envelopes do not normally support information about message formatting as this is usually left to the receiving mail user agent to sort out. The Exchange X.400 connector has a "Remote clients support MAPI" check box on the General properties page—see Figure 7.21. If checked, the X.400 connector will code the extended features into TNEF and include the data as part of the message envelope before a message is sent. This is OK as long as an Exchange client is at the receiving end, because it will be able to make sense of the extended features and it will allow a recipient to see the message content and format exactly as it appeared on the originator's PC. However, if the recipient uses a different user agent that doesn't know how to deal with the extended features it's likely to cause some problems. In these cases it's best to force the X.400 connector to strip off the extended features before sending the message by not checking the box. The most obvious effect of not using TNEF is that rich text memos will be translated into simple text, losing any formatting that may have been used.

7.6.12 Setting up an X.400 connector

We've spent a lot of time on X.400 concepts, let's proceed to use the X.400 connector to do some real work. A certain amount of information needs to be collected before the new X.400 connector can be created. Much of the necessary information can be gained by asking the questions listed in Table 7.9.

Table 7.9 *Questions to ask when setting up an X.400 connector*

Question/Area of investigation	When connecting is required to another Exchange site	When connecting to a foreign MTA
What is the name of the remote MTA? Does it have a password?	A password is seldom, if ever, required when two sites connect over X.400	A password should be used when connecting to a foreign MTA
What MTA transport stack is going to be used	TP4, TCP/IP, or X.25	TP4, TCP/IP, or X.25
Do lines in messages have to be wrapped?	No	It depends on whether the mail systems behind the X.400 connection are able to handle long lines of unwrapped text.

Table 7.9   *Questions to ask when setting up an X.400 connector (continued)*

Question/Area of investigation	When connecting is required to another Exchange site	When connecting to a foreign MTA
Will remote clients be able to support MAPI message contents?	Yes	Unlikely.
When can messages be transferred?	Exchange servers should be able to transfer messages on a demand basis	Scheduled transfer is often the most appropriate mechanism when connecting to foreign MTAs.
What OSI TSAP, SSAP, and PSAP[a] information is required	Pass blank values or an agreed value up to 4 characters in each field.	You can decide what Exchange will pass, but have no control over what the incoming MTA will provide.
Will delivery restrictions be enforced?	Unlikely when using X.400 to connect two sites.	Possible to restrict the transfer of messages outside the company, or restrict whom you'll receive messages from.
Degree of X.400 compatibility?	Full 1988.	1984 or 1988
Send MAPI-encoded messages?	Yes. It's best to use MAPI when connecting two sites together as this avoids any conversion overhead.	No. Foreign MTAs require messages to be presented in P2 or P22 format.
Allow two-way alternate communication	Yes. Exchange servers are happy to send and receive messages alternatively during one connection.	Perhaps. Some MTAs prefer to send all messages and then receive any messages.
Limit on message size?	Unlikely when connecting two Exchange sites, unless the network link is very slow.	Many companies restrict the size of outgoing messages when sent to external agencies.
X.400 Global Domain Identifier OK?	The default GDI can be used.	May need to restate GDI for the remote MTA.
Connected sites?	Other sites may be reached through this connector.	Not applicable when connecting to a foreign MTA

a. TSAP, SSAP, and PSAP are OSI Transport Service, Session Service, and Presentation Service Access Points representing the different layers in the OSI model that are used by the Exchange X.400 connector.

If you're unsure about the answers to any of these questions you should review the connection with the administrator who looks after the MTA you want to connect to. The Exchange administrator's guide also contains a lot of useful information, particularly in respect of the different settings that can be defined for a connector.

Two separate references to MAPI are made in Table 7.9. First, should MAPI contents be sent to remote clients. If the X.400 connector is configured to pass MAPI message contents for eventual delivery to clients it means that all of the rich text formatting in messages (bold, underline, different colors, and so on) will be retained. Attachments, and icons for those attachments, will be positioned where they were placed in the message. If the remote mail system can't handle MAPI contents the X.400 connector will convert rich text to plain text and convert embedded attachments into normal X.400 attachments. The rendering information, used to position an embedded attachment within a message, is also discarded. An extra attachment (the infamous WINMAIL.DAT) is added to the message. This file includes information about the rich text information that has been lost during conversion.

The second point relates to the internal format of the messages passed from one MTA to the other. If you're connecting Exchange sites together you can safely leave the messages in their native format (MDBEF). This avoids any need for the MTA to convert messages and attachments into the X.400 P2 or P22 formats and reduces the demand on system resources.

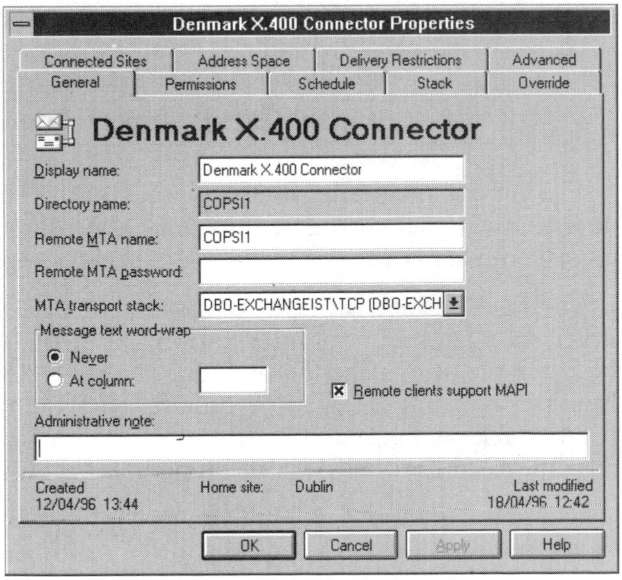

Figure 7.21
General properties for an X.400 site connector

7.6.13 Connecting two sites with an X.400 connector

The most popular connection (and easiest to set up) is using the TCP/IP stack, so that's what we'll use as an example. The two sites we want to connect are Dublin and Denmark. The sites are in different European countries with a reasonable network link between them. It's a good idea to use an X.400 connector to link sites across wide geographical distances where it is costly or impractical to create the type of high-speed link required by the standard site connector. If there are a number of sites in each country the X.400 connector can be used as the glue in the middle, with site connectors used to link all the sites within each country.

Figure 7.22
Stack properties

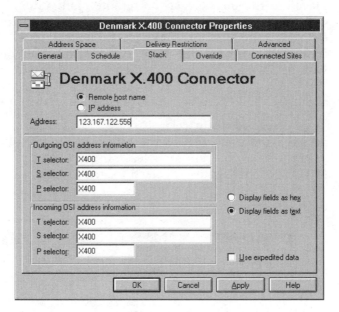

The general properties for the connector are shown in Figure 7.21. Note that no password is required for the remote MTA. This is the normal course of events when connecting sites together.

The stack defined is TCP/IP as installed on the DBO-EXCHANGEIST server. We can see more information about the stack by clicking on the Stack property page (Figure 7.22). Note the IP address entered for the server we want to talk to. If you refer back to the OSI settings for the TCP/IP stack configuration illustrated in Figure 7.10 you'll see how the outgoing OSI information is determined.

Examining Figure 7.22 you'll see that a fixed IP address is specified for the remote server. This approach is a bad idea in production environments. Using a host name is preferable because it insulates you from any change in the underlying IP address for the remote server. IP addresses have been known to change in the past! On the other hand, fixed IP addresses do reduce the dependency on DNS, a service that has proven troublesome in a number of implementations over the past few years.

The fields used for the outgoing and incoming OSI information can be entered as text or hex values. Hex values are a throwback to the past, when older X.400 implementations wallowed in configuration information that was very difficult for human beings to understand. Computers certainly understand hex, but I haven't met many humans who can read it fluently. It's best to enter values in text format so that you can see and understand what you've entered, but don't be too quick to write hex off because it can help, sometimes.

Figure 7.23
X.400
interoperability
options

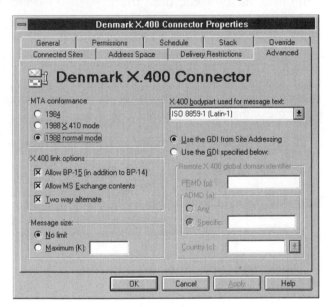

There have been situations when, as in Figure 7.22, an agreement was made between two sites to use a string like "X400" as a default value for all the OSI information. Adopting a default string like this is a good idea when the X.400 connector is used internally. You'll probably end up with different OSI information for external connections, but there's no point in making things more complicated than you have to, so pick a default string and use it for all internal X.400 connectors. The default string helps makes connections easy to establish as long as everyone enters the same string. I have known instances where a connection proved remarkably difficult to debug because one site had entered "x400" instead of "X400" in all the OSI fields. A lowercase "x"

is very different to an uppercase "X", but a quick glance doesn't always detect the problem, especially when you might be worried about the more esoteric things that can go wrong when setting up X.400 connections. Reverting back to hex revealed the problem, because the exactitude of hex showed up the different values.

The Advanced property page contains all the settings to control the level of interoperability this connector will have with the remote MTA. In the case of two Exchange sites the interoperability, as expected, is extremely high, as shown in Figure 7.23. Refer to the earlier discussions regarding body part types or the Exchange Administrator's manual for the meanings of BP15 and BP14.

Many people have shied away from X.400 because it accumulated a reputation for unfriendliness in the past. It's certainly true that it's all too easy to lose your way if you are forced to resort to poking around under the hood and have to speak in the somewhat convoluted terminology the X.400 recommendations foster. The graphical interface presented by the Exchange administration utility eases the pain somewhat, even if there still are eight property pages to deal with, so the task of setting up an X.400 connector is easier in Exchange than most other messaging systems.

Figure 7.24
Connecting a site using the X.400 connector

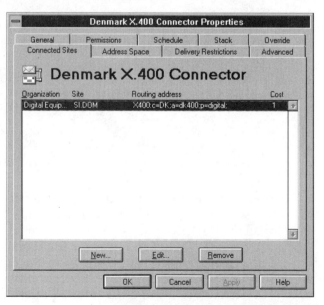

The final thing to do to complete connecting a site in over the X.400 connector is to define the address space for the site or sites you want to communicate with. A valid X.400 address, or enough of the address to allow Exchange to route messages to addressees in the site, is entered. Figure 7.24 shows that the site "SI.DOM" is connected using an address C=dk;A=dk400;P=Digital, meaning that any message to a person whose X.400 O/R address begins with these attribute values can be routed using this connector.

Remember that setting up a connector is only one part of connecting sites. Messages can certainly be routed through the new connector, but users will have to enter in full X.400 addresses to get the messages to their correspondents. A directory replication connector is required to replicate directory information between the remote site and your server. For more details, see the discussion on directory replication connectors in chapter 8.

7.7   The Internet Mail Service

The Internet Mail Service (IMS) is a connector to enable messages to be sent and received using SMTP (simple mail transfer protocol), the predominant standard for electronic mail within the Internet. A subtle renaming exercise was performed in Exchange V5.0, where the V4.0 Internet Mail Connector (IMC) became a fully-fledged service. One reason for this was the much closer relationship between the IMS and the Information Store. Instead of depending on a set of directories to host messages going to and from the Internet, the Information Store is used for this purpose. The same mechanism is used by the other connectors that are integrated with the MTA (the site and X.400 connectors) and establishes a point of differentiation between these connectors and others, like the Microsoft Mail or Lotus cc:Mail connectors, which both use the file system to hold messages in transit. Because the Information Store is used for storage a dependency exists between it and the IMS. If you stop the Information Store service for any reason, the IMS must be closed down too.

Exchange V4.0 and V5.0 are both very capable Internet mail servers, with good support for the required SMTP and MIME protocols. The early teething problems that were seen in Exchange V4.0 were addressed in some of the early service packs and hot fixes and Exchange V5.0 provided most of the missing functionality demanded by administrators who wanted Exchange to act as more than just a simple SMTP server. The routing capabilities introduced then have now been supplemented with better security, support for additional protocols, and the ability to block off loathsome spammers. The general focus on performance that led to increased throughput in the Information Store and MTA has also helped the IMS. Interestingly, the changes have delivered much better inbound performance (246% improvement in the number of messages processed[3]) than outbound (a

---

3.   These results are those reported by Microsoft at the 1997 Exchange Conference. You may wish to run your own tests.

mere 5% improvement). Clearly better scalability and SMP support has helped, and the new database engine is probably at the root of the massive improvement in the ability of the IMS to introduce new messages into the store as they arrive.

Microsoft intends Exchange to be an "effective, inexpensive messaging switch" The broad reach of connectors certainly helps to attain this goal, and the smart-host routing capabilities of the IMS make a major contribution in this respect.

7.7.1　Internet Standards

Within the Internet world a set of standards for communication have been established through a series of generally agreed papers called Request for Comments, or RFCs, generated by the Internet Engineering Task Force (IETF), a volunteer group made up of representatives from major organizations and institutions. The Internet Mail Service supports the RFC 821 and RFC 822 standards that define the SMTP server-to-server protocol and the format of messages sent between servers. As the name implies, SMTP began life as a very simple messaging format, basically marking the lowest common denominator for messages that could be sent between servers manufactured by different software vendors using different operating systems.

The original RFC 822 standard defined in 1982 considered messages that could only contain 7-bit ASCII text characters, and supported lines that could not contain more than 1,000 characters, not to mention a restricted overall message size. All these limitations appeared perfectly acceptable in a world where telex machines still generated the majority of electronic communications. These limitations have long been lifted.

7.7.2　SMTP and MIME

SMTP messages are always transmitted as text. Clearly the restrictions imposed by the original RFC 822 standard could not be maintained in a world where PC formats are now the norm. A new set of features were originally defined in RFC 1521 and RFC 1522 (now updated in RFCs 2045 to 2049) to allow for an agreed encoding standard for non-text attachments. These standards are referred to as MIME (Multipurpose Internet Mail Extensions), and are supported by the IMC. MIME allows users to send complex objects across an SMTP link up to and including multimedia files. The Internet Mail Service also supports UUENCODE, an earlier encoding scheme for handling non-text attachments. Messages generated by Exchange are not simple ASCII text as the basic editor produces files in Rich Text Format. Lots of messages include embedded files. One of the functions of the Internet Mail Service is to encode the Rich Text Format memos and any embedded files using MIME before the messages are sent out via SMTP. Upon receipt any foreign messaging system that understands MIME should be able to unpack the MIME-encoded parts and rebuild the message as it was originally sent.

Coding a message's bodyparts according to an established scheme is a great step towards being able to send complex files anywhere throughout the world via SMTP. But the world doesn't use an ASCII character set everywhere; different cultures use different character sets, so international mail servers must be able to support a range of character sets when messages are encoded or decoded. Exchange server supports US-ASCII, the Western European ISO 8859-1 set, Scandinavian IA5, and character sets support for Korea, China, Taiwan, and Japan.

Exchange V5.5 supports RFC 1869 and RFC 1870, also known as ESMTP. The two RFCs describe how SMTP systems communicate to relay information about delivery status and size of messages (DSN and SIZE commands). The DSN command is important, because it addresses a major weakness in SMTP's capabilities, the inability to provide a satisfactory indication that a message has reached its intended destination.

The combination of SMTP and MIME have laid the foundation to allow companies to build messaging backbones comparable to those constructed with X.400 but at lower cost and with less technical effort. The combination has gone from the original proposals to world-wide deployment within the Internet in just a few years.

7.7.3 SMTP conversations

SMTP depends on TCP/IP networks to send and receive messages. The IMS uses TCP/IP to create the connection to the remote mail server, conduct a conversation with the remote server to transmit message header information and contents, and then break off the connection. All SMTP communication generated by the IMS is channelled through TCP port 25, the port number defined in the SMTP standard.

A common set of steps forming a structured conversation between two SMTP systems is used to pass messages between SMTP mail servers. The conversation occurs between one computer acting in the role of the client and another acting as a server. The client initiates and drives the conversation and the server responds to the demands from the client. These steps are illustrated in Figure 7.25 and proceed as follows:

1.   The conversation is started by the client though a connection to port 25 on the server.

2.   After the network connection is established the client sends an

SMTP "Hello" command to the server. The server responds with "OK" to indicate that it is willing to accept an SMTP message. Exchange V5.0 and V5.5 are able to send a "EHLO" command instead of the normal "HELO", indicating that Exchange supports ESTMP.

3.   The client proceeds to pass originator information in a "Mail From" command. The server checks the information to ensure that it is willing to accept the message from the originator.

Figure 7.25
*Steps in passing
an SMTP
message*

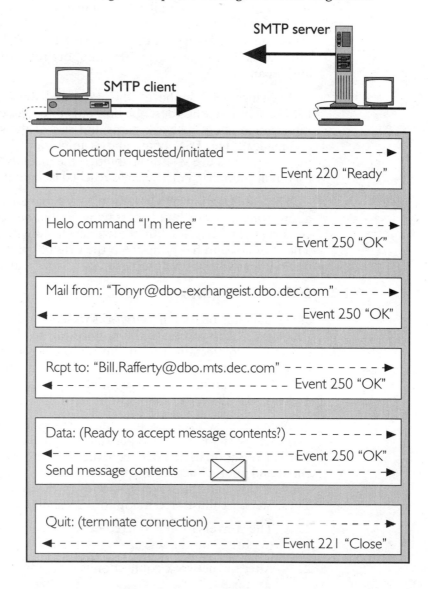

4.   The client then sends a list of recipient information in the form of a set of "Rcpt To" commands. Note that only SMTP recipient information is transmitted. Information about non-SMTP recipients will be passed later in the general body of the message.

5.   After all the header information is exchanged the client begins the process of sending content. A "Data" command is sent to indicate that the client is ready to begin, followed by an acknowledgement from the server. The data is transmitted in 7-bit ASCII characters, which may include files encoded previously into MIME or UUENCODE format.

6.   Once all the content has been sent the client signs off and terminates the connection by sending a "Quit" command. However, if the client has another message to send it can start to send the next message by returning to step 3. This process continues until all messages have been sent.

You can trace a conversation between the IMS and another SMTP server by looking at the log files kept in the \EXCHSRVR\IMCDATA\LOG directory. Indeed, by turning the diagnostic setting to maximum, full and complete transcripts of all the communication between the IMS and other SMTP servers will be captured.

7.7.4   Added security in Exchange V5.5

Client connections to an SMTP server could always be protected using SSL, the Secure Sockets Layer, but there was no previous way to protect the traffic passing between Exchange servers over an SMTP link. Exchange V5.5 supports SSL over SMTP to provide for server to server encryption. All the data in messages can be encrypted before transmission, and decrypted when the messages arrive at the destination server.

Support is also included for SASL, which is the method by which SMTP clients can be forced to provide authentication before an SMTP client to server connection is established. Administrators can use SASL to choose to accept or reject connections from other SMTP hosts if those hosts cannot provide credentials, similar to the approach taken for X.400 connections, where a password is sometimes required. SASL is further able to provide a method to avoid "spoofing" by requiring clients to provide credentials before they are allowed to submit messages from or on behalf of the addresses specified in the message header.

7.7.5   The Internet Mail Service and SMTP

The Internet Mail Service provides a full-function SMTP service. Transport, message routing, translation, and delivery are all handled by the connector, giving this service a reasonable amount of work to do if a heavy volume of incoming or outgoing SMTP traffic is to be handled. If you expect a heavy volume of messages, perhaps based on the volume seen coming in or going out of a previous messaging system, or because you have decided to operate an SMTP-based corporate messaging backbone, then implementing specific servers to handle the SMTP traffic should be considered. Routing messages out of the system is not a very demanding activity; the majority of the potential system load is generated by the need to convert messages from the internal format used by Exchange server into the appropriate SMTP format. Converting large attachments from PC file formats and the message's MAPI properties over to the appropriate MIME encoding is not a simple affair, especially when OLE objects are included.

The process of content conversion from Exchange's internal format can have some unforeseen side effects. One example is the rendering of rich text format content into simple ASCII for messages sent to SMTP recipients that aren't connected to an Exchange server. Any formatting effects inserted by users into messages such as bolding, underlining, italics, different colors, and typefaces are all reduced to simple non proportional fonts. The advantage here is that the conversion creates content that can be read by almost any messaging system. The disadvantage is that the layout of messages may suffer greatly, leading to a situation where users become dissatisfied with the way the system treats "their" messages.

7.7.6   And if you can't use MIME?

MIME is the de facto standard for bodypart encoding exchanged between e-mail systems across the Internet. However, sometimes it's just not possible to use MIME and another encoding scheme is more appropriate. The most likely situation is that the intended recipient isn't able to handle MIME attachments. The solution is to create a PAB entry for the recipient and use the send options to define exactly how the contents should be encoded. As shown in Figure 7.26, the options available in Exchange V5.5 include plain text (any mail system should be able to read plain text) and HTML. Macintosh mail clients usually understand BINHEX, so that option is available too. The actual encoding is done by the Internet Mail service when the message is taken from the queue and processed for sending. Exchange V5.5 further supports MHTML (MIME encapsulated HTML), which essentially wraps HTML content with a MIME wrapper to allow the format of HTML pages to be 100% preserved if included in a mail message.

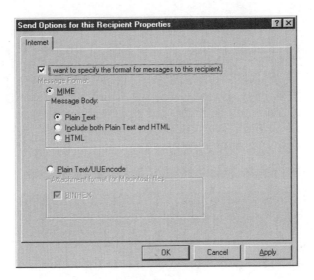

Figure 7.26 Send options for a PAB recipient

7.7.7   Using the Internet Mail Service

Exchange is able to use the Internet Mail Service in a number of different ways. These are the three most common options:

- Making a direct connection to another SMTP mail server in the Internet or within a corporate Intranet.

- Using an external SMTP relay host for routing purposes.

- Using an internal SMTP backbone to link Exchange sites together. This option is slightly more complex than the preceding two because it usually involves directory replication in addition to interpersonal messaging. See chapter 8 for more information on directory synchronization and replication.

In all cases the IMS depends on Windows NT being correctly configured for TCP/IP. Use the Network option from the Windows NT Control Panel to allocate important TCP/IP parameters such as the IP address of the computer and a FQDN (Fully Qualified Domain Name[4]). In fact, the IMS will not start if you don't provide a FQDN. A test is made to see whether the computer's host name can be resolved during IMS initialization, and if a FQDN cannot be resolved the IMS will terminate. A Windows NT error is logged if this happens and you can see details of the error through the Windows NT event. The event viewer is the first place to look if you ever discover problems starting the IMC.

---

4.   An FQDN is basically the domain name containing all the pieces necessary to route data back to a particular computer.

Making a direct connection to the Internet or an Intranet allows Exchange to send messages to any other SMTP server. The basic requirements for such a connection include TCP/IP and a static IP address for the server. The computer's IP address is used in conjunction with your system's host name[5] by other SMTP mail servers to address messages to Exchange users. If you use DHCP to allocate IP addresses you must take out a permanent lease for the IP address allocated to the server and not permit dynamic reallocation as this will prevent incoming messages finding the correct destination.

7.7.8   Notes about Internet Mail Service operation

If a single server equipped with the Internet Mail Service is established to handle all SMTP mail for the organization, the routing cost for all SMTP addresses can be set to 1. You also need to define the set of SMTP addresses that the connector is able to process. The Internet Mail Service processes addresses in the following order:

1.   Exact match

2.   Wildcard match

3.   Partial substring match

4.   No match

For example, if you put "*.com" into the address space for the Internet Mail Service it means that the connector is able to send messages to any SMTP address ending in ".com", such as my normal address:

```
Tony.Redmond@digital.com
```

In the example where "*.com" is defined in its address space the IMS will reject any SMTP address ending in any other form. So in this instance if I was to attempt to send to:

```
Tony.Redmond@zyz.net
```

The message would be rejected and returned to me.

If the IMS address space is left blank it indicates that the IMS is able to handle any form of SMTP address, subject always to the ability of the local DNS to resolve the host's address and provide the appropriate TCP/IP address for onward routing. Note that there is a difference between a blank SMTP address space and one that specifies "*" or "*.*", both of which are deemed to satisfy a wildcard match. If there's

---

5.   If the name of the host for the IMC is not the same as the electronic mail domain an entry must be added to the local domain name server (DNS) to map the domain name to the IMC host name.

only one IMS operational the difference doesn't matter, because a blank or wildcard address space will effectively allow any SMTP address to be processed by the connector.

Things get a little more complex when multiple Internet connectors are in place because the SMTP:"*" or SMTP:"*.*" address space is resolved as a wildcard match whereas a blank address space is a partial substring match. Why is this important? Well, let's assume you have sites in London and Paris, each of which has an Internet connector. The London connector has an address space of SMTP:"*" and the Paris site one of SMTP: (blank). If no routing restrictions (see page 502) are imposed, the GWART in both sites will list the two Internet connectors as viable routes for SMTP messages. When the MTA comes to route a message it examines the address spaces, and the result will be that all SMTP traffic will be routed to the IMS in London because it provides the best possible match. It is therefore important to use the same address space for all Internet connectors within an organization, or impose routing controls via address scoping.

When SMTP hosts are already active within an enterprise the IMS can connect to them for routing purposes. This is a variation on the theme above where the work is split between Exchange and the SMTP host. Exchange takes care of preparing messages for SMTP transmission (format conversion and so on), while the SMTP relay host actually sends the messages to other systems after they are delivered to the SMTP relay host by Exchange. The only difference between this option and the first is that the Message Delivery property for the connector is set to forward all messages to a single nominated host.

If lots of small messages are dispatched into the Internet this configuration offers a potential performance gain over letting Exchange do its own routing. But if the messages are large and complex then the additional routing cost incurred by Exchange to transmit messages to their final destination will largely be overshadowed by the work necessary to convert them from Exchange internal format to SMTP/MIME.

Many enterprises, most commonly in the United States, already operate SMTP-based corporate messaging backbones to unify disparate electronic mail systems running on different platforms as well as to provide a single point of external contact (an SMTP "smart" host) for the enterprise. To external recipients all the messages coming from the enterprise appear to be generated from a single domain. For example,

```
Tony.Redmond@xyz.com
```

Rather than what might be the case where the full routing address required to reach my mailbox is:

Tony.Redmond@exchange.xyz.com

The SMTP host uses a set of proxy addresses to map the addresses on incoming messages to full routing addresses. The host is regarded to be "smart" because it is able to reroute messages using proxies. You define the correct proxy for Exchange by creating an outbound proxy in the IMS Connections property page. The Message Delivery property for the connector is set to forward all messages to the "smart" host.

In all cases, external SMTP addressees can be created as custom recipients in the Exchange directory. Creating a set of custom recipients is a convenience for users, who then don't have to remember to add sometimes complex SMTP addresses to their personal address book (or type the addresses in directly from memory). If you choose to put custom recipients into the directory a certain implied responsibility is assumed to ensure that the recipients' addresses are kept up to date. Keeping internal addresses updated is a task that can be approached with a certain air of confidence (assuming that directories of mail addresses are available from the other SMTP-compliant systems). Keeping external addresses updated is quite another matter because so much is out of your control. You should also identify these external recipients so that users receive some sort of visual indication that they are exchanging messages with these recipients. One easy way to do this is to include the recipient's company name in their display name as in "Tony Redmond (Digital)" or "Bill Gates (Microsoft)". This simple step means that the recipient's company name is displayed whenever an incoming message is read, or a new message is addressed.

7.7.9   Exchange as a relay host

We've already discussed the use of an external (outside the Exchange organization) host computer to route messages to and from the rest of the SMTP world. At present, those computers tend to be UNIX systems, mostly because of the history of UNIX and its close association with SMTP. However, what steps can you take if Exchange is the only mail system in use within the company, and you don't really want to learn UNIX just to do some routing?

Exchange V5.0 or V5.5 are both capable relay hosts. The Internet Mail Service is now able to route messages as they arrive onto a server. Indeed, this function must be set up to allow POP3 or IMAP4 clients to send mail to recipients outside the organization. When routing occurs, the Internet Mail Service is able to selectively reroute messages to other SMTP hosts without performing any other processing.

Smart routing is controlled through the routing properties of the Internet Mail Service, as illustrated by Figure 7.27.

Figure 7.27
Setting up a routing table.

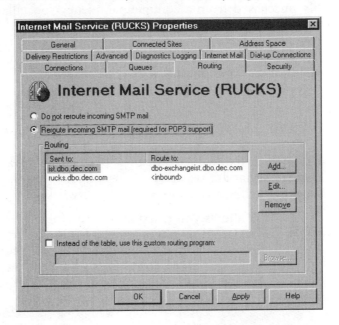

The screen shot is taken from the server called RUCKS. Two entries are in the routing table. The bottom entry tells the Internet Mail Service that it should handle any mail addressed to a domain called rucks.dbo.dec.com. The top entry is a selective reroute because it causes any mail coming in that's addressed to a domain called ist.dbo.dec.com to be rerouted immediately to the server dbo-exchangeist.dbo.dec.com. This is a good example of how the Internet Mail Service can now act as a single point of contact between a company's mail environment and the Internet, a capability that just didn't exist before Exchange V5.0.

If the "do not reroute incoming SMTP mail" radio button is clicked the Internet Mail Service will only deliver messages to recipients that can be found in the GAL. Any other message presented to the Internet Mail Service will generate a non-delivery report.

7.7.10 Stopping spammers

Unsolicited commercial email (UCE) is the polite term for SPAM, a feature of the Internet that drives many usually mild-mannered people wild. Spamming means that someone sends out a message offering to sell a product or service to a distribution list of people who have never asked for such information to be sent. The distribution lists are usually massive, featuring thousands of email addresses that have been harvested from newsgroups, mailing lists, or other public forums, or simply purchased from a commercial agency specializing in distribution list building and maintenance. Spammers often "borrow" someone else's mail address and insert it into the header of the message to mask the real sender (and block all the annoyed replies sent back as the result of their message).

Unlike paper flyers and letters that arrive at your "real" mailbox, all of which can be easily dispatched with little effort into the nearest bin, UCE messages impose a real cost on their recipients. People with POP3 or IMAP4 mailboxes on ISP systems must pay for the messages to be downloaded, while companies pay for the network, disk, and CPU resources that are wasted to transport, store, and process these messages once they arrive into a private network.

The IMS allows you to establish a list of servers or addresses that you will not accept messages from. This is an effective mechanism to stop all messages from a specific server. Unfortunately, the people who engage in spamming don't always use the same server name or IP address, so the technique illustrated in Figure 7.28 won't work.

Figure 7.28
Specifying hosts that you don't want to accept messages from

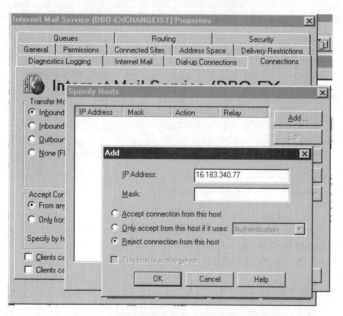

The answer is found through the implementation of a "turf table". I am not exactly sure where this term arose, but can only imagine that it means that if any message arrives that matches an entry on a list the message should be "turfed" (discarded) from the system. No user interface is available to control or set up turf lists. Everything is done through registry entries. You can find documentation in the readme file in the \server directory on the Exchange CD. Other information is available from article Q155683 in the Microsoft Knowledge Base.

In Exchange V5.5, you need to go to the following location in the registry to define a turf list:

```
HKEY_LOCAL_MACHINE\SYSTEM\CurrentControlSet\Services\
MSExchangeIMC\Parameters
```

Then, add two new parameters called TurfDir (type REG_SZ) and TurfTable (type REG_MULTI_SZ). The TurfDir parameter defines a directory where copies of any rejected messages are kept. It's useful to set up a directory to establish the effectiveness of the turf table. You don't have to set up a directory, but if you don't, any rejected messages will be instantly deleted and leave no trace on the system.

The TurfTable parameter provides the IMS with a list of addresses to watch for. You can specify that:

- Messages are not accepted from a specific domain. For example, to block off any message from people in digital you'd specify #@digital.com.
- Messages are not accepted from a specific domain and any of its sub domains. For example, @digital.com.
- Messages are not accepted from a specific user. Simply put someone's full email address on the list (like Tony.Redmond@digital.com) and any messages from this person will be rejected.

The parameter values are not case sensitive. The IMS must be stopped and restarted to make them. Another set of registry entries is available to prevent the IMS acting as a relay host for UCE—there is a known bug in V5.5 for the relay flags that is described in:

```
http://support.microsoft.com/support/kb/articles/q179/2/89.asp
```

A hot fix is available. This is important if Exchange is acting as a connection point to the Internet and accepts messages for non-local recipients. POP3 and IMAP4 clients are counted as non-local recipients, but routing onwards to other servers (Exchange or otherwise) is possibly a higher concern. Details of these parameters can be found in the readme file, which also includes details of a set of registry values to control unauthorized mail relaying. Unauthorized mail relaying is a technique used by spammers to find a random relay host on the Internet and use it to send their messages instead of submitting mail via their ISP. Often this is done by making a connection to port 25 (the port used by SMTP) on your server, and feeding in the commands to create and send messages to large distribution lists. If someone decides to take over your Exchange server and use it to send a million messages to Internet recipients you will definitely notice the effect on performance, disk space, and network resources.

The need to edit registry values to block UCE and unauthorized mail relaying is avoided in Exchange V5.5 SP1, which provides the user interface required to manipulate the registry.

7.7.11   ETRN and ISPs

RFC 1985 describes the ETRN command, an extension to standard SMTP. ETRN is used to instruct a mail relay to dequeue messages waiting for delivery to a server, and is supported by Exchange V5.0 SP1 onwards. Message dequeuing is a common requirement when an ISP is used as an Internet access point. If you're in this situation you should check with your ISP to see whether they support ETRN, and if so, what steps they suggest to connect Exchange and fetch messages from the ISP mail system. Now that Exchange supports ETRN this method is the easiest and most straightforward to set up. For reference, all versions of sendmail (the most common mail utility used by ISPs) from 8.8.x onwards support ETRN.

Here's a basic checklist of the major points related to ISP communication.

- The ISP will have to allocate a static IP address to the Exchange server that is used as the point of connection between your organization and the Internet. This is a requirement of both DNS and SMTP.

- The ISP will also create DNS "MX" and "A" records for your domain name and Exchange server to indicate to the outside world that any messages for your organization should be sent to this server. The ISP will intercept the messages and hold them on your behalf until a connection is established between Exchange and the ISP to dequeue the messages. The server must be configured for TCP/IP (host name and domain). Don't forget to configure Site Addressing so that appropriate SMTP reply addresses (routed via the ISP) are generated on all outgoing messages.

- The firewall between you and the ISP must be able to pass SMTP traffic through port 25. For more information about Exchange and firewalls, see:

```
http://www.microsoft.com/exchange/deployment/
techsupport/exchsec.htm.
```

- The IMS must be configured to route all mail for Internet addresses to the ISP. Mail sent to internal SMTP addresses (inside your firewall), such as those going to other Exchange servers, can be routed directly and certainly should not travel via the ISP (unless you like to encourage long reflective periods between mail transmission and delivery).

- ETRN is the preferred method to dequeue messages. There are other methods. See:

```
http://www.swinc.com/resource/exch_smtp.htm
```

for a useful summary of these methods.

- Some method to automatically dial the ISP to fetch mail must be established. The easiest way is to configure RAS and Dial-Up Networking, along with a phonebook entry for the ISP. A dial-on-demand router can be used instead (see below).

- SMTP traffic may be very heavy. If you have a slow link (less than 64 Kbps), consider tuning the IMS to reduce the number of inbound and outbound connections and the maximum number of messages sent in a single connection. For example, if the IMS is only used to connect to the ISP, it is quite safe to set inbound and outbound connections to 1 and increase the maximum number of messages sent to 40 or more. If the IMS connects to internal mail systems you may not be able to reduce the number of connections as this can interfere with the server's ability to connect to multiple systems concurrently.

- The Mail Retrieval button on the Dial-Up Connections property tab for the Internet Mail Server instructs Exchange how to fetch mail from an ISP. Earlier versions of Exchange that don't support ETRN can use other methods, such as dequeue.exe available from http://www.swinc.com. However, you really should upgrade servers to Exchange V5.0 SP1 or V5.5 (preferred) to take advantage of ETRN, along with all the additional features of these releases.

Exchange V5.5 adds a registry key to force the IMS to send an ETRN command each time it connects to an ISP to dequeue messages. This is useful when you have a dial-on-demand router, such as one used to establish an ISDN link to the ISP. Dial-on-demand routers are used to ensure that outgoing messages are delivered to the ISP as quickly as possible, and it is logical to attempt to fetch any queued messages that are waiting after the outgoing messages are sent.

The registry key is:

```
HKEY_LOCAL_MACHINE\System\CurrentControlSet\Services\
MSExchangeIMC\Parameters\AlwaysUseETRN
```

It is a DWORD value that can be set to 0 (off, don't send an ETRN command) or 1 (on, always send an ETRN command). Of course, mail will only ever be fetched after an outgoing message is sent. It is possible that no messages are sent over extended periods (overnight, for example) but you want to collect queued messages regularly. Regular collections avoid large queues building up and ensures that messages arrive promptly. You can create dummy messages with a command line utility like MAPISEND (from the Exchange Resource Kit) and send them regularly using a batch scheduler like WINAT. The dummy message might be addressed to go out and come back in again, and it will effectively force the dial-on-demand router to connect, send messages, and clear the queues.

Other tuning suggestions, such as a mass of registry values that control SMTP time-outs, can be found in the Microsoft Dial-up FAQ[6].

7.7.12 Using the Internet Mail Service instead of a Site Connector

Within an internal TCP/IP network you have a choice as to the connector to use when linking sites together. Site connectors are the optimum choice and should be used whenever possible, but the IMS offers a viable alternative to the normal site connector when the link between sites is often interrupted and prone to failure.

Figure 7.29
Sites connected by the IMC

---

6.   http://www.microsoft.com/exchange/support/deployment/techsupport/dialfaq.asp

Site connectors use direct RPC communication to send and receive messages in real time. The data transmitted is in native Exchange format and requires no manipulation when it is received by the target system. Thus, site connectors provide the most efficient use of system resources but they depend on highly available bandwidth (> 64 KB).

While not as efficient as the RPC-based site connector because of the requirement to translate messages into SMTP/MIME, the IMS permits store and forward messaging. Messages can be sent to a smart host that collects messages from many different SMTP-based mail systems, and retrieved from the smart host when available. The SMTP version of a site connector still works even if part of the communications path to the other site(s) is unavailable for whatever reason. However, store and forward messaging via SMTP is bought at the price of the overhead required to translate messages into SMTP/MIME, an overhead which may be unacceptable on a heavily loaded system or one that must handle a high volume of messages.

7.7.13 Communicating with the Internet

The ease by which the Exchange IMS facilitates communication with recipients dotted around the Internet is a double-edged sword. On the one hand you get good interoperability and messages flow easily, but on the other, you possibly don't want all the information that might flow to escape outside your enterprise. The IMS includes a number of interesting features that allow system administrators to exercise some control over outbound and incoming connections. These include:

- Stopping out-of-office notifications going out to Internet users. People can use the Out of Office Assistant to create helpful messages for other users to know that they are unavailable and won't be able to process any messages they receive. It's not always a good idea for this information to be broadcast externally. Do you really want people to know when senior management are traveling? You should set up the IMS to prevent these notifications going outside. Use the interoperability dialog (see the Internet Mail property page) for the connector to stop out of office notices and automatic replies going to Internet correspondents.

- The ability to accept or reject connections based on IP addresses. The Internet Mail Service can be configured to only permit messages to be sent to particular hosts, or only accept messages arriving in from others. These restrictions can help you restrict communications to a set of hosts that are deemed essential to the business, or stop unwanted inflows of large quantities of messages from overactive Internet mailing lists, and so on. Stopping unwanted connections also helps to stop potential hackers probing your system for holes by which they can gained unauthorized and unwanted entry.

■ You often don't want to give everyone the ability to access the Internet. Why should temporary staff or contractors have the chance and the tools to transmit confidential data (extracted, for instance, from an unguarded public folder) to people outside? Use the Delivery Restriction property page for the IMS to restrict any users you'd prefer not to have free and easy communications. Along the same line, you can restrict the size of messages that either go out to the Internet as well as those that come in. Restricting the size of outgoing messages can stop large chunks of data being transmitted (like strategy documents), and restricting the size of incoming messages can stop a "denial of service" hacker strike, basically an attempt to send a system so much mail that disk space is exhausted and the system has to be taken off the air.

Figure 7.30
Internet
interoperability
options

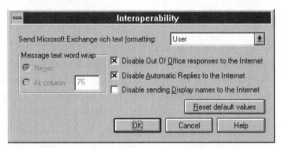

These features should be operated in tandem with a well-configured and secure firewall. There is no situation when the IMS should be connected directly to other Internet hosts unless you want to create a truly open system (in terms of its ability to be attacked).

7.7.14 Interaction with the Domain Name Server

Another item to consider is how to enter records for Exchange servers into your organization's Domain Name Server. The basic function of DNS is to act as a distributed database that translates host names to and from IP addresses. The contents of the DNS database include entries for specific systems within your own network as well as the points of contact for other organizations. All organizations which connect to the Internet have "bastion hosts", systems which connect to the Internet directly. Another term much used is a "relay host", a system that is able to process or reroute messages for a domain, directing them from the time messages enter a domain down through the internal network to the correct server and recipient.

DIGITAL, for instance, has a couple of systems acting as bastion hosts and relay hosts. Collectively these systems process all messages sent to "dec.com" (the public DIGITAL domain). Addresses on arriving messages are examined by these systems, checked against the DNS database to see whether the addresses are valid, and then routed on their way to the eventual recipients. Large, distributed messaging networks incur a fundamental requirement to ensure that all mail servers are correctly entered into DNS as otherwise there'll be no chance of messages ever being delivered.

A request to PING a named computer, such as System1.xyz.digital.com results in a look-up against DNS to resolve the host name that's provided into its base IP address, unless of course the host name and IP address have been entered in the system's local "hosts" file. Windows NT computers can also resolve host names using WINS or by looking up its local LMHOSTS file.

Apart from the straightforward host name to IP address mapping records DNS holds information specific to mail servers. These records are "MX" (Mail Exchanger) records, and serve to identify which systems are able to accept mail, or act as "relay hosts", systems that accept incoming messages for a domain and relay it onwards to their final destination.

MX records can also be used to give a different name to a computer being used as a mail server, in effect an alias that the outside world can use to send messages to that computer. You might want to do this if you didn't want the FQDN of your computers published to the Internet. This is not a good reason really since people can still look up both records in DNS. In any case most companies operate two name spaces—one internal and one external—so the actual address of the email server can't be accessed via the Internet. Better reasons include protection from a physical change of server (i.e. my mail address stays the same even if the mail services move to another machine), or the ability to have a distributed mail system with one e-mail domain). For example, a system called Internet-gateway.xyz.com might have the following records in DNS:

```
Internet-host.xyz.com IN A 16.240.111.111

Internet-host.xyz.com IN MX 10 Internet-host.xyz.com
```

These DNS records associate the IP address 16.240.111.111 with the FQDN of a computer that we'll use to host an IMC. The second DNS record tells us that the system is able to accept mail messages.

The example host name I've chosen to use here may be very accurate in a purely technical sense but "Internet-host@xyz.com" isn't going to win any prizes for brevity. Adding a different MX record to DNS allows us to substitute our longwinded name with a shorter version:

```
Mail.xyz.com IN MX 10 Internet-host.xyz.com
```

Now we've associated the alias mail..xyz.com with the system's FQDN, allowing external correspondents to address mail to people within our organization as:

```
username@mail.xyz.com
```

rather than

```
username@Internet-host.xyz.com
```

Putting both "A" and "MX" records into the DNS database speeds up message delivery by giving the system less work to do to figure out whether a computer is able to accept messages or not. This explanation is purposely kept simple. Several MX records might be involved to route a message from its originator to the final destination.

If an Exchange server is going to accept messages from external Internet systems you'll have to ensure that two records for the Exchange server are entered in your local DNS database. The first maps the host name for the Exchange server with its IP address, the second identifies the Exchange server as a mail system.

When you configure the IMS you can decide to provide it with the IP address for the DNS to query to resolve addresses for messages. This allows the IMS to resolve the IP address itself and send messages on their way without further intervention. However, you might not want to have every Exchange server in an organization to generate messages in this manner, preferring instead to route all messages to one or more systems dedicated to the task of external mail connectivity. These systems might, for instance, be fully equipped with a range of gateways to enable messages to be exchanged with a wide range of other messaging systems. They might also serve as the point of connection with an Internet Service Provider (ISP); the company who provides the necessary link between your organization and the rest of the Internet. In this case you can configure the IMS to route all messages to a specific system.

There are many tips, tricks, and techniques that can be applied to DNS and the way external connections are handled. Certainly far too much information to be discussed in any comprehensive manner here. If you're in charge of Internet connectivity make sure you have a firm grasp of the techniques that can be applied. Messaging is a critical part of connectivity, but it's one that needs to be controlled, so make sure your implementation is well planned.

7.7.15 Sending rich text message contents

In an Exchange-pure environment all of the clients connected to the network are able to read rich text format messages. The same is true when an Exchange client sends a rich text message across an SMTP network to another Exchange client. Problems begin to occur once you begin to communicate with other mail systems.

The cover notes (initial body part) of rich text messages sent to external mail systems through the IMS will be translated into plan text. At the same time the IMS will attach a copy of the formatted text as an extra binary attachment. Depending on how the IMS is set up the extra attachment is provided as a UUENCODE file (called WINMAIL.DAT) or a MIME-encoded file with a MIME type of MS-TNEF (see the discussion about TNEF earlier).

Recipients who expect a simple message can be quite confused when they see the extra attachment. There's no indication as to what the attachment might contain. It might be an exciting picture, a financial spreadsheet, a copy of their job plan, or details of an important project. All they see is the attachment. Naturally people are curious and won't just let the matter rest there, so they'll call the help desk and pester them with questions like "what's in the file," "why have they sent me something I can't read?", or "what application should I use to see inside the file?" All good questions, but something that the help desk can do without.

If you're in the situation where you expect a lot of mail to go out via the IMS to non-Exchange recipients you can configure whether rich text messages are sent to recipients on a per-domain basis. For instance, if you know that lots of messages go to a domain called xyz.com you can configure the IMS to never send rich text messages to a recipient in that domain. Recipients in users' personal address books[7] or custom recipients in the directory[8] can be configured to always receive messages in rich text format, but if you instruct the IMS to send plain text messages to specific domains the settings in personal address books or the directory are overridden. This step effectively stops Exchange adding the extra attachment and stops users worrying about the contents of the mysterious attachment. Note that if the IMS is used to connect sites together you should always allow rich text messages to flow unimpeded between the sites.

---

7. Via the SMTP Address property page for personal address book entries
8. Via the Advanced properties for custom recipients

7.7.16 Managing the message flow from the Internet

If you haven't been used to communicating via the Internet the amount of message traffic generated once a link is established may come as a shock. As soon as people realize they have been released from the boundaries imposed by the internal e-mail system and can send e-mail to friends, relatives, and other correspondents throughout the world they'll start doing it. Be prepared to see outgoing traffic volumes mount up at a fairly rapid rate.

Letting users subscribe to Internet list servers is a good way to generate lots of incoming messages. Many of the active lists handle well over a hundred messages per day, all of which will be sent to list subscribers unless they have opted to receive a daily digest (a concatenated set of all the submissions to the list server sent as a single message). Exchange V5.0 allows you to redirect mailing list activity towards the new Internet News Service (see next section), but it's unlikely that any such changeover will happen quickly. The sheer number of people who maintain individual subscriptions to news groups and mailing lists is probably the major limiting factor.

If users do subscribe to Internet list servers make sure that you don't allow out of office notification messages being sent through the IMS (the default is to prohibit them). Apart from annoying the other people who subscribe to the list server, out of office messages can often convey business sensitive information to people you wouldn't really wish to share it with. It's OK to compose an out of office message to let fellow workers know that you're off to Australia for two weeks to work on an important deal, but do you really want this information going outside?

Having a single point of contact for Internet mail makes things easier to manage, but it also introduces a potential bottleneck into the messaging system. Any organization generating or receiving more than a thousand SMTP-type messages per day should consider spreading the load by implementing multiple Internet connectors. It is possible to configure multiple connectors so that each handles different domains. In other words, the IMS on one server deals with everything sent to "*.com" and "*.gov" whereas another handles messages sent to "*.edu". Configuring connectors in this manner is really only possible if you have a good idea about the volume of traffic sent to different domains, so an easier solution is to let all connectors process messages to any domain and let the Exchange MTA balance the load across the available connectors.

Some of the heavier messaging sites have found it convenient to dedicate servers purely to Internet mail. In fact, some have gone so far as to dedicate one server to handle outgoing mail and another to handle incoming mail. Dedicated IMS servers don't need a high-end hardware configuration. A system equipped with a 100 MHz Pentium, 64 MB of memory and at least 2 GB disk is a good starting point. Better performance will be gained if the system is equipped with an uprated I/O subsystem, principally by spreading the I/O load generated by the processing of SMTP messages across several disk spindles. Such a system is more than capable of handling the load for most organizations, and if you find that message queues build up you can divide the load across two servers or enhance the hardware configuration. Overall, this is a convenient and practical solution for Internet messaging and avoids the need to run multiple connectors across an organization.

7.8   The Internet News Service

The Internet News Service, newly introduced in Exchange V5.0, can be closely associated with the Internet Mail Service, if only because the same underlying communications paths support both services. The big difference is that the Internet News Service uses the NNTP protocol to transport its messages while the Internet Mail Service uses SMTP.

Mail protocols do not generally lead themselves to threaded or group discussions. Protocols like SMTP are much more focused on getting messages from one place to another. Each message is treated as a standalone entity, with no real relationship to another message or set of messages. Messages sent to a large number of people are often sent in a scattergun fashion, with copies dispatched to all points of the network. Thus, using messaging as the basis for discussions or structured forums is inefficient and makes ineffective use of scarce network bandwidth. Lotus Notes addresses the issue by keeping all items relating to discussions inside databases, with each discussion being allocated its own database. A similar approach was taken with Digital Equipment Corporation's VAX Notes product, a forerunner of Lotus Notes. Both suffer from the same problem: before you can take part in a discussion, you must be able to access the relevant database.

Usenet, a distributed bulletin board system, is the oldest of the Internet solutions to the problem of how to handle discussions. Newer technologies are becoming available, such as Alta Vista Forum, but for the moment Usenet reigns supreme. Usenet provides a topical hierarchy of threaded discussion newsgroups. Communication between the newsgroups is accomplished using the NNTP protocol, which permits messages to be exchanged over TCP/IP. Public-domain news servers support the majority of the active newsgroups within the Internet, but this situation is changing as Microsoft and other software vendors create commercial newsgroup products. For example, Microsoft has its Internet News Server, in direct competition with similar products like

Netscape News Server. And anyone running Exchange V5.0 is now able to use the Exchange Internet News Service to correspond with the many and varied newsgroups scattered around the Internet.

NNTP is designed to hold news articles in a central database (on a server). Subscribers can browse through the contents and select the articles they wish to read, ignoring the rest. Articles can be indexed and cross-referenced for further convenience. In structure and functionality the NNTP protocol is much like SMTP. Commands are available to send messages between the set of NNTP servers that collectively form the Usenet, and other commands are available for servers to query and update each other with details of newly formed newsgroups. The Exchange implementation of NNTP in the Internet News Service positions the Public Information Store as the NNTP database. Public folders act as the repositories for individual newsgroups, and users access information in exactly the same manner as they would other public folders. Figure 7.31 shows a newsfeed being configured. In this case the newsgroups all relate to computer subjects.

Knowing what to do with the Internet News Service is the major issue in corporate deployments. Many companies will simply ignore NNTP completely. Either they have no need for newsgroup functionality or they already have an application in place to provide similar functionality. Indeed, there is some competition within Exchange itself because it is possible to use public folders as the basis of discussions. Public folders are still somewhat Exchange-centric whereas newsgroups are platform-independent, so perhaps the argument for public folders can only be made when everyone (or at least a sizeable majority of the user community) is connected to Exchange.

Figure 7.31
*Selecting
newsfeeds for
public folders*

Some companies will seek to replace individual subscriptions to newsgroups (maintained by users) with a form of "corporate" subscription. In essence this means that a single feed will come into the company from the Internet and the information will then be distributed and accessed through public folders. As noted earlier, I don't think it will be easy to replace individual subscriptions purely because it is nearly impossible to track down all such subscriptions. Where do you start? However, I think the idea of a corporate subscription has great merit because it can act as a catalyst for people to realize the quantity of information available in the Internet. Of course, selecting the right type of newsgroups to feed into public folders is an important part of the catalyst. If rubbish flows into public folders user opinion of the value of newsgroups in general will be pretty low.

NNTP has been around for many years. Its incorporation into Exchange provides more evidence that Exchange is becoming more and more open. Before considering any deployment I suggest that you read the appropriate section in the Exchange documentation set, and consult some of the FAQs covering NNTP and newsgroups that are available on the Web.

7.8.1   TCP/IP ports used by Microsoft Exchange Server

Sometimes Exchange servers need to communicate through a firewall. Perhaps sites are linked together using X.400 connectors over the public Internet, or maybe you want to enable client connectivity from insecure locations. In these and other instances you'll need to enable different TCP/IP ports on the firewall to let traffic through. Table 7.10 details the ports used by the different services associated with Exchange.

Table 7.10   *TCP/IP ports used by Exchange*

TCP/IP Port	Service	Description
25	SMTP	Simple Mail Transfer Protocol (Hosts and Clients—like POP3 and IMAP4)
53	DNS	Domain Name Service
102	X.400	MTA/X.400 RFC 1006 Port for communication
110	POP3	POP3 Client protocol listen port
119	NNTP	RFC977 "News" Protocol (NNTP)
135	RPC	Microsoft RPC Service Locator Port (End-Point Mapper)
137	NetBIOS	Windows Internet Name Service (NetBIOS over TCP/IP)
138	NetBIOS	NetBIOS datagram service (used for browsing)

Table 7.10 *TCP/IP ports used by Exchange (continued)*

TCP/IP Port	Service	Description
139	NetBIOS	NetBIOS Session Services (used for connections)
143	IMAP	IMAP Server Listen Port
389	LDAP	RFC1777 LDAP Listen Port
636	LDAP (SSL)	Secure LDAP SSL Port
993	IMAP (SSL)	Secure IMAP SSL Port
995	POP3 (SSL)	Secure POP3 SSL Port

Note the difference in ports when a client protocol is secured with SSL authentication. For example, IMAP4 clients normally use port 143 to fetch message contents, but when SSL is used, the port changes to 993.

7.8.2 Handling RPC redirection

Exchange monitors port 135 for incoming MAPI client connections over RPC. After a client connects to a socket, Exchange allocates two random ports to use to connect to the Information and Directory stores. Random remapping of ports can be an issue for firewalls as clearly you don't want to have to open up large arrays of ports just to facilitate MAPI clients. To solve the problem, registry settings can be set to allocate suitable static ports for both the Information and Directory Stores. See Q1555831 in the Microsoft Knowledge Base for details. The static ports can be selected from the set of "well known ports" (values below 1023) or the "ephemeral ports" (values between 1024 and 65535). However, the selected ports should clearly not conflict with any port allocated to services such as FTP, or with those allocated to another application.

Port 135 also comes into play when a firewall is used between Exchange servers in the same site. All communication within a site is performed via RPCs. The MTA and the Directory need to communicate with their peers to pass information between servers. When a server receives an incoming RPC connection, it allocates two random ports for use by the MTA and the Directory. Clearly the same issue arises as with client connections, so a further change can be made to the registry to instruct the MTA to use a fixed port (see Q161931 in the Microsoft Knowledge Base). A static port must also be allocated to the Directory, as described above.

Finally, RPCs are used across the site connector, so if a firewall is deployed between two sites you'll have to allocate a static port for the MTA to handle RPC traffic (Q161931). In all cases where static ports are defined, configure the firewall to pass traffic to port 135 as well as the static ports. Also, make sure that all of the servers involved use the same set of ports.

The Microsoft Exchange Directory Service

The Exchange Directory Service is responsible for managing information held about an enterprise's messaging structure—user mailboxes, servers, distribution lists, and the configuration data used to route messages and map address types. All of this information is kept within a single directory. The directory is relatively sophisticated when compared to other messaging directories, if only for the amount of detailed configuration data held and the way that the data is shared between all of the servers in an organization. Distributing the configuration data in this manner allows a server to view the entire configuration and structure of an organization even when working off-line, disconnected from the network. Of course, it is impossible to change any part of the configuration of a remote server without a network connection, but it is always possible to view the data.

Like other entities within Exchange server, all of the items held within the directory are treated and manipulated as objects. An object like a server has properties that define the specific characteristics of the object. Properties also specify the users who are able to manage objects. All management activities on the Directory Store are carried out through the Exchange administration program.

8.1 Of directories, Exchange, and Windows NT

In the Windows NT V4.0/Exchange V5.5 environment NT has one directory (the SAM), and Exchange has another (the Directory Store). The connection between the two is limited at best, with the basic link being established by the fact that each Exchange mailbox is associated with a Windows NT account.

The Windows NT directory is designed as an authentication service. Users must be authenticated against the directory by logging on before they are allowed to access the services offered by NT. Exchange depends on that authentication and does not enforce any special log-on of its own. The NT directory cannot be extended to hold application-specific information, so Exchange must provide its own directory to hold data about objects such as sites, servers, custom recipients, and the configuration of an organization.

The Active Directory is a major and pervasive feature of Windows NT V5.0[1]. The Active Directory provides features such as a hierarchical view, an extendible schema, scalability, distributed security, and multimaster replication. Compare these features to those already available in the Exchange Directory, which also uses a hierarchical view of the directory (organization/site/server/mailbox), scales to hold hundreds of thousands of objects, offers distributed security through certificates held in the directory and replicated like any other data, and a replication model that deals with sites as peers. Sites, a concept introduced in Exchange, also feature in the Active Directory. You could define an Exchange site as an island of high-quality network connectivity. Sites in Windows NT V5.0 reflect network locality in a slightly different, if tighter, manner by using TCP/IP subnets to create site boundaries. Like Exchange sites, information about NT V5.0 sites is known throughout the domain through replication to all domain controllers.

Of course, the Active Directory must be able to satisfy the demands of other applications and provide better authentication than the existing NT directory, so it is a more complex structure than the Exchange Directory. The NT developers have had the opportunity to view the Exchange Directory in many production environments, so while the Active Directory is similar in many respects it is also a big step forward. For example, when objects are changed or added to the Exchange Directory, the complete object must be replicated out to all other servers. In comparison, the Active Directory only replicates the properties of an object that have been changed.

The Active Directory borrows a lot of ideas from the Internet. The concept of a name space is integrated with NT user accounts. This allows data for many other objects to be stored and manipulated in a common directory through a common interface (ADSI). These objects include files, peripheral devices like printers, databases, users, mailboxes, and other objects like application services. The Active Directory provides a single point of contact to manage all objects.

LDAP is very important to the Active Directory as LDAP provides the basic access protocol to tie together multiple name spaces and systems.

---

1. For more information about the integration between Exchange and the Active Directory, see http://www.microsoft.com/exchange/guide/papers/directinteg.asp

The X.500 access protocols are not supported, but just as the Exchange Directory looks and feels very close to X.500, the X.500 information model is supported as one of the valid storage schemas.

Unlike the PDC and BDC setup used by Windows NT V4.0, no notion of a primary controller exists in the Active Directory. Domain controllers exist, but all domain controllers are peers. Like Exchange servers, each domain controller maintains a piece of the overall directory, and knows how to navigate amongst the other domain controllers to build a complete picture. Domain controllers continue to authenticate user log-ons, but now an administrator can make changes at any controller and that change will be replicated to all other controllers, in much the same way as an administrator can make a change the configuration on an Exchange server and have that change replicated to all other servers. To facilitate transition, mixed environments of Windows NT V5.0 controllers and V4.0 controllers are supported. In these situations the NT V5.0 controller can take the place of the V4.0 PDC and continue to communicate with all the BDCs until they can be migrated to NT V5.0.

We've already discussed how companies like DIGITAL are probing the outer limits of NT V4.0 domains with more than 30,000 accounts in a single domain. The limit is 40,000 or thereabouts, but the design goal for the Active Directory is to increase this to around 10 million total objects in a single domain. Domains can be combined into a domain tree, so the theoretical total objects that could be supported is much more than anyone would want to use. Companies that operate multiple domains may well use the scalability and easier management provided by the Active Directory to reduce the number of domains, preferably to a situation where only one domain is used. That unified domain can consolidate all the master and resource domains used in a typical corporate deployment of Exchange.

Windows NT V5.0 replaces the current domain controller authentication mechanism in favor of a new scheme based on MIT Kerberos V5 (RFC 1510). Like Exchange advanced security, Windows NT V5.0 supports X.509 public keys, and stores the keys in the Active Directory. The keys are mapped onto user ids by the directory to allow users to authenticate themselves when they connect to a computer. It is conceivable that the same X.509 certificate might be used as the basis for both user authentication and electronic mail encryption.

The effect of these changes on Exchange and the exact degree of integration that is then possible will emerge at the same time. It is certainly possible that the Active Directory will provide a solution to the problem of inter-organization communications we have today; will allow sites to be split and merged in a reasonably automatic manner; and may even be able to accommodate different Exchange organizations within a single directory structure. All of these operations are required for Windows NT domains today, so the advance in functionality for Exchange organizational management is both logical and inevitable, given that the Active Directory is delivered.

In all this flux around directories and their futures we can be sure of two things. First, an upgrade to Windows NT V5.0 will be required before any use can be made of an extended, expanded, merged directory service. The initial upgrade might just be to migrate the account domain PDC to an NT V5.0 server running Active Directory, but eventually all the other controllers will have to be migrated. The "Platinum" release of will use the Active Directory. Platinum will use other NT V5.0 features, so a fair amount of time and attention is going to be required to assess the tasks involved in the migration, prepare a plan, and then execute. If NT V5.0 ships in late 1998 and Platinum follows in early 1999, then the planning and design work will happen during the remainder of 1999 and into 2000. Pioneers will certainly be running Exchange with the Active Directory in 1999, but I think that prime time will come about much later.

8.1.1   Exchange and X.500

As described earlier in this chapter, X.500 is a set of ITU recommendations describing the interconnection of different information systems or directories. Two sets of X.500 recommendations have been issued to date, in 1988 and 1992. The central X.500 concept is the directory, an information system that holds data about a set of objects of interest. An object of interest is something that somebody might want to consult the directory to discover more information about. Recipients are practical examples of an object of interest. Clients consult the directory to discover information about recipients, such as correct address to use when sending messages to a particular recipient.

X.500 information is collectively stored in a DIB, or Directory Information Base. The DIB provides an interface between the users of the directory and the services that provide and maintain the information within the directory. You can think of objects, such as recipients, being stored as records within the DIB in much the same way as transactional information is written into an accounting database. The DIB imposes certain rules on the objects stored in the directory to ensure that a degree of consistency is maintained. The overall set of rules for the DIB is known as the directory schema. Objects are classified by type, known as object classes. The DIB imposes consistency by only allowing objects to be created according to the rules stated for a particular object class. For example, if you attempt to create a new custom recipient (a new directory object) and the Administration program is not currently positioned in a "Recipients" container (an object class), Exchange signals an error and offers to move into a container that allows custom recipient objects to be created there.

The internal hierarchy and structure of an X.500 directory is determined by the Directory Information Tree (DIT). Beginning from the root, or top of the directory the DIT allows navigation through entries called containers and leaves. The basic difference between a container and a leaf is that a container acts as a repository for leaves and other containers whereas a leaf normally represents an object of interest. Think of the Exchange Administration program. You can see a containers such as "Configuration" and "Recipients". "Configuration" holds other containers such as "Monitors" and "Servers", but the "Recipients" container only holds objects of interest, actual recipients or mailboxes. In this example I am purposely ignoring distribution lists which are stored in "Recipients" and can be regarded as containers, albeit not in the true meaning of the X.500 term.

The directory used within Exchange is based upon the X.500 recommendations, meaning that the directory schema used to represent an Exchange organization within the directory is very similar to the model defined in the X.500 recommendations. Microsoft decided not to implement a true, fully compliant X.500 directory because the Exchange directory is designed to store items not supported by X.500 such as titles, organizational information (manager and reports), and the customizable attributes that a system administrator can define for recipients. Despite hints about future support for the X.500 access protocols it has become clearer over time that LDAP has become more and more important to Microsoft. At this stage it must be deemed unlikely that the X.500 protocols will ever be supported by Exchange.

Figure 8.1 illustrates how the objects within the Exchange directory are mapped on top of X.500 object classes. Both directory schemes organize objects into a well-defined hierarchical structure, the DIT. The concept of the DIB is also supported, as are container and leaf entries.

The full Exchange directory schema consists of:

- Object classes representing different types of objects such as mailboxes, servers, connectors, monitors, and so on.
- Sets of attributes for each object class. For example, a common name, the name of the object class itself, the distinguished name, the date and time when the object was created.

- Details of the hierarchical structure within the directory. For example, Organization → Site → Recipients → Mailbox.
- The consistency rules governing which objects can be added to which containers.

Figure 8.1
*X.500 Object
Classes used in
the Exchange
Directory*

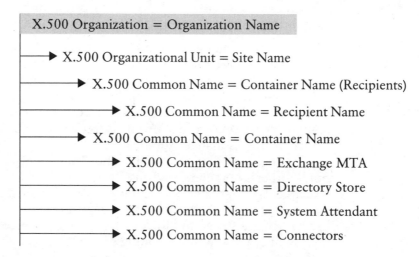

X.500 Organization = Organization Name

→ X.500 Organizational Unit = Site Name

→ X.500 Common Name = Container Name (Recipients)

→ X.500 Common Name = Recipient Name

→ X.500 Common Name = Container Name

→ X.500 Common Name = Exchange MTA

→ X.500 Common Name = Directory Store

→ X.500 Common Name = System Attendant

→ X.500 Common Name = Connectors

Apart from recipients, the Directory holds entries for the other objects that form Exchange including the System Attendant, the MTA, and user mailboxes and public folders. Thus, all objects in Exchange are addressable, so you can see how this provides the basis for information to be transmitted between components in the form of specially formulated messages. Directory replication is an excellent example of this concept in action as messages containing the information to be replicated are exchanged between the Directory Store objects in all the sites within an organization.

Like the Public and Private Information Stores, the Directory Store is physically represented by a database (DIR.EDB). The size of DIR.EDB is much smaller than either the private or public stores. For example, a 15-site organization with approximately 15,500 entries for mailboxes and custom recipients occupies just 40MB. This data is as valuable as the Information Store and it should be accorded the same degree of protection.

How many entries can be stored in the directory? According to Microsoft sources, they have tested the directory with more than 10 million entries. Will a directory ever be constructed to hold such a number of entries? Probably not—and from a practical perspective it's fair to say that the Exchange directory is more than capable of handling the largest corporate directory in use today.

8.1.2   X.500 naming

Within an X.500 DIB each object is uniquely identified by a name called the X.500 Distinguished Name. A distinguished name is constructed from the ordered set of object names representing the path through the DIT that must be taken in order to arrive at a specific object. The set of names within a distinguished name is referred to as relative distinguished names, or RDNs. Each RDN provides the name of a container or leaf entry within the DIT. Within the Exchange directory Distinguished Names are made up from the name of the organization, the name of the site, the name of the recipients container, and the name of the user's mailbox.

Figure 8.2
Navigating through the Exchange Directory Information Tree

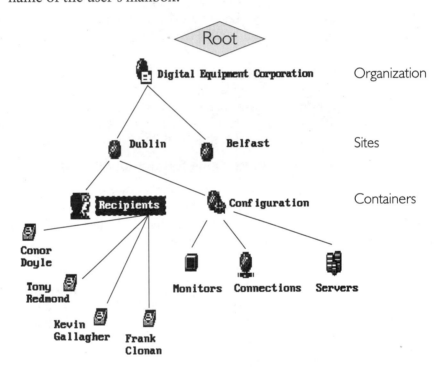

Thus, based on the graphical representation of the Exchange DIT shown in Figure 8.2, the different RDNs necessary to form my X.500 distinguished name (and thus locate my mailbox within the directory) are:

```
Organization = Digital Equipment
Site = Dublin
Common Name = Recipients
Common Name = Tony Redmond
```

Amalgamated together in the format used by an X.500 directory the entry becomes:

```
o=Digital Equipment, ou=Dublin, cn=recipients, cn=Tony Redmond
```

In the Exchange directory the last RDN in a distinguished name is normally the mailbox alias. In my case this might be something like "TonyR". If you're getting confused by all these terms you could think of RDNs as simply fields in the database that makes up the Exchange directory. Many fields can be held for each mailbox, custom recipient, or distribution list object. A quick glance at the database schema (we'll find out more about how to work with the schema in a little while) reveals that there is nearly 500 available fields for each object. You can discover the full distinguished name for a mailbox or custom recipient by examining its Obj-Dist-Name attribute through the object's raw properties.

In passing it is worth noting that Exchange attempts to make effective use of space within the directory; if a field does not hold a value for an object no space is reserved for a value until it is first populated. Thus, the directory does not have a whole mass of blank space in it representing fields that could be filled but aren't.

8.1.3   The Ambiguous Name Resolution Process

RDNs are important because they are used when Exchange attempts to check a name presented to it for resolution, normally when a user addresses a mail message. The resolution process is known as ANR, or Ambiguous Name Resolution. In other words, the directory is searched against a number of different fields to find any or all-matching addresses. If a number of addresses are found we have an ambiguous name, and the addresses are presented to the user in a dialog for them to make the final selection. Fields such as the first name, surname, display name, and mailbox alias are checked during the ANR process.

An automatic check on addresses is performed when messages are sent, but you can always force a directory look-up through the CTRL/K shortcut. Being underlined when displayed in message headers indicates addresses that have been resolved.

How do you know which fields are checked during the ANR process? The answer is simple. Each field in the directory can be indexed. Clearly not all fields are indexed as this would mean that the indexes for the directory would potentially be larger than the directory itself, and any time a field was added or updated the directory would have to also update an index, adding an unacceptable overhead to processing. Exchange has a search flags property to indicate which fields are to be searched by the ANR process; the same flags dictate whether the field is indexed or not. Three values can be passed:

0   Do not index this field, and it is not checked during ANR

1   Index the field and so enable fast searching, but do not include the field in the ANR process

2   Index the field and include it in the ANR process.

So now we have our answer. All the fields in the database that have the search flags property set to 2 are automatically checked when a mail address is resolved. By default these fields include the display name, first name, surname, and even office. I have no idea why anyone should want to address mail to someone based on their office code, but the Exchange directory accommodates such weird and wonderful thoughts. You can, if you like, amend the value in this property for any field you like, a subject that we will deal with later on in this chapter.

Obviously the distinguished name is very important to Exchange, in some ways surprisingly so. Let me give you one example. Let's assume you have two sites—London and Chicago—with an Internet Mail Service configured in each site. A user in London creates a message and addresses it by selecting an Internet recipient from the Global Address List, which just happens to come from a custom recipient entry made in Chicago. The message is duly sent. Instead of routing the message via the local Internet Mail Service Exchange examines the address, finds that the distinguished name (from the Global Address List) references the Chicago site, so the message is sent to Chicago for processing by the MTA there. Eventually the message is sent and will be delivered to the right place, but its route via Chicago is curious to say the least.

8.1.4 DUAs and DSAs

Having a directory stuffed full of information isn't very interesting if that information can't be easily and quickly retrieved. In the X.500 world Directory User Agents (DUAs) and Directory Service Agents (DSAs) accomplish the retrieval of data from the directory. A DUA is responsible for initiating a request for some information from the directory, while a DSA takes charge of responding to any requests that arrive in to the directory. The DSA retrieves the information directly or corresponds with other DSAs (if the directory is distributed throughout a network) to satisfy the request.

Figure 8.3
*X.500 DSAs
and DUAs in
Exchange*

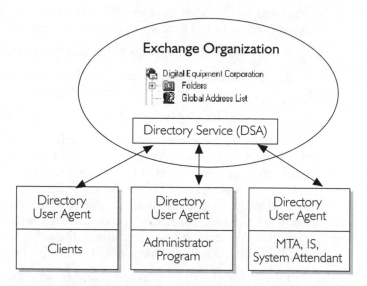

Figure 8.3 illustrates the Exchange implementation of X.500 DUAs and DSAs. Exchange clients, the Administrator program, or behind-the-scene components such as the MTA, Information Store, or System Attendant initiate requests for directory information. A client might, for instance, request the directory to supply a mail address for a custom recipient. The Administrator program corresponds with the directory when information is added, amended, or deleted about mailboxes or custom recipients. The System Attendant uses the directory to store the certificates used by advanced security, among other things.

In all instances requests for directory information are processed by the Exchange Directory service, which fulfills the role of an X.500 DSA. Because the Exchange Directory is distributed and replicated across all sites in an organization the chaining from one DSA to another to retrieve directory information when required is accomplished in a transparent manner.

8.1.5   Multiple address storage within the directory

Exchange server automatically creates a distinguished name within the directory when a new mailbox is created. At the same time a number of proxy addresses may be created, one for each connector that's available for sending messages. For example, if the MS-Mail, X.400, and SMTP connectors are operational, three separate proxy addresses will be created for a new mailbox. Each proxy address represents the address format used by another messaging system to reach an Exchange recipient (via a connector). So the proxy address for MS-Mail is therefore in MS-Mail format and looks and feels just like a regular MS-

Mail address when viewed by an MS-Mail user. The same is true for an SMTP or X.400 address, and so on for all the various connectors. In fact, Microsoft requires vendors who sell connectors for Exchange server to create well-formed proxy addresses for recipients when connectors are plugged into an Exchange server. Adding a template to the directory proxy table when the new connector is installed does this.

Figure 8.4
Multiple e-mail
addresses

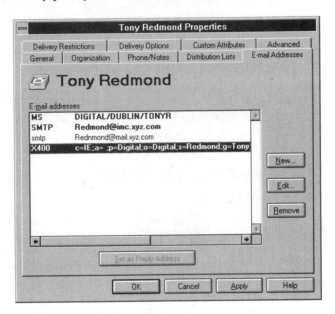

It's also possible for the directory to hold multiple addresses of the same type for mailboxes. This is a useful feature when you have modified an X.400 or SMTP addressing scheme, or when users have migrated to Exchange from another system. Let's look at an example to see if it clarifies things. Assume that you have migrated some users from a UNIX system to Exchange. The form of SMTP address used to direct messages to the Internet Mail Service is *user@imc.xyz.com*. The SMTP address used for the UNIX system was *user@mail.xyz.com*. Default addresses for the IMS are generated automatically as mailboxes are created, and we can generate new Internet addresses for each mailbox afterwards. New addresses are added through the E-Mail Addresses property page for the mailbox. After you add a new address you'll see that some of the addresses are bolded and some aren't (see Figure 8.4). The bolded addresses are the primary address used by each connector type, in other words, the address that will be placed on ongoing messages (and therefore used by external recipients when they reply to the messages).

You can delete any of the addresses for a user if you like, but never succumb to the temptation to delete the X.400 address, even if you don't like X.400 and see no reason to keep X.400 addresses around. Exchange uses the X.400 addresses for internal routing, so if you remove them you'll stop messages being delivered.

Having a number of potential mail addresses seems confusing and wasteful but it allows Exchange to meet a goal of the Universal Inbox concept. That is, to allow users to receive messages generated from many different mail systems into a single mailbox. This can only be done by providing a range of mail addresses for correspondents to send mail to. As it happens, Exchange automatically checks the addresses on incoming messages against all possible recipient addresses held in the directory, so messages sent to any valid address actually end up in the same mailbox. Users remain blissfully unaware of the fact that messages have been addressed differently.

8.1.6   Maintaining directory information

The Exchange Directory holds much valuable information. Data like this must be carefully protected, but unfortunately Exchange has gone overboard on this point and stops users updating even the most mundane of the information held about them in the directory. There are no client options to allow people to update fields such as their internal telephone number, office location, or other attributes that can hardly be regarded as strategic data. All changes to the directory must therefore be made by administrators, an unwelcome overhead and addition to the list of day-to-day tasks already cluttering busy days.

It is possible to write a client extension to allow users to access and update directory information, and indeed a number of programs like this already circulate amongst the general Exchange community. All extensions written to date seem to follow the same route—a client MAPI extension (new menu option) to allow users to browse directory information and make changes which are then handed over to a background Windows NT service running on the server. The service takes responsibility for applying the changes to the Exchange directory. Why two steps and not make immediate updates to the directory? Control is one possible response—it is easier to filter entries through a separate process, rejecting the changes or making small alterations before the changes are applied (with an e-mail to the user confirming the update).

8.1.7   X.400 addresses

Confusion often arises between X.400 addresses and X.500 directory entries. At first glance both can appear similar, but they are different.

This is especially so within an Exchange environment where the X.500 distinguished name is used primarily to locate recipients or other objects within the directory and an X.400 address is just one of the proxy addresses that may exist for a recipient.

The X.400 recommendations set a standard whereby the electronic mail address for a recipient can be constructed in a perfectly unambiguous manner. This means that the address given to any one person should be built in such a way that it is guaranteed to be unique, and the quest to achieve the level of uniqueness necessary to achieve the goal has arrived at the somewhat strange and unwieldy address format used by X.400 systems today.

An X.400 e-mail address is built up in stages from the country where the MTA is located through the name of the organization responsible for the MTA and down eventually to the personal details of the user who actually composes and sends messages. The full address is referred to as an "O/R address", or "Originator/Recipient address", meaning, in effect, that the address of the originator (sender) can be taken from the message and used to address a response back without interfering with the address in any way. An O/R address is composed of a set of attributes. Each attribute has a value and the collective set of attributes and their values enables a messaging system to deliver messages to a person.

Let's look at how an X.400 O/R address is built up using the following example:

```
C=IE; admd=EIRMAIL400; PRMD=XYZ Corporation; O=RETAIL;
OU1=Sales; CN=Tony Redmond
```

Each of the component parts of an X.400 address has its own special meaning. The first term refers to the country where the recipient is located and each country has its own two-character code as defined in the ISO 3166 standard. In this case the code "IE" refers to Ireland, so according to the standard this recipient must be located somewhere in Ireland. However, this isn't strictly true as some organizations group everyone under a single country code no matter where they are located in order to have a single common entry point into the organization.

The next component refers to the administrative domain (ADMD) while the third refers to the private management domain (PRMD), the two major types of X.400 management domains. An X.400 address must contain one or both domains.

A private administrative domain can be thought of as the collection of electronic mail systems within an organization. Within a single organization that never makes connections to the outside world you would only ever use the private administrative domain. The X.400 addresses created by Exchange server use the Exchange organization name as the private administration domain, another good reason for getting the design of your organization, sites, and servers well thought out before you start an implementation.

On the other hand, administrative domains are typically managed by a PTT or other public telecommunications provider (such as those operated by MCI, Telecom Eireann, British Telecom, or AT&T) and serve the function of relaying messages between other management domains. A PTT is often used to connect together the administrative domains of organizations working within a single country, and then, on a somewhat higher level, to connect into the domains managed by other PTTs. The collection of administrative domains currently operated throughout the world forms an international message transfer backbone.

The "O" attribute holds the organization name and in the case of the example it's XYZ Corporation. This should be the same top-level name used when Exchange is implemented for your organization. Up to four organizational units (the "OU1" through "OU4" attributes) can be specified to provide further definition. In most cases only a single organizational unit is ever used, and for our purposes we can equate the first organizational unit to a Microsoft Exchange site. The final attribute in the example (CN) defines the "common name", literally the name used to identify a certain recipient within an organization. Many other attributes are available to help identify a recipient including initials and a generation qualifier. If all the attributes are spelt out it's certainly possible to create very long and complex X.400 addresses.

8.1.8   Lightweight Directory Access Protocol (LDAP)

The introduction of Internet clients in Exchange V5.0 meant that the directory had to expand the set of protocols supported for directory access. Outlook clients use MAPI to browse the directory and retrieve information, but it is highly unlikely that you'll find an Internet client that supports MAPI, and certainly not any of the shareware clients.

The University of Michigan in conjunction with the IETF developed LDAP. Exchange V5.5 supports LDAP 3.0. Many other software vendors support LDAP. Netscape uses LDAP in its Directory Server; Novell has announced its intentions to support LDAP as an access point to NetWare Directory Services; DIGITAL has Infobroker software that uses LDAP to communicate with its X.500 directory. Most importantly Microsoft will support LDAP as the primary access interface to the Windows NT V5.0 Active Directory. Exchange V5.5

includes support for ADSI, the Active Directory Services Interface or the programmable interface to the Active Directory. In turn, ADSI supports LDAP as a mechanism to manipulate directory information. LDAP is therefore a very important protocol in the future of both Exchange and Windows NT.

Figure 8.5 *LDAP access by the Outlook Web client*

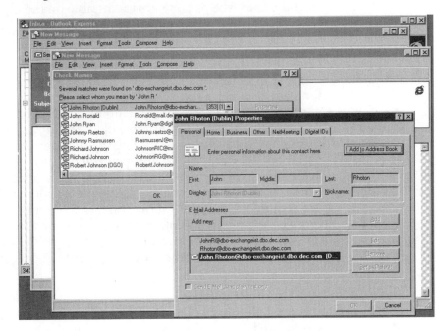

Obviously, because LDAP can communicate with the Exchange Directory Store, the protocol supports much more than just X.500 directories. As designed, LDAP can communicate with any hierarchical, attribute-based directory. LDAP does, however, assume that the X.500 naming model is used within the directory being accessed. The Exchange directory, based on X.500, is very hierarchical, supports the X.500 naming model, and maintains many different attributes for objects held in the directory, so LDAP and Exchange are a good match.

Figure 8.5 is an excellent example of a client using LDAP to browse the Exchange directory. In this case it's the Outlook Express client, but any LDAP client is able to execute exactly the same type of commands. The functionality enabled by LDAP is minimal, but this is understandable when you understand that the very reason LDAP evolved in the first place was to build a streamlined interface to access and update directory information, avoiding the necessity to support a full-function interface to interrogate X.500 directories.

When used by Exchange, LDAP is primarily a query interface. In other words, clients provide some search criteria and LDAP will query the directory for entries matching those criteria. In the example illustrated by Figure 8.5, LDAP was used to query the directory after "John R" was input into the TO: field of a message. In LDAP terms, the query is "Find any entries whose First Name begins with John and Surname starts with R". In this instance, the client restricts the result of a search to 100 names (the parameter is adjustable on the client), which is more than enough for someone to browse through to find the right name. Clicking on the properties of an individual entry displays the detail shown in Figure 8.5.

Fetching directory entries through queries is relatively efficient, as long as the criteria stated in the queries allow a reasonable filter to be applied to the search. For example, searching any reasonably large directory for a common surname like "Smith" or "Jones" might return over a hundred entries. Searching the directory for anyone whose surname begins with "M" would probably return even more. All of the entries must be fetched from the server and stored (in memory) on the client, leading to potential performance problems if very many entries are requested. As noted above, clients like Outlook Express can customize the number of entries that are returned from a search, but better still, the administrator on an Exchange server can override a client request by restricting the number of entries the directory will return from a search.

There isn't much else to say about LDAP. The protocol is simple and well defined. The implementation in Exchange is simple and works well. The most important points that can be made are that LDAP is an important protocol for the future, and that its implementation is an excellent example of the ease in which new protocols can be absorbed by the Exchange architecture.

8.1.9   Blocking access to some directory attributes

It's great to be able to share directory information with different clients, but sometimes you don't want everything that's in the directory to appear in open view. Anonymous users, who might well connect to the directory using LDAP, are certainly not candidates to access items like internal telephone numbers, reporting relationships, or even job titles. The DS Site Configuration allows you to determine which attributes are available to different user communities, and even to reduce the amount of traffic generated between sites for directory replication.

Figure 8.6 shows a filter being applied to the attributes replicated between sites. Notice that you can apply similar filters to authenticated requests (clients that have connected to a known mailbox) as well as anonymous requests. The normal situation is to restrict the attributes available to anonymous clients to items like the display name. If you look through the list of attributes you'll see items like "Best friend" and "Birthday", neither of which are attributes provided with Exchange. These are customized attributes, added on a site basis. We'll discuss how to add customized attributes to the directory later on in this chapter.

Figure 8.6
DS Site
Configuration

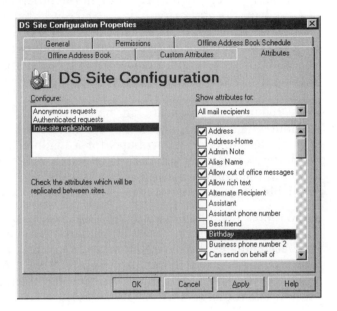

Reducing inter-site replication traffic is a useful feature if you operate a site that is primarily used for directory synchronization activity. Feeds from other messaging systems are unlikely to support all the attributes in the Exchange directory. There's no real point in Exchange attempting to replicate blank or missing information after a directory import operation has occurred. Eliminating the missing attributes from the set presented here allows Exchange to replicate on a more efficient basis.

8.2   Directory synchronization and replication

Given that Exchange is a messaging system designed for distributed operation it is critical that the mailbox entries which are stored and managed by the directory service can be quickly and easily synchronized between the different servers in an organization. Exchange automatically synchronizes address information within a site after changes are made to the directory from any server in the site. You don't have to do anything to initiate the process; the directory service knows that it must update all other servers if something changes in its store. New servers automatically inherit contents of the site directory after they join the site.

8.2.1 Intra site directory replication

In Exchange terminology the intra-site directory synchronization process is known as a multi-master full-mesh environment. All servers within the site automatically participate in directory synchronization. Each server is regarded as equal to all the others, so all servers within the site have the authority to update an object belonging to the site, no matter which server first created the object. For example, a new mailbox can be created or an update applied to an existing mailbox can be made at any server, and the new data will be shared with all the other servers in the site. Field level replication is not supported. Complete objects are replicated after they are changed. The exact amount of data required to replicate an object depends on the number of attributes held for that object. For example, if administrators populate a minimum number of attributes for a mailbox (display name, alias, Windows NT account), then approximately 3.5Kb is required to transport information about the mailbox. On the other hand, if many of the available attributes are populated, then up to 5.8Kb is used.

Within a site, updates about new or changed directory information is not sent out to other servers immediately. Instead, the directory service accumulates the information and replicates it via RPCs with the other servers every five minutes (a push model). A component of the Directory Service called the Directory Replication Agent (DRA) is responsible for all replication activities.

Servers authenticate themselves to each other before data is exchanged. All servers in a site share the same service account, and the password for the service account is used as a "shared secret" that a server must know before it can participate in intra-site directory replication. In addition, when an RPC connection is made to perform replication, a check is made to ensure that the incoming account holds replication permission over the site configuration object.

The alternative to holding updates for a period is to send changes immediately after they are made. However, while this approach means that all servers are updated very soon after a change, it runs into significant performance problems whenever a large quantity of changes are made in a short period. For instance, the administration program can be used to import a CSV file containing instructions to create new Windows NT accounts and Exchange mailboxes, or add custom recipients to the directory. The CSV file might contain data for 500 or 1,000 new directory entries. Or think of what happens when entries from a remote site arrive to be synchronized into the directory. If the importing server sends an update for each entry, the site would be swamped with messages between the servers. Accumulating the entries and sending them together at one time is a sensible compromise.

Regardless of the normal intra-site replication process, each server conducts a full backup replication at a regular interval to ensure that its directory is totally consistent with every other server in its site. The default interval is 6 hours, which is reasonable unless you are attempting to connect servers in a site using network capacity that is often saturated and wish to remove as much optional traffic as possible. An attribute called "Period-Rep-Sync-Times" is maintained in the directory for each naming context (see page 587). The attribute can only be edited using the administration program in raw mode and its content (168 hex digits) are somewhat obscure. Each bit corresponds to 1 fifteen minute period during the week. Setting a bit (digit) to "0" stops Exchange from starting backup replication at that hour, while setting a digit to "1" instructs Exchange to start backup replication at that time. If you use the administration program in raw mode to view the "Period-Rep-Sync-Times" attribute, and then select the editor button followed by the schedule option, you can use the normal schedule page.

Backup replication is designed to fill in the gaps in the directory, so the amount of actual updates that are generated should be reasonably small. Traffic is generated through the form of question and answer session that each server conducts with its peers. A separate update request is generated for each naming context. A response is created and sent back, and any updates are applied. The interaction continues until each of the five naming contexts is complete. The next server in the site is then selected and the question and answer session begins again. If a server is unavailable the DSA will move onto the next server, but if a server cannot be contacted within 35 minutes an error is written into the system's Application Event Log.

A backup replication cycle can generate a reasonable volume of traffic inside large sites. If each exchange between servers requires 20 Kb (each way), then a site such as the Americas site in the DIGITAL organization (64 servers) will generate:

(Number of Servers − 1) × Amount of data × (Number of servers)

or

$(64 − 1) \times 20\text{Kb} \times 64 = 80.64\text{MB}$

of traffic during a backup replication cycle. Sites based in LANs or on a high-capacity WAN probably won't notice this data flowing, but sites based on lower-capacity WAN connections may.

8.2.2   Inter site directory replication

Directory synchronization between sites is performed through a replication scheme similar to that used to distribute the contents of public folders. Unlike intra-site directory access, external servers receive read-only copies of directory objects. Changes to an object must always be applied at an object's home site.

Synchronization (or replication) between sites is accomplished through specially formatted mail messages. Following a schedule, the bridgehead server in each site sends request messages to adjacent bridgehead servers. The messages request the receiving bridgehead to generate a reply message containing directory changes that have occurred since the last sychronization cycle. The Directory Service (or DSA) generates a message containing change information and sends it back, via the bridgehead, to the DSA at the requesting site. The message only contains information about changes that have occurred to objects maintained by the site. In situations where transitive connections are made to sites, bridgehead servers ask adjacent servers for changes from downstream sites. This is the only instance where a site can provide change information for objects that it does not own.

When the message containing the change information is received by the DSA at the requesting site the changes are applied to the directory. Updates are then distributed from the bridgehead to the other servers in the site using the normal intra-site replication mechanism. The schedule for inter-site directory replication normally operates at much less frequent intervals than intra-site replication. It doesn't make sense for sites to request updates from each other every five minutes[2] as this would only lead to the network being clogged up with unnecessary replication traffic.

Inter-site replication uses a pull method based on request messages from bridgehead servers. Everything depends on an operational mail connector being available between the sites, one of the main reasons why the directory service in each site is allocated a mail address. In itself the DSA takes no great interest in the underlying details of how its messages are transported between sites. The assumption is made that because a mail connection is available it can be used to transport messages containing directory information from the DSA in one site to its counterpart on another. The MTA, in its turn, regards these messages as any other and does not allocate any great importance to them. If you look at MTA queues you are quite likely to see messages originated from the DSA—notification messages to say that a change has occurred, or data messages containing directory information to be applied to a directory on a remote site.

---

2.   Within the push model used for intra-site replication communication between servers only occurs every five minutes if changes exist.

Once a valid mail connection is available between sites you can configure a directory replication connector. Two approaches can be taken:

1. The connector can be configured on each site. In this case all you need is the ability to send messages to the remote site, This option is very useful when the systems in the remote site are not part of the same Windows NT domain and no trust relationship exists between your domain and the remote domain. The disadvantage is that a certain degree of co-operation and synchronization must take place between the system administrators in the two sites before directory replication works.

2. The connector can be configured in a single operation from either site. This option is only possible within the same domain or when trust relationships exist within the two domains. In addition, the account being used for configuration must possess administrative permissions for the remote site.

Figure 8.7
*Configuring a
directory
replication
connector*

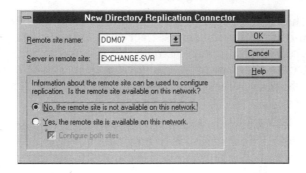

Figure 8.7 illustrates a directory replication connector being configured. In this instance we have elected to configure each site separately.

8.2.3 Naming contexts

As we've seen earlier in this chapter, the Exchange directory is organized in a hierarchical structure similar to an X.500 schema. A number of naming contexts are described within the hierarchy as listed in Table 8.1. Exchange V5.x supports five contexts whereas Exchange V4.0 used four (address book views were added in V5.0). Directory modifications always take place within a specific context, and separate notifications and requests are generated for each context.

For example, if you generate a new address book view and add a new mailbox to a server, two different contexts have been changed. The DSA will therefore generate two separate notifications to update the other directories in the site.

Table 8.1   *Directory Naming Contexts*

Naming Context	RDN in Directory
Organization	/O=Digital Equipment Corporation
Site	/O=Digital Equipment Corporation/OU=Dublin
Schema	/O=Digital Equipment Corporation/OU=Dublin/ CN=Microsoft DMD
Configuration	/O=Digital Equipment Corporation/OU=Dublin/ Cn=Configuration
Address Book Views	/O=Digital Equipment Corporation/ OU=_ABViews_

8.2.4   How directory changes are tracked

Exchange uses USN (Unique Sequence Numbers) or change number to monitor replication status. Every server maintains its own USN list and allocates every change it makes in its directory a different USN. Each object in the directory holds a number of different USNs, depending on its source and its current replication status. These USNs are maintained as attributes for the object and are:

- **USN-Changed:** The last USN change number allocated to the object. This attribute is automatically updated by the local DSA when a change is applied, even if the change was generated on a remote site.

- **USN-Created:** The USN allocated when the object was created.

- **USN-Source:** The value of the USN-Changed attribute on the server where the object was last changed.

USNs start at 1, representing the first change made to the directory during a server's lifetime, and go up to a maximum value of 2,147,483,647. There is no way to query the directory directly to discover the value of the last or next USN. Some insight can be gained by amending an object and then checking its USN-Changed attribute, as explained below. However, determining what might be the next USN through a process of examination is largely guesswork, as other processes might be busily incrementing the USN while you look at directory objects.

In addition to USNs, an Object-Version attribute is maintained for each object. When an object is first created the value of the attribute is set to 1. Whenever a change is made afterwards the DSA increments the attribute by 1. The Object-Version provides the primary checking mechanism for the DSA to discover whether an object has been changed in two places at the same time to cause a replication conflict. If an incoming update for an object holds the same value for the Object-Version attribute but has a different DSA-Signature then the DSA assumes that the object has been updated by two servers at the same time. Because servers batch updates before transmission to other servers within a site it is quite easy to visualize a situation where a mailbox or custom recipient is updated on two servers within a short period of time, which would lead to a replication conflict. When a conflict occurs, the DSA checks the time signature for the change (maintained in the When-Changed attribute), and the latest update discovered is accepted.

Figure 8.8
Viewing the DSA-Signature for an object

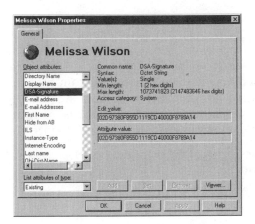

Each server is allocated a signature for its directory, referred to as the Invocation-Id. Whenever an object is updated in the directory the server's Invocation-Id is written into the object's DSA-Signature attribute. This signature or stamp is used to identify the server that last changed an object. Attributes like Invocation-Id or DSA-Signature are not immediately obvious because there is no reason for the user interface of the administration program to reveal them. After all, what interest would a human being have in the change numbers and signatures used to track inter-server communication? The DSA-Signature is especially obtuse, as is obvious from Figure 8.8.

The administration program must be run in raw mode if you want to see the Invocation-Id, DSA-Signature or USN information. It is interesting to look at the USN attributes to see how they change as an object is replicated within the organization. For example, let's assume you create a new object in the directory. When this happens, the directory on the home server applies its own DSA-signature to the object and generates a new USN. The same USN is placed into the USN-Changed, USN-Created, and USN-Source fields.

Figure 8.9 *The
USN-Changed
attribute on the
server where an
object is created*

Figure 8.9 *The
USN-Changed
attribute on the
server where an
object is created*

Figure 8.9 shows what the value of the USN-Changed attribute for a newly created object, in this case, a custom recipient. When the object is replicated to another server in the site the USN-Source attribute remains the same, but a different value is given to the USN-Changed and USN-Created attributes, as shown in Figure 8.10.

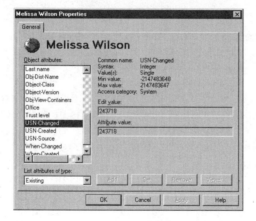

Figure 8.10 *The
USN-Changed
attribute on
another server
in the same site,
after replication
has occurred*

If you check the DSA-Signature on the object on another server in the site you'll see that the attribute retains the same value as it received when the object was first created on its home server. This is because the object was last modified on its home server. If the object is modified on another server its DSA-Signature is inserted and replicated out along with the changed data. The USN-Changed attribute is also updated, let's say from 243718 (the value shown in Figure 8.10) to 243750 and the new USN is sent out with the replicated data. When the update arrives on the home server it updates the DSA-Signature attribute with the signature from the server where the change occurred. The USN-Source attribute on the home server is then updated with the value of USN-Changed from the server where the change occurred. Together, the USN-Source and DSA-Signature attributes are enough to identify a particular change and the server where that change was made.

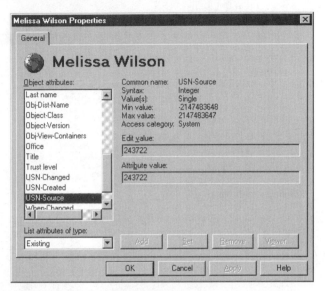

8.2.5 Replication Bridgeheads

The Directory Replication Bridgehead is a term describing the server within a site that takes charge of managing the synchronization process for a connector between that site and another. There can be multiple replication bridgeheads active in a site, one for each operational site that we need to connect to. However, a site cannot have two replication bridgeheads configured for any other particular site. This is logical—each site has a directory, and if multiple replication connects were made between one site and another there would be clear potential for synchronized chaos occurring within the directory. Preventing chaos or inconsistency within a distributed enterprise-wide directory is important because you want to encourage users to believe that the directory represents a definitive statement of user mail addresses for the organization. If erroneous or duplicated entries are registered users will lose faith in the directory, which is bad. Even worse, errors in the directory will rapidly lead to messages not being delivered.

Figure 8.12 illustrates the general properties for a directory replication connector. The local bridgehead server for the site is the DBO-EXCHANGEIST server, whereas the bridgehead on the remote site is the TCHOUP1 server. Directory replication is accomplished through a request process. Bridgehead servers generate request messages to the remote sites that they service rather than pushing or force-feeding changes in directory information to remote sites. Thus, the DBO-EXCHANGEIST server will issue requests to TCHOUP1 whenever it wants to be updated about the directory entries managed in the site where TCHOUP1 is located.

Figure 8.12
*Directory
Replication
Connector*

When a directory has changes (additions, deletions, or updates to existing entries) notification messages are generated and sent to all the other servers within a site. Remote sites do not receive updates until they issue update requests. USNs, explained earlier in this chapter, are used to track the status of directory updates between servers. Servers keep track of the USNs on other servers and the messages contain a note of the last USN known by the requesting server. In effect, the requesting server is saying "here's what I know you had, give me any changes since this USN". For example, if the current USN in the London site is 182754, and the New York site sends a request message noting that the last USN it knew of from London was 180031, then the update message sent back from London to New York will contain details of all changes corresponding to USNs 180032 through 182754. This is a process similar to public folder backfill.

Replication is performed on an object basis. In other words, if any part of a directory entry (configuration information, mailbox, custom recipient, or distribution list) is changed, complete details of that object are replicated across whatever directory connectors are available. It is not possible, with today's directory, to replicate at the field level. Distribution lists are a special case. In most cases, the changes made to distribution lists only affect one or two entries, so the change (add or delete a mailbox to a list) are made at mailbox level as well as the distribution list object.

8.2.6   Understanding the replication schedule

Changes and new directory entries are normally replicated every three hours, unless overruled by the schedule property page for a directory replicator. Updating remote sites every three hours may not be satisfactory in the early stages of an Exchange implementation where the directory is likely to be in a state of flux as mailboxes and custom recipients are added at frequent intervals. Later on, when the system has stabilized, updates every three hours (or at even longer intervals) are more acceptable because there won't be so much traffic.

Figure 8.13
Directory
Replication
Schedule

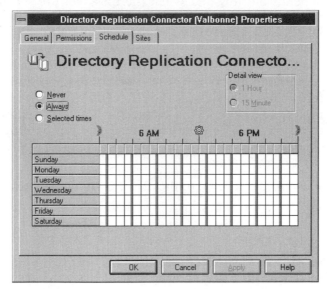

A replication schedule can be set at two levels of detail: 1 hour and 15 minutes. Apart from the obvious ability to determine exactly when replication occurs an important difference exists between the two views. If you select a particular hour for replication, as used in Figure 8.13, replication messages will be generated every 15 minutes during the hour long slot (4 times during the hour). In most cases, it is sufficient to replicate once during each selected hour, especially if network resources are scarce, so it's better to opt for the 15 minute view and decide exactly when replication messages will be created. Figure 8.13 is an example of the worst possible replication schedule for a message based system, like Exchange. "Always" means that changes are replicated according to the default interval for the directory, normally every 15 minutes. Take care to review every directory replication connector from time to time to check that its replication schedule is set at appropriate times.

You should also remember that the directory replication schedule is a property that only applies to the connector it is configured for. Take the example of the organization with sites in Dublin, Belfast, and London that we discussed earlier. Directory replication occurs every three hours between Dublin and Belfast, and every three hours between Belfast and London. It doesn't follow that changes made in Dublin will turn up in London three hours afterwards, courtesy of the transitive connection through Belfast.

Replication is performed through messages, so everything really depends on how and when the messages are sent between each site that lies along the path. When a change is made or new object added in Dublin no action is taken to provide details until a remote site requests change information. The bridgehead server in Belfast generates change requests according to its replication schedule, and Dublin responds to the change request with a message containing the relevant information after the DSA in Dublin has received and processed the request. The messaging connector between Belfast and Dublin may operate on a scheduled basis that may not be synchronized with the change requests, so delays start to creep into the process. Let's see what might happen:

- A change is made to the directory in Dublin at 1:00 p.m.

- The replication schedule in Belfast generates change requests for Dublin at 1:30 p.m. and places the messages on the MTA queue for Dublin.

- An X.400 connector is used to link Belfast and Dublin on a scheduled basis, and messages are sent every 30 minutes. The connector is activated at 1:45 p.m. and the request message is sent to Dublin.

- The DSA in the Dublin site receives the change request at 1:47 p.m. Details of all the changes that have occurred in the Dublin directory since the last time Belfast requested an update are packaged together into a message and sent to the DSA in Belfast at 1:48 p.m. The message is placed on the MTA queue for Belfast.

- The message is eventually sent to Belfast at 2:00 p.m. and is received by the DSA, which unpacks details of all the changes and applies them to the directory. Changes are finally available to users in the Belfast site at 2:02 p.m.

The directories in Belfast and Dublin are now synchronized. However, the change made in Dublin has not yet appeared in the London directory. A separate set of request messages must be sent by the DSA in London to the DSA in Dublin to force the updates. If messages are routed from London to Belfast and then to Dublin it follows that extra time is required to get the messages from DSA to DSA and back. If the replication schedule in London generated the change requests at 2:00 p.m. and scheduled X.400 connectors were used from London to Belfast and then Belfast to Dublin, the change made at 1:00 p.m. in Dublin might not get to London before 2:30 p.m. In a distributed organization with transitive connections the opportunity clearly exists for long delays between updates being made and applied.

If required, you can force directory replication to occur, but only on a server by server basis. Forced updates are desirable in situations where you have applied many different updates to the directory and now want to have this information distributed throughout the organization. The "Update Now" command button on the General property page for the Directory Service object sets off the process of forced directory updates. As directory propagation only happens one step at a time you may need to initiate several update processes, beginning at the bridgehead server furthest from the server you want to be updated. Think of this process as "pulling" the updated directory information one step at a time, from server to server, through the organization until you reach the point you want the information to reach. The process isn't particularly graceful and it's easy to miss something along the way, so hopefully Microsoft will come up with a better way to start a forced directory update from every site in the organization, perhaps through the equivalent of an "all points bulletin" message sent to all bridgehead servers requesting an immediate update in reply.

8.2.7 Transitive connections

Directory information never propagates more than one "hop" (link between two servers) at a time. The connector can be direct, or transitive. In other words, directory replication is possible when two sites are linked by a direct site connector, or when two sites are linked indirectly, with another site in between. Take the example of three sites, Dublin, Belfast, and London. Dublin and Belfast are linked with a direct site connector, and Belfast and London are linked with an X.400 site connector. Dublin and London have no direct connection, but the intermediate link established via Belfast is enough to enable directory replication to proceed. In this instance the messages containing directory information are routed in two "hops"; from Dublin to Belfast and hence to London, and vice versa in the other direction. The important point to understand is that as long as a path exists for messages to travel along, that same path can be used for directory replication.

Transitive directory replication is configured automatically by the Knowledge Consistency Checker (KCC). Basically, the KCC process makes a list of all the directly connected sites, and then looks in the replicas of those sites for their replication connectors. A merge is then performed of all the known sites connected throughout the organization, and updates are made to the appropriate replication connectors. Finally, stub objects for any newly-discovered sites are created in the directory.

Figure 8.14 *A common site layout based on a low-bandwidth network*

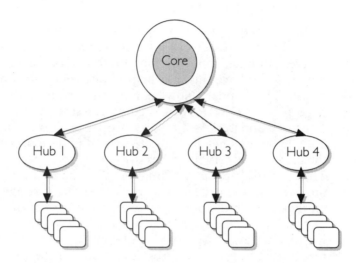

Figure 8.14 illustrates a common design problem faced outside North America where network resources are often hard to come by. This design features a core site, often located at corporate headquarters, connected to four hub sites, each of which links a number of much smaller sites. These sites might each contain one or two servers. Reasonable bandwidth (128Kbps or greater) is usually available between the core and the four hubs, but the links to the smaller sites is often restricted and perhaps Exchange is going to be only one of many applications expected to share the same link. There is no prospective of connecting the servers together to form large sites. Either sufficient bandwidth is unavailable, very expensive, or the company sees no good justification in a major upgrade of an existing network "just for email".

Directory replication connectors are established between the core and the four hub sites. Each hub maintains directory replication connectors in turn to all of its subservient sites. Everything works, but the volume of replication traffic will become more and more pressing as the number of sites increase. A number of considerations now come into play, being dependent to a certain degree on the others.

■ The amount of traffic generated during a synchronization cycle.

- The number of synchronization cycles each day.
- The length of time it takes to synchronize the entire organization.

The number of messages generated by a bridgehead server during each synchronization cycle depends on the number of sites retrieved through the connector. The bridgehead sends two messages to each site (remember, only a site can provide up to date information about the objects it owns). One message requests an update for configuration data (for example, the connectors), the other requests updates for recipients (mailbox, custom, or distribution lists) in the site. A final message requesting address book view information is also sent. The messages are quite small (2K), but the sheer number of messages is what we need to be concerned about. Take the example of the site design illustrated in Figure 8.14. Each hub site is connected to the Core, and each of the four hubs supports eight downstream sites. The bridgehead in each downstream site therefore generates 73 requests during each synchronization cycle. The 73 messages are calculated as follows:

$(2 \times 31$ other downstream sites$) + (2 \times 4$ hub sites$) +$
$(2 \times 1$ core site$) + 1($address book views$)$

$= 73$

The bridgehead server in each site sends the messages to the site it is connected to. Thus, each downstream satellite site sends all its messages to its hub site, which then processes the requests on behalf of itself and its downstream sites. While the messages are not very big and the MTA can process them very quickly, the fact remains that the core site in this organization must process 2,701 request messages for each synchronization cycle (each site in the organization generates 73 messages, and there are $32 + 4 + 1 = 37$ sites).

The bridgehead server in each site checks incoming update requests and generates responses in return. Each request generates a response. If no changes are unnecessary the response message is very small, but traffic is still generated. If changes exist, the details for the relevant objects are collected together and sent in a single message. The contents in an update message may be compressed, but only if the size of the message is greater than 50Kb (there is little point in wasting CPU cycles if the messages are smaller). Generally, the compression ratio is 5:1. Incoming messages are decompressed by the bridgehead server before the updated objects are passed to the DSA. Compression is not used for intra-site replication.

The number of messages and the volume of data that must pass across the network grows in line with the number of sites in an organization. This is one of the reasons by Microsoft recommends that you should deploy as few sites as possible. However, if adequate network resources aren't available the number of sites grows quickly as single-server sites are implemented. A number of examples exist where over 200 sites have been deployed in hub and spoke networks. Exchange V4.0 and V5.0 (prior to SP1) supported a maximum of 212 sites in an organization, but you can now deploy over 1,000, if you have the network and the necessary hardware to power such an organization. The largest Exchange organizations that I know of in production today have around 300 sites.

Organizations with hundreds of sites must pay careful attention to the number of directory replication cycle each day. Usually one or two replication cycles per day are often enough to distribute amendments, but transitive connections can lengthen the time required to get an update from one side of the organization to the other. Care must also be taken to ensure that replication traffic occurs outside peak working hours, as otherwise the request and response messages may interfere with the flow of interpersonal mail. These are points often overlooked during the design and pilot phases of an implementation as the problem only becomes apparent after a lot of sites have been deployed. The exact threshold when the problem is evident differs from organization to organization and is directly related to the capabilities of the underlying network. For more information on how to control the replication traffic within an Exchange network, see the Microsoft white paper "Understanding and Controlling Background Traffic in Microsoft Exchange Server 5.*x*". The paper is available on TechNet.

Finally, designs based on low-bandwidth hub and spoke networks also need to consider the impact of public folder replication messages. In Exchange, replicated data doesn't just come from one source. It would be frustrating to tune the directory replication cycle only to discover that the network hubs are still being swamped by messages generated through excessive public folder replication.

8.2.8   Limiting the data that's replicated

The DS Site Configuration object allows you to manipulate the set of attributes that are replicated to other sites for each directory entry. The same screen (Figure 8.15) allows you to determine the attributes which are available to anonymous and authenticated LDAP queries.

Normally there's no reason to be concerned about the number of attributes that are replicated as the default set is sensible. Also, blank attributes are not replicated and as we've already discussed, replication data is compressed when large amounts of entries are sent between bridgehead servers.

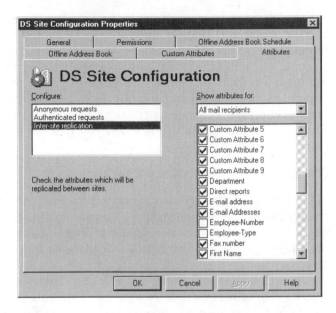

Figure 8.15
Configuring
attributes for
inter-site
replication

You only need to be concerned if one of the following conditions exist:

1.   Some of the attributes contain sensitive information that you don't want to share with other sites. For example, the custom attributes might be used to store department or site-specific information.

2.   For whatever reason, changes are made to directory entries on a very frequent basis and you want to reduce the amount of data that needs to be replicated. Because replication occurs on an object basis rather than at field level, objects will be replicated even if one of the "restricted" attributes is changed. This is because the DRA only knows that something about the object has changed and that it must therefore replicate the changes to other sites.

3.   The network is struggling to keep up with demand and all possible steps must be taken to reduce load.

Eliminating attributes is a final-gasp tuning step. Getting the replication frequency right is far more important.

8.2.9   Replication at start-up

Restarting the Directory Service on a bridgehead server forces a complete synchronization cycle to begin. This is understandable because it means that the directory has an opportunity to be updated with changes that have occurred while the Directory Service on the bridge-head was inactive. In a similar way the Information Store broadcasts requests for public folder updates when it is restarted. However, in situations where the these services are regularly stopped to take off-line backups, it is easy to generate unwanted replication cycles. It must be said that given the wide choice of backup products that support on-line backup for Exchange, there is no good reason to take an off-line backup. The sole exception is when you prepare to upgrade software on the server[3].

8.2.10 The Knowledge Consistency Checker

With the possibility that servers, sites, and connectors constantly change within an organization it's easy to imagine how Exchange might lose track of some details within the organization's structure. If such a thing happened, problems would inevitably occur when routing directory updates from site to site. To avoid this problem Exchange uses a component called the Knowledge Consistency Checker (KCC). The KCC usually runs as a background thread on a server every three hours, but it can also be activated directly through the general property page of the Directory Service object for a server. The KCC is often activated in this way to review the hierarchy after a directory replication connector is removed.

To give you a flavor of what the KCC does, let's look at some of the processing that's performed when the KCC is invoked:

- The KCC connects to the local directory.

- The names of all servers in the local site are retrieved and checked.

- A connection is made to the Directory Service on another server and the list of servers in the local site is retrieved there. In general, the KCC uses an alphabetic order to determine which server it should connect to. If the selected server is not available (for instance, it is down for maintenance), the KCC will select the next server in alphabetical order and attempt to bind to it.

- The two lists are checked to make sure that they match. In other words, that the organizational information shared by servers in the same site is identical. If the data does not match the KCC proceeds to synchronize the configuration data for the site between

---

3.   There are a number of registry parameters that prevent directory and public folder replication cycles when the services start. Preventing replication may cause inconsistencies in the directory and public folder hierarchy. In any case, stopping replication is only necessary in situations where Exchange is operated without any public folders at all. For these reasons the registry values are not detailed here. Contact Microsoft support for further information. The parameters are only valid for Exchange V4.0 SP5, Exchange V5.0 SP2, and Exchange V5.5 SP1 onwards.

the servers until the data matches. The process is repeated with the other servers in the site.

- After the KCC is sure that all the servers in the same site contain the same organizational data, the directory on the local server is checked and a list of all of the known naming contexts is established.

- Each naming context in the list is checked to establish whether links exist to exchange directory information with the context. Any missing links are fixed.

- The local directory replication container is searched to build a list of directory replication connectors. Each connector is checked to verify that there is a matching directory replication connector in the remote site. This information should be replicated to the local site along with other configuration data. If a local copy is found, the list of inbound sites for the connector is updated to match the remote connector's outbound sites.

- The list of connectors is then reviewed to ensure that the right sites are replicated across each connector. Any inconsistencies (missing or obsolete data) are fixed. Checks are also performed to ensure that any information from Intersite replicas that exists on the local server has been replicated to all other servers in the site.

In essence, the KCC has a simple role to play in the life of the Exchange directory in that it makes sense of all the configuration data exchanged between sites to determine what links have been set up between the different sites. Determining the site connection topology prevents multiple directory replication bridgeheads being created between two sites, avoiding the problems discussed above. The KCC checks configuration information when it is first supplied (when a site is joined to an organization), and continues to review configuration information as it is replicated between sites at regular intervals. If new sites are discovered from replicated data the KCC attempts to figure out how the sites are connected into the organization and whether other sites are connected in via the newly discovered sites. Transitive directory replication, or propagation across multiple links, is enabled through knowledge of these indirectly connected sites.

New sites are inserted into the organizational hierarchy when directory replication connectors are created. At this stage the new site contacts the site that it is connected to and sends some initial information—the site name and some skeletal configuration data. Immediately after a new site is inserted into the hierarchy its containers appear to be empty, but fairly soon afterwards their contents will be populated via normal directory replication.

The process of populating directory information from containers in newly connected sites is known as backfill. If containers for a new site are visible but their contents are not available three hours afterwards the site first appears (the actual delay depends on the directory replication schedule) it's a good indication that problems exist in the mail connection between the two sites.

For example, compare the two site views extracted from the administration program in Figure 8.16. The view of the Belfast site is complete, because we can see the different recipient containers within the Belfast configuration. However, the view of the Valbonne site is incomplete because only the configuration container can be seen. In this instance backfill has not occurred and we need to check whether the connector between the two sites is operational.

Figure 8.16
Successful directory replication with Belfast, but not with Valbonne!

8.2.11   Successful directory replication

Putting everything together we can see that successful directory replication across multiple sites depends on a number of steps:

1.   Synchronization must be active between all servers within a site. This implies that the nominated bridgehead server in each site must know all the servers within its own site. Fortunately the synchronization between the bridgehead server and its peers within a site is totally automatic and requires no human intervention.

2.   Sites must be able to communicate together. In other words, a site connector (direct, X.400, or RAS) must be configured and operational to allow configuration data to be exchanged between the different sites.

3.   The KCC in each site must be able to create the site and configuration containers for other sites to form an accurate picture of the complete replication environment.

4.   Once the configuration containers have been established normal directory replication can proceed to request data from bridgehead replication connectors. The data is populated into the recipient containers for each site. Remember that there can be several recipient containers active for each site. Replication will ensure that the appropriate recipient information is placed into the various recipient containers.

Once replication is operating smoothly it is not a good idea to make changes that would force a large amount of data to be replicated within the organization. For example, it's not a good idea to decide on a whim to reassign connectors from one site to another and affect the flow of replicated information to transitive sites. You will certainly be able to delete the relevant connectors and recreate them wherever you wish, but, depending on the number of sites, the size of the directory, and the available network resources, it may take up to a week to replicate the new structure to all sites again. During that time users will be unable to "see" recipients in some sites.

It is best to spend the necessary time to consider how directory information will flow across replication connectors in the early stages of a deployment and make any required adjustments then. As the directory grows and the number of sites increase the effect of any change intensifies.

8.2.12   Tombstones

Tombstone entries are used to mark objects in the directory after they have been deleted. An object is never removed immediately. Like messages and other items from mailboxes and public folders that are kept in the deleted items cache, deleted objects are soft-deleted by setting its "IsDeleted" property to "True", and is hidden from view (address book or administration program). In addition, a tombstone property composed of the date and time that the deletion occurred is added to the object. The fact that the object is updated in the directory forces the change to be replicated out to other servers, so that eventually all servers in an organization will be informed that the object has been deleted.

In large or distributed organizations, or where sites connect intermittently over dial-in connections, replication of a changed object might take several days, or even longer. Tombstones are designed to allow deleted items to be purged completely from an organization, even if extended replication intervals are in use.

Every 12 hours, a background thread (known as the "garbage collector") executes within DSAMAIN.EXE to check for deleted objects whose tombstones have expired. This interval can be changed through the Garbage Collection Interval property on the DS Site Configuration object (Figure 8.17). The garbage collector examines objects with the "IsDeleted" flag set to decide whether or not the tombstone has expired and the object should be permanently removed from the directory. A tombstone expires when its timestamp is older than the current date and time minus the tombstone lifetime defined for the site (normally 30 days). The tombstone lifetime is defined as a property of the DS Site

Configuration object. Assuming the tombstone lifetime is 30 days, the garbage collector will remove any object that was first deleted 30 days ago. It's not a good idea to reduce the tombstone lifetime from 30 days unless you are absolutely sure that all directory replication messages will reach every server in an organization within that time. Given the nature of messaging systems such a guarantee is not always possible, so it's best to play safe and use the default lifetime.

Figure 8.17
Viewing the
tombstone
lifetime and
garbage
collection
interval via the
DS Site
Configuration
object

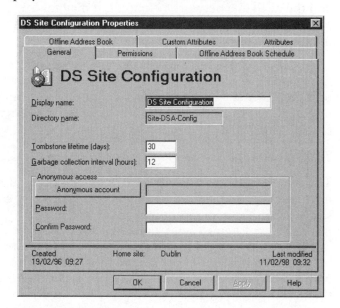

Orphaned objects are created when updates for deleted objects do not reach some sites before the tombstone lifetime expires. In effect, the sites never discover that an object has been deleted in its home site and continue to treat it as before. Once the object is permanently removed in the home site the only writeable copy of the object has been removed from the organization. All of the copies in the directories in the other sites are read-only, so they cannot be deleted there. There are usually two reasons why deleted objects turn into orphans. First, extended replication intervals or breaks in replication traffic might not distribute object deletes before a tombstone expires. Or, messages containing object deletes might be removed from a server somewhere along the route between the server where the delete occurred and another server. For example, the MTACHECK utility might be run with the /RD switch (remove all directory replication messages) to help clear a backlogged MTA queue. No backfill mechanism exists to ensure that a deleted object is removed everywhere, so don't rush to remove replication messages from an MTA queue unless you are certain that you know what you're doing.

Orphaned objects often pass unnoticed, especially those for custom recipients or mailboxes. It is more common to discover an orphaned object for something like a connector. If an orphan is discovered it can be traced back to its original home by viewing the Obj-Dist-Name attribute in its raw properties, as this will reveal the full path to the object within the directory. The orphans are read-only, so before the orphan can be removed a writeable copy must be recreated in the original home site. The new object must be given the same Obj-Dist-Name as the original, and you then need to alter the object's raw properties to increase its Object-Version attribute to a value higher than any other copy held elsewhere in the organization. The recreated object can then be deleted and normal replication should occur to remove all of the copies (the orphans) throughout the organization. For further information, see the section on how directory changes are tracked earlier in this chapter (page 588).

8.2.13 The need for synchronization

Synchronization with directory information other mail systems raises a very important question. What is your strategy for an organization-wide directory?

If you are moving to a homogeneous implementation of Exchange throughout the enterprise then the answer is easy. In these situations the strategy for directory synchronization should be based around the Exchange directory. But if you foresee a heterogeneous messaging environment composed of multiple e-mail systems you also have the option to select a common directory such as X.500. The number of directory synchronization tools available from third parties will inevitably increase as the number of Exchange installations climb in the corporate world. Synchronization gets more and more important as the size of the user community increases and the number of mail systems involved with the synchronization process grows. Corporate messaging environments usually support many thousands of users and are prone to the operation of many different mail systems, hence the requirement for synchronization.

8.2.14 Synchronization with other Exchange organizations

Exchange does not currently support automated directory replication between different organizations. This would be useful in an environment where a corporation is not able to form an Exchange organization for one reason or another but still wishes to share directory information. Microsoft is aware of the issue and an Exchange-to-Exchange inter-organization directory replication connector is included in the Exchange V5.5 Resource Kit. The code for the connector has been available on a case by case basis for some time, and it has had a chance to settle down in operational environments.

If you're not happy to use a tool from the Resource Kit, there's always a manual workaround to the problem. Exchange offers a feature to export and import directory entries in the form of CSV (comma separated value) data files. Thus it is possible for organizations to export their directory to a file and arrange to swap their exported data with other organizations. Addresses in exported files are treated as custom X.400 or SMTP recipients by the importing organization, so an appropriate connector will also be required to send messages to the recipients after they've been imported. It is convenient to create a new recipients container for imported directory information, clearly separating custom recipients from native Exchange addresses (mailboxes and distribution lists). If you import data from multiple sources you may like to have separate recipients containers for each source. For example, an organization that imports data from PROFS and Internet (sendmail) systems might have a set of containers named as follows:

- Recipients (to hold native Exchange addresses)

- PROFS Recipients

- Internet Recipients

Apart from anything else, it is convenient for users to be able to select and browse through a specific recipients container if they know that the person they wish to send mail to uses a certain mail system. The extra recipients containers are not created on each server and every site. They are only required on the server used to import directory information from the foreign mail systems.

8.2.15 Synchronization with foreign directories through DXA

Synchronization is also possible with non-Exchange sources through a Windows NT service called the Directory Synchronization Agent (DXA). The service operates in conjunction with the DXA database (XDIR.EDB), built using the same database engine as the information and directory stores. The DXA database is used to track changes that have been made in the Exchange directory between the times when synchronization occurs with foreign directory sources. The database also maintains records of the synchronization operations it has recently performed. Unlike the Information or Directory Stores, no transaction logs are maintained for XDIR.EDB. If the database is lost or corrupted it must be rebuilt from scratch.

The protocol used by DXA is the well tried and tested mechanism implemented by Microsoft Mail V3.2 directory synchronization. This allows any system that performs directory synchronization with Microsoft Mail to also support Exchange server.

Microsoft Mail post offices synchronize the contents of their Global Address List (GAL) through a relatively complex series of events which, in outline:

- Generates directory information from individual post offices
- Collects the directory information from the post offices to a central directory synchronizer
- Merges the directory information into a new GAL
- Distributes the new GAL to the different post offices

Within this scheme Microsoft Mail post offices act as either a DirSync Server or a DirSync Requestor. The server acts as the central directory synchronizer while the requestors provide directory information and accept the merged GAL back afterwards. Through the DXA Exchange is able to assume either role, but an individual server cannot be configured to act in both roles.

When the Exchange DXA assumes the role of the DirSync Server all the Microsoft Mail post offices must be reconfigured to identify the Exchange MS-Mail Connector post office as the DirSync Server. Only one DXA Server can be configured per site, and it takes charge of propagating the addresses for the MS-Mail users (attached to the post offices it synchronizes) to other Exchange sites via normal directory replication.

When DXA acts as a DirSync Requestor it means that DXA will receive copies of the MS-Mail GAL from another DirSync Server, and then propagate the addresses in the GAL to other Exchange sites. Multiple DirSync Requestors can be active within a site, but this configuration would only be used if there were multiple available sources of MS-Mail address information. For example, if there were two or more separate MS-Mail networks. In this case you could create a separate DirSync Requester to receive the GAL from the DirSync Server acting in each MS-Mail network.

8.2.16 Synchronization with foreign mail directories using load files

As we've seen, automatic synchronization for Exchange directories is seamless within an Exchange organization, and relatively painless for Microsoft Mail directories or systems that supports the Microsoft Mail directory synchronization methodology. Outside of these scenarios the picture isn't so clear and the work required to achieve high fidelity within a synchronized directory is very demanding. In this context, a high-fidelity directory means one that has a low incidence rate of invalid directory entries introduced as a result of synchronization operations. Large corporate directories, those with over 20,000 entries, can expect to have an invalid entry rate of between 2% and 4% at any time, chiefly due to the inevitable number of changes that occur within large corporate entities all the time. Staff turnover and transfers, especially in international organizations, is normally the reason for the largest number of invalid entries. The challenge is to reduce the rate down as low as possible so that the user community is willing to depend on the directory.

Unfortunately the mechanisms available to achieve directory synchronization are limited. If you can't go along the Microsoft Mail/DXA route you're limited to using the administration program to load import files containing directory data. The general approach taken in these instances normally includes:

1.   Establish a separate container within the directory to hold the imported entries. All the imported entries become custom recipients within the Exchange directory. It is generally unwise to mix different recipient types within the same directory container whenever synchronization is required. Exchange allows you to create a clear differentiation between recipient types within the directory, and you should use this facility.

2.   Extract an export file from all the mail systems that need to be synchronized with Exchange. The format of the import file is defined by Exchange, and the best way to discover what that format should be is to export the entries for some custom recipients from the Exchange directory. You don't need to complete all fields. In general, minimize the number of fields that you synchronize to those that are really essential.

3.   Import the export file from the source foreign mail systems into Exchange. The administration program can be used for this purpose. You can either use the Tools.Directory Import option through the normal GUI (Figure 8.18) or run the administration program in batch mode to import the contents of the file. See the sidebar for more information on how to use the administration program as a directory import/export command line utility. Before you attempt any batch runs, make sure that any files you create can be processed using the GUI. This simple step eliminates a lot of common formatting problems with files generated from other messaging systems.

4.   Create an export file from Exchange to provide to the other mail systems. There's no real point in doing one-way directory synchronization. Exchange will create an export file for you, but you'll probably need to perform some text manipu-

lation on its contents to prepare it for the other mail systems. PERL, a text-manipulation language originally for UNIX and now available for Windows NT, is often used for this purpose. It is highly unlikely that the other mail systems will understand the syntax and format of the export files generated by Exchange!

5. Import the duly amended directory information from Exchange into the directory of the other mail systems. The exact mechanism to perform these operations is highly specific to the individual mail system and cannot be described here. Make sure that the import procedure ignores any directory information that originated from the target mail system, as otherwise you will end up with duplicate addresses in the directory.

The steps outlined above will accomplish a basic synchronization process. Three important decisions must be taken before you can achieve a more refined synchronization process.

Figure 8.18
Exporting some directory information

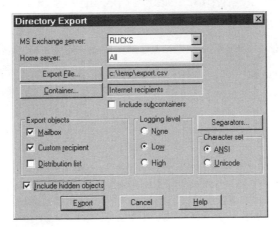

The first question is how the directory entries should be inserted into Exchange. There is no problem whatsoever inserting a new directory entry. The question is what to do with that entry thereafter. The easiest approach is to delete all entries relating to a specific mail system from Exchange before importing any data. This method avoids the need to worry about making amendments to directory entries that are already in the directory, but it's rather crude and can take longer to process. There are usually relatively few amendments to perform when compared against the requirement to first delete one or two thousand entries followed by the recreation of the same (or more) entries. The directory database will also become a little less efficient with each series of delete/import operations, so you'll need to consider whether the directory should be compacted with the ESEUTIL utility from time to time. Executing amendments to the directory requires a lot more intelligence to be built into the synchronization process. It must be possible, for example, for the synchronization process to be able to first check for an entry before it either amends it with new data or inserts a brand new entry into the directory.

The second issue that must be decided is how often directory synchronization should occur. Generally speaking, during the early stages of an implementation, when it is quite likely that many changes are occurring in the directory as users migrate to Exchange, the need for frequent directory synchronization is more prevalent than when the messaging systems have stabilized (in terms of their user communities). The more frequently synchronization occurs the more up to date the directories (Exchange and the other messaging systems) will be, and the less Non-Delivery Notification messages will be generated to be sent to users (and promptly referred to the Help Desk). However, it may not be possible to perform directory synchronization very frequently (nightly, for instance) because of other operational requirements such as staff not being available to supervise the procedure.

Directory Import/Export command line interface

Export

```
ADMIN/E export-file /D=server /N /O=options
```

Import

```
ADMIN/I import-file /D=server /N /O=options
```

In both cases the options file creates a specific context for the import or export operation to proceed. For example, the container to operate against. The server indicates the name of the Exchange server that will either export or import the directory data. The /N switch indicates that you don't want to see a progress bar on-screen. The only mandatory switch is either /E or /I. Usually import or export operations are carried out on the server hosting the relevant directory information.

Most installations find that a weekly synchronization is sufficient, although it is a good idea to allow for special synchronization runs to occur, such as immediately after a workgroup is moved to Exchange. In all cases the procedure to migrate a user to Exchange should incorporate directory updates for both the source and Exchange directory. In terms of Exchange the old custom recipient entry should be removed and replaced with the mailbox entry. The directory for the source mail system should be updated, if possible, with an autoforward or redirect address to force messages sent to the "old" address to be sent on for eventual delivery to the new Exchange mailbox.

Within any typical Exchange organization a network of directory replication connectors distributes directory updates. Any plan for synchronization must consider how long it will take for the newly-synchronized updates to be dispatched to all sites within the organization, taking due note of the time delays that may occur due to replication schedules for sites downstream of major hubs (see the discussion about transitive directory connections earlier in the chapter. Ideally synchronization should be performed so that all sites in the organization are fully refreshed with up to date directory information within 6 hours of the new data being imported into the synchronization server. Large directory updates, those involving 20,000 entries or more, can generate a considerable amount of network traffic to fan out the updates to all sites, so make sure that synchronization occurs at a time when the network is not fully occupied with other (more important) work.

The final, but perhaps most strategic decision to take is whether Exchange or another directory should be the focal point for synchronization. I've already made the point that if you are going towards a homogeneous Exchange messaging environment the wisest decision is to base synchronization around the Exchange directory. On the other hand, if there is a continuing requirement to operate multiple systems then Exchange might not be such a good choice, primarily due to the lack of user-friendly or highly functional synchronization utilities (some might define the situation a little more harshly, and say "non-existent synchronization utilities.)

If you're in the latter situation it's probably best to spend some time looking at what's currently available on the market. Writing your own set of synchronization routines is guaranteed to be a time-consuming and expensive business. One project to create a set of bespoke routines to synchronize directory data from Novell GroupWise, Microsoft Mail, DIGITAL ALL-IN-1, and Exchange took over six months elapsed time to complete. The job could have been done a little quicker, but it would have had a number of rough edges that might have led to invalid addresses creeping into the directory. The resulting synchronization worked automatically with a great deal of success for over 50,000 entries, but it was expensive. Selecting an off-the-shelf package is always going to be cheaper and transfers problems to someone else. Dealing with changes in directory structures in new versions of any of the contributing messaging systems is one obvious example of a problem waiting to happen.

8.2.17 Understanding Directory Import/Export files

As noted earlier, Exchange supports simple text comma separated, or CSV files for directory import and export operations. CSV files use the comma character as a delimiter between each field in a record. The major value of using CSV files is that they can be easily generated and manipulated by many different systems. Each record occupies one line in the file, although the records are often wrapped when viewed in a text editor.

Figure 8.19
Header section for directory import/export file

```
Obj-Class,First Name,Last name,Display Name,Alias
Name,Directory Name,Primary Windows NT Account,Home-Server,
E-mail address,E-mail Addresses,Members,Obj-Container,Hide
from AB
```

Directory import/export files are divided into two parts. The first record in the file is the header (Figure 8.19) used to define the directory attributes that might be stated for each record thereafter. The attributes are stated in the order they will occur in the other records.

Note that the header does not have to state all of the attributes that can be held for directory entries. There is certainly a requirement to state enough of the attributes to create a reasonably complete entry in the directory, so some of the attributes, like the directory name and e-mail address, can be regarded as mandatory. All of the records following the header are deemed to contain directory information, a sample of which is shown in Figure 8.20. This record was obtained by exporting details of a recipients container from a server and editing the resulting CSV file to extract details of a custom recipient created using the GUI of the administration program.

Figure 8.20
Import entry for a custom recipient

```
Remote,Owen,Doyle,Owen Doyle,OwenD, OwenD,,,
SMTP:Owen.Doyle@IRFU.IE, MS:DIGITALEQU/EXCHANGEIS/
OwenD%X400:c=IE;a=eirmail400;p=digital;o=digital;s=Doyle;g=Ow
en;ou1=Exchange IST;%SMTP:Owen.Doyle@IRFU.IE,,Internet
recipients,
```

In addition to its cross-platform support, the CSV file format is understood and supported by many Windows applications, making it possible to use these applications to manipulate or clean up directory information before it is imported into the directory. It is not recommended to manually check files using any application before every import operation. If you find that the directory import files created by your synchronization process are flawed and need attention before they can be given to Exchange you should track down the reason for the problem and fix it. Using a tool like Excel (see Figure 8.21) to check directory information should really only occur when an unforeseen problem arises. The old adage that rubbish in results in rubbish out is especially true for directory information, and inaccurate directory entries are very irritating (and worse than useless) to users.

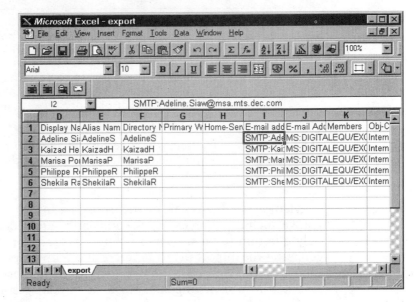

Figure 8.21
Using Excel to work with directory import information

Using a sample directory CSV file exported from Exchange is a good starting point, but you don't need to populate all the fields (or, more correctly, directory schema attributes) to create custom recipient entries for mail addresses from other systems. The fields in a header file for a typical import operation are described in Table 8.2.

Table 8.2   *Fields for a directory import file*

Header Field	Use
Obj-Class	Remote (for custom recipient), or Mailbox (for an Exchange recipient)
Mode	The default mode is Add, in which case the column is left blank. Other valid modes are Delete and Modify.
Directory Name	The internal RDN used by the directory to identify the recipient. If omitted the alias name will be used to create a directory name. Normal practice is to make the directory name the same as the alias (which is what Exchange does) or the display name.
Alias Name	The unique nickname or alias for the custom recipient. This is a mandatory value.

Table 8.2   *Fields for a directory import file (continued)*

Header Field	Use
Display Name	The display name shown to users in the GAL. This is a mandatory value because there's no point in adding an entry to the directory unless users are able to select it.
E-Mail Address	The mail address to use to route messages to. The e-mail address is prefixed with a known term (like SMTP) indicating the type of address. Naturally, this is also a mandatory value.
Obj-Container	The name of the recipients container to operate on (import/delete/modify). If omitted, the default recipients container is used.

Many more fields can be incorporated into the import file. Once you've included the really essential attributes (detailed above), the only question to be answered is how easy it is for the procedure that generates the import file to generate and output appropriate values for each attribute. Some attributes may not be available or cannot be generated if you're taking data from a human resources database or another messaging directory.

The CSV header therefore looks like this:

```
Obj-Class, Mode, Directory Name, Alias Name, Display Name,
E-Mail Address, Obj-Container
```

And a sample data line for a custom recipient with an SMTP mail address to be inserted into the "Internet Recipients" container is:

```
Remote,, Jim Smith, JimSmith-970601, Jim Smith,
SMTP:Jim.Smith@abc.com, Internet Recipients
```

It's best when unique aliases are created in the directory. If the import files are generated automatically by a program or other procedure it's easy enough to insert logic to generate a unique alias for each entry. In the example shown above the load date (970601 = 1st June 1997) is appended to the display name to create a unique value. Other algorithms may be more appropriate for your company.

Creating entries is the easiest task you have. The CSV header for delete operations is slightly more complicated:

```
Obj-Class, Mode, Directory Name, Alias Name, Obj-Container
```

If passed, the mode command must be stated in the second column. If this is not done the operation will fail. Events that occur during import or export operations are written into the system event log for object MSExchangeDSImp (import) or MSExchangeDSExp (export). For example, if the mode command wasn't in the second column event id 222 is reported. The start and finish of import operations are reported as event ids 31 and 32, while the start and finish of export operations are event ids 36 and 37.

The data lines look like this:

```
Remote, Delete, Jim Smith, JimSmith-970601, Internet Recipients
```

Modifications are accomplished with a similar header file, albeit with fields added for each attribute to be changed. The data lines contain values for each field to be changed or just a comma if the field is to be ignored. For example:

```
Obj-Class, Mode, Directory Name, Alias Name, Display Name, E-
Mail Address, Obj-Container
```

```
Remote, Modify, Jim Smith, JimSmith-970601, Jim (New) Smith,
SMTP:Jim.Smith@xyz.com, Internet Recipients
```

Commands to add, modify, or delete custom recipients can be combined together into a single file. The same header can be used, providing it contains the mode command in the second column. Combining all directory commands into a single file delivers an advantage in that the administration program must only be initialized once. It does make recovery a little more difficult if something goes wrong such as a system crash (unlikely, but possible over the lifetime of a system). In these cases it is easier if the various operations (adds, updates, and deletes) are spread across a set of files, one for each type of operation. Further information about the complete set of valid schema attributes as well as general advice on directory synchronization can be found in the Exchange migration guide, part of the product documentation set.

8.2.18 Batch synchronization procedures

Automating synchronization operations is clearly desirable. No one wants to be tied down to a set of manual procedures, so you should investigate how best to create a batch job to do all the work when the system is quiet (and system administrators asleep). Here's an example of a batch procedure in use within a real production environment:

```
REM Synch.Bat — Synchronize files from X.500 with Exchange
REM First copy the necessary files from the UNIX system
ECHO *** Preparing to synchronize ***
CHDIR C:\EXCHSRVR\SYNCH
DEL *.CSV
ECHO *** Copying commands to delete entries ***
```

```
COPY X:EX-DEL.CSV EX-DEL.CSV
ECHO *** Deleting old entries ***
ADMIN/I EX-DEL.CSV
ECHO *** Deletions finished ***
ECHO *** Copying commands to create new entries ***
COPY X:EX-NEW.CSV EX-NEW.CSV
ECHO *** Now processing modifications ***
ADMIN/I EX-NEW.CSV
ECHO *** New entries added to Exchange ***
ECHO *** Copying commands to modify entries ***
COPY X:EX-MOD.CSV EX-MOD.CSV
ADMIN/I EX-MOD.CSV
ECHO *** Modifications complete ***
ECHO *** Please check System Event Log ***
EXIT
```

This procedure assumes that drive X is connected before anything starts. The CSV files are generated from an external X.500 directory that serves as a common synchronization point for a number of different messaging systems. Using an X.500 directory is convenient, but it's not important. All that matters is to establish a repository for directory information that can be provided to Exchange. A similar procedure can be used to export information from Exchange before importing details of Exchange mailboxes into the common directory. The export procedure is much easier when all Exchange mailboxes are gathered together into a distinct container, isolated from the entries created by the import operations. If this is not the case then a certain amount of pre-processing will be necessary to eliminate data lines containing information about distribution lists and custom recipients before the export files can be processed by the common directory.

8.2.19 How long will directory synchronization procedures take?

Directory synchronization operations vary greatly. The factors influencing the time required to process import files include:

- The capability of the server where the import operations are being processed. The faster the processor, the faster the import operations will happen. High-end processors such as Alpha systems are good choices for directory import servers.

- The other workload that the server is handling during the import operation. Clearly the less work the server is doing, the less contention will occur with the import operation. This is the best reason to schedule directory imports for night-time when systems are normally at their quietest.

- The number of directory entries to process. The larger the amount, the longer the import will take. Restricting the amount of data to the entries that definitely need to be added, changed, or deleted is a good tactic to adopt. Never include entries that don't have to be processed. If necessary, do some pre-processing to eliminate any entries that shouldn't be included in the import.

- The number of attributes for each directory entry. The smaller the number of attributes the quicker each entry is processed. However, this factor has the least impact in the elapsed time for import operations so it is not an excuse or reason not to include attributes such as telephone numbers if you have this data available.

As an indication of directory updates in a real-life situation, Table 8.3 contains details of synchronization operations performed for a large customer that I have worked with.

Table 8.3 *Timings for synchronization operations*

Influencing factor	Details
Import Server	175 MHz Pentium Pro, 196 MB memory, 2GB system disk, 2GB transaction log, 8GB RAID-5 set for stores (including directory).
Workload	Low (operation occurred at night)
Import data	50,000 entries, each containing 11 attributes. Average entry size 176 bytes, total data to process 8.38 MB.
Average import rate	13 entries/second
Time to process entire file	67 minutes

Delete and modify operations produce similar results. The results show that synchronization operations are pretty resource intensive. Importing 50,000 entries generates a fair amount of replication load for the organization afterwards, with updates being sent to other sites according to the replication schedule for the import server. All of the other servers in the site where the import server is located should be fully updated between ten and fifteen minutes after the import server processes the last entry. The time taken to ripple the new directory information out throughout the organization greatly depends on the replication topology you have implemented. Considerable delays (more than a couple of hours) may be experienced if a number of transitive connections are used.

8.2.20 Other uses for directory import files

Directory import files are not only used to for directory synchronization operations. They can also be used to create a set of new mailboxes for users before a migration begins (in this case, you use "Mailbox" as the object class you wish to create). Manually creating 50 or 100 mailboxes is a boring task, but it's just about bearable if it only needs to be done on an irregular basis. If you're faced with the need to create a thousand mailboxes the task is much more daunting. You can automate mailbox creation for a group of new users by creating a CSV load file with Excel before feeding it into the administration program. Everything, including Windows NT accounts, will be set up for the new users, and all in much less time than you'd be able to create the accounts manually.

The CSV header and the data specified for each entry is slightly more complex than for custom recipients. In this instance you have to specify the name of the Exchange server where the mailbox is to be created as well as the name of the Windows NT account to use. Note the "Hide from AB" attribute. This controls whether or not the new account is shown to other users when they browse the address book. If you're creating a set of new user accounts you may not want to reveal their existence until the new users have received training and are ready to use Exchange. Setting the "Hide from AB" attribute to "N" hides the new account from the GAL. You can modify the directory entry later on and set the switch to "Y" when everything is ready to go.

Let's look at an example of adding a new account:

```
Obj-Class, Mode, Directory Name, Alias Name, Display Name, E-
Mail Address, Obj-Container, Home-Server, Assoc-NT-Account,
Hide from AB
```

```
Mailbox, Create, Tony Redmond, TonyR, Tony Redmond,
SMTP:Tony.Redmond@dbo-exchangeist.dbo.dec.com, Recipients,
DBO-EXCHANGEIST, OFFICESI\T_Redmond, N
```

Although the data provided is similar, creating mailboxes isn't as straightforward as custom recipients, especially when Windows NT accounts are involved. In fact, an import options file is required to override the default options that the administration program takes when it processes import files. One of the important options we need to use allows us to create new Windows NT accounts. The option file looks like this:

```
[Import]
```

```
DirectoryService=
Basepoint=
Container=Recipients
InformationLevel=Minimal
```

```
RecipientTemplate=
NTDomain=OFFICESI
OverwriteProperties=No
CreateNTAccounts=Yes
DeleteNTAccounts=No
ApplyNTSecurity=Yes
GeneratePassword=Yes
RawMode=No
CodePage=0
```

The important fields are CreateNTAccounts, ApplyNTSecurity, and GeneratePassword. In the example I create an NT account called T_Redmond in the OFFICESI domain. A password is automatically generated for the new account, with the password set to the same value as the account name. The user will be required to change the password the first time they log-in to the server.

Always import CSV files to create new mailboxes on the server that will host the mailboxes. If you want to create new Windows NT accounts, make sure that the primary domain controller is available (in other words, don't attempt to create new accounts if the server is disconnected from the network or a backup domain controller is all that's available).

In addition to mailboxes and custom recipients, distribution lists can also be created, modified, and deleted through import files. For example, to create a distribution list called Management Team, you might use the following CSV file:

```
Obj-Class, Mode, Directory Name, Members, Obj-Container

Dl, Create, Management Team, Recipients/cn=FrankC%Recipients/
cn=FrankB%Recipients/cn=TonyR, Recipients
```

This file creates the distribution list and populates it with three members. The distribution list must not already exist, and all of the members specified must already exist in the directory in the specified container. I've used the standard "Recipients" container for the example, but you can specify other containers if you need to fetch recipients from them. The directory alias name for recipients is the best way to include them in a distribution list. Exchange only needs a pointer to each member in the distribution list because that's what a distribution list is—a set of pointers to directory entries. Those entries can be mailboxes, custom recipients or other distribution lists. Note the % (percentage sign) used to separate each member in the list.

I've already recommended Excel to you as a good tool for composing CSV files. Distribution lists pose a particular challenge for Excel and other spreadsheets because the possibility arises that we may exceed the maximum limit for a spreadsheet cell. In Excel V7.0 that limit is 255 characters, a value that can easily be encountered with large distribution lists.

To amend the same distribution list and add a new member we can use the following CSV file:

```
Obj-Class, Mode, Directory Name, Members, Obj-Container

Dl, Modify, Management Team, Recipients/cn=PhilipI, Recipients
```

I don't honestly believe that many people will create distribution lists using import files. The exception is when you need to migrate a mass of distribution lists from another system, where the choice is either to create the lists from scratch or to generate the lists using a program. The latter option is preferable if there are more than 20 or so lists to move. In this case the program (which is not yet written and certainly not available off the shelf) will read list members in the format used by the legacy system and write out an import file in Exchange load format. Remember that all the entries in the list must already exist in the directory before you attempt the import.

8.3   Expanding the set of Address Book Service Providers

X.500 (or other corporate-type) directories don't have to remain hidden from Exchange users. MAPI extensions can be built to make a directory available as another source of address information, along the same lines as the Exchange directory or the Personal Address Book. DIGITAL personnel have always enjoyed a facility called ELF (for Employee Locator Facility) which can be consulted to find out details about other employees—their mail stop, electronic mail address, phone number, and so on. ELF data is stored in an X.500 database distributed across a set of UNIX servers, and the Exchange implementation within DIGITAL uses a MAPI Address Book Service Provider to map ELF as an additional source of directory information for Exchange clients.

Figure 8.22
DIGITAL's
Employee
Locator Facility
accessed by an
Exchange client

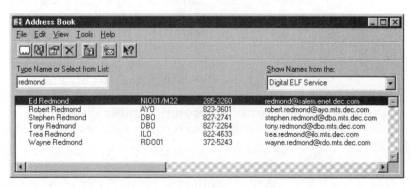

Figure 8.22 shows the results gained by consulting ELF to discover the DIGITAL employees with the surname "Redmond". Apart from anything else, making a corporate directory accessible to all users via their mail client helps the client to be accepted quickly. It also leverages the information in the corporate directory and prevents any requirement to rekey information or otherwise transfer entries into another directory.

To complete this discussion on corporate directories I'll take the opportunity to note that Digital offers a number of different synchronization tools that can help to keep DIGITAL DDS (Message Router Distributed Directory Service) and X.500 directories in line with Exchange. If you're moving from a DIGITAL system or simply trying to integrate Exchange into an existing DIGITAL messaging environment you should check out DSU, XDSU, and X.500 synchronizer. DSU and XDSU enable synchronization between DDS and other directories, X.500 and other directories, while the X.500 Synchronizer product links Exchange and AltaVista Directory Service.

In the future, when Exchange offers direct support of external directory access products such as DAP, it may be possible to build a more elegant directory synchronization scheme, possibly using features built into Exchange but more likely through third party add-ons.

In all cases the critical selection factor is which directory service supports the highest degree of automatic synchronization (once everything is set up—it's too much to expect totally automatic directory synchronization) across all potential directory sources. There's no point in performing manual synchronization if you can at all avoid it.

8.4   The Off-line Address Book

The Off-line Address Book is a snapshot of a subset of the Exchange directory that can be downloaded to clients so that they can work when disconnected from the server. When clients are working in offline mode they perceive no difference between the off-line address book and the directory held on the server; both are used to validate the addresses entered into message headers, and both can be browsed to retrieve information about mailboxes, distribution lists, and custom recipients.

Figure 8.23
*DS Site
Configuration
properties for
OAB generation*

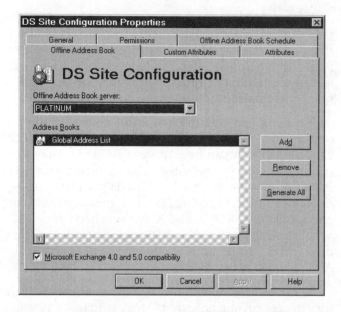

Each site nominates a single server to generate the OAB along with a schedule to define when the OAB is generated. The DS Site Configuration object (see Figure 8.23) from the site Configuration container is used to determine:

- The name of the server within the site that will generate the Off-line Address Book

- The schedule used to generate the Off-line Address Book

- The containers from the server Address Book that will be included in the Off-line address book

Note the "Microsoft Exchange V4.0 and V5.0 compatibility" checkbox. This controls whether the OAB is generated in a format that can be used by older MAPI clients (Exchange V4.0 or V5.0 or Outlook V8.0 through V8.02). Tick the checkbox unless all the clients used for remote working have been upgraded to any release from Outlook V8.03 onwards.

When the OAB is generated it is stored in a hidden folder in the Public Information Store of the server. Clients retrieve the OAB with the Tools.Synchronize.Download Address Book option. At this point the data is fetched from the server and downloaded to a set of five .OAB files in the client's Windows directory. The data is highly compressed to limit the time taken to perform the download, and you can speed things up even more if you elect to download the address book without "details information". However, this option is not recommended because, while you'll save a little on disk space, you won't be able to see a lot of valuable information (such as phone numbers) when you browse through the address book. You also won't be able to send encrypted messages because the public keys for Exchange recipients aren't available. Public keys are amongst the attributes downloaded for mailboxes when detailed information is retrieved together with the bare minimum mail addresses.

How compressed is the data downloaded from the server? Well, Microsoft quotes the example of its own off-line address book that holds 51,000 entries (mailboxes, distribution lists, and some custom recipients). This address book is 6MB when compressed, and 12MB when it is uncompressed on the client to create the .OAB files. Another example is a customer with a 95,000-mailbox directory. The off-line address book in this case is 13MB when compressed and 23MB when uncompressed.

Downloading such a large data file is OK when you're attached to a LAN (although things might get interesting if lots of users tried to download the file at the same time). Even if you have such a large directory there's no requirement to create an off-line address book that contains everything. The DS Site Configuration properties allow you to determine exactly what container from the directory is used to create the off-line address book. In most situations where the GAL is a reasonable size it's best to select the GAL because this means that off-line users will be able to access all the addresses they can when working online. With large directories you might want to select another container, such as the recipients container for the local site.

Most installations schedule the off-line address book for generation at least once a day. I like to schedule generation to occur twice. Once in the morning and once just before close of business each day. That way an up-to-date off-line address book is almost always available, and the generation towards the end of day helps people who are packing up ready to go on a road trip because they can always pick up a new copy that includes any directory changes made during the day. Generation does not place much strain on a server, nor does it take very long, so generating the off-line address book twice a day is no big deal. If necessary, you can generate the off-line address book whenever you need by clicking on the "Generate Off-line Address Book Now" command button in the DS Site Configuration object.

8.4.1   Differential downloads

Downloading an off-line address book is fine as long as it's small. Once the Exchange organization grows the download can take many minutes, even with a fast modem. Exchange V5.5 supports the concept of differential downloads, basically allowing users to opt to only download details of entries that have changed since the last time the local copy of the address book was synchronized with the server. The net effect is a drastic cut in the time required to download the OAB. For anyone who spends a lot of time working remotely, like I do, this is a great feature that was long overdue.

Figure 8.24
*Differential
OAB downloads*

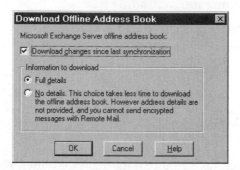

Important people generate stories about themselves. It is rumoured that Bill Gates said some very rude things when he discovered that Exchange didn't support differential downloads, something that greatly affected the speed in which the engineers generated the necessary code to include the feature. If the story is true, it surely must have occurred after Gates had spent some fruitless minutes staring at the animated graphics that serve as a progress gauge. Even with differential downloads, it would be nice if the graphics were less animated and more informative, and displayed some indication of how long more the download could be expected to take. Maybe this will come about after Bill Gates uses differential download for the first time!

8.5   Address Book Views

Address Book views were first introduced in Exchange V5.0. My personal observation is that not many implementations have yet used address book views to any great extent, possibly because views are deemed to be something that can wait until other, more important aspects of the implementation are complete. This is somewhat of a pity, because address book views have some interesting potential.

Address Book views attempt to make navigation within large directories easier. A view is a logical grouping of directory entries (mailboxes, custom recipients, distribution lists and even public folders) according to a common set of criteria. For example, a view might incorporate all the entries in the directory that are located in Dublin. Immediately we meet the first issue. Address Book views are only useful if the directory is populated with a reasonable selection of attributes that can be used to create views. If the data held in the directory is minimal, for example, just alias, first name, last name, and display name, then the views that can be created aren't going to be very useful. To create viable views you need first to review and update directory entries with information that could be used to create views, such as the names of cities, countries, departments, offices, or other attributes that make sense within your organization. Processes that feed information into the directory, perhaps as part of directory synchronization with external directories, also need to be reviewed to ensure that any new entries are created with enough information to make address views work properly.

Figure 8.25
Creating a new
address book
view

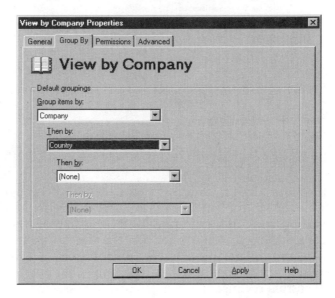

Figure 8.25 shows the grouping properties of an address view. Grouping defines how Exchange orders the directory entries. As you can see, four levels of grouping are supported. In this case the view is being created on the basis of company names, with country names used as a second level grouping. Thus, when the address view is opened we should see directory entries ordered first by company name and then sub-divided into countries. Such a view is very appropriate for a company like DIGITAL, which operates in over 80 countries around the world. It possibly wouldn't be appropriate for a company based in a single country, especially if custom recipient entries for external correspondents are also located in the same country. In this instance you'd be better off creating a view based on company and then city. Like sites, geographical terms are a good basis for the creation of views. Countries and cities don't tend to change often whereas other organizational terms, like department names, do.

Figure 8.26
*Browsing an
address book
view*

The result of the address view ordered by company and then country is shown in Figure 8.26. The screen shot is taken from my group's own production server and illustrates some of the points that I have just made. First, you can see that the view is reasonably effective. The company "Digital Equipment Corporation" is sub-divided neatly by country, and expanding the "Belgium" container exposes the entries, all custom recipients in this case, whose directory entry specifies "Belgium" in the country attribute. While the view is reasonably effective we can see a flaw too. Look at the list of company names. There are duplicate entries for "Butterworth Heinemann", one with a hyphen separating the two parts of the company name, and one without. There are two entries for DIGITAL, this time resulting from a misspelling of the word "corporation". Without accurate directory information the old adage that rubbish in equals rubbish out will be proved. In this instance the damage is obvious and easily rectified, but this might not be the case always.

Address views are replicated to all sites in the organization. Some agreement or discipline is therefore required amongst system administrators to assure that everyone works together to create an appropriate set of views. It does not make sense for each site to do their own thing, as all you'll create is a mess.

The results of address views are available to users through the client Address Book. The Show Names From drop-down list (displayed at the right top-hand corner of the window) allows users to select a view to browse for names.

8.5.I Address Book views versus Multiple Recipient Containers

If you view the GAL you'll notice that it is organized into a set of containers. Each site must have at least one container to hold recipient details, so the structure is broken down into recipient containers organized by sites. Address Book views take precedence and are shown at the top of the GAL.

Implementations that don't use address book views often look at recipient containers and consider using a number of different containers to segment their user population. For example, a separate container might be created for each department. This scheme certainly works, and if you browse the GAL you'll see each one of the containers shown. However, the approach comes with an almost fatal flaw that only becomes apparent over time.

Each recipient is allocated a unique distinguished name within the directory. The container where their details are held is part of that name. Therefore, if a recipient is to move from one container to another their unique name must change. This means that the recipient entry must be deleted and then recreated. There is no way to simply drag and drop a recipient from one container to another.

Address book views are logical rather than physical separations. Changing directory attributes is all that's needed to effect a change to a view. For example, to move a recipient from one department to another, just change the name of the department held in their directory entry. This is much easier than deleting and recreating recipient information. Address book views are therefore a much more practical approach to GAL segmentation than separate recipient containers.

There are situations when separate recipient containers are totally appropriate. For example, if you have some directory synchronization code for importing and exporting information to and from Exchange, it's probably best to isolate all of the entries (custom recipients) for the foreign directories in separate containers.

8.6   Directory customization

The Exchange directory is designed for corporate deployments. It would be unreasonable to expect that every company in the world is exactly the same in terms of the information they'd like to hold in a directory, so Exchange allows its directory to be customized in a certain degree in two ways.

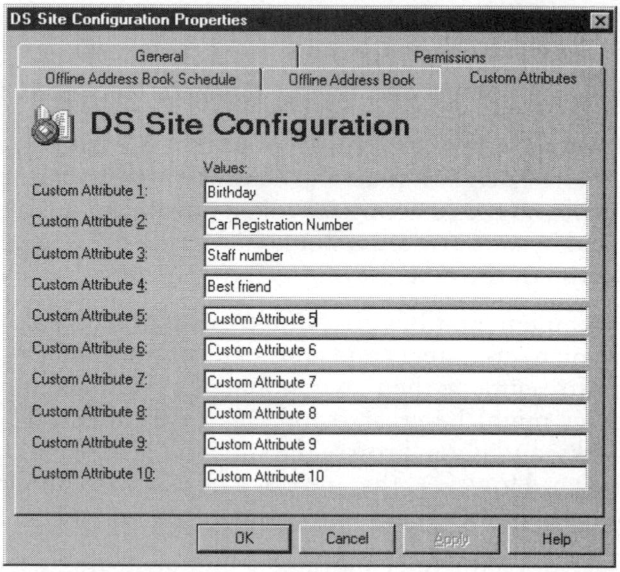

Figure 8.27
*DS Custom
Attributes*

First, there are 10 pre-defined custom attributes (or fields) provided for mailbox or custom recipient entries in the directory (no custom attributes are available for distribution lists). The default names for the custom attributes are quite boring—"Custom Attribute 1", "Custom Attribute 2", and so on. But you can easily change the names to whatever you want. For example, you might want to store everyone's car registration number so you can quickly find out who's left their lights on in the car park, or perhaps people's birthdays so you can send them a cheery message on the day in question, or even something boring like their staff number. The custom attributes are accessed through the "Custom Attributes" page of the DS Site Configuration object (see Figure 8.27).

Changing the name of a custom attribute is one thing. The second customization is used to let people see the newly renamed attributes. Administrators are always able to insert data into the attributes and see what's been put in because the administration program has a "Custom Attributes" page to view mailbox or custom recipient properties. Regular users will be left in the dark unless you customize one of the templates used by Exchange to present attribute information to users, or to allow people to use attributes, for example, to perform a search against the directory. These templates are stored in the Addressing container of a site's Configuration container (see Figure 8.28). Single language servers will have templates just for that language while multilanguage servers will have templates for all the languages used by clients that connect to that server.

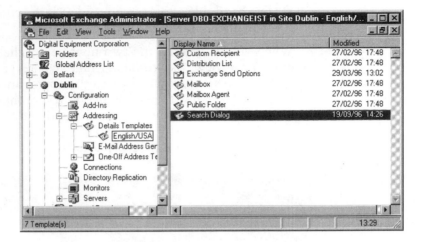

Figure 8.28
Address
Templates

Let's assume that we have modified one of the custom attributes to be "Birthday". The following steps would be taken to add this attribute to the set of attributes presented to users when they searched the directory:

1.   Open the set of templates for the client language. On US systems this will be English/USA.

2.   Click on the "Templates" page. After a brief pause to load in attribute details from the directory schema the set of attributes that users are shown is displayed. Each attribute is defined in terms of its X and Y co-ordinates on a page or set of pages, together with its width and height. All of these definitions are in pixels. Most attributes are 12 pixels high and between 50 and 100 pixels wide. No graphical tool is available to position the new attribute on the page; getting it right is mostly a matter of trial and error.

3.   You need to make two additions to the set. One of these is a label, the other the actual "box" that will be used to display the attribute's information.

4.   Each page (in the dialog presented to users) must start with a page break. Click on a field below the first page break in the set and then click on the New button. A set of field types will be presented. Select "Label" and enter "Birthday" into the text box. Click on OK to add the new label to the set.

5.   Repeat the operation to add the text box to display the attribute information, this time selecting "Edit" from the set of field types. You'll need to spend a little time playing with the X and Y co-ordinates and the height and width of the fields. As a tip, 10 is the X co-ordinate that lines up labels on

the left-hand side of the screen, and 65 is the corresponding X co-ordinate to line up the text boxes.

6.   When you've entered the two new fields, click on the Test button to view the results. Make whatever changes are required to satisfy yourself as to the appearance of the form until you're happy, then click on OK to save the updated template. Clients will be able to see the updated template immediately, as they will fetch it from the server whenever they attempt to perform a directory search.

Figure 8.29
Modifying a template

Figure 8.29 shows the set of fields for the Search Dialog template together with the set of field types you can add to the dialog. You can see the X and Y co-ordinates and the width and height settings for all the fields. It's pretty easy to work out how things mesh together to create the screen presented to users, but it would have been much nicer if a more graphical tool was available

8.6.1 Modifying directory Search Flags

Earlier we discussed Ambiguous Name Resolution (ANR), the process used by Exchange to search the directory to find addresses that match information provided by users. It may be advantageous to alter the directory schema to include our customized field in the ANR process. Each field has a Search-Flags property, and the value in this field determines whether the field participates in the ANR process. Normally we can't access or change directory properties through the administration program, but we can through "raw mode", activated by starting ADMIN.EXE with the /R command line qualifier (Figure 8.30).

Figure 8.30
*Starting
ADMIN.EXE in
raw mode*

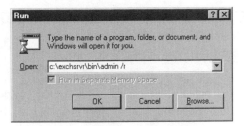

When the administration program runs in raw mode you have direct access to the directory schema and properties. Having access is great, but it's also slightly dangerous in so far as it's easy to make mistakes. Normal administration mode attempts to prevent mistakes by presenting directory information through a well-designed user interface. Raw mode circumvents the user interface and therefore avoids its protection.

After starting the administration program in raw mode all of the attributes in the directory can be viewed by selecting View.Raw Directory, an option that's not available in normal mode. At this stage the "Schema" container appears in the left-hand pane and the directory fields are listed in the right hand pane. As you can see from Figure 8.31, the "Birthday" customized field is listed amongst all the others. The raw properties of the attribute are accessed through File.Raw Properties, another option that's only available when working in raw mode.

Figure 8.31
*Viewing the
Directory
Schema*

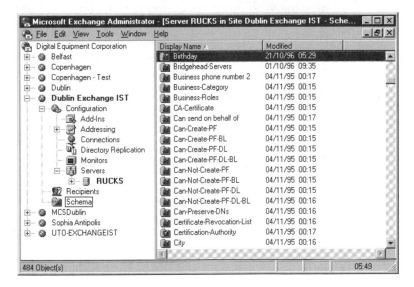

Figure 8.32
*Amending the
Search-Flags
property*

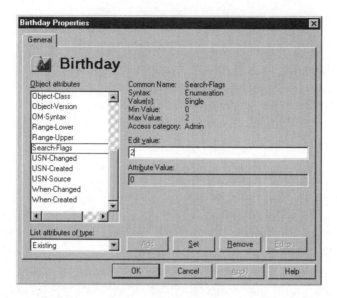

Move to the Search-Flags attribute by selecting an attribute in the left-hand list box and typing "s". The attribute value should be 0 (zero), meaning that this field does not participate in the ANR process. To allow people to search against birthdays (somewhat weird, but useful to illustrate the point), enter 2 into the edit value field and click on the "Set" button (Figure 8.32). At this stage you'll be warned that messing with directory contents is an activity that shouldn't be undertaken without reference to Microsoft product support. Clicking on OK twice will convince Exchange that you really know what you're doing, and the server will proceed to create an index to use during the ANR process.

Note that any changes you make to the directory are replicated within the site, but no further. This is because the schema is a container within the site container, so its contents are not replicated outside the site. If you want the same changes to be effective at other sites, the changes must be made at a server at those sites.

Testing that the customized fields participate in the ANR process is easy. Select a recipient mailbox, go to the Custom Attributes property page and enter some data into the custom attributes, for example, a birthday of 1-Dec-1961. Create a new message and type the data you just entered into the To: box, and then press CTRL/K. Exchange should take the data and use it to search the directory, returning the name of the recipient whose birthday it is.

8.6.2   Changing display names for LDAP clients

Adding birthday information to the directory is an interesting example of how the directory can be customized, but it doesn't solve any business problems. Changing information provided for LDAP lookups is much more practical.

By default, Exchange provides LDAP clients with the common name attribute any time a client requests information. The common name attribute is normally taken from the directory name, not the display name. However, the directory name differs across recipient types (mailboxes, custom recipients). The directory name is not always what you want displayed, especially if it has been automatically generated through a directory synchronization process, something that often happens when custom recipients are loaded from address information taken from another messaging system.

Exchange allows any directory attribute to be mapped as an LDAP attribute. The normal situation is for the Directory Name attribute to be mapped as "cn", so we need to remap this to point to the Display Name attribute. Do this as follows:

- Start the Exchange Administration program in raw mode.
- Select the Schema container.
- Select the Directory Name object and double click to expose its attributes. Modify the "Description" attribute and change it from the default value ("cn") to something else, such as "ExDirectoryName". Click on OK and confirm that the action should proceed.
- Select the Display Name object and change its "Description" attribute to "cn". Click on OK.

The display name is now mapped to the LDAP common name attribute. Remember that this modification is site-specific and must be made on all sites that provide directory access to LDAP clients.

9

Conducting a Pilot for Exchange

9.1   Introduction

Conducting a pilot will be easier for some companies than others, and everyone will find that different aspects of the Exchange server (or clients) and its interoperability with various components of already installed systems have to be covered.

The easiest pilots will be those for sites who already have a Microsoft Mail network up and running. Exchange server is the natural and evolutionary path for Microsoft Mail installations and anyone who is operating this mail system should look at Exchange with a very serious eye to a quick introduction to production status. Exchange addresses the majority if not all of the architectural weaknesses of the technology embodied in the Microsoft Mail Post Office and provides a great deal of new functionality at the same time. In addition, Exchange allows you to connect Microsoft Mail clients with the new server fairly easily so users don't have to be retrained when the new server is initially introduced. Finally, the migration wizards that are available for Microsoft Mail are much more developed and functional than the equivalents for any other mail system. The wizards enable Microsoft Mail users to migrate all their messages to Exchange private folders with ease. The fact that the migration wizards for Microsoft Mail are so good isn't altogether surprising but is welcome as it eliminates much of the pain otherwise felt at the user level during any migration process.

Longer and more complex pilots will have to be conducted if you currently operate a non-Microsoft mail system. The degree of complexity will vary considerably and no hard or fast rules can be given yet, but logic indicates that a pilot to assess the technical issues involved in the introduction of Exchange into a Windows-based user community that's already running a LAN-based e-mail system, such as Novell GroupWise or Lotus cc:Mail, might well be easier than the altogether different issues that will come up during an analysis of a similar situation involving a system delivering "more than just mail" already, such as Lotus Notes. In general in these circumstances you won't, for example, have to sort out basic problems like PC networking and connectivity. However, often other non-technical issues like user unwillingness to move to a new system have to be addressed.

9.1.1   What do I want to prove in a pilot?

A pilot implementation of any product seeks to prove that the product is suitable for deployment into a particular production environment. An Exchange pilot is no different. You want to validate many different aspects of your deployment plan to catch and solve any potential problems before they get a chance to occur in production. Amongst the most important aspects to be validated during the pilot are:

- Windows NT domain design
- Other elements of the Windows NT infrastructure, including items like WINS.
- Network capacity and throughput
- Exchange organization design
- Server and client hardware sizing and installation
- The desktop environment, including support for roving and mobile users, if these issues are important to you
- The ease and effectiveness of your migration strategy and the impact on users
- Disaster recovery plans
- Third party software add-ons
- Mobile access

If you accept that the purpose of the pilot is to validate the items listed above it logically follows that the pilot must accurately reflect the production environment that you are attempting to create. In reality this means that the pilot systems must actually be "early deployments", servers that operate under the same Windows NT domain model as intended for the roll-out. The servers should comply with the same organizational model, use the same types of messaging and directory replication connectors, and operate the same software and hardware configurations that you want to use in production. In other words, the pilot is not going to be discarded when it is over. Instead, the pilot systems will evolve into the full-scale deployment and become production servers immediately the pilot period finishes. If you choose to run in any other type of environment you can't be sure that the pilot will accurately validate your design.

Classic pilot systems are usually discarded once the pilot is over, if only to allow the lessons learnt from the pilot to be incorporated into a deployment design that is executed from scratch. You can certainly discard the Exchange servers used in a pilot and start over again, but I would only do this if the pilot revealed some fundamental flaws in your design.

9.2 Approaching a pilot

In the world of monolithic, centralized computer applications specifying the boundaries of a pilot was pretty easy. The new mini- or mainframe computer was rolled in, the software was installed, and you connected a number of video terminals to run the application. Between ten and twenty-five terminals were enough to generate a realistic test load for the application's functionality, and you could confidently scale up the results gained from the test to get a good idea of the size of system required to support the eventual user community.

With client/server systems the situation isn't as clear-cut. It is easy to take client software out of the shrink-wrap and install it on individual PCs, then connect the clients to the server to check out the functionality. But this isn't really fulfilling the purpose of the pilot by generating a realistic load to check whether the application will function when it's scaled up. Consider the following questions:

- Are the client platforms used in the pilot representative of the PCs actually used by users? Are the systems covering the range of CPU types and speeds and is the memory configuration the same?

- Are all the client operating systems represented in the pilot—Windows V3, Windows 95, and Windows NT as well as any other non-Windows platforms. In conjunction with this topic I would consider whether you intend to upgrade to a Windows 95 or NT desktop environment in the near future and, if so, what impact this will have on the client configurations under test. How are you going to configure desktop clients so that they can connect to Exchange? Do you have a WINS and DHCP environment to set up?

- What clients are you going to consider for deployment? Are all of these clients going to be adequately tested during the pilot so that a full and fair comparison of the different capabilities can be arrived at? Are you going to use Outlook instead of the standard Exchange client? How will client software be distributed during the pilot and then eventually during the full implementation?

- Are all connectors going to be tested in the pilot? If you plan to use the X.400 connector to connect sites together in production there's little point in using the Internet Mail Service or site connector for this purpose during the pilot. If you plan to use connectors to foreign messaging systems such as PROFS, SNADS, Lotus Notes, or FAX then these should be factored into the pilot too.

- What will you do to satisfy people who use systems like Apple Macintosh, IBM OS/2 or UNIX workstations? There is an Outlook client for the Apple Macintosh, but it's not suitable if you don't have PowerPCs. The obvious solution is to deploy either POP3 or IMAP4 clients for these platforms, or to use Outlook Web Access if you can use a browser that supports frames and scripting. But you have to make a choice and test one or both options. Will these clients be used in other circumstances than non-Wintel platforms?

- Are the network connections between the clients and servers the same as will be used in production? For instance, do you need to check out remote access over an asynchronous telephone connection?

- Is the software installed in the same method as you want to use for full deployment? For example, do you want to test the difference (if any) in start-up time for client software loaded from a network file service and local hard disks?

- Are all third party add-ons going to be tested during the pilot? Backup products such as Cheyenne ArcServe or Seagate's Backup Exec provide significant advantages over the standard Windows NT backup software, but they have to be tested during a pilot in order that you can take maximum advantage of their capabilities when they go into production. For example, you need to ensure that your disaster recovery plan (which, of course, you also have ready to go) incorporates the installation of third party backup software.

- Can the client software be deployed and managed easily? Microsoft's solution is System Management Server (SMS), another part of the Back Office suite, but you may already have another PC management tool in place. How will this work with Exchange?

Another point to consider is the type of personnel taking part in the pilot. To provide an accurate assessment of any application's value in real life it's important that a good cross-section of the user population is included in the pilot. If you have people who have never seen PCs in their lives before then clearly the pilot is going to take a long time before any worthwhile data becomes available. On the other hand, you don't want to staff the pilot with too many technical people because they tend to be either too forgiving or too critical of a product's performance depending on whether they "like" the product. Liking a product often comes down to whether someone approves of the technical nature of the product, the vendor, or any associated reasons that come to hand during coffee room debates!

All of the above points could be made for any PC client/server product. Because Microsoft Exchange is a messaging system there are some other important points that must be considered during a pilot. These include:

- How will the entries for Exchange mailboxes and custom recipients be synchronized with other directory sources? This is only going to be really important if you already have a messaging system in production. If you do, you better make sure that it is possible to achieve an easy synchronization of addresses between Exchange and the other system, using an automated procedure if at all possible. Can the same synchronization procedure handle address information from all the potential sources within your organization? Is the synchronization bi-directional or only one-way?

- How will Exchange send and receive messages to and from any other messaging system that's in place internally or externally? What connectors (SMTP, X.400, etc.) are going to be operational and how will you test the connection between Exchange and other messaging systems? Do you have a full list of all the connections already used by people within your organization? How will you test that multi-bodypart messages are able to flow from one side to the other while preserving their essential attributes?

- Can the content of messages generated and sent by Exchange be read after they have been delivered to people using the other messaging systems in place within your organization? Outlook clients usually create messages in Rich Text Format (RTF), while Outlook 98 supports both RTF and HTML. It is indeed wonderful to be able to send your thoughts out to the world in bold red 24 point Arial, or any of the other interesting formatting possibilities offered by these content types. Connectors can render the RTF and HTML output back to plain ASCII, which provides a base line for interoperability, but perhaps you'd like to test to see whether external recipients can handle RTF or HTML content?

Asking these questions, even if you think you're pretty sure of the answers, is a good way to make sure that all the essential issues are covered during the pilot. Possibly even more important it's a way to isolate potential costs so that you can factor them into a deployment budget. Software components like directory synchronizers, format converters, and mail gateways are expensive to buy or build. It's important that you uncover all the situations where additional costs might be incurred before Exchange can be put into full production. If you don't you'll find that your deployment schedule and budget will be afflicted by complexities that arise and have to be dealt with when you should really be concentrating on delivery. Good preparation is half the battle in achieving good deployments.

Failure to ask the correct questions both when considering a migration and during a pilot implementation inevitably ends up in an exercise that's a waste of time, energy, and money, and one that will lead to a shoddy deployment that delivers a low level of service to the user community.

9.2.1   The numbers involved in the pilot

Anybody can set up a single Exchange server and connect a few clients to it. A single Exchange server is not an accurate or even useful pilot for a corporate deployment because you're not reflecting the production environment. Here are some guidelines to consider in terms of the number of systems and users that should participate in pilots to validate plans for large corporate deployments.

- **Servers and Sites:** You need to test messaging connectivity and directory/public folder replication. This requires at least three servers, in at least two sites. The sites should be connected using the connectors you intend to use in production. If you only have two sites but intend to use more than one type of connector in production you can configure the different connectors to link the two sites for different periods during the pilot. If the final design calls for sites to be connected across different Windows NT domains then reflect this fact in the pilot and make sure that you test items such as public folder affinity and message tracking.

- **Users and Clients:** You need to place a real load on the servers, and test Exchange across a wide variety of user types and client platforms. Confining the pilot to a group of technical users from the MIS department, all of who run well-configured Windows NT workstations is not a true test if the majority of target users are currently running Microsoft Mail on low-end 80486-class systems. It's best to look for a reasonably large user population (between 50 and 100) spread across several types of people (technical, non-technical) who use the complete range of clients that need to be supported in production. Non-technical users will tell you how much training is really required to help their peers once Exchange is being rolled out to everyone, and the problems they encounter during the pilot will assist the help desk to determine how they can best support the user community.

Engaging in such a comprehensive pilot may seem like a lot of effort, but you should remember two things. First, getting your design for Exchange deployment right is a critical success factor and, to some degree, it's a one-time operation. If you get your design wrong it might mean that you have to re-implement some or all of your deployment. Second, my attitude is that pilot systems are just an early deployment and will not be thrown away after the pilot. Thus, any work that's done to make the pilot a success is even more valuable than it seems at first.

9.3   Training

I don't believe anyone can pick up the documentation set for Exchange server and become a trained expert by close study of its contents. It's good to read the documentation, including the release notes, but some degree of formal training should be part of the project plan for any pilot.

Initially you'll want to cover training focused towards system management and administration. Programming, including the whiz-bang aspects of Exchange like Outlook electronic forms and MAPI, can be left until the next phase (formal deployment) begins. It's essential to master the basics of any subject, and the basics of Exchange include topics like planning the network, defining how servers are placed into sites, the relationship with the Windows NT security model, and other aspects of system management.

Your pilot shouldn't ignore user training. The people participating in the pilot will need some training, otherwise they won't be able to properly exercise the product's functionality, so make sure that at least one formal training session is made available to pilot users. It's likely that you won't have in-house skills to be able to run this course so you need to contact a local Microsoft qualified training centre (ATEC) and get them involved.

9.3.1   Helping users form good habits

The opportunity to give people good e-mail habits is one major advantage gained through well-planned user training. If people learn how to do things properly right from the start they'll work with the system in an intelligent and constructive manner. Table 9.1 lists eight good user habits that you may want to encourage. Use this table as a base to build on, adding your own ideas to the list.

Table 9.1 *Good user habits to encourage*

1	Make a decision to delete or keep a message as soon as you've read it. If you're keeping the message move it into an appropriate folder.
2	Check the "Empty Deleted Items folder upon exiting" option. This deletes unwanted mail and stops it accumulating in the Deleted Items folder.
3	Don't include the text of original messages in replies as this increases the overall size of messages within the system.
4	Don't include documents in messages unless you really need to. Send pointers to documents (the name of the file in a shared file service, a suitable public folder, or a short-cut to the document) if at all possible. Alternatively, use a compression program like WinZIP (see http://www.winzip.com) to shrink large files before they are attached.
5	Don't use messaging as a way to broadcast information to people who may not want to receive it. In other words, try and keep the distribution list for messages as short as possible.
6	Don't add graphics to Auto Signature files as this will drive up the overall size of messages and create a demand the network may not be able to handle.
7	Compact personal folder files on a regular basis to reclaim space on your hard disk.
8	Don't leave an unattended PC logged into your Exchange account. Protect your work with a password-protected screen saver or log-out of Exchange if you have to leave your PC alone.
9	If you travel with your computer remember to download the off-line address book before you leave for a trip. This makes sure that any message you create while traveling will be addressed correctly. Remember to synchronize some or all of the folders in your mailbox before you travel as otherwise you won't see up-to-date information when you work off-line.
10	Use the Out of Office Assistant to notify people whenever you won't be able to respond to messages for any reason.

Many installations print up "cheat sheets" for users to publicize hints and tips. Users can keep the cheat sheets beside their PC and if you take the opportunity to inform people about good working habits amongst the other hints and tips there's a fair chance that users will actually follow the advice. Another good idea I have seen is to print up the most important tips onto mouse pads, and give a mouse pad to each user after they attend training. Apart from anything else, this method ensures that good habits are constantly under users' noses.

Good habits aren't just set once. They need to be worked on constantly. Every time a new version of the client is available people should be told how to make effective use of new features. Help users share ideas, tips, and techniques too. Set up a public folder (make it available via the web and NNTP so that all clients are accommodated) and use it as a repository for information that's useful and interesting to users. A number of good books that focus on client technology (always more important to users) rather than Exchange itself have been published recently. Client documentation isn't easily obtained from Microsoft, so consider selecting one of the independent books and use it as the basis for client training.

During the pilot it's a good idea to check with the people who received training and see whether the training was relevant and helpful. After reviewing feedback from users who have received training you can decide whether or not the same training can be used during the roll-out phase. Bear in mind that off-the-shelf training is often delivered at a lowest common denominator level so the content of the initial course will often need to be adjusted to reflect your organization's computing infrastructure as well as how you intend to use Exchange in day-to-day life. Some people are happy enough to go with standard training, perhaps supplementing the course material with a booklet covering site-specific details while others design and deliver their own tailored training. Cost, as always, has some bearing on the decision, but remember that good training will invariably repay its cost several times over by driving down the number of calls that support personnel have to deal with.

9.3.2 Programmer and administrator training

User training is a critical part of the pilot, but it's a mistake to concentrate totally on this aspect alone. Programmers and system administrators will also need training and this need should be factored into an overall training plan that begins in the pilot stage and continues on through implementation.

Consider the skills necessary in an Exchange environment. In your environment they might include:

- Windows NT server including Apple Macintosh client andnetworking support (if required)

- The basics of Exchange Server (creating and maintaining mailboxes)

- Monitoring the correct operation of Exchange Server

- Creating and configuring connectors to other messaging systems

- Managing connections from MAPI, POP3, and IMAP4 clients and web browsers

- Configuring the Internet Information Server for web access

- TCP/IP utilities such as WINS, DHCP, and DNS

- SMTP, X.400, and the site connectors, plus knowledge of any other messaging systems you want to connect to

- Associated technologies such as Windows NT workstation

- Directory synchronization with external directories

- Migration tools and utilities

- Windows 95, Windows 98, Windows V3.11, DOS, UNIX utilities associated with SMTP-based messaging such as sendmail, and Internet firewalls

- Visual Basic, Vbscript, Visual C++, and other development tools used to build or enhance electronic forms applications

- General networking experience

Few people have the ability to master all of these skills, neither time nor the wide experience required to achieve a good understanding of them all. This means that you'll probably need to spread skills across a team of individuals engaged in the pilot or use expertise bought in externally.

Don't forget other associated developments that may be happening at the same time as they may affect your pilot or the implementation by introducing new skills that must be factored into a training plan. For instance, SMS might be used to manage the deployment of Exchange clients and other desktop applications. Or your company may well have decided to use the Microsoft Internet Explorer (client) and Microsoft Internet Information Server for World Wide Web access and home page management. Who's responsible for these issues?

9.4   Was the pilot successful?

At the end of the exercise all pilots have to come up with some results, the most fundamental of which is an assessment of whether the product under trial is suitable for widespread deployment. Attached to this assessment are many caveats that determine the degree of success the deployment is likely to have. You may find that network links between servers need to be upgraded, that new hardware needs to be installed, client systems need more memory, or even that the whole thing should be put off for six months or so to allow you to sort out some other aspect of the overall infrastructure. You'll definitely need to have carefully built a draft plan for the roll-out in order to gauge whether a roll-out is feasible. The plan should include details of the Exchange sites and servers that are proposed together with details of how the Exchange structure is layered on top of the Windows NT security and network models. Finally, you should have a technical and end-user training plan laid out. All of these conclusions need to be documented and reviewed so that all possible issues are fully covered.

At the end of the day your management are likely to ask a number of basic questions that you'll need to have good answers for. Amongst the normal questions in this category are:

- How much will the deployment cost in total—software (server and clients), hardware (including upgrades), training, systems management, day-to-day operations, and consultancy?

- How long will the complete roll-out take from beginning to end?

- What benefits will the new messaging environment deliver to the organization (in general) as well as the end users?

The final question is whether or not it is worthwhile to move from an existing messaging infrastructure to a new one, albeit one as interesting as Microsoft Exchange. That question deserves far more attention than a brief paragraph or two here, so I'll cover it in detail in a separate chapter.

9.5   Summary

Running a pilot is always an interesting and important activity because it's the place where marketing hype is discarded and technical reality comes into focus. A good plan for the pilot that identifies all the important questions for your organization is an essential aid to producing accurate results and eventually a productive long-term implementation. Hopefully this chapter has managed to identify some of the challenges that you're likely to meet along the way if you make the decision to look at Exchange and its clients.

10

Migrating from Other Messaging Systems

Computer applications evolve in either of two ways. One route is to continually update, applying software and hardware upgrades as they become available. The other is to migrate from one system to another. The former is less painful than the latter, but sometimes a migration is deemed to be imperative and so it proceeds. In this chapter we'll look at some of the aspects of messaging systems that migrations bring to the fore, with particular reference to the tasks involved in planning for and then executing a migration of a messaging system to Exchange.

10.1   An end, or a beginning?

I hate migrations. It's a fact of life that a large number of Exchange installations will involve a migration in some form or other. Any migration I have ever been involved with has been painful, and many have left a bad taste in my mouth. No migration is or can be seamless and users always experience some impact. So it's important to be sure that a migration is justified, feasible, and the right thing to do. Asking yourself some questions and making sure you have answers, and then analyzing the content of the answers is an excellent way of verifying that a migration is the right thing to do. In my opinion, amongst the first questions that must be answered in relation to a migration from an existing electronic mail system to Exchange are:

- Why are we considering a migration away from our existing system?
- What benefits are going to be delivered to the user community after the migration is accomplished?
- Can the benefits be quantified in terms of finance or extra functionality that can now be provided to users?
- When do we want the migration to be completed by?
- What data will be involved in the migration?
- How will the data be migrated?

Different organizations will place varying degrees of importance on the questions listed above, and no doubt everyone has their own specific questions that they'll want to add. I feel it's important to have absolute clarity about all the issues before plunging into a migration so that those involved can justify the time, expense, and other costs to both users and management.

Perhaps another question that should be asked at this time is whether a better and more effective job can be done with the messaging system that you're considering moving from? I have seen many situations where a messaging system is badly managed and doesn't deliver a good level of service to user communities. It may well be the case that replacing the current system with a new system, like Exchange, will draw a line underneath all of the ineffective management that has gone before, but it's more likely that the old bad habits will be transferred from one system to another. Clearly if you're aware of the danger steps can be taken to ensure that current problems are addressed and eliminated as part of the migration project.

If a mail system is in operation today you should take advantage by extracting various operational statistics to help understand:

- The volume of messages being processed by the system.

- The amount of data (messages) being stored in shared system areas and user (or personal) areas.

- Details of any other application that depends in any way on the messaging system. Workflow systems are obvious examples of systems which often depend on electronic mail, but there can be applications that make sporadic use of electronic mail, possibly to generate warning or other status messages, and you need to know about these.

- The service levels being delivered to users. For example, how long does it take to transfer a message from one side of the organization to another? How long does it take for a message to arrive within the same physical site?

Migrations are unsuccessful if the new system cannot meet the same service levels as the existing system once the migration process is complete. If the hardware installed cannot cope with the volume of messages, if applications are disabled because they cannot communicate using the messaging system, if user data is lost or otherwise becomes inaccessible, or message delivery times are not improved then you really have to ask why you are even considering a migration in the first place.

10.2   Why migrate at all?

Are you migrating to Exchange because:

- You think it's a good idea, and anyway, everyone else seems to want to do it.
- Windows NT is the strategic computing platform for your organization, or at least Windows NT is the strategic choice for distributed application servers.
- Microsoft are the preferred software vendor for desktop and other applications.
- Exchange offers a significant increase in the functionality you already enjoy from your existing system.
- Exchange is the natural upgrade path for your existing mail system.
- The operation of an Exchange server will help to achieve a return on the additional investment required to perform the migration.

Not many people will openly agree with the first response listed above. Thinking something is a good idea is not a rational argument to back up a major change in any technical or computing infrastructure. The old adage "There goes the crowd; I must be with them" springs to mind here. Are you proposing to migrate because someone else says that it's a good idea.

I often wonder about the ideas and opinions expressed in the content of reviews written in computer magazines as well as the conclusions reached at the end of product reviews. There's no doubt that many journalists are very competent individuals with a broad range of expertise, but it's difficult to write knowledgeably about a mail system unless you've lived and breathed with the system in an operational environment over a period of time. Running a messaging system for ten or twenty users is easy, running the same software for hundreds of users exposes the weak points as well as the strengths. The lesson here is simple. Never take someone else's opinion as fact. You know your computing environment best so accept input from many sources and then make your own mind up.

10.2.1   Dealing with the existing investment

Many companies find themselves in a situation where they have a huge financial investment in their current mainframe or mini-computer based electronic mail system. The investment is represented by hardware, software licenses, knowledge (programming, administration, and user), data, any associated applications which may use the system in one form or another, the infrastructure put in place to enable the electronic mail system to operate, and whatever connections exist to other messaging systems. Quite a shopping list when the time comes to justify a migration!

If you find yourself in a situation where your company really must continue to leverage off its existing financial investment and can't afford to engage in a total migration the best tactic to adopt is to establish Exchange as the "new" platform. If any opportunity arises to move users off the older system, perhaps as hardware maintenance contracts expire or systems reach their end of life, or new user communities request an electronic mail server they can be attached to an Exchange server. This tactic establishes a situation where two "islands" of electronic messaging exist within the company—the old established system and Exchange. Gradually, over time, the aim is to grow the Exchange island and diminish the other and get to a stage where a total cut-over can be justified.

An approach like this minimizes the additional investment required to introduce Exchange while it maximizes the investment represented by the existing system. It also allows the Exchange implementation to progress at a comfortable, well-controlled pace. On the other hand, you will have to devote a lot of time and attention to ensuring that the best possible connectivity is maintained between the two messaging islands.

Electronic mail is a highly visible application because it affects almost every desktop in a company. Everyone from the Chief Executive Officer down to the newest entrant might well be using e-mail, so when something goes wrong its effects are felt everywhere, including in the job continuation prospects of system administrators. Accordingly it is essential that the migration is done right no matter what tactics need to be adopted in order to achieve eventual success.

10.2.2 Strategic computing platforms

The decision about the strategic computing platform for your organization is often not surrounded in clarity. The larger the organization and the more autonomous the divisions within the organization the harder it is to enforce strategic decisions. In these situations you'll often find tactical compromises being made to facilitate the requirements of specific applications or organizational entities.

Windows NT grows in capability and functionality all the time. The original version (V3.1) was slow, lacked applications, and needed lots of hardware. Even so, V3.1 created a clear differentiation between

Windows, the user-oriented desktop operating system, and a much more robust and interesting high-end server specifically designed for applications. Each release since has added functionality to the point where Windows NT workstation is a more than viable option for deployment as a generalized desktop platform, and Windows NT server is probably the most flexible distributed application server available today. It's important not to engage in too much hype however. Windows NT is good, but there are lots of situations where it would be inappropriate or just plain foolish to even consider NT. The time when Windows NT takes over from mainframes when applications like airline booking systems is probably not yet with us!

If your organization has determined that Windows NT is a strategic computing platform the decision to migrate towards Exchange is easy. But what happens if the strategic platform is UNIX (any variant), or a proprietary operating system such as OpenVMS or IBM MVS? How then does Exchange fit into the overall picture? Can the implementation of an electronic messaging system on Windows NT be represented (and agreed) as a tactical solution? And how will the Windows NT servers fit into other aspects of the computing infrastructure such as network security or integrated network management?

Even if Windows NT is the nominated choice for a strategic organization-wide computing platform you must ensure that the implementation of Exchange accommodates the Windows NT domain and network infrastructures that might already be in place. Or if you're only starting with Windows NT, as we've mentioned before, the initial implementation of Windows NT must take the requirements of Exchange into account. Remember that it is very difficult to change items such as server and site names once the implementation starts, so it's important to take these factors into account in your migration plan.

If Windows NT is new to your organization a migration is easier because you can plan the introduction of Exchange and Windows NT together as an integrated entity rather than having to retrofit Exchange on top of an existing NT infrastructure. However, the purely practical aspects involved in the introduction of any new computer platform such as physical security, data backups, and communications might well be impacted by the requirements of Exchange. For instance, how will the Exchange data structures be backed up, when will this take place, and will it stop people using the messaging service while backups are taken?

The question of Microsoft as the preferred vendor for software applications is linked, in some respects, to the decision about Windows NT. If Windows NT is your strategic computing platform then there are strong and compelling reasons to select other Microsoft applications in the areas they are available. All of the products in the BackOffice and Microsoft Office sets fall into this category.

10.2.3 Will Exchange provide more functionality than my existing system?

Determining whether a move to Exchange will provide more functionality than an existing system depends on:

- The functionality in Exchange that your users will actually use. For example, there's no value at all in replication of public folders if this type of information sharing is not going to be used.

- Whether any commonly-used or otherwise desirable features available in the existing system are not available in Exchange. Workflow is one example. Even with the introduction of Exchange Routing Objects, it's probable that the out-of-the-box workflow features currently available in Exchange are not as well developed or mature as those available in the latest releases of Lotus Notes (for example). If you currently run a Lotus Notes shop and have a number of workflow applications deployed and in use on a day-to-day basis to solve real business problems, you'll have a challenge to move the people who depend on those applications if you can't come up with a replacement. A further challenge is posed by a potential requirement to have a method to access old data represented by workflow items that have been processed in the past.

Knowledge of the features the user community deem to be important is essential when you compare one system against another. You might get excited about the prospect of the latest whiz-bang-wallop feature that's only available in a specific product. However, how many people actually use all of the features provided in the products they have today and will your users feel the same way about the features you now propose to introduce? Will the feature make them more productive, assuming they'll ever use it?

The AutoSignature and Rules Wizard features offered by Outlook clients are two good examples of what I mean. AutoSignature allows users to add a piece of text to messages before they are sent to provide additional information about the originator. In the UNIX messaging world this text is known as a signature. The Rules Wizard can act as a filter against new mail messages as they arrive, taking action for messages that meet preset criteria. For instance, refile all new messages from my manager into the wastebasket, or send anything that references a particular project to another user because they've taken responsibility for that project now.

10.2.4 Following the upgrade paths

Microsoft Mail is the only mail system that Exchange can reasonably be regarded as the natural or evolutionary upgrade path. Indeed, the primary market for the initial implementations of Exchange were the many thousands of Microsoft Mail post offices running around the world. With over 10 million active users of Exchange, things have moved on a little now, and now I encounter more and more Lotus cc:Mail post offices being migrated to Exchange now, so maybe Exchange can be regarded as a natural evolutionary path for cc:Mail?

So if you're running Microsoft Mail now you have the easiest argument to make for a migration. Exchange servers can be installed to take the place of the Microsoft Mail Post Offices, and the Microsoft Mail clients can be replaced by Exchange clients. Because the two clients come from the same vendor they share many common features, at least on the surface and in terminology, so the visual and immediate impact on day to day use after a switch-over is reasonably limited. Exchange includes a migration wizard to help users transfer the contents of their Microsoft Mail file cabinets into Exchange, so most of the important points in relation to a migration can be taken care of in an almost automatic manner.

If you're running another mail system the situation is different. No other vendor is going to be happy to see customers migrating away from their software (not to mention hardware), so you can hardly expect to see glowing recommendations for Exchange as the upgrade option of choice. You can also expect to incur more costs during the migration because the movement of user information, messages, and documents is not going to be as automatic or straightforward.

10.2.5 Achieving a return on your investment

Messaging often becomes a mission-critical application. In other words, if messaging is not available to users business suffers. Even after messaging is acknowledged to be a mission-critical application you want to get good value for the investment made to build and operate the messaging environment. If you now propose to migrate from one system to another then ideally the total value gained from the exercise should exceed the costs by a considerable margin.

Determining an accurate total for the costs of migration is not an exact science as there are many factors that will influence the outcome. Migrations tend to be difficult to cost to any exact degree. In fact, migrations are rather like household do-it-yourself exercises in that hidden costs reveal themselves after a start is made on a job. For instance, you decide to change the wallpaper in a room only to find that there are holes behind the existing wallpaper, so you need to fill them in. Once the paper is up it looks good, but the woodwork looks dull and blemished in comparison so you really need to apply a new coat of paint. And if the woodwork is done the ceilings should be done to match. All additional costs.

To avoid unpleasant surprises I think it's a good idea to set down a list of bullet points to cover the major cost headings. Here are some common areas of cost that might be met during a migration:

- Installation and configuration of all the necessary hardware, including upgrades to existing computers.

- Installation and configuration of Windows NT on the hardware according to the domain and security models you have chosen to use.

- Licensing and installation of Exchange on all relevant Windows NT computers.

- Payment of client access licenses for all active clients.

- Training people to use the client functionality (this is more expensive if you have to support a number of clients), including details about how to get to data that might remain on other systems. Ideally, the training will also focus on the differences between Exchange and the old messaging systems, and clearly explain how to perform the most common tasks. If functionality is available in the old system and not in Exchange that fact should be covered too, along with any workaround if one is available.

- Migrating user messages and documents from the existing mail system.

- Running a pilot and then proceeding with a roll-out.

Apart from the financial aspects of a migration I think it is also wise to consider the question of the long-term future for your current electronic mail system. Ask the vendor whether plans exist for new versions, when the new versions will be available and what features will be delivered in the new releases. If there is little future in the current mail system then the financial aspects of a proposal to migrate to Exchange may quickly become a moot point. If a migration is going to be required anyway at some point in the future it makes sense to take the pain now to establish a new messaging system and go forward so that maximum benefit can be gained from the new system. On the other hand, if detailed plans exist to develop and enhance your existing electronic mail system the question of how much it will cost to upgrade to new releases should be asked. If you don't have a maintenance or other type of support contract you may have to purchase server and client software again, albeit possibly at a discounted price, but even if the software upgrades are free what another possible costs might be incurred?

Table 10.1 *Comparing the cost of upgrading or migrating*

Potential area of cost	$ cost of migration to Microsoft Exchange	$ cost to evolve existing electronic mail system
Client software		
Server software		
Ongoing support costs for client software. For example, the cost to upgrade to new releases of the software or the right to report problems to a support centre.		
Ongoing support costs for server software		
User training. Remember that moving to a new version of any software may impact users and require some degree of retraining.		
Programmer/system manager training.		
Any additional or new hardware costs (memory upgrades, disks, etc.) for user PCs.		
Any additional or new hardware costs for the servers involved in the electronic mail system.		
External consulting or other personnel costs.		
Messaging gateways. Some gateways may only be required during the migration period.		
File format converters or viewers either for PC clients or elsewhere in the network.		
Associated applications (e.g. time management, workflow), both servers and clients. Costs might include rewriting or replacing applications.		
Directory synchronization, both initial costs to implement synchronization plus ongoing costs to ensure that synchronization occurs on a regular and predictable basis.		
Ongoing system management/system administration		
Operating a user Help Desk.		
Remote access (telephone communications, RAS systems and whatever other infrastructure is required).		
LAN/WAN networks and other communications. For example, will you require new telecommunications links?		
Overall Total Costs	$	$

The points above list some of the areas where costs may arise. It's often a useful exercise to compare the costs of migration against the costs of staying with an existing mail system, as shown in Table 10.1. There are two ways to approach this exercise. First, you can assume that the existing system will stay in place in much the same shape as it is today. Or, more realistically if users are complaining about the features and service provided by the current system, you can factor in the costs to evolve the system so that it provides approximately the same level of functionality as you can expect from Exchange.

Listing the potential areas of cost is easy, but putting a real degree of exactitude on these costs is not. Costs are likely to occur over an extended period of time and the amounts involved will differ from site to site. The desired (or required) rate of return on investments will also vary from organization to organization. Technical people might sometimes wish that financial issues would go away but you have to be able to answer the question about how much the whole exercise will cost, and what additional value will be delivered to the organization once the migration is complete. Saying that everything will be better, more up to date, more robust and compliant with standards, messages will be transmitted more securely and faster or that the Exchange architecture is much more impressive than the current system will surely cut no ice with the financial wizards. It's better to come up with some realistic figures for the work, factor it into an operational budget, and seek to justify the expenditure through reasons like:

- Lower cost of ownership (based on deployment on Windows NT systems rather than mini- or mainframe computers) over a reasonable period, say three years. The cost here includes initial purchase plus depreciation.

- Lower power consumption.

- Less real estate is needed to build expensive air-conditioned computer rooms. Production NT servers should be housed in proper conditions, but their requirements are usually less stringent than mainframe or mini-computers.

- Enabling the organization to achieve higher levels of quality through the deployment of work-group applications rather than the purely interpersonal nature of simple electronic mail. Give some examples to illustrate the point such as the use of replicated public folders to automatically distribute up to date marketing information across the enterprise.

- Implementation of other valued-added applications enabled by Exchange that solve business problems. For instance, integrating a voice mail system with Exchange to replace an existing voice mail system that may be standalone and perhaps showing signs of age.

Whatever logic you come up with to justify the decision you must be realistic. Use figures intelligently to show costs benefits and illustrate your points with examples of how new functionality will enable people to work together more effectively. If your logic is not reasonable and cannot be backed up to other peoples' satisfaction the decision to progress with a migration is probably not a good one and you should take another hard look at your situation before going on.

10.3   When will the migration be over?

Migrations, like all other techniques, occupy a spectrum defining the different approaches that can be taken to the actual process. At one end you have the "Big Bang" approach, moving all users as quickly as possible from the old system to the new. Right at the other end of the spectrum is the phased, gentle movement, generally involving the migration of groups of users over an extended period of time.

Few experienced system managers like the risk factor involved in one-shot migrations. The one-shot technique is only ever practiced when the number of users and data involved is small, certainly at levels where people are comfortable that the migration can be carried out in a single day or over a weekend. Extended migration periods can be difficult to manage, and more often than not involve the introduction of potential bottlenecks as messages pass through gateways. Directory synchronization for addressing information is also an issue to be managed during migrations. We'll discuss these points in more detail later on in this chapter.

Most organizations will conduct a pilot for Exchange before engaging in widespread deployment. Even if you have taken a strategic decision to use Windows NT and Exchange as your future messaging platform it's still a good idea to run a pilot. To reinforce the advice offered throughout this book, consider these good reasons for including a pilot implementation of Exchange server and clients in your migration plan:

- A pilot allows technical staff to get to know the capabilities and weaknesses of the new server in a real-life environment. You can use this experience to plan for:
  - The hardware configuration for server deployment. Determine how many servers will be required to support the total user population and where those servers will be located, as well as how they will form sites within the Exchange organization. You should make a first pass at allocating users across

the servers. You should consider the hardware and software required for client deployments too!

- The operational rules to be followed by system administrators and operators. For example, when will backups be taken and how will the backups be secured?

- The network links required to connect servers and clients. Do you need to reconfigure any parts of the network?

- The way Exchange will be installed on top of the Windows NT domain and security models deployed within the organization. If problems are detected the models may need adjustment, work that must be carried out before general deployment of Exchange begins.

- What third party software will be used in conjunction with Exchange. There is no point on planning to use different backup software, or a fax connector, or a full text retrieval package or virus checker in production if you don't include it in the pilot. The pilot will reveal the good and bad points about the add-on software, allowing you to make a more intelligent decision about its deployment into production environments.

- The order in which different groups within the organization will be moved to Exchange. In general it's best to plan to move groups that share a high degree of data commonality at one time in order to maximize the usefulness of functionality like public folders and to minimize the message flow outside the Exchange environment. This part of your plan will also help you identify when older systems can be switched off and hardware removed (and hardware and software maintenance contracts for the old systems terminated).

- Which Exchange servers will act as messaging servers and which will fulfill special roles such as points of connection with foreign messaging systems or public folder servers.

- Which clients will be used—Outlook, POP3, IMAP4, Windows CE, Web browsers?

- Migration of documents and users. Perhaps some special tools are required to extract, manipulate, and then import data from the system you are migrating from? If so, can these tools be obtained from external agencies or will they have to be written internally?

- Users need to be trained as they move from the older system to an Exchange client. A training plan should be prepared so that the user community is ready to move. The pilot allows the plan to be developed and verified. The training plan should answer questions like:

- What training will they receive? Will you provide users with customized quick look-up guides or cheat sheets for items specific to your environment such as electronic forms applications? Are there any good habits (for example, how to effectively use disk space within the Private Information Store) that you want to enforce during training sessions?

- Do users need to be told how to deal with data migrated from the old system? For example, how to deal with distribution lists that contain a mixture of people using the old system as well as Exchange?

- Who will deliver the training? Do you have an internal training department that can do the work or will an external training provider come in to deliver courses? How much will the training cost? Do you have a proposal to charge departments for the training their personnel will receive or will the total cost of the training be rolled up into the overall migration plan?

- When is the training available? Make sure that training is synchronized with the movement of users to Exchange. Training people too early is nearly as bad as training them too late.

- Support must be put in place so it's important to involve those who deliver end-user support in the pilot. Support personnel need training too, and this requirement should be addressed in the overall training plan. Experience gained in the pilot will help you identify exactly what form and content that training should take.

A proper pilot cannot be rushed. There's always a temptation to take a short cut on the basis that the sooner the new system goes into production the better, but this is a short-term view that inevitably leads to tears. The old adage that fools rush in where angels fear to tread comes to mind here.

Several times during 1995 Bill Gates was widely quoted to say that Exchange would not ship until its customers told Microsoft that it was ready (the same was said about Windows 95). Customers in this sense are the technical community, not end-users, and the judgement as to when the software was ready was made in a technical context and not related in any sense to corporate deployments. Make sure you are ready on all fronts by conducting a comprehensive pilot before proceeding with the migration. How long will this take? That depends on your organization, but allow at least two months.

After a good pilot you should have much of the information necessary for the deployment. You won't have everything, and you can expect to encounter unforeseen problems as you proceed, but at least you should be confident enough to plan for a fairly aggressive roll-out schedule. Migrating 50 to 100 users a week is certainly a sustainable rate over a prolonged period of time. Going any faster will place strain on everyone the implementation team, technical support, help desk, training department, and the users themselves. At 50–100 users per week you'll be able to migrate between 2,500 and 5,000 users in a year while maintaining service levels to users.

10.4   Migrating information

Messaging systems, or rather messaging systems that are not well managed, have a remarkable tendency to accumulate vast quantities of data. Even when systems are managed and the amount of messages users can keep are restricted there will still be a fair amount of data to deal with when migration time comes around.

All messaging systems have some degree of junk mail. By this I mean messages that have no relationship to any business activity. Invitations to lunch, to meet after hours, to engage in a social activity, or just people exchanging views on the major topics of the day all generate message traffic, tying up valuable disk space and possibly even preventing users sending business messages because some system limits are reached. Clearly junk mail should not be migrated and the first step before attempting to perform any migration is to strip any such message from the system.

The largest folder I ever saw in active use in a mail system held 14,000 messages, while the largest file cabinet held 225,000 objects. Migrating message containers that hold such a large volume of documents is clearly a challenge, but maybe you don't have to migrate them at all? Can the older file cabinet system remain in situ for an agreed length of time after users begin to use Exchange as their default messaging system? Can the documents be accessed in a mode that allows users to perform read, fetch, and delete operations, perhaps from a customized version of the application that they were originally created with? If you decide to leave the older system operational, albeit in a read-only mode, it's a good idea to clearly set a date in the future at which time the older system will be disconnected. Turning off a system, albeit it on a clearly advertised date is hard for users as it irrevocably removes their access to documents that may well contain valuable information and this is the point when migration utilities need to be considered.

10.4.1 Migration wizards and other tools

Microsoft has provided a tool called the Migration Wizard to move messages and other information created in foreign messaging systems to Exchange. The Migration Wizard always runs on a Windows NT workstation or server, so the information it processes must be made available to the Wizard. This is done in two ways:

- Direct access (perhaps via a networked drive) to PC files. This is the approach taken when migrating messages from Microsoft Mail and Lotus cc:Mail post offices.

- Stripping information from a messaging system and writing it out into files in a highly structured manner. These files are then moved to the Windows NT system and processed by the Migration Wizard. This is the approach used to migrate host-based electronic mail systems.

Figure 10.1 *The Migration Wizard*

The Exchange Migration Wizard is able to migrate messages from the following messaging systems:

- Microsoft Mail
- DIGITAL ALL-IN-1
- IBM PROFS
- Lotus cc:Mail
- Novell GroupWise
- Netscape Collabra

- Verimation MEMO

Exchange V5.5 SP1 introduces support for the migration of mail-boxes and calendars from Lotus Notes and Lotus Domino servers. Administrators can migrate from Notes and Domino releases 3.x and 4.x running on Microsoft Windows NT Server, IBM OS/2, Novell NetWare and UNIX.

The Exchange resource kit includes unsupported migration utilities to help migrate users of UNIX systems that use the sendmail utility. Even though they are built around a standard utility, the nature of UNIX means that sendmail-based messaging systems vary greatly in implementation. The sendmail migration utilities might therefore be regarded as a starting point, something that may require additional effort to get right in any particular set of circumstances.

While all migrations eventually use the same Migration Wizard to import data there are fundamental differences between e-mail systems built around PC LAN file-sharing architectures and those that run on mini- or mainframe computers. When dealing with a PC LAN-based mail system, like Microsoft Mail or Lotus cc:Mail, the extract and load operations can sometimes be carried out on the same server, or at least the extract files can be created and immediately accessed by the migration wizard on a network file location that's accessible from the Windows NT computer where Exchange is running. This makes the whole process much easier as you don't have to copy files around the network during the transfer. Because data held in host-based systems (PROFS, MEMO, and ALL-IN-1) is not normally directly accessible from Windows NT the basic approach to the task of migration is evolved a little into three phases, illustrated in Figure 10.2.

1.   Create the extract files on the host system. Procedures for the supported operating system are provided as part of the Exchange kit and can be used to create the extract files. The procedures are written in languages (interpreted or compiled) appropriate for the operating system. For example, some of the procedures to migrate information from Verimation MEMO systems are written in the JCL (Job Control Language) for IBM MVS mainframes while forms, scripts, and some VMS Macro code are provided for ALL-IN-1 systems.

2.   Transfer the extract files to the target Exchange server. Some form of network connection can be used or the information can be transferred using magnetic media.

3.   Run the Exchange Migration Wizard.

Apart from the ease of data access (for PC based migration utilities), the potential volume of data that may need to be migrated often marks another difference between host- and PC-based electronic mail systems. As I've mentioned before, there are known instances of single user accounts storing hundreds of thousands of messages. Of course, such accounts are unusual and the majority of system managers impose strict quotas based on the number of messages a user can store or the amount of disk space they can occupy on the server. Nevertheless, my own personal observation is that users on host-based systems are more prone to the accumulation of old or unwanted messages, what you might call "file cabinet debris", especially if they've been using the host system for years. Clearly steps should be taken to eliminate as much of this debris before the migration process begins as otherwise the whole procedure will take much longer and will use more resources than necessary.

Figure 10.2
Steps in migrating host-based messages

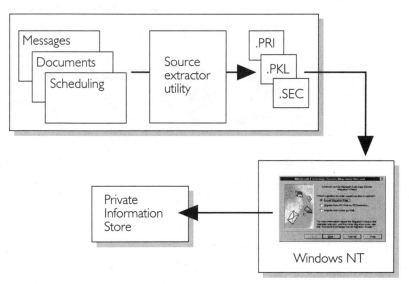

10.4.2 **Extracting and importing**

In simple terms, the Exchange migration wizard works by analyzing the contents of one or more files generated from a source messaging system. Typically three different types of files are extracted from a source system:

- The packing list file. This file contains some information about the data that is being migrated, such as the code page for the character sct used to create the contents, plus the names of all the other files associated with the extract.

- Primary intermediate files. These files contain the data necessary to create new Exchange mailboxes or custom recipients. They also contain message headers, entries for the personal address book, and pointers to data used by secondary intermediate files.

- Secondary intermediate files. These files contain the bulk of the data to be imported into Exchange and include message bodies and attachments and any data that can be extracted from an older time management or scheduling system.

Packing list files are usually given a file extension of .PKL. For example, TREDMOND.PKL. Primary intermediate files use a file extension of .PRI while secondary intermediate files use the file extension .SEC. There are no hard and fast rules for naming the files and each source extractor is free to name files whatever way it wishes. The intermediate files must be located in the same directory as the packing list. The Exchange migration wizard is not able to search disks for intermediate files, so if they can't be found in the same directory the import operation will fail.

Figure 10.3
Selecting an extract file for the Migration Wizard

The source extract files are formatted according to a set of rules specified by the Exchange developers. Failure to follow the rules when extracting information from a source system will inevitably lead to problems when the time comes for the Exchange migration wizard to process the badly-formatted data. The old rule of "rubbish in leads to rubbish out" is very true in this case.

The basic approach to the migration process for host-based messaging systems is:

- Extract files from the source messaging system
- Run the migration wizard

There can be a period of elapsed time between the two steps, but this is undesirable because the users involved cannot participate in messaging communications until their mailboxes have been transferred to Exchange. An important part of the planning for migration is to establish when mailboxes can be moved with the least impact on users.

For best results the migration wizard should be run on the server where the Private Information Store for the new mailboxes is located. As the import operations require a fairly heavy level of processing it's wise to schedule some time when the server is relatively inactive. Attempting to import thousands of messages for newly migrated mailboxes in the morning when users are arriving and logging in to their mailboxes to read their new mail will not guarantee good system responsiveness.

10.4.3 How long will the wizard take?

Depending on the capacity of the server and its current workload the migration wizard can take some time to import files for a user who's been a prolific generator of messages and documents on their previous system. Rough measurements taken for a range of users migrated from a host-based system show that on a lightly loaded server powered by an Intel 120 MHz Pentium CPU the migration wizard processes between 15 and 40 messages per minute. Messages range in size from small 2K files to 2 MB or more (including attachments), so clearly the throughput achieved in your environment greatly depends on the average size of message and the capacity of the server to unpack the messages from the source files. Farsighted system administrators include trial imports in the list of tasks for a pilot.

Apart from the length of time taken to import a user's files system administrators should be aware of two other side-effects of the import process. First, importing a large quantity of information from a legacy system can quickly blow any limit that has been set on the space allocated in the Private Information Store for a user's mailbox. The migration wizard ignores space limitations on user mailboxes, the logic apparently being that it's best to get the information into the mailbox and then let the user sort out what they should discard in order to get back under the limit. Second, importing large quantities of information gives the Exchange databases a lot of work to do and generates a significant load on the system, which may impact response times for other users. Before starting any import operation make sure that enough disk space is available to allow the Private Information Store to expand as files as imported. If you're about to import ten users, each of whom has generated source import files amounting to 30 MB or so (which isn't really a lot for many heavy mail users), make sure that the disk holding the Private Information Store has 300MB (plus at least a 10% margin for error) available. This is basic system management, but it's amazing how many people forget to look after the simple things and are surprised when things go wrong.

10.4.4 The effect of migrating data on the Private Information Store

To a certain degree, migrated data is like a millstone around the neck of the Private Information Store. There is no guarantee that users will ever review, visit, use, or process the data that the implementation team migrates so carefully on their behalf. Some data will be used, and that data will no doubt prove valuable to the people concerned, but previous experience of migrations indicates that the majority of migrated data will remain largely untouched until users take it upon themselves to clean it all out, probably when they begin to receive warnings that their allocation within the store is about to be exceeded.

Why describe data taken from a previous mail system as a millstone around the neck of the Private Information Store? What harm does it do to migrate data and import it into the Private Information Store? Consider the consequences of migration:

- Unless users delete portions of the migrated data it cannot be compacted by the ESEUTIL utility. Thus, the Private Information Store will grow from a base represented by the data that's been imported and will fill available disk space faster than if everyone had started off with an empty mailbox. I know several installations where migrated data occupies 6GB or more in a store.

- The migrated data must be backed up along with the rest of the store. There's no way to say "only backup new stuff,", as everything must be written out to tape. The time required to backup the Information Store is therefore greatly extended, and restore operations (which hopefully will never be necessary) are also complicated by longer restore times.

- Users are affected too. The migrated data occupies their quota within the store, leaving them less to work with. This assumes that you place limits on the amount of space people can occupy within the store.

The top two points are operational considerations that affect day to day server management. The last point only affects users, but it's easy to spend a lot of time cleaning up mailboxes just to get under a user's limit. Inevitably the messages that are cleaned out are never the data that was migrated, perhaps because users don't want to delete items that they brought across from their "old" system.

10.4.5 How long will it take to migrate a user?

Experience of a large number of migration projects involving different mail systems shows that it takes a surprising amount of time to migrate a single user. Consider the tasks that are involved:

1. Creating the new Windows NT account and Exchange mailbox.

2. Adjusting the contents of distribution lists on both the legacy system and Exchange.

3. Extracting data to be migrated from the legacy system.

4. Transferring the data to the Windows NT server where the Migration Wizard will run.

5. Running the Migration Wizard.

6. Checking that data has been loaded correctly into the user's mailbox.

7. Checking that the user profile is correctly configured and that the user can log-in to the mailbox.

8. Setting up an auto-forward or auto-direct on the legacy system so that new messages will be forwarded to Exchange.

9. Disabling the old user account on the legacy system so that the user can't revert back to using the legacy system after their data is migrated.

10. Updating the corporate directories so that the migrated user is correctly identified as an Exchange user.

11. Contacting the user to tell them that their new mailbox is ready to go.

Each step takes its own amount of time and it's difficult to trim it down. Extracting data, transferring it across the network to the new server, and running the migration wizard takes the most time, but even if the amount of migration data is minimized it's hard to get the average time per user under 25–30 minutes. Taking this figure as the basis for calculation, over a sustained period of time a system administrator can probably transfer 16–20 users in a working day. However, the amount of time to process a user is greatly dependent on the volume of data to be processed. For example, large Microsoft Mail MMF files (greater than 100 MB) can easily take 30 minutes to process, and it is not unknown to encounter MMF files larger than 400 MB. Processing a huge amount of data will extend the time to migrate any user to several hours and extend the overall migration period. For this reason alone it is wise to aggressively encourage users to reduce the amount of data to be migrated. Murphy's Law (the 22nd in the series) states that the users with the largest amount of data occupy the most senior positions within a company, and if this is true in your case you're probably going to have to grin and accept the challenge.

If other steps are included, like having to configure the user PC with a new TCP/IP address, DHCP or WINS information, then the number of users that can be migrated in a single day will drop to between 8–10. Your mileage will vary, but you'll only know exactly how when you begin the actual migration.

Inexperienced or low-level staff cannot carry out all of the tasks listed above. Privileged access is required to the legacy mail system, Windows NT, and Exchange. A certain knowledge of networking is required, and a fair knowledge of Exchange. Using valuable system administration time to migrate hundreds of users over hundreds of hours of work isn't perhaps the most effective use of your system administrators, so attempts have been made to reduce the average time required to process a single user. Amongst the most valuable tactics are:

1.   Reduce the amount of data to be migrated to nil, or as close as possible to that figure. Encourage users not to take any of their old messages over to Exchange. There is no auto-magic function in the migration tools. Data that is processed by the migration wizard isn't automatically upgraded in the value of its content so that it becomes essential business data once it's imported into Exchange. A non-delivery notification message in one messaging system is the same everywhere, but it still surprises me to find that people are quite content to allow users to move anything they want, including all the junk mail in their old mailbox, to Exchange. Apart from slowing down the migration process, the old junk reduces the space available in the Private Information Store and increases the time required to take system backups.

2.   Provide tools that can be run by users rather than system administrators. If a MAPI service provider exists for the legacy system it can be used to allow users connect back to the old system from an Exchange client. They can then drag and drop any items they wish to keep over to Exchange. After a specified period of time access to the legacy system should be turned off, so the user has an interest in doing the work themselves before their old account is discarded. Apart from MAPI service providers there are other specialized migration tools

that can be controlled by users. A quick scan of the Web to see what's available now would be a good thing to do. Document format conversion is the major issue encountered with these tools. If the legacy system stored items in a particular format then the tool must be able to convert the items to a more suitable format (simple text, RTF, or Word for Windows) as the items are moved to Exchange.

3.   Stage PCs and ready a "hot-swap" of the user environment. If you're moving from Windows V3.11 to Windows 95 or Windows NT, upgrading your office application suite, and changing a network protocol in addition to migrating to Exchange, then big benefits can be gained by preparing a PC off-line before swapping it in when the time comes to migrate the user. The configuration can be fully tested before it is presented to the user and should therefore work without any difficulties when installed on the user desktop. This tactic is particularly useful if you intend upgrading desktop hardware.

Everyone's experience of Exchange migrations is growing all the time. Talk to other system administrators and consultants to see how they have handled the situation, and then make your own decision based on the requirements of your site.

10.4.6   The quality of the migration tools

The quality of the source extractors and their ability to deal with different items of data that may be stored in the repositories on the host systems varies greatly. I don't find this situation to be surprising at all because it is very difficult to build generic extract utilities capable of handling the situation at every installation. In general it seems that if you've restricted your use of the host system to pure messaging you shouldn't have any problems, but if you've built applications on top of the host messaging system then those application objects may not be processed correctly by the source extractors. And of course, even if the source extractor can process the application objects there is still the issue of what should be done with that object after it is imported into Exchange.

The evolution of a host-based system to incorporate PC clients can also cause problems. Host systems accessed through video terminals typically only store simple text messages and attachments, but PC clients introduce PC format objects as attachments to messages or electronic documents stored on the host in preference to a DOS device. PC clients such as TeamLinks (for DIGITAL's ALL-IN-1 or MailWorks servers) leverage the central storage capabilities of a host system and off-load processing to intelligent clients, and have become more and more popular over the last few years. The question that arises when PC clients join the equation is whether the source extractor is able to deal with PC format documents, messages, and attachments, and if they are, will the information written into the files for the migration wizard make any sense after it is imported into Exchange? I have certainly encountered some significant problems with the standard source extractors when they attempt to process PC format files, especially with ALL-IN-1. If you're interested in migrating from ALL-IN-1 be aware that the Macro code provided with Exchange V4.0 to populate the source extract files is only able to run on VAX processors. Exchange V5.0 updated the code to support Alpha.

These issues point to a general need to test the migration utilities in your own environment before making any assumption that just because the utilities come along with Exchange they're going to perform perfectly. My own experience with the migration utilities indicates that problem areas do exist and need to be worked around. Reducing the amount of data to be migrated helps. The less data there is to migrate, the less chance there'll be that problems will be encountered.

10.4.7 Breaking up the migration into achievable steps

It is wise not to attempt to transfer too many users at one time, unless you know that the users have very few messages to move. Some of the migration tools impose a limit, but even if they don't you should think the whole operation through. Breaking up the user population into groups of 50 or 100 creates more extract and move operations, but it also creates a much more manageable situation. For instance, if you attempt to move 500 users at one time:

- Do you have enough disk space for all the temporary files required for extracted data?

- Will you be able to move the volume of data represented by the extract files over to the Exchange computer in a reasonable time?

- Will the Exchange migration wizard be able to import all the data in the extract files in a reasonable time?

- Will your training department be ready to train so many users in a short period of time?

It may be possible that everything can be accomplished in one weekend, but it is the case that everything can be done provided it all goes exactly to plan without any errors creeping in? In other words, do you have any redundancy built into the plan just in case something goes wrong?

Host systems that provide purely messaging functions are easier to migrate than those which take a broader view of office automation. MEMO and PROFS are both good electronic mail systems, and offer some degree of other functionality like scheduling. But neither takes the concept of an electronic file cabinet much further than the level necessary to store and access messages. Systems which enable distributed shared drawers or folders, such as Exchange, are more difficult to migrate because the shared elements of the file cabinet may not have an equivalent in Exchange, or the migration utilities may not be able to process the data stored in these repositories. Further complications arise if the file cabinet is used as a base for applications such as workflow or EDI, especially if users are allowed to mix and match application-specific objects with mail messages and documents within their mailboxes.

All messaging systems differ in one way or another, so it is more than possible that some of the information held about messages by your current mail system may not migrate across to Exchange. The migration wizard is easy to use and provides reasonable functionality, but it doesn't attempt to resolve conflicts between Exchange and the source system. The general rule is that if a reasonable match can be made between Exchange and the other system regarding message attributes the information will move across. Some message attributes are generic and shared across all systems, such as message subject. Others, such as the X.400 concept of a reply-to-list, are more esoteric and will not be migrated.

10.4.8 Getting help on migrations

Lots of people are going to migrate other messaging systems to Exchange. In turn this means that there should be plenty of experience recorded in public forums dedicated to Exchange like the Internet Exchange mailing list. It would be unreasonable to expect that the migration utilities will be able to handle 100% of all the different types of messages and other objects held on messaging systems, so you can expect to encounter some problems or adventures along the way. In these situations it can be very profitable to browse through the contents of whatever sources of information are available to you, or to send a message to the Exchange mailing list.[1]

10.4.9 Migrating without a wizard

It's nice to have some automatic wizards available to migrate data to Exchange, but what happens if you have a mail system that Microsoft

---

1.   The address of the Internet mailing list for Exchange is given in the appendix at the back of the book.

don't provide a migration wizard for? The wizards packaged in Exchange are carefully targeted to facilitate migration of the most popular electronic mail systems, but over the last decade almost every computer manufacturer has developed one or more electronic mail systems. For example, DIGITAL's electronic mail systems include ALL-IN-1, MailWorks for OpenVMS and MailWorks for UNIX, not to mention the free VMSmail utility packaged with every OpenVMS computer. A migration wizard is only available for ALL-IN-1, so anyone migrating from one of the other systems is on their own.

What options exist for a do-it-yourself migration? The most obvious answer is to establish a connection via SMTP or X.400 and ask users to mail selected messages and other items of interest to their new account on the target Exchange server. This approach is practical and workable, but only when the quantity of messages involved are fairly limited. Most users rapidly lose patience if they are forced to mail more than a few dozen files, and no-one will be happy to be faced with the prospect of having to mail several hundred items before the connection is removed or their old account is deleted. Remember that mailing documents to Exchange is a two-part operation. First the messages have to be created and sent, and then they must be processed when they arrive into Exchange.

Some electronic mail systems have APIs or script languages and these can be used to develop automated procedures to export medium to large quantities of old messages and documents. One way to approach this task is to look at a sample load file generated from one of the source messaging systems supported by the Exchange migration wizard, and then proceed to work out how a similar load file can be created by extracting messages from your mail system. Make sure that all the necessary formatting information is included. There's no good rule to say what formatting information is mandatory and which is optional, so to avoid any messing around it's wise to create a load file that looks exactly the same as one prepared by an "official" extractor. Be prepared to go through a certain amount of trial and error before everything works all the time. Depending on the richness of the source system's APIs and the availability of experienced programmers accustomed to the APIs, expect to devote three to four weeks of hard work to produce a robust source extractor.

If your current electronic mail system runs on a DOS platform it may be enough to just export the messages out to DOS and leave them there, letting users import the files into Exchange as they are required (or missed). Importing files is easy—a simple drag and drop operation from the Windows Explorer or File Manager direct to the folder where the files should go. It's so easy that users may be tempted to drag and drop a little too much information, thus clogging up the Information Store with data that isn't really valuable any more.

Any do-it-yourself migration procedure will cost time and money. The question has to be asked whether all the energy devoted to migrating old messages could be used in a more productive manner elsewhere, and whether the cost involved in moving old information to Exchange can be justified by the content. Sites that have taken the radical approach to migration, that is to turn off the old system as the new system is turned on, often experience a period of confusion immediately after the change-over. But costs are lower and users quickly get used to the fact that the old messages are no longer available. As with many other aspects of a migration what users demand and how you react to the demands really depends on the situation pertaining within the installation. The golden rule is not to do any more work to migrate information than is strictly and absolutely necessary.

10.4.10 Migrating other data

An existing system may be used for more than just electronic mail or document management. DIGITAL's ALL-IN-1 office system is a good example of a popular office system in use world-wide since 1982. One of the reasons for ALL-IN-1's popularity is its application development capabilities which have allowed many organizations to build reasonably complex data processing applications which can be totally integrated with the electronic mail subsystem. While a migration wizard exists to move documents and messages from ALL-IN-1 file cabinets into Exchange folders, the wizard's magic cannot cope with any application-specific data.

In cases where a messaging system has been used as the basis for applications arrangements will have to be made to migrate the application completely or move the data into a format that is understood by an application available for Windows NT. In the latter case the usual tactic is to try to output the data into a format that's understood by the target application. One instance of where I've been able to do this is with 20/20, a spreadsheet application sold by Access Technology and it was quite common in its day, due to its multi-platform nature. 20/20 is able to write information out in WK1 format, and most Windows spreadsheet programs such as Lotus 1-2-3 or Excel are quite happy to import WK1 data. Spreadsheets can contain complex formulae. Retrograding content to a format like WK1 may retain data (the actual values in the cells) at the expense of losing the computations that link the cells. Test the effect of such a downgrade before making it the preferred option.

While it is often possible to output data from an older application in a compatible format the data may not be immediately reachable from Windows NT. This situation usually occurs when the source system is a mini- or mainframe computer. Moving data between computer systems is an area fraught with pitfalls, but there are at least three obvious methods to investigate:

1.   Using a common network protocol to transfer data from source to target system. FTP (File Transfer Protocol) is the protocol that offers most potential because it is supported on a very wide range of computer systems, including Windows NT. Be careful to ensure that data originating on systems with different character sets (for example, mainframes running the IBM MVS operating system) is converted before or after the transfer is performed.

2.   Moving the migration data to somewhere available to both source and target systems. For example, logical network-based disk drives that can be directly accessed by Windows NT. Novell NetWare or DIGITAL PATHWORKS network drives are both good examples of network devices that can be mapped by Windows NT and other computer systems.

3.   Using manual transfers via magnetic media. This method relies on a common type of media (disk or tape) being supported by both source and target systems as well as Windows NT having the ability to correctly interpret the data on the media once it is presented for reading.

In all cases don't assume that a method works just because you are able to transfer a small file, or even a selection of small files. Test all methods with real data and try and build an automated procedure to speed up the process. It's common to suddenly discover that the method you've chosen, or the procedure that's been carefully written, works quite happily with small amounts of data but falls over or takes an inordinate amount of time to complete when confronted with the data generated by more prolific users.

10.4.11 Cleaning up after the migration

It's obvious that disk space will be used during the migration process. You can't expect to extract information from the source messaging system to feed into Exchange without occupying some type of transient storage. Make sure that your preparations for the migration take transient disk space requirements into account. It's a good idea to thoroughly analyze the current disk space occupied by user messages and other files due to be moved before the migration process begins, and plan to make the total storage determined by the analysis plus an extra 20% margin for error available during the migration. The margin for error should also take care of the slight additional overhead imposed by the "format wrapper" created around messages by the Exchange migration tools.

Calculating the disk space used by an individual user is pretty easy if the current messaging system delivers separate copies of messages to all users. All you have to do is see how much disk space is allocated to message files in any user's account to know what figure to use for planning purposes. Calculating the requirements when a shared server-based message model (like Exchange) is used is harder unless utilities exist to report how much space a user is responsible for within the shared message store. This figure isn't always easy to get, nor is it obvious as to how you might go about getting it, so you may even end up writing some utilities to analyze data structures and extract the relevant information.

Before the migration process gets under way it's important that you take whatever steps are feasible to reduce the amount of data to be moved. If the source system provides facilities to remove unwanted or obsolete messages and documents from user mailboxes they should be used before any extracts are created. There isn't much point in moving all the contents of users' wastebasket (deleted) folders across into their new Exchange mailboxes, for example.

Depending on the space available on the source system you even may have to install an additional drive to use during the migration period. Of course, if small groups of users are to be moved you'll only have to ensure that the total disk space occupied by these users (plus the safety margin) is available. The disk space used for this activity should be reclaimed as soon as possible after the extracted data has been loaded into Exchange.

Apart from space used for migration purposes, it's also important to recognize that removing user-specific files from the system after a user has been successfully migrated to Exchange can reclaim disk space. You may want to leave a gap of a week or so after a user has been moved before taking the plunge and deleting their files, as you never know when problems might occur and the user has to be moved back to their original system. When the time comes to clean up you'll find that the task is purely manual as there is no functionality to do this included in the migration wizard.

10.5   Maintaining quality of service during the migration period

The migration period imposes stress on all layers within the messaging system. Backbones and connectors have more messages to process; the network is generally handling more data; users are struggling to cope with change brought upon by new applications; help desk staff are running harder to keep up with requests for help from users; and the system designers and implementation team are overseeing the migration process. The strain makes it difficult to maintain the overall quality of the service delivered to users, but keeping quality as high as possible should be a concern for the migration team, if only to avoid the "coffee machine" syndrome.

The coffee machine syndrome describes how easy it is for rumors and misconceptions about any change can arise. People gathering around the coffee machine, or water fountain, to discuss various happenings can quickly decide that a new computer system or application isn't much good, coloring the view of other users including those who have never even used the system! The very worst thing that can be said is "Everything worked with the old email system, but now that I've moved to Exchange email to my friends and colleagues just isn't delivered...." The migration team wants to make the implementation of Exchange a complete success, and the best way to do this and stop rumors spreading is to maintain or increase the level of quality delivered by the messaging service.

In this respect the entirety of the messaging service is composed of the legacy mail system or systems, backbones and connectors, the corporate directory, and Exchange. The focus may be on migrating to Exchange, but many companies make the mistake of concentrating on Exchange to the expense of the other components. Once the migration is complete then absolute concentration can be devoted to the exploitation of Exchange, but until the migration is over we've got to deal with the entire service as a whole.

There are a number of important areas to consider:

- The speed in which messages are delivered throughout the whole system and the degree of fidelity for message contents and attachments
- The accuracy of the corporate mail directories
- The satisfaction of users with the migration process
- The ability and willingness of the help desk staff to handle questions for both Exchange and the legacy mail systems until the migration is complete

- Mail-enabled applications
- Operation of the legacy mail systems

When two or more messaging systems are joined together it is inevitable that gateways and connectors must be used to achieve the join. Messages can be slowed as they pass through gateways, so the first goal to achieve is to maintain the overall transfer time for messages between different systems. People perceive transfer time differently to the stark technical detail. As long as users perceive that their messages are transported between systems as fast as they were delivered by the legacy system they'll be happy. Exchange will not deliver a message to recipients on foreign mail systems as quickly as local messages. The aim therefore is to ensure that people don't realize that extra time is required to transport a message from IS to MTA to connector to the foreign system and eventually to the recipient. If messages arrive within ten minutes people are usually happy, but if delivery intervals extend out towards twenty minutes, or worse again, to an hour or more, users will begin to lose faith in the system. Fortunately, the Exchange connectors are fast and capable of handling a large volume of messages on a daily basis, so providing adequate network links are available between the two systems and the gateways are configured with sufficient power to process the load, messages should flow at a sufficient speed.

Gateways will be loaded as migrations proceed. A good pilot deployment will give you some indication of how much traffic flows in both directions. You should note this data and try and predict what the likely volume will be when the migration demands most of the gateways, usually at the half-way mark, when an equal number of people use each mail system. Make sure that the gateways are configured to handle surges in demand and are still capable of processing messages quickly at peak times. Training plays its part to keep messages flowing too. Users should be discouraged to send very large messages, or those with multiple bodyparts, through gateways if at all possible. Many gateways are single-threaded, and large or complex messages can block smaller, possibly more important messages, getting through.

Preserving message contents is a different matter. The gateway should be able to preserve the format of attachments, but this will only be possible if Exchange and the legacy system share a common understanding of message structure and formats. Conversion may be required as messages pass between the systems, and users are usually only satisfied if they don't see extra attachments (such as the infamous WINMAIL.DAT), and are able to work with the contents when they arrive in Exchange, or when an Exchange message arrives back at the legacy system. Remember the 80/20 rule—80% of all messages are typically sent to people you work with, so ease this aspect of migration by migrating complete departments or workgroups at one time. If you split a department between different mail systems you're only creating problems for yourself.

We've already discussed the dissatisfaction that arises when messages are not delivered because mail addresses are incorrect through no fault of the user. If a corporate directory is consulted and a mail address retrieved, and that address proves to be inaccurate, then users have a real and justifiable cause for complaint. Every effort should be made to ensure that the corporate mail directories—those used by the legacy systems as well as Exchange—are up to date. Any large corporate directory (over 20,000 entries) will have some degree of inaccuracy, but over 1% (200 inaccurate entries in the 20,000 entry directory) is unacceptable. Directories with more than 10% inaccurate entries are basically useless and will be an irritation for users. Directory synchronization on a regular basis during the migration period should be built into all migration plans. It is probably too difficult to track down every distribution list and personal address book and try to update the addresses contained within against the corporate directory, so using a redirect or auto-forward feature (if available) on accounts that have been migrated to Exchange is the only practical way to address the issue. Most redirect or auto-forward functions disappear when an account is removed from a system, so it's better to disable user accounts on legacy systems instead of deleting them.

Users believe that all the information they hold on the legacy system is valuable. Their starting point is to require all information to be migrated, but as we've already seen, this approach is impractical. The migration team must therefore convince users that they don't need the old data and will be much better off to start afresh with a new account. This is a difficult proposition to sell, and it requires a certain amount of propaganda to convince people that the pain of moving to Exchange will be repaid by all the great new functionality that's available in Exchange. Addressing the coffee machine syndrome by training people, making them aware of new functionality, and not allowing users to focus on what they might have lost but concentrate on what they've gained is an effective tactic. Back this approach up with a team of super-users, specially trained on the advanced features of Exchange and so able to answer user queries immediately, or debunk incorrect assertions about Exchange and stop rumors before they get going. A supportive and knowledgeable help desk to support the help desk is a pre-requisite.

Out of the box Exchange is a messaging system. If the legacy system included some mail enabled applications then the migration project must seek to provide replacement functionality as quickly as possible. If Exchange can't provide the functionality then maybe another application can be used in conjunction with Exchange. For example, if an expense reporting application built around electronic forms is available on the legacy system, maybe an Exchange e-form can do the same job, or if not, perhaps a combination of an Excel template and Exchange messages will do the trick. Migrating people who work together won't address the problem, but it will stop you getting into a situation where people are attempting to use incompatible mail-enabled applications between Exchange and the legacy systems.

A temptation exists for operations staff to concentrate on Exchange once it's put into production. After all, Exchange is the new technology and people want to learn. Concentrating on Exchange can lead to the legacy systems being ignored, so good system management practices are not kept up. System tuning, backups, monitoring (especially of gateway queues), software upgrades, and all the other day-to-day tasks may not be carried out as well as they were done before, inevitably leading to a degradation of service from the legacy system. If this happens the users who remain on the legacy system will not be happy and they will relay the feeling of discontent to their peers. Also, a legacy system that is not maintained will probably affect some of the other aspects of service quality discussed in this section. Inaccurate entries will end up in the corporate directory; the legacy system may become unreliable and suffer system failures; the gateways operating on the legacy system may experience bottlenecks, queues, or failures to the detriment of message transfer times. Users will not understand that these problems are due to mismanagement of the legacy system. They will perceive the problems as being due to the introduction of Exchange—after all, everything worked just fine before the migration project started, didn't it?

The search for quality in all aspects of life is a difficult path to follow. Achieving real levels of quality during a messaging migration project is one of the more difficult things to do, but it can be achieved if real attention is paid to the issue by the migration team.

10.6   Coexisting with other messaging systems

The vast majority of migrations do not happen overnight. In fact, if you are moving from another system supporting thousands of users the migration period is often extended over months or even years. During this time Exchange and its predecessor mail systems will need to coexist and cooperate within a single, logical messaging environment.

It's obvious that the most basic need to coexist can be defined on the level of interpersonal message interchange between the two systems. One of the Exchange connectors or a link to an SMTP or X.400 backbone will probably solve this problem, albeit perhaps after a degree of testing to ensure that all message body parts can be successfully transmitted from one electronic mail system to the other.

After messages, what are the issues that may prove to be of concern during the period of coexistence? Here are a few of the issues I have encountered.

- **Directory Synchronization.** The Exchange directory is no doubt different to the one used by the existing system. How will the address information contained in the two directories be synchronized so that people are able to address messages to anyone within the organization without having to remember complex address syntaxes?

- **Transferring users from Exchange back to the older electronic mail system.** During a migration phase the normal operation will be to transfer a user from the older system to Exchange, but there may be instances where someone is transferred from a department that uses Exchange to a department where they don't. In these cases there will be problems extracting user data from Exchange and transferring it to the "old" mail system, mostly because no wizard or "backward migration" tools are probably available (unless you build your own).

- **Interchange of scheduling information.** Interchange of scheduling information. Outlook calendaring provides excellent scheduling functionality in an Exchange environment but it's difficult to schedule meetings and appointments with anyone else, even people using older versions Microsoft calendaring software like Schedule+!

- **Mail-enabled applications.** Workflow applications built on top of the electronic mail system are compromised if everyone who may be part of a document's routing cycle cannot be reached through the electronic mail system. Even if they can be reached with a message, the recipient may not be able to interact with the contents and participate in the workflow.

- **Guest users.** With a single consistent mail system throughout an organization it's normally possible to access your mail from any workstation, provided that your access can be authenticated from the workstation. If some parts of the organization are still using the old mail system will Exchange users be able to access their mail when they visit? Outlook Web Access may well provide a solution here. On the other hand, will users of the older

mail system be able to read their mail when they visit a department that uses Exchange?

■ **Distribution lists.** Maintaining the contents of distribution lists
so that the addresses contained in the lists are up-to-date, accurate, and don't lead to undelivered messages can be a nightmare.
How do you make sure that distribution lists are updated as
users migrate from the older system to Exchange? Can the
selected techniques cater for personal distribution lists as well as
those shared between groups of users or system-wide? Can you
apply the same technique to solve the problem posed by mail
addresses held in nickname files or personal address books?
While you can take some steps to enable local users to continue
to use old addresses problems may still arise for external messages delivered from other organizations.

Human beings generally like a settled environment and often resist
change. It's fair to assume that greater problems will be encountered at
the beginning of the migration when users struggle to cope with new
ways to address messages to colleagues, transfer documents from one
system to the other, find equivalent options on client menus, or even
just cope with the trauma of moving from a different style of computing and user interface to client/server Windows. Help desk and programming staff will experience the same transition pressures but their
extra technical knowledge will assist their personal migration, so the
overall impact on these people shouldn't be as great. Migrations proceed more smoothly (and usually quicker) when everyone recognizes
that problems will occur, and steps are taken to lessen the impact of
the problems before users meet them. This is one good reason why a
thorough and extensive pilot is essential to pinpoint the specific areas of
interoperability which may affect your users most. Knowledge gained
through pilots is a great help in achieving non-traumatic migrations.

10.6.1 Operating Mail Gateways

Gateways have been a fact of electronic messaging life since the earliest
days of e-mail. Following the same line as operating system development, no great efforts were initially made to ensure that messages could
be sent to other systems. Everything was focused on optimizing the messaging design and architecture for the computer and operating system it
ran on. Some of the IBM mainframe e-mail systems written in APL, a
unique symbol-driven programming language in many respects, provide
eloquent examples of the approach taken when developing e-mail.

With a wide range of e-mail systems in production, each having
their own idea about how to create and send messages, gateways rapidly became a necessary evil of a messaging administrator's life. Gateways are a necessary evil because they delay messages en route to their

final destination and so degrade some of the raison d'être for e-mail, the desire to send information quickly from one person to another. Gateways often impose restrictions on users, for instance limiting their ability to send anything but simple text messages to users contacted via the gateway. Attached or embedded documents are often stripped out as messages transit the gateways, and generally speaking the message that leaves an originator's desk arrives in a fairly bent shape at its final destination. Of course, it's a mistake to blame gateways for all the restrictions. Target e-mail systems mightn't be able to cope with embedded documents or rich text format cover memos, or many of the other advanced features of modern systems. In these cases gateways merely act as a negotiator between different e-mail systems, transforming messages arriving at the gateway into a form that's acceptable to the other systems.

Any medium to large-scale migration usually requires a gateway between the old system and the new, in this case, Exchange. Smaller migrations that can be done in a "big bang" or over a short period of time may remove any need to install and operate a gateway. Once you have to deal with more than a few hundred users the sheer logistics of migration determine that the period of migration extends to such an extent that a gateway is needed to facilitate communication between the two user communities.

Given that one or more gateway is necessary during an extended migration period it follows that it is sensible to take any necessary steps to ensure that the best possible interoperability for all types of messages is achieved. Important points to consider include:

- Can a common messaging standard be used by the gateway to transfer messages from the older system to Exchange? The two obvious options are SMTP/MIME and X.400.

- What features are supported by the gateway? Is it limited to simple (single-bodypart) messages or can attachments in different file formats be sent through the gateway? Does the gateway preserve attachment information such as file formats and titles? Is the gateway able to handle attachments in a format that it doesn't recognize, for instance, a compressed file produced by the PKZIP or WINZIP applications.

- What happens when a message generated by a mail-enabled application arrives at the gateway? Remember that this situation can arise from either direction. In other words, a message can be generated and sent from the older system or an electronic form can be generated and sent by Exchange. The important thing to consider is whether the fact that a message arrives at the gateway influences the immediate and future processing by the mail-enabled application? For example, if the message is part of a workflow cycle that consists of a number of serial steps, each of which involves a message being sent to the next person in the cycle, can the cycle be re-established after the message is sent to a user via the gateway?

If the responses to these questions are largely negative it is time to consider whether another gateway should be used. There is no point in operating a gateway that enables a minimalist degree of interoperability between the two systems because this only leads to additional strain on the help desk staff and system administrators, who get to explain to users the reasons why their messages sometimes don't get through. Buying a cheap gateway with a low level of functionality can be a case of engaging a low up-front cost while incurring higher costs over the lifetime of the gateway.

Sometimes the most demanding users, those who will place most strain on the gateway's capabilities, can be identified before the migration begins, or they become obvious quickly afterwards. If this is the case it's reasonable to concentrate on migrating these people first to avoid the problems they may encounter. For example, if you know that a specific group of people, perhaps spread across several departments, communicates on a regular basis via a workflow application it makes little sense to split them across different migration stages. Move them together instead. This is an example of where it's good to ignore organizational or corporate divisions when considering when users should be moved.

Hopefully a gateway is a transient component in your messaging environment, one that can be discarded once the migration is complete. Of course, larger migrations can take many years to arrive at the last user, so gateways can quickly become a semi-permanent fixture. Even if the gateway is temporary don't take short cuts. Pay attention to gateway details and avoid lots of problems in the future.

10.6.2 Maintaining addressing sources

After gateways electronic directory services and other sources of address information are the most common problem areas that must be addressed during the migration period. People hate receiving non-delivery notifications, and the potential for "bad" electronic mail addresses greatly increases as people are moved to any new messaging system. Exchange is no better or no worse than any other mail system. It offers no panacea for badly addressed messages and during the course of the migration the chances are that you won't be able to avoid some undeliverable messages due to invalid addresses. Over the long term you can take steps to significantly reduce the number of invalid addresses within the system.

Most electronic mail systems in use today have some form of directory service. This may be a simple list of subscribers (mailboxes) or it might be something more complicated, such as an X.500 or similar distributed directory service. In all cases the repository holds information about other users' electronic mail addresses which people can consult when they wish to send messages. Some systems validate all addresses entered in message headers against the directory to ensure that a user cannot attempt to send a message to an undeliverable address. The personal address book is a form of directory service, in this case, a purely personal service totally under the control of an individual user.

When people are migrated from a system to Exchange two basic courses of action in respect to the directory can be taken by a system administrator.

1.   The directory entry for the user is removed. This can be frustrating for users who remain on the older system because they will no longer be able to "see" the migrated user in the directory. Also, messages sent to the old address, perhaps those originating from another connected system will be undeliverable unless they can be redirected.

2.   The entry for the user is altered so that any new messages addressed to the user are redirected to their new Exchange mailbox. Not all systems support message redirection, and this approach assumes that the system is capable of sending messages to Exchange, normally via a gateway. A further complication is that redirection may require that the user's old mailbox or account is retained. If this is the case you should disable access to the account so that no one can log into it.

Enabling directory synchronization between Exchange and the old system is a more sophisticated but costly answer. It requires the older system to support the MS-Mail directory synchronization facility or a utility program to provide directory information to Exchange and import directory information originating from Exchange. Despite the almost inevitable costs involved, maintaining a fully synchronized directory is the best solution and will stop users becoming unhappy during the migration process because they can't address messages to their friends, or their friends' messages don't arrive.

One final point. Unless absolutely necessary (for example, if the company changes its name), whatever you do, take steps to maintain the mail addresses that people use for external communications. It is a mistake to force people to publish new mail addresses and will cause discontent. They won't like doing it, mostly because their friends and business contacts already have an e-mail address that's in use today and there is no immediately obvious benefit from a changeover so why do it? There is a relatively high potential for mistakes to be made in the transmission of new mail addresses to external contacts, so further potential exists for confusion to be introduced. The net result is user discontent, something to be avoided at all costs.

Using something like a smart relay host as the external point of contact for your company is generally a better approach to take. Smart relay hosts are able to examine and rewrite mail addresses as messages arrive. Old addresses can be quickly reformatted into new addresses and directed away from legacy systems to arrive to Exchange for eventual delivery to recipients. Using computers like this relieves users of an irritating task and greatly enhances accuracy, thus contributing to the overall stability and reliability of the messaging infrastructure.

11

Keeping Your Exchange Server Healthy

11.1   Introduction

To a certain degree, Exchange can be said to be self-maintaining. The engineers attempt to improve matters through knowledge is gained from operating Exchange in real-life environments. In Exchange V5.5, for instance, the MTA tunes its own internal demands and the Information Store attempts to manage memory better. You shouldn't have to continually perform system tuning to make everything run smoothly, but there are going to be times when things go wrong. In this chapter we'll look at some of the utilities that come with Exchange that help system administrators keep servers in shape.

11.1.1   Performance Optimizer

The Performance Optimizer utility is a somewhat intelligent program designed to analyze the current status of an active server and make changes based on:

- Information about the intended role for the server as input by a system administrator before the analysis begins (Figure 11.1). This allows the utility to consider what changes are required to enable the server to support an increase in the user community or the way the server is used. For example, a change in server workload from "messaging only" to a situation where messaging and public folders are supported.

- The I/O subsystem and disks installed on the server.

- The set of internal parameters currently in operation and performance data gathered by Exchange as it runs. Exchange continues to improve its ability to tune the internal workings of many of its services. For example, the advent of dynamic buffer allocation in Exchange V5.5 has made the adjustment of memory-related parameters for the Information Store less of a necessity than before. However, the Performance Optimizer is able to adjust a wide variety of parameters across all components.

One useful, but sometimes overlooked aspect of the Performance Optimizer is its ability to move the work directories for the MTA and Internet Mail Service away from the location where the directories are first installed (on the same disk as the Exchange executables). Any system expecting to deal with a large volume of traffic through the MTA or IMS should move these directories onto a different disk.

The Performance Optimizer cannot run with Exchange in an active state. All services must be halted before any analysis can begin. Run the utility early in the morning or late in the evening when users will feel the least impact.

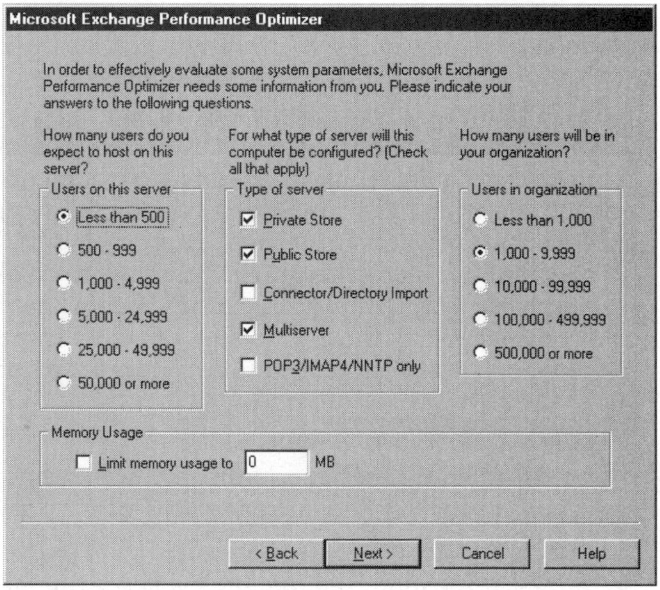

Figure 11.1
Setting parameters for a Performance Optimizer run

Note the checkbox available to limit memory usage. This is a hangover from previous versions that has been rendered largely unnecessary by dynamic buffer allocation. Do not limit memory usage on an Exchange server unless you have very good reason to do so.

By default Performance Optimizer reveals little of the internal calculations it makes and offers no opportunities for experienced system administrators to selectively tune one or more settings before new parameters are created. You can request (or force) Performance Optimizer to show you more options to change by running the program with the -V option enabled. To do this, select the desktop icon for the "Microsoft Exchange Optimizer" and then change the properties to include the -V parameter. The resulting command line should look something like this:

C:\EXCHSRVR\BIN\PERFWIZ.EXE —V

Each run of the Performance Analyzer creates a log called PER-FOPT.LOG in the \WINNT35\SYSTEM32 directory. The log file can be reviewed at leisure after the analyzer has run, and any corrections that seem necessary can be made afterwards.

Logged information from two separate Optimizer runs are illustrated in Figure 11.2. The first set of entries comes just after Exchange is first installed on the server, while the second set comes from the same server after it had been in use for a number of months.

Figure 11.2
Performance
Optimizer Log

```
------------------------------------------------------------------
Microsoft Exchange Server Performance Optimizer log file opened.:
11/5/97 - 4:16:33 PM
------------------------------------------------------------------
Detected 1 processor(s)
Detected 100061184 bytes physical memory
Found fixed logical disk C:
Found fixed logical disk D:
Found fixed logical disk F:
The database file C:\EXCHSRVR\MDBDATA\PRIV.EDB is consistent.
The database file C:\EXCHSRVR\MDBDATA\PUB.EDB is consistent.
The database file C:\EXCHSRVR\DSADATA\dir.edb is consistent.
Performance Results (Smaller values better)
DiskRA(ms) Seq(ms)
------------------------------------------------------------------
C: 45499   82219
D: 45984   81765
F: 19844   18328
Microsoft Exchange Server Information store log files was moved
  from C:\EXCHSRVR\MDBDATA to D:\EXCHSRVR\MDBDATA
Microsoft Exchange Server Private information store file was moved
  from C:\EXCHSRVR\MDBDATA to F:\EXCHSRVR\MDBDATA
Microsoft Exchange Server Public information store file was moved
  from C:\EXCHSRVR\MDBDATA to F:\EXCHSRVR\MDBDATA
Microsoft Exchange Server Directory service log files was moved
  from C:\EXCHSRVR\DSADATA to D:\EXCHSRVR\DSADATA
Set # of information store buffers from 1000 to 24429
Set # of directory buffers from 1000 to 24429
Set Minimum # of information store threads from 8 to 10
Set Maximum # of information store threads from 20 to 100
Set # of directory threads from 48 to 50
Set # of background threads from 25 to 47
Set # of information store gateway in threads from 1 to 2
Set # of information store gateway out threads from 1 to 2
Set Buffer Threshold Low Percent from 5 to 3
Set Buffer Threshold High Percent from 15 to 3
Set Maximum # of pool threads from 10 to 50
Set # of information store users from 500 to 50
```

```
Set # of dispatcher threads from 1 to 2
Set # of transfer threads from 1 to 2
Set # of kernel threads from 1 to 3
Set # of database data buffers per object from 3 to 6
Set # of RTS threads from 1 to 3
Set # of concurrent MDB/delivery queue clients from 3 to 10
Set # of concurrent XAPI sessions from 80 to 30
Set # of MT gateway clients from 8 to 10
Set # of retrieval queue clients from 2 to 10
-----------------------------------------------------------------

Microsoft Exchange Server Performance Optimizer log file closed.:
11/5/97 - 4:28:15 PM


-----------------------------------------------------------------
Microsoft Exchange Server Performance Optimizer log file opened.:
2/9/98 - 11:57:21 AM
-----------------------------------------------------------------
Detected 1 processor(s)
Detected 100061184 bytes physical memory
Found fixed logical disk C:
Found fixed logical disk D:
Found fixed logical disk F:
The database file F:\EXCHSRVR\MDBDATA\PRIV.EDB is consistent.
The database file F:\EXCHSRVR\MDBDATA\PUB.EDB is consistent.
The database file C:\EXCHSRVR\DSADATA\dir.edb is consistent.
Performance Results (Smaller values better)
DiskRA(ms) Seq(ms)
-----------------------------------------------------------------
C:  45797   106797
D:  47640   106406
F:  19344   19391
Set Maximum # of information store threads from 100 to 50
Set # of background threads from 47 to 37
Set # of information store users from 50 to 500
Set # of concurrent MDB/delivery queue clients from 3 to 10
Set # of concurrent XAPI sessions from 80 to 30
Set # of MT gateway clients from 8 to 10
Set # of retrieval queue clients from 2 to 10

-----------------------------------------------------------------

Microsoft Exchange Server Performance Optimizer log file closed.:
2/9/98 - 12:10:42 PM
```

Before beginning any analysis, Performance Optimizer takes a snapshot of the system to locate physical drives and make sure that the databases are consistent. The analysis then begins. From the log files we can see that:

- The optimizer attempts to discover which disks deliver the fastest performance. Note that the Performance Optimizer cannot detect the difference between multiple partitions on a single physical drive. Each partition is analyzed separately, so this is one reason why you might want to adjust the results of the Performance Optimizer after it is complete. For example, it's always a good idea to separate the databases used by the Information Store and Directory by placing them on separate physical drives. In addition, keep the transaction logs away from the databases. The analysis cannot tell whether the data on a disk is protected by a RAID array or simple mirroring, so this is another piece of added value that humans can give once the Performance Optimizer suggests suitable file locations.

- The initial run is just after Exchange is installed for the first time. The Performance Optimizer therefore moves the databases and transaction logs away from the place where they are first created (normally on the C: drive). However, moving files automatically is not default behaviour. The Performance Optimizer always asks before files are moved.

- Performance Optimizer then proceeds to review a set of internal counters and parameter settings that are maintained by Exchange in order to determine whether any parameters need to be changed to accommodate the workload observed to date on the server. The parameters are maintained in the system registry, so it is entirely possible to tweak one individually, but only if you understand the relationship between one parameter and the rest, and like living dangerously. The initial parameters are "best guess", and set according to guidelines established by the development team. The parameters set during the second run after the server has been in use reflect the actual workload that the server has been handling.

- If you've run the Performance Optimizer in verbose mode, you will be allowed to view and modify the parameter changes before they are committed (Figure 11.3).

- After the new parameter values are set all of the Exchange services are restarted.

The Performance Optimizer has encountered some problems with new hardware in the past. For instance, when 9GB disks were first introduced the utility could cause corruption because it wasn't able to handle disks larger than 8GB. This problem was fixed long ago but given the speed that hardware evolves it's an indication that new hardware should be tested before it's introduced into a production environment.

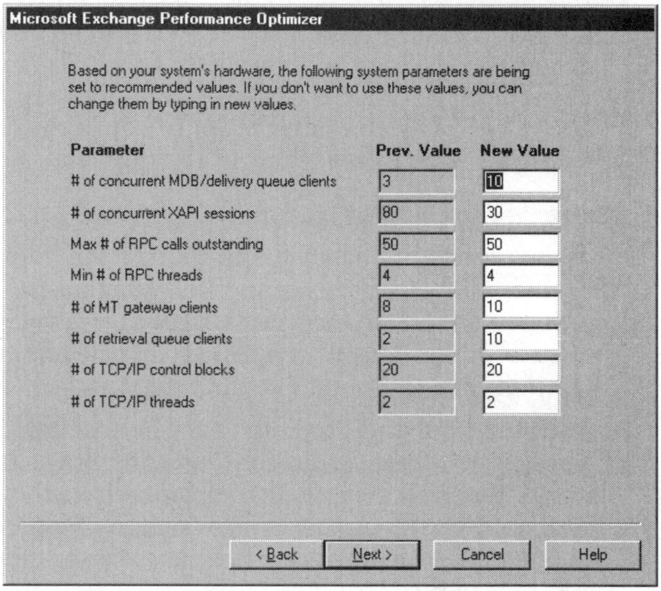

Figure 11.3
*Running the
Performance
Optimizer in
verbose mode
allows many
individual
parameters to
be set*

A server's workload changes over time for many reasons, including increases in the user community, different client protocols, new applications, and the additional load imposed by add-ons like virus checkers, fax connectors, and so on. For these reasons you should consider running the Performance Optimizer on a fairly regular basis.

As always with automated tools, it's unwise to accept their conclusions without considering whether or not the software actually understands the situation it is dealing with. For example, in large Exchange networks, bridgehead servers don't typically host many mailboxes, so the parameters fed to the Performance Optimizer will reflect this fact. However, the MTA on bridgehead servers need to cache information about the routing data for the organization. Performance Optimizer determines the size of the MTA cache by comparing the number of mailboxes on a server, a calculation which is perfectly acceptable for the majority of servers, but results in caches that are too small for dedicated bridgehead servers. You can adjust the size of the MTA cache afterwards[1], but this is a manual operation that must be performed each time the server is tuned.

---

1.   The size of the MTA cache is held in the registry value:

    Hkey_Local_Machine\System\Services\MSExchangeMTA\Parameters\MDB users.

If there are less than 5,000 mailboxes in the organization set the value to the number of mailboxes, else set the value to be approximately 25% of the mailbox population. Changing the MTA cache in this way is only required on dedicated bridgehead servers.

11.1.2 Server monitors

Server monitors are used to determine whether specified Exchange services are operating correctly on target servers. The entire set of core services—System Attendant, Information Store, Directory, MTA as well as any optional connectors can be monitored.

Figure 11.4 *An Exchange server monitor*

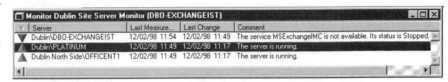

Each server monitor operates on a set of servers that you select from any site in your organization. However, server monitors use RPCs to communicate with the servers being monitored, so if a suitable network link is unavailable you won't be able to use a server monitor. When you add a server to the monitor you can determine which services you wish to monitor. Three essential Exchange services (the Directory, Information Store, and MTA) are added for each server, and the System Attendant is also monitored automatically. Any valid NT service can be added to the monitor. The status of each service is detected by sending an "are you there" message over the link to the target service and seeing whether the message arrives.

The results of server monitors are recorded in two places—graphically and in a log file. The graphic display (Figure 11.4) shows one line for each server being monitored. The beginning of each line displays an icon to flag the current server status. A red down arrow means trouble. It's obvious that a problem has occurred on the DBO-EXCHANGEIST server because the monitor is reporting that the MSExchangeIMC service is unavailable (MSExchangeIMC is the internal name for the Internet Mail Service). Note that the server monitor could be configured to automatically restart a service if a problem is detected. However, the default action is to do nothing but signal the error.

Automatically attempting to restart a missing service is probably the correct course of action to take in the majority of cases. It won't, however, address situations where a physical problem on the system has caused the service to stop in the first place. For example, a disk failure on the array where the Information Store databases are located, or the disk where the transaction logs or MTA database is located has less than 10MB of free space remaining. These situations require human intervention and should be guarded against by monitoring for multiple conditions, as in the amount of free space remaining on all disks used by the Exchange together with the existence of the Exchange services.

Figure 11.5
*Detail of services
being monitored*

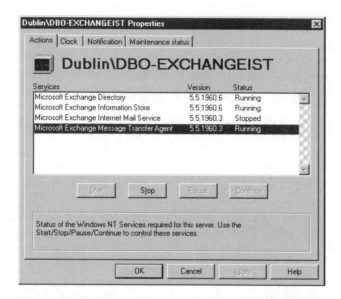

Double-clicking on the server with the problem reveals more detail, as shown in Figure 11.5. Note that this screen includes command buttons to allow an administrator to stop or start a selected service. A service is stopped or started by sending commands via RPCs to the server. However, this is only possible if the user account issuing the command (the account that the administration program is logged into at the time) can be authenticated and has the appropriate permissions. For this reason it is not possible to monitor servers across domain boundaries, unless trust relationships are in place and the accounts used for monitoring are granted "Admin" or "Service Account Admin" permission. Authentication failures will prevent monitoring as access will be denied to the services. Failures are reported in alert messages similar to that shown in Figure 11.6. Alerts can also be signalled through standard NT alerts or sent to pagers or other devices.

Figure 11.6 *An
error message
generated by a
server monitor*

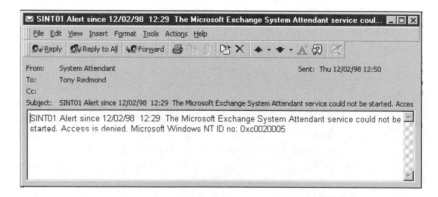

Red icons displayed in server monitor windows are certainly capable of indicating that a problem has happened, but only if someone regularly checks the display. Not every installation can afford the luxury of having a system administrator engaged in nothing but monitoring all the time. To make sure that all problems are detected you should:

- Run one or more server monitors all the time to observe the most important servers in each site. The most important service to monitor is the System Attendant, as without it Exchange has no chance of ever working correctly. Bridgehead servers and those that host external connectors to other messaging systems (X.400, Internet, PROFS, SNADS, cc:Mail, MS-Mail, and Lotus Notes) should be a priority for monitoring in order to detect possible blocks in message transmission or reception.

- Have alert messages generated and sent somewhere where they will be responded to. For example, send the messages to a distribution list containing all system administrators. It's better for everyone to hear about a problem and have someone respond quickly rather than to send a message to a specific individual or subset of administrators who may be unavailable when the problem happens.

- Make sure that the server monitors actually do something useful. It's better to attempt to restart a missing or failed service rather than just signal the error (which may be missed).

- Stop server monitors during planned maintenance so that a monitor doesn't attempt to restart something like the Information Store service during a software upgrade or file-level backup operation.

- Review the server monitor log files on a regular basis, if possible once a day but at least once a week. A different log file is created for each monitor. You can find out the name of the server monitor log by viewing the general properties of the monitor.

Apart from making sure that essential services are running, monitors can also check the system clock on servers to see whether any inconstancy exists between the expected and actual time. This is important because a server with an incorrect time can generate message time-stamps that cause concern to users. Receiving a message that appeared to be sent two days ago or a day in the future does not generate a great level of confidence in the messaging system.

Creating server monitors and making them active should be one of the first actions you take after deploying Exchange servers into an operational status. Server and link monitors form an important part of a proactive attitude to problem detection that can pay back great benefits from just a little effort put in at the start.

11.1.3   Link monitors

Link monitors operate by sending probe messages similar to those produced by the PING utility to a set of servers. The idea behind link monitors is simple. Messages are dispatched at regular intervals to the system attendant service on each target server, which returns the message back to the originating server. Calculations are then performed to determine the round-trip time between the originating and target servers. Figure 11.7 shows how servers are added to a link monitor. Note that the servers can come from many different sites as the probe messages only need to make a simple network connection to be able to do their job.

Monitors are run as child windows within the Exchange administration program. The window for a link monitor lists the target servers together with the time when a probe was last sent and the time taken for the round trip. If monitors are active when the administration program is closed down they will be reactivated the next time the program is started.

Figure 11.7
*Defining the
server links to
be monitored*

Links to distant servers or those over extended network connections will clearly take longer than a round trip to a local server. Figure 11.8 illustrates a link monitor in operation. In this example, the monitor is being used to ensure that network connectivity is present between servers in a set of European sites. Everything seems OK apart from the link to the server in the "BRO-WGSALP" site. This somewhat strange name is explained by the fact that a link monitor uses the directory name rather than the display name. In this case, the server is actually located in the Brussels (Belgium) site.

Figure 11.8 *A
Link monitor in
operation*

The failure of message probes is a good indication that some sort of network problem exists. The actual link may be congested or broken. In either situation it's something that deserves further investigation. Large MTA queues are likely to build up quickly if you leave things alone in the hope that everything will sort itself out. Double-clicking on the problem server reveals some further information (Figure 11.9).

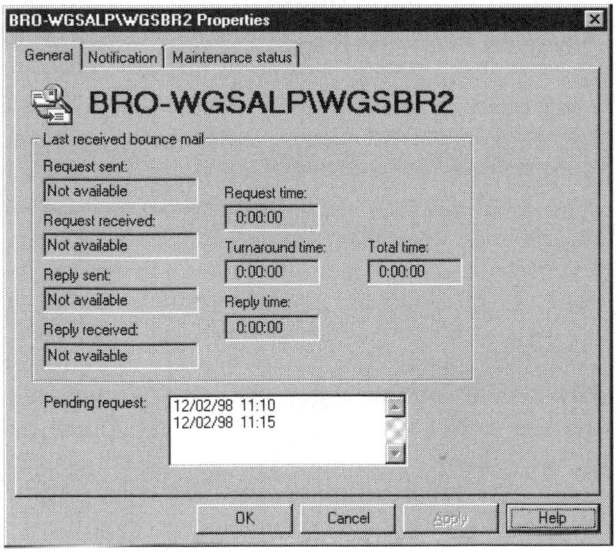

Figure 11.9 *Link
Monitor detail*

Figure 11.9 shows that a probe has never succeeded in getting to the target server. Indeed, two probe messages (issued at 11:10 and 11:15) are outstanding. In other words, probe messages were sent at those times but the target server has not yet responded. The network link could be functional, but perhaps the system attendant service is not running. Even if the network link is available the fact that the system attendant has not responded indicates that the other Exchange services are not operational on this server. Therefore, no mail can be sent to users on the server.

Administrators can configure the frequency and threshold times for messages and the notification list for any alarms generated as a result of a message not being returned or arriving outside the predetermined threshold.

It's a good idea to run a link monitor on all the important sites in your organization from a central server. No human intervention is required as automatic alarms are generated if anything goes wrong. Alarms can be notified by standard Windows NT alerts, which flash a message up onto the server's screen, or by sending a mail message to a designated individual or distribution list. The latter is preferable in most cases, especially when a number of people share the task of managing the Exchange infrastructure.

II.I.4   Moving outside the Exchange administration tools

In my opinion, the Exchange administration tools are designed for small to medium deployments. The tools provide sufficient functionality for organizations that span 5–10 sites, involving up to 15–20 servers. Outside these ballpark figures you should look at other options and decide whether the standard administration tools can be supplemented with purpose-designed management utilities from third parties.

A wide range of utilities exist. Here are three examples I have encountered in large deployment projects:

- NetIQ AppManager (http://www.netiq.com)
- Mailcheck from Baranof Software (http://www.baronof.com)
- Unicenter TNG from Computer Associates (http://www.ca.com)

NetIQ regularly connects to servers to extract information and statistics, which is then logged into an SQL database. A graphical representation of the servers being monitored is always available through the AppManager "command console", which can combine many different data streams into a graph. Different graphs can be displayed as required. The console is also used to control and configure the execution of "Knowledge Scripts", which specify the events to monitor, the data to collect and retain, and the actions that should be taken should specified conditions occur (like a large MTA queue building up). A set of scripts is supplied for each module monitored by AppManager, including Exchange and Windows NT. You can decide to use the supplied scripts or write your own in Visual Basic.

Mailcheck enables you to verify that round-trip times for messages meet service level agreements. The utility sends automated messages out to different destinations in your email environment and checks the delivery time. In essence, MailCheck can be regarded as a more sophisticated version of the Exchange link monitor. Instead of just polling remote servers, MailCheck is able to collect data and generate reports that can be used to validate agreed service levels. MailCheck is, of course, also able to deal with many other messaging systems than just Exchange and can be used as the basis of a company-wide email reporting system.

Similar in many ways to NetIQ, the Exchange option for the Unicenter TNG management suite uses an agent process to collect information about Exchange servers from a running network. The information is collected in real-time and compared against a set of predefined procedures to verify that activities such as directory replication are proceeding normally. Using other products from the Computer Associates range, further options can be installed for backup (ArcServe) and anti-virus protection (InnocuLAN).

The continuing success of Exchange ensures that new system management products appear all the time. For example, Tivoli announced the availability of an Exchange module for their GEM (Global Enterprise Manager) product in February 1998. The exhibition area at the annual Exchange Conference, which takes place in early fall, is a great place to see all the different products in action. Further information on tools for managing Exchange can be found in "Monitoring Microsoft Exchange"[2].

11.2   Message tracking

Users send messages at the drop of a hat, but sometimes those messages don't get through and when this happens it falls on the head of the system administrator to try and find out just what happened to the message. Was it delivered to someone else? Did a gateway reject the message? Maybe the message is stuck somewhere waiting for a connection to be established to a remote system.

The majority of messaging systems allocate a unique identifier to messages as they are generated. Exchange is no different in this respect. Complete identifiers are built for Exchange messages as follows:

2.   Author: Jim Pringle et al., Digital Press, (1998), ISBN 1-55558-215X.

1.   The country code for the server. For example, "IE" means Ireland.

2.   The administrative X.400 domain for the server, if defined.

3.   The private X.400 administrative domain. For example, "Digital".

4.   A unique identifier built from the name of the server, the date and time when the message was created, and a computer-generated suffix to ensure uniqueness.

The first three parts of the complete message identifier (collectively called a GDI, or Global Domain Identifier) come from the X.400 site address. An example message identifier generated at 2.29 p.m. on 14th March 1998 on the server called DBO-EXCHANGEIST is:

```
C=IE;A= ;P=Digital;L=DBO-EXCHANGE980314142937FA000101
```

You can view the message identifier generated for a message from an Outlook client as follows:

- Open the message
- Select the File.Properties menu option
- Select the Message Id property page

In general, the message identifier property page is only shown if the message originated on another Exchange server, normally in the same organization. I have seen instances where the message identifier property page is available for messages delivered from another Exchange organization, but this is not always true. Messages delivered from other messaging systems such as an SMTP server or America On-Line normally bear their own type of message identifiers that is not recognized by Exchange, and is not therefore displayed as a property of a message.

Generating unique message identifiers provides the fundamental basis for message tracking but identifiers are of little use in themselves if they are not recorded somewhere as a message makes its way through the different links in the system. Exchange will record the necessary data, but only if it is instructed to do so. Message tracking is enabled by setting properties for all the components that handle a message on its path through a organization and outside via an external connector. Message tracking is set as a property on objects in the site configuration container, meaning that when message tracking is set, logging occurs for the relevant components on all servers within a site. The components are:

- The Information Store service, which handles delivery of messages to local recipients (mailboxes on the same server).

- The Message Transfer Agent (MTA), which handles message fan-out, the process by which copies of messages are provided to all of the connectors required to transfer messages to recipients. Screen 1 shows message tracking being enabled on the MTA Site Configuration object.

- The set of connectors used to route messages to destination such as Microsoft Mail, the Internet, and Lotus Notes.

Note that enabling message tracking for the MTA automatically logs messages processed by the Site and X.400 connectors. These connectors are integrated into the MTA and run as threads within the EMAMTA.EXE process. Message tracking is enabled to help you trace the path of messages as they are transferred from the Information Store to the MTA and then to another site or foreign mail system. It doesn't make much sense to enable just one component, so once the decision is made to enable message tracking, make sure that it is enabled on all components. Writing tracing information to the log files does not create a major system overhead. I wouldn't even consider the effect unless a server runs at more than 80% CPU load regularly. If your server is under such a load it's time to tune system performance or think about replacement hardware.

11.2.1   Message tracking logs

After message tracking is enabled Exchange records details of messages as they are processed by the MTA. Details are held in a set of tracking log files stored in the \EXCHSRVR \tracking.log directory on each server. This directory is automatically made available to other servers as an NT file share called tracking.log. This point is important, because message tracking from server to server is only possible if the Message Tracking Center is able to access the tracking.log file share on each server. If you want, you can change the location, but only by changing a registry parameter:

```
HKEY_LOCAL_MACHINE\CurrentControlSet\Services\MSExchangeSA\
Parameters\LogDirectory
```

The change becomes effective the next time the System Attendant service is started. A new tracking log is created at midnight, so each log holds details of all the messages processed in a single day. Tracking logs are named in a YYYYMMDD.LOG format. For example, the tracking log created on 20th April 1998 is called 19980420.LOG.

Tracking logs quickly grow to large sizes on even moderately busy Exchange servers. You might expect to accumulate up to 100MB of log data on moderately busy servers dedicated to user mailboxes. A greater volume of data is usually produced on systems that serve as messaging or replication hubs, and have active connectors. Lower volumes will be seen on public folder servers.

Figure 11.10 *A*
set of message
tracking logs

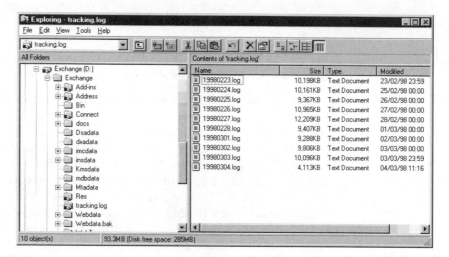

A server running the Internet Mail Service to link Exchange to other SMTP messaging systems might generate between 30 and 40MB of log data on a busy day. My own server, which supports a relatively small population of mailboxes (30 or so), but acts as a public folder host and as the hub site in a 16-site organization usually generates up to 15MB of data each day. Expect lower volumes of data inside smaller organizations. These volumes are not excessive and do not provide an excuse not to implement message tracking. Apart from anything else, the message tracking logs provide the raw data for statistic gathering and reporting programs like Crystal Reports, which is able to export data in a number of different formats appropriate for reporting purposes.

Figure 11.11 is a chart (generated by Excel) of hourly message traffic through one of the largest Exchange servers operated by DIGITAL. The chart clearly illustrates the spread of message traffic over the hours in the day (18 February 1997), peaking at nearly 14,000 message transactions between 4 and 5 o'clock GMT, or between 11 and 12 o'clock in the morning, US Eastern Standard Time. The data used to create the graph comes from the message tracking log for the day. Each message can generate a number of transactions as the server processes it, so the actual number of unique messages handled in any particular hour is less than the numbers in the chart. For example, the 14,000 message transactions were generated by approximately 4,500 messages, still a large number for a server to handle in one hour.

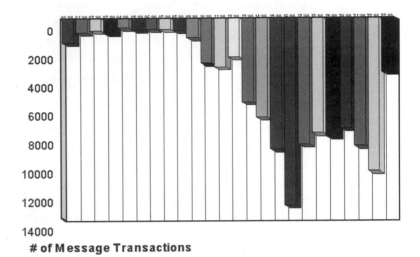

Figure 11.11 *A sample chart of data in the message tracking logs*

It is possible to edit or read the contents of tracking logs with a text editor and because the fields in the logs are tab-delimited they can be loaded into a spreadsheet, such as Excel. Once in the editor or spreadsheet the contents of the log reveal the interaction between the MTA and messages, and how messages proceed as they are submitted by users, delivered to other mailboxes, or pass off the system via a site or other connector. Given experience and knowledge of the codes and fields used in tracking logs it is feasible to use the raw logs as the basis for satisfying user requests to discover where messages went. We'll discuss how to do examine the raw logs later on in this chapter.

Examining raw logs is an activity that might be enjoyed by masochists, but the more sanguine system administrator quickly learns to appreciate the standard "Track Message" option featured on the Tools menu of the Exchange Administration utility.

Apart from their obvious use in message tracking exercises there is no formal requirement to keep tracking logs for any length of time. If you find that tracking logs are occupying too much storage you can delete some or all of the logs to free up some space. However, if something with relatively low storage demands is causing disk storage problems perhaps it is a good hint that now is an excellent time to buy another disk?

11.2.2   Using the Track Message command

Browsing through large amounts of tracking log data is an interesting once-off experience, but not something you want to do every day. The Track Message command provides an easy to use graphical interface to the data contained in message tracking logs and the steps necessary to interpret the data and follow the message from server to server. As an example we'll use the graphical interface to track a message I sent to a distribution list and see what happens.

Tracking a message is a two-stage process:

1.   First, select the message to be tracked.

2.   Track the selected message via the "Message Tracking Center".

Selecting a message means that you provide Exchange with search criteria to filter the contents of message tracking logs in order to find messages that meet the stated criteria. You can elect to search the current tracking log (the default option) or search back through as many tracking logs as are available on a server. Searches can also be carried out against tracking logs stored on remote servers, an operation that can be quite slow if the network is occupied or the remote server is busy. Once a message is being tracked the logs on all the servers in the relevant site are automatically searched.

Figure 11.12
Selecting a message to track

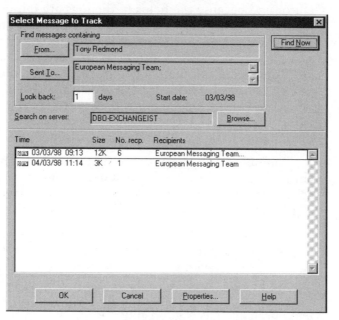

Clearly the better and more focused the search criteria the less messages will be discovered and the bigger chance that the messages found will actually be the ones you are interested in. The message we're interested in was sent by Tony Redmond to the European Messaging Team distribution list. This information can be entered into the form (see Figure 11.12) as the initial search criteria. We weren't quite sure when the message was sent, so the logs for the last two days are to be scanned (in other words, go back one day). After the search is executed we find that two messages meet the criteria. Any of these messages can then be selected for tracking. Once a message is selected we return to the Message Tracking Centre where the actual tracking process can begin.

Tracking begins after the "Track" button is pressed and is accomplished by scanning the tracking log files to interpret the actions performed for the message. Each action is then displayed to the screen to allow the system administrator to see exactly how the message was processed. If you look at Figure 11.13 you'll see a graphical view of the conclusions we reached when the extract of the tracking log was analyzed earlier. As you can imagine, it's a lot easier to click a few buttons than it is to delve into the depths of a tracking log.

Figure 11.13
Viewing the path of a message

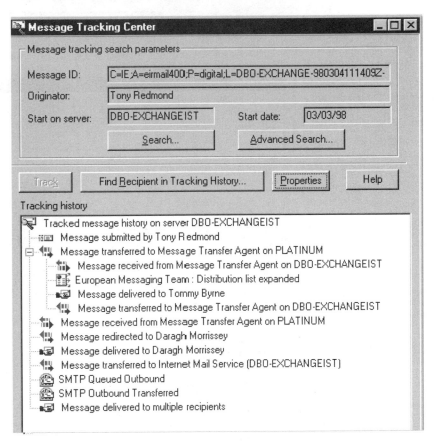

At the bottom part of the routing steps displayed in Figure 11.13 you can just see that several attempts were made to reroute the mes-

sage to the MTA on a server called PLATINUM. This is because the
message was sent to a distribution list, and the PLATINUM server is
used in this site to expand distribution lists into the set of individual
recipients. After PLATINUM is finished, the set of recipients is
returned to the original server and message delivery begins.

Selecting one of the steps in the message's path and clicking on the
properties button reveals additional information, as shown in Figure
11.14.

Figure 11.14
*Displaying
details of the
recipients list*

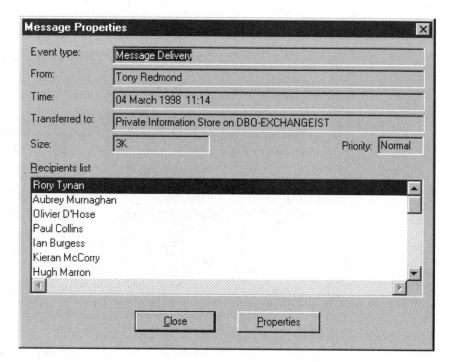

No message tracking system is ever perfect in the eyes of everyone
who tries to use it. It's either too simple and doesn't display enough
information or too complex and can't be used by normal human
beings. The messaging tracking system in Exchange walks a line down
the middle and as such will satisfy the vast majority of system administrators. If you're not happy with the out-of-the-box facilities you can
always write a bespoke own tracking utility based on the data collected in the message tracking logs.

11.2.3   Matching message tracking logs to the graphical interface

A graphical interface is great, but sometimes you need to examine raw
data to discover exactly what's gone on as a message passes from the
Information Store to the MTA to a connector, or wherever else it goes.
The tracking logs can be edited with the WordPad editor (they are too

large for NotePad). Take a copy of the log you want to examine before you start, just in case.

Table 11.1 lists some of the most common event numbers that you'll see in a message tracking log. For full details, see chapter 17 of the Exchange Administration Guide.

Table 11.1 *Common event numbers in message tracking logs*

Event Number	Meaning
0	A message was received from a server or connector.
4	A local client submitted a message. Clients can be mailboxes or system components such as the Directory Service Agent (DSA) or the Public Information Store, which generate replication messages for the directory and public folders respectively.
7	A message was transferred out to another server or connector.
9	A message was delivered to one or more local recipients (mailboxes).
26	A distribution list was expanded.
28	A message was redirected to a destination other than the original set of recipients.
1010	A message was accepted by the Internet Mail Service and placed on its outbound queue.
1011	The Internet Mail Service successfully sent a message.

Now that we know some of the events that we'll meet in a tracking log, let's examine the entries for the message traced by the Message Tracking Center shown in Figure 11.13.

Every message has a unique identifier, which is clearly obvious in the Message ID field shown in Figure 11.13. The relevant tracking log can be identified from the date coded into the Message ID (980304 or March 4, 1998 in this instance). To locate the entries examined here, I loaded the tracking log into WordPad and searched for the string "980304111409Z". For clarity, I have edited some of the data to remove superfluous information.

Event 4

The message is sent from the Private Information Store (/CN= Microsoft Private MBD) on behalf of the mailbox with alias TonyR to the "Exchange IST" recipient. In this case, "Exchange IST" is the alias for a distribution list with the display name of "European Messaging Team". As you can see, full distinguished names are used to identify recipients throughout the tracking log.

```
C=IE;A=eirmail400;P=digital;L=DBO-EXCHANGE-980304111409Z-23655
41998.3.4 11:14:10/O=DIGITAL EQUIPMENT CORPORATION/OU=DUBLIN/
CN=CONFIGURATION/CN=SERVERS/CN=DBO-EXCHANGEIST/CN=MICROSOFT
PRIVATE MDB

/o=DIGITAL EQUIPMENT CORPORATION/ou=DUBLIN/cn=RECIPIENTS/
cn=TONYRO2302 001

/o=DIGITAL EQUIPMENT CORPORATION/ou=DUBLIN/cn=RECIPIENTS/
cn=ExchangeIST
```

Event 7

The MTA on this server routes all distribution lists to be expanded by the MTA on another server (PLATINUM, shown as /CN=PLATINUM). It is more usual to expand distribution lists locally, but dedicated servers are often used when organizations depend on very large or nested distribution lists.

```
C=IE;A=eirmail400;P=digital;L=DBO-EXCHANGE-980304111409Z-23655
71998.3.4 11:14:10/O=DIGITAL EQUIPMENT CORPORATION/OU=DUBLIN/
CN=CONFIGURATION/CN=SERVERS/CN=PLATINUM/CN=MICROSOFT MTA
```

Event 0

The MTA on the PLATINUM server has expanded the list and responds with the set of recipients. In this case, the list actually contains 27 recipients (not all are shown in the extract) and the expansion server responded in approximately one second. The expansion server is in the same site, so all communications are performed via RPCs over a LAN. Exchange V5.5 is much faster at distribution list expansion than previous versions.

```
C=IE;A=eirmail400;P=digital;L=DBO-EXCHANGE-980304111409Z-23655
01998.3.4 11:14:11

/O=DIGITAL EQUIPMENT CORPORATION/OU=DUBLIN/CN=CONFIGURATION/
CN=SERVERS/CN=PLATINUM/CN=MICROSOFT MTA/o=DIGITAL EQUIPMENT
CORPORATION/ou=DUBLIN/cn=RECIPIENTS/cn=TONYRO230200 27

/o=DIGITAL EQUIPMENT CORPORATION/ou=DUBLIN/cn=RECIPIENTS/
cn=TYNAN

/o=DIGITAL EQUIPMENT CORPORATION/ou=DUBLIN/cn=RECIPIENTS/
cn=AUBREYM

/o=DIGITAL EQUIPMENT CORPORATION/ou=DUBLIN/cn=RECIPIENTS/
cn=D'HOSE
```

```
/o=DIGITAL EQUIPMENT CORPORATION/ou=DUBLIN/cn=RECIPIENTS/
cn=PAULC
```

```
/o=DIGITAL EQUIPMENT CORPORATION/ou=DUBLIN/cn=RECIPIENTS/
cn=IANB
```

Event 28

One of the recipients (alias = DaraghM) has an Inbox Assistant rule set to autoforward any new messages to another address. The Information Store detects the rule and redirects the message.

```
C=IE;A=eirmail400;P=digital;L=DBO-EXCHANGE-980304111409Z-23655
281998.3.4 11:14:12/o=DIGITAL EQUIPMENT CORPORATION/ou=DUBLIN/
cn=RECIPIENTS/cn=TONYR0230200 1
```

```
/o=Digital Equipment Corporation/ou=Dublin/cn=External People/
cn=DaraghM
```

Event 9

Redirection via an Inbox Assistant rule does not prevent a message being delivered to the recipient's mailbox, so the Information Store goes ahead and delivers a copy.

```
C=IE;A=eirmail400;P=digital;L=DBO-EXCHANGE-980304111409Z-23655
91998.3.4 11:14:14/O=DIGITAL EQUIPMENT CORPORATION/OU=DUBLIN/
CN=CONFIGURATION/CN=SERVERS/CN=DBO-EXCHANGEIST/CN=MICROSOFT
PRIVATE MDB/o=DIGITAL EQUIPMENT CORPORATION/ou=DUBLIN/
cn=RECIPIENTS/cn=TONYR0230200 1
```

```
/o=DIGITAL EQUIPMENT CORPORATION/ou=DUBLIN/cn=RECIPIENTS/
cn=DARAGHM
```

Event 7

The rule set on the DaraghM mailbox forwards messages out of the Exchange organization, so a copy of the message is now delivered to a connector, in this case the Internet Mail Service (IMS).

```
 C=IE;A=eirmail400;P=digital;L=DBO-EXCHANGE-980304111409Z-
2365571998.3.4 11:14:15/O=DIGITAL EQUIPMENT CORPORATION/
OU=DUBLIN/CN=CONFIGURATION/CN=CONNECTIONS/CN=INTERNET MAIL
CONNECTOR (DBO-EXCHANGEIST)/o=DIGITAL EQUIPMENT CORPORATION/
ou=DUBLIN/cn=RECIPIENTS/cn=TONYR0230200 1
```

```
/o=DIGITAL EQUIPMENT CORPORATION/ou=DUBLIN/cn=RECIPIENTS/
cn=DARAGHM
```

Event 1010

The IMS accepts the message and places it on its outbound queue.

```
c=IE;a=eirmail400;p=digital;l=DBO-EXCHANGE-980304111409Z-23655
10101998.3.4 11:14:16/o=Digital Equipment Corporation/
ou=Dublin/cn=Configuration/cn=Connections/cn=Internet Mail
Connector (DBO-EXCHANGEIST)
<E081F44FDB37D011A5480020AFF54A23B10FD4@dbo-exchangeist.
dublin.dbo.dec.com> [FXCJ98NV]
```

Event 1011

The IMS successfully sends the message to the specified SMTP address (removed here).

```
c=IE;a=eirmail400;p=digital;l=DBO-EXCHANGE-980304111409Z-23655
10111998.3.4 11:14:17/o=Digital Equipment Corporation/
ou=Dublin/cn=Configuration/cn=Connections/cn=Internet Mail
Connector (DBO-EXCHANGEIST)ml.com
<E081F44FDB37D011A5480020AFF54A23B10FD4@dbo-exchangeist.
dublin.dbo.dec.com> [FXCJ98NV]
```

Event 9

The Information Store delivers copies of the message to all of the other local recipients.

```
=IE;A=eirmail400;P=digital;L=DBO-EXCHANGE-980304111409Z-236559
1998.3.4 11:14:27/O=DIGITAL EQUIPMENT CORPORATION/OU=DUBLIN/
CN=CONFIGURATION/CN=SERVERS/CN=DBO-EXCHANGEIST/CN=MICROSOFT
PRIVATE MDB/o=DIGITAL EQUIPMENT CORPORATION/ou=DUBLIN/
cn=RECIPIENTS/cn=TONYRO230200 26

/o=DIGITAL EQUIPMENT CORPORATION/ou=DUBLIN/cn=RECIPIENTS/
cn=TYNAN

/o=DIGITAL EQUIPMENT CORPORATION/ou=DUBLIN/cn=RECIPIENTS/
cn=AUBREYM

/o=DIGITAL EQUIPMENT CORPORATION/ou=DUBLIN/cn=RECIPIENTS/
cn=D'HOSE

/o=DIGITAL EQUIPMENT CORPORATION/ou=DUBLIN/cn=RECIPIENTS/
cn=PAULC

/o=DIGITAL EQUIPMENT CORPORATION/ou=DUBLIN/cn=RECIPIENTS/
cn=IANB
```

Hopefully walking through the contents of the message tracking log has revealed some of its secrets. This shouldn't be something you have to do often, but it certainly helps to know where to know to look when someone (normally important) wants to find out whether a message was delivered or not.

11.3 The Exchange Load Simulator

In chapter 4 we reviewed how the different hardware components interact in a server that runs Exchange. Selecting suitable hardware configurations is clearly an important part of a deployment. If the hardware can't handle the workload users will complain and it will eventually be replaced, driving up overall costs. Over-configured hardware will certainly support users but accountants won't be happy at the heavy price tags. Over the long term it is better to over-configure than under-configure, mostly because a return on the initial investment will be realized because the servers will last longer. This is a comforting thought, but it still doesn't answer the question as to how can you be sure that a particular configuration will perform under any given load? Do you depend on figures supplied by hardware vendors, or do you attempt to carry out your own tests, preferably in the same type of environment that you expect a production server to operate in?

Microsoft supplies (but does not officially support) a tool called LoadSim (the Exchange Load Simulator) to help assess hardware configurations. The tool is supplied "as is". In other words, Microsoft builds the software and keeps it up to date, but you won't get support for it through the normal support channels. LoadSim kits can be downloaded from the Microsoft web site[3]. A new version (for both Intel and Alpha platforms) is available for Exchange V5.5. Older versions are available, but you should use the most current version

Using LoadSim is easy. Create a new directory on the server to hold the files contained in the kit, and then double-click on LOADSIM.EXE and you'll be started. Before that, let's consider what the tool is designed to do and the different steps you have to go through in order to use it properly.

In simple terms LoadSim allows you simulate the workload generated by multiple concurrently connected clients. Multi-threaded processes running on one or more computers (usually Windows NT workstations), each of which has MAPI client software (either the Exchange or Outlook client can be used) installed to generate the workload. Windows 95 clients can be used to place additional load on the server during the test but Windows 95 doesn't offer the operating system features necessary to support such a simulation. Up to several hundred clients can be simulated from a single computer, meaning that it's easy to conduct your own tests on different hardware configurations. You certainly

---

3. The exact location for downloading the LoadSim kit may change over time, so the best place to start looking is the generic home page for Exchange at http://www.microsoft.com/exchange.

don't have to create a hugely complex testing laboratory to test hardware with LoadSim.

LoadSim works by generating a number of processes, typically no more than 30. Each process represents a set of clients, each represented by a separate thread within the process. During the simulation the client threads generate MAPI function calls to emulate common actions performed by real users. Commands are issued to create and send messages, to add recipients and distribution lists to messages, to read messages that have arrived in user mailboxes, to create and respond to appointments, and so on.

11.3.1   Workloads and clients

The current load simulation workload is biased towards the Exchange client (which is no longer shipped) and does not take Internet clients into account. If you're interested in using these clients you need to adjust the results from the simulation or generate a load with a tool called InetLoad, which is part of the BackOffice Resource Kit. InetLoad is able to generate user loads with Internet protocols such as HTTP, LDAP, NNTP, and POP3.

If you want to use LoadSim without InetLoad you can adjust the results to arrive at some rough conclusions. In the interim, let me suggest some adjustments you might like to use as a starting point.

- Outlook tends to generate more load on a server than the standard Exchange client. If you use Outlook, reduce the number of supported clients by 10%. The logic here is that Outlook makes more extensive use of Exchange server folders to store data like calendar and contact information.

- If using POP3 or IMAP4 clients, increase the number of supported clients by 30%. Internet clients use a much simpler messaging model so they should decrease the load each client imposes on the server. 30% is an arbitrary figure selected to be safe rather than setting an expectation that Exchange might be able to support twice the number of POP3 clients as it can MAPI clients. This might well be the case, but I want to see firm evidence first.

- If using Outlook Web Access, decrease the number of supported clients by 10%. As explained in chapter 2, Outlook Web Access is a server-side application where the browser acts chiefly as a display device. All of the active pages that contain the code that fetches and process data, and then renders HTML output to create the user interface for Outlook Web Access must be processed on the server. Usually, Internet Information Server runs on the server too, creating an additional workload. While the operations performed by Outlook Web Access clients are simpler than full Outlook clients, the demand they create more server-side load and you must adjust for this fact. Note that the functionality available to web browsers grows all the time, and each new feature adds load for the server.

- If using a mixture of clients, the figure reported by LoadSim can probably be taken as is. The extra load imposed by one client type will offset the advantage gained by using one of the other clients.

These recommendations are generic and arbitrary. Depending on client mix and user demands, your mileage will vary.

11.3.2   Load Simulator Test phases

A LoadSim test is broken down into a number of phases:

1. *The topology for the test is defined.* In other words, what elements of an Exchange organization (specifically the servers) will be used to conduct the test. You can define how many accounts for simulated clients will be allocated to each server used for the test. You can also define the type of users profile to use during the test, whether public folders are used, and if so, how many are stored on each server. If you want the test to include the extra processing required to expand distribution lists you can specify that these should be configured into the test. Distribution list configuration means specifying parameters such as the minimum, maximum, and average number of recipients per list.

2. *Generation of user accounts.* LoadSim uses a specific naming convention for the user mailboxes employed during the simulation. Details of these mailboxes have to be generated into a file suitable for importing into the Exchange directory on the system under test. When the file is imported the mailboxes are created in a new "LoadSim" recipients container. Note that you don't need to create separate Windows NT accounts for each mailbox because the import file grants access to all accounts to the Windows NT "Domain Users" group, enabling any account in the local domain to access all LoadSim mailboxes. If you want to run a test across multiple domains or you have other reasons to force LoadSim to use specific accounts you can edit the import file to specify other account permissions. Three separate import files are created— the directory import (to set up the mailboxes) and separate import files to set X.400 and SMTP addresses for each mailbox. You only need to import the directory import file if you conduct tests within a single Exchange organization (the norm).

3.   *User and public folder initialization.* LoadSim needs to place some messages into user mailboxes for use during the simulation. The user initialization (known as the "UserInit" test) phase cycles through all the mailboxes and creates the necessary messages in each one. If you have included public folders in the simulation you should run the public folders initialization test. This step populates public folders with some test data. Before running these tests you can specify various parameters through property pages. For example, what recipients to use.

4.   *Execute the load simulation test.* This can only be done properly after all the other steps are complete. You can give a name to each test scenario you create. The scenario defines how long the test should last (it can last forever, meaning that the test can be stopped at any time), the length of a typical user day, whether users should log off at night-time (a test can span several working days) and empty their deleted items folder, and whether clients log-off during the working day. You can even compress the standard length of day from 8 hours to 4 or less, creating an effect of very busy users who place more stress on the system.

All of the information you enter to specify settings for a test (topology, number of users, parameters, etc.) is stored in a file with a .SIM extension. This allows you to repeat tests under the same conditions across multiple LoadSim sessions. The parameter file also allows you to run LoadSim from a command line prompt or from a batch file as follows:

```
C:> LoadSim simulation_file_name test_name /q
```

for example:

```
C:> LoadSim LargeServer.SIM FullTest /q
```

This command instructs LoadSim to recreate the simulation scenario described in the LargeServer.SIM file and then proceed to run the test called FullTest. If the name of a test is not specified LoadSim will open but won't attempt to run a test. The /Q parameter instructs LoadSim to terminate after the specified test is complete.

During the test the actions being simulated for clients are echoed to the LoadSim window, allowing you to see exactly what's going on. Running the NT Performance Monitor during the simulation allows you to see how different system components respond to the test load. Test results are logged by LoadSim to a file for later analysis. If multiple client computers are used each produces a log file. All of the log files from a test can be merged together at the end in order to create a single file for analysis.

You don't have to have a dedicated test system to run LoadSim. The utility will run happily on any Exchange server. If you decide to run a simulation on a production system be aware of several side effects:

- The test recipients are created in the special LoadSim container.

- Details of the test recipients are automatically added to the global address list. Of course, data for the container and all the mailboxes will be replicated to all other servers in the site and all other sites in the organization, which is not a good idea. For this reason alone it is unwise to run LoadSim on a production server.

- The volume of messages created and sent during the test will impact the Private and Public Information Stores. The databases expand as all the test messages are created and sent, and a large series of transaction logs are also written. It is possible to exhaust disk space if you're not careful, so make sure that the Performance Optimizer has been run before the test to distribute Exchange files across all available disk spindles. Also check that there's sufficient disk space free where the databases and transaction logs are located.

It's a good idea to take a backup of the Information and Directory Stores before starting the test and compact them afterwards with the ESEUTIL utility. You may want to restore the backup before beginning a new simulation. This step means that the database environment is the same for each test.

A simulation can be stopped at any time or allowed to run through to its designated completion time. If you elect to stop a test the results are only indication of the events processed up to that time. Not all client processes may have connected, only a subset of message types might have been sent, and perhaps only some of the public folder manipulations may have been carried out. Stopping a test too early leads to unreliable results. You have to let the test run for long enough for the simulation to stabilize and have produced enough results to be meaningful when analyzed. Microsoft's performance group and major hardware vendors conduct tests for between six and eight hours when they measure hardware configurations, a good indication of what they feel is an appropriate timespan.

11.3.3   Using the LSLOG utility

LsLog, the LoadSim Performance Log Parser, is a command line executable that can be found in the same directory as LoadSim. The major function of this utility is to analyze the log files recorded during a simulation test. The results or answer delivered by LsLog after it has analyzed the logs are 95[4] percentile results for all of the actions tested during the simulation as well as a weighted average 95th percentile for all actions. The results are reported in milliseconds, so lower values are better because the system has taken less time to respond to a client request to perform an action. If you compare two similar hardware configurations with the same test and one configuration delivers better results than the other it should be a fair indication of which one to use for production purposes. Don't accept results always without question. In a situation where you compare two similar configurations and find one performs significantly better than the other by a wide margin (more than 10%), ask the question whether the two configurations are really so similar. Are the network controllers identical? What disk controllers are used? Is there more memory cache in one system than the other? Because errors can arise during the set-up of test scenarios knowledge of Exchange and PC hardware is invaluable when conducting tests and then interpreting results afterwards.

The steps to use LsLog to analyze a performance log file are as follows:

- Merge the performance logs from each computer participating in the test. Ignore this step if only one computer is used.

- Extract a specific time window from the log. This is an optional step as the default is to analyze the entire log. Extracting a time window allows you to focus on a period after the test scenario has stabilized.

- Use the LsLog "answer" option to generate the 95th percentile results for the actions recorded in the performance log. The results are displayed to the screen, but can also be redirected to a file for inclusion in a report or distribution by mail. Figure 11.15 illustrates results achieved from a simulation

Figure 11.15
Sample results from a simulation run, as reported by LsLog

Category	Weight	Hits	95th Percentile
SEND	1	27	11084
Sub-weight	16	6	48640
Sub-weight	2	1	1863
Sub-weight	5	2	721
Sub-weight	60	15	2914
Sub-weight	4	3	991

---

4.   In other words, 95% of all response times recorded were equal to or below the reported value. 95th percentile measurements are often found in statistical analyses.

```
READ            10     535     801
REPLY            1       6    1412
REPLY ALL        1       5    2103
FORWARD          1      56    1222
MOVE             1     104     490
DELETE           2     206     411
SUBMIT           0      94     942
RESOLVE NAME     0      83     560
LOAD IMSG        0      41    1712
DELIVER          0     236     660
Weighted Avg    17    1393    1479
```

Some sample LsLog commands:

```
C:> LsLog Merge System1.Log System2.Log > Systems.Log

C:> LsLog Truncate Systems.Log 2 4 > Test.Log

C:> LsLog Answer Test.Log > Results.Txt
```

These commands merge System1.Log and System2.Log (performance log files from two client computers) to form Systems.Log, which is then stripped of data spanning four hours' testing (for 2 clients). The stripped test log is then analyzed and the test scores written into Results.Txt.

11.3.4   Simulating connector workload

LoadSim generates lots of messages as it loads the server under test. The messages are generated to local recipients and do not measure the load that a connector can impose on a server as it converts message content to the format demanded by a foreign mail system. In addition, the MTA has a much easier time when local mailboxes are addressed as it doesn't have to get involved with message transport. Everything can be handled within the Information Store. Not many servers will never send remote messages so it's important to factor some load into tests. This is easily done as follows:

- Create a number of custom recipients with addresses that will force messages to be sent through a connector. You don't need a lot of custom recipients. It's enough to create one custom recipient for each connector to be tested.

- LoadSim generates mailbox entries to use during the simulation. Before the simulation begins, select a percentage of the mailboxes and modify their entries to redirect any incoming messages to the custom recipients. If you expect that 10% of all messages will be sent off a server when it is in production, redirect 10% of the mailboxes. If 25% of all messages go to other systems, redirect 25% of the mailboxes, and so on. Take care to spread the load across all the different connectors according to the traffic patterns you expect to see in production. For example, 20% might be redirected to a FAX connector, 50% to the Internet connector, and 30% to Microsoft Mail.

During the simulation LoadSim will create and send test messages as normal. The difference is that a percentage of the messages will be redirected to the custom recipients and force the MTA and connectors to do some work and generate additional load. Thus, the results of the simulation will more accurately reflect a real-life environment.

Executing a test for Exchange only is only useful if you want to compare one hardware configuration against another, as in the case when you might want to compare two Intel Pentium-powered systems from different vendors against each other. Depending on the other components wrapped around the CPU, two systems with apparently the same CPU type and clock speed can differ in real delivered performance by 10% or more.

11.3.5   Putting results into context

After carrying out a successful simulation it's important to put the results into a realistic context. To achieve realistic results the server should run the same set of applications during the test that you expect to run in production. For example, if you expect to use a virus checker that connects to the Information Store on production servers, then this must be active during the test. If your servers will host Internet, Lotus Notes, cc:Mail, or Microsoft Mail, or a FAX connector, then these connectors should be installed on the test server too. We've already discussed how to generate traffic through the connectors and this step should be taken to increase the level of realism.

If you're going to use the Event Service, then create some scripts and associate them with events on some of the folders used during the test. And if you want to run workflow, document management, or full text retrieval products that are integrated with Exchange you need to install and run these on the server under test.

Many LoadSim tests are run with both client workload and server functions executing on a single computer. That's fine, but in a production environment clients will connect to servers over the network, so the LoadSim results need to be adjusted because they don't account for any network latency or fallibility. It's important to ensure that the network bandwidth available to servers is sufficient to handle client connections in real life.

The type of messages used during the test is another item to bear in mind. Unless you customize the test by adding a set of messages you have determined to be typical, the set of default messages is quite simple. Some of the default messages contain Word and Excel attachments, and there's even one with an embedded bitmap image. Useful as these messages are they may not reflect the type of messages sent by your users, and they don't test the impact of users sending very large messages or messages with lots of complex attachments. They do, however, deliver a reasonably weighted average of the type of messages seen in general messaging, which is possibly the type of system you'll operate.

LoadSim runs in an artificial environment. That's obvious because real human beings are not producing the load placed on the server under test. Aside from the human factor there's another huge influence that is never seen in a load simulation. No real network activity is ongoing. You might try and create the same type of Exchange organization (sites, connectors, directory replication connectors, and so on) to run the servers in while they are under test, but it is impossible to generate exactly the same stress that will be seen in production. You might well get to a 70% level (my best guess), but it's awfully difficult to move on from this point. There's no way, for instance, to simulate the complex RPC-driven interaction that occurs between servers in a site as they communicate with each other to update the directories and process interpersonal mail. The impact of a fax or other connector is difficult to simulate as well.

In some quarters LoadSim has attained almost saint-like status and is treated as the de facto standard for Exchange benchmarks. This is indicative of a problem that I think has grown up around LoadSim since it was first made available. The main advantage of LoadSim is its ease of use, but this is also its major disadvantage because the results generated by one LoadSim test cannot be compared to another unless both tests are performed in exactly the same, almost laboratory-like conditions. In my experience, few companies go to the bother to produce truly comparable results for each LoadSim run.

Different people have different needs from LoadSim. Marketing departments from major hardware vendors love to see the headline figures generated by running LoadSim on the latest and greatest servers, especially if they can boast that more simulated users can be supported than on competitor hardware. IT departments use LoadSim for a comfort factor, to assure themselves that a certain specification will handle a predicted workload. The lack of exactitude is staggering but understandable. As long as the workload is handled everyone is happy that a system configuration will perform in a production environment. But will it? Will the same performance be seen when real human beings create demand instead of computer-simulated clients? Do computer clients do incredibly silly things like sending a 25MB attachment to large distribution lists? Is a virus checker in use during the simulation? What about a FAX connector, and a full text retrieval product, and maybe some electronic forms applications, or some document management functionality? And is directory and public folder replication incorporated into the simulation? All of these things are factors that influence real-life performance. Most are ignored during simulations, so is it any wonder that your mileage will vary?

11.3.6   Using LoadSim to validate newly arrived hardware

PC hardware is not perfect. Many systems suffer problems with one component or another when they are delivered. Some of the problems are small and quickly fixed. Others, such as a motherboard or controller failure, are more serious and need specialist attention. The most annoying failures are those that occur several days after delivery, usually after all the software has been installed and maybe even after the server has been put into production.

Putting a system under load is one way to test all its components thoroughly. LoadSim is a convenient tool for this purpose because it is easy to set up and can run without much human intervention. You can therefore use LoadSim to test whether a system is running properly after Windows NT and Exchange have been installed and before the server is put into production. This takes a little more time, but it makes sure that everything works.

Here are some simple steps to use LoadSim to validate hardware:

- Install Windows NT and Exchange, including all service packs. Exchange should be installed into a special test organization.
- Install LoadSim.
- Configure a test for 200 clients. The test can last as long as you like. 24 or 48 hours of solid load should certainly identify any hardware problems.
- Run the test. Check the results and compare them against the results you would expect from the system configuration (it helps to have a set of sample results for several different configurations to compare against).
- If everything seems OK, run SETUP to remove Exchange from the server.
- Reinstall Exchange, this time using real organizational details.

This approach takes time, and is only useful if you incorporate the effort required to test servers as they are delivered.

11.4   Using the Windows NT Performance Monitor

The Windows NT Performance Monitor provides a graphical interface to allow many different aspects of a Windows NT system to be monitored. The utility provides charting, alerting, and reporting capabilities to report live data as it is generated by applications or to capture performance data to log files for later analysis. Performance Monitor depends on applications having probes or points of measurement buried in the code, ready to provide information to the monitor should the need arise. Windows NT refers to the items being monitored as objects, and objects can be:

- aspects of the system itself such as memory usage
- an individual process
- a section of shared memory
- a physical device

In the case of Exchange you'll be interested in monitoring aspects of the many services that collectively deliver functionality to users. Important Exchange objects that can be monitored include:

Table 11.2 *Important Exchange Services for Performance Monitor*

Service Name	Meaning
MSExchangeDS	The Directory Store
MSExchangeISPriv	The Private Information Store
MSExchangeISPub	The Public Information Store
MSExchangeDX	Directory Synchronization
MSExchangeMTA	The MTA
MSExchangeIMC	The Internet Mail Service

Each object is broken down into "counters". Monitoring tracks the counts of specific events and allows system administrators to report what it's found. Normally reporting is done graphically, as shown in Figure 11.16, perhaps on a dedicated workstation. Any counter supported by the Windows NT Performance Monitor can be exposed to and collected by an SNMP network-based monitoring service (such as HP's OpenView product). Exchange V5.5 supports the commonly-used MADMAN MIB (an SNMP Management Information Base). The MADMAN MIB allows the performance data collected about Exchange to be reported and monitored by these popular SNMP management tools. All of the counters used in this MIB are documented in the "Books Online" provided with Exchange.

If you're not happy with the prepackaged MADMAN MIB, the PERF2MIB utility (from the Windows NT Resource Kit) can be used to generate HP OpenView or IBM NetView compatible MIBs from any set of Performance Monitor counters. It's worth noting here that the version of PERF2MIB in the Windows NT V4.0 Resource Kit is a huge improvement over its V3.51 counterpart. Apart from some bugs being eliminated, PERF2MIB works almost all the time now.

When you start a Performance Monitor session you must tell it what objects and counters you're interested in. This process involves selecting from a list of available objects and counters and adding them to the "workspace", a description of the current monitoring environment.

Figure 11.16
"Server Health"
Performance
Monitor

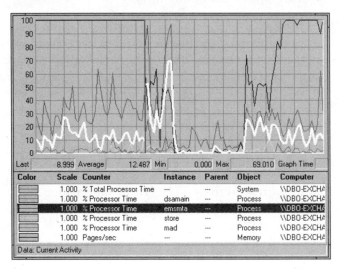

When you're happy with a set of parameters that record whatever data you need to log the whole scenario can be saved in the form of a workspace file. When you install Exchange onto a Windows NT computer a number of prepackaged performance monitor workspaces are installed into the \EXCHSRVR\BIN directory. The set of workspaces is divided between five that are useful on all servers and three specifically for servers running the IMC.

Because the performance monitor scenarios have been developed as Exchange evolved through the different stages in the product's development process, they therefore capture the most important statistics based on knowledge of server and system behavior. The workspaces describe scenarios that are very usable and useful in their own right and provide an excellent starting point for system administrators who wish to develop performance monitor workspaces tailored to fit their own server environment.

For example, EXHEALTH.PMW holds the parameters for the "Server Health" workspace illustrated in Figure 11.16. To make things easier for system administrators, pointers to each workspace are created as icons in the Exchange Server program group. A full list of the prepackaged workspaces is shown in Table 11.3.

Table 11.3 *Pre-Packaged Performance Monitor workspaces*

Packaged Performance Monitor workspace	Important statistics tracked in workspace
Server Health	Overall % processor time; % processor used by Directory Store; % processor used by MTA; % processor used by Information Store; system paging.
Server Load	Rate messages are delivered to recipients; rate messages are submitted by clients; number of connections to other MTAs; address book activity.
Server History (since server was last stated)	Total messages delivered and submitted to users; total messages sent by MTA; total recipients for messages; number of users connected to the server; length of work queues (messages waiting to be processed by the MTA); system paging.
Server Users	Number of users currently connected to the Information Store.
Server Queues	Number of items in the MTA work queue; number of items in the send and receive queues for the private and Public Information Stores.
IMCTraffic	Number of inbound and outbound connections to other SMTP hosts; number of messages awaiting conversion to and from SMTP/MIME format.
IMCStatistics (since server was last started)	Total number of messages delivered to the Internet Mail Service and the total number of messages sent out to the Internet.
IMCQueues	Number of messages coming in from the Internet; number of messages going out to the Internet; number of messages waiting final delivery to recipients.

In cases where message submission and delivery activity is being tracked it is normal to collect separate figures for the Private and Public Information Store. Private Information Store activity relates to interpersonal messaging, that is, messages generated and sent between people. Public Information Store activity relates to messages and other documents posted to public folders. On most servers it would be safe to expect that the Private Information Store gets more work to do than the public, the exception being those servers dedicated to public folder storage.

Which of the pre-packaged workspaces are most useful? It all depends on the workload of your servers, but my favorites are:

- Server Health
- Server History
- IMCTraffic

All servers should have some indication that the system is running smoothly. I find the "Server Health" workspace provides a good overall picture of what's going on at any particular point in time.

Figure 11.16 is a good example of the active workspace. You can see that there is a lot of activity in one of the counters because its line is at the top of the chart at the left-hand side (most recent figures). It's not obvious from the screen shot (because the different colors used for the counters are not reproduced), but the very active counter is system paging, expressed as paging operations per second. The other lines, including that for the MTA counter (shown as the white line), display a fair amount of activity, so clearly this computer is doing a reasonable amount of work. If system paging exhibited the same rate of activity during normal daily operations a system administrator would be worried because it's delivering a strong indication that the computer is overloaded. In this instance there's a reasonable explanation: the screen shot was taken shortly after the computer was rebooted, and all the system services, including the Exchange services, had just been restarted. Just listen to the disk activity after a system is rebooted and you'll immediately realize that a great deal of work is done in this period, as reflected in the results charted by the counters in the "System Health" workspace.

As to my other favorites, I like running "Server History" from time to time just to see what workload the computer has processed since it was last restarted. The figures reported in this chart vary greatly and depend on the number of days since the last reboot. However, a browse through the different counters sometimes provokes questions that should be answered. For example, is there any reason why the computer has processed a larger number of messages than normal?

Systems running the Internet Mail Service, especially those that connect internal messaging networks to the big (sometimes-bad) world of the Internet, need careful monitoring if reliable message delivery times are to be guaranteed to users. The "IMCTraffic" workspace captures and displays details of all the most important IMC-counters.

Feel free to disagree with my opinions. Play around with the pre-packaged workspaces and make changes if you like, but don't add too many counters to any workspace as the chart will become very cluttered and difficult to interpret. The important thing is to ensure that monitoring is a part of day-to-day system administration and not just an activity that's engaged in whenever problems appear on the horizon.

11.5   Logging and viewing Windows NT events

Like all other BackOffice applications, Exchange uses the Windows NT Event log to record information specific to the processing performed by its services such as the MTA, Key Management Server, and Internet Mail Service (to name but a few). All Exchange events are deemed to be "application" events rather than system or other events. The Exchange Resource Kit contains some tools to help you filter, understand and store event information related to Exchange.

Figure 11.17
*The Windows
NT Event Log*

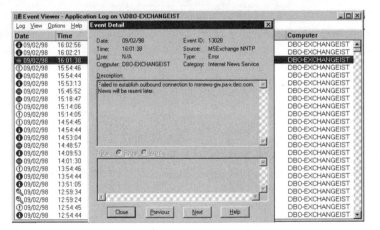

Windows NT logs a great deal of information about different events that occur during applications and system processing. Event information is initially logged internally, and can be written to a file if required for later analysis, or to be used as evidence relating to a problem. The Windows NT Event Viewer (Figure 11.17) allows you to view event logs on any server you have access to. On any moderately large server many events are generated each day, so filters can be applied if you know you're looking for a particular problem. For example, you could apply a filter to view only events relating to the MTA, or look for problems with an NNTP news feed, such as that shown in Figure 11.17.

You can influence the amount of information logged through the diagnostics property of these components, but be aware that it is all too easy to generate vast amounts of data if you enable maximum event logging. Few people have the patience and knowledge to be able to make very much sense of the huge quantity of events logged at full flow by the Exchange MTA (Figure 11.18). The quantity of data produced when full diagnostic logging is enabled has the capacity to exhaust the space reserved for the Event Log after a couple of minutes on any reasonably sized server. You will be forced to clear the log and save existing data to a file if you want to continue to record information. For these reasons it's best to leave diagnostic logging at minimal levels in day-to-day operation and reserve full diagnostic levels for the times when it's justified, for instance, when requested by a support center to help track down the root cause of a problem.

Figure 11.18
Setting MTA diagnostics

Even when minimal diagnostics are enabled the Event log should be browsed on a daily basis to ensure that problems aren't being recorded and then missed. Any event associated with Exchange that is not information status (shown as an "i" surrounded by a blue circle) must be investigated and the reason why the event was logged determined to your satisfaction. Failure to do this might lead to a situation where a small problem develops into something that's rather more serious. Automated tools like NetIQ AppManager or Unicenter-TNG can check events and monitor system processes automatically on a regular basis. For this reason alone these products take a great deal of work off the shoulders of administrators in large Exchange networks.

Event logs should also be checked immediately after a system has been restarted. This step is to ensure that all the Exchange services have started correctly.

11.6   The Exchange Resource Kit

Not all good ideas end up as features in a fully supported product offered for sale to customers. Sometimes the ideas aren't quite fully developed, the code not quite fully debugged, or perhaps a new feature has no obvious place to fit in alongside the existing code base. Engineers occasionally develop code to test features in a product, and the test modules prove useful elsewhere. And people not directly involved with the engineering of a product exploit the APIs to develop features required for particular projects. In all these instances it has long been common practice to bring code that works, but isn't integrated into a product, together in the form of a resource kit, which is then made available to customers on an unsupported basis. Customers then have the freedom to decide whether to use any of the code to help with their deployments, albeit in the full knowledge that if any problems occur, no formal support channel is available. The Exchange Resource Kit (ERK), published as part of the Microsoft BackOffice Resource Kit (BORK), provides many useful and sometimes essential utilities that make system administration easier.

A resource kit is different to a software development kit (SDK) in many respects. The most obvious difference is that a resource kit is composed of fully-functional programs whereas a development kit contains many code fragments that are intended to show programmers how a particular API works. The ERK does not contain any code fragments, so programmers need to look at the Platform SDK for information on the internal workings of APIs like Collaboration Data Objects or MAPI.

The ERK is now in its third iteration, and has matured enormously since its first release. For a resource kit, maturity can be gauged in terms of the number of utilities, the robustness of the utilities, and the availability of utilities across both Intel and Alpha platforms. The third version of the ERK sets new standards in all respects. New versions appear some time after a new version of Exchange is released. For example, the ERK for Exchange V5.5 was made available on the Microsoft web site at the end of March 1998, five months after the product shipped.

At the time of writing there are well over 40 utilities in the ERK. Table 11.4 lists my favorite ERK utilities, some of which, like as the

Mailbox Cleanup Agent should really be part of the product. Some utilities included in previous resource kits, such as the Preview Pane Extension, are now part of a standard product (in this case, the Outlook client), so there's every chance that some of the utilities in the current ERK will find their way into a future release of Exchange after they have been developed a little more.

Table 11.4 *Favourite ERK utilities*

Utility	Comments
Mailbox Cleanup Agent	Useful for helping user mailboxes stay within preset quotas by automatically removing old messages from folders.
MAPISEND	Command-line utility to send a message. Useful for automating system management procedures by sending messages when preset conditions occur, or for automatic distribution of reports, etc.
Inter-organization directory sychronization	Synchronizes the directories of multiple Exchange organizations together.
PFADMIN	Documents and maintains the public folder hierarchy in a number of useful ways.

It's fair to assume that the code and documentation provided in the ERK has not gone through the same quality assurance process imposed on the Exchange product. If you elect to follow the suggestions in the documentation or use code that hasn't been fully tested you have to live with the consequences of those actions. The majority of the code I have used from the ERK is of high quality (certainly of a higher quality than I could create), but that still isn't a recommendation to use any of the ERK utilities without fully testing the code in your production environment. You should also take the time to document the integration of any non-standard utility for operations and help desk staff, so that they know how first to recognize a non-standard utility, and then how best to deal with any problems.

12

The Exchange Event Service

12.1   Introduction

From its inception, Exchange was designed to be a platform for more than just electronic mail. Groupware always featured in the design goals for Exchange. Alas, reality and good intentions have not been a 100% match in this area, and Exchange V4.0 and V5.0 never quite delivered an extendible base for application development. Exchange V5.5 unveils the Scripting Agent, a process to allow server-side application code to be executed when events occur in folders, code that can be used to automate business processes and build real groupware and applications. Microsoft hopes that the Scripting Agent will close a gap between Exchange and Lotus Notes, which commentators have always regarded as having a lead in terms of groupware and document routing capabilities.

Server-side execution is not an unknown quantity for Exchange installations. Outlook Web Access uses exactly the same approach to execute the code in active pages to generate content for web browsers. And like Outlook Web Access, the Scripting Agent is built around CDO (Collaborative Data Objects), a reusable set of messaging and calendaring objects that allow code written in VBscript or JScript to access components within Exchange.

12.2   Events and Folders

The combination of public folders and purpose-built electronic forms was usually positioned as the cornerstone of Exchange V4.0 and V5.0 groupware applications. However, several difficulties became apparent with this approach once Exchange deployments began. Public folders are excellent repositories for static information but are less capable when you want those repositories to be a little more active or intelligent about how the information they hold is controlled or managed. Document management or workflow applications can use public folders to store items, but how do these applications "notice" that conditions have changed in a folder? For example, a user drags a Word document from Windows Explorer and drops it onto a public folder that is under the control of a document management application, or a manager approves a purchase order that's waiting in a public folder designated to hold such items.

A manual solution might be applied. Users could monitor folder contents and take appropriate actions to invoke the document management or workflow application, but this is not real integration and it certainly doesn't leverage the storage capabilities offered by public folders. Writing a server process that constantly monitors folder contents is a more automated solution, but why should every application designer have to recreate the wheel? Developers have been able to use notification mechanisms provided by interfaces like MAPI in the past, but these have required a substantial amount of bespoke code. A standard method to notify applications that an event has occurred in a folder is what's needed, and that's exactly what the Exchange developers have provided in V5.5. The advantage is obvious. Any programmer who knows Visual Basic will be able to write applications that use data held in public folders without having to resort to C++ code or writing their own NT service.

12.2.1   The Event Sink

The Scripting Agent can be used to call applications when 4 types of events occur in public or private folders. These events are:

- New: an event that fires when a new item is created.
- Changed: an event that fires when an item is updated.
- Deleted: an event that fires when an item is deleted.
- Scheduled: an event that can be fired according to a specific time or schedule.

EVENTS.EXE is a new Windows NT server process (the Event Service) that must be active on all servers before scripts can be processed. EVENTS.EXE is what's known as "a generic event sink", capable of invoking COM objects as a response to events as they happen. Exchange-specific script processing is provided by SS.DLL, a new COM object.

The Event Service is an optional part of Exchange and is not required unless you want to experiment with scripting. It's best to avoid installing the Event Service on production servers until you are quite certain that you know what you want to use it for, and have some debugged code ready to go. Installing the Event Service on test or pre-production servers will allow programmers and other interested parties to try their hand at this new development environment.

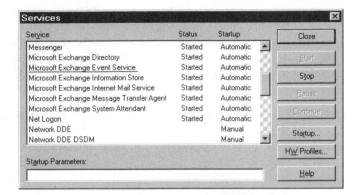

Figure 12.1 *The Exchange Event Service*

The Event Service is automatically included in all new installations but you'll have to specify it as a sub-component of Exchange during server upgrade installations. When it is the service operates under the control of the Exchange service account in exactly the same way as other Exchange services, such as the MTA and System Attendant, as shown in Figure 12.1.

When events are fired through an action occurring in a folder, the event is handed off to an event handler, also known as an "Event Sink", basically a process responsible for making sure that the correct actions are performed. Exchange V5.5 provides a default Event Sink in the form of an ActiveScript engine that can run interpreted VBscript or JScript code on the server, and this is what is referred to as the Scripting Agent. Scripts can call code from other COM-compliant applications, so they're not restricted to interpreted code. The Event Service begins to monitor folders dynamically immediately event code has been added.

12.2.2 The Events Root Folder

The installation of the Event Service creates a new branch in the System Folders hierarchy. System Folders are used to hold items such as the Offline Address Book and Free/Busy schedule and aren't visible to users. The new branch is called the Events Root, and a separate folder is created in the branch for every server that will run the Event Service. Figure 12.2 shows the System Folder hierarchy. You can see that only one server is configured here for script processing.

The events system folder serves two purposes. First, it is used to hold details of script "bindings" or the registration list of scripts for a particular server. Second, its properties include an access control list (ACL), just like any other folder. The ACL defines who is able to execute scripts on a server. By default no-one can, so the first thing you've got to do is select the folder, view its properties, and then use the "Client Permissions" dialog to nominate the users who will be able to submit scripts. Users must have at least author permission on the events system folder before they can run code. It makes sense to restrict access to as few users as possible on the basis that the less people who can create code the fewer potential culprits to look for when things go wrong.

Figure 12.2
*The Events
system folder*

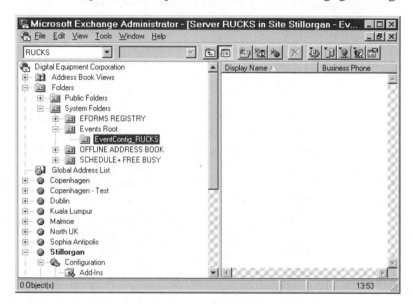

12.3   Script creation

Not every user can associate code with folders. Before you're able to write any code you must first be a folder owner and then be listed in the ACL for the events system folder on one or more servers in a site. You cannot register (or bind) a script to a folder unless you have owner permission for the target folder. In a broader sense, before a user can view or write code for folders they do not own an administrator must first grant them the new "run script on server" permission. The ability to associate code with a folder is only valid for the servers that a user has permission for. For example, if there are three servers in a site and you have author permission on the events system folder for only one server, then you can only register scripts for that server.

After permission is given, folder owners are able to see the Agents tab when they view folder properties, and can then click on the tab to view any existing code or add new code for folder events. It would be very undesirable if people could suddenly begin to write code that, after all, is executed on the server without some controls being in place, so this is a sensible restriction.

Don't expect references to agents or how to write scripts to process folder events in user documentation. There's a brief mention about the event service in the release notes and the What's New guide, and the Exchange V5.5 Administration Guide describes how to grant permission to run scripts on a server, but that's it. Anyone needing more information must consult the Platform SDK. Alternatively, you can register for MSDN (http://www.microsoft.com/msdn) and access programmer documentation for the scripting agent free of charge there.

Application developers can leverage the Scripting Agent by creating code to fire when events occur in public folders used by their application. Consider the document management example. When a new item is added to the folder event code might fire to place a copy of the item into a separate database that's used to track changes that occur to the item during its lifecycle. As changes are made in the public folder the "change" event code can update the external database, and so on. In the workflow scenario, after a purchase order is approved the "change" code can fire to validate that the approval is valid (the person attempting to approve the item might not have the correct authorization). If authorization is given the change code could then route the purchase order into the next step in the purchasing cycle (electronic or otherwise).

Users do not have to be online to fire events. For example, an Outlook client might post a new item to a folder when working in off-line mode. The next time the client connects to its home server and synchronizes the contents of the folder, the new item is posted the server-based folder and thus causes the "create event" to fire. Conceivably the off-line posting might eventually result in a whole series of transactions within a workflow or document management application, all occurring under the control of the code linked to the create event.

12.3.1   How Scripts are created

Initially, script code can be written using Notepad (or Visual Notepad, the name given by Jim Reitz, a Microsoft program manager, to this ancient utility when deployed in its new development role). You'll only be able to do this if you're running Outlook V8.03 or later. Although Outlook has a special role to play in the creation and management of script code for agents it's important to note that events are triggered by the interaction of any client—MAPI, IMAP4, POP3 or Web —with a folder that has associated agents. In this respect Outlook is no better nor worse than any other client that can be connected to Exchange.

Figure 12.3 *The
Agents tab in
folder properties*

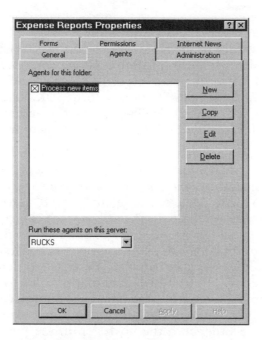

Outlook exposes scripts through a new "Agents" tab that's added
to folder properties. As noted earlier, the Agents tab is only visible if
you're the folder owner and have been granted the necessary permission on the events system folder on one or more servers. Figure 12.3
shows what you might expect to see when the Agents tab is clicked.
One script or agent is listed for the folder.

Improved client performance was a goal of the Outlook 98 release,
and the engineers attempted to eliminate any unnecessary client-
server communications. A side effect is that the Server Scripting add-in
is loaded by default into Outlook 98's Add-In Manager, but it is not
enabled. When enabled, the add-in causes an extra network RPC to
the server whenever the client executes a File.Properties look-up on a
folder. Only a tiny percentage of users will ever want to create or view
scripts, so disabling the add-in is a very sensible step. However, it does
mean that anyone who starts working with scripts with Outlook 98
must enable the Server Scripting add-in. Do this through the
Tools.Other.Advanced.Add-In Manager menu option. If you used
Outlook 8.03 to work with scripts the add-in is automatically enabled
during the upgrade process.

Clicking on the edit button reveals the dialog illustrated in Figure
12.4. Note the way you can associate the selected agent with each one
of the four potential events that might occur in a folder. What we've
seen so far are agent properties. Clicking on the "Edit Script" button

reveals the actual script code associated with the agent. Whenever a new script is created Exchange generates some prototype VBscript code. The code is divided into a set of procedures, one for each of the events that the agent might have to handle.

Figure 12.4
Defining the events to fire script code

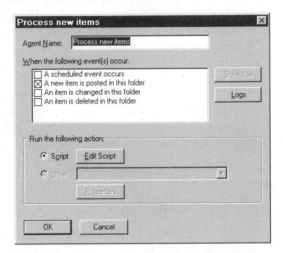

12.3.2 Sample scripts provided with Exchange

New code can be inserted into the appropriate section as required. It's perhaps easier to begin by making some minor changes to one of the sample scripts supplied with Exchange[1]. These include:

- **Folder count:** a script that counts the number of items in a folder and sends a message with the count back to the person who last posted in the folder.

- **Bank Post script:** a script that shows how to call Microsoft Transaction Server (MTS) objects. The script interprets the subject and body field of messages posted into a folder as bank account numbers and amounts, and then calls a COM object (called Bank.Account) to post the transaction.

- **Auto-categorize script:** a script to search message bodies for a set of defined keywords. If the keywords are found the keywords field of the message is updated. Clients like Outlook can then use the keyword information when they categorize items.

- **Auto-accept script:** a script to monitor the inbox of a resource mailbox like a conference room. Incoming meeting requests are checked against the resource's schedule and if the requested time is free the meeting is automatically accepted and a note sent back

---

1.   See the \Server\Collab\Sampler\Scripts directory on the Exchange Server CD.

to the requester. If the time isn't free the meeting is declined and a refusal note issued.

Because it solves a real-life problem and adds some useful functionality to the calendaring subsystem, the auto accept script is probably going to be a favorite for early use. Going through the code in the script and enhancing its functionality provides an excellent introduction to scripts and CDO. Examining the code with NotePad will also convince you that serious programmers need something more sophisticated if they are going to write scripts for Exchange. In fact, it's important that you review and test any sample script, no matter its source, before you introduce it to users. Sample scripts do not receive extensive testing under different sets of conditions as their purpose is merely to illustrate the concepts behind a technology.

Here are some ideas for changes that could be made to the auto-accept script:

- Reject meeting requests if they occur more than six months in the future
- Reject meeting requests for recurring meetings, unless you explicitly want groups to be able to take large chunks of a schedule with such meetings
- Auto accept requests to cancel existing meetings (in fact, just include some code to handle cancel requests)
- Process requests to reschedule a meeting by moving the date and time forward or backwards to a new slot.
- Provide feedback to users on the capabilities of the conference room (size, contact name, etc.)

Further details about the auto-accept script can be found in Q178351 of the Microsoft Knowledge Base.

Even in a relatively small set of four, the sample scripts still manage to cover a range of situations. Expect more sample scripts to appear over time, probably posted through the web-based Microsoft Exchange application farm.

12.3.3   Writing code

By default, Notepad is used whenever Outlook is used to create or edit code (Figure 12.5).

A more sophisticated script editor is available through Microsoft DevStudio (the IDE component of Microsoft Visual Studio). If the Outlook V8.03 Setup program detects Visual Studio is installed on a computer the necessary extension to access Exchange is copied to your disk. You'll then have to load in the macro file for Exchange using the Tools.Macro option in Visual Studio. The extension allows programmers to browse, edit, and save VBscript or JScript programs into Exchange folders.

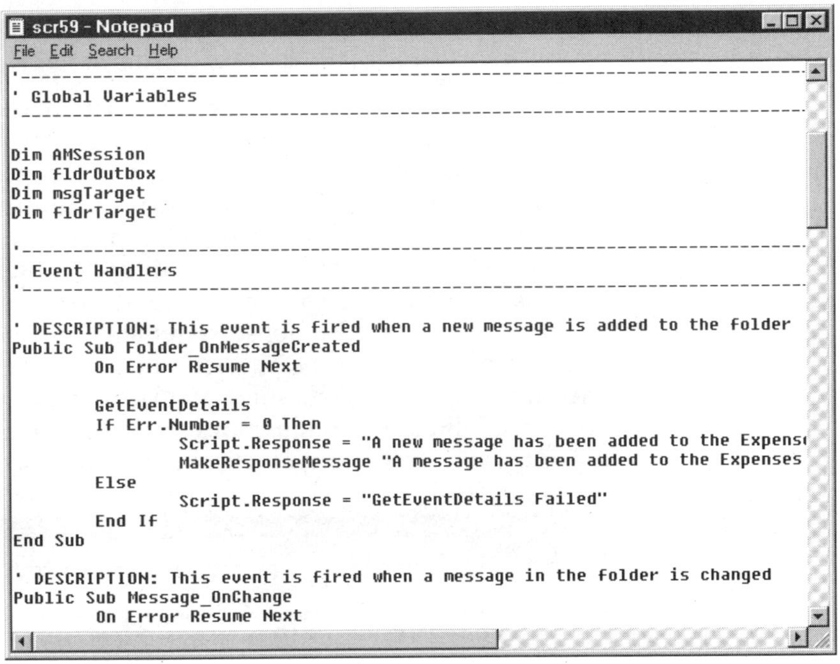

Figure 12.5
*Editing script
code with
Notepad*

```
scr59 - Notepad                                                  _ □ ×
File  Edit  Search  Help

'------------------------------------------------------------
' Global Variables
'------------------------------------------------------------

Dim AMSession
Dim fldrOutbox
Dim msgTarget
Dim fldrTarget


'------------------------------------------------------------
' Event Handlers
'------------------------------------------------------------

' DESCRIPTION: This event is fired when a new message is added to the folder
Public Sub Folder_OnMessageCreated
        On Error Resume Next

        GetEventDetails
        If Err.Number = 0 Then
                Script.Response = "A new message has been added to the Expens
                MakeResponseMessage "A message has been added to the Expenses
        Else
                Script.Response = "GetEventDetails Failed"
        End If
End Sub

' DESCRIPTION: This event is fired when a message in the folder is changed
Public Sub Message_OnChange
        On Error Resume Next
```

The Event Service passes several useful intrinsic objects to a script when it is executed. These include a prelogged-on Exchange connection or session (connection to the mailbox of the last script editor), the identity of the mailbox, the folder identity of the folder where the event happened, and the identity of the message that triggered the event (this identity is null for timer events). Equipped with this information it's possible to select a message in a mailbox and process its contents, and all without having to create special queries to locate a particular message.

12.3.4   Debugging scripts

In some respects scripts execute in a void. No user interface is available to flash "Working ..." progress messages to as code is executed. You can insert Script.Response statements to write information out into a log that's maintained for each script, but this technique harks back to the days of COBOL and FORTRAN when programmers inserted code to print the value of variables to a terminal as a program executed. I was, at one time, quite comfortable with this technique as the print output provided a certain amount of reassurance that a program was executing. Of course, that was when I had to beg 17K of core memory to compile a COBOL program, and things progressed a little slower than they do today. Inserting print statements (or their equivalents) is now a throwback to a previous programming epoch and is something that I am quite sure will be improved over time. The logs, by the way, can only be viewed by the Outlook client and are limited to 32K. Log entries are overwritten after log file space is filled.

Crude as they are, Script.Response statements are a useful starting point on the debug trail, but only that—a starting point, and only to track down logic errors. Clicking on the "Logs" button on the agent properties dialog (Figure 12.4) accesses the information held in the log file, again using the ever-reliable Notepad utility. As is obvious from the log file, the information that's captured is highly dependent on the effort an individual programmer extends to report error conditions. If the necessary Script.Response statements are not incorporated into scripts the log file will be perfectly blank, unless of course the script encounters some fatal run-time errors, in which case the error details are logged. Figure 12.6 illustrates some good examples of the type of log entry you see when syntactical errors are encountered.

Figure 12.6
Script processing errors captured in a log file

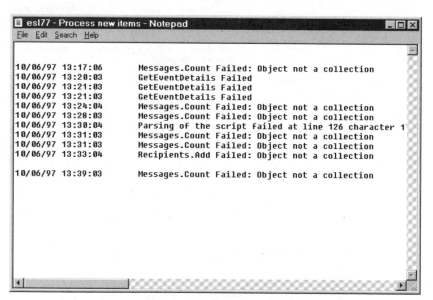

STOP (for VBscript) or Debugger (for JScript) statements can be inserted into a script to force a halt to execution if a debugger is active. In this respect STOP statements act as simple breakpoints. If the Microsoft Script Debugger (available as part of IIS V4.0 and IE V4.0) is running when a script is invoked by the Event Service the debugger will interrupt script execution and allow you to examine what's going on. For example, you can look at the value of different variables and compare them with whatever you'd expect them to contain at a certain point. However, while it's great to have a debugger its effect is somewhat limited because you must run the tool on the server where the script is executing (in other words, no remote debugging can be performed). Also, when a script is halted by the debugger the processing of all other scripts pauses too. This is not something you want to do in situations where several active scripts might be executing.

With these limitations in mind it is obvious that no script should be installed on an operational server unless it has first been thoroughly tested on a trial server. You don't want to get into the situation where a script encounters an error, falls through to a section of code, and proceeds to execute that code with unforeseen consequences.

12.3.5   Executing scripts

As you can see from the drop-down list on the bottom of Figure 12.3, scripts are assigned to run on specific servers. There is no automatic load-balancing, so if you want to spread the load generated by agents across multiple servers you'll have to modify the properties of each folder to define where agents are to run. It is possible to direct all agents to a specific server within a site, and that server could be minimally configured with no mailboxes, connectors, or public folders. This might be a good way to use a low-end server that may have been replaced by a more powerful configuration.

Because the Event Service (in turn logged by the Exchange Service Account on during service start-up) is used to execute scripts, they normally run under the same NT security context as the Service Account. This is not always a satisfactory state of affairs, and if you'd prefer not to use the service account you can use Microsoft Transaction Server to specify which Windows NT account should be used to run the script engine.

A mechanism called ICS, or Incremental Change Synchronization, is used to track successful completion of scripts. If a script runs and encounters a fatal error (for example, the event service crashes), the master counter (or change number) on the folder that is used to track successful executions will not be incremented. The next time the folder is examined by the event service, normally due to a timer or event occurring, the event service will notice that it has not yet handled the change number associated with the incomplete script and will proceed to execute it. Scripts are executed in their change number order, so there's no danger that scripts will be executed out of step.

It's important to remember that agents are built from code that is interpreted on the server. That code isn't going to be anyway near as fast as compiled code. The requirement to interpret code and the inevitable delay in inter-process communication (how fast does the service realize that a script should be executed?) mean that events are never processed in a synchronous manner. It is quite possible for something to occur to change a folder's contents before an agent is called. For example, someone might delete a new item from a folder before an agent ever gets to execute its "on new item" code.

12.3.6 Extending the Event Service

Developers can write their own Event Sink to provide processing required by an application. Any COM-compatible language can be used. Documentation is included in the Platform SDK (see the Exchange/BackOffice section), but only from October 1997 onwards. The SDK includes some sample scripts that are useful building blocks or starting points for projects. Conceptually, implementation of an Event Sink is relatively simple and can be done by creating an in-proc COM object with a single required interface and method.

12.4   Exchange Routing Objects

Microsoft describe Exchange Routing Objects as a set of tools designed to simplify the development of e-mail based routing and approval applications. For example, if a new travel request is created and posted to a "Travel Requests" public folder, the item can be routed to a manager for initial approval, then to the Travel Department to have flight and hotel bookings confirmed, and finally to the Accounting Department as a note to authorize payment. This application uses a simple serial route to move the item from recipient to recipient. Items for processing are delivered to recipients like normal e-mail, and Outlook voting buttons are used to approve or disapprove their contents. Separate routing steps can be invoked when an item is approved or disapproved.

Routing Objects are included in a new Collaborative Data Objects (CDO) library provided with Exchange V5.5 SP1. However, the new CDO library and the associated routing engine can be retrofitted to any Exchange V5.5 server[2].

12.4.1 Routing components

As discussed earlier in this chapter, the Event Service is based on Microsoft COM. Routing Objects is also built on top of COM, and

---

2.   A kit is available from http://backoffice.microsoft.com/downtrial/moreinfo/exchrouting.asp

provides a purpose-built event handler to process stages in an item's routing lifecycle. Three major server-side components are provided:

1.   The Routing Engine, or event handler, that communicates with the Event Service. The routing engine is a simple state engine that processes the items in folders marked as holding routing items. Each item in the folder has a state (initiated, rejected, approved, and so on), and the routing engine takes charge of tracking the state and executing the appropriate code. The routing engine contains all the necessary functionality to route an item via email, and it is able to call purpose-built Vbscript functions for bespoke processing.

2.   A set of CDO objects used to control routing behaviour. The CDO routing objects enable programmers to create and control process maps, which define the steps an item can pass through in a routing cycle, and the activities to be performed at each step.

3.   A set of Vbscript functions to build the steps commonly found in routing applications. These functions include steps like sending and receiving an item for approval, consolidation (checking approvals from multiple recipients), and evaluation activities such as an item timing out after it has been in a recipient's mailbox for a certain period of time. Programmers can build their own Vbscript functions and incorporate them into routing applications.

In addition, Microsoft provides a Routing Wizard sample application to demonstrate how routing applications can be quickly built. Routing applications often attempt to encapsulate a paper-based business process into an electronic form. After they've worked in an office for a while, people instinctively know how to process paper forms, but it's often difficult to capture the knowledge people have of a paper-based process and turn it into the code and functions required to emulate the process to a routing engine. The Routing Wizard generates simple serial or parallel routes for free-text workflow items. The applications aren't very complex, and it's easy to pick holes in their functionality, but it's very easy to get an application up and running, which is the major purpose of the wizard.

Once people realize that routing applications are useful the desire is created to learn more about the technology. Managers will be prepared to invest programmer time to investigate the Routing Objects interface, learn how it operates, and discover how complex routing applications can be built. The initial travel request application generated by the Routing Wizard can be enhanced to incorporate electronic forms for data entry, multiple-step parallel processing, and so on.

There's no doubt that Routing Objects is an important step forward for Exchange. Simple email becomes intelligent email when can be routed and used to automate business processes. Automated processes are easier to cost-justify than a simple email service, so everyone, including the accounting department, is happy. I expect major developments and enhancements in CDO (in general) and workflow capabilities in Exchange over the next few years, and it will be very interesting to see how things develop.

12.5   What the Event Service might be used for

It's early days yet for the Event Service, but Microsoft is actively suggesting what the service could be used for and, even more importantly, what it is not well suited to. Amongst the suggested applications are document routing for review or approval, list automation (like sending everyone on a distribution list updates from a public folder once a day), newsfeed processing (possibly associated with an NNTP feed into a public folder), and the automation of common administration tasks. For example, you could allow users to post requests to leave or join a distribution list in a public folder and have an agent carry out the task in the background. Microsoft is working on a sample agent that will auto-accept meeting requests for resources like conference rooms, something that will be very useful and remove an irritation from today's scheduling environment.

But there are places where scripting is not a good fit. I've already mentioned that events are not synchronous with store contents. Applications that absolutely depend on an item being retained in a folder until its contents can be processed could get into trouble with agents, unless you ensure that no one can interfere with a folder until an agent has dealt with incoming items. The Event Service is completely separate to the Information Store so an agent that attempted to process every piece of outgoing mail would experience horrible performance characteristics as the interpreted script code is called for each message. Essentially, you'd be reducing the performance of your Exchange server to the execution speed of VBscript. Not good!

Finally, scripts have to be installed into folders on an individual basis. There is no facility to distribute scripts to multiple folders within a site so the creation and installation of agents is a strictly manual affair. This isn't a huge problem where you only need to create script code to a couple of folders but it would become tiresome if you wanted to use the same code for a certain folder in everyone's mailbox.

13

Bringing It All Together—
How to Proceed

13.1 Things you'll enjoy about Exchange Server

These are the best things I've enjoyed when working with Exchange. Selecting aspects of a product that are pleasing is a very personal activity, so feel free to disagree... The points are not listed in any order of importance because they're all important.

- *MAPI*. The power and flexibility of the Messaging Application Program Interface can be seen in Microsoft's own clients as well as the MAPI service providers appearing from other vendors.

- *Exchange clients* are easy and powerful to use, even if they require fairly substantial hardware resources for truly satisfactory performance. Microsoft have followed their own user interface standards to good effect. Outlook is an interesting alternative to the standard client and is the right choice for 32-bit desktops. Outlook Web Access is a splendid example of excellence in user interface design for Web applications, although its splendour has to be paid for by network bandwidth.

- *Single point of administration*. Maybe it's missing some features that I'd like to see included, but the Exchange Administration program is the most integrated messaging administration utility I've ever encountered to date.

- *The transactional nature of the Information Store* is a huge advance on Microsoft's previous file sharing architecture. It's also at the center of Exchange's ability to scale up for corporate implementations. The single-file-entity nature of databases poses challenges of its own, but good planning minimizes these while optimizing the store's capabilities.

- *The Exchange MTA* almost manages to bring plug and play capabilities to the e-mail world. It also co-ordinates connectors for different messaging systems in a very nice manner.

- *The Exchange connectors* are generally reliable, robust, and extremely fast. The Internet Mail Service deserves special mention.

The array of connectors in Exchange now qualifies it for messaging-switch status.

- *The Exchange Resource Kit* is a mine of useful information. It's backed up by TechNet. Together a lot of knowledge and useful tools on Exchange, Windows NT, and other products is available for those who care to search it out.

- *Advanced security* delivers encryption and digital signatures for those who really need it. You have to invest time and energy to deploy advanced security, but once it's implemented advanced security delivers what it promises.

- *Integration between a messaging system and its host operating system* has moved to a new level with Exchange. Account management, performance monitor, event logging, backup, and all the other points of integration make Windows NT and Exchange work together in a great combination act.

- *The Load Simulation utility* is something every messaging system should provide. Being able to conduct your own automated benchmarks is great!

13.2   Some things that aren't so good

Nothing in life is ever perfect, and Exchange certainly doesn't attain that unreachable standard (despite the best efforts of Microsoft's undoubted marketing muscle). I have my own black list of pitfalls and imperfections. I imagine that Microsoft will address many of these as new versions of Exchange are rolled out over the next few years. At least, I hope they will. In the meantime you can avoid these areas of difficulty!

- *Directory synchronization* is the black hole of Exchange because lots of system administrators will spend many aimless hours wandering around unless they run a pure Exchange environment or only ever have to synchronize with Microsoft Mail. Moving away from the antiquated scheme used to synchronize the Microsoft Mail global address list to support a standard (and API) for directory synchronization is an essential step for the future. Directory synchronization should occupy many hours of Exchange administrators' time and be a happy hunting ground for third party tools.

- *The migration source extractors* vary in quality. I wonder how some managed to get through Microsoft's normally excellent QA cycle. They are certainly nowhere near the same level of quality achieved elsewhere in Exchange.

- *Inter site mailbox transfers* are a complex manual process. Why can't it be as easy as moving a mailbox within a site?

- *Inter organization communications* (aside from messaging) doesn't appear to have been considered necessary. But people will move between operating companies within a group, or from an organizational unit in one country to another where each country wants to do its own thing. In short, it's not always going to be possible to go with a single organizational unit so it would be nice to be able to have items like advanced security, scheduling, user mailbox moves, and public folder replication supported on an inter-organization basis.

- *Conflict handling* for updates applied to multiple copies of a document in a replicated public folder is not neat. Surely it should be possible to lock a document for exclusive write access without having to set permissions on the entire folder each time?

- *Backups are great, but restores aren't.* Accidents will happen and restores will be necessary. Restoring a user mailbox without having to restore the entire Information Store would save a lot of time and money. In fact, needing to restore the entire Information Store when problems arise is going to cause a lot of system managers sleepless nights. Be sure you have a "hot-box" server waiting to swap in to replace failed hardware, and practice restore. All Exchange implementations need a well thought-out disaster recovery plan, just in case.

- *The integration and dependency with Windows NT is a double edged sword* because it's all too easy to mess up an Exchange implementation by not paying enough attention to the underlying Windows NT infrastructure. Microsoft can't do much about this point, but I make it yet again in the hope that a loud and clear message goes out—get Windows NT right first before trying to do anything with Exchange. As we go towards Windows NT V5.0 the importance of getting NT right before starting with Exchange increases.

- *There is a lack of enterprise wide monitoring and management tools* so knowing exactly what's happening on your Exchange servers is quite difficult. Capturing information like statistics (number of messages in the store, who owns them, number of messages sent in a period) or configuration data (human-friendly routing tables, details of connectors and other setup data) is too hard for a system aspiring to be a true enterprise solution. It is also far too difficult to split sites up, or merge them together.

- *Network planning for Exchange requires too many finger in the air type guesses.* The amount of network traffic within a site is unpredictable, especially when there are more than 10 servers.

Communication between sites can be controlled, but only if you go to the trouble of setting schedules for public folder content and directory replication.

13.3   10 essential points to get right when implementing Exchange Server

Distilling the content of a complete book into a single page is not easy, but lots of people demand a road-map to follow when planning the implementation of Exchange. With this request in mind I have created my own "Top-10" issues to consider and decide upon before an implementation begins.

	Issue	See chapters
1	Design the Windows NT infrastructure	3
2	Plan how Windows NT will be layered onto the internal network	3
3	Chart out the Exchange organization in terms of the sites and servers. Determine how the sites will communicate in terms of message flow, public folders, and all aspects of replication.	3
4	Determine what platforms are to be used for both servers and clients. Will you use Windows 95, 98 or NT on the desktop? Also, what hardware configurations will be used for both clients and servers?	4
5	Design the naming conventions for use within the Exchange organization – sites, servers, and mailboxes.	3, 6
6	Determine where the points of external communications will lie and what connectors (SMTP, X.400, Microsoft Mail, others) will be used to connect Exchange with other mail systems. Also, do you need to create a corporate mail directory by synchronizing with other mail directories?	3, 7, 8
7	Look at how public folders can be used to address business needs and requirements within your enterprise. What folders are needed? Where will they be located? Who will control their content? Will electronic forms be required?	5
8	Consider how the Windows NT computers will be managed. What system administration policies will be implemented to cover important topics such as backups?	5
9	If you are migrating from another electronic mail system what plan are you going to follow to migrate users and their data to Exchange?	10
10	Create a training plan that accommodates the needs of users, programmers, and system administrators so that the true power of Exchange can be unleashed.	9

These issues are not presented in order of importance. However, it's obvious that the first three issues should be tackled before anything else. While I encourage you to conduct a pilot so that you gain valuable experience with Exchange, experience that will enable you to build a better plan afterwards, it is critical to have a clear and well thought-through plan before you commence a full implementation. Experience is a hard master, but it tells that taking short cuts just to get a system into operation can have disastrous consequences afterwards!

13.4   The Exchange manager's toolkit

Managing any computer system is a challenge. Having the right set of tools to hand makes everything go a lot more smoothly. Here's my list of the items I think should be in the Exchange manager's toolkit.

Item	Reason
Windows NT Resource Kit	The kit contains many interesting and useful tools to help keep Windows NT systems running smoothly.
Exchange Resource Kit	Less interesting than the Windows NT resource kit, but still valuable!
Site Disaster Recovery Kit	When things go wrong you'll need your kit. It should include Windows NT repair disks, software distribution CDs (including all service packs), valid backups, documentation on the system configuration, and a cool head.
Subscription to TechNet	The CDs hold an unbelievable amount of information (but be sure to put the ideas in context for your own company), including the Knowledge Base. When things go wrong the Knowledge Base is the first port of call.
Third party products	Windows NT and Exchange system administration tools are OK, but there are some gaps, like enforcing disk quotas for users. Third party products, including backup utilities, full text retrieval systems, and virus checkers help move the system from a 95% solution towards a 100% fit.
Performance Monitor, Link and Server Monitors	Something to keep running so you know when problems arise before your users point this salient fact out to you!
Event Viewer	Check this every day!
Training vouchers	Keep on being trained! Go to the Exchange Deployment Conference and keep up to date with new versions of Windows NT and Exchange. Lots is happening at a bewildering pace.

14

Acronyms

The language of electronic messaging technology is full of acronyms. This appendix describes many of the acronyms used in a Microsoft Exchange environment.

BDC: Backup domain controller. A Windows NT server allocated the task of acting as a backup to the Primary Domain Controller (PDC) in case a problem arises with the PDC.

CA: Certification Authority. The Key Management Server is the Exchange component which acts as a certification authority to control X.509 security certificates.

CAST: A proprietary encryption algorithm developed by Northern Telecom.

CCITT: In English, the International Consultative Committee on Telephony and Telegraphy, a body concerned with the formulation and definition of standards for electronic communications. The CCITT is a sub-delegation of the International Telegraph Union (ITU).

DDA: Domain Defined Attribute. A DDA can be encapsulated in an X.400 O/R address to allow routing to occur through an X.400 network to a gateway which takes the DDA and uses it to deliver the message to its final recipient. In such cases the DDA holds the recipient's address in the format used by the mail system serviced by the gateway.

DES: Data Encryption Standard. An encryption algorithm developed by the US National Bureau of Standards.

DHCP: Dynamic Host Control Program.

DIB: X.500 Directory Information Base.

DIT: X.500 Directory Information Tree.

DMD: Directory Management Domain. The collection of DUAs and DSAs within an X500 directory. In an Exchange organization the DMD is represented by the set of directory services run in all sites.

DN: X.500 Distinguished Name composed of a set of RDNs.

DNS: Domain Name Service. The part of TCP/IP networks that contains and provides information about networked computer systems, basically by looking up computer names and providing the IP addresses for those that can be resolved.

DSA: Directory Service Agent. An X.500 concept of a computer process responsible for handling directory queries initiated by a DUA. The DSA will either satisfy the request itself or consult with another DSA.

DUA: Directory User Agent. An X.500 concept of a computer process that makes queries against an X.500 directory on behalf of a user.

DXA: Directory Synchronization Agent. The Exchange component responsible for synchronizing the contents of MS-Mail Global Address Lists and the Exchange directory.

FQDN: Fully qualified domain name. An Internet (or Intranet) name for a computer which contains all the necessary pieces to allow data to be routed back to the computer.

GAL: Global Address List.

GWART: Gateway Address Routing Table. The internal routing table used by the Exchange MTA to determine how messages can be routed through all the connectors and gateways operating within an organization.

HTML: Hypertext Mark Up Language. A standardized set of mark-up codes used to format pages for display by a World-Wide Web browser such as Netscape.

HTTP: Hypertext Transport Protocol. The protocol used to communicate between Web browsers and servers.

IMAP: Internet Mail Access Protocol.

ISP: Internet Service Provider. A company which provides Internet connectivity to other companies or individuals.

ISO: International Organization for Standardization.

ITU: International Telegraph Union.

KCC: Knowledge Consistency Checker. An Exchange component responsible for tracking the various links and connections that exist between different sites.

KMS: Key Management Server.

LDAP: Lightweight Directory Access Protocol. A protocol used by clients to access X.500-based directory services.

MAPI: Microsoft's Messaging Application Programming Interface.

MIB: Management Information Base for SNMP systems.

MTA: Message Transfer Agent.

MX: Mail Exchanger. A type of record stored in DNS databases.

NDR: Non Delivery Report. A special form of message sent back to users if a message they send can't be delivered.

NNTP: Net News Transfer Protocol.

PDC: Primary Domain Controller. The Windows NT server that validates all authentication and security requests within a domain. The PDC also maintains the definitive copy of the security database for the domain.

POP: Post Office Protocol.

RAID: Redundant Array of Inexpensive Disks.

RAS: Remote Access Server. The component of Windows NT that permits dial-in or asynchronous connections to be made between a client and a Windows NT computer.

RDN: Relative Distinguished Name. A name used to navigate within the Exchange directory.

RFC: Request for Comment. An Internet standard.

RSA: A public key encryption standard developed by Ron Rivest, Adi Shamir, and Leonard Adleman at the Massachusetts Institute of Technology in 1977.

SMTP: Simple Mail Transport Protocol. SMTP is the de facto standard for electronic mail within the Internet.

SNMP: Simple Network Management Protocol. A protocol allowing applications and other components to be managed across a distributed network.

SPI: Service Provider Interface.

WINS: Windows Internet Name Service.

X.400: The international standard for electronic mail interchange.

X.500: The international standard for electronic directory services.

XAPI: X/Open Application Programming Interface.

XDS: X/Open Directory Services.

15

Useful Points of Reference

15.1   World Wide Web sites

Much useful information about Exchange or associated products is available from World Wide Web sites.

http://www.microsoft.com/exchange/	Microsoft Exchange Server home page
http://www.exchangeserver.com/	Microsoft Exchange Community Web site—news, resources, events, and so on.
Http://www.microsoft.com/Exchange/eval.htm	Microsoft Exchange Server evaluation tools
http://www.microsoft.com/syspro/technet/boes/bo/ mailexch/exch/tools/appfarm/default.htm	Microsoft Exchange Server "application farm"
http://www.microsoft.com/win32dev/mapi/	Messaging development information (MAPI)
http://www.microsoft.com/exchange/meia/meia.htm	Microsoft Exchange Server in action —(case studies, corporate experiences and deployment, etc.)
http://www.microsoft.com/exchange/workflow.htm	Microsoft Exchange Server workflow page
http://www.microsoft.com/outlook/	Microsoft Outlook home page
http://www.microsoft.com/OutlookDev/Features/ outlook97.htm	Microsoft Outlook 97 development
http://www.microsoft.com/scheduleplus/	Microsoft Schedule+ home page
http://www.microsoft.com/security/	Microsoft Security Advisor

http://www.microsoft.com/exchange/reskit.htm	Microsoft Exchange Server Resource Kit Home Page
http://www.slipstick.com/exchange/exsfaq.htm	Slipstick Systems Exchange Resource center
http://www.ema.org/ema-home.htm	Electronic Messaging Association
http://www.eema.org/	European Electronic Messaging Association
http://www.computek.net/public/Sgutknec/exchfaq	Microsoft Exchange Server FAQ (not affiliated with Microsoft)
http://www.ms-exchange.com/	Microsoft Exchange trial server (brought to you by Microsoft, USConnect and Digital)
http://www.halcyon.com/goetter/widgets.htm	Ben Goetter's Exchange Widgets
http://www.angrygraycat.com/goetter/mdevfaq.htm	MAPI FAQ (unofficial and unsupported by MS)
http://www.donadams.com/exchange/default.htm	Don Adam's Microsoft Exchange Page (contains a downloadable Exchange Admin guide in PDF format)
http://backoffice.bhs.com/borc/satellite.idc?satellite=exchange	Beverly Hills Software Exchange Resource Center
http://www.msexchange.org/	Information about the unofficial Microsoft Exchange Server public listserver msexchange@insite.co.uk.
http://domen.uninett.no/~hta/x400/	Index to X.400 Web pages
http://terminator.rs.itd.umich.edu/projects/imap/imap.html	University of Michigan's IMAP/POP E-mail Service (lots of IMAP/POP3 info and links to many IMAP/POP3 sources)
http://home.istar.ca/~anthony/	Microsoft Exchange Server/Outlook resource pages
http://www.orca.bc.ca/win95/faq10.htm	Windows 95 Messaging Client FAQ (unaffiliated with Microsoft)
http://www.windows95.com/apps/mailutils.html	Windows95.com mail utilities page

http://ourworld.compuserve.com/homepages/ marcse/groupwar.htm	Microsoft Exchange Server groupware collateral
http://www.rsa.com/rsa/S-MIME/	S/MIME Central (specs, FAQ, links to 3rd parties)
http://www.delconet.com/em/	"Exchange Manager" newsletter home page
http://www.r2m.com/MAPIutils/	Microsoft Exchange Freeware MAPI Utilities GetMail and MAPI Logon
http://www.zerosix.nl/cgi-bin/rfc.new/	Fuzzy Search the RFCs
http://www.worldtalk.com/html/msg_resources/ email_ref.html	Worldtalks's E-Mail References, lots of great links and information!
Http://www.sover.net/~hawthorn/schedfaq.html	Schedule + FAQ page (unaffiliated with MS)
http://www.amrein.com/eworld.htm	Comprehensive Microsoft Exchange Server resource site from Amrein Engineering
http://www.mokry.cz/windows/exchange/	Ludek Mokry's Microsoft Exchange Client Add-Ins
http://nitty.rmit.usf.edu/usfit/exchange/ exchange1.shtml	University of South Florida (USF) Microsoft Exchange Server information page
http://www.fed.gov/	Government wide Electronic Messaging Program Management Office
http://www.imap.org/	The IMAP Connection—hosted by University of Washington
http://www.casahl.com/rawp.html	Casahl Technology's Replic-Action and Microsoft Exchange Server 5.0 white papers
http://eml01.usace.army.mil/	U.S. Army—Electronic Mail Center of Expertise
http://www.imc.org/	The Internet Mail Consortium
http://www.neosoft.com/internet/paml/	Publicly Accessible Mailing Lists
http://www.imc.org/mail-standards.html	Complete list of mail-related Internet standards

http://www.dejanews.com/	Deja News—The Source for Internet Newsgroups
http://andrew2.andrew.cmu.edu/cyrus/email/index.html	E-Mail Resources Web Index
http://web2.airmail.net/ncouch/modem.html	Microsoft Mail Modem Scripts
http://www.meer.net/~davidb/emapi.html	The Unofficial Extended MAPI Resources Page (maintained by David Boreham)
http://www.cs.ruu.nl/wais/html/na-dir/mail/.html	Internet Messaging FAQs
http://www.cs.ruu.nl/wais/html/na-dir/pgp-faq/.html	PGP (Pretty Good Privacy) FAQ
http://www.outlook.useast.com/	Outlook Developer's Resource Center
http://www.cauce.org/	Coalition Against Unsolicited Commercial Email
http://www.bqm.org/	Business Quality Messaging home page
http://www.swinc.com/resource/exch_smtp.htm	Simpler-Webb's Microsoft Exchange Server and SMTP resources

Just like much of the web, sites evolve all the time. Some grow old and become obsolete, others simply disappear, and new ones appear to distribute more information. Use your favorite search engine (like www.altavista.digital.com) to look for more sites associated with topics linked to Exchange.

15.1.1   Internet Mailing List for Exchange

The Internet Mailing List for Microsoft Exchange is available by sending an electronic mail message to:

```
msexchange-request@insite.co.uk
```

- The word "SUBSCRIBE" should appear in the body of the message. Do not include any other text.
- Leave the subject line blank.

File name index

ADMIN.EXE 7
AT.EXE 342
AUTOTEXT.SIG 237
DB000001.DAT 484
DB000002.DAT 476
DBBITMP.DAT 484
DBREFS.DAT 484
DEFAULT.PRF 402
DIR.EDB 250
DIR.PAT 344
DSAMAIN.EXE 244
DXA.EXE 244
EDB.CHK 253
EDB.DLL 251
EDB.LOG 253
EMAMTA.EXE 701
EMSMTA.EXE 244
ESE.DLL 251
ETEXCH.DLL 446
ETEXCH32.DLL 446
EVENTS.EXE 730
EXCHANGE.INI 395
EXCHANGE.PRO 396
EXCHINS.EXE 244
EXCHNG32.EXE 247
GWART0.MTA 489
GWART1.MTA 489
ISINTEG.PRI 366
ISINTEG.PUB 366
KMSPWD.INI 441
KMSERVER.EXE 244
KMSMDB.EDB 446
KMSPWD.INI
MAD.EXE 244
MSEXCIMC.EXE 244
MTACHECK.TXT 507
MTA.LOG 505
NEWPROF.EXE 401
NTBACKUP.EXE 338
OUTLOOK.EXE 247
OUTLOOK.INI 395
PERFOPT.LOG 689

PROFGEN.EXE 401
PRIV.EDB 250
PRIV.PAT 344
PROFGEN.EXE 401
PS19UPG.EXE 417
PUB.EDB 250
PUB.PAT 344
REGEDIT.EXE 395
REPAIR.EDB 375
RES1.LOG 269
RES2.LOG 269
SAMLIB.DLL 135
SAMSRV.DLL 135
SCANPST.EXE 430
SECADMIN.DLL 446
SECKM.DLL 446
SS.DLL 730
STORE.EXE 185
TEMPDFRG.EDB 376
TREDMOND.PKL 664
WINAT.EXE 342
WINMAIL.DAT 535

File type index

.ASP 88
.DAT 480
.EPF 439
.OAB 623
.OST 423
.PAB 399
.PFX 459
.PKL 664
.PMW 723
.PST 416
.SEC 664
.SIM 714
.TPL 472

Main index

A

Access Control List (ACL)
   for public folders 299

X